A Note from the Author

The developers at Microsoft did programmers a big favor when they released Visual Basic 5. Not only is VB5 easier to use than ever before, but it contains more power and features. Programmers who want to access the Internet with their applications or want to write their own ActiveX controls will have a difficult time finding a better programming platform than Visual Basic 5.

Visual Basic 5 Night School takes advantage of that power and ease by teaching you Visual Basic with a new approach. The book not only uses the latest in publishing technology to bring you the most effective training style, but the book's Internet connection constantly keeps the book fresh.

Each one-hour lesson ensures that you can master a topic in a single sitting. Also, the extra quiz questions and exercises give you feedback so that you'll know whether you've mastered the content. The book's evolving Web site keeps you updated with the latest of Visual Basic's tips and traps and—more importantly—keeps you in touch with me. I'll stay abreast of the Visual Basic arena and post the items that readers of *Visual Basic 5 Night School* need the most.

I look forward to being part of your Visual Basic training. I wish you much luck and I hope that you enjoy Visual Basic as much as I do!

Greg Perry

Greg Perry

Visual Basic® 5

NIGHT SCHOOL

QUE'S

Visual Basic® 5

NIGHT SCHOOL

Written by Greg Perry

Application developed by Bob Reselman

Visual Basic® 5 Night School

Library of Congress Catalog No.: 97-65534

ISBN: 0-7897-0921-X

99 98   6 5 4 3

Interpretation of the printing code: the rightmost double-digit number is the year of the book's printing; the rightmost single-digit number, the number of the book's printing. For example, a printing code of 97-1 shows that the first printing of the book occurred in 1997.

Contents at a Glance

Table of Contents

/// **PART III: INTERMEDIATE VB PROGRAMMING   355**

15 INTERACTING WITH USERS   357

Credits

PRESIDENT
Roland Elgey

PUBLISHER
Stacy Hiquet

DIRECTOR OF MARKETING
Lynn E. Zingraf

PUBLISHING MANAGER
Fred Slone

SENIOR TITLE MANAGER
Bryan Gambrel

EDITORIAL SERVICES DIRECTOR
Elizabeth Keaffaber

MANAGING EDITOR
Caroline D. Roop

ACQUISITIONS EDITOR
Tracy Dunkelberger

PRODUCT DIRECTOR
Erik Dafforn

PRODUCTION EDITOR
Susan Shaw Dunn

EDITORS
Kelli M. Brooks, C. Kazim Haidri,
Patricia Kinyon, Juliet MacLean,
Julie A. McNamee, J. Christopher Nelson

PRODUCT MARKETING MANAGER
Kristine Ankney

ASSISTANT PRODUCT MARKETING MANAGERS
Karen Hagen, Christy M. Miller

STRATEGIC MARKETING MANAGER
Barry Pruett

TECHNICAL EDITORS
Lowell Mauer, Tim Monk

TIME EDITORS
Dan Berkowitz, Al Valvano,
Jerry L. Dunn, Jeff Hilton,
Vache Krikorian

WEB CONTENT PROVIDERS
David Sherman, Guy Thompson,
Robert Houghtaling

TECHNICAL SUPPORT SPECIALIST
Nadeem Muhammed

SOFTWARE SPECIALIST
Brandon K. Penticuff

ACQUISITIONS COORDINATOR
Carmen Krikorian

SOFTWARE RELATIONS COORDINATOR
Susan D. Gallagher

EDITORIAL ASSISTANT
Andrea Duvall

BOOK DESIGNER
Ruth Harvey

COVER DESIGNER
Jay Corpus

PRODUCTION TEAM
Erin M. Danielson, Trey Frank,
Bob LaRoche, Tony McDonald,
Angela Perry, Nicole Ruessler

INDEXERS
Sandy Henselmeier, Greg Pearson,
Tim Tate, Chris Wilcox

Composed in *Frutiger* and *Caliban* by Que Corporation.

For Mr. John Barnett, a husband and father who exemplifies Heaven's best on Earth.

About the Author

Greg Perry has written more than 45 books. His forté is taking computer topics and bringing them down to the beginner's level. Perry has been a programmer, trainer, and speaker for the past 18 years. He received an undergraduate degree in computer science and a master's in corporate finance. Among the books he has written are *C By Example*, *Special Edition Using Visual J++*, *Access CD Tutor*, and *Visual Basic for COBOL Programmers*. In addition to books, he's written articles for several publications, including *Software Development*, *Access Advisor*, *PC World*, and *Data Training*. In his spare time he manages rental houses, helps produce a national television program, participates in local political campaigns, and constantly strives to hone his fractured Italian.

About the Application Developer

Bob Reselman, who developed the VBScheduler application used in this book, is a senior software engineer at Gateway 2000, where he's involved with designing platform architecture. He also teaches object-oriented programming with Visual Basic at Western Iowa Technical Community College. Bob has been programming with Visual Basic since version 1.0. He lives in Sioux City, Iowa, with his wife, Dorothy Lifka, and two daughters, Genveiève and Alexandra. He likes motorcycles and reggae.

Acknowledgments

My thanks especially go to Que's hard-working editorial staff, which transforms my words into writing. Tracy Dunkelberger led this project from its inception—a difficult task with the Internet-based training approach that had to go along with this work. Fred Slone often lent a hand when his expertise was needed, and to both Tracy and Fred I am grateful.

In addition, I want to thank two fine technical editors, Lowell Mauer and Tim Monk, for turning my bugs into working code. I also want to thank the editors and production staff who made this book work, especially production editor Susan Dunn. If problems still exist with this tutorial, the problems are mine; if you find something good here, it's because of the job that the editorial and production staff did.

As usual, Bob and Cheryl Enyart helped me retain my sanity (what was left of it) during this project's hectic writing. Denver is blessed to have the Enyart family. My family stays at my side through ups and downs. My precious bride, Jayne, is my beautiful encourager, helper, and friend. My parents, Glen and Bettye Perry, make me the most fortunate and loved son on Earth.

Tell Us What You Think!

As the reader of this book, *you* are our most important critic and commentator. We value your opinion and want to know what we're doing right, what we can do better, what areas you'd like to see us publish in, and any other words of wisdom you're willing to pass our way.

As the Executive Editor for the Programming team at Macmillan Computer Publishing, I welcome your comments. You can fax, email, or write me directly to let me know what you did or didn't like about this book—as well as what we can do to make our books stronger.

Please note that I cannot help you with technical problems related to the topic of this book, and that, due to the high volume of mail I receive, I might not be able to reply to every message.

When you write, please be sure to include this book's title and author, as well as your name and phone or fax number. I will carefully review your comments and share them with the author and editors who worked on the book.

Fax:	317-817-7070
E-mail:	**vb@mcp.com**
Mail:	Executive Editor
	Programming
	Macmillan Computer Publishing
	201 W.103rd Street
	Indianapolis, IN 46290

You can also visit our home page on the World Wide Web at

http://www.mcp.com

INTRODUCTION

WELCOME TO *Visual Basic 5 Night School*, a project that combines the best of book-learning, night school, and the Internet to give you a complete course on Visual Basic, and that will turn you into a Visual Basic programmer in about a month of nightly one-hour lessons. This tutorial is designed to meet today's programming needs. You not only will get to hands-on work right away, but you'll also understand the theory behind that hands-on training.

Unlike most tutorials, if you have questions, you can ask the author and other support staff! Surf the Internet to this book's Web page and view updates, quiz answers, additional links, explanations, tips, traps, and special offers. Leave questions and suggestions for the support staff. Once every month or so

during this book's print life, you'll be able to chat with the author so that you can personalize your skills and approach the Visual Basic language asking for answers that you need.

Is This Book for You?

This book is aimed at novice VB programmers with hectic schedules, but who are willing to set aside an hour a night to learn a new programming language that will help them at work. This book is targeted at the same people who are willing to sacrifice their evenings or weekends to take continuing education classes or seminars to further their careers. Rather than go to class, however, you stay at home and follow the class that we bring into your home with this tutorial and the Internet.

If you've worked with Visual Basic before—whether a little or a lot—you will appreciate this book's Fast Track approach. The final five lessons jump head-first into the ocean of Visual Basic programming and help you develop a complete application from scratch. As you read about the application's development, you can refer to specific sections in the earlier lessons that teach each topic in more detail. If you are new to Visual Basic, you will see what the rest of the book teaches; if you're an old pro, you will gain lots of insight into version 5's tools and programming treasure chest.

The Book's Training Format

Several books on the market exist for novice programmers and new Visual Basic programmers. None of them, however, are designed specifically to help readers learn Visual Basic in the environment in which they are learning at home, at night, in less than an hour a day, or crammed into a weekend.

Each lesson consists of three topics that help you focus on specific areas. Each topic is arranged in a three-step approach: explaining the concept, providing a relevant example, and providing reinforcement of the example to guarantee that you actually understand the concept.

In addition to the typical approach to teaching programming, this book provides Fast Track sections to point those of you who are more advanced—or more adventuresome—to building a scheduling and contact application. You can jump back to the relevant reference sections whenever you need more assistance.

The CD-ROM

On the CD

The CD-ROM included in *Visual Basic 5 Night School* is filled with valuable Visual Basic 5 resource material. Included on the CD-ROM are the following Que titles: *Special Edition Using Visual Basic 5*, *HTML By Example*, and *Special Edition Using VBScript*, and *Special Edition Using ActiveX*. There's a stand-alone CD-ROM version of the *Visual Basic 5 Night School* Web site, providing you with interactive quizzes, a Visual Basic FAQ (Frequently Asked Questions document), and the sample application from the book. The CD also contains all source code used in the book in electronic format, providing you with a great cut-and-paste source of Visual Basic code.

The Virtual Classroom Web Site

One of the truly unique features of *Visual Basic 5 Night School* is that you can get the simulated effects of learning Visual Basic along with a group of your peers. How is this possible? Through the interactive Web site that we have created for this book—the Visual Basic Virtual Classroom. At this Web site (**http://www.quenightschool.com**), you can talk with fellow *Visual Basic 5 Night School* readers about the book and VB programming in general, attend a monthly real-time chat hosted by the author, and even have your VB questions answered in real time by the many experienced programmers on the Night School IRC (Internet Relay Chat) channel.

The Web site boasts a wide range of features designed to help you in your Visual Basic 5 education. Interactive quizzes are available to test your knowledge and reinforce your learning. Along with the real-time discussion features, you also have access to a Visual Basic FAQ, providing you the wisdom of other programmers' experiences. You can also submit your own programs for review by your fellow "classmates" in the showcase section of the Web site. A complete virtual classroom awaits you, providing you with invaluable Visual Basic resources and information.

Conventions Used in This Book

This book uses several special conventions that you need to become familiar with. These conventions are listed here for your reference.

This book uses a `monospaced typeface` for Visual Basic code, to set it off from standard text. If you're told to type something, what you are to type appears in **`monospaced boldface`**.

When discussing the syntax of Visual Basic commands, this book uses some special formatting to distinguish between the required portions and the variable portions. Consider the following example:

```
If conditional Then
    Block of one or more Visual Basic statements
End If
```

In this syntax, placeholder information is presented in *italic*; information that must be typed exactly is not in italic. The word *conditional* indicates a placeholder—that is, in actual code, the word is replaced with whatever condition you actually want the `If` statement to work with. `If`, `Then`, and `End If` are required because they're keywords within the statement.

In some cases, command information is optional—that is, it's not required for the command to work. Square brackets (`[]`) enclose optional parts of the command syntax. Consider the following example:

```
intResponse = MsgBox(strPrompt[, intStyle][, strTitle])
```

Here, `MsgBox` is the function name and is neither optional nor a placeholder. The *intStyle* and *strTitle* parameters are both variable and optional (they're in italic and enclosed in square brackets); this means that you can type any character string in place of *strTitle* (without the brackets), or type nothing at all. *intResponse* and *strPrompt* are placeholders, but they aren't optional; you must supply a response and a prompt.

Also in this book, you may see a ➡ character at the beginning of a line of code. This character indicates that the line continues the code line above it. For example,

```
For intSub = 1 To 35
    strFamilyName(intSub) =
    ➡InputBox("What is the family member's name?")
```

shows that the `strFamilyName(intSub)` = line was too long and had to be moved down to the next line. You also occasionally may see an _ at the *end* of some VB code lines; the underscore is Visual Basic's own code-continuation character:

```
Private Sub cmdChangePic_Click()
   picPicture.Picture = LoadPicture("VB\Graphics\MetaFile\ _
                          Business\Computer.WMF")
End Sub
```

Tips, notes, and cautions appear throughout the book in special formats to make the information they contain easy to locate. Longer discussions not integral to the flow of the lesson are set aside as *sidebars*, with their own heading.

Introducing Visual Basic

WELCOME TO NIGHT SCHOOL with Visual Basic! You've decided to go the extra mile and learn Visual Basic programming in your extra time. *Visual Basic 5 Night School* encompasses a power-packed course, amplified by the Internet, so that you can learn to program with Visual Basic and make your time investment worthwhile.

Microsoft Visual Basic can be simple or complex, depending on your background. To truly master Visual Basic, you have to tackle both the easy and difficult parts. This hour's lesson gets you started by describing the background you need to understand where Visual Basic fits in with other programming products.

Topic 1: The Programming Process

Why bother with Visual Basic? After all, if you want your computer to do something, you only have to go to the store and buy a program.

Visual Basic enters the picture when you can't find a program that does exactly what you want done. For example, you might want a program that manages your company's accounting records exactly the way you've done business for years, yet all the accounting programs you find in the stores manage books slightly differently. You might want to play a certain kind of computer game that you've thought of but nobody else has come up with, so you're stuck without it unless you write the game yourself.

In this section, you'll learn why programming is important, the history of programming languages, and why Visual Basic offers benefits over other languages you might choose. This first section is the longest in this hour because, despite the short history of programming compared to other fields, programming has evolved through several distinct stages that are still important if you want to understand why programming tools work today the way they do.

▶▶ **FAST TRACK**

If you already know what programming languages do, jump to this lesson's second topic section, "Visual Basic's Nature" (p. 19), to learn the specifics of Visual Basic.

Overview   Before diving into Visual Basic, you should take the time to learn a little about the history of computer development tools that came before Visual Basic. Visual Basic (sometimes called VB) is one of the most advanced programming systems on the market today—yet Visual Basic is one of the simplest ones to use.

This topic section won't look at the specifics of Visual Basic yet. At this point—especially if you've never written computer programs before—it would be difficult to see the overall picture if you began studying Visual Basic's details. Therefore, this topic section begins by exploring the need for development systems such as Visual Basic, and explains the historical events that led to Visual Basic's development.

Looking at Programs

You already know what a program is. When you purchased your computer, the seller probably loaded it with lots of introductory programs, such as card games, personal finance programs, and system-related programs.

When you want your computer to do something, you must supply a program for it. Before learning about the programming process in more detail, you need to understand what a program is from the computer programmer's perspective (as opposed to a computer user's perspective): A *program* is a set of detailed instructions that tells the computer what to do.

Someday, you might be able to talk to a computer, and the computer will do what you want. In the meantime, you can't even type commands into the computer unless those commands follow a rigid *syntax* (grammar and spelling), and the computer can then handle only single instructions as you type them (such as MS-DOS commands). A program lets you group such instructions together to do more than a single task.

▼ COMPUTERS ARE DUMB

Even the most powerful and expensive computers built today lack intelligence. They lack *all* intelligence. Your computer is no more capable of doing something on its own than your car is capable of driving to your office without you.

Computers are just boxes with wires that connect millions of switches to each other. Without a program, your computer wouldn't know how to do anything.

A program is really only temporary in most computers. The program loads into memory and teaches the computer how to do something, such as be an electronic worksheet. Then, when you turn off the computer, its memory is erased and the computer comes back on with a fresh (and dumb again), blank program space. Although you can set up your computer to start certain programs when you power it up, such action hides the fact that the computer begins each power-up with empty memory. ▲

If you want the computer to perform a fairly complex task, such as balance your checkbook or play a game, you must enter lists of instructions. Those instructions make up a program, and the program is the instruction collection that does a job.

▼ **NOTE**

A program can be complex, and you have to get the program just right before Visual Basic runs it. Expect mistakes! Visual Basic makes it easy to locate and correct mistakes. One of the most common new-programmer misconceptions is that a computer is broken when it's the programmer's *program* that has problems, and the programmer needs to fix the mistakes. ▲

The History of Programming

Over the years, tools have been developed to help make computer programming easier. In the old days of the 1940s and '50s, programmers often entered cryptic instructions called *machine language* and *assembler language* that made the computer do work. Computers were difficult to program in those early days, even though the computer programs were much less complex than today's programs. The old programming methods were time-consuming and difficult to get correct, so lots of computer errors (called *bugs*) appeared.

▼ **NOTE**

Machine language is a language with only two commands: *on* and *off*. A machine-language program is nothing more than a collection of 1s and 0s representing the states of the millions of two-state (*binary*) switches inside the computer.

Don't worry too much about machine language, because if you're lucky, you'll never need to learn it! Today's tools—especially advanced development systems such as Visual Basic—make using machine language obsolete and a waste of time, except for the deep understanding of computers such language might produce. ▲

Machine language and assembler language are called *low-level languages*. Developers needed easier ways to program computers than the low-level languages provided. The problem, however, is that computers understood only machine language. (Assembler language is just a superset of machine language that hides the fact that a programmer is using binary values to create a program. Therefore, assembler language is only a slight improvement over machine language.) How would you enjoy writing a program that calculates a square root by using machine language's 1s and 0s? The program might start like this:

```
01000111
10100011
01110110
10010010
10011001
```

Such programs obviously lend themselves to trouble and are extremely difficult to understand. Even today, computers understand only machine language at their lowest levels. Nevertheless, computer developers have put
buffer languages between you and the machine language, so that you can
enter high-level instructions and let the computer convert those instructions
to the needed machine language. Only after converting the language you
use into machine language can the computer eventually follow your instructions and do the program's job. (This lesson's final topic section,
"Compiling and P-Code," explains the process of this conversion in more
detail.)

Although computers can't understand spoken languages yet, we can program computers by using *high-level programming languages*. One such
high-level language is Visual Basic, but Visual Basic is so much more advanced than the early high-level languages were. Perhaps you've heard of
some of the following high-level programming languages:

FORTRAN

COBOL

Pascal

BASIC

C

Each of these languages is much easier to work with than the machine and
assembler languages, because high-level languages use commands that you
can understand, such as `Print` and `Get`. You must admit, typing `Print` is
much simpler than entering a bunch of 1s and 0s.

All these languages (and additional less-common ones) worked well and
were used as the major high-level languages through the 1980s. The late
1980s, however, brought new computer challenges that these languages
couldn't handle well. Windowed environments, such as Microsoft Windows, made writing programs in these older languages difficult, compared
with the day's text-mode environment. You'll learn why windowed graphical environments present challenges as you progress through your Visual
Basic night-school training.

As you might suspect, Microsoft based Visual Basic on the older BASIC programming language. The next section explains why Microsoft gambled on BASIC for Visual Basic's foundation.

BASIC: Visual Basic's Roots

Whereas BASIC is a language suited *solely* for text-mode environments and *sorely* suited for graphical environments, Visual Basic includes almost the full original BASIC language. Although Visual Basic goes far beyond BASIC and makes BASIC suitable for windowed environments, one of Visual Basic's greatest strengths is its BASIC foundation.

The name BASIC is an acronym for *Beginner's All-purpose Symbolic Instruction Code*. In the 1960s, some Dartmouth College professors designed BASIC for their students. Students balked at learning some of the more detailed programming languages of the day, such as FORTRAN and COBOL, because—understandably—those languages are often difficult for non-computer students. The Dartmouth professors wanted their non-computer students to be able to write quick-and-simple programs without worrying too much about the details required from the other languages of the day.

Throughout the years, companies added to the original BASIC language and made it more powerful while still keeping the ease of use. Businesses and technical programmers rarely adopted BASIC, however, because it was known as a beginner's language and too simplistic for real-world programming. Just when it looked as though BASIC might become obsolete, Microsoft made a fateful decision—rather than toss BASIC, Microsoft recharged the language with these goals:

- Keep the original simple programming style
- Add a full-screen editor
- Revamp the input and output (I/O) statements to work inside the Windows operating environment
- Add response elements needed for the Windows environment so that the new BASIC could respond to graphical *controls* (controls can be command buttons, check boxes, dialog boxes, data-entry text boxes, scroll bars, and all the other on-screen items that a Windows user interacts with)

The result was Visual Basic. Although Visual Basic is based on BASIC, a high-level computer programming language for beginners, you have several nights ahead of you before you'll grasp all the Visual Basic concepts and before you'll be very productive with Visual Basic. Nevertheless, unlike most other Windows programming languages, such as C and C++, Visual Basic retains enough of BASIC's ease of use to make it one of the simplest tools to learn for the Windows programming environment.

▼ **NOTE**

Visual Basic isn't easy just because of the underlying BASIC-like language. Visual Basic is simple because so much of your program development will consist of arranging graphical icons and controls on-screen while using a Paint-like program editor. In older languages, you'd have to write detailed input commands; a Visual Basic programmer, on the other hand, simply drags and drops a control such as a text box, scroll bar, or command button to a Visual Basic screen, adjusts a few details about the control, and lets Visual Basic take care of all the tedium. Much of a Visual Basic program's development requires designing the user interface and choosing the right tools needed. ▲

Microsoft Visual Basic is the official name of the programming language you'll learn here, but Visual Basic isn't just a language—it's a complete development environment that includes the language, editor, program test environment, graphical controls, and online help. Therefore, when you learn Visual Basic, you must learn more than a new set of commands, but you must also master the development environment. Fortunately, Microsoft makes mastering the Visual Basic environment easy!

Example   Back when computers had only a few bytes of memory, programming in machine language didn't actually pose the same problems that machine-language programming produces today. Perhaps the most difficult job needed for those early computers might be to average a list of numbers. Many early computers had a couple of hundred bytes of memory at most. To write a program in machine language, you wouldn't even sit in front of a keyboard; you would sit in front of a switch panel, such as the one in Figure 1.1.

FIG. 1.1
Early program-mers used a switch panel to program computers.

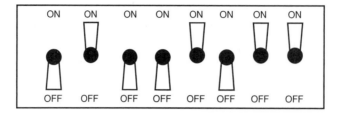

As computer designers learned how to add more memory to the comput-ers, machine language became too complex, so they added a keyboard and began using assembler language to help mask the 1s and 0s. Listing 1.1 shows a sample from an assembler language program. The codes, called *mnemonics*, represent a different pattern of 1s and 0s that make the computer do something. The mnemonics each stand for something. For example, `MOV` represents a combination of 1s and 0s that instruct the computer to move data from one memory location to another. `MOV` is easier to remember and less bug-prone than having to type the specific series of 1s and 0s that represent the data-movement command.

Listing 1.1   Sample Code from an Assembler Language Program

```
FDIVR    DWORD PTR [BX+DI+001E]
REPZ
STOSB
MOV      [D82E],AX
MOV      [D724],AX
XCHG     DI,AX
AND      [SI],BX
OR       [BX+0021],DX
ADD      [BP+SI],AH
ADD      [BX],CH
DAS
OR       AL,FD
ADD      DH,[BP+SI]
XOR      AL,00
JL       0141
```

Assembler language was a huge step forward and further promoted com-puter purchases. Businesses and government installations began buying computers and putting them to use. The widespread growth of computers required a better programming system than assembler language. Although assembler language was one step closer to spoken language than machine language, the one-to-one correspondence between assembler language and machine-language instructions made the low-level assembler language too bulky to use for the larger applications than institutions needed.

Therefore, developers began writing high-level languages, such as FORTRAN, C, and BASIC, that weren't closely linked to the underlying machine language. Although the computer has to convert the high-level language to machine language before running the program, programmers don't have to do as much work to write and enter programs. Listing 1.2 shows a simple BASIC program. Although the language is still somewhat cryptic, the commands make much more sense than assembler language and especially more sense than machine language.

Listing 1.2 A More Easy-to-Understand BASIC Program

```
10 PRINT "This program will calculate the area of a circle."
20 PRINT
30 INPUT "What is the circle's radius"; R
40 P = 3.14159
50 A = P * R * R
60 PRINT "The circle's area is"; A
70 END
```

▼ NOTE
The 7-line BASIC program in Listing 1.2 might require 100 lines of assembler language or—worse—several thousand machine-language 1s and 0s to perform the same work! Obviously, high-level languages make a programmer's job easier. ▲

Visual Basic takes the ease of BASIC a step further. Not only is Visual Basic a language that's greatly improved over BASIC (and most other modern and classic programming languages), Visual Basic includes the following components:

- A complete full-screen editor with which you can write your program and which works a lot like a word processor
- A runtime environment that lets you see the results of your program with the click of a button
- A project manager that lets you create multiple-file Visual Basic Windows applications

- An interactive testing platform that helps you locate and find program bugs
- Visual tools that let you manage the controls and icons that make programs function properly under the visual Windows environments

Before I explain any of the details of Visual Basic programming, Figure 1.2 gives you a hint of things to come. It shows the Visual Basic development system during the creation of a program. Things got busy fast, didn't they? The BASIC language that was making things simpler now seems to become convoluted with Visual Basic!

FIG. 1.2

The Visual Basic screen includes lots of things happening.

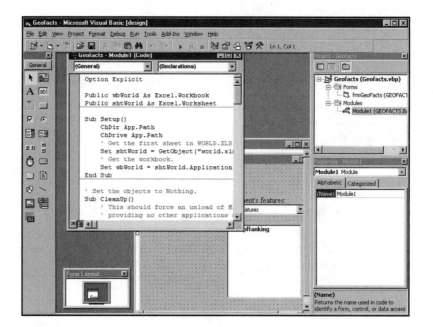

Visual Basic really didn't complicate programmer's jobs. Despite Figure 1.2's complex-looking screen, Visual Basic helps *streamline* Windows programming jobs. Windows brings many new requirements to a program that non-windowed environments don't require. With those requirements, however, comes a ton of benefits that the rest of this book will explore.

Next Step   To prepare you for "thinking in Visual Basic," consider the following differences between a text mode (non-Windows) and a Windows environment.

In a text-mode environment,

- Users use a keyboard to make selections
- Users answer questions as the program asks the questions
- Users have little control over the program flow
- Multitasking doesn't take place
- Users run one program at a time
- The screen shows one program's output

In a Windows environment,

- Users use a keyboard and mouse to make selections
- Users click buttons, enter text, display lists, and select from menus whenever they feel like doing any of those things
- Users have major control over the program flow and generally dictate the selection of controls and screens
- Several tasks might happen at once in multiple windows
- Users might run several programs at once
- Each running program's output might appear in a window at the same time on users' screens

A development system such as Visual Basic can handle the potential complexities that a Windows graphical interface hands to the programmer. Whereas graphical environments are often easier for users than text-based environments, graphical environments offer tremendous challenges to program writers due to the windowed environment's multitasking, multi-window, multicontrol nature.

Topic 2: Visual Basic's Nature

▶▶ **FAST TRACK**

Have you used Visual Basic before? If so, jump to the next topic section, "Compiling and P-Code" (p. 29), to learn about Visual Basic 5's new compilation option.

Actually, you've already been exposed to the nature of Visual Basic in the previous topic section. To get you up and running as quickly as possible, however, we must spend the rest of the hour discussing today's benefits of Visual Basic and the nature of Visual Basic.

Overview   This topic explores the nature of Visual Basic programming more thoroughly. In this and the next topic section, you'll learn the final introductory preliminaries that you need before diving into Windows programming. By the time you get to the next hour's lesson, you'll be ready to dive head first into a Visual Basic application.

Visual Basic Wears Many Hats

As you learned in the previous topic section, Visual Basic isn't just a language, but an applications development system. Although you'll have to master Visual Basic's language, you must also master Visual Basic's environment, including all the windows you saw in Figure 1.2.

Even though Visual Basic sometimes resembles a programming language when you're buried in the middle of code (*code* is another word for program instructions), Visual Basic resembles several software packages in that you use menu items, toolbars, and the graphical user interface to develop applications. You'll develop Windows programs that look and act just like the Windows programs you see all the time.

TIP   As you develop your Visual Basic applications, keep in mind that Windows programs follow a common pattern. Most Windows programs have File, Edit, and View menus; online help; and toolbars. You'll want to make your program as standard as possible by following as many of the other Windows products in style. You aren't plagiarizing but *standardizing*; in a Windows program, standardizing is so vital that Microsoft recommends that you match the company's own style with the Microsoft Office products' menus and toolbars. Microsoft realizes that the more that programmers standardize on common Windows components that exist in most programs, the less fear users will have and the more quickly users will adapt to the graphical environments.

Not a Windows Expert?

If you don't feel as though you've mastered the Windows 95 interface (the Windows 95 interface appears on different Microsoft operating systems, such as Windows NT and, of course, Windows 95), keep in mind that you don't have to be a Windows wizard to learn to program well with Visual Basic. However, you should be comfortable with using Windows, including these elements: window moving and resizing, menu bars, scroll bars, buttons, system menus, files, file names, icons, and dialog boxes (often called *property sheets* in Windows 95 terminology because of the multiple pages on many dialog boxes).

▼ **NOTE**

If you're unfamiliar with the Windows elements just mentioned, you should put aside Visual Basic for a short while and get acquainted with the Windows 95 interface. This book can't take time out of your Visual Basic night-school tutorial to cover Windows fundamentals, but here are two great resources that should help you learn Windows 95 quickly: the user-friendly *Using Windows 95* or the more comprehensive *Special Edition Using Windows 95*, both published by Que Corporation. ▲

Visual Basic Is Object-Oriented

Visual Basic is an *object-oriented programming* (OOP) language. OOP purists would cringe at that last sentence because Visual Basic doesn't contain a few of the advanced but needed requirements for a truly technically pure OOP language; nevertheless, Visual Basic is about as object-oriented as a language can get in many ways.

Object-oriented programming languages began springing up in the late 1980s as C++ and SmallTalk made a splash in the programming community. OOP programmers began rejoicing that, finally, their work backlog would be behind them because OOP would make programming virtually trouble-free. Today, the programming backlog in most computer departments is at least twice that of the late 1980s. Current OOP implementations are proving to be too difficult, and OOP proponents overestimated OOP's promise.

In many ways, Visual Basic, although not a pure OOP language, lends itself to the OOP spirit more so than many of the true OOP languages out there. Visual Basic instantly offers you a set of predefined objects that you'll recognize right away, such as command buttons that you can add to your program just by dragging them there with your mouse. Hooking these objects into your Visual Basic code is typically much simpler than doing the same from within a true OOP language such as C++.

Also, Visual Basic contains not only the standard Windows controls such as command buttons, but third-party developers are making new controls for you to plug into your own Visual Basic programs all the time. If you need to insert a spreadsheet or calendar in your Visual Basic program, you don't have to write the code; someone else has written a control that can embed itself as a spreadsheet right in the middle of your accounting program, and you can add a calendar feature to your Visual Basic program by dragging a calendar tool that's available in many flavors.

You can download many of these *Visual Basic controls*, or VBXs, from the Internet and other online services. Also, Visual Basic supports OLE Control Extensions (OCXs) and ActiveX controls, the newest controls that might help pave the way between desktops and Internet applications, among other functions.

The proliferation of VB control support makes Visual Basic popular. When you program, you don't want to be the only kid on the block who writes in your programming language. You want to use what everybody else uses so that you can share skills, discuss problems, and trade code. Visual Basic is one of the world's best-selling programming languages out today, so you won't be alone when you begin writing Visual Basic programs.

TIP Not only do you learn Visual Basic, but as a bonus, you'll also learn *Visual Basic for Applications*, a Visual Basic-like language that Microsoft has added to the Office 97 products. VBA is a close superset of Visual Basic, so you can use VBA to automate your Office 97 work immediately after mastering Visual Basic.

Event-driven programming requires that you understand events. In the world around you, an event might be the birth of a child, an Olympic meet, or a football championship. In addition to these once-in-a-lifetime events, an event can be an ordinary happening, such as a doorbell ringing or a car running out of gas. Events happen to you in life all the time, and you must make a decision every time an event occurs: Do you handle the event, ignore the event, or put off a response until the event occurs again? You handle events by prioritizing them and ranking your responses according to the events' purpose.

Computer events occur all the time as well. As in the real world, a computer event might be important or trivial. One of the most important parts of a Visual Basic program is deciding which events to respond to and specifying what that response should be.

When users run a Windows program, they do lots of things—press the keys, move the mouse, click screen icons, drag objects, cut, copy, paste, and so on. Your programs must run inside this multitasking environment. Some events occur for your program's sake (such as a user's answer to a question that your program asks), and some events occur that have nothing to do with your program (such as the user clicking the taskbar's Start button to start another program while yours is running).

Your programs must recognize what the user just did (that is, what event just occurred) and respond rationally to those. Given the variety of possible events, your program's job can be great just filtering through all the events that take place during execution.

Handling Events the Old-Fashioned Way

Before the advent of windowed environments, programs fell into one of two categories:

- **Batch.** Programs that execute without user interaction, such as a payroll year-to-date update program. Batch programs typically respond only to a single event—the event that started the program. On receipt of the start command, the batch programs execute without user interaction and run to completion or bomb due to a bug.
- **Online.** Programs that assume that a person is sitting in front of a computer screen with a keyboard (but no mouse, touch screen, or elaborate devices such as voice-recognition systems).

From its inception, the microcomputer has been interactive in nature with a single user and a single CPU (let's ignore parallel processing now, because the subject is still in its infancy and not prevalent among most microcomputer users quite yet). Therefore, most PC-based programs are online programs because there's always the user at the keyboard, and because batch processing is much less likely to take place except in rare situations.

Online text-based programs are designed to run with the user at the keyboard answering questions and responding to the program at the program's rigid prompting. These programs usually require users to select from a limited set of choices by pressing certain keys. Such systems often present the user with a menu of choices such as these:

1. Create an invoice
2. Post a payment

3. Send out late notices

4. Exit the program

Although users have limited control over the program's flow (they might select any one of the four choices), the users can't control the method of interaction; the keyboard is the only input allowed. Also, users can't change options and many times can't easily back up to previous menu items if desired, unless the program is specifically written to allow that.

Handling Events the Windows Way

Graphical user interfaces provide so much more functionality and usability than text-based systems. When color graphics first appeared on PCs, many software developers took the text-based menu and placed the menu on the graphics screen. The result was little changed from the older pre-visual programs.

As graphics boards became more powerful and as developers began integrating more and more graphics and less text onto program screens, it soon became clear that the old menu approach to program control couldn't work in the new environment because the keyboard by itself wasn't enough. Users had to have a way to manipulate graphic images as though they could grab an image on-screen and drag that image to another location. Although touch screens never really took off, the mouse made graphical interactions finally possible.

Unlike keyboard text, the mouse pointer isn't limited to the current input area on-screen. Users can move the mouse to any screen location and click any object. Users liked pointing, drawing, clicking, and dragging, so Microsoft developed the Windows operating environment to give customers what they wanted. Of course, with the invention of the mouse, a new programming challenge was born: How would a program handle all the complicated interactions that the new graphics hardware allowed? The next topic section explains everything.

Example Figure 1.3 shows a running Visual Basic program. The running program is the window titled "Bibliography Database Browser" in the middle of the screen. As you can see, you can execute Visual Basic programs from within the Visual Basic environment. The window is a complete stand-alone

Windows application that you can run inside the Visual Basic environment and by itself in a stand-alone mode.

FIG. 1.3

A Visual Basic program window often shows several controls.

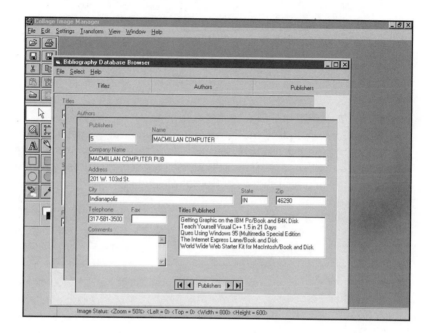

Almost every element you see in the application's window is a control. You'll find text boxes (such as the ones labeled Name and Address), command buttons (such as the wide ones across the top labeled Titles, Authors, and Publishers), and even scrolling controls (labeled Publishers at the bottom of the window).

Visual Basic supplies many controls for you to use. Not only will you be able to develop Windows programs with common Windows controls such as the ones you see here, but from a variety of sources you can also purchase (many are free) and download several additional controls called *custom controls*. You can obtain custom controls that perform specific calculations (such as advanced scientific calculations), motion picture controls, dissolve graphic controls, grid controls, wild spin buttons, and list-selection controls that may not match anyone's idea of a Windows standard, but they do make for interesting applications.

The best thing about Visual Basic controls is that you don't have to do a lot to put them in your application. Simply install the control (if you want to use one that doesn't come with Visual Basic) and drag it onto your Visual Basic application's window. Throughout this book, you'll learn all about programming with Visual Basic controls. In the past, you would have to spend countless hours tediously programming the user interface for your programs. Today, with Visual Basic's power, you simply design the visual interface with your mouse.

▼ **NOTE**

After you place the control on your application, you'll see that you can change the control's behavior from its default behavior. For example, you can set special colors, adjust scroll bar scrolling areas, and modify the way the graphic-related controls display images. ▲

Figure 1.4 shows a menu on a text-based computer screen. Now that you're used to Windows, such screens are rather boring, aren't they?

FIG. 1.4
A traditional text menu is outdated today.

```
                    Invoicing System
                    ----------------

            What do you want to do?

                1. Create an invoice

                2. Post a payment

                3. Send out late notices

                4. Exit

            Enter your choice: |
```

Figure 1.5 shows a simple example of how a Visual Basic programmer might design such a program. Although users still must control the order of the program execution with the choices on-screen, other controls appear on-screen that modify the way the program behaves. Without powerful and simple programming tools such as Visual Basic, the program behind such a screen would be complicated because of the large number of events that might happen in any order.

FIG. 1.5

Menu selections take on new meaning in a Windows program.

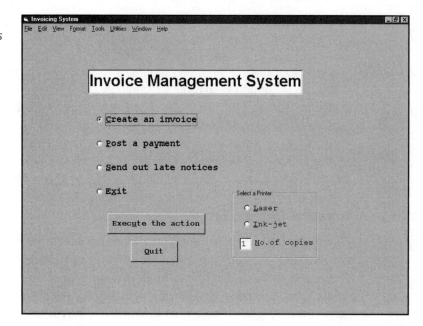

Here are some of the possible events that users can trigger in Figure 1.5:

- Select one of the four option buttons with the mouse or by pressing a hotkey such as Alt+C
- Press the top command button to execute the selected option (with a mouse click or hotkey)
- Terminate the program by pressing the bottom command button (with a mouse click or hotkey)
- Move the mouse on-screen
- Click or double-click the mouse button anywhere on-screen

- Display and possibly select from a menu that the user pulls down with the mouse or keyboard
- Select the type of printer on which to print invoices
- Change the default number of printed invoice copies
- Restore the maximized program window
- Minimize the window
- Move the program window
- Display and select from the program window's Control menu

Next Step   Look at your favorite Windows programs to see how they're alike and how they vary. Although each program's primary purpose might be different (such as Microsoft Word and Excel), many Windows programs share commonality in menus and toolbars. Therefore, when you master one Windows program, you're that much ahead when you want to master another. Before the standard Windows environment came along, you would have to learn how to interact with several different kinds of programs; with Windows, you must learn only a single interface, and you know almost every other Windows program interface as well.

If you use Visual Basic to write a Windows program and the program must use a data file, you should add a File menu to your program's menu bar and put Open and Save commands on the File menu. (Where else would you want such file-related commands?) Although you might want to use the term *Load* instead of the Windows standard *Open*, resist the temptation to change the standard. Your users will appreciate that they don't have to learn a new interface to use your program.

Figure 1.6 reviews the event-driven nature of Windows. As you can see, one of many possible events can happen at any time. Windows filters the events and sends to the proper program the event that belongs with that program. It's then your program's job, if you've programmed the code correctly, to respond to that event or to ignore the event altogether.

FIG. 1.6
Windows filters out some events before the events get to your program; your program must handle the rest.

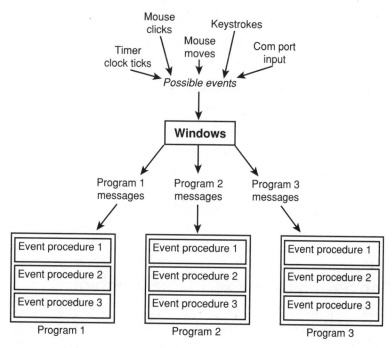

Topic 3: Compiling and P-Code

After you write a program, your computer can't magically execute the program until you issue the order. This topic section explains how your computer takes the Visual Basic program you develop and converts that code into machine language (the only language your computer really understands at its core) behind the scenes with only the click of a button.

▶▶ **FAST TRACK**

Want to know Visual Basic's most impressive feature? You'll appreciate version 5's new compile capability. Jump to the section "Converting to an Executable Program" (p. 30) for more information.

Overview No matter if you use Visual Basic to write small programs that calculate averages or gigantic applications that run corporate businesses, the overallprogram-development cycle looks something like this:

- Determine your needs
- Plan the program requirements that will fulfill those needs

- Design the user interfaces for the program
- Design the program's output
- Write the Visual Basic code that ties the interface and output elements together
- Convert the Visual Basic application to machine-readable form
- Test the program and correct the bugs

Although the rest of your night-school training will address each topic, this hour's lesson has spent considerable time explaining the differences between today's high-level languages that you write and the low-level machine language that your computer actually runs. The following sections briefly show why learning all that was vital to understanding the new version of Visual Basic.

Converting to an Executable Program

To run a Visual Basic program, you only need to click a toolbar button. Visual Basic does the rest of the work, and then interactively runs your program. You'll notice a brief pause right after you run a program before you see the results. The Visual Basic system converts your application into an intermediate file called *p-code*. P-code (which stands for *pseudocode*) isn't machine language and isn't a high-level language. P-code is a Visual Basic-specific language that requires a *runtime module* (a collection of common routines that your programs access).

Although I could get really technical here, there's no reason to do so. The bottom line is that when you run a Visual Basic program, the Visual Basic system first converts your program to p-code, and then runs the p-code through a runtime module. The runtime module quickly converts the p-code—one line at a time during the execution—into machine language and executes those converted machine language instructions.

Until version 5.0, Visual Basic wasn't a *compiled language* but was an *interpreted language* by using the p-code system. An interpreted language isn't as efficient as a compiled language because of the on-the-fly interactive conversion of your program's p-code to machine language. Therefore, Visual Basic has been fairly efficient in the past due to a tight p-code conversion process and efficient runtime module, but it hasn't been able to compete with speedy languages such as C++.

Starting with version 5.0, the Visual Basic system includes a true language compiler. When you compile a Visual Basic program before running the program (as opposed to simply running the program), the Visual Basic system takes the time to convert your entire application to a machine-language file called an *executable file*. You then can run the executable file, and the file runs *much* more quickly than an equivalent interactively converted p-code-based language.

TIP Perhaps you've seen file listings with files that end in the .exe extension. Those files are usually fully converted machine-language programs that run as efficiently as possible. Until version 5.0, you couldn't run a truly compiled Visual Basic program.

▼ NOTE

Just because compiled programs run faster doesn't mean that you'll forsake p-code now. The easiest way to see the results of the Visual Basic you write is to run them without first compiling them. Visual Basic automatically uses the p-code conversion process (you never have to specify p-code or even know it's there). During testing, executing your programs interactively provides the best means for testing and feedback. **▲**

Program Maintenance

As you learn to program, this night-school course would be doing you a disservice if you didn't learn about *proper coding techniques* as you learn the Visual Basic language and development system. There are many ways to write the same program. In today's changing world, you need to realize that the program you write today will probably need changing in the future. Therefore, when you write programs, you'll do so with future *program maintenance*, or updates, in mind.

As you learn topics throughout this course, you'll see ways to improve on techniques so that you'll be more easily able to maintain the program at a later date.

Example   Companies grow, merge, consolidate, and spin off every day. If you write Visual Basic programs for a company, you'll be more valuable to that company if you write clear and concise code. For example, in Part II of this Visual Basic night-school course, you'll learn how to document your programs. Documentation resides *inside* a Visual Basic program to offer explanatory remarks about the code and explain what the code does at different places in the program.

Documentation isn't required. You can write any program and never document the program. Your computer won't care. Nevertheless, if someone is assigned to change your program later, the more you can document what you did inside the program, the more quickly the programmer can understand your code, make the updates, and move to another project. If you don't document your code, the programmer must spend extra time figuring out what much of your program is doing.

If you write programs for yourself and only for yourself, you *still* need to document! The program explanatory remarks that you add today will save you time when you need to make a change to a complicated set of instructions a year later. Programs can become lengthy, and you won't always be able to remember why you did something; a simple remark here and there will aid in your program maintenance process.

Next Step

At this point, you're probably looking forward to the next hour's lesson, when you can create your very first Visual Basic program. You have the groundwork out of the way and understand much more about what's required as a programmer. You also understand what a program is really all about, and how the computer takes your Visual Basic program and converts it down into the low-level machine language code needed by your machine. Fortunately, the days of 1s and 0s are over; your computer and Visual Basic do all the work. Your dragging of a control onto your Visual Basic window might take you one-half second, whereas programming the same control from scratch in machine language might take a week or more. We've come a long way, baby!

Perhaps one of the best ways to round out this hour's lesson is to review some important terms related to programming and Visual Basic. Here is a list of terms that you should master as soon as possible. You've seen some of the terms already in this lesson; others you may have already known. Some might be new to you, but you'll face them shortly as you master the fundamentals of Visual Basic.

- **Application.** A completed program. Often, a Visual Basic application is more than a single file and might consist of 10 or more related files.

The term *application* seems a little more appropriate for such files. Nevertheless, you'll often see the term *program* used to refer to the entire application.

- **Compile.** The process of converting a high-level programming language (such as Visual Basic) to machine language.

- **Controls.** Tools that appear on the user interface that let users respond to the program, enter data, and view images and other kinds of output data.

- **Custom Controls.** Controls you can purchase or download from Internet sources that add new features to Visual Basic's user interface.

- **Event.** An activity that occurs during an application's execution. Users normally trigger many events, such as keypresses, mouse clicks, or mouse movements. The Windows operating environment can also trigger events such as timer clicks and data transferred from other running programs.

- **Event-Driven Programming.** The process of writing programs that respond to triggered events, as opposed to older text-based programs that were sequential in nature and followed a predetermined flow. Events can come from many sources, and your program must know which events to respond to and which to ignore.

- **Executable File.** The machine-language program your high-level Visual Basic program becomes when you compile and run the program.

- **Icon.** A little picture that represents an application or other object. Icons often appear on toolbar buttons to let you know what the button does.

- **Object.** An element of your Visual Basic application that typically—but not always—represents a data item. Objects, as opposed to non-object data, contain properties, methods, and events that activate the objects. Visual Basic objects can be forms, printers, windows, controls, pictures, and program data items such as data records and totals.

- **Project.** A collection of files that work together to create your working application program. You can manage your application's files from the project's window.

- **Source Code.** The high-level program instructions that you write in a language such as Visual Basic. Although your computer can't understand source code, people can understand source code, and the compiler can convert the source code to the computer's machine language (all behind the scenes, thankfully!) when you run the program.

- **Tools.** Classes of objects that can appear in Visual Basic programs. A tool supplies the pattern for the controls you drag onto your Visual Basic application.

- **User Interface.** Part of the computer program that users respond to. The user interface is the graphical windows in which your program users retrieve and enter information and control program flow.

- **Window.** A rectangular screen area that contains an application or part of an application. The window is analogous to a sheet of paper lying on a desktop. You can overlay one window with another, get rid of the window, return a buried window to the top of a window stack, and make program entries in the window.

Summary

The first night is now over! You just received an hour's introduction not only to Visual Basic, but to the programming process in general. You're starting at Hour 1's lesson if you've never programmed a computer before. Although this hour's lesson has provided a summary of the programming history and process, you're *much* better prepared to tackle Visual Basic's specifics.

In Hour 2 you'll learn about Visual Basic's environment so that you can create your very first program.

Hour 1 Quiz

You can find the answers for the following questions on the accompanying CD-ROM and on the Virtual Classroom Web site.

On the CD

1. **True or false:** Your computer can't understand high-level spoken languages such as English.

2. What language is the only language a computer can actually understand?

3. Why is Visual Basic more than just a computer language?

4. Explain why Visual Basic is easier to learn than many other languages.

5. Describe how Visual Basic adds visual impact to programs.

6. Which process produces more efficient and faster programs—an interpreter or a compiler?

7. Why should you conform to the standard Windows program interface as closely as possible when you write your own programs?

8. **True or false:** Controls are commands that control the way your Visual Basic program behaves.

9. **True or false:** Visual Basic has been a compiler and an interpreter since its inception.

10. What file-name extension do executable programs usually have?

Hour 1 Homework Exercises

1. Start Visual Basic, press Enter when you see the dialog box, and display the File menu by clicking Alt+F. Does the menu look familiar to you? Many options on the menu match the same File menu you'll see in Microsoft Word and Excel. Visual Basic looks and feels like a true Windows program and contains most of the common Windows elements you're used to seeing. Stick to the same! Keep the program menus and toolbars on the programs you write similar to equivalent options on other programs' menus and toolbars. Don't add a Quit option to your program's File menu when most other Windows programs use Exit. (By the way, choose Exit from the File menu to close Visual Basic and return to Windows.)

2. Start the Windows 95 or Windows NT Explorer and look at file extensions. You'll see lots that end with the .exe extension, meaning that those files are executable programs. Look in your Windows directory for files with names that look something like these: Vbrun300.dll, Vbrun400.dll, and Vbrun500.dll. These files are Visual Basic runtime modules that execute p-code generated from Visual Basic versions 3, 4, and 5, respectively. If you don't compile your application, you'll have to distribute the version 5 runtime module along with your program so your users can run the program's p-code. If you compile your programs, the programs will have no need for the runtime modules, and your programs will also execute more efficiently.

Creating Your First Application

NOW THAT YOU UNDERSTAND all about programming languages, event-driven programs, and how Visual Basic fits into the Windows picture, in this lesson you'll get your feet wet by learning about Visual Basic's programming environment. After you learn how to use the environment, you'll develop your very first Visual Basic application. Although this first application is extremely simple, it demonstrates event-driven programming.

When you finish this hour's lesson, you'll have a clearer understanding of event-driven programming and why Windows requires such programming, as opposed to the more traditional text-based environments.

Topic 1: The Visual Basic Development Environment

The Visual Basic development environment is simple yet powerful. The advanced features stay out of your way until you're ready for them. Therefore, you'll be able to get started in this hour's lesson by creating an application. But before digging into the nitty-gritty, you need to understand the Visual Basic development environment's windows and capabilities.

▶▶ **FAST TRACK**

Have you worked within Visual C++ or Visual J++'s development environment? If so, you should have little trouble working within Visual Basic's development environment, so you can skip to Topic 3, "Your First Application!" (p. 56).

Overview Visual Basic newcomers might find the Visual Basic development environment confusing. When you first start Visual Basic, you see a dialog box that may make little sense. When you get past the dialog box, the next step in program creation isn't obvious either. This topic section will try to make you comfortable within Visual Basic's environment, so you'll be ready to create an application with the development environment's tools in this hour's final topic section.

Starting Visual Basic Properly

When you first start Visual Basic, you'll see the New Project dialog box (see Figure 2.1). As you learned last hour, Visual Basic is a project-oriented development environment. Multiple files often comprise a Visual Basic application. When you first start Visual Basic, VB needs to know the kind of project you want to work with.

TIP If you don't want to see the New Project dialog box in subsequent sessions, click the option labeled Don't Show This Dialog in the Future. You still can create and load any kind of project with Visual Basic's menus. Without the dialog box, however, you have to tell Visual Basic what you want to do first.

FIG. 2.1
The New Project dialog box determines the kind of project you want to build.

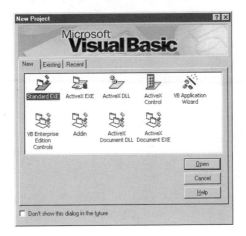

▼ NOTE

If you choose not to show the New Project dialog box at Visual Basic's startup, you won't be able to display that exact dialog box from elsewhere in the program. You can, however, create any of the dialog box's applications by selecting from Visual Basic's menus. **▲**

The tabs near the top of the New Project dialog box determine the actions you want to perform. The tabs correspond to the following actions:

- **New.** Lets you create new applications. As you can see from the icons shown on the New page, Visual Basic creates several kinds of new applications. Most of the applications that you create will be Standard EXE applications (the first icon). These standard applications are stand-alone Windows programs, such as a payroll program you write in Visual Basic. Also, you can create ActiveX-related controls and DLLs (*Dynamic Link Libraries*, which are sharable routines that multiple programs can use), or *add-in* routines that let you extend Visual Basic's capabilities. You also can start the Visual Basic Application Wizard, which helps you create programs.

- **Existing.** Lets you open a current Visual Basic project to edit or change (see Figure 2.2).

- **Recent.** Displays a list of recent Visual Basic projects that you've worked on. Often, you'll work on the same projects over a period of time, so you can return to your current work in progress easily.

FIG. 2.2

The Existing page in the New Project dialog box lets you open existing projects.

▼ NOTE

The applications you create with Visual Basic are true 32-bit applications that take advantage of the newest hardware supporting 32-bit-wide data paths. ▲

If you've just started Visual Basic and see the New Project dialog box, click the Cancel button to close the dialog box and return to Visual Basic's development environment so that you can review the environment in the next section.

▼ NOTE

Remember that Visual Basic programmers often use the terms *application*, *project*, and *program* interchangeably. ▲

Working Within the Development Environment

Visual Basic's development environment includes a complete windowed platform from which you can create Windows applications. The menus, toolbars, windows, and other tools that the development environment provides help you create applications as painlessly as possible—although with all those windows, the process is rarely *pane*-less.

Although the development environment can be fairly complex to newcomers, you don't need to learn all the development environment's ins and outs to write Visual Basic applications. In fact, you'll see in this hour's final topic section that you can create complete Visual Basic applications without ever using much of the development environment.

▼ **NOTE**

You can use wizard technology to create application shells. You see in this hour's final topic section, however, that the application shells don't have much functionality. To add punch to your applications, you need to learn more of the development environment. ▲

Figure 2.3 points out many of the components of Visual Basic's development environment. Take a moment to review the parts of the development environment screen.

FIG. 2.3

The development environment contains many components.

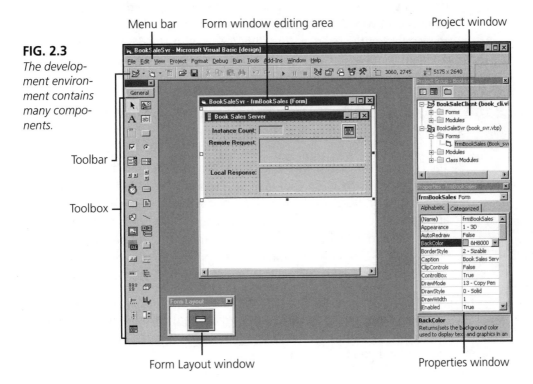

Menu bar   Form window editing area   Project window

Toolbar

Toolbox

Form Layout window   Properties window

▼ **NOTE**

Visual Basic supports many more screen components than Figure 2.3 shows. For example, your application may require *property pages*, which describe advanced properties for controls in your application. Visual Basic also supports an extensive debugger that includes a complete set of debugging windows. (You'll learn all about Visual Basic's debugging tools in Hour 36, "Debugging and Testing.") As you need these and other additional components, this night-school tutorial will explain them. For now, learn the basics so you can get your first Visual Basic application up and running quickly. ▲

The development environment is nothing more than a Windows program. Therefore, if you understand how to work with common Windows elements such as windows, toolbars, menus, status bars, and window-resizing buttons, you'll feel at home within the development environment.

Most of Visual Basic's windows are dockable and resizable. You can drag the development environment windows to different locations. When you *dock* a window to another, the combined windows act as though they are one window, and remain uncovered and visible if you open additional windows. If you want to close a window that you don't need now, such as the Form Layout window, you can close it and then redisplay it when you need to by selecting the window from the <u>V</u>iew menu. The development environment contains lots of windows, so you'll often rearrange and resize windows while programming.

TIP You can move toolbars and hide toolbars. You also can modify the size and scope of the development environment's tools.

The Form window contains the backdrop for your program's visual development. The Form window holds your application's forms, which can each contain one or more windows and additional forms. When you add to your application a control, such as a command button, you drag that control from the Toolbox (which generates tools you can use) to the Form window and place the control where you want it. You specify the controls' properties, such as their color and caption, inside the Properties window.

This process becomes clear almost immediately as soon as you begin creating applications within Visual Basic's development environment. For now, just familiarize yourself with the development environment and its components so that you feel comfortable there.

Example Visual Basic comes with several sample applications. One of the best ways to familiarize yourself with the development environment is to load a sample program and look at the windows. Follow these steps to load a sample application:

1. Start Visual Basic if you don't have Visual Basic running now.

2. Click the New Project dialog box's Existing tab to display a directory folder. You should see a listing of folders within the Visual Basic directory. If you don't see Visual Basic's directory, search for it by clicking the Up One Level toolbar button and opening program folders until you find it.

3. Double-click the Samples folder to display a list of sample application folders.

4. Double-click the PGuide folder to open additional sample folders. Each folder contains a complete Visual Basic project.

5. Double-click the ATM folder to open the ATM project. The dialog box will display only the ATM project name. The ATM project simulates an international automatic teller money machine.

6. Double-click the Atm.vbp name to open the project. Visual Basic opens the ATM sample application by loading the project into memory. As Figure 2.4 shows, the Form window doesn't appear when you first open a project because you don't always begin working on the form first.

FIG. 2.4
The ATM project is loaded.

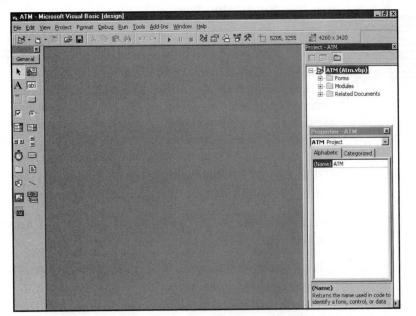

Pt I
Hr 2

At this point, you've loaded a sample Visual Basic application project into the development environment. The project doesn't look like much yet, primarily because of the closed Form window. Keep in mind that the Form window contains the primary application background and is what your users see when they eventually run the program.

The Project window shows three elements in the ATM project: forms, modules, and related documents such as resource files the program uses for external storage. You can expand and collapse the Explorer-like view by clicking the plus signs and minus signs that appear in the window. When you click the plus next to Forms, you see that ATM contains three forms: `frmAmountWithdrawn`, `frmInput`, and `frmOpen`. When you expand the Modules element, you see only a single module named `modATM`. The Related Documents folder contains a *resource file* named `atm32`. The resource file holds text and controls that make program maintenance more efficient. Although many projects contain multiple forms and possible multiple modules, simple applications may not contain more than a single form.

You already know what the forms hold (the elements the user sees, such as text and controls). Visual Basic modules hold VB programming code that tie the other elements together.

▼ NOTE

Each component resides as a separate file on your disk. The component's file name appears in parentheses to the right of the element. Therefore, the form named `frmAmountWithdrawn` is a file on your disk named frmamoun.frm, and the `modATM` module resides on your disk under the name of atm.bas. Forms always have the .frm extension, and modules always have the .bas extension. You can use uppercase or lowercase letters in file and component names. Often, the Visual Basic component name is shorter than the file that holds the component, so that you can tell more clearly from the name what the element does. **▲**

Follow these steps to view the Form window and to familiarize yourself with Visual Basic's screen components:

1. Double-click the Project window's `frmOpen` entry to open the Form window. Figure 2.5 shows the Form window that holds the form. (Now *that* looks more like a Windows program!)

FIG. 2.5

The Form window displays the application's primary features.

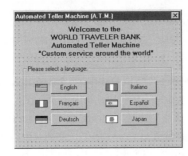

2. From the <u>V</u>iew menu choose <u>F</u>orm Layout Window to display the Form Layout window. This small window shows you where the form will eventually appear on-screen when the user runs the program. If you drag the miniature form inside the Form Layout window, Visual Basic changes the starting position of the form when the user runs the program. Previous Visual Basic programmers had to position the initial form through code or through Properties window settings.

3. Practice using the Toolbox by double-clicking the Command Button tool. A command button appears in the center of the form, but you can drag the new control down and to the left so that it's out of the way. Notice that the Properties window displays the new tool's properties. (The Properties window always shows the currently selected tool's properties.)

   Figure 2.6 points out each Toolbox control. You might see additional controls, depending on your Visual Basic setup; Figure 2.6's tools are the standard tools that always appear. If you forget what a Toolbox control is, put the mouse pointer over the tool to see a ToolTips message with the control's name.

FIG. 2.6

The Toolbox window's controls generate tools for your application's form.

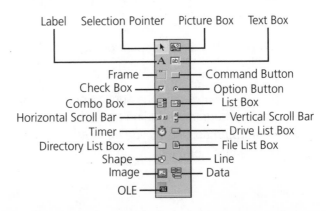

4. Delete the form's command button by clicking it once and pressing the Delete key. Visual Basic removes the command button, and you're back where you started.

5. Double-click the `modATM` entry in the Project window to see the Visual Basic code inside the module file. Scroll through the code to see what's ahead for you as a Visual Basic programmer. Although you may not "speak" the language yet, you'll be fluent in Visual Basic when you graduate from night school. Don't be concerned if the entire window contents confuse you—you're just looking around Visual Basic's Code window.

6. Close the module's Code window by clicking the Close window button above the Project window. Double-click the form's title bar to maximize the module window. The three window control buttons there apply to the open window in the middle of the screen, whereas the three control buttons to the right of Visual Basic's title bar apply to the Visual Basic system as a whole. Therefore, don't click Visual Basic's Close button, or you'll shut down Visual Basic.

7. Drag the Project window's title bar to the center of the screen to move the window.

8. Double-click the Project window's title bar to dock the Project window to Visual Basic's toolbar edge. By docking the window, you've ensured that the window remains on-screen.

9. Double-click the Project window's title bar again to undock the window, so you can move it back to the upper-right corner again. If you move the window to the Properties window, you'll dock both windows together. You then can drag the edges to resize the combined window and adjust the amount of each that appears at the same time.

Leave the ATM project open for the next section.

Next Step   Now that you've seen the application, why not see the results? Remember that the program, including all the forms and modules, comprise the computer instructions. Until you or another user runs the program, the instructions remain dormant.

To run a program from the development environment, click Visual Basic's toolbar's Start button. You can also choose Start from the Run menu or press F5 to run the program. Figure 2.7 shows the running program. Click one of the language buttons to start your ATM transaction.

FIG. 2.7
You're ready to make an ATM withdrawal with VB.

After you learn how to compile programs, you can run them from Windows without the Visual Basic development environment's interface. For most of this night-school series, however, you'll run your programs from within the development environment because you'll need the tools the development environment provides. To stop any running program, click the Close window on the running program's window, or click the development environment toolbar's End button. When you stop the program, Visual Basic returns you to the development environment.

▼ NOTE
If you exit Visual Basic or open another project, don't save any changes you made to the ATM project. Even moving around project windows can modify an application enough to make Visual Basic ask whether you want to save your changes. The ATM project is a sample project that demonstrates Visual Basic and comes with the system, so you should probably keep changes out of the samples by telling Visual Basic that you don't want to save changes when prompted. ▲

Topic 2: Get Help from Visual Basic

If you've used online help before, you may not think you need to read this section. Although you might be able to figure out Visual Basic's online help yourself, the help is fairly advanced and varies from most other online help you may be used to. This topic section describes some of the help tools available from within Visual Basic.

▶▶ **FAST TRACK**

Have you used online help until you're blue in the face? If so, you may really be tempted to skip this section. Visual Basic's online help includes a new Internet interface that you might want to know about. Therefore, you should skim the "Web Support" section (p. 52) to see how the Internet plays a role in providing Visual Basic help. If you truly don't want to mess with online help at this time, you can skip to the next topic section, "Your First Application!" (p. 56), to begin building your first Visual Basic application.

Overview Visual Basic's online help is so advanced, it often seems to offer more help than you'll ever need. Not only does Visual Basic offer the usual Windows online help selections—including context-sensitive help that looks at what you're doing and provides appropriate help—but the Visual Basic help system also uses Microsoft's Books Online references to place multiple reference titles on your disk. (To save disk space, you can access the Books Online from the Visual Basic CD-ROM by indicating that intent when you install or reinstall Visual Basic.) Also, Visual Basic's help system extends to the Internet, as you'll see in this topic.

Visual Basic's Online Help

Unlike most Windows programs, Visual Basic requires that you not only learn a new program interface, but also a new language. Microsoft designed Visual Basic's online help to give you help with the product as well as the language. You'll see that Visual Basic's help goes far beyond that of a regular Windows program, such as Microsoft Outlook.

The content-sensitive nature of Visual Basic's help system extends to almost every menu option, screen element, control, window, and language command. When you want help and aren't sure exactly where to turn first, press F1 and let Visual Basic give it a try. For example, if you think you need to use the Picture Box control but want to read a description first to make sure that you have the right control, click the Toolbox's Picture Box control and then press F1. Visual Basic sees that you've clicked the Picture Box control and returns with the help screen shown in Figure 2.8.

FIG. 2.8

Click any screen element and press F1 for help.

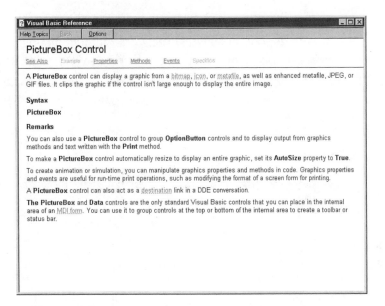

Throughout the help screens, Microsoft has scattered numerous links to related topics. When you click any underlined word or phrase inside a help window, Visual Basic responds with a pop-up definition or an additional help screen. Often, so many related topics appear throughout the help system that when you click a link, Visual Basic displays a scrolling Topics Found list (see Figure 2.9), from which you can choose the description that most closely matches the topic you need.

FIG. 2.9

Help links often provide several alternatives.

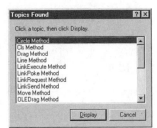

Often, Visual Basic not only *describes* a topic but also *prescribes* a solution! For example, if you click a control or property, Visual Basic not only displays a help screen when you press F1, but it also gives you an Example link.

When you click an Example hypertext link, Visual Basic displays a window similar to the one shown in Figure 2.10. Although the help might look ambiguous at this point, you'll grow to appreciate the helpful suggestion when you begin learning the Visual Basic language. The Example help link shows you real Visual Basic language code that uses the item you've requested help for. As a programmer, you'll therefore see how to implement the item inside your own Visual Basic code by looking at the sample Visual Basic provides.

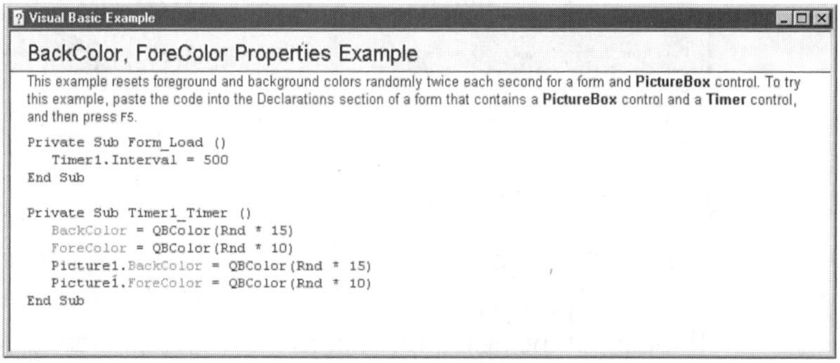

FIG. 2.10

Visual Basic shows you sample code that uses the property or control.

```
Visual Basic Example                                          _ □ ✕

BackColor, ForeColor Properties Example

This example resets foreground and background colors randomly twice each second for a form and PictureBox control. To try
this example, paste the code into the Declarations section of a form that contains a PictureBox control and a Timer control,
and then press F5.

Private Sub Form_Load ()
    Timer1.Interval = 500
End Sub

Private Sub Timer1_Timer ()
    BackColor = QBColor(Rnd * 15)
    ForeColor = QBColor(Rnd * 10)
    Picture1.BackColor = QBColor(Rnd * 15)
    Picture1.ForeColor = QBColor(Rnd * 10)
End Sub
```

The Help Menu

When you choose the first topic on the Help menu, Microsoft Visual Basic Topics, Visual Basic displays a help dialog box (see Figure 2.11). This dialog box contains the usual Windows-like help tools. You can open and close the book icons on the Contents page to read about different Visual Basic topics. You can search for a particular topic in the index by clicking the Index tab. To locate every occurrence of a particular help reference word or phrase, you can click the Find tab to build a comprehensive help database that returns multiple occurrences of topics.

When you need technical advice on Visual Basic, Microsoft has included a special Help menu option labeled Obtaining Technical Support that produces a dialog box similar to the one shown in Figure 2.11, and helps you locate the best technical advice. The technical support advice centers around your Visual Basic installation. If you experience bugs or if Visual Basic doesn't seem to be working the way it should, check out the Help menu's Obtaining Technical Support option to see whether you can find a solution.

FIG. 2.11

The Help menu produces a standard Windows help system.

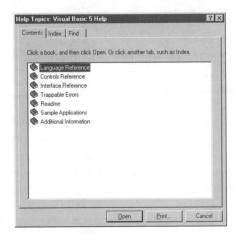

▼ **NOTE**

As you'll see from the technical support topics, Microsoft offers different levels of support—from free to pay-per-question support, depending on your needs and priorities. ▲

The Help menu's Books Online option is perhaps the greatest help asset in the system. Software packages and programming languages, such as previous versions of Visual Basic, often came with a truckload of heavy and bulky manuals that not only added to the software's price but also to your closet space.

At one time, Microsoft decided to offer these manuals separately—in bookstores and by mail order—to people who wanted them, and Microsoft reduced the number of manuals in its software packages. Users, however, often resented buying manuals separately when they were getting the manuals free (so it seemed) before. Fortunately, the CD-ROM gave Microsoft the needed cost-effective solution. Microsoft designed Books Online, a CD-ROM crammed full of reference and user manuals, as well as additional manuals that wouldn't ordinarily come with the program.

TIP The best feature of the combined online references comes when you need to look for a topic but have no idea where that topic is. When the documentation came printed, you might have had to search through several volumes' worth of indexes before you found your topic. Now, you only have to perform a search with Books Online's search tool to search one, some, or all of the Books Online references for your subject.

When you choose <u>B</u>ooks Online from the <u>H</u>elp menu, Visual Basic responds with Figure 2.12's Books Online screen. The left pane lets you open the books to see additional topics. The right pane provides the detail from your left-pane selection.

▼ **NOTE**

Microsoft does offer the references in printed volumes, and you can often order the references if you want them. Before ordering three tons of manuals, however, give Books Online a try. You'll probably find that you really don't need printed reference manuals anymore, especially after mastering this night-school course! ▲

FIG. 2.12
Books Online puts many reference volumes at your fingertips.

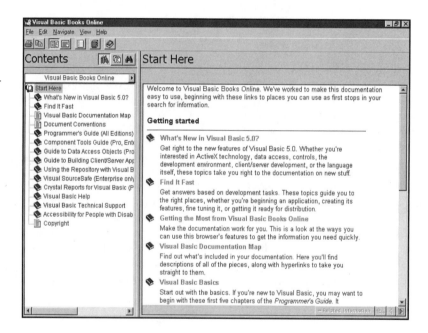

Web Support

As with this night-school series, Microsoft integrated Visual Basic's help topics on the Web so that you can get the latest and greatest information about Visual Basic as it happens. For example, Microsoft might opt to put Visual Basic updates on the Web or provide extra help not found in Visual Basic's online help systems. Also, Microsoft might provide corrections and bug workarounds. Whatever Microsoft decides to put on its Web sites, you can access those sites by choosing Microsoft on the <u>W</u>eb from the <u>H</u>elp menu.

▼ NOTE

Obviously, you must have access to the Internet and have a Web browser before you can access the Web's help topics. **▲**

Visual Basic uses a Web browser such as Internet Explorer to log on to the Internet and access Microsoft's Web sites. Before Microsoft integrated Web support into software, you were limited to the documentation and online help, unless you wanted to wait on hold for a long time while asking for advice on the telephone. The Web lets you access additional off-site help 24 hours a day when you need it.

When you choose Microsoft on the <u>W</u>eb from the <u>H</u>elp menu, Visual Basic starts your Internet browser and goes directly to the topic you selected, such as Figure 2.13's Online Support Web page.

FIG. 2.13

You now have 24-hour-a-day online help from within Visual Basic.

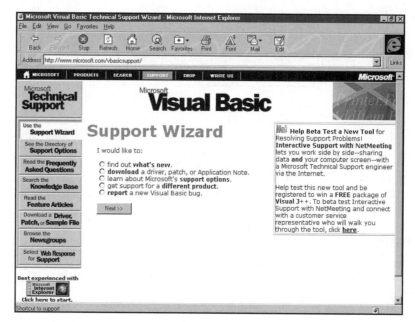

▼ NOTE

Visual Basic uses your default Web browser. Microsoft has particularly fine-tuned its Web sites for Internet Explorer, however, so the Microsoft Web pages seem to work best with that browser. **▲**

Example Start Visual Basic. Select Standard EXE in the opening New Project dialog box to close the dialog box and open a blank project. Click one of the Toolbox controls, such as Shape. Press F1 to view help on that control. Visual Basic sees which control you have just clicked and offers context-sensitive help.

While viewing the help window, look for links to other help topics. The links appear as underlined topics. Visual Basic offers two kinds of links:

- Definition links, indicated by a dotted underline. These links provide a pop-up definition for a term such as the one shown in Figure 2.14.

- Hyperlinks, which take you to additional help windows or to topic lists from which you can select.

Close the help window by clicking the window's Close button.

FIG. 2.14
Get an instant definition for help links with a dotted underline.

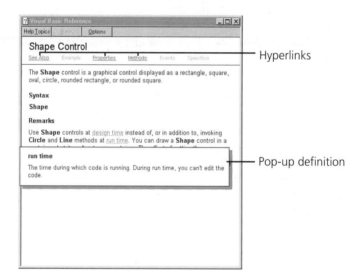

Next Step From the Help menu choose Books Online to display the Books Online opening window. Adjust the dividing line between the two window panes so that you can see more of the first column. You might notice that some topics in the left window (the book list) offer help for all Visual Basic editions, while others offer help only on the Professional or Enterprise Edition.

Although Visual Basic offers all the reference books for all Visual Basic versions, you can implement only the help topics in the version you have. (If you own the Enterprise edition, you automatically have the Professional and Learning editions.)

The Programmer's Guide applies to all editions, and you'll perhaps use the Programmer's Guide more than the other online books. To see the contents of the book, double-click the book icon at the left of the Programmer's Guide entry in the left pane. Visual Basic opens additional topics, or sections, within the book. Double-click the book labeled Part I: Visual Basic Basics; an additional set of topics opens. Open the book titled Introducing Visual Basic 5.0. Finally, double-click the topic labeled Welcome to Visual Basic to see a page icon, as Figure 2.15 shows.

FIG. 2.15

You've now opened the Books Online to an information page.

The page with details —

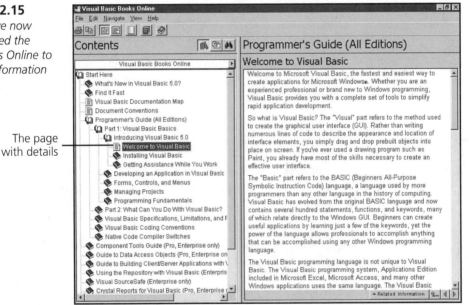

As you can see, you keep opening the book icons by first selecting a book and then selecting topics until you get to detail pages. The right pane then shows the detail for the topic you've selected. You can read the right pane (use the scroll bar, if necessary) and navigate through the topics in the left pane or by clicking the appropriate buttons on the small Books Online toolbar at the bottom of the Books Online window.

Pt I

Hr 2

TIP Check out the Books Online toolbar beneath the menu bar. Click the Print icon if you want to print any detail page you've read. The Copy button copies selected text to the Clipboard. To devote more screen room to your help topic, click the Topic Only button and then click the Navigation & Topic button to return to the summary and detail view.

One of the neatest toolbar buttons is the Notebook button. When you want to add your own notes to a topic, click Notebook, then click Add to Notebook, and type your text. After closing the notebook window, you can see your own notes if you ever return to the Books Online topic and click Notebook again.

The Glossary button offers an alphabetical glossary for every term related to Visual Basic programming in the Books Online.

Finally, one of the most important Books Online features is the View menu's Find command. Although you can read Books Online sequentially to learn about a particular topic, you'll almost always be hunting for information about a particular word or phrase. Type the word or phrase into the text box and press Enter to start a search. You can limit the search to book contents or to the topic details by clicking the appropriate toolbar buttons above the search text box.

Topic 3: Your First Application!

When you finish this short topic, you'll have created and run your very first Visual Basic application. Even though you may know nothing yet about Visual Basic application development, you can use Visual Basic to generate a simple Windows program. Granted, the program won't do a lot, but you'll see how to generate a working Windows program shell to which you can later add code and forms.

▶▶ FAST TRACK

Have you already mastered enough of Visual Basic's environment to develop fundamental programs and are comfortable enough to develop an application that uses several Windows controls? This lesson creates an initial application, but the application is little more than a shell built automatically by the wizard. If you've seen the wizard technology develop program shells (such as Visual C++'s AppWizard, which generates an application framework) you'll want to move onto Hour 3's lesson, "Adding Controls to a Program" (p. 63), which begins to describe specific details of application development.

Overview The VB Application Wizard generates a Windows program shell. By following a series of dialog boxes, you can tell Visual Basic to generate a Windows program with a menu, toolbar, title bar, status bar, and resizable window. Although the program will have no detailed functionality, you'll be able to run and exit the program just as you can run and exit other Visual Basic applications.

Pt **I**
Hr **2**

▼ **NOTE**

Until now, the Windows wizards that you've run have probably helped you use a program. For example, Microsoft Word contains a wizard that helps you set up a mail-merge system. The Visual Basic wizard doesn't really help you use Visual Basic; rather, it helps you generate your own program. The wizard walks you through a step-by-step process, asking you questions about the application shell that you want to create, and eventually creates the application according to your answers. ▲

Why a Wizard?

Visual Basic versions before 5.0 didn't include the Application Wizard. Therefore, you would have to create an application from scratch, creating all the forms and adding all the code for each application you wrote. The Application Wizard does the dirty work for you; most Windows programs have a menu and toolbar, so why not let the Application Wizard generate the fundamental program and then you fill in the details later?

The wizard creates a working Windows application shell. The Application Wizard is a great place to begin the programming process. Surprisingly, however, you won't use the Application Wizard throughout much of the Visual Basic night-school course! One of the best ways to learn Visual Basic is by creating applications from the ground up without the help of the wizard. When you understand the necessary programming fundamentals, you can add appropriate code to an Application Wizard program shell much more quickly, and know where and what to add to make the program work the way you need it to.

Starting the Application Wizard

You start the Application Wizard from the New Project dialog box or by choosing New Project from the File menu. Click the VB Application Wizard icon to start the wizard. Figure 2.16 shows the Application Wizard's opening dialog box.

FIG. 2.16

The Application Wizard begins to create your first application.

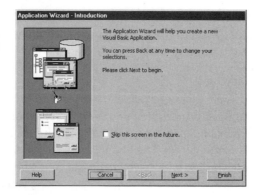

Application Wizard - Introduction

The Application Wizard will help you create a new Visual Basic Application.

You can press Back at any time to change your selections.

Please click Next to begin.

☐ Skip this screen in the future.

| Help | Cancel | < Back | Next > | Finish |

TIP Click the check box toward the bottom of the opening wizard dialog box if you want to bypass the opening and informational dialog box in the future.

Example Assuming that you started the Application Wizard in the previous section, follow these steps to build your first application:

1. Click the Next button to display the Interface Type dialog box. The wizard can generate one of three types of user interfaces for the application you're generating:

   - **MDI (Multiple Document Interface)** lets you create a program window that contains embedded windows called *child windows*.

   - **SDI (Single Document Interface)** lets you create a program with one or more windows that exist at the same level (not windows within windows).

   - **Explorer Style** lets you create programs that somewhat take on the Books Online appearance, with a summary of topics or windows in a left pane and the matching program details in the right pane.

   The MDI option should already be selected. If not, click it.

2. Click Next to display the menu selection dialog box. You can select certain menu options that will appear on your application's menu bar. By using the dialog box's options, you can help ensure that your application retains the standard Windows program look and feel. (You can add your own menu options after the wizard generates the program's initial shell.) For now, leave these options selected: File, Edit, Window, and Help.

3. Click Next to display the wizard's Resources dialog box (see Figure 2.17). A *resource* might be a menu, a text string, a control, a mouse cursor, or just about any item that appears in a program.

FIG. 2.17
Determine how your application's text resources appear.

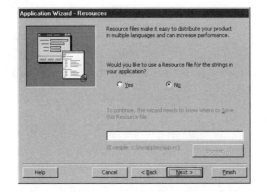

Resources that you might want the Application Wizard to store separately from your program are the text string resources. Visual Basic stores all your program's text in a separate, stand-alone resource file (which you can view, edit, and manage from the application's Project window). You can more easily translate your program's text that appears to the user into other languages, because all the text resides in the single resource file. If you don't create a resource file, you'll have to hunt through your program, looking for all the text if you want to translate the program into additional languages.

Despite the resource file's advantages, keep the No option selected for this example so that you don't have to enter a storage location for the resource file.

4. Click Next twice. The second time you click Next, you'll bypass the Internet connectivity dialog box because you don't need to add such

connectivity to your first application shell. The second dialog box, Standard Forms, determines which forms appear in your application:

- A *splash form* is an opening title form that your users see when they first run your application.
- A *login form* requests the user's ID and password, in case you want to add security features to your application.
- The *options dialog box* gives users the ability to modify certain application traits.
- The *About box* is accessed from most Windows <u>H</u>elp menus and provides your program description and version.

Check the <u>A</u>bout Box but leave the other options unchecked.

5. Click the <u>N</u>ext button twice to display the final Application Wizard dialog box. (You'll bypass the database access dialog box because you won't be retrieving database data in this first application.)

6. Click the <u>F</u>inish button. The wizard generates the application before your eyes. You'll see the wizard generating forms and titles; without the wizard, you would have to perform these steps yourself. When finished, the Application Wizard displays a dialog box to tell you that the application is completed.

7. Click <u>O</u>K to close the final Application Wizard dialog box. A summary report appears, to describe the generated program.

8. Click <u>C</u>lose to close the summary and return to the development environment.

Next Step In the preceding section, you generated your first application. Although the generation was simple and required only that you answer a series of dialog box questions, you need to see the results to make sure that the application did its job. Therefore, run the program by clicking the Start toolbar button. Visual Basic executes the generated application after asking that you save it.

Figure 2.18 shows the Visual Basic development environment with the running application that you generated. Although the form is empty, check out these features that work already:

- A working menu bar with several options
- Resizable program and child windows

- Window control buttons on the program and child windows
- A splash dialog box that appears when you choose <u>A</u>bout from the <u>H</u>elp menu (try it!)
- Scroll bars in the child window, in case text that you later add consumes more information than will fit in the window

FIG. 2.18
The generated application, although simple, contains several features already.

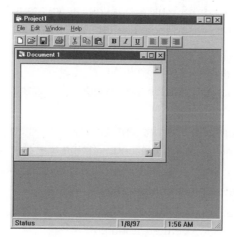

Close the program window. If you want to save your first application, use the <u>F</u>ile menu's <u>S</u>ave command. You've digested a lot of material in this hour's lesson, so take a break!

Summary

You're now a true Visual Basic programmer! You've mastered enough of Visual Basic's development environment to understand how to manage much of your application. Also, you can run the VB Application Wizard to generate program shells. Although the programs you can now create are extremely simple and have no specific details, this is just your second hour! You'll build on your skills every night you study Visual Basic.

In the next hour you'll learn more about Visual Basic's controls and build a more complete program from scratch. By bypassing the wizard, you'll learn more about the Visual Basic application development process. Controls make up the most important components of a program, because they perform interaction between the program and the user through the program's keyboard and mouse.

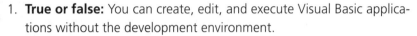

Hour 2 Quiz

You can find the answers for the following questions on the accompanying CD-ROM and on the Virtual Classroom Web site.

On the CD

1. **True or false:** You can create, edit, and execute Visual Basic applications without the development environment.

2. What are the kinds of applications you can create from the New Project dialog box and ultimately from within Visual Basic?

3. **True or false:** You can dock two Visual Basic development environment windows and move them as one.

4. Which development environment window holds the application's background?

5. Which development environment window generates the controls your application will use for interacting with the user?

6. **True or false:** You can execute Visual Basic applications only from within the development environment.

7. **True or false:** You can execute Visual Basic applications only from outside the development environment.

8. What two kinds of links does Visual Basic's online help support?

9. Why might you want to store an application's resources in a separate file?

10. **True or false:** Although the Visual Basic Application Wizard generates a program shell, you can't run that program shell until you add functionality to the program.

Hour 2 Homework Exercises

1. Start Books Online. Locate all the topics that contain the word *wizard*. Books Online will find several (the search is *case-insensitive*, so it doesn't matter if you type the search word in uppercase, lowercase, or a combination of uppercase and lowercase letters). Read through some of the topics, especially the one titled "What Are the Top 20 New Features?"

2. Generate another application with the VB Application Wizard. Change the options along the way—perhaps creating an Explorer Style—and run the application to see how it varies from the other application you generated in this lesson's third topic section.

Adding Controls to a Program

THIS LESSON IS one of the most important hours in your Visual Basic tutorial. In this lesson, you'll create a new project and add a new form to that project. The form will contain controls that interact with the user (the user is *you*, in this case) who runs your application. You'll create this application without the help of the Visual Basic Application Wizard. By creating the application from scratch, you'll learn important Visual Basic fundamentals that you'll use almost every time you work with Visual Basic.

The user interface is vital to your Windows programs, because the programs visually interact with users. In the text-based programs of old, programmers had to write tedious code every time they wanted to display information for users or request information from the

user. Visual Basic virtually eliminates all coding for I/O (input/output). Visual Basic takes care of the tedious details so that you can concentrate on your program's more important and application-specific details.

Topic 1: Creating New Applications

Without the VB Application Wizard, you need to control more of your application's creation details. For example, you'll size the Form window, add controls to the form, add possible extra forms, and specify the behavior of the application.

▶▶ FAST TRACK

Have you used a previous version of Visual Basic to add controls to forms? If so, you'll want to skip to the third topic section, "Setting Property Values" (p. 74), to see how Visual Basic 5 improves the control process.

Overview   Visual Basic creates empty projects that contain only one form when you create new applications from scratch. After you learn to create these initial projects, you'll need to add the details to the form so that your application does the work you need done.

The New Application Project

As you already know, a Visual Basic application contains at least one form and possibly several other files, such as extra forms, modules, and resources. Therefore, when you want to create a Visual Basic application, you'll need to create a new project. New projects are blank slates that you can change and build on as you create your final application.

TIP   Don't start a new application until you have a good idea what you want the application to do. Sketch the forms that the user will see, get a good idea of the data you want to produce, and design the output (such as reports) that you want the application to generate. Although Visual Basic offers a flexible programming environment that lets you change your mind after you begin building a new application (unlike former programming tools that made modification more difficult than it was worth), you should have a good idea where your application is headed before going to the keyboard to begin your project.

Creating the New Application

Follow these steps to start a new application:

1. If you've just started Visual Basic, double-click the Standard EXE icon to tell Visual Basic that you want to create a standard Windows program. If Visual Basic is already running, from the File menu choose New Project; then select Standard EXE from the dialog box that appears. Visual Basic creates a new project.

   Your screen should look similar to Figure 3.1. As you can see from the Project window (which displays all the application's components), the new project now holds only a single form, Form1.

Pt **I**
Hr **3**

FIG. 3.1
Visual Basic just created a new project.

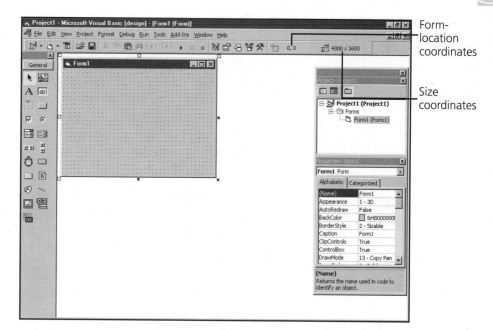

Form-
location
coordinates

Size
coordinates

2. In the Form window, drag the lower-right resizing handle down and to the right to expand the size of your application's form. Coordinates on the right side of the toolbar describe the width and height of the application's form. The coordinates appear in a twip measurement (a *twip* is one screen dot). Size your form so that it measures approximately 7,400 by 5,200 twips. This first application's form won't take much of the screen, so the resulting application will appear in a small window.

▼ **NOTE**

The toolbar not only shows the form's coordinate sizes, but also the placement of the form on the end user's screen. The default form location is 0,0, which means that the form will appear in the upper-left corner of the screen when you or someone else executes the application. The first coordinate measures the number of twips from the left of the screen; the second measures how far from the top of the screen the form's upper-left corner appears. Although you can change the location of the form by specifying properties as described in this hour's last topic section, you'll probably move the form's screen placement with the mouse from the Form Layout window. For this lesson, don't change the form's location. ▲

Standard Naming Prefix Conventions

One of the most important and useful tasks you can perform when you see a new application element is to name that element. The default name that Visual Basic supplies is usually a bad one. For example, the name Form1 is a lousy name for a form. If you were to add nine more forms and followed Visual Basic's naming conventions, your project would contains forms named Form1, Form2, and so on. By changing the default name to a more descriptive one, you'll better remember the purpose of the form later when you must work with multiple form lists.

Visual Basic programmers often use a naming prefix before such Visual Basic components as forms and controls. The prefix tells you what the component is. Therefore, you can distinguish between a form and a label control when you name the components `frmDataEntry` and `lblSaleCode`, whereas the underlying component type isn't obvious without the prefixes.

Table 3.1 contains a list of the common Visual Basic naming prefixes. When you assign a name to a Visual Basic element, use the prefix to clarify the underlying element's nature.

Table 3.1 Common Visual Basic Naming Prefixes

Prefix	Element Named
cbo	Combo box
chk	Check box

Prefix	Element Named
cmd	Command button
dir	Directory list box
drv	Drive list box
fil	File list box
fra	Frame
frm	Form
grd	Grid
hsb	Horizontal scroll bar
img	Image
lbl	Label
lin	Line
lst	List box
mnu	Menu
mod	Module
ole	OLE
opt	Option button
pic	Picture box
res	Resource
shp	Shape
tmr	Timer
txt	Text box
typ	User-defined data type
vsb	Vertical scroll bar

Pt I

Hr 3

Example   Study the callouts in Figure 3.2. Notice that the form's title bar contains the form name (Form1) and that the name also appears in the Project window. The Properties window also describes the form, as you can see from the name at the top of the Properties window. You should be getting familiar with how projects and their components go together to form a Windows application.

FIG. 3.2
The project names and property locations.

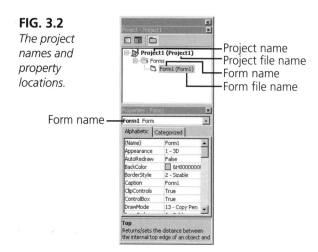

NOTE

Don't give a prefix to file names. The file-name extension describes the file type. For example, the .frm extension tells you that the file is a form file. Visual Basic uses the .vbp extension for Visual Basic project file-name extensions. Rarely will you need to work with individual Visual Basic files outside the Visual Basic environment, but you should understand the file-name extensions so that you'll be able to recognize what the file is for when looking through a directory of Visual Basic files. ▲

Although you won't begin working with the Properties window until Hour 4's lesson, you can use the Properties window to change the name of your form now for practice. Notice the top entry in the Properties window named (Name). (If you don't see the entry, scroll the Properties window to the top.) The current name is Form1, but you can change the name to frmMyFirst by clicking the (Name) entry and typing the new name.

NOTE

The Properties window describes all your application's components, including controls and forms, so the description to the right of each name helps you verify the Properties window's item now being shown. ▲

After you type the new name, notice that the Project window now reflects the form's new name (as does the Properties window text box).

The default file name that Visual Basic gives to all forms is the Visual Basic form name with the .frm extension. Therefore, when you eventually save the form to disk, Visual Basic will add .frm to the form's file name for you.

Next Step   Before adding more to your new application, save the project to disk—from the File menu choose Save *ProjectName*. The Save *ProjectName* command saves, in one step, your entire project and all the items in the Project window. (Before saving your project files, be sure to select an appropriate directory.) The Save *ProjectName* command first saves your forms (if you've yet to save them before now) and then the project itself.

Save *ProjectName* asks for a form name and a folder. The command uses the new form name you added in the previous section but uses Project1.vbp for the project name, which, as you might guess, is a bad name. Change the project's name to MyFirst before clicking OK to carry out the save (you don't need to type the .vbp extension; Visual Basic adds the extension for you). Visual Basic places the project's new name on VB's title bar at the top of your screen as soon as you name and save the project.

Pt **I**

Hr **3**

Now that you've saved the initial project, you can save later by using the Save *ProjectName* command, and Visual Basic won't prompt you again for the name.

> **TIP**   If you make extensive changes to a form and want to save the form but not the rest of the project, choose Save *ProjectName* from the File menu (Visual Basic replaces *ProjectName* with your current project's name on the File menu's Save *ProjectName* option).

Topic 2: Adding Controls to the Application

The new form is rather dull looking, but you'll change that in a hurry. This topic section explains how to add controls to your new form. Although the controls will arrive on your form in their generic format, you'll learn how to place and size them in this topic section, and then how to specialize the controls in the next topic section so that they look the way you want them to look.

Overview   Visual Basic offers several ways to place controls on your form. Generally, you'll double-click or drag a Toolbox control to your form. After you place a new control on the form, you then can size and move the control where you want it. Keep in mind that you'll place controls on your form during the design of your application. The controls won't behave as they will when users eventually run the program, but you'll see what the controls look like from within the development environment.

The Toolbox generates controls for your Form window. When you place a control on the form, that control comes from the Toolbox. The Toolbox holds an unlimited number of controls; you can get as many labels, text boxes, and other controls from the Toolbox as you need for your form. If you add additional forms to your application, the Toolbox supplies controls for those forms as well.

To place a control on the form, you can do one of two things:

- Double-click the Toolbox control. Visual Basic places and centers the control on your form. You then have to move and size the control to your preferences.
- Click the control and move the mouse pointer to the Form window. Drag to draw the control's outline on your form in the placement and size you need.

After you place a control on the form, you'll want to modify the control so that it behaves the way you expect.

Example   In this example, you create a simple application from scratch that you'll complete in Hour 4's lesson. Your first from-scratch application won't be fancy, but you'll learn Visual Basic fundamentals that you'll use every time you write subsequent applications. This application's Form window will contain the following controls:

- **Label.** A control that displays text on the Form window.
- **Command button.** A control that offers pushbutton capabilities to the Form window.
- **Image.** A control that holds and displays a graphic image on your Form window.

You'll start with the blank form you created in the previous topic section. Follow these steps to add controls to the form:

1. Double-click the Label control. Visual Basic puts a new label in the center of your Form window. Move the control higher on the form to the approximate position in Figure 3.3.

FIG. 3.3
You've placed and moved your first control.

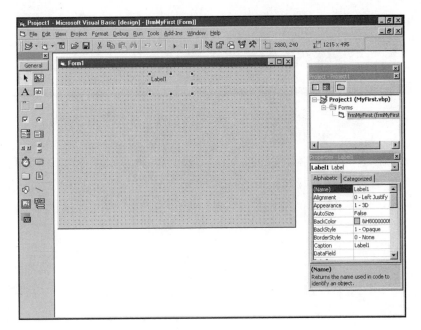

The control doesn't look like much, does it? You'll rectify that after adding other controls, as described next.

2. Double-click the Command Button control to place a command button in the middle of your Form window. Leave the command button where it appears for now.

3. Click the Image control *once*. Move your mouse to the Form window. The mouse pointer appears as a plus sign to show that you've selected a control.

4. Drag your mouse to outline the new Image control on the Form window. Figure 3.4 shows where you should place the control. Try to get close to the figure's placement and size.

As you can see from the measurements, Figure 3.4's Image control measures 2,175 twips wide and 1,825 twips in depth. The control starts (in the upper-left corner) at twip measure 2,520 (the number of twips from the left of the form) and 2,880 (the number of twips from the form's top edge). As long as you come close to these measurements, you'll have placed the control where it goes.

The Image control will hold a graphic image, but not until you specify the image's file name that will appear in the Image control's property.

FIG. 3.4

*The third control
is now placed at
the bottom of
the Form
window.*

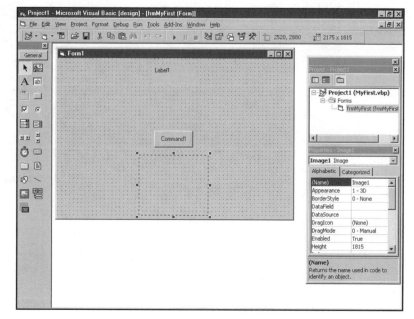

5. Open the Form Layout window by selecting <u>F</u>orm Layout Window
   from the <u>V</u>iew menu. You can see from the Form Layout window that
   your form will appear in the upper-left corner of the user's window at
   runtime.

6. Center the Form Layout window's form image on-screen by dragging
   the image with your mouse. You won't see the form itself move yet
   because you're not moving the form on Visual Basic's development
   environment screen with the Form Layout window; rather, you're
   specifying the location where you want Visual Basic to display your
   form at runtime.

This would be a good time to save your project (choose Sa<u>v</u>e *ProjectName*
from the <u>F</u>ile menu). You've already named and saved everything before, so
Visual Basic won't prompt you for form and project file names this time.

▼ **NOTE**

If you were to exit Visual Basic without saving your project, Visual Basic
would warn you that you haven't saved and give you one more chance to
save your work. Never turn off your computer while working with an open
Visual Basic project. Always exit Visual Basic to make sure that you've
saved all your recent changes. Actually, you should be in the habit of

shutting down Windows properly before powering off your computer so that Windows can safely store settings and close files correctly. ▲

Next Step   You've now added three controls to your form. The Form window may not look like much of an application, but you're close to making the controls look much better in the next topic section. Before sprucing up the controls and your application, this might be a good time to run your new application. That's right—even though you haven't done much, you *have* created a working application.

When you click the Start button, Visual Basic checks your application for errors, generates runtime codes, and runs your program. Figure 3.5 shows the result. Visual Basic still resides in the background, but you could run your program outside Visual Basic if you first compiled the code (which you won't do until Hour 6's lesson).

FIG. 3.5
You've created a running application.

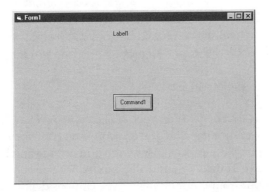

Although the control text isn't centered and you can't even see the Image control, you've learned the most important part of Visual Basic programming—placing controls. Much of a Visual Basic programmer's job takes place by managing controls on the Form window.

▼ NOTE
Don't worry, your Image control *does* appear on your Form window—you just can't see it. An image's default state is to show nothing and display no borders. You'll change the image's properties in the next topic section so that the Image control displays a picture when you run the program. ▲

Perhaps you're beginning to see why the controls are your program's path to the outside world. Users will use the controls to read your program's output and respond with program input. Therefore, you've created a working application with a full user interface without writing one line of Visual Basic code. Of course, the application won't do much until you put code behind the controls and write code that can tie the application's tasks together, but you've built much of the user interface already.

The Picture Box control works a lot like the Image control. You placed the Image control in this lesson's application because the Image control is much more efficient than the Picture Box control. The Image control responds more quickly by displaying its image faster than the Picture Box. Hour 19's lesson describes the Picture Box and explains how it varies from the Image control.

Click the command button a few times. See what happens? Visual Basic added all the code necessary to show the command button pushing in when you click it. You're triggering a Windows event as a result. The application does nothing to respond to that event, however, because no event code appears behind the command button. You'll add some code in Hour 4's lesson. For now, close your program by clicking the Close window button.

▼ **NOTE**

The grid of dots that appears on your application's form at design time doesn't appear at runtime. This grid lets you align controls with each other. You can hide the grid or change the grid dot spacing by choosing the General page of the Options dialog box, which you can display by choosing Options from the Tools menu. The Options dialog box contains the Align Controls to Grid option, which forces your form controls to move to the nearest grid dot when you place controls on your form. If you deselect this option, the grid can still appear as a guide, but you can place controls between grid dots. ▲

Topic 3: Setting Property Values

Properties, or property values, determine how controls are unique to one another. Without changeable properties, every command button would be the same size and color, contain the same caption, and be indistinguishable from any other command button on your form. Most of the controls support these common properties:

- Size
- Location
- Color (foreground and background)
- Border
- Caption
- Font

This topic section explores some of these more common control properties and ends by letting you modify your application to make the form's controls look better. Figure 3.6 shows a form with eight command buttons. All the command buttons work the same—that is, when you click a command button, you trigger an event that causes each button to look pushed in. As you can see, however, the different properties of the eight command buttons make them look completely different from each other.

FIG. 3.6
Command button properties distinguish controls from one another.

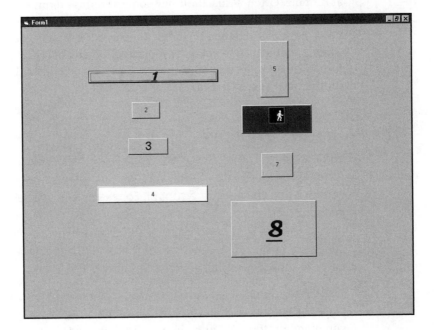

Overview   You're used to working with properties in everyday life. Some people are thin, some are fat, some honest, some dishonest, some law-abiding, some law-breaking, some nice, some mean, and so on. Each description is a *property* that you can attribute to some people. The properties that you set for controls gives each control a "personality" and look, just as character traits give each person a different personality and look.

You can set some properties at design time, some at runtime, and some at both times. When you want to change the appearance or behavior of a control during the program's execution, your Visual Basic code will change that control's properties. If a control doesn't change during a program's execution, you'll set that control's properties when you write your program (at design time). If certain properties—such as items in a list box control—aren't available at design time, you'll have to set those properties at runtime with code.

▼ DESIGN TIME VERSUS RUNTIME

Visual Basic programming requires a special thinking mode. You need to distinguish between *runtime* events and *design-time* requirements. You write and modify your application at design time. You run the application at runtime. Often, Visual Basic newcomers confuse terms such as *events* and *properties*. The job becomes more confusing when you learn about Visual Basic *methods* and *modules*. Keep in mind that an *event* occurs when you or someone else runs your program and performs some action, such as click a command button. A *property* is a descriptive fact about a control, such as the control's size or color. ▲

The Properties Window

You'll see each control's property in the Properties window. The Properties window changes to display every design-time property available for a control when you select the control. For example, if you select your application's command button, the Properties window displays properties unique to command buttons and lets you set specific values for the selected command button. If you then select the label, the Properties window updates to show you the label properties now set.

Visual Basic automatically assigns default values to each control when you place the control on your form. For example, Visual Basic assigns the first command button the `Caption` property `Command1`. That's why you see the `Command1` caption on the control that you placed on your application's form.

Many of the default values work fine, but you'll almost always change some of the values. For example, the `Top` and `Left` properties indicate where the control appears on your form. If you drag the control to a

different location, Visual Basic automatically updates these location properties for you. Rather than drag the control, you could enter their twip locations directly in the Properties window, and Visual Basic moves the controls
to the specified location as soon as you enter the property value.

> **TIP** You don't have to select a control to work with that control's properties.
> Rather than click a control, you can select a control from the Properties window's
> drop-down list box. Figure 3.7 shows the Properties window's control-selection
> drop-down list box.

FIG. 3.7
*Select the
control whose
properties you
want to modify.*

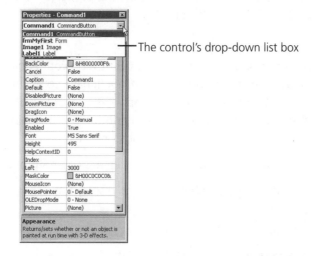

The control's drop-down list box

Notice that Visual Basic displays a description of the selected property at
the bottom of the Properties window. Therefore, you don't have to display
help if you forget what a property specifies. Also, if you click the Properties
window's Categorized tab, you see the selected control's properties organized by such categories as appearance and screen position. By collapsing
categories you don't want to see, you can hide the properties that you're
not interested in at the moment.

Form Properties

Controls aren't the only Visual Basic items with properties. Notice that Figure 3.7's Properties window drop-down list includes the form as well. Forms
have properties.

Think about how one form might vary from another. One form might be blue, whereas another is red. A form's title bar could hold a title that describes the form's contents. The form might support the use of a control menu and icon, or no control menu. A form's window might be resizable, or you may not want to give users the ability to resize the form's window.

You're rarely finished with an application until you specify the form's properties. If you look at the sample application from the previous two topic sections, notice that the form's title bar shows `Form1`, even though you've assigned the name `frmMyFirst` to the form. The form's title—called a *caption* in Visual Basic terminology—is a control property you'll change before you complete this hour's lesson.

Example   It's now time to add properties to the controls on your application's form. Before you complete this hour's lesson, you'll have completely improved the appearance of your application. The application still won't do anything (other than let you click the command button), but the application will contain a proper form caption and control properties.

Follow these steps to modify your application's control properties:

1. Click the control named `Label1` to display the label's properties in the Properties window.

2. Click the Properties window's `Caption` entry.

3. Type **Have a happy day!** As you type, you'll see the label's caption change.

4. Click the Properties window's `Font` entry. A font name doesn't appear, but an ellipsis does. Ellipsis after a property value always indicates that you can select from a list of choices rather than type the value directly into the Properties window.

5. Click the `Font` entry's ellipsis to display the Font dialog box. A font supports multiple properties, so you must use the dialog box to specify the font name, size, and style.

6. Select the Courier New font, with a Bold style and a 36-point size.

7. Close the Font dialog box. Resize the label's caption to see more of it. Although you can drag the label's edges, you'll instead enter location

and size values directly in the Properties window so that your application matches the one in this book.

8. Set these Properties window values: `Left`, 1,320; `Height`, 1,695; `Top`, 120; and `Width`, 4,695. You can now read the new label's caption, but the caption is still left-justified. Expand the Properties window's width if you need more room to read the property values.

9. Click the label's `Alignment` property. Click the drop-down list box arrow to open the list box and you'll find three values: Left Align, Right Justify, and Center Justify. Select Center Justify, and the label straightens up nicely.

Pt **I**

Hr **3**

▼ **NOTE**

Notice that Visual Basic displays numbers to the left of each property. You could type a number to select the number's corresponding alignment style. Also, you'll use the numbers inside Visual Basic code to set property values without having to type the entire description, such as **Right Justify**. ▲

At this point, your screen should look something like the one in Figure 3.8.

FIG. 3.8

The label now contains a nice caption.

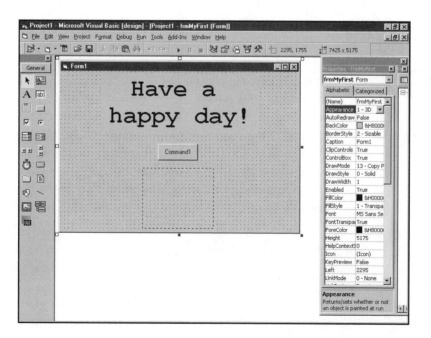

10. Select the form's command button, click the **Caption** property, and then type **Click Here** for the caption.

11. Save your project. You're not going to do anything with the image until Hour 4's lesson, when you'll add some code to surprise users with a pop-up image.

As you learn Visual Basic, you'll also learn about several *literals* (sometimes called *named literals* or *named constants*) that correspond to property values. For example, Visual Basic recognizes a constant named **vbLeftJustify** that corresponds to the **Alignment** property's Left Justify value. In addition to assigning 0 to the property when you want to change a control's alignment to left-justified through code, you can assign **vbLeftJustify** to the control. When maintaining the program later, you'll recognize what **vbLeftJustify** means more quickly than you would remember what 0 stands for, even though both mean the same in this control's **Alignment** property. This night-school tutorial will keep you posted on the best use of the named constants when you begin programming.

Next Step   As your applications become more complicated, you'll learn ways to make the program creation run smoothly. As your applications become more powerful, you'll use Visual Basic code to access controls and properties. To make that access more manageable, you should assign names to your controls. Although Visual Basic assigns default names, such as **Command1** and **Label1**, you should assign names that use the naming prefix followed by a description of the control. For example, you could change your application's label name (specified by the **(Name)** property at the top of the Properties window) from **Label1** to **lblHappyApp**. Change the command button name from **Command1** to **cmdGetHappy** (you'll see why that name is good in Hour 4's lesson). Although the Image control still is invisible, go ahead and change its name to **imgViewHappy**.

Taking the time to change control names might seem a waste of time at this point, but the names pay dividends later as you add to your programs. In Hour 4's lesson, you'll add Visual Basic event code to your controls, and your code will be clearer if you rename your controls now. You'll have no ambiguity, especially if you later decide to add additional command buttons and labels to your project.

In addition to the controls, you should modify the form's properties. The only property that really needs changing is the form's caption; change it to **Happy Face**. Also, select `False` for the `MaxButton` property, so the user won't be able to maximize the application's window to full screen and the controls will stay centered on the form.

When you run your application, you'll see the application's window appear like the one in Figure 3.9. The window's maximize button is grayed out, so users can only minimize the window.

FIG. 3.9
*Your appli-
cation's window
is looking better.*

Save your project so you can continue adding functionality to it in Hour 4's lesson.

▼ NOTE
Unlike this lesson's example, you won't always add all your form's controls before setting their properties. Usually, you'll add a control and set many or all of its property values before adding additional controls. After you add several controls to a form and see how they look together, you may need to change additional properties, such as their sizes and locations. ▲

Summary

You can now place controls on your form and modify the control properties. The user interface is vital to an effective end-user application. Fortunately, Visual Basic takes care of the tedious details and handles the user interaction; your job is to place those controls and make them look and behave the way you want them to look and behave.

How are you supposed to know every property that exists for every kind of control? Actually, very few Visual Basic programmers know all the control properties because there are too many properties to remember, and you rarely change many of them. The Visual Basic online help system displays a list of properties if you click **Properties** on any help screen that describes a control. You'll see more controls than you'll see in the Properties window because of the controls that you can modify only at runtime with code.

In Hour 4 you'll learn how to teach your application to respond to events. At the end of the lesson, your application will be complete, and your program will respond directly with users at the keyboard.

Hour 3 Quiz

You can find the answers for the following questions on the accompanying CD-ROM and on the Virtual Classroom Web site.

On the CD

1. What's the default name that Visual Basic assigns to a new project's form?

2. Why do you not use prefixes for Visual Basic component file names?

3. What file-name extension does Visual Basic use for project files?

4. **True or false:** Visual Basic property values describe the costs of owning real estate.

5. Why does the form have properties?

6. What's the name of the command button title's property?

7. **True or false:** You can't change some properties at design time.

8. Why do some property values have an ellipsis after their Properties window entry?

9. Why should you change the control names from their default values?

10. How can you keep users from using your application window's maximize button?

Hour 3 Homework Exercises

1. Save this lesson's project under a new name, perhaps *Homework3*, so that this exercise won't change the book's application. Modify the new project as follows: Change the command button's **Background**

color property to blue. Run the application to see what happens. The result might surprise you because the command button won't be blue! Some properties, such as command button colors, require that you set additional properties. Change the command button's `Style` property to Graphical; the command button turns blue when you run the application.

2. Create a new project and add two command buttons to the form. Make the buttons look different by using a different font and color on each. Add a label between the two buttons that reads *A button above and below*. Name your controls and change the form title to *My 2nd Application*. Although this exercise is simple, you'll be reviewing this hour's lesson well if you create this application.

Pt I

Hr 3

Activating Controls

THIS LESSON PUTS ACTION into the controls you learned about in Hour 3's lesson. Although your first application has several nice-looking controls, the controls don't do anything. You'll add code this hour to activate those controls so that something happens when users use one of them.

In this hour, you'll gain some insight into the Visual Basic language. When you activate a control, you do so with VB programming code. The code goes in a special program section called an *event procedure*. If you write an event procedure for a certain event, such as a mouse click, the code inside that event procedure executes.

Topic 1: Control Events

Each control has its own set of events that the control supports. You can probably predict many control events. For example, one obvious command button event is the click event, called—appropriately enough—`Click`. Even forms have their own set of events, such as `Click`, `DblClick`, `Resize`, and so on. As you become more familiar with events, you'll learn which events go with certain controls.

▶▶ **FAST TRACK**

Are you familiar with Windows events? If so, move to the next topic section, "Event Procedures" (p. 91), to learn how to implement event controls in Visual Basic.

Overview Almost anything users can do on a form or with controls on a form is an event. A huge number of events exist simply because of the huge number of user possibilities. Not only does an event occur when you move your mouse but also when you drag your mouse. Some actions trigger multiple events. When you double-click your mouse, a single click occurs then as well and a mouse up event occurs when you release your mouse button.

Visual Basic must be able to distinguish among various similar and different events so that Windows passes as many detailed events to your program as possible. Your program can respond to none, some, or all events. Rarely will you ignore all events or handle all events that Windows passes to your program. Instead, you'll handle those events that apply to your program, and the form and controls in your program, and you'll ignore the rest.

▼ **NOTE**

Not all events are user-triggered. In Hour 23's lesson, "Enhancing Your Program," you learn that your computer's internal clock triggers an event at every tick. ▲

The following sections explain some of the events possible with the form and the three controls you've added to Hour 3's application.

▼ **NOTE**

These sections review only the bare-bones fundamental and most common events. When you learn how to deal with these events, you'll have no trouble accepting additional events described throughout the rest of this night-school tutorial. ▲

Form Events

Generally, you don't capture very many form events in applications. Often, the form events that you deal with are the events that occur when your user starts or quits your application. Here's a list of common form events:

- The `Activate` event occurs every time the form gets the focus.
- The `Click` event occurs when users click the mouse over the form.
- The `DblClick` event occurs when users double-click the mouse over the form.
- The `Deactivate` event occurs when another form becomes the active window.
- The `Initialize` event occurs when Visual Basic generates the form.
- The `Load` event occurs when the form first loads.
- The `Paint` event occurs when Windows must redraw the form because you moved or closed a window that was hiding all or part of the form.
- The `Resize` event occurs when users resize the form (not available if you've hidden the form's control menu).
- The `Unload` event occurs when your application unloads the form from memory. The `Unload` event automatically occurs when users close your application.

Command Button Events

Although almost every application you create will contain one or more command buttons, the command button doesn't support as many events as most of the other Visual Basic objects, such as forms and text boxes. The command button is simpler than many of the other controls.

Here's a list of common command button events:

- If the `Cancel` property is set to `True`, the command button is the button clicked when users press the Esc key. Only one command button can have its `Cancel` property set to `True`; all the rest must be `False`. A command button with a caption of `Cancel` or `Exit` usually has the `Cancel` property set to `True`.
- The `Click` event occurs when users click the command button.

- If the `Default` property is set to `True`, the command button is the button clicked when users press Enter. Only one command button can have its `Default` property set to `True`; all the rest must be `False`. A command button with a caption of `OK` usually has its `Default` property set to `True`.

- The `MouseDown` event occurs as soon as users click and hold the mouse button over the command button.

- The `MouseUp` event occurs as soon as users release the mouse button.

Label Events

Labels usually are dormant and simply display text such as titles and instructions. Users can't enter text in a label or change the label's text directly. (The label's text changes only through Visual Basic programming code.) Labels can be the result of an event, however. Here's a list of common label events:

- The `Change` event occurs when the label's text (held in the `Caption` property) changes.

- The `Click` event occurs when users click the label.

- The `DblClick` event occurs when users double-click the label.

- The `MouseMove` event occurs when users move the mouse over the label.

Image Events

You'll see in the next topic section that the Image control displays graphic images. Although your sample application has yet to do anything with its image, such as make the image display a picture, you can probably imagine that the Image control supports several events. After all, the Image control is a lot like a Label control, except that the Image displays a graphic image and not text.

Here's a list of common Image control events:

- The `Click` event occurs when users click over the image area.

- The `DblClick` event occurs when users double-click over the image area.

- The `MouseDown` event occurs whenever users click and hold the mouse over the image area.

- The `MouseUp` event occurs whenever users release a mouse button with the mouse pointer over the image.

- The `MouseMove` event occurs when users move the mouse over the image.

Triggering Events

Almost any event that you want triggered can be. Both keyboard and mouse users can trigger many of the keyboard and mouse events. Consider, for example, the number of ways you can trigger the `Click` event. You already know that the `Click` event occurs whenever users click the left mouse button. The `Click` event also can occur in response to a number of other events:

- On certain controls, pressing the right mouse button triggers the `Click` event. This happens when the object under the cursor at the time of the click is the form itself. If, however, the object is a command button, a check box, or an option button, only the left mouse button will produce the `Click` event.

- When a command button has the focus—as it always will in your application that contains only a single command button—pressing the space bar triggers the `Click` event.

▼ NOTE
The active control on the form is the one with the *focus*. You'll learn more about focus in this lesson's third topic. ▲

- If a command button's `Default` property is set to `True`, pressing Enter triggers the event.

- If a command button's `Cancel` property is set to `True`, pressing Esc triggers the event.

- You can set a command button's `Value` property to `True` with code and thus trigger the event.

- If a shortcut key has been defined in the `Caption` property of an object (such as `&Help` on a help button), pressing Alt+H triggers the event.

▼ NOTE

If you see an underlined letter in a command button's caption, you know that you can "click" the command button by pressing the Alt key along with the underlined letter. The ampersand (&) before any character in a caption specifies that character as the shortcut character. Users won't see the ampersand in the label's caption but will see an underlined letter instead. **▲**

Example As with the control properties, you'll learn many control events just by using Visual Basic. The true goal of your application hasn't yet been revealed to you, but you've probably almost figured out what the application will do, especially after you add the suggested names from last hour's lesson.

This hour, you'll set up your application to display a happy face in the image area when users click the center command button. Figure 4.1 shows what the finished application will look like when users click the button.

FIG. 4.1

The application displays a happy face when users click the command button.

TIP Visual Basic comes with several graphic images. The happy face is actually an icon that you'll stretch to the Image control's measurements.

Obviously, you're going to have to handle the command button's `Click` event. The label doesn't need to respond to any events, and neither does the image. (This application is staying fairly simple because you're still new to Visual Basic.)

Visual Basic supports a special mechanism for handling the events you want to handle and for ignoring all the others. You'll have to see some Visual Basic programming code first, and then learn how to complete this application in the next topic section.

Before moving onto event code, give your application's command button the Alt+C shortcut keystroke—in other words, change the `Caption` property to read `&Click Here`. As soon as you type the caption, you'll see that the command button's first letter is underlined, indicating the shortcut keystroke's designation.

▼ **NOTE**

Any letter, not just the first letter, can be a command button's shortcut key. You can also apply shortcut keystrokes to other controls, such as option buttons and check boxes. ▲

Pt **I**

Hr **4**

Next Step   Your application can use the `Load` form event. When Visual Basic loads the form, you can request that Visual Basic center the form inside the screen's coordinates automatically.

You used the Form Layout window last hour to center the form within the screen's boundaries. However, Visual Basic can position the form more accurately within the screen's coordinates and can even center the form, no matter what kind of monitor end users have.

The users' screen is a special fixed object that's always available to your Visual Basic program. Your program can access the screen by using the `Screen` object name. As with Visual Basic controls, the `Screen` object has properties that you can access. Two helpful `Screen` properties are `Width` and `Height`. By calculating the center of the screen from the `Screen`'s `Width` and `Height` properties, you'll ensure that Visual Basic will center your form on every computer your application runs on. The next topic section centers the form through Visual Basic code.

Topic 2: Event Procedures

Windows sends to your application all events that apply to the application. Handling or ignoring Windows events requires only that you

- Write an *event procedure* for all events you want to handle
- Don't write event procedures for any events you want to ignore

This topic describes what event procedures are, how to specify them, and how to implement event procedures in your sample application.

▶▶ FAST TRACK

Have you written Visual Basic code before? If so, skip to this topic's example section (p. 96) to learn about Visual Basic 5's Auto Quick Info pop-up help. You'll wish you had that feature sooner!

Overview   An event procedure contains Visual Basic code. The Visual Basic code describes the instructions that your computer is to follow when the event occurs. For example, if you write an event procedure for the command button's `Click` event, Visual Basic executes that event procedure only if users click your application's command button. If users never click the command button, the event never occurs, and the code in your command button event procedure never executes.

Event Procedures

Before looking at event procedure specifics, look back at the preceding topic section's event lists. Notice that the form, command button, label, and image all support the `Click` event. In other words, if users click the mouse over any of these four objects, a `Click` event occurs. Your program, however, must know *which control* (or form) users were clicking over.

Remember that every handled event requires an event procedure. The event procedure name is a special name that not only names the event handled, but also *the control name that received the event*. All event procedures have names; the names describe *both* the control and event that produced the event.

Here's the format of event procedure names:

```
ControlName_Event ()
```

To write an event procedure for a mouse click over the command button, you would name that event procedure `cmdGetHappy_Click ()`. The underscore separates the control name from the event.

▼ **NOTE**

The parentheses aren't actually part of the event name, but you'll always see parentheses after every event procedure name. The parentheses are often empty, but they sometimes hold items that you'll learn about as you progress through your Visual Basic night-school training. ▲

Therefore, in the application you're creating, if users click the command button that you've named `cmdGetHappy`, the application will execute any code you've stored in an event procedure named `cmdGetHappy_Click ()`. If you don't write the event procedure, however, your application would do nothing when users click the command button.

▼ **NOTE**

You must know the control's exact name (through its `Name` property listed at the top of the Properties window as `(Name)`) and the name of the event you want to handle if you want to know the name of that control's event procedure. Fortunately, Visual Basic can automatically generate event procedure names for you, as you'll see in a moment. Thus, you don't even have to type the special event procedure name because Visual Basic generates the name for you and automatically separates the control name from the event with the required underscore character. ▲

A Sample Event Procedure

Here's the complete event procedure that you'll add to your application's command button:

```
Private Sub cmdGetHappy_Click()
  imgViewHappy.Picture = LoadPicture("C:\My Documents\
                    ➥VB NightSchool\Happy.bmp")
End Sub
```

The code is only three lines long, and the first and last lines really do nothing more than identify the event procedure's starting and ending points.

> **TIP** Indent the *body* (the code lines between the first and last lines) of event procedures so that you can quickly locate executable code from a listing of event procedures.

Almost every event procedure that you write will begin with `Private Sub`. The `Private` keyword is optional; if you don't specify `Private`, Visual

Basic assumes that the event procedure is private anyway. By specifying `Private`, however, you clarify your intention to leave the procedure as a private procedure. When a procedure is private, only other procedures within the current module have access to the procedure.

Visual Basic supports two kinds of procedures: functions and subroutines. Although both look similar, they vary in how they terminate. A *function*, indicated by the `Function` keyword, always returns a value to somewhere. *Subroutines*, indicated by the `Sub` keyword, don't return values. A control's event procedure doesn't return a value, so control event procedures are subroutines. Hour 13's lesson explains the differences between subroutines and functions in much more detail.

▼ **NOTE**

A *keyword* is a built-in Visual Basic language command or routine. When programming, as you'll learn in this book's second part, you often need to assign names to various program elements. You can't assign keywords to your own program elements. ▲

The name of the subroutine, `cmdGetHappy_Click`, tells you that this subroutine is the command button's `cmdGetHappy` click event procedure. The event procedure executes *only* when users click over the command button named `cmdGetHappy`. If this is the only event procedure in the entire application, the application will ignore all other events that Windows passes to it. Therefore, if users move the mouse over the command button or click the label or the image control, the program will ignore these events sent to it.

Event procedures can range from one to several hundred lines. Generally, event procedures are short, from three to 10 lines. If an event procedure grows to more than 20 or so lines, most Visual Basic programmers will break up the event procedure code into external smaller procedures and trigger those procedures from within the event procedure.

This event procedure's body is only one line long. Not much has to happen when users click the command button. During design time when you write the program, the image control's `Picture` property stays blank (indicated by `(None)` in the Properties window). When users click the command button, the Image control displays the happy face, a bitmap graphic image that comes with Visual Basic.

▼ **NOTE**

Notice how you specify properties in Visual Basic code. Type the control name, followed by a period, followed by the property name. Therefore, `imgViewHappy.Picture` refers to the `Picture` property for the control named `imgViewHappy`. If the form contained another Image control, the other control wouldn't be affected by this line. ▲

If you were to assign a picture to an image at design time, you can type the path name and bitmap file name into the Properties window's `Picture` property. However, if you want to assign a bitmap picture to the Image control at runtime, you must use the `LoadPicture()` built-in function. Remember that functions return values, and the `LoadPicture()` function returns a bitmap image. The end result of the event procedure's middle line is the loading and assignment of the picture to the image. As soon as the assignment takes place (when users click the command button), you see the image on the running form.

▼ **NOTE**

You *must* assign the full path name of the Happy.bmp file to the file's location on your own disk; otherwise, the application won't find the bitmap. Therefore, change `LoadPicture()`'s path name from this lesson's \My Documents\VB NightSchool directory folder to the location of Happy.bmp on your computer. You can use the Windows Start menu's Find command to locate the file. If the file is buried deeply inside multiple directories (as is probably the case), you should copy the file to a simpler location. ▲

Visual Basic must know where your event procedure ends. All subroutine procedures end with the `End Sub` *statement* (a code line); all function procedures end with the `End Function` statement. The command button event procedure is a subroutine, hence the termination of the code with `End Sub`.

You'll create this event procedure (with your computer's Happy.bmp's path name) in the example that follows the next section.

The Code Window Editor

Now you understand the event procedure. But how and where do you enter the code? Visual Basic makes it easy. VB uses a *Code window* to hold code that you write and edit. The Code window contains Visual Basic's

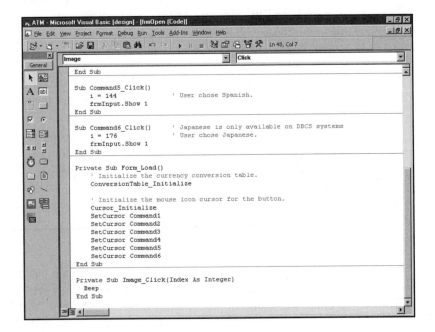

editor. Figure 4.2 shows an example Code window. As with most windows, you can resize the window and place it where you want it to appear.

FIG. 4.2

Enter and edit VB code inside the Code window.

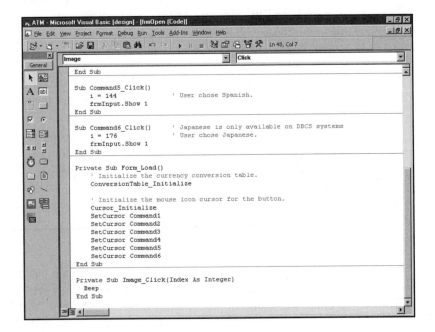

The Code window's editor works like a word processor, except that the editor doesn't wrap lines of text. You need to press Enter at the end of each line of code that you type. You can insert and delete text just as you can inside word processors, and the Windows Clipboard operates as you expect. If your line gets too long to read inside your Code window, put an underscore at the end of the line and continue the statement on the next line.

Example To complete the application with the happy face, you first might want to locate and move the Happy.bmp file to your application's disk location, if you haven't already done so.

Also, you must modify one Image control property that isn't set properly for this application. By default, the **Stretch** property is set to **False**. If you leave the **Stretch** property set to **False**, the happy face won't stretch to the control's full size but will appear as the bitmap's actual size, which is much smaller than the control. Change the **Stretch** property value to **True**. When the image subsequently displays the happy face, Visual Basic stretches the happy face to the size of the Image control's boundaries; the happy face appears on your application's form stretched larger than its disk image.

After you change the image's `Stretch` property to `True`, you must add the event procedure for the command button's `Click` event in the Code window. To open the Code window from the Form window, simply double-click the form's command button. Visual Basic opens the code editor shown in Figure 4.3.

FIG. 4.3
Complete the event procedure with the Code window.

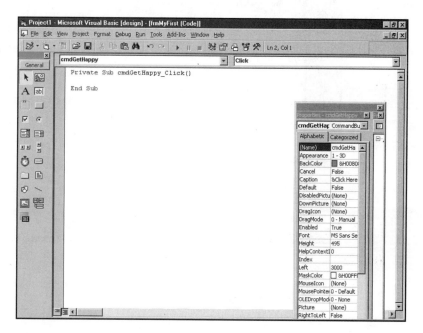

One of the truly nice things about the Code window is that Visual Basic automatically writes the first and last lines of the event procedure for you and opens a space for the body of the code. Type the following line between the first and last lines (be sure to insert your own path name) to complete your application's single event procedure:

```
imgViewHappy.Picture = LoadPicture("C:\My Documents\
                    ➥VB NightSchool\Happy.bmp")
```

When you type `LoadPicture()`'s opening parenthesis, Visual Basic displays Auto Quick Info pop-up help (see Figure 4.4). Whenever you type the first part of a built-in routine or keyword, Visual Basic displays Auto Quick Info to describe the entire statement's format. For the `LoadPicture()` function, Auto Quick Info tells you that the center part must be a file name, followed by an `As` clause. (The `As` clause turns out to be optional, because Visual Basic assumes the correct clause for you.)

FIG. 4.4

Visual Basic helps you complete program statements.

Auto Quick Info's help

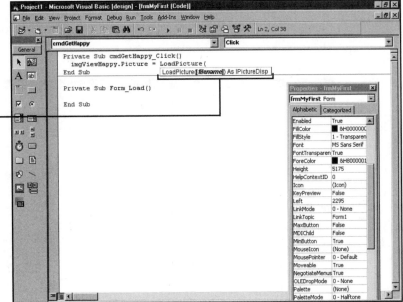

Because Visual Basic is a fairly large programming language, the Auto Quick Info feature comes in handy, especially if you need to use some obscure functions and don't remember the exact format of the functions.

▼ DEFAULT EVENT PROCEDURES

How did the Code window know that you needed the `Click` event procedure and not `DblClick`, `MouseMove`, or any of the other event procedures that you could write for the command button? When you double-click any control on the Form window, Visual Basic opens the Code window and writes the first and last lines for the *most common* event that takes place for that control. The most common event that a user performs on a command button is the `Click` event. If you double-clicked on the Form's background rather than the command button, the Code window would display the `Form_Load()` event procedure, the most common event programmed for forms. If you want to write an event procedure for an event that isn't the `Click` event, you have to select that event from the Code window's drop-down list of events (see Figure 4.5). ▲

FIG. 4.5
Select the event for which you want to write an event procedure.

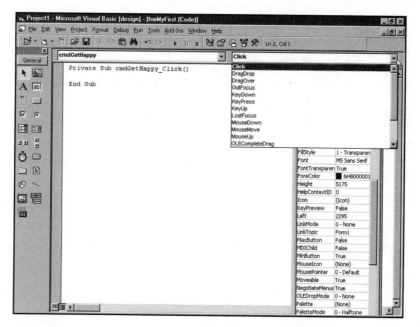

Close the Code window and run your application. You'll see the Form window you're now used to. Click the command button and watch the happy face appear. Congratulations! You've written your first event-driven Visual Basic application!

CAUTION If you get an error dialog box that looks something like the one in Figure 4.6, you haven't set the happy face bitmap image's path name properly inside the event procedure's code. (You've just written your first Visual Basic bug.) Click End to terminate the error message and program and correct the path name. Use Windows Explorer or the Windows Find command if you need help finding the exact location of the file named Happy.bmp. If the Code window doesn't appear when you close the error's dialog box, return to the Code window to fix the bug by choosing Code from the View menu or by double-clicking the command button again.

FIG. 4.6
A bug appears in the application.

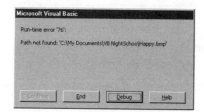

Pt I
Hr 4

Just for fun, run the program again. But rather than click the command button, press Alt+C to display the happy face. Alt+C is the shortcut key for the command button. As explained earlier in the section "Triggering Events," a command button's shortcut key triggers the same event as clicking the command button.

Next Step Now add a second event procedure to the application. Follow these steps to make the form automatically center itself on-screen, no matter what kind of graphics adapter or screen size users have:

1. Return to your application's Form window if you're not there now.

2. Double-click the form's background to open the `Form_Load()` event procedure. As Figure 4.7 shows, the Code window lists the current code (from the command button's `Click` event procedure) and the new procedure's first and last lines.

FIG. 4.7
The Code window holds all your event procedures.

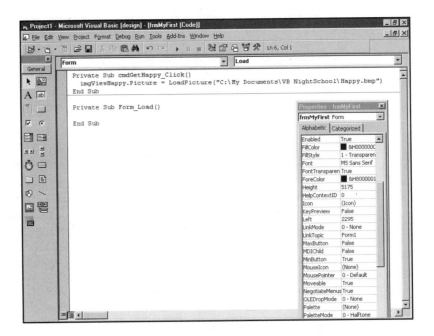

When the Code window displays several procedures, you have to scroll the window to locate the procedure you want to edit. You can also select from the drop-down list at the top of the Code window if you want to locate a particular procedure within your event procedures. With only two procedures, however, you don't need to worry about searching for procedures.

You'll adjust the form's center position during the `Load` event because you want to center the form as it appears, not after the form appears. If you centered the form in another form event, such as the `Click` event, the centering would come way too late or never.

3. Begin typing the following line:

```
frmMyFirst.Left = (Screen.Width - frmMyFirst.Width) / 2
```

As soon as you type the period after the form's name (`frmMyFirst`), Visual Basic displays the Auto List Members drop-down list, which lists all the properties available for the control name you've just entered (see Figure 4.8). The Auto List Members list comes in handy, especially for long properties, because rather than have to remember all the properties available for a control, you only need to select from this list.

FIG. 4.8

Let the Auto List Members drop-down list help you locate properties.

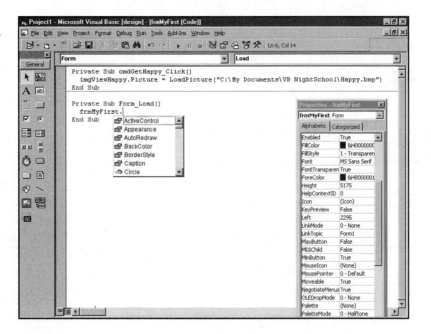

To select from the list, you can scroll to the item you want or just type the first letter or two. Type **Le** to find `Left`; then press the space bar to select `Left` and to have the Visual Basic Code editor fill in the remaining letters, `ft`.

4. Finish typing the form procedure's body:

```
frmMyFirst.Top = (Screen.Height - frmMyFirst.Height) / 2
```

5. Run the application to see the centered form. If you ported your application to another computer whose monitor resolution and size were different, your form would also appear centered on that monitor because of this procedure's calculation.

> **TIP** You can save time by omitting the form name from the form's event procedure body. The following two lines are identical to the ones you typed for the form load's event procedure:
>
> ```
> Left = (Screen.Width - Width) / 2
> Top = (Screen.Height - Height) / 2
> ```
>
> By specifying the form name, however, you lessen ambiguity in your code but have to type more to finish the procedures.
>
> Again, don't worry about the specifics of this code just yet. Although you can probably figure out what the code is doing, subsequent lessons will explain all the details for you.

Save your application. The final topic section in this lesson will add one additional item to the application.

Topic 3: Textbox Controls and Focus

Now that you're mastering the placement of controls and their event procedures, you have a jump-start on the rest of your Visual Basic learning. Although each of the remaining Toolbox controls varies from the Label, Command Button, and Image controls, you place them on the Form window by using the same steps used to place the other controls. You also can write event procedures for them in the same manner as the controls you now know. This topic section concludes this hour's lesson by introducing you to the Text Box control and explaining how to manage a form's focus.

Overview Whereas users can't type values directly onto a Label control, the Text Box control allows data-entry by users. When you want users to enter a name, address, or other word or phrase, place a text box on your form. The Text

Box control can display initial default text, or you can leave it blank for the users. You also have a choice as to how the text appears in a Text Box control.

As you begin to place additional controls that require user interaction, such as command buttons and text boxes, you have to begin determining the form's Tab order or focus. When users execute the application, they can press Tab to move the highlight from control to control. The control now highlighted is said to have the focus, and all applications have at least one control in focus at any one time (if the application contains user-input controls, such as command buttons and text boxes).

Text Box Controls

Text Box controls work like interactive labels—you display text in text boxes, but users can change or enter entirely new text. Also, users can leave your original Text Box control text, so your program can continue working with the default text.

▼ **NOTE**
Don't use text boxes for asking users yes/no questions. You'll use input boxes for such questions when you get to Hour 9's lesson. ▲

The Text Box control properties are important for understanding how Text Box controls work. Read through these common Text Box control properties that you'll work with:

- `Alignment` justifies text (left, right, or centered) inside the Text Box control.
- `BackColor` is the background color on which the text sits.
- `BorderStyle` is the kind of border that surrounds the text.
- `DataChanged` is automatically set to `True` if users change the text.
- `Font` determines the text's font name, style, and point size. (Other related properties that take on `True` or `False` values are `FontBold`, `FontStrikethru`, and `FontUnderline`.)
- `ForeColor` is the text color.
- If `Locked` is set to `True`, users can't change the text; if `Locked` is set to `False` (the default), users can change the text in the Text Box control.

- **MaxLength** specifies the maximum number of characters that users can type into the Text Box control. If **MaxLength** is set to 0, users aren't limited to a specific length.

- If **MultiLine** is set to **True**, the control can display more than one line of text.

- If you specify a character for the **PasswordChar** property, the character appears in the Text Box control as users enter text, although your program will receive the text that's actually typed. Use **PasswordChar** for password entries so that nobody can read the actual password as users type it. The asterisk (*) is the most common character programmers use for the password character.

- If **ScrollBars** is set to 0, no text box scroll bars appear; 1 specifies that a horizontal scroll bar appears; 2 specifies that a vertical scroll bar appears; and 3 specifies that both horizontal and vertical scroll bars appear.

TIP When you design text boxes, you must decide whether you want users to have multiline capabilities. If you want the text box to hold multiple lines of text (via a **True** **MultiLine** property), you should also set the **ScrollBars** property to one of its possible values. The scroll bars let users move back and forth between the Text Box control's lines of text.

- **Text** is the starting value that you place in the Text Box control at design time.

▼ NOTE

The Text Box control has no **Caption** property. The **Text** property holds the text that users initially see. **▲**

Here are some common Text Box control events that you'll frequently use:

- The **Change** event occurs when the text box's text (held in the **Text** property) changes.

- The **Click** event occurs when users click the text box.

- The **DblClick** event occurs when users double-click the text box.

- The **KeyDown** and **KeyUp** events occur when users press or release a key while working within the Text Box control.

- The **MouseMove** event occurs when users move the mouse over the text box.

> **TIP** Be sure to label your text box to tell users the information you want in the Text Box control. Don't just put an unlabeled text box on a form and expect users to know what to type.

Control Focus

One control on your form will have the focus, and user actions can move the focus to other controls. The *focus* is the currently highlighted control. Some controls, such as labels, can't receive the focus, but any control that interacts with users can receive the focus.

Figure 4.9 shows an application similar to yours that contains three command buttons. Notice that the third command button has the focus because of the dashed box around the control. Pressing Enter, therefore, would "click" the third command button. If users press Tab, another command button would receive the focus and the highlight would move to that command button.

FIG. 4.9
The focus moves between controls.

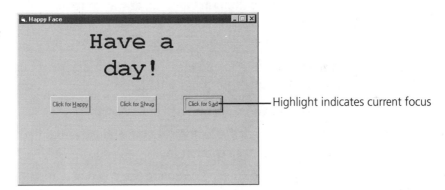

Highlight indicates current focus

▼ **NOTE**
Why do you think Figure 4.9's third command button uses the letter *a* as the shortcut key and not the letter *S*? You should not give two or more controls the same shortcut key. The second command button already uses the S, so the third command button had to use a different letter. If you give two or more controls the same shortcut key, the key with the lower `TabIndex` property will always receive the shortcut keystroke. ▲

The `TabIndex` property determines the focus order. Visual Basic automatically uses 0 for the `TabIndex` of the first control you place on the form,

1 for the second control you place, and so on. When users run the application, a Tab press sends the order through the controls determined by the sequential `TabIndex` values. Changing the `TabIndex` sequence changes the order of the focus.

Some controls can't receive the focus, but you can still set a `TabIndex` property for those controls. The `TabIndex` property simply sends the focus to the next control in line for the focus.

> **TIP** Give your text boxes a `TabIndex` value that's one less than the label that describes the text box. If you assign a shortcut key to the label, users can press the label's shortcut key to jump to the text box. Labels can't receive the focus, so the label sends the focus (obtained by the shortcut key) to the next control in line to receive the focus, which will be the text box.

Example Until now, you've had to exit your application by clicking the application's Close window button in the upper-right corner of the form. Clicking the Close window button isn't an elegant way to terminate a running program, however. This example adds an additional command button that you can use to exit the program.

Follow these steps to add the command button and set up the application to respond to the new command button:

1. Display your application's Form window.

2. Double-click the Toolbox's Command Button tool to send a command button to the center of the Form window.

3. Drag the command button to the coordinate position 2,295, 1,755. If you can't place the button there, simply type **2295** for the `Left` property and **1755** for the `Top` property. (Never type commas in such values.)

4. Change the command button's `Name` property to `cmdExit`.

5. Change the command button's `Caption` to `E&xit`. The ampersand makes Alt+X the shortcut key for the button. (By the way, both Alt+X and Alt+x work for the command button's shortcut key. Visual Basic ignores the case.)

6. Change the command button's `Cancel` property to `True`. You've now given users several ways to exit the program, including pressing Esc, Alt+X, and clicking the new command button.

7. Double-click the new command button to open the Code window to the `cmdExit_Click()` procedure.

8. Type **End** as the only statement inside the procedure's body. (Remember that indenting the code body makes the code easier to read in a long listing of code if you later add to the program.) The **End** command tells Visual Basic to terminate the program. Therefore, Visual Basic—actually, Windows—terminates the program as soon as you trigger this `Click` event.

9. Close the Code window and save your project.

10. Run the program and display the happy face.

11. Press Tab several times to move the focus back and forth between the command buttons. Figure 4.10 shows the running application.

12. Press Esc to exit the program.

Pt I

Hr **4**

FIG. 4.10
The new command button gives you an exit.

▼ **NOTE**
Windows programs rarely have such an exit command button. Generally, standard Windows programs use the File menu's Exit command for the program's exit. Hour 5's lesson, "Creating Menus for User Ease," explains how to add menus to your applications. ▲

Next Step Load and run the sample application named Controls that comes with Visual Basic. (You should find the Controls project inside Visual Basic's \Samples\PGuide\Controls directory.) The sample application demonstrates single-line and multiline text boxes extremely well. When you run the application, click the command button labeled *Text Box*; Visual Basic displays the window shown in Figure 4.11.

FIG. 4.11
Practice with the sample Text Box control.

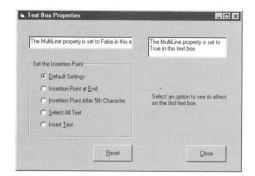

The sample application demonstrates that you can, through Visual Basic programming, manage the location of the Text Box control's text cursor (often called the *insertion point* or *caret*), select text, and restore saved text.

▼ NOTE
Type several lines of text into the sample's multiline text box, and you'll see why scroll bars come in handy. To see the text toward the top of the multiline text box, you have to press the up-arrow key several times to scroll back up when you don't have scroll bars.

Also, if you have a large monitor (at least 17 inches), you'll see why centering forms is a good idea (the Controls project fails to center the form). ▲

Summary

In this hour, you learned how to activate your controls. By entering code into event procedures with the Code window, you can set up your controls to respond to one or more events. Visual Basic helps get you started by writing the first and last line of your event procedures. If you double-click over a control, Visual Basic takes you to that control's default event procedure, but you can select from the event's drop-down list if you want to work with another event for that control.

As you begin to improve the power of your applications, you need to worry about the focus order of the controls. Users rely on the focus order so that they can use the keyboard rather than the mouse to step through the controls at times. You should place the first focus on the control that users will most likely select and use first.

In Hour 5, you'll learn how to add menus to your application. Visual Basic creates menus that add a professional Windows appearance to your applications.

Hour 4 Quiz

You can find the answers for the following questions on the accompanying CD-ROM and on the Virtual Classroom Web site.

On the CD

1. How do you assign a shortcut key to a command button's caption?
2. What's the difference between the `Cancel` property's action and the `Default` property's action?
3. **True or false:** Users can trigger the `Click` event by using the mouse or keyboard.
4. How can you tell which control holds the current focus?
5. What would be the name of a double-click event procedure for a control named `txtGetName`?
6. **True or false:** Alt+X differs from the Alt+x shortcut key.
7. Is `LoadPicture()` a subroutine, function, or event procedure?
8. What's the difference between a Text Box control and a Label control?
9. What would happen if you assigned 0 to the new command button's `TabIndex` property in the third topic section's exercise?
10. Why can't users see text entered into a Text Box control that uses a `PasswordChar` property?

Hour 4 Homework Exercises

1. Create an application with three multiline text boxes. Make the text boxes tall enough to display three or four lines of text. Give the first one a vertical scroll bar, the second a horizontal scroll bar, and the third one both kinds of scroll bars. In all three text boxes, supply the

initial text **Type here**. In addition to the text boxes, include an Exit command button on the form. Run the application and enter text in the three text boxes. Notice that you can enter multiple lines of text. The text boxes accept the Enter keypress, so you can send multiple paragraphs of text to the text boxes.

2. Create a password-entry form that contains an appropriate title, a label that reads **Type your secret password**, and a single-line text box that uses an asterisk (*) as the password character. Clear the text box's **Text** property in the Properties window so that no text initially appears in the text box. Also, add an Exit command button that terminates the program when users click the button or press Esc. Run the program and type characters into the password text box to see your password character appear.

When you learn more Visual Basic program commands, you'll learn how to test the password text that users type. As far as this program is concerned, the text box is getting your text, but you see only the password character on-screen for security reasons.

Creating Menus for User Ease

HOUR 5

During this hour you will learn

▶ What the Menu Editor does

▶ How to start the Menu Editor

▶ Which event responds to a menu selection

▶ What extras you can add to your application menus

MENUS ARE PART OF nearly every Windows application that you buy. Even when the application is equipped with a toolbar, those toolbar buttons are nothing more than shortcuts that duplicate menu actions. Clicking the Print toolbar button is often faster than choosing Print from the File menu and then clicking OK; however, menus provide more choices than will fit on a toolbar and provide a standard interface to most Windows programs.

Fortunately, Visual Basic lets you create menus without programming. VB creates completely interactive pull-down menus that respond to user selections. Your job, as you'll learn in this hour, requires only that you determine the menu bar item names and specify which options (or submenus) appear on each menu bar item; Visual Basic does the rest, creating a working menu for your application.

Topic 1: The Menu Editor

Visual Basic's Menu Editor is the tool you use for creating your application's menus. This topic section teaches you how to use the Menu Editor to build menus. When you learn the fundamentals, the next topic explains how to assign events and code to menu options.

▶▶ FAST TRACK

Are you familiar with Microsoft's Menu Editor? Visual Basic 5's Menu Editor hasn't changed significantly from earlier versions. If you've used menu editors in previous editions, or in Visual C++ or Visual J++, you can move on to Hour 6, "Understanding the VB Program Structure" (p. 133).

Almost every application you create will have menus. Menus require no programming to create, but you'll have to write program code that executes when users select from your menus.

Overview If you want to make your users at home with your application, supply a menu. The closer your menu matches that of other Windows programs, the more quickly your users will adapt to your application. Therefore, if you place a program termination option on your application's menu bar, use the industry standard Exit option on the File menu instead of something like a Quit option on the Tools menu.

The words on your menus comprise your application's menu bar. Normally, the words that appear on the menu bar aren't menu items, but menu names. If you click one of these menu names, you get a pull-down menu with two or more items. You can think of these items as command buttons that support only one event—the `Click` event. Because the only event related to menus is `Click`, your programming job is simple. You'll focus most of this hour mastering the Menu Editor because responding to menu events is straightforward. (Even a keyboard-triggered menu selection triggers the `Click` event.)

▼ **NOTE**

Recent Microsoft applications turn the menu bar into a kind of pushbutton bar as you pass the mouse pointer over the menu items. In other words, if you move your mouse over Visual Basic's Edit menu name, the word Edit becomes a button that you can click. The button appearance helps you know when you've selected the correct menu and helps reduce errors that result from clicking between two items and selecting the wrong choice.

Unfortunately, Visual Basic's Menu Editor doesn't support this menu item pushbutton feature. Perhaps Microsoft will add the pushbutton look to Visual Basic's next version. ▲

Introducing the Menu Editor Window

The Menu Editor is a dialog box that helps you design and create menus. Surprisingly, Microsoft hasn't changed the Menu Editor much in several years. (The Menu Editor has existed in many Microsoft products, including previous versions of Visual Basic and Visual C++.) The length of time that Microsoft has used the Menu Editor, and that the Menu Editor has remained relatively unchanged, is a testament to the Menu Editor's ease and power.

Pt **I**

Hr **5**

Menus appear on forms. Your application can contain a single form or multiple forms. You can place a menu on any or all of the forms. You can't access the Menu Editor until you display a form in your Form window. The Menu Editor then creates a menu for that form.

TIP The Menu Editor makes it easy to change your mind. If you don't like the menu that you created, you can change it. You easily can add or remove menu items later as your application's needs change.

To invoke the Menu Editor, choose Menu Editor from the Tools menu; press Ctrl+E; or click the toolbar's Menu Editor button. Figure 5.1 shows the Menu Editor.

FIG. 5.1

Create and edit menus in the Menu Editor.

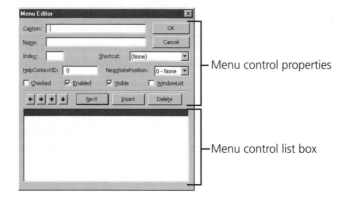

Menu control properties

Menu control list box

The top half of the Menu Editor, called the Menu control properties area, lets you set specific properties about your menu items and the overall menu bar. The large blank area at the bottom of the Menu Editor, the Menu control list box, displays the current menu structure as you build the menu. Table 5.1 describes the options you'll find on the Menu Editor.

Table 5.1   The Menu Editor's Options

Option	Description
Caption	The menu item name that you want to appear on the menu bar
Name	A control name that you assign to each menu item
Index	A value you assign if you create a *menu control array*, which lets you work with multiple menu items simultaneously through programming code
Shortcut	The Ctrl+*keystroke* combination that triggers the current menu item
HelpContextID	A reference value that lets you connect online help to each menu item
NegotiatePosition	A reference value that determines how and where the menu item falls within a special *container form*, where you can store a repository of controls
Checked	An option that determines whether a check mark appears to the left of menu items (choose Toolbars from VB's View menu for an example)
Enabled	An option that determines whether the menu option is temporarily disabled (indicated by the option being grayed out)
Visible	An option that determines whether the menu item is now visible or hidden on the menu

Option	Description
WindowList	An MDI (Multiple Document Interface) option that determines whether the menu contains open MDI forms
Arrow buttons	Controls that let you change the indentation level of selected menu items
Next	A command button that moves the selected menu item in the Menu control list box to the next line
Insert	A command button that lets you insert new menu items between two existing items
Delete	A command button that lets you remove menu items you no longer want

One of the best ways to learn the Menu Editor is to use it. The following example builds an imaginary menu structure. Because the menu you build isn't going to conform to any Windows menu bar standards, you can concentrate on the Menu Editor and not worry about programming details.

Pt **I**

Hr **5**

Example Create a new project so that you can practice with the Menu Editor. Choose Standard EXE from the New Project dialog box; Visual Basic creates the sample form named `Form1` for you. For this example, don't worry about renaming the form because you'll discard it after you're done.

Table 5.2 describes the menu structure you're going to create in this example.

Table 5.2 The Example's Menu Structure

Menu Name	Menu Option	Name	Event Procedure
Fly		mnuFly	
Fly	Delta	mnuFlyDelta	mnuFlyDelta_Click
Fly	American	mnuFlyAmerican	mnuFlyAmerican_Click
Fly	United	mnuFlyUnited	mnuFlyUnited_Click
Fly	Southwest	mnuFlySouthwest	mnuFlySouthwest_Click
Drive		mnuDrive	
Drive	Truck	mnuDriveTruck	mnuDriveTruck_Click
Drive	Car	mnuDriveCar	mnuDriveCar_Click
Drive	Tractor	mnuDriveTractor	mnuDriveTractor_Click

At first, you may not understand how all of Table 5.2's columns work together to create a menu, but they make sense when you think of how menu structures often appear:

- The Menu Name column, holding values such as Fly or Drive, is the name of the menu bar items. No event procedure is associated with these names in this example; you don't specify event procedures for top-level menu bar items because Visual Basic takes care of displaying the pull-down menus when users click menu bar items.

- The Menu Option column represents the name of the menu item that triggers an event procedure. As the programmer, you choose that name.

- The Name column contains the name of the menu item as it appears in the code. When you choose this reference name, you normally follow a set naming convention. The prefix `mnu` indicates that the item inside the code is a menu; you follow `mnu` with the menu name and the menu item's name.

> **TIP** Search Visual Basic's Books Online for *Menu Title and Naming Guidelines* for additional menu option naming conventions you should follow.

- The Event Procedure column displays the name of the event procedure that will match the menu item when selected. The procedure always ends with the `Click` event.

▼ NOTE

Although the menu item and event names are lengthy, you'll be able to remember them when you begin programming their events because their names describe exactly to which menu bar items and options they refer. ▲

Follow these steps to create a menu with the Menu Editor:

1. Type **Fly** in the Caption text box.

2. Type **mnuFly** in the Name text box.

3. Click the Next button without entering other Menu Editor values, because the Fly menu bar item is already complete. Notice that clicking Next moves the highlight bar down the Menu control list box area.

4. Type **Delta** for the next Caption and **mnuFlyDelta** for the Name and click Next. Your Menu Editor window should now look like the one in Figure 5.2.

FIG. 5.2
The sample menu is taking shape.

Pt I

Hr 5

▼ **NOTE**

Don't be confused that you didn't type **Fly** again for the Menu Name. Fly is a menu bar item, but Delta won't be after you fix the menu in a later step. ▲

5. Click OK to see the menu as it appears so far (see Figure 5.3).

FIG. 5.3
The menu bar as it appears so far.

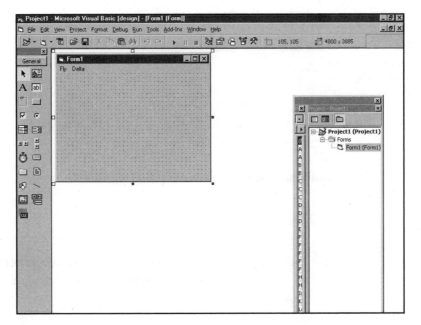

Because Delta is directly beneath Fly in the Menu Editor's control list box area, Visual Basic thinks Delta is a menu bar item instead of a submenu item (as you can see by the menu bar shown in Figure 5.3).

However, Delta is supposed to appear as an option on Fly's pull-down menu. Indentation tells the Menu Editor which items are menu bar items and which are submenu items. If you indent Delta to the right, the Menu Editor knows that Delta is a submenu item for Fly.

6. Open the Menu Editor again and click the row with Delta.

7. Click the right arrow button. The Menu Editor indents Delta to the right, showing that Delta is now a submenu item under Fly.

   If you ever need to turn a submenu item into a menu bar item, click the left arrow's button to move that submenu item up to the menu bar. Also, the up and down arrow buttons move items up or down the menu without changing the item's subordination to other menu items. You can also use the Insert and Delete buttons (as explained in Table 5.1) to insert and delete items from the menu. Next simply moves the highlight down the list.

8. Continue building the menu with Table 5.2's entries until you've added all the Fly submenu items. Your Menu Editor window should look like the one in Figure 5.4.

FIG. 5.4

You've now entered all the first menu's items.

9. With the highlight in the new position under your menu items, click the left arrow button to move the subordination up a level so you can enter the second menu bar item.

10. Type **Drive** in the Caption text box and **mnuDrive** in the Name text box. Make sure that Drive aligns with Fly at the left of the Menu Editor, so they both appear on the menu bar.

11. Enter the rest of the menu items. When you finish, your Menu Editor should look like Figure 5.5. Make sure that your Menu Editor's indentation matches that of Figure 5.5's. If you've added a blank, indented menu item at the bottom of the Menu Editor, highlight the blank item and click Delete.

FIG. 5.5
You've completed the menu structure.

Next Step You've built your first menu structure! Click OK to see the menu bar on the form. Menu design is simple because VB activates the menu while you work at program design time; that way, you can see what users will see when the application runs. To test your menu, click Drive to see Drive's pull-down menu (see Figure 5.6). You can drag the mouse up and down the menu to see what happens when you run the application.

To review, each menu item—whether on the menu bar or on a submenu—has a caption and name. If you indent the item in the Menu Editor window's list box, Visual Basic puts the item on a submenu for the most recent menu bar entry.

FIG. 5.6
You can review your menu while working inside the development environment.

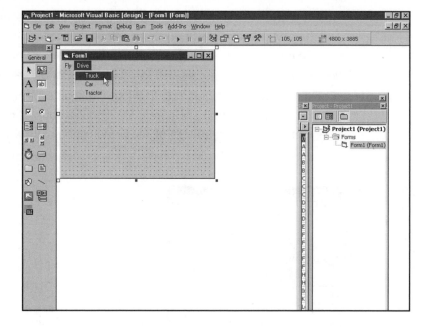

Topic 2: Responding to Menus

Each time users select a submenu item, a Windows `Click` event occurs. You're responsible for writing the event procedure code that responds to your menu options. If you ran the sample application that you created in the previous topic section, nothing would happen because no event procedures appear in the code.

Overview   In this topic section, you'll add code for the menu items. As with most of this lesson, you may not understand all the code details that you put in the menu's event procedures, but that's fine for now. Part II of this course, "Programs That Do Work," explores the Visual Basic language in depth. This part of your training simply gives you the overall "big picture" so that you'll learn, hands-on, how to operate inside the Visual Basic environment and how VB program components go together to create a working application.

The Menu Events

Although Table 5.2 listed the event procedures needed to respond to the menu item selections, you never typed one of the event procedure names during the creation of the menu. The Menu Editor doesn't deal with event procedures. Remember, the Code window is where you type and edit *all* event procedures. The Menu Editor's job is simply to help you design and create the menu bar and its options.

You generate the name for each menu option's event procedure every time you name a menu option. The only event procedure for a menu option is the `Click` event, so as soon as you enter the menu item name in the Menu Editor, you've indirectly specified the name of the event procedure for that item. Therefore, the event procedure for the Car option on the Drive menu is `mnuDriveCar_Click` because the name of the option (if you followed Table 5.2 when you created the sample menu) is `mnuDriveCar`. The only event available for menus is `Click`.

The following example explains how to open the Code window so that you can add executable code to make the menu options work.

Pt I

Hr 5

Example   Opening the Code window for a specific menu item event procedure is simple. From your Form window, display a pull-down submenu and click the item whose event procedure you want to write. For example, if you click the menu bar's Fly option, you'll see the submenu. Clicking United opens the `mnuFlyUnited_Click()` procedure shown in Figure 5.7's Code window. Just as VB opens the Code window when you double-click a form's controls, Visual Basic opens the Code window for menu items when you select those items from within the form window.

Press the space bar to indent the first line of code that you enter and type the following for the United event procedure:

```
Dim Msg As String, Title As String, Style As Integer
Msg = "You chose United"
Title = "United Air"
Style = vbOKOnly
Response = MsgBox(Msg, Style, Title)
```

FIG. 5.7
*Visual Basic
prepares to
receive the
menu code.*

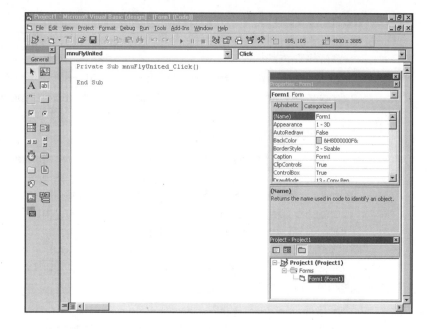

The second, third, and fourth lines set up a *message box*, a pop-up window that displays messages in Windows applications. (You'll learn about message boxes in Hour 9's lesson, "Working with Interactive Keyboard and Screen I/O.") The fourth line displays the message box on-screen.

Close the Code window and run the application. Choose United from the Fly menu; Visual Basic displays the message box shown in Figure 5.8. After you verify that the event procedure works, you can create event procedures for the remaining items, if you want. Click OK in the message box to return to the running application, and then close the application so that you can work on the application's design again.

FIG. 5.8
*The menu
selection
triggered
the code.*

> **TIP** Copy the event procedure's code body to the Clipboard. When you click the other menu options to add event procedures from the Form window, you can paste the Clipboard into the Code window. The only change you have to make is to the airline name or the type of driving vehicle.

Next Step The menu doesn't look anything like a standard Windows menu because I wanted you to concentrate on menu-building specifics, not on menu items themselves. Nevertheless, you'll gain additional practice if you add a File menu-bar item with an Exit option to end the application. You'll then have a graceful way to exit the application without clicking the Close window button; you'll also gain additional Menu Editor practice.

Follow these steps to add the File menu and Exit option:

1. Open the Menu Editor again. The highlight will rest on the menu bar's Fly option.

2. Click the Insert button to insert a new menu item before Fly.

3. Enter **File** in the Caption text box and **mnuFile** for the Name. Make sure that the Menu Editor is inserting the File entry with no indentation, because File is to be a menu-bar item.

4. Click Next to save the File entry and open a new entry below File.

5. Type **Exit** for the Caption and **mnuFileExit** for the Name.

6. Click the right arrow while Exit is still highlighted to turn it into File's submenu option.

7. Click OK to see the resulting menu. Now you need to add the Exit option's procedure code.

8. Choose Exit from the File menu to open the `mnuFileExit_Click` event procedure. (You'll see your other menu event procedures as well.)

9. Indent two spaces and type **End** so that your entire event procedure looks like this:

```
Private Sub mnuFileExit_Click()
  End
End Sub
```

The **End** command, as you might remember from Hour 4's lesson, terminates the running program.

10. Close the Code window and run the program. Display a few menu message boxes and then choose Exit from the File menu to terminate the program.

Your menu isn't quite finished because no shortcut keys exist. The Menu Editor supports several other options, such as hotkeys, shortcut keys, and separating lines. You learn about those menu extras in the following topic section.

Topic 3: Advanced Menu Options

Although you can now create menus, the Visual Basic Menu Editor supports several additional menu features that you can add to your applications. You want to make your application as easy as possible for your users. Therefore, you'll want to give your users many options. By providing hotkeys, shortcut keys, and cascading menus, you can help add a professional touch to your applications—plus, you'll gain the users' respect.

Overview This topic section explains how to add hotkeys and shortcut keys to your menus as well as use checked, enabled, and other attributes on your submenu items. Specifying these extras requires little more than clicking the correct option for that entry in the Menu Editor.

Hotkeys

In Windows, it's common to use keystroke combinations instead of mouse manipulation to accomplish some tasks. For example, to save a file, you can either choose Save from the File menu of most applications, or press Alt+F+S. These key combinations are called *hotkeys* or *accelerator keys*. A menu item's underlined character indicates the hotkey. Thus, the File menu's hotkey is Alt+F; if you press Alt+F in most Windows applications, Visual Basic opens the File menu.

As with command-button hotkeys (as discussed in Hour 4), you only need to place an ampersand (&) before the hotkey letter in the menu item's caption. When you run the application, you'll see that Visual Basic assigned the underlined hotkey to that letter. When you develop Visual Basic applications, you can add hotkeys to make your menus easier to traverse.

▼ **NOTE**

If you don't assign a hotkey to a menu item, Visual Basic uses the item's first letter as the hotkey. Therefore, if you display the Fly menu and press the letter A, Visual Basic selects the American option, even if you haven't turned the A in American into a hotkey. ▲

Shortcut Keys

Similar to hotkeys are the *shortcut keys*. You've already mastered shortcut keys for command buttons; when you press Alt plus a command button's underlined letter, you trigger that command button's `Click` event. By adding shortcut keys to menu items, you eliminate the users' need to display a menu-bar menu to choose an option. When you add shortcut keys to menu items, Visual Basic lists the shortcut keystroke on the menu so that your users can more quickly learn the shortcut key.

You'll optionally designate a shortcut key for your menu's items inside the Menu Editor in the next example.

▼ **NOTE**

Hotkeys are used to navigate the menus; shortcuts bypass the menus. A properly designed menu *must* have a hotkey for each menu item so that users can effectively navigate through the menu options with the keyboard instead of the mouse. Shortcuts, however, are generally reserved for most-used commands; they're easier than hotkeys to remember and to key in, but assigning them to every menu item would be overkill. ▲

CAUTION Most current Windows applications place a toolbar button's icon next to the matching menu item so that you can learn the buttons that go with the menu options. Therefore, if you open Visual Basic's File menu, you'll see icons on the menu that correspond to matching toolbar icons. Unfortunately, Visual Basic doesn't yet support menu icons in the Menu Editor, so your applications will contain menus that have shortcut keystrokes but can't display icons.

Other Critical Features

A few other Menu Editor features appear that you can now master. The check boxes labeled Checked, Enabled, and Visible determine the default value for the menu when a form is loaded. Checked means that a check mark appears beside the menu option when users display the submenu.

Enabled (selected by default) means that the option is available and not grayed out. Visible (selected by default) means that the option appears in the menu when the application starts.

During the application's execution, your program might change one or more of these menu properties. For example, if no data exists to print but you normally provide a Print option on a File menu, you may want to gray out the option until users enter data that your program can print.

▼ **NOTE**

Programmers can disable or hide temporarily unavailable menu options. Generally when an option isn't currently available, users appreciate seeing the option grayed out rather than find that the option has disappeared. If you hide unavailable options, users can more easily forget where that option is when you make the option visible again. By graying out an option, users know that the option is available but just not now. ▲

You'll use the HelpContextID option when you add online help to your application. (Hour 29's lesson, "Building a Help Subsystem," explains how to add online help to menus.) The Index, NegotiatePosition, and WindowList options are useful only in special situations. You can check the online help if you want to know more about these rarely used menu options.

TIP   One of the most helpful style modifications you can apply to your menus is a separator line that separates groups of menu options from one another. On Visual Basic's File menu you'll see seven lines that separate the parts of the menu form one another. To add separator lines, simply type a hyphen (-) for the Caption value and add a unique name, such as mnuSep1, to each separator line that you create. When you run the application, Visual Basic won't let you choose the separator line; VB uses the separator line just to group menu options.

Example   Follow these steps to add hotkeys to the File menu name and the Exit option:

1. Open the Menu Editor.

2. Click the File entry if File isn't highlighted in the bottom of the Menu Editor.

3. Click the F in the Caption text box to insert the text cursor before the word File.

4. Press the ampersand key to make the F the hotkey.

5. Click the Exit entry.

6. Make the letter x the Exit option's hotkey. (The Windows standard always makes x the Exit hotkey on the File menu.)

7. You can now add a shortcut key to one of the other menu options for practice. Highlight the Car entry.

8. Open the Shortcut drop-down list (see Figure 5.9).

FIG. 5.9

Select a shortcut key from the list.

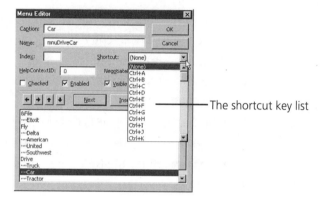

The shortcut key list

9. Select Ctrl+C for the shortcut key.

10. Click OK to close the Menu Editor.

11. Run the application.

12. Press the Ctrl+C shortcut keystroke to simulate the Drive menu's Car option. The Car message box should appear.

13. Press Alt+F to open the File menu, and then press the X letter key to exit the program.

Next Step *Cascading menus* are submenus within submenus. The Windows Start menu is a great cascading menu model because when you select one menu, another usually pops up next to it. The Menu Editor can easily create cascading menus. All you need to do is indent the subordinate menus with the right arrow button.

Add the following submenu options to the Fly menu's Delta option:

- L1011
- MD88
- 747

Follow these steps to add the new options:

1. Open your Menu Editor if you don't have it open already.

2. Click the American entry.

3. Click the Insert command button to insert a blank area for a new menu option before the American entry.

4. Click the right arrow to indent the option more than the Delta entry. Indented options that fall under Delta will be subordinate to Delta; therefore, they will comprise Delta's submenu.

5. Type **L1011** for the Caption and **mnuFlyDeltaL1011** for the Name.

6. Click Next and Insert to open a new option. Type **MD88** for the Caption and **mnuFlyDeltaMD88** for the Name. Be sure to indent the entry directly under the previous one.

7. Click Next and Insert to open a new option. Type **747** for the Caption and **mnuFlyDelta747** for the Name. Be sure to indent the entry directly under the previous one.

8. Click OK to close the Menu Editor.

   You now have to correct a possible problem. If you were to run the application and choose Delta from the Fly menu, you wouldn't see the new submenu! Remember that you've written an event procedure for `mnuFlyDelta_Click()`, and that event procedure will override the submenu.

9. From Visual Basic's View menu choose Code to display the Code window for your event procedures.

10. Delete the lines that comprise the `mnuFlyDelta_Click()` event procedure (you may have to scroll the window to see the procedure). Select the lines (highlight them by clicking and dragging your mouse from the start of the procedure to its final character) and press Delete to remove the event procedure.

11. Close the Code window and run the application. The Fly menu shows a triangle next to Delta that indicates that a submenu appears from that option. When you choose Delta from the Fly menu, you'll see your new cascading submenu, which should look something like the one in Figure 5.10.

FIG. 5.10
A menu option can produce additional submenus.

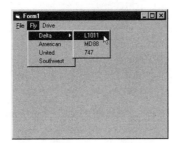

Summary

Your Visual Basic applications aren't complete until you add menu bars to them. Fortunately, the Menu Editor makes adding menus simple because you design, create, and edit your application's menus directly inside the Menu Editor. You don't have to know how to program to create menus, but you'll need to add event procedure code to the menu selections to activate the menus.

▶▶ FAST TRACK
Have you seen pop-up menus that appear when you right-click over an item? You'll learn in Hour 23's lesson, "Enhancing Your Program" (p. 535), how to create pop-up menus.

This hour's lesson ends Part I of your night-school training. In Hour 6 you'll begin to study the details of the Visual Basic programming language. Now that you've seen the fundamentals of Visual Basic development, the Visual Basic commands that you learn in the next part are needed before you can tackle additional controls. (Many of the Visual Basic form controls require runtime programming before you can use them.)

Hour 5 Quiz

You can find the answers for the following questions on the accompanying CD-ROM and on the Virtual Classroom Web site.

1. What event corresponds to the selection of a menu item if users click the mouse to select from the menu?

2. What event corresponds to the selection of a menu item if users use the keyboard to select from the menu?

3. **True or false:** You can design your menu as well as enter event procedure code with the Menu Editor.

4. What's the difference between the <u>V</u>isible and <u>E</u>nabled options in the Menu Editor?

5. What does the name of the menu item do?

6. What's the difference between a hotkey and a shortcut key?

7. What's the purpose of the <u>C</u>hecked option in the Menu Editor?

8. What is a cascading menu?

9. Which has priority—a cascading submenu or an event procedure?

10. Describe how to open a menu bar option's Code window from the development environment.

Hour 5 Homework Exercises

1. You didn't get a chance to use the Menu Editor's up and down arrows to rearrange menu options. Use the up and down arrow buttons to reverse the Fly and Drive menu options.

2. Extend the Delta menu three more levels.

▼ NOTE

Although this exercise is great practice, you normally don't want to cascade four or five levels. Generally, three levels are the most you should ever include. If you need more levels, you should probably add additional menu bar options to eliminate some nested menu levels. ▲

3. Write a program that creates the same menu structure that's in the Windows Paint program. By working through this entire menu, including the shortcut keys and hotkeys, you'll know the Menu Editor inside and out. Be sure to add separator lines where needed to group related menu options together as Paint does.

Understanding the VB Program Structure

THIS LESSON INTRODUCES YOU to Visual Basic programs. Now that you've worked with Visual Basic's Form window and learned the fundamentals of placing controls and setting control properties, it's time to add punch to your programs. Learning a programming language—especially the Visual Basic programming language—is much easier than learning a foreign language! To make the language easier, this lesson describes the structure of Visual Basic programs and shows how to document your programs to make them easier to maintain later.

Topic 1: Project Structure

Until this lesson, you've only scratched the surface of Visual Basic application development, as you might guess. Nevertheless, you've already come a long way, and you can already create simple Windows programs. When you add Visual Basic code, you can turn simple programs into powerful programs that process data and perform the work you need done.

Before you learn the Visual Basic language details, take a few minutes this hour to see the "big picture." This topic section introduces you to the structure of Visual Basic programs. Every VB application's Project window describes the application's structure.

▼ NOTE

Have you programmed before? If you've programmed strictly in a text-based language, such as COBOL, FORTRAN, or QBasic, you should study this hour's lesson. If you've programmed in a windowed high-level language such as Visual C++, you can probably scan this lesson to make sure that you understand the concepts unique to Visual Basic. No matter what your programming background is, this lesson is critical because you need to understand Visual Basic's structure fully before learning the language. ▲

Overview Before Windows came along, an application primarily consisted of one long text-based program without any graphical additions such as a form with controls. Through the years as computers and software advanced, programmers began breaking their code into small sections, called *modules*, *subroutines*, or *procedures* (Visual Basic uses all three terms today), so applications began changing formats from one long program to several small routines that worked together as a single program.

When Windows came along, the visual interface had to be part of the picture. Somehow, programmers had to combine text-based instructions with a graphical interface. Sadly, programmers had to work with several different tools—some for the text program parts and some for the visual parts. For a time, a Windows program was an awkward collection of files that programmers had to glue together into a working Windows application.

Visual Basic not only supplies the glue, but keeps things organized for you. Visual Basic gives you a platform on which you work with a Windows application that's a collection of organized forms, event procedures, and other code that work together in a common development environment.

Code Everywhere

You've already seen code in event procedures such as the following:

```
Private Sub cmdGetHappy_Click()
  imgViewHappy.Picture = LoadPicture("C:\My Documents\VB
                           ➥NightSchool\Happy.bmp")
End Sub
```

The event procedure code is a small portion of any Visual Basic application. The more forms your application has, the more controls your application will likely have. The more controls your application has, the more event procedures your application will likely have to make those controls respond to events.

Event procedures aren't the only place where you'll find Visual Basic code. In most applications, VB code also appears inside one or more Visual Basic modules. The module code is data-processing code that doesn't respond to events, but performs the specific work you need your application to perform.

Pt II

Hr 6

▼ **NOTE**

Not everything in this hour's lesson will be applicable right away. Keep in mind that this lesson is a preview of details to come, especially in this and the next part of this tutorial where you'll learn language specifics. ▲

Projects In Depth

An application consists of a single project. No application will contain multiple projects, because a project is a single application's collection of files that work together. (No project will contain multiple applications, either; Visual Basic maintains the one project/one application relationship.) Table 6.1 describes the kinds of files that can appear in a project.

Table 6.1 The Files That Make Up Projects

File	Extension	Description
ActiveX control	OCX	Appears if your application contains ActiveX controls.
Class	CLS	Appears if your application contains a *class* (a description of a user-generated Visual Basic object). Hour 20's lesson explains more about classes.
Project	VBP	A record-keeping file that maintains the project contents. Visual Basic updates this file for you and displays its contents in the Project window.
Form	FRM	A form description file.
Form properties	FRX	Contains the control that properties appear on the form.
Resource	RES	A file that holds the application's resources, such as the menus, icons, and accelerator keys.
Standard module	BAS	A file that holds non-event procedure code.

▼ **NOTE**
A single project may contain multiple form files, form properties files, standard modules, class modules, and ActiveX control files. ▲

The Project window constantly updates as you add and remove files to your applications. It lets you navigate your projects by selecting the file that you want to work with. The Project window, such as the one in Figure 6.1, displays your project files by using an Explorer-like format, with folders and icons that represent the different kinds of files available in the Project window.

▼ **NOTE**
Often, Visual Basic programmers call the Project window the "Project Explorer" due to the interface it shares with Windows Explorer. ▲

When you want to work on a Visual Basic application, you'll open the project file to gain access to the project's components. When you save the project, you save every file in the project. If you want to edit a component, such as the form inside the Form window, double-click the form to open it for editing.

FIG. 6.1

A Project window can contain several files.

From the <u>P</u>roject menu choose *<project name>* Prop<u>e</u>rties to display Figure 6.2's Project Properties dialog box. From this dialog box, you can specify the startup file (usually, but not always, the application's primary form is the startup file specified in the option labeled <u>S</u>tartup Object), compile options, and version control if you want to maintain different running versions of an application.

Pt **II**

Hr **6**

FIG. 6.2

Customize the project from the Project Proper-ties dialog box.

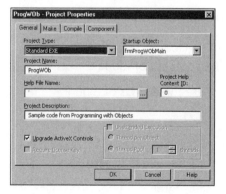

As you begin creating more advanced Visual Basic applications, you'll work as much or more within modules (some applications have several code modules) as you do with controls on the form. You'll begin to add code to your application's modules so that the application can work with general-purpose code that often works with the form controls.

▼ **NOTE**

All event procedure code resides in a module called the *form module*, as you'll see in the following example section. Event procedures aren't the only kind of code that can appear in a form module. You can also write *general procedures* that work with the event procedures. ▲

For example, if you want several different controls to respond in much the same manner, you could type common code inside each event procedure. If you add a general procedure to the code module, however, you can put the common code inside the general procedure. Each event procedure can then trigger the general procedure's code (by using a method known as *calling* the procedure). When the general procedure's code completes, Visual Basic returns control to the event to clean up anything that's left and to close the event procedure. The general procedure acts as a detour for the event procedure's code.

TIP By putting common code in a module's general procedures, rather than duplicate the code throughout your event procedures, you need to change the code in only one location if the application's goal changes. On the other hand, you would have to change every occurrence of the code if you kept multiple copies of the code throughout several event procedures.

Example This topic section has been loosely discussing modules. Now is a good time to learn about the different kinds of modules that you can write.

Visual Basic supports these three kinds of modules:

- Form
- Standard
- Class

All the code you've seen so far in this book—the event procedure code—has resided inside a form module. A form module's code goes with the form. Therefore, if your application contains several forms, your application will contain several form modules. The form modules contain event procedures related to its form's controls. As you've learned in this topic section, a form module might contain code inside a general procedure as well as in event procedures.

A form module not only contains event procedures, but also general procedures and possibly class procedures. Also, a form module can contain data declarations. Figure 6.3 shows a form module's makeup. A general procedure contains many of the same kinds of code details that an event procedure contains and even includes parentheses after its name.

FIG. 6.3

A form module contains event procedures, general procedures, class procedures, and a Declarations *section.*

The Form's Form Module

```
┌─────────────────────────────────────┐
│ Declarations                         │
├─────────────────────────────────────┤
│ Private Sub Event_Proc1 ()           │
│   'Body of first event procedure     │
│ End Sub                              │
├─────────────────────────────────────┤
│ Private Sub Event_Proc2 ()           │
│   'Body of 2nd event procedure       │
│ End Sub                              │
├─────────────────────────────────────┤
│ Private Sub Event_Proc3 ()           │
│   'Body of 3rd event procedure       │
│ End Sub                              │
├─────────────────────────────────────┤
│ Private Sub Gen_Proc ()              │
│   'Body of a general procedure       │
│ End Sub                              │
├─────────────────────────────────────┤
│ Private Sub Class_Proc ()            │
│   'Body of a class procedure         │
│ End Sub                              │
└─────────────────────────────────────┘
```

Pt **II**

Hr **6**

You'll write general procedures when your program needs them, so you're responsible for naming them. Unlike event procedures, general procedures don't follow any preset naming pattern. General procedures appear with the declarations in a module section named General. All these sections (such as Declarations and General) appear in the Code window, as you'll see in the third topic's "Next Step" section at the end of this lesson.

▼ NOTE

Keep the Visual Basic overall picture in sight here. The rest of the book discusses the nitty-gritty details of the code lines that reside inside these procedures and declaration areas. This hour's topic is clearing the way for the details so that you know how code fits together. ▲

▼ **NOTE**

Hour 20's lesson, "Understanding Objects and Using the Object Browser," explains class procedures. You can write advanced, fully working Visual Basic applications without using class procedures, so their coverage isn't critical at this time. ▲

Next Step The form procedures, general procedures, and class procedures that you studied in the preceding example section included a section named `Declarations`. The `Declarations` section of any module holds data descriptions that belong *only* to that module. The procedure's data is said to be *local* to the procedure. Therefore, if you declare data-holding areas (called *variables*, as you'll see in Hour 7) in one form module's `Declarations` section, only the procedures inside that form module can store and access the data locations.

If your application contains several forms and, thus, several form modules, one form module can't access the data in another form module unless you make specific arrangements to share the data, as you'll learn to do throughout this course.

▼ **NOTE**

All modules have one `Declarations` area each but can contain multiple procedures of every kind. ▲

A standard module looks a lot like a form module. Standard modules are separate files within your application's project (with the .bas extension) that contain code. Standard modules have no event procedures, but they have a section named `General` that holds a `Declarations` section and procedures that you write. You'll see throughout this tutorial how to use a standard module to hold processing code that applies to multiple forms. Whereas code inside one form module can't easily access variable data in another form module, a standard module's code can access all form variable information within your complete application.

TIP As you work more with Visual Basic, remember that a standard module doesn't have to be tied to any one application. Suppose that you produce some accounting calculations that you want to use in several applications. Put those accounting calculations inside a standard module. You can then add that module (by using the Project menu's Add Module option) to any application that needs to access the accounting routines. Of course, you'll want to keep specific form and control names out of such standard modules that you use across applications; otherwise, the standard module will work only with a single application.

To look at a fairly comprehensive project that includes all three kinds of modules, follow these steps:

1. Open Visual Basic's sample application named ProgWOb (stored in the \Samples\PGuide\ProgWOb directory folder).

2. Double-click the Project window to expand it to your entire editing area. The Project window displays forms (which each contain form modules to hold the event procedures for the form controls), standard modules (listed in the Modules folder), and class modules.

3. Open each folder by clicking the plus sign next to each one. After you adjust the bottom edge of the Project window, you'll see all the forms and modules shown in Figure 6.4.

FIG. 6.4

You can display objects within different modules.

4. Now that you've seen the large Project window, double-click the window's title bar again to resize the window to a smaller size.

5. Drag the Project window to the right edge of your screen to make room for the Code window.

6. Double-click the form named `frmImplements` to select and display it.

7. From the <u>V</u>iew menu choose <u>C</u>ode. Visual Basic displays the selected form's Code window. A lot of code goes with the form, so you'll see lots of procedures. The editor automatically separates procedures from each other by using dividing lines.

8. Although you can scroll through the Code window, Visual Basic's editor is smart; the two drop-down list boxes at the top of the Code window search and find specific procedures for you. The left drop-down list describes an object, whereas the right drop-down list describes procedures. The `General` object contains the `Declarations` section and any general procedures that appear in the form module. Open the right drop-down list, as shown in Figure 6.5, to see a list of the `Declarations` section and the general procedures. You won't see event procedures in this list.

Select the `General` object's procedure that you want to view

FIG. 6.5
This drop-down list shows your form module's `Declarations` *and general procedures.*

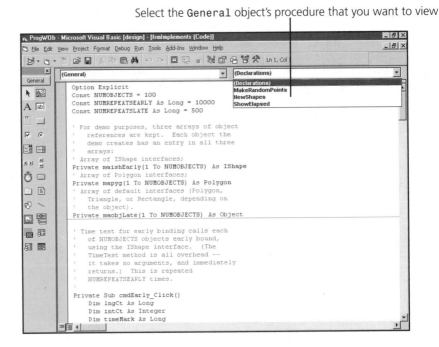

9. Select `Declarations` from the list to move the text cursor to that area in the form module. Nothing seems to happen, but as you'll see, Visual Basic moves the text cursor to the top of the form module to

the `Option Explicit` statement. All code in that section (down to the first dividing line) is part of the `Declarations` section that applies to the entire form module.

10. Select `NewShapes` from the list now. The Visual Basic Code window jumps to the subroutine general procedure named `NewShapes`. (Although you could have scrolled down to the procedure, can't you see how selecting the procedure is easier?) `NewShapes` is a general procedure, and you know that because it's listed in the `General` object section.

11. Click the arrow next to the Object drop-down list (on the left) to open the list of form module objects that appear in the form module. Figure 6.6 shows this list.

FIG. 6.6
This drop-down list shows your form module's General *section and the form's objects.*

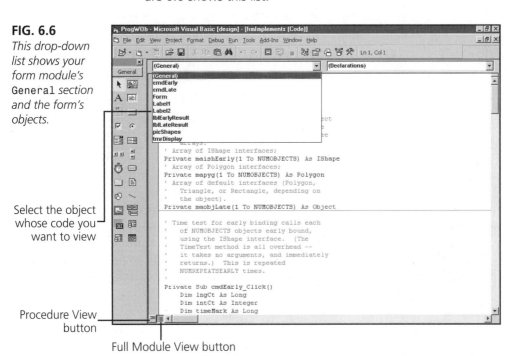

Select the object whose code you want to view

Procedure View button

Full Module View button

12. You already know what the `General` section contains, so select `cmdLate` from the list. As you can tell from the name, `cmdLate` is a command button on the form. As soon as you select `cmdLate`, Visual Basic updates the procedure drop-down list on the right to contain only those procedures related to the `cmdLate` object.

13. Scroll through the procedure list. You'll see that Visual Basic boldfaces only the `Click` event in the list. The list contains all possible events for command buttons. Visual Basic boldfaces `Click` to tell you that *only* the command button's `Click` event has an event procedure.

14. Select the `Click` event; Visual Basic displays the rather lengthy `cmdLate_Click ()` event procedure. As you can see, the two drop-down lists let you select the `Declarations` section and the general procedures (both in the `General` object section), as well as the event procedures that are available for the control objects on the form.

15. Double-click the Project window's `modFriends` entry to display the standard module named `modFriends` in the Code window. If you click the object drop-down list, you'll see only a `General` section. Why? Remember that a standard module never contains event procedures, but *only* a `Declarations` section and standard procedures that aren't tied to any event.

16. Open the procedure drop-down list to see all the general procedures in the module (including the `Declarations` section).

17. Scroll through the procedures and close the application when you're finished. You now should have a better idea of Visual Basic's Code window capability to display event procedures, `Declarations`, and general procedures.

> **TIP** If you click the Code window's Procedure View button on the bottom left, Visual Basic displays only the selected procedure. If you click the default Full Module View button, Visual Basic displays the list of procedures separated by the dividing lines. Because you can display whatever procedure you want to see and edit with the drop-down list boxes, the Procedure View button keeps the other procedures out of your way.

Topic 2: Program Documentation

Visual Basic totally ignores the most important statement you'll write: *remarks*. Remarks provide program documentation. Remember that you write a program once but read, maintain, and update that program many times. The easier you make it to understand the program code you write, the easier it will be for you to understand that code later when you have to make changes. As you write, you'll want to embed program documentation by using Visual Basic remarks. In this topic section, you'll learn how to code remark statements and document your code.

Overview   When you add program documentation, you're telling yourself—and anyone else who might work on your program in the future—about the program details. Although any Visual Basic programmer can scan Visual Basic code and decipher the details, remarks will speed and simplify that understanding because you write remarks by using the same language you speak with.

The Need for Remarks

You know that a program exists to give the computer instructions to read and follow. You need to understand the programs you write, however. After writing a program, you can't always remember parts of the program when you're making changes later. When someone else writes a program, working on that program is especially difficult.

Someday, computer instructions might be written in a spoken language such as English. Until then, you must learn to speak and understand the computer's language.

The Remark Statement's Format

The `Rem` statement makes Visual Basic code more understandable to humans, although the computer ignores `Rem`. `Rem` is short for *remark*. The format of the `Rem` statement is

```
Rem Any message you choose
```

You can have as many remarks in your program as you want. Many programmers scatter remarks throughout a program. You can insert remarks in event procedures, general procedures, declarations sections, and class procedures. The computer completely ignores remarks. Remarks produce no output, store no data, and require no data.

If a computer completely ignores remarks, you probably wonder why you should bother to use them. `Rem` statements are for *people* to use so that they can understand programs better. For example, a Visual Basic program that produces a fancy colored box with flashing lights around it and your name inside (like a marquee) would take some cryptic Visual Basic graphic and text commands. Before those commands, you might put a remark like this:

```
Rem The next few lines draw a fancy colorful boxed name
```

This remark doesn't tell Visual Basic to do anything, but it makes the next few lines of code more understandable to you and others; this statement explains—in your own language, not in Visual Basic—exactly what the program is going to do.

Rem statements also are helpful for putting the programmer's name at the top of a program. In a large company with several programmers, it's helpful to know who to contact if you need help changing the original code. Remember that Rem doesn't display that name on the form or anywhere else when you run the program (printing is done with other Visual Basic commands), but the name is there for anyone looking at the program's listing.

You also might consider putting the module file name of the program in an early Rem statement. For example, the statement

```
Rem Programmer: Pat Johnson, Module: ComputeSales.BAS ()
```

tells who the programmer is, as well as the program's module file name. When you're looking through many printed program listings, you quickly can load the one you want to change with Visual Basic's editing tool by looking at the Rems at the top of the program.

Rem's Shortcut: The Apostrophe

Because Rem statements appear so often in programs, the authors of Visual Basic supplied an abbreviation for the Rem statement. Rather than type **Rem**, you can type an apostrophe, **'**, and Visual Basic interprets the line as a remark. Unlike Rem, apostrophe remarks can appear to the right of program lines to help explain each line. Rem statements have to go on separate lines.

The following two lines are identical:

```
Rem This is a remark
' This is a remark
```

Using Helpful Remarks

Although a program without remarks can be difficult to understand, you should use only helpful remarks. Remarks explain what the program code is doing. Therefore, the following remark isn't helpful:

```
' Put the value 3 into the variable named intNumKids
intNumKids = 3
```

Although the preceding remark is lengthy, it doesn't explain why the value 3 is placed in the statement. Consider the following improved example:

```
' Save the number of kids for dependent calculations
intNumKids = 3
```

This remark gives a better idea of what the program's statement (the assignment) is used for. Someone trying to figure out the program would appreciate the second remark more than the first remark.

This example was simple. However, many Visual Basic statements don't require remarks. For example, including a remark to explain the End statement might not be worth much because there's little ambiguity about what's going on; End terminates the running application.

Remember to put remarks in your programs as you write them. You're most familiar with your program logic when you're typing the program in the editor. Some people put off including remarks in their programs until after they write the programs. As a result, the remarks never get included, or the programmer makes only a half-hearted attempt to include them.

Most of this tutorial's examples include remarks that explain the code.

Pt **II**

Hr **6**

> **TIP** Visual Basic lets you insert blank lines in your code to separate sections of code from each other. Visual Basic programs are also known as *free-form*, meaning that statements can begin in any column. Most Visual Basic programmers include lots of *white space* (blank lines and extra spacing here and there) to make programs more readable than they would be if the code were scrunched together.

Example Suppose that you write several standard accounting procedures that you want to use in different applications. Here's a great introductory remark that you can place in the standard module's Declarations section (the Declarations section always appears before any procedures):

```
'''''''''''''''''''''''''''''''''''''''''''''''''''''''''''''''
'                    UTILITY FUNCTIONS                         '
'                                                              '
' This module contains useful functions that you              '
' can use in expressions on your forms and reports.           '
'''''''''''''''''''''''''''''''''''''''''''''''''''''''''''''''
```

The apostrophe looks cleaner and is easier to type than a bunch of `Rem` statements.

The following section of code contains remarks that appear on lines by themselves, as well as to the right of other programming statements:

```
For intPtr = 1 To Len(strAString)    ' Go through string char
                                     ➡by char
    strCurrChar = Mid$(strAString, intPtr, 1) 'Get the current
                                     ➡character.

    Select Case strPrevchar          'If previous char is a
                                     'letter, this char should
                                     'be lowercase.
```

Because the apostrophe is easier to type and can be used where `Rem` can't be used, the rest of this tutorial uses the apostrophe remark rather than `Rem`.

Next Step Sometimes you may write code but want to temporarily block that code from executing. Rather than delete lines of code that you'll have to add later, insert the apostrophe remark before each line. The next time you run the program, Visual Basic will ignore that section of code. When you're ready for the code to execute properly, remove the remarks, and the lines will execute again. Remember that Visual Basic ignores *all* remarks, even if those remarks contain valid Visual Basic code, so remarking out code lets you modify the execution of the program.

Topic 3: Code Window Extras

Hour 7's lesson dives head first into Visual Basic program code. Therefore, this hour's lesson wraps up with a few Code window features that you should learn now so you can implement them as you write code for your applications.

Overview With each version of Visual Basic, Microsoft has improved Visual Basic's features, commands, and development environment. With version 5, Microsoft made some of the most significant Code window improvements since VB's inception. You've already seen how Visual Basic can pop up event lists when you type control names followed by a period so that you can select from the list rather than have to type the control name. The Code window sports many additional features. Some of them you won't be able to learn until you get to certain programming topics later in this course; you can master a few extras in the Code window now to speed your code entry later.

Multiple Code Windows

If your application contains multiple modules, you can open multiple Code windows for each module. Therefore, you can view and edit your form's event procedures at the same time you view and edit your standard module's `Declarations` section.

The multiple Code windows let you edit more than one module's procedure at once. Perhaps you can resize the two Code windows on your screen to see both at once. You can easily copy and move text between the two windows, and you don't have to close one when you want to make a minor change to another module.

Set the Editor Options

Figure 6.7 shows the Options dialog box (choose Options Editor from the Tools menu). As you work with the Visual Basic editor, you'll return to this dialog box to modify the way the editor behaves. Especially if you're new to Visual Basic, you'll want to try some of the options to see which ones fit well within your programming abilities and which detract from writing code.

Pt **II**

Hr **6**

FIG. 6.7

You can set several Code window editor options.

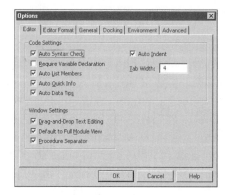

Table 6.2 describes the options you can turn on or off with the Options dialog box.

Table 6.2 The Editor Options You Can Control

Option	Description
Auto Syntax Check	Checks your code as you type it and indicates an error in Visual Basic language spelling or grammar (called *syntax*) while you're typing rather than wait until you run the program.
Require Variable Declaration	Requires that you first tell Visual Basic about all storage locations before you use them (discussed in depth in Hour 7's lesson).
Auto List Members	Lets Visual Basic display the pop-up list of items (such as control events) that can complete the statement you're starting to type. Rather than type the rest of the command or statement, you can select from a list of choices.
Auto Quick Info	Displays pop-up help automatically that shows you the format of lengthy code you're about to enter.
Auto Data Tips	Used during debugging to show the value of storage locations you're pointing to with your mouse.
Auto Indent	Automatically indents your code to align with the previous line to eliminate pressing Tab for subsequent code lines.
Tab Width	Lets you specify exactly how many spaces the Code window's editor should insert when you press Tab.

Option	Description
Drag-and-Drop Text Editing	Lets you drag and drop objects from elsewhere in the development environment into your code.
Default to Full Module View	Sets the default to show the full module's procedures or just one section at a time.
Procedure Separator	Lets you display or hide the separator lines that divide procedures from one another when viewing the full module.

Example Open the ProgWOB sample project that you opened in this lesson's first topic section. Open the Project window if it's not already open, and then open the Forms folder to display all the forms. In this short example, you're going to open two Code windows at once to see how easy Visual Basic editing can be.

Double-click the form named `frmEvents` to display the form. From the View menu choose Code to see the code in the form module. Now, double-click the form named `frmSticks` to display that form and again choose View Code. At first, it appears that Visual Basic closed the first Code window when you opened the second window, but if you pull down the Window menu, you'll see two sets of code: one for the `frmEvents` code and one for the `frmSticks` code.

Click the Code window's Restore button (the center button on the far right of the title bar). Visual Basic resizes all the open windows, as shown in Figure 6.8.

After you resize and move the Code windows, you can position both open Code windows so that you can see both sets of code at once. (You can click each Form window close button to close the Form windows, because they will probably get in your way.) Clicking in one window and then the other moves the text cursor to the next window and activates that window for data entry. You now can work within one Code window and view code within the other for reference, or you can use the Windows Clipboard to copy and move code between the windows.

FIG. 6.8
Working with multiple Code windows.

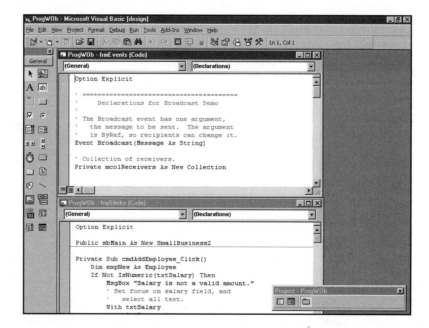

CAUTION If you make changes with the code, do *not* save anything when you close Visual Basic or attempt to open another project. If you inadvertently type something over a sample application, you'll have to reinstall the samples from Visual Basic's installation CD-ROM.

Next Step Scroll through the code windows that you have open from the last example. Study the way the Visual Basic programmers used remarks. You won't see the **Rem** statement because most programmers use the shorter apostrophe remark. Also, the apostrophe is cleaner and lets programmers add remarks to the right of existing lines of code.

Do you notice something about the colors inside the Code window? The remark color varies from the other code. Some code is black (variable, control, and procedure names), some is green (remarks), and some is blue (reserved keywords). The colors give you clues to the type of code you're typing. As you press Enter after typing a line, Visual Basic colors the code according to a present plan. For example, if your remarks appear in green, you'll get used to seeing green remarks. If you type a remark but Visual

Basic doesn't color the remark green by the time you get to the next line, you'll have a good idea that you did something wrong, such as omitted the apostrophe.

Summary

This hour's lesson begins the second part of your Visual Basic night schooling. You've seen an introduction to Visual Basic, created simple applications, placed controls, set properties, and now understand more about how code fits into the Visual Basic picture.

This hour's lesson shed some needed light on Visual Basic code. You learned that not every application contains the same sets of code. Some applications contain form modules, whereas others contain two other modules—standard and class. A standard module often resides in several applications because of the common code you can put there.

Not only should you worry about your code's content, but also the code's documentation. Be sure to add remarks throughout your code, describing the code's duties along the way. The `Declarations` section (always the first section of any module) is a great place to put a remark with your name, so other programmers can contact you later if they have questions about the program you wrote.

In Hour 7, you'll begin learning more of the Visual Basic language so that you can begin to add power to your programs.

Hour 6 Quiz

You can find the answers to the following questions on the accompanying CD-ROM and on the Virtual Classroom Web site.

On the CD

1. **True or false:** You'll find Visual Basic code in event procedures and general procedures.

2. **True or false:** General procedures contain no event procedure code.

3. **True or false:** A form module contains only form design contents and controls but no code.

4. What kind of code can you put in a standard module?

Pt **II**

Hr **6**

5. To what specific application code is the `Declarations` section available?

6. What object name do you see in the Code window when you display the `Declarations` section?

7. Why does Visual Basic not boldface every event in the procedures drop-down list?

8. What are the two kinds of remark statements? Why would a programmer use one over the other?

9. What do the Code window's two drop-down list boxes do?

10. Name one advantage of multiple Code windows.

Hour 6 Homework Exercises

1. Open the Code window for one of the sample applications. Look at the class module to see whether you see differences between it and the form module. (Some sample applications don't have class modules.)

2. Find three sequential lines that contain no remarks but contain executable code. Turn these lines into remarks with three apostrophes. (Don't save the file if it's a sample file.)

3. Click the Code window's view buttons to see the difference between the Full Module View and the Procedure View. From the Full Module View, scroll through the entire module. If the module is lengthy, you'll see why most Visual Basic programmers select code sections that they want to work on from the procedure drop-down list box.

Handling Data

COMPUTERS ARE ALL ABOUT data processing. The computer blindly follows the programmer's orders and manipulates the data so that reports and other meaningful results can follow. Therefore, you must learn how to construct and work with data inside your Visual Basic programs. The Visual Basic programming language helps you transfer data back and forth between controls, the printer, the disk drives, the screen, the keyboard, the mouse, and the CPU (the brain of your computer). Therefore, to master the Visual Basic language, you must master the data that forms the program's foundation.

This hour's lesson explains what kinds of data Visual Basic recognizes and how to specify that data in Visual Basic terms. This lesson won't have much

hands-on at the machine, because you'll be learning theory that you can't quite put into practice yet until you learn a few additional parts of the Visual Basic language. Nevertheless, this lesson provides the language fundamentals that the rest of this course will build on. By the time you finish this lesson, you'll be writing straight Visual Basic code like a pro.

Topic 1: Introducing Data Types

Data comes in all shapes and sizes. Your applications will work with text, numbers, pictures, sounds, and video. Also, your programs will manage combinations of the various kinds of data as well. This topic introduces you to the Visual Basic *data types*. Visual Basic supports a fixed number of data types. When your program works with any kind of data, you have to tell Visual Basic the data type. If you want your program to generate data, you have to tell Visual Basic the kind of data to generate.

▶▶ **FAST TRACK**

Are you familiar with QBasic or previous versions of Visual Basic? If so, you'll see that Visual Basic 5 doesn't introduce anything new into the data type assortment. You might want to skip to the next topic section (p. 165) to review variable storage.

▼ **NOTE**

Every programming language supports certain kinds of data types. When you familiarize yourself with data types, you'll begin to see how programming languages process data. You'll also begin to recognize the flow of data between program components. In a Visual Basic program, a control might send data the user entered to the running program for disk storage. (You'll learn about special holding places in memory that hold data in the second topic section, "Variables Hold Data.") Not all data types can work together, so you'll have to make sure that you don't try to store one data type in a storage location designed to hold a different data type. ▲

Overview Visual Basic supports 12 data types. VB also supports *user-defined data types* that you can create (which are explained in Hour 21's lesson, "Accessing Files"). This topic section introduces you to the 12 data types and shows you examples of the different kinds of data that fit within those types. When learning a new language, you must learn how the language internally stores different data types because you sometimes can gain efficiencies when you know how the language stores data. Visual Basic categorizes the data types into numeric, text, and special data type groups.

▼ **NOTE**

This topic section concentrates on *literal* data, sometimes called *constants*. Literals are unchanging data values such as the number 823. When you know how to work with literals, you can easily comprehend how Visual Basic supports literals as well as *variables*, or data that changes. You learn about variables in the second topic section, "Variables Hold Data." Generally, VB programmers use the term *literals* rather than *constants* because Visual Basic includes some special named constants, such as those you find in the Properties window (for example, the three values in the Label control's `Alignment` drop-down list), that you can use in your programs when you want to designate special values. ▲

Numeric Data

Visual Basic supports eight numeric data types. You'll see all of them at one time or another, so even if you don't consider yourself a "math person," you should get to know these data types. When you have to write a program that deals with ages, prices, counts, or virtually any other kind of numeric quantity, it will be your job to figure out the correct numeric data type to use. Visual Basic will do all the math, but you'll have to set up Visual Basic's data properly so that VB can do its job.

Numeric data generally falls into two categories: integers and decimals. An *integer* is a whole number that doesn't have a decimal place. The following values are integers:

454   0   −191   47

Notice that 0 is an integer, and negative numbers can also be integers. As long as the number contains no fractional portion with a decimal point, you can think of the value as an integer. Common integers are ages, month and day numbers, counts, and other numeric values that you work with that typically contain no decimal part.

Decimal values, however, contain a fractional portion that follows a decimal point, even if that fractional portion is 0. Here are some sample non-integer decimal values:

Pt **II**

Hr **7**

534.2233	0.0	−12.3454	10000.000001
5.434E+12	−93E+1	6.5348729012D−5	
8.52918300009D+3			

Decimal values always have decimal points. Even if the decimal value ends with one or more zeros to the right of the decimal, the value is still considered to be a non-integer decimal value. The decimal point indicates a precision. In other words, the value 1.23 means that the value is precise to two decimal places. When you need to represent a numeric literal in your program, you'll type the literal inside the Code window. (You'll see later this hour how to type other kinds of literals.)

▼ **NOTE**

Decimal values are often called *floating-point values*. ▲

▼ **SCIENTIFIC NOTATION**

You were probably reading along just fine until you saw the E's and D's in the preceding list of decimal values. The E stands for *exponent*. Because computers use exponents all the time, now would be a good time to familiarize yourself with them. The D stands for *double-precision exponent*, which provides more precision than the regular exponent. (The regular exponent is often called a *single-precision exponent*.)

Both data types represent a shorthand numeric notation called *scientific notation*. (You may see scientific notation with uppercase or lowercase E's and D's because the notation's letter case is insignificant.) Scientific notation lets you represent extremely large and extremely small decimal numbers without typing lots of zeroes or other digits to the right of the decimal point.

You can convert a scientific notation value to its real meaning by multiplying the number to the left of the D or E by 10 raised to the number after the E or D. Therefore, 3.120E+7 represents 31,200,000; you multiply 3.120 by 10 raised to the 7th power, or 10,000,000. If the exponent is negative, divide the number by 10 raised to the power. Therefore, 5.128172356D−4 represents .0005128172356, or 5.128172356 divided by 10,000. Use a double-precision exponent when you need Visual Basic to track decimal places that extend past seven digits.

If you don't use scientific programming, you may still see scientific notation occasionally. Visual Basic might display a value as a scientific notational amount to save room in certain situations. Data tables, such as ones you'll see throughout this hour's lesson, frequently use scientific notation to show extreme values within a limited amount of space. ▲

Often, you'll need to know how much storage Visual Basic uses to hold numeric values. Although memory is cheaper than ever before, and although most computers have ample RAM these days, you'll want to write efficient programs and not use more memory than necessary to hold program data. Integers generally consume less memory space than decimal values because your computer doesn't have to keep track of the extra precision required by decimals. As you learn more about data types in this lesson, you'll learn how much memory each type of number consumes.

▼ NOTE

Generally, you can't determine how much memory a value takes by the number itself. Surprisingly, the number 1.1 consumes more memory than 32,766. Fortunately, you won't have to bother too much with numeric literal storage requirements, but you'll need to be aware of how much memory each data type takes when you learn about storing numbers in your program variables later in this hour's lesson. ▲

Integer Types

If the distinction between integers and decimals weren't enough, Visual Basic separates values into different kinds of integers and decimals. Table 7.1 describes the three kinds of integers.

Table 7.1 The Integer Data Types

Data Type	Storage	Range
Byte	1 byte	0 to 255
Integer	2 bytes	–32,768 to 32,767
Long	4 bytes	–2,147,483,648 to 2,147,483,647

▼ NOTE

Byte values are always zero or positive. ▲

A *byte* is one memory location. Visual Basic uses the keyword **Byte** to represent the data type that holds very small integers ranging from 0 to 255. Therefore, if you need to hold people's ages, you might consider using **Byte** values because a person's age will never be negative or more than 255. However, if you need to keep track of integer measurements that go negative or go as high as 32,767, you must use an integer (represented in Visual Basic with the keyword `Integer`) or long integers (represented by `Long`).

Why not just use long integers for *all* integer values? After all, long integers hold virtually any integer you'll work with. But using longs for all integer data would be extremely inefficient. Visual Basic would have to store all data in 4 bytes and move 4 bytes every time the data moved or changed. Reserve such long integers for those data values that might require the extra range.

Decimal Types

Table 7.2 lists the decimal value data types that Visual Basic supports.

Table 7.2 The Decimal Data Types

Data Type	Storage	Range
Single	4 bytes	$-3.402823E+38$ to $-1.401298E-45$ for negative values; $1.401298E-45$ to $3.402823E+38$ for positive values
Double	8 bytes	$-1.79769313486232E+308$ to $-4.94065645841247E-324$ for negatives; $4.94065645841247E-324$ to $1.79769313486232E+308$ for positives
Currency	8 bytes	$-922,337,203,685,477.5808$ to $922,337,203,685,477.5807$
Decimal	14 bytes	$+/-79,228,162,514,264,337,593,543,950,335$ if you use no decimal; $+/-7.9228162514264337593543950335$ with up to 28 decimal places

▼ NOTE

Technically, the `Currency` data type is known as a *scaled integer* and stored as an extremely large integer value and converted to dollars and cents when needed. The scaling keeps the precision that you want for currency amounts, because you never want calculations to round currency values but always work out exactly to proper dollar-and-cent values. For practical purposes, however, you and Visual Basic can treat currency values as though they're decimals. ▲

> **CAUTION** At this time, Visual Basic doesn't support the data type that the `Decimal` keyword represents except in special situations. Future versions may do more with this extremely precise decimal value.

For most applications, you'll use single-precision values (represented by the `Single` keyword) for most of your decimal values, unless your program requires extremely precise values that might take an extraordinary range as found in scientific and mathematical situations. Use double-precision (represented by the `Double` keyword) only for those extreme values. Of course, you'll use the currency data type for all monetary values so that Visual Basic can track the cents portions correctly.

▼ **NOTE**

Visual Basic is designed to work in any country that Windows supports. Therefore, if your International settings are set to Italy, Visual Basic prints your currency values with commas and decimal points reversed from the North American standard. ▲

Text Data

As mentioned in Hour 1's lesson, Visual Basic's roots are in the BASIC programming language. Although BASIC was considered a beginner's language, its ease of use was the strength that kept it in use for a long time. When Microsoft decided to improve on the language, the company kept the fundamentals there so that new programmers would take to programming more quickly than otherwise would happen.

In addition to its ease of use, BASIC had another technical advantage over all other languages of its time and over just about all languages developed since: BASIC and its descendants fully support text data and provide a large collection of text-manipulation tools that other languages only dream about.

Computers simply don't work with text internally as well as numbers, especially large streams of text known as strings. (A *string* is a collection of zero or more characters considered to be one unit, such as a name, sentence, paragraph, or any other collection of characters a program needs to track.) BASIC's creators took the pain out of string programming by adding string processing to BASIC's core functions.

Pt **II**

Hr **7**

As an incarnation of BASIC, Visual Basic holds true to its roots by providing much text support. Table 7.3 describes the two kinds of text data types that Visual Basic supports. In almost every case, VB programmers refer to text, whether the text is a single character, or 200 characters, as *string data*.

Table 7.3   String Data Types

Data Type	Storage	Range
`String` (fixed length)	Length of string	1 to about 65,400 characters
`String` (variable length)	Length of string plus 10 bytes	0 to 2 billion characters

You always enclose string literals in quotation marks. A string can contain *any* character. Therefore, the following are all valid string literals:

```
"I love Rome"      "Z"     "w20kd-x302,m,x-222"      ""
```

Enclosing numeric digits inside quotation marks tells Visual Basic that the literal is a string, not a numeric literal. You can never perform math calculations with string literals, even if those literals contain valid numbers, unless you first convert the strings to numbers by using standard Visual Basic conversion methods that you'll learn about in later lessons (especially in Hour 14, "Using the Supplied Functions"). Quotation marks with nothing between them represent a zero-length string literal. Surprisingly, string literals with nothing in them, called *empty strings* or *null strings*, are used a lot as Visual Basic placeholders for future text.

▼ **NOTE**

Visual Basic supports a keyword called `Null` that you can store in strings and other kinds of data holders. `Null` indicates that the data contains no valid information, and you might initialize a storage area with `Null`.

The keyword `Empty`, if stored in a data location, indicates that you've not initialized the value yet. Empty numeric values contain `0` (or `0.0`); empty strings contain `""` and are zero bytes long. ▲

As you can see in Table 7.3, Visual Basic uses the same keyword, `String`, to represent both fixed-length and variable-length strings. When working with string literals, the distinction isn't as critical as it will be when you work with string storage, as you learn in the next topic section.

Special Data

Table 7.4 lists the remaining data types that Visual Basic supports. Although one tends to think of data as falling into the numeric or string categories, Visual Basic's extra data types let you do more with today's kinds of data values such as dates and even object data such as graphic and sound files.

Table 7.4 Special Data Types

Data Type	Storage	Range
Date	8 bytes	January 1, 100 to December 31, 9999
Boolean	2 bytes	True or False only
Object	4 bytes	Any embedded object
Variant (with numbers)	16 bytes	Any value up to Double
Variant (with text)	Length of text plus 22 bytes	Same as variable-length String

The Variant data type can represent *any* kind of data, except fixed-length strings. Variant data (used with the Variant keyword) offers VB programmers all kinds of programming flexibility that didn't exist before Visual Basic arrived on the scene. Originally, the VB designers added the Variant data type to support data coming from form controls that had no real data type or that may take just about any form in many instances. As you work through this night-school tutorial, you'll learn more ways to use variants in your programs.

The Date data type holds the time as well as the date. Visual Basic lets you specify date or time value literals in several forms, as long as you enclose the date literal within pound signs (#). The following are all valid literals that represent the Date data type:

```
#April 6, 1937#
#4:54 am#
#23:01:21#
#1-2-1998#
#4-Mar-2004#
```

Basically, any date or time format that your computer recognizes, respecting the International settings you've set in Windows, the Date data type will represent.

Pt II

Hr 7

▼ **NOTE**

Occasionally, your Visual Basic programs will have to convert a date value to a number or a numeric data type. Visual Basic stores the `Date` data type as an 8-byte floating-point number, so the conversion is possible. The value to the left of the decimal represents the date; the value to the right of the decimal point represents the time, where .0 is midnight and .5 is noon. ▲

Visual Basic uses either a 24-hour clock or `am` and `pm` indicators, depending on the value of your Windows International date and time settings that you can adjust in your Windows Control Panel.

The `Boolean` data type represents true or false states. For example, if you needed to represent a past-due flag, you'd use the `Boolean` data type and store `True` or `False` (both are keywords) in the `Boolean` storage location. Occasionally, you may convert a Boolean value to a numeric data type; in that case, `False` becomes `0` and `True` becomes `-1`.

Example   Although this data type topic is one of the longest single topic sections in the book, the material is theory. In many cases, you don't have to worry about all the specific cases. In other words, if you need to send a number to a control inside a Visual Basic program (as opposed to doing so in the Properties window), you just type the number with the appropriate assignment statement and not worry whether the literal number is an `Integer` data type or `Double` data type or anything else.

Perhaps the most important lesson you can glean from this topic is the characters that must enclose certain literals. Never enclose numeric data types inside any characters; just type them directly like this:

```
45
-6756.4322
```

Also, never use commas inside numbers, unless your Windows International settings use the comma for the decimal position (in which case you should not embed points inside numbers).

You can use scientific notation any time you want (for example, for 6756.4322 type **6.7564322E+3**). However, you should save scientific notation for extremely small or extremely large numbers because scientific notation wouldn't save coding time otherwise.

"343", "Terry", "", "January 5, 2031", and "6104 West 2nd Street, #7" are all string literals due to the quotation marks. #January 5, 2031# is a Date literal because of the pound signs.

Next Step   In certain situations, you need to ensure that Visual Basic interprets a numeric literal as one of the specific data types. For example, you might type the literal **16** and need Visual Basic to store or display the value as a Long data type, even though 16 fits within a Byte or Integer data type.

Therefore, Visual Basic supports the *data-type suffix characters* in Table 7.5. These suffix characters let you specify the data type for numeric literals when you need to. Occasionally, Visual Basic also uses the data-type suffix characters when displaying numeric information. Therefore, if you type **16#**, Visual Basic treats the number 16 as a double-precision value.

Table 7.5 Numeric Data-Type Suffix Characters

Suffix Character	Data Type Described
&	Long
!	Single
#	Double
@	Currency

The scientific notation's E represents a single-precision value and D represents double-precision value, so the corresponding letter indicates the scientific notation data types.

Pt **II**
Hr **7**

Topic 2: Variables Hold Data

Now that you've mastered data types, you'll have little trouble understanding how to store that data inside programs. Whereas literals don't change, storage locations do. For example, you might designate a storage location to hold the hours worked in a payroll application. The number of hours worked each week might change, so you can't use a literal (such as 40) to represent the current number of hours worked for each employee. Instead, you designate a variable to hold the value. *Variables* are named storage locations inside your program that hold values that can vary.

Overview You, the VB programmer, are responsible for creating and naming variables in your programs. You need a variable for each storage value you want to track. If you need to keep track of a customer's name, account number, and balance, you'll need three variables.

Variables hold specific kinds of data. `Integer` variables hold integers and `Byte` variables hold byte values and so on. Visual Basic lets you create variables for every data type (except for the special `Decimal` data type, which Visual Basic doesn't support as fully as the other data types). This topic section teaches you how to declare variables. Before you can use a variable, you must *declare* the variable so that your program knows you need the variable storage later. Visual Basic lets you declare as many variables as you need. In many cases, the first few lines of a procedure list variable declarations.

▼ NOTE

You must give variables different names so that Visual Basic can distinguish one variable from another. Two variables can't have the same name within the same procedure. **▲**

TIP Think of a variable as a box in your computer that holds only one value at a time. You can store a number in a numeric variable or a string in a string variable. No matter how long the string is, the string variable can hold the string but only one string at a time. If you store one string and then later store another string in the variable, the second string replaces the first one.

Declaring Variables with *Dim*

You must declare a variable before you can use it. When you declare the variable, you specify the variable's name and data type. A variable's name and data type never change. Visual Basic contains several statements that declare variables, but the most common statement is `Dim`, which stands for *dimension*. Although the `Dim` statement takes on many forms, here is a standard `Dim` statement format for declaring variables:

```
Dim VarName As DataType
```

VarName is a variable name that you declare. *DataType* is any of the data types you learned in the previous topic section (except `Decimal`). Here are several variable declarations:

```
Dim Age As Byte
Dim Salary As Single
Dim FirstName As String
```

These statements declare three variables. If you typed these statements at the beginning of a procedure (immediately following the procedure's first line), any line in the rest of the procedure could use the variables. (The variables are known to be *local* to the procedure.)

CAUTION Declaring strings can be confusing because of the two string data types. You'll see a more complete explanation of declaring string variables in this topic's "Next Step" section. If you want to review the Declarations section, look at Hour 6, "Understanding the VB Program Structure."

TIP If you declare one or more variables at the beginning of a module (outside the procedures inside the Declarations area), the variables are available to the entire module. Good programming practices dictate that you keep data as *local* as possible, meaning that procedure-level variables generally protect values better and make for more maintainable programs. If a variable is needed in several procedures, however, you might choose to make the variable less local by declaring it in the Declarations area. If you replace Dim with Public, the variable is available to the *entire application*, even if the application contains multiple modules. Such *global* variables, however, often lend themselves to programming troubles if you use them for variables that don't need such a global scope. You might accidentally change a variable in one procedure that another procedure has initialized. You can safely declare and use variables without having to review variable names in every other part of your program if you stick to local variables only.

Pt **II**

Hr **7**

The variable's name must follow these naming rules:

- It must begin with an alphabetic letter.
- It can contain letters or numbers. Some special characters, such as the underscore (_) are allowed, but if you stick to letters and numbers, you'll never use a special character that's illegal.

TIP Some programmers use underscores to separate words inside a variable name, as in First_name. However, more modern programming techniques prefer mixing uppercase and lowercase letters to distinguish between such words, as in FirstName.

- It can range from 1 to 255 characters.
- Never embed spaces in a variable name.

The following are all valid variable names:

```
AmtDue      SalesTotal     Count      Qtr1      Year98Sales
```

Many Visual Basic programmers prefix each variable name with a data-type prefix (see Table 7.6 for some prefix suggestions). If you prefix a variable with its data-type abbreviation, you'll rarely forget a data type and attempt to transfer a `String` variable to a `Double` variable some time. (Such transfers would cause problems.)

Table 7.6 Suggested Variable Name Prefixes

Prefix	Data Type	Example
bln	Boolean	blnIsOverTime
byt	Byte	bytAge
cur	Currency	curHourlyPay
dtm	Date	dteFirstBegan
dbl	Double	dblMicroMeasurement
int	Integer	intCount
lng	Long	lngStarDistance
obj	Object	objSoundClip
sng	Single	sngYearSales
str	String	strLastName
vnt	Variant	vntControlValue

CAUTION Never do calculations with string variables, even if those variables hold numerical digits that look like numbers. If you need to work mathematically with a value stored in a `String` data type variable, convert and transfer the variable's value to a numeric variable before you perform the calculation.

▼ **NOTE**

Visual Basic does let you make several transfers that cause no conflict, such as putting a `Single` value into a `Double` variable or assigning a `Byte` value to an `Integer` or `Double`. Such assignments don't cause any problems because the target variable is large enough to hold the value.

Also, the target variable is numeric, so the number transports well to the more precise data type. Transferring a `Double` to a `Byte`, however, could cause problems because `Byte` can't hold the range of values that a `Double` can. ▲

If you don't declare variable names, one of two things will happen:

- Visual Basic assumes that the variable is a `Variant` unless you use one of the data-type suffix characters listed in Table 7.7.
- Visual Basic issues an undeclared variable error if the `Option Explicit` command appears in your module's `Declarations` section, or if the Editor page of the Options dialog box (accessed via the Tools menu's Options command) has the Require Variable Declaration option checked (see Figure 7.1).

Table 7.7 Visual Basic's Variable Data-Type Suffix Characters

Character	Data Type	Example
%	Integer	Amount%
&	Long	Length&
!	Single	Sales!
#	Double	Measurement#
@	Currency	Cost@
$	String	CompanyName$

Pt **II**

Hr **7**

FIG. 7.1

The Require Variable Declaration option requires that you declare all variables before you use them.

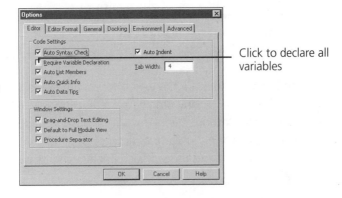

Click to declare all variables

Although you can voluntarily declare all variables before you use them, the `Option Explicit` statement or the checked Require Variable Declaration option tells Visual Basic to issue an error if you fail to declare a variable. Such safeguards are recommended; without them, if you inadvertently typed the `amtGiven` variable as `amtGaven`, your program won't work properly. What's more, the bug can be difficult to trace if your application is large and contains lots of code.

If you don't declare variables and if you don't have one of the declaration requirement options set, you can specify the data type of an undeclared variable by suffixing the variable name with one of the suffix characters in Table 7.7. Nevertheless, defining a variable as the `Single` data type with `Dim` is clearer and less error-prone than simply making up the variable at the time you use it with an add-on `!` at the end of the name.

Example   Suppose that you need a variable that will hold the number of days worked in a month. The following statement declares such a variable:

```
Dim k As Integer
```

Although `k` is a valid variable name, the name has no relationship to its usage. Why not be more creative and name the variable as follows?

```
Dim intDaysWorked As Integer
```

Although this variable name requires more typing, you later can modify and maintain the program and know exactly what `intDaysWorked` holds and that the variable is an integer.

> **TIP**   Good Boolean variable names usually can be phrased as questions or statements that their `True` and `False` values will describe, such as `blnIsWorking`, `blnGetsTaxed`, or `blnPaidOvertime`.

If you didn't explicitly declare the variable, you'd have to use the data-type suffix character any time you referenced the variable, such as `intDaysWorked%`. Without the suffix, Visual Basic would treat the variable as though it were of the `Variant` data type. Generally, you write better code if you stay away from the suffix characters and use `Dim` to declare all variables explicitly.

If you declare `intDaysWorked` at the top of a procedure, the variable is available only to that procedure. If you declare `intDaysWorked` in the module's `Declarations` section, `intDaysWorked` is available to every procedure in the module, but loses some of the protection from inside the procedure scope that it would have if you declare it at the top of a procedure. If you replace `Dim` with the `Public` keyword, the variable is available to the entire application, including other modules, but is vulnerable to accidental changes from elsewhere in the code.

When you protect a variable by limiting its scope, you keep other procedures from changing the variable's value. Also, if you happen to give two variables the same name in two different procedures, those variables won't conflict if they're local just to their own procedure.

> **CAUTION** Try to avoid giving two variables within the same application the same name, except for work variables that hold temporary counts and totals. If the variables are global, you'll overwrite one with the other's value; if the variables are local to different procedures, you might get confused when you later modify the code.

If you want to declare two or more variables on the same line, you can do so like this:

```
Dim intNum1 As Integer, intNum2 As Integer
```

You *must* list the `Integer` keyword on both declarations. If you omit a `Dim` variable's data type, Visual Basic declares that variable as a `Variant` data type. Therefore, the following statement declares only one `Single` (`sng4`) and three `Variant` variables (`sng1` through `sng3`):

```
Dim sng1, sng2, sng3, sng4 As Single
```

Pt **II**
Hr **7**

Next Step   The `Dim` statement works well for all data types, but strings add one extra problem. If you're declaring variable-length strings, you can use `Dim` as you might expect. The following statement declares a string variable named `strCity`:

```
Dim strCity As String
```

`strCity` is a variable-length string. Therefore, you can store any string of any length into the variable. (The next topic section explains how to store data in variables that you've declared.) When you store a string in `strCity`, such as `"Miami"` (the quotation marks don't get stored into the string variable but serve only to delimit the string literal), you can later store a different string, such as `"Indianapolis"`, in `strCity`. Visual Basic expands and contracts a variable-length string *during runtime* as needed to hold the strings you transfer to the variables.

> **TIP** Use string variables for ZIP codes, phone numbers, and Social Security numbers. Although these kinds of values contain only numeric digits, you never perform math on them. When you must track such strings of digits, be sure to use string variables to hold the data.

If you want to declare a fixed-length string, you have to tell Visual Basic at the time that you declare the string exactly what maximum length the string will ever be. Add the `Dim` option * *length* like this:

```
Dim strCity As String * 15
```

The `strCity` string can now hold only strings up to 15 characters long (from zero to 15 characters).

▼ NOTE

Variable-length strings are certainly easier to work with than fixed-length strings, and take less effort to declare. Nevertheless, you may need to declare fixed-length strings when dealing with communications or disk file data, or when storing data that will appear in a fixed-length control such as a label. ▲

Topic 3: Working with Variables

When you declare variables, Visual Basic creates the variable; reserves the name for that variable's scope; designates the variable's data type; and initializes the variable with a `0` for numeric variables, null strings (`""`) for variable-length strings, zeros for fixed-length strings, and the special keyword `Empty` for `Variant` data-typed variables. Your program then changes the variable's value right away, perhaps by using the variable for a total or a counter. The data that your program stores in variables might come from a control, a dialog box, a literal that you type in the program, another variable, or a calculation.

Overview This topic section explains how to use Visual Basic's assignment statement. The *assignment statement* transfers values into variables. You must declare the variables before assigning values to those variables; otherwise, you get an error unless you've turned off the explicit declaration options mentioned in the previous topic section.

The assignment statement is simple to use. All you must ensure is that you transfer the appropriate kind of data to the variable.

The Assignment Statement

Here is the assignment statement's format:

```
[Let] VarName = Expression
```

The square brackets indicate that the `Let` keyword is optional; hardly any VB programmer types `Let`. *VarName* is any valid variable that you've declared or defined with a suffix data-type character. *Expression* refers to a literal, a variable, a control, or a combination of such items in a manner that Visual Basic can convert to the correct data type.

If you wanted to assign an hourly pay rate to a variable that you've declared to be a `Currency` data type, the following statement would do just that:

```
curHourRate = 12.75
```

Of course, you could also write the following, but `Let` requires extra typing:

```
Let curHourRate = 12.75
```

Remember that you can apply data-type suffix characters to literals, so you could also write this:

```
curHourRate = 12.75@
```

Such literal data-type suffix characters aren't required. If you had omitted the @ on the currency literal, Visual Basic would convert the `12.75` to a `Currency` data type automatically before storing the value in `curHourRate`.

▼ **NOTE**
Make sure that you don't assign strings to any kind of numeric variables or numeric values to any kind of string variables. Visual Basic can't perform the automatic conversion on such data-type differences. ▲

Pt **II**

Hr **7**

Be sure to remember the quotation marks if you assign a string literal to a string variable:

```
strMyState = "Oklahoma"
```

Keep in mind that a variable can hold only one value at a time. Therefore, if another statement in the program assigned another string to `strMyState`,

```
strMyState = "Indiana"
```

`strMyState` would now hold `"Indiana"` (without the quotation marks).

The *Expression* might be another variable. Therefore, the following statement would also store `"Indiana"` in the variable, because `strMyState` holds that value:

```
strNewState = strMyState
```

CAUTION Don't treat the assignment as a *move* operation. The assignment sends a copy of whatever is on the right side of the equal sign to the variable on the left. The right side's variable *still* holds its value after the assignment finishes. Therefore, unlike a move operation, the assignment ensures that *both variables* hold the same value after the assignment takes place.

As a general rule, control values take on the `Variant` data type. Visual Basic performs the needed data-type conversion if you assign a control value to a variable, as in

```
IntBookCount = txtBook.Text
```

Always remember to separate the control name from the property with the period, as shown.

This topic section has assigned only literals, controls, and variables to declared variables. The next hour's lesson explains how to assign more complex expressions to variables.

Example When assigning literal dates and times to a `Date` variable data type, enclose the literals in pound signs. The following assignment statements assign a starting date and time to two `Date` data-typed variables:

```
dteDateStarted = #6-Jul-1992#
dteTimeStarted = #08:30#
```

You can assign `True` and `False` directly to Boolean variables as follows:

```
blnGetsDiscount = False
blnTaxed = True
```

The `True` and `False` literals are Visual Basic keywords that you can use both in assignments and elsewhere. Although you can assign numeric values to Boolean variables (and if you do, `0` converts to `False` and anything else converts to `True`), stick to the literals to make your programs as clear as possible.

Next Step The assignment statement always takes the right side of the equal sign and transfers that side to the variable on the left. The assignment statement works for controls as well. If a variable holds a value you've defined and you want to send that variable's value to a control's property, you can put the control's property on the left of the equal sign to receive the assignment. Therefore, the following statement assigns a literal to a control property inside a Visual Basic procedure:

```
cmdClickMe.Caption = "Press &Here"
```

The following statement assigns a variable named `strEntered` to a label:

```
lblTitle.Caption = strEntered
```

If you put the first assignment inside the command button's `Click` event procedure, the command button's caption would change as soon as the user clicked the button. The event procedure might look something like this:

```
Private Sub mnuFileExit_Click()
  cmdClickMe.Caption = "Press &Here"
End Sub
```

Summary

You're on your way to writing advanced Visual Basic programs! Although you didn't work hands-on with Visual Basic in this chapter, you learned programming theory that applies not only to Visual Basic, but to all other programming languages to some degree. This hour's topic taught you the importance of data types so that you can declare the correct kinds of data that your program needs to process.

After you declare your variables, your program can work with those variables by assigning values to the variables and using the values inside variables for other assignments. The assignment statement transfers data to and from controls as well as variables.

In the next hour, you'll learn how to complicate the assignment's right side somewhat. By writing expressions that Visual Basic evaluates to specific values, you can store the results of calculations inside variables.

Hour 7 Quiz

You can find the answers for the following questions on the accompanying CD-ROM and on the Virtual Classroom Web site.

On the CD

1. What kinds of numeric data does Visual Basic support?
2. Name the two kinds of string data Visual Basic works with.
3. What's the difference between a literal and a variable?
4. **True or false:** "July 7, 1998" represents a Date data type literal.
5. What's the difference between a fixed-length string and a variable-length string?
6. Which of the following are valid variable names?

   ```
   X        Boolean     MrBoolean      Amt1998      1998Amt
   DoRight        My Age
   ```

7. Why do we sometimes use scientific notation?
8. What characters must enclose string literals?
9. How can variable-name prefixes help you reduce program data conflicts?
10. **True or false:** You can assign a literal to a control but not a control to a literal.

Hour 7 Homework Exercises

1. Convert the following scientific notational values to their actual values and tell the data type of each:

   ```
   1.234E+12     −9.01D−4     7.123E−1
   ```

2. Write the code that declares four variables: one for your first name, one for your last name, one for your age, and one for your ZIP code. Limit the first name's storage space to 10 characters. Make sure that you use the correct data type for the ZIP code.

3. Write the declarations for two string variables: your country and your mother's first name. Limit each string to a maximum of 15 characters.

4. Write assignment statements that fill your variables in exercise 2 with appropriate data.

Understanding Fundamental Expressions

HOUR 8

During this hour you will learn

▶ What operators are

▶ In which order Visual Basic computes expressions

▶ How to override the operator order

▶ Why you should use conditional operators

▶ How to combine operators to create compound expressions

THIS HOUR'S LESSON FURTHERS Hour 7's lesson by showing you how to formulate Visual Basic expressions. An *expression* is a math- or string-related set of variables, literals, and control values that combine with math- and string-related operators to produce a resulting value. Visual Basic assigns that produced value to the object to the left of the assignment's equal sign.

Reread the definition of expression above. Now that you have that out of the way, you'll be pleased to know that working with expressions is simpler than describing the process! Often, you'll put together fairly complex expressions in your assignment statements, even if you don't consider yourself a math wizard.

Topic 1: Understanding Operators

An *operator* is a symbol used for addition, subtraction, multiplication, division, and other calculations. In addition to symbols, the Visual Basic language includes some abbreviations that work as operators as well.

Operators aren't just for mathematical calculations. Visual Basic has operators that work with string expressions as well.

▶▶ FAST TRACK

If you know all about computer operators that manipulate data, such as * and /, read through this hour's operator tables to brush up on the ones that are new to you. Then move to Hour 9's lesson, "Working with Interactive Keyboard and Screen I/O" (p. 203), where you learn how to enter and display data by using special built-in Visual Basic routines. In particular, make sure that you understand Mod and Like, because both are limited to Visual Basic and other recent BASIC language descendants.

Overview   This topic section explores the operators through tables that explain many of Visual Basic's more common operators. You'll see that Visual Basic does all your math for you, but you must set up the operations correctly.

The Common Operators

Visual Basic's operators are similar to those you use to do arithmetic. Table 8.1 lists Visual Basic's common operators and their meanings.

Table 8.1   Visual Basic Common Operators

Operator	Meaning
*	Multiplication
/	Division
+	Addition or concatenation
-	Subtraction
^	Exponentiation
\	Integer division
Mod	Modulus

▼ **NOTE**

Most of these fundamental operators are mathematically related. The plus sign (+) sometimes operates on both string and numeric values (as you'll see), but you'll apply the rest of the operators to only mathematical calculations. ▲

The Four Primary Operators

The four primary Visual Basic operators (*, /, +, and –) operate just as their counterparts in mathematics do. Multiplication, division, addition, and subtraction operations produce the same results as when you do these math functions with a calculator. The four examples in Table 8.2 illustrate each operator.

Table 8.2   Results of Calculations Done with Primary Operators

Formula	Result
4 * 2	8
95 / 2	47.5
80 – 15	65
12 + 9	21

For multiplication, you must use an asterisk rather than an × (a common multiplication symbol). Visual Basic reads × as a variable named x.

You can use the addition and subtraction operators by themselves, in which case they're called *unary operators*. (The unary addition operator is optional because Visual Basic assumes a positive value unless you tell it otherwise.) By using the unary plus or minus, you can assign a positive or negative number to a variable or assign it a positive or negative variable, as the following code shows:

```
a = -25   ' Stores a negative 25 in a
b = +26   ' Stores a positive 26 in b
c = -a    ' Stores a positive 25 (the inverse of a)
d = +b    ' Stores a positive 26 (the value of b)
```

▼ **NOTE**

This topic's "Next Step" section explains how to use the plus sign to work with string values. ▲

▼ MATH INSIDE THE COMPUTER: DOES IT ALL ADD UP?

Internally, your computer can perform addition only. This fact might seem strange, because computers are used for all kinds of powerful mathematical computations. Addition, however, is all that your computer needs to know.

At the binary level, your computer can add two binary numbers. Your computer has no problem adding 6 + 7. To subtract 6 from 7, however, your computer must use a modified form of addition, in which it adds a negative 6 to 7. When your program stores the result of 7 − 6 in a variable, your computer interprets it as 7 + −6. To simulate subtraction, all your computer needs to do is add and compute the negative of any number (called the *two's complement*).

Multiplication simply is repeated addition. Therefore, 6 * 7 is interpreted as 6 added to itself seven times, or 6 + 6 + 6 + 6 + 6 + 6 + 6.

Division is repeated subtraction. When you calculate 42 / 6, the computer repeatedly subtracts 6 from 42 until it gets to zero, and then adds the number of times it did that. This becomes 42 − 6 − 6 − 6 − 6 − 6 − 6 − 6 = 0. Reaching 0 takes seven subtractions of 6 (actually, seven additions of −6). Thus, the result of 42 / 6 is 7. Because division doesn't always result in a whole number, when the repeated subtraction results in a negative number, the computer uses that number to produce the remainder.

With the capability to add and to simulate subtraction, multiplication, and division, your computer has the tools required for every other math function as well. ▲

Integer Division, Modulus, and Exponentiation

The three remaining fundamental operators—integer division (\), `Mod`, and exponentiation (^)—might be new to you, but they're as easy to use as the four operators in Table 8.2.

Use integer division to produce the integer (whole number) result of a division. Integer division always produces an integer result and discards any remainder. You don't have to put integers on both sides of the backslash (\); you can use floating-point numbers, integers, or both on each side. Table 8.3 shows the results of some sample integer-division code.

Table 8.3 Integer-Division Results

Formula	Result
8 \ 2	4
95 \ 2	47
95.0 \ 2	47
95 \ 2.0	47
95.0 \ 2.0	47

The Mod operator is one of the few Visual Basic operators that doesn't appear in the form of a symbol. Mod produces the *modulus*, or integer remainder, of division. Table 8.4 shows the results of some simple Mod operations.

Table 8.4 Results of Simple *Mod* Operations

Formula	Result
8 Mod 2	0
8 Mod 3	2
8 Mod 7	1

Use the exponentiation symbol (^) when you want to raise a number to a power. The number to the left of the caret (^) is the *base*, and the number to the right is the *power*. You can put integers, floating-point numbers, or a combination of both on each side of the caret. Table 8.5 shows the results of some exponentiation calculations.

Table 8.5 Exponentiation Results

Formula	Description	Result
2^4	2 raised to the fourth power (2^4)	16
16^2	16 raised to the second power (16^2)	256
5.6 ^ 3	5.6 raised to the third power (5.6^3)	175.616
144^0.5	144 raised to the .5 power ($144^{1/2}$)	12

Example The procedure in Listing 8.1 illustrates a payroll computation. It assigns to three variables the hours worked, the pay per hour (the rate), and the tax rate. It then uses those variables in calculations to create three new variables: the gross pay, the taxes, and the net pay. The procedure ends by assigning these values to labels so that the values appear on the users' form.

Listing 8.1 CalcPr.BAS: Payroll Computation

```
Private Sub Calc_Pr()
' Computes three payroll variables.
  Dim intHoursWorked As Integer
  Dim sngRate As Single, sngTaxRate As Single
  Dim curTaxes As Currency, curGrossPay As Currency
  Dim curNetPay As Currency

  ' Initialize the variables
  intHoursWorked = 40    ' Total hours worked
  sngRate = 7.80         ' Pay per hours
  sngTaxRate = .40       ' Tax rate percentage

  ' Calculate the amounts
  curGrossPay = intHoursWorked * sngRate
  curTaxes = sngTaxRate * curGrossPay
  curNetPay = curGrossPay - curTaxes

  ' Display results in labels
  lblGrossPay.Caption = curGrossPay
  lblTaxes.Caption = curTaxes
  lblNetPay.Caption = curNetPay
End Sub
```

▼ **NOTE**

Whew, that's a long procedure! Actually, this procedure's length is fairly typical. You're beginning to see how a procedure's code does work inside a Visual Basic application when that procedure isn't an event procedure. ▲

TIP Notice the blank lines throughout Listing 8.1. These lines help separate parts of the procedures and make procedures more readable. Add as much of this white space to your own programs as you need to make your programs easy to read and maintain. For more information about code remarks, you may want to review Hour 6, "Understanding the VB Program Structure."

Notice that the code in Listing 8.1 mixes `Single` data type calculations with `Currency` data types in the same expressions. This mixing of data types isn't critical here because Visual Basic rounds the tax calculations and stores the results in the `Currency` data type format with the appropriate dollars and cents. The tax rate can't be `Currency` because a tax rate may need more than two decimal places; the pay rate per hour, however, could have been data-typed as a `Currency` value. The choice won't affect these calculations.

In Listing 8.1, the labels `lblGrossPay`, `lblTaxes`, and `lblNetPay` are assumed to be on the form and set up with appropriate preceding label descriptions so users know what the three values represent.

When sending data to labels, you'll often format the output so that the labels display values in an appropriate format, such as with a dollar sign and commas in large numbers. You learn in Hour 14's lesson, "Using the Supplied Functions," how to format numeric data.

TIP You can assign expressions to labels. In other words, you could have assigned the gross pay expression directly to the gross pay label in this example procedure. Nevertheless, the variables help you separate the calculations from the data display. Such separation often lends itself to more maintainable programs when your calculations change or when you must add additional calculations.

Pt **II**

Hr **8**

Next Step When you perform *string concatenation*, you merge two strings to form a single string. Perhaps you need to take a user's first name and concatenate his last name onto the end of the first name and store the composed string into a third string. You can concatenate as many strings as needed to form single strings.

> **CAUTION**   Make sure that the target string that's receiving the concatenated strings (the string on the left of the assignment) is a variable-length string or, if fixed-length, long enough to hold the concatenated strings.

Visual Basic uses the plus sign (+) for string concatenation. Therefore, the following statement sends `"Grant Holdorf"` into the string named `strFullName`:

```
strFullName = "Grant" + " " + "Holdorf"
```

Without the center space, `strFullName` would receive `"GrantHoldorf"` because Visual Basic would never insert a space between two merged strings automatically. Be aware that your merged strings will appear next to each other when you concatenate and insert spaces if needed.

The plus sign is known as an *overloaded operator*, because it performs two separate operations: addition of numbers and concatenation of strings. Therefore, to reduce ambiguity, Microsoft added to Visual Basic a concatenation operation, **&**, that performs only string concatenation. Therefore, most Visual Basic programmers now use the plus sign only for numeric calculations and the ampersand (**&**) for string concatenations. The following statement performs the same concatenation as the preceding statement:

```
strFullName = "Grant" & " " & "Holdorf"
```

Topic 2: The Order of Operators

Knowing the meaning of the math operators is the first of two steps toward understanding Visual Basic calculations. You also must understand the order of operators. The *order of operators* (sometimes called *operator hierarchy* or *operator precedence*) determines exactly how Visual Basic computes formulas. The order of operators is exactly the same as that used in high-school algebra.

Overview   To see how the order of operators works, try to determine the result of the following calculation:

```
2 + 3 * 2
```

Many people would say that the answer is 10, but 10 is correct only if you interpret the formula from left to right. What if you calculated the multiplication first? If you first calculate the value of 3 * 2 to be 6 and then add 2 to that value, your answer for the calculation is 8. Visual Basic uses the latter technique to calculate the problem and therefore would produce 8 as the answer.

The Table of Operators

Visual Basic performs any exponentiation first, and then performs multiplication and division. Finally, it performs addition and subtraction. Table 8.6 shows this order of operators.

Table 8.6 The Order of Operators

Order	Operator
1	Exponentiation (^)
2	Unary positive and negation
3	Multiplication, division, integer division, Mod
4	Addition and subtraction

You easily can follow Visual Basic's order of operators if you follow the intermediate results one at a time. The two calculations in Figure 8.1 show you how to follow Visual Basic's order of operators.

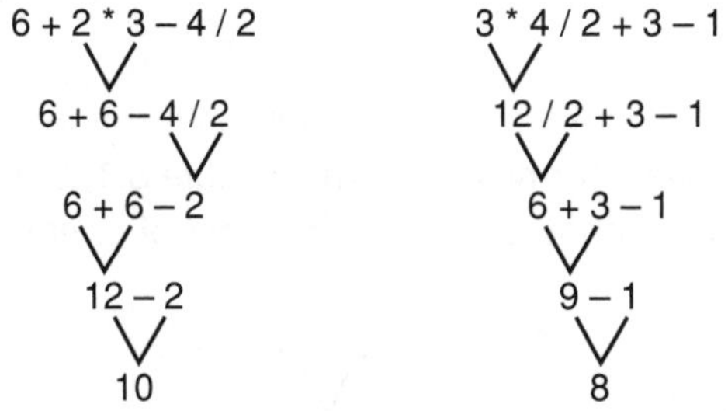

FIG. 8.1
Visual Basic follows an operator order for calculations.

```
6 + 2 * 3 – 4 / 2
    \/
6 + 6 – 4 / 2
        \/
6 + 6 – 2
\/
12 – 2
    \/
    10
```

```
3 * 4 / 2 + 3 – 1
\/
12 / 2 + 3 – 1
    \/
6 + 3 – 1
    \/
9 – 1
  \/
  8
```

Parentheses Override the Order

If you want to override the order of operators, use parentheses in the calculation. Parentheses are operators just like + and *, except that they appear higher in Visual Basic's order of operator table. Thus, Visual Basic always performs calculations inside parentheses before any other operations in the expression. By using parentheses, you can write expressions in the order you prefer and specify the calculation order yourself.

The formula **2 + 3 * 2** produces 8 because multiplication is performed before addition. But if you put parentheses around the addition, as in **(2 + 3) * 2**, the answer becomes 10 because Visual Basic computes the calculation between the parentheses first.

If expressions with parentheses are inside other parentheses—for example, **((5 + 2) – 7 + (8 + 9 – (5 + 2)))**—Visual Basic calculates the innermost parenthetical expressions first.

Example Consider the short expression evaluation shown in Figure 8.2. Although the expression is short, its result may at first surprise you.

FIG. 8.2
Be careful when performing integer arithmetic.

```
20 \ 3 ^ 2
      V
   20 \ 9
      V
      2
```

The first step is probably no surprise. According to Table 8.6, the exponentiation must calculate first. But look at the second line carefully; notice that the expression contains an *integer division* operator, not a regular division operator. Therefore, Visual Basic will calculate **20 \ 9** as an integer division and throw away any remainder that may appear. 20 divided by 9 is 2 with 2 left over. When Visual Basic discards the remaining 2, the result is simply the integer 2.

For another example, look at the expressions in Figure 8.3. The formulas in the figure are the same formulas shown in Figure 8.1, but the calculations vary because the parentheses override the order of operators.

FIG. 8.3
The parentheses take precedence over the operators.

```
6 + 2 * (3 – 4) / 2          3 * 4 / 2 + (3 – 1)
         V                            V
  6 + 2 * –1 / 2              3 * 4 / 2 +  2
        V                            V
   6 + –2 / 2                 12 / 2 + 2
         V                          V
      6 + –1                     6 + 2
        V                          V
         5                          8
```

Next Step   In Table 8.6, notice that multiplication, division, integer division, and Mod appear on the same level. This arrangement implies that no hierarchy exists on that level. If more than one of these operators appears in a calculation, Visual Basic performs the math from left to right. The same is true for addition and subtraction; Visual Basic does the leftmost operation first if two or more addition or subtraction operators appear in an expression. Figure 8.4 shows an example of left-to-right division and multiplication. In this example, because the division appears to the left of the multiplication (and because division and multiplication are on the same level), Visual Basic computes the division first.

FIG. 8.4
Operators on the same precedence level calculate from left to right.

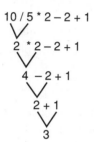

See if you can spot a potential problem with the following procedure fragment:

```
sngGrade1 = 86.0
sngGrade2 = 98.0
sngGrade3 = 72.0
sngAverage = sngGrade1 + sngGrade2 + sngGrade3 / 3
lblAverage.Caption = sngAverage   ' Oops!
```

The problem with this code results from the fact that Visual Basic performs division before addition. Therefore, the third grade is divided by 3 and then the other two grades add to that result. To fix the problem, you can add a set of parentheses, as shown in the following corrected code:

```
sngGrade1 = 86.0
sngGrade2 = 98.0
sngGrade3 = 72.0
sngAverage = (sngGrade1 + sngGrade2 + sngGrade3) / 3
lblAverage.Caption = sngAverage   ' Now displays correctly
```

This average calculation illustrates why the parentheses can keep you out of trouble. If you find that a Visual Basic program won't return a result that you expect, scan all the expressions in the program's code to make sure that you've specified your expressions so they respect the order of operator table.

> **TIP** Use plenty of parentheses in your programs to make the order of operators clear to anyone who reads the program. Even if you don't need to override the order of operators, the parentheses make the calculations easier to understand if you modify the program later.

Topic 3: Conditional and Logical Operators

Believe it or not, not every Visual Basic statement should execute every time users run the program. Because your programs operate on data, they're known as *data-driven programs*. In other words, the data should dictate what the program does.

For example, you wouldn't want the computer to print a paycheck every pay period for every employee who works for you; some employees might have taken a leave of absence, or some might be on a sales commission and might not have made a sale during the pay period. Printing paychecks for no money would be ridiculous. You want your program to print checks only to those employees who have pay coming to them.

Overview This topic section introduces *conditional* and *compound logical operators*. Unlike math operators, conditional operators don't perform calculations but instead compare data values against one another. Conditional operators form the basis for several Visual Basic statements. In fact, after you learn the Visual Basic statements that depend on the conditional operators, you'll know much of the Visual Basic language.

▼ **NOTE**
Conditional operators are sometimes called *comparison operators* because they compare data values. You'll also see them called *relational operators* occasionally. ▲

Compound logical operators (often just called *logical operators*) let you combine two or more conditional expressions. By learning the compound operators now, you can see a more complete order of operator chart at the end of this topic.

Conditional Operators

The conditional operators compare data values against one another, and then tell your program the result of the comparison. Your program then can use control commands (which you'll learn about throughout this nightschool course) to make decisions based on the conditional operator results. Table 8.7 lists VB's conditional operators.

Table 8.7 Conditional Operators

Operator	Description
=	Equal to
>	Greater than
<	Less than
>=	Greater than or equal to
<=	Less than or equal to
<>	Not equal to

These six operators form the foundation for comparing data in VB applications. The operators always appear with two literals, variables, controls, expressions—or a combination of the four—on each side. You should know these operators as well as you know the ^, +, -, *, and / mathematical operators.

The result of a mathematical operation is a number; the result of a conditional operation is a **True** or **False** data-typed result. (This result is often called a *Boolean result*, corresponding to Visual Basic's **Boolean** data type.) Depending on that result, your Visual Basic application code might take one of two possible execution paths.

Assume that a procedure initializes four integer variables, as follows:

```
A = 5
B = 10
C = 15
D = 5
```

The following statements are true and illustrate how the conditional operators compare data and return the **True** result:

● A is equal to D   so   A = D

● B is less than C   so   B < C

- C is greater than A   so   C > A
- B is greater than or equal to A   so   B >= A
- D is less than or equal to B   so   D <= B
- B isn't equal to C   so   B <> C

These statements aren't Visual Basic statements, but they demonstrate the conditions tested by the conditional operators. Conditional logic is simple because it always produces a true or false result.

> **CAUTION** If the value on either side of the conditional operator is `Null`, Visual Basic returns `Null` for the comparison's result. If one side contains the `Empty` value, numeric comparisons assume that `Empty` is 0 and string comparisons (see the next section) assume that the `Empty` value is a null string (`""`).

▼ WHAT'S HAPPENING INSIDE?

Did you know that a conditional's `True` or `False` result occurs internally at the bit level? Look at the following conditional:

```
(A = 6)
```

To determine the truth of the relation (`A = 6`), the computer takes a binary 6, or 00000110, and compares it bit by bit with the variable named A. If A contains 7 (a binary 00000111), the result of the equal test is `False` because the right bit (called the *least-significant bit*) is different from the 6's least-significant bit. ▲

▼ DON'T BE ANXIOUS!

Many people say they suffer from "math anxiety"—you might even be one of them. As mentioned earlier this hour, you don't have to be good at math to be a good computer programmer because Visual Basic does all the mathematical work. Don't be frightened by the term *conditional logic*; you use conditional logic every day. Nevertheless, some people see the conditional operators and get confused about their meanings.

The two primary conditional operators, less than (<) and greater than (>), are easy to remember. You might have been taught which is which in school but forgot. Actually, their symbols tell you exactly what each means. Notice that in the previous true examples, the small part of the operator (the point) always points to the smaller number. The large, open part indicates the larger value.

The relation is false if the arrow points in the wrong direction. In other words, 4 > 9 ("4 is greater than 9") is false because the small part of the operator points to the 9. ▲

String Comparisons

In addition to comparing numeric data with conditional operators, you can compare character string data. Comparing strings is useful for alphabetizing, testing answers, comparing names, and much more. Generally, strings compare uppercase before lowercase, and special characters and numbers before alphabetic characters. This comparison technique, called a *binary compare*, results in case-sensitive and accurate alphabetizing of strings.

▼ **NOTE**
If you include the following statement in your module's Declarations section,

    Option Compare Text

Visual Basic compares with a case-insensitive sequence, and *A* compares equally with *a*. ▲

You know that A comes before B. Therefore, it's true that A is less than B. When comparing more than one character at a time, Visual Basic scans each character of each string being compared until it finds a difference. For example, "Adam" and "Adam" are exactly equal. "Jody" is less than "Judy", however, because *o* is less than *u* according to the normal Visual Basic binary comparison. Also, a longer string such as "Shopping" is greater than "Shop" because of the extra characters. The null string, "", always compares less than any other string except another null string.

All of the following string comparisons are true (assuming that the Option Compare Text statement doesn't appear in the module's Declarations section):

    "abcdef" > "ABCDEF"

    "Yes!" < "Yes?"

    "Computers are fun!" = "Computers are fun!"

    "PC" <> "pc"

    "Books, Books, Books" >= "Books, Books"

Pt II

Hr 8

TIP Use string comparisons to check for a correct password entry. After users type a password, compare the control holding the password to an internal password string or one that your program reads from a file to see whether they match.

Compound Logical Operators

At times, you might need to conditionally test more than one set of variables or controls. You can combine more than one conditional test into a *compound conditional test* by using the following logical operators: And, Or, Xor, and Not. The logical operators combine two or more conditional expressions into one expression.

These might not seem like typical operators because they aren't symbols, but like Mod, the logical operators are word abbreviations that work as operators. The logical operators always appear between two or more conditional operations within the same expression.

Tables 8.8, 8.9, 8.10, and 8.11 show how each logical operator works. These tables, called *truth tables*, show how to achieve true results from a conditional test. Take a minute to study the tables.

Table 8.8   The *And* Truth Table (Both Sides Must Be True)

True	And	True	=	True
True	And	False	=	False
False	And	True	=	False
False	And	False	=	False

Table 8.9   The *Or* Truth Table (One Side or the Other Must Be True)

True	Or	True	=	True
True	Or	False	=	True
False	Or	True	=	True
False	Or	False	=	False

Table 8.10   The *Xor* Truth Table (One or the Other Must Be True, But Not Both)

True	Xor	True	=	False
True	Xor	False	=	True
False	Xor	True	=	True
False	Xor	False	=	False

Table 8.11 The *Not* Truth Table (Negates the Comparison)

Not True	=	False
Not False	=	True

The logical operators are difficult to describe in more detail until you get to Hour 10's lesson, which studies the `If` statement. Nevertheless, consider the following expression:

```
(1 < 3) And (9 > 3)
```

The expression doesn't comprise a complete Visual Basic statement, but it does test your knowledge of logical operators. The `And` truth table tells you that both sides of the `And` logical operator must be true before the entire expression is true. Therefore, because `(1 < 3)` returns a `True` result and because `(9 > 3)` returns a `True` result, the result of the entire expression is `True`. The following, however, is *not* true because of the first conditional expression:

```
(3 <> 3) And (5 <> 6)
```

If you replaced `And` with `Or`, the expression produces a `True` result again:

```
(3 <> 3) Or (5 <> 6)
```

Although the left side of the `Or` compares with a `False` value, the right side returns a `True` value. The `Or` truth table tells you that `False Or True` produces a `True` result.

> **TIP** The parentheses around individual conditional expressions of a compound conditional statement help you distinguish the sides of the logical operator. Also, the parentheses take precedence over both mathematical and compound conditional statements.

The `Xor` (for *exclusive or*) is often used as a mutually exclusive comparison, when one side or the other must be true but not both. The `Not` operator reverses comparison results. Visual Basic programmers generally use only `And` and `Or` in their applications because `Xor` and `Not` can produce confusing code.

▶▶ FAST TRACK

Do you understand file name wild-card characters? If so, you'll appreciate Visual Basic's `Like` operator. `Like` works like an equality comparison, with

continues

continued

one exception—you can use wild-card characters on either side of Like to compare a variable, control, literal, or expression to a pattern. Use ? to compare against any single character match, * to compare against zero or more characters, and # to compare against numeric digits. You also can place brackets ([and]) around a character list you want to use for the comparison, and start a bracketed list with a ! if you want to compare against a single character *not* in the list. Therefore, "Bettye" Like "Be*" returns True, as does "A" Like "[ABC]" and "A" Like "[!XYZ]".

If you've programmed a lot before, the Like comparison operator is probably one of the few new operators for you. Now that you've seen Like, you may want to skip ahead to Hour 9's lesson, "Working with Interactive Keyboard and Screen I/O" (p. 203).

The Complete Order of Operators

The order of the math operators that you saw earlier in Table 8.6 didn't include the conditional and logical operators. You need to be familiar with the entire order, shown in Table 8.12. As you can see, the math operators take precedence over the conditional and logical operators, but parentheses override any of the defaults.

Table 8.12 Complete Order of Operators

Order	Operator
1	Parentheses
2	Exponentiation (^)
3	Unary negation and the unary positive
4	Multiplication, division, integer division, Mod
5	Addition, subtraction
6	Conditional operators (=, <, >, >=, <=, and <>) and Like
7	Not logical operator
8	And
9	Or
10	Xor

You might wonder why the conditional and logical operators are included in the order. The following expression helps show why:

```
curSales < curMinSales * 2 And intYrsEmp > 10 * intFactor
```

Without the complete order of operators, it would be impossible to determine how Visual Basic would interpret such a statement. According to the operator order, this expression would evaluate as follows:

```
((curSales < (curMinSales * 2)) And (intYrsEmp > (10 *intFactor))
```

This expression still is confusing, but it's less confusing than the preceding expression. The two multiplication operations would be performed first, followed by the conditionals < and >. The logical **And** is performed last because it's lowest in the order of operators.

> **TIP**   To avoid problems with reading such code, use ample parentheses, even if you want the actions to be performed in the default operator order. Also, don't combine too many expressions; break them up, if you can.

Example   Again, return to these four integer variables initializations:

```
A = 5
B = 10
C = 15
D = 5
```

Each of the following conditional operations would result in *false* results:

```
A = B

B > C

D < A

D > A

A <> D

B >= C

C <= B
```

Study these statements to see why each produces a false result. A and D are equal to the same value (5), so neither is greater than or less than the other.

Next Step You deal with conditional logic in everyday life. Think of the following statements that you might make:

- "The generic butter costs less than the name brand."
- "My child is younger than Suzie."
- "Our salaries are equal."
- "The dogs aren't the same age."

Each statement can be *only* true or false—there are no other possible outcomes.

As is true of other relational operators, you use logical operators in everyday conversation, as in the following examples:

- "If my pay is high and my vacation time is long, we can go to Italy this summer."
- "If you take the trash out or clean your room, you can watch television tonight."
- "I can go to the grocery or go to the flower shop, but not both."

The first two examples are straightforward. The last example illustrates the Xor operator. Notice from the Xor truth table that one side of the Xor or the other side of the Xor can be true for the final result to be true, but not *both* sides. You're often faced with two choices, but you can do only one thing or the other; you don't have the time or resources to do both. The same is true sometimes with computer conditional tests. You might need to print an exception report if a customer's payment is late or if the customer's debt is forgiven, but not if both events occur.

Summary

After this hour's lesson, you now can write almost any math operation that you'll ever need. By understanding the order of operators, you know how to structure your formulas so that Visual Basic computes the answers the way you intend for them to be computed. You always can override the order of operators by using parentheses.

Computers do more than calculate arithmetic expressions, however. This hour's final topic introduced you to Visual Basic's conditional operators.

With the conditionals, you'll be able to learn a lot of Visual Basic commands in Hour 10's lesson. At this point, you know only a few of Visual Basic's commands, especially how to code remarks and assignment statements (and remarks aren't even runtime commands). In a couple of lessons, you'll know several more statements and can begin to make Visual Basic perform complicated logic.

In Hour 9, you learn how to produce input and output by using special Visual Basic routines called *input boxes* and *message boxes*. At this point, you can display and accept user information with controls on a form, but form controls are limiting when you want to display messages for only short periods of time. The input boxes and message boxes will let you interact with users as your program runs without changing the form's appearance.

Hour 8 Quiz

You can find the answers for the following questions on the accompanying CD-ROM and on the Virtual Classroom Web site.

On the CD

1. What are the results of the following expressions?

   A. `1 + 2 * 4 / 2`

   B. `(1 + 2) * 4 / 2`

   C. `1 + 2 * (4 / 2)`

   D. `9 \ 2 + 1`

   E. `(1 + (10 - (2 + 2)))`

2. Convert each of the following formulas to their Visual Basic equivalents:

   A. $a = \dfrac{3 + 3}{4 + 4}$

   B. $x = (a - b) * (a - 2)^2$

   C. $f = \dfrac{a^{1/2}}{b^{1/3}}$

   D. $d = \dfrac{(8 - x^2)}{(x - 9)} - \dfrac{(4 * 2 - 1)}{x^3}$

3. Why is the plus sign considered to be an overloaded operator?

4. Which operator is preferred for concatenating strings?

5. What logical operator returns `True` if either expression is `True`?

6. State whether the following conditional tests are true or false:

    A. `4 >= 5`

    B. `4 >= 4`

    C. `165 = 165`

    D. `0 <> 255`

7. State whether each of these expressions produce a `True` result or a `False` result (assume that the normal binary compare is in effect):

    A. `"Que" > "QUE"`

    B. `"" = "0"`

    C. `"yES" < "Yes"`

8. What's the result stored in `N` after the following two lines execute? (*Hint:* If you reuse the same variable name on both sides of a mathematical operator, you're updating the value in that variable.)

    ```
    N = 0
    N = N + 5
    ```

9. Determine whether the following compound conditional tests return a `True` or `False` result:

    A. `Not(True Or False)`

    B. `(True And False) And (False Xor True)`

    C. `Not(True Xor True)`

    D. `True Or (False And False) Or False`

10. Assuming that w=15, x=7, y=5, and z=2 what would be the value of the Boolean `blnResult` after each assignment is complete?

    A. `blnResult = w < 20 Or y > 5`

    B. `blnResult = Not y < 20`

    C. `blnResult = z < w And y > z`

    D. `blnResult = x > y Xor y > z`

Hour 8 Homework Exercises

1. Write the assignment statements that calculate each of the first eight powers of 2 (that is, 2^1, 2^2, 2^3...2^8) and store the results in eight variables.

2. Change the `Calc_pr()` procedure in Listing 8.1 so that it computes and prints a bonus of 15 percent of the gross pay. Don't take taxes out of the bonus. Display the four values in labels.

3. Write a single expression that compares three numbers for equality.

Working with Interactive Keyboard and Screen I/O

THIS HOUR'S LESSON takes a break from the programming theory of the last few lessons. You're in for a treat. This lesson shows you how to program message boxes and input boxes. *Message boxes* let you display information for the user without changing the form on-screen. *Input boxes* let you get interactive user input without using a form's control. By saving the form controls for more standard I/O (input and output), your program can ask your user questions and display error messages by using pop-up dialog boxes that users can control.

Tools such as message boxes and input boxes also will help you master the next few hours' lessons. By learning how to create and respond to message and input boxes, you can write small applications that test the programming controls that you learn in subsequent lessons.

Topic 1: The *MsgBox()* Function

You should be concerned with the way your output looks and also with the way users enter data. The `MsgBox()` function is one of the best ways to display a message for your users during the execution of the program. Unlike controls on a form, the message box that appears will pop up as a dialog box. After users read the message in the message box, they can click the message box's OK button and continue with the program.

▶▶ **FAST TRACK**

Have you programmed in Microsoft Access or any other Windows-based programming environment? If so, you've no doubt used message boxes and input boxes, and this hour's lesson will be familiar to you. Visual Basic uses all the standard icons and responses you're used to. But even though you've seen message and input boxes before, you still need to read through this lesson to learn how the Visual Basic language hooks into these interactive dialog boxes.

Visual Basic uses internal functions to interact with users, and you need to familiarize yourself with Visual Basic's tables related to these I/O dialog boxes. When you learn how Visual Basic produces the boxes, including the named constants that Visual Basic uses to test users' return values from these dialog boxes, you can move on to Hour 10's lesson, "Creating Logical Programs" (p. 217), to learn how Visual Basic produces conditional control through `If` and related statements.

Microsoft wants you to begin using the `MsgBox()` function exclusively because the `MsgBox` statement doesn't let you test for button clicks.

Overview The `MsgBox()` function not only displays data in a pop-up dialog box, but optionally displays an icon and response buttons for users. `MsgBox()` can write string data to the screen. The string contains the message you want to send to users.

Figure 9.1 shows a sample dialog box generated with `MsgBox()`. From the figure, you see that you control both the message and the title of the dialog box. You also can determine which icon is displayed and how many buttons appear on the box.

FIG. 9.1
A message box is like a miniature dialog box.

Users can move or close message boxes but not resize them. This topic section explains how to display such message boxes. After you master message boxes, the next two topics build on that knowledge and show you two additional kinds of dialog boxes your user may need to see and respond to.

The *MsgBox()* Function

Although you won't fully master Visual Basic's predefined built-in functions until Hour 14's lesson, "Using the Supplied Functions," the message-box function and its cousin, the input-box function, work so well and give you so much to learn with that now is the best time to see how to work with those functions.

▼ **NOTE**

Just like a function procedure that you write, a built-in function always returns a value. MsgBox() is no exception. The second topic section explains how to work with MsgBox()'s returned value. ▲

Here is the MsgBox() function's syntax:

```
intResponse = MsgBox(strPrompt[, intStyle][, strTitle])
```

This hour's second topic explains how you work with the *intResponse* value; you can ignore it for this topic section. You must include such an integer variable at the left of the MsgBox() function if you want the function to work correctly.

strPrompt is a string expression (a constant string enclosed in quotation marks, a string variable, or a text-control value) that you want displayed in the dialog box. If the string is long, the dialog box expands to hold the whole string, properly breaking each line between words. Figure 9.1's *strPrompt* would be "This is a message box".

▼ **NOTE**

The message box prompt can be no longer than 1,024 characters. ▲

The last two values to the `MsgBox()` function are optional, as indicated by the brackets. The easiest kind of dialog box to display is one with only a message and an OK button. If you want to display a message box such as the one shown in Figure 9.2, you don't have to specify the second and third values. Whenever you see a statement or function format, such as the one shown at the beginning of this section for `MsgBox()`, the values inside the brackets indicate optional values. Don't include the brackets; as part of the `MsgBox()` function's syntax, they simply indicate optional parts of the function.

FIG. 9.2
Simple message boxes require only a prompt.

> **TIP** While you type inside Visual Basic's Code window, as soon as Visual Basic realizes that you're coding a `MsgBox()` function, VB pops up the Auto Quick Info help that describes the function's values for format. You can review the Auto Quick Info feature in Hour 6, "Understanding the VB Program Structure."

If you specify only a `MsgBox()` prompt string with no other values, Visual Basic displays the prompt and the project name in the message box's title bar. The following `MsgBox()` function displays Figure 9.2's message box:

```
i = MsgBox("This is a message box")
```

Assume that `i` is an integer variable that's been declared previously. As you can see, a simple message box that requires only that users click OK is simple to produce. When a program needs to display such a message, pop up a message box at the place in the code and users will get the message.

Extending Message Boxes

`MsgBox()`'s *intStyle* value is a numeric value or expression that controls the number of buttons as well as the icon that appear in the message box. *strTitle* is the string that appears at the top of the box in the title bar. (As mentioned earlier, if you don't specify a title, Visual Basic displays the project name for the message box title bar.)

The value you use for *intStyle* is made up of several things. Tables 9.1, 9.2, and 9.3 contain values that comprise *intStyle*. The tables include several named constants, such as vbOKOnly. Visual Basic makes these named constants available to you from any procedure in any module, no matter how global or local the procedure is. Therefore, rather than code a 3 for the message box's style value, you can use vbYesNoCancel. Internally, vbYesNoCancel is set to a 3; however, vbYesNoCancel is easier for you to understand later if you have to change the program. vbYesNoCancel is self-documenting and tells you that the value means the three buttons (Yes, No, and Cancel) will appear in the message box.

Table 9.1 Controlling the Buttons

Named Constant	Value	Description
vbOKOnly	0	Displays OK button only
vbOKCancel	1	Displays OK and Cancel buttons
vbAbortRetryIgnore	2	Displays Abort, Retry, and Ignore buttons
vbYesNoCancel	3	Displays Yes, No, and Cancel buttons
vbYesNo	4	Displays Yes and No buttons
vbRetryCancel	5	Displays Retry and Cancel buttons

Table 9.2 Controlling the Icons

Named Constant	Value	Description	Icon
vbCritical	16	Displays Critical Message icon	
vbQuestion	32	Displays Warning Query icon	
vbExclamation	48	Displays Warning Message icon	
vbInformation	64	Displays Information Message icon	

Pt **II**

Hr **9**

Table 9.3   Controlling the Default Buttons

Named Constant	Value	Description
vbDefaultButton1	0	First button is default
vbDefaultButton2	256	Second button is default
vbDefaultButton3	512	Third button is default

Table 9.1 describes the layout of the buttons on the dialog box. When you decide it's time for a message box, consider the set of buttons the message box needs. Figure 9.2's message box didn't specify a *intStyle* value, so Visual Basic used the default value of 0 that sends only a single button—OK—to the message box. (The message box in Figure 9.2 contains only an OK button because it has 0 for *intStyle*.) If you want a style of buttons different from the single OK button, use a different value from Table 9.1.

If you want an icon to appear inside the dialog box, *add* one of the values from Table 9.2 to the *intStyle* value from Table 9.1. In other words, if you want the OK and Cancel buttons to display (an *intStyle* of 1) and want the Warning Query icon to display (an *intStyle* of 32), you specify 33 for the *intStyle* (both table values added together).

A dialog box always contains a default button, which appears outlined to look as though someone is selecting it. (In other words, the button has the focus.) If users press Enter without selecting another button, the button defined as the default is selected. Therefore, if you want the Cancel button (the second button described in the preceding paragraph) to be the default button when the dialog box appears, add an additional 256 to the 33 to get a total of 289.

▼ **NOTE**
Message boxes respect the Windows Sound settings. Therefore, if users have set up a specific sound for one of the message box icons, such as the critical warning icon, the sound will broadcast along with the message box. ▲

Example   Suppose that you want to display the dialog box shown in Figure 9.3. (Notice that the center button is the default.) Use the following `MsgBox()` function to create this dialog box:

```
i = MsgBox("Is the printer on?", 291, "Question Box")
```

FIG. 9.3
Message boxes can become rather complex.

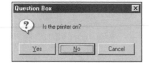

Next Step   Adding the *intStyle* values together can be cumbersome, but thanks to Visual Basic, you don't even have to add. Use an expression that adds the named constants shown in this topic section's tables. The following `MsgBox()` function works just like the preceding example because the function totals the *intStyle* values:

```
i = MsgBox("Is the printer on?", vbYesNoCancel + vbQuestion +
➥vbDefaultButton2, "Question box")
```

Again, such statements are a bit cumbersome to type initially, but you'll appreciate the self-documenting code if you ever have to modify the message box.

Topic 2: Working with *MsgBox()*'s Return Values

The `MsgBox()` function is useful for displaying messages, but you'll want to know which buttons users clicked when they close the dialog box. If the message box displayed only an OK button, your program knows that users clicked only the OK button to close the message box. If, however, the message box contains additional buttons, your program should respond according to the button the users click.

▼ NOTE
Keep in mind that your application basically comes to a halt during the display of the message box. The `MsgBox()` function triggers the display of the message box, and no other line in the code can execute until users close the message box by clicking one of its buttons. **▲**

The message box function's return value indicates the button clicked by users. Therefore, after the function displays multiple buttons, your program can determine which button users chose by testing the return value.

Pt **II**

Hr **9**

TIP   You may have already guessed that the conditional operators you learned in Hour 8 help test the message-box return values. In Hour 10, you'll learn how specifically to use the conditional operators to test for which button the users clicked.

Table 9.4 describes the return values that come from `MsgBox()`.

Table 9.4 *MsgBox()* Return Values

Named Constant	Value	Description
vbOK	1	Users clicked OK
vbCancel	2	Users clicked Cancel
vbAbort	3	Users clicked Abort
vbRetry	4	Users clicked Retry
vbIgnore	5	Users clicked Ignore
vbYes	6	Users clicked Yes
vbNo	7	Users clicked No

Example   The following assignment statement does a lot:

```
intButton = MsgBox("Are you ready?", vbYesNoCancel +
        ➥vbQuestion)
```

When Visual Basic reaches this statement, the program waits for users to answer the `MsgBox()` prompt by choosing one of the message box buttons. The result of the button choice, a numeric value from Table 9.4, is then assigned to the variable `intButton`.

`vbYesNoCancel` sends the Yes, No, and Cancel buttons to the dialog box, and `vbQuestion` displays the Warning Query icon. If the users choose Yes, the `intButton` variable is assigned the value 6. `intButton` gets a 7 if the users choose No and gets 2 if the users choose Cancel. Although your program will work with this return value, you'll want to use Table 9.4's named constants instead of the actual values.

▶▶ **FAST TRACK**

How many buttons can users click for each message box your program displays? No matter how many buttons the message box displays, users can click at most one button in response. Users *must* click a button to get rid of the message box (or click Cancel or the message box's Close window button, which selects one of the buttons by default). Therefore, every `MsgBox()` function that your program issues will get only one button click in response to the message box. Not coincidentally, *every* function returns only one value. The value might be any one of the data types, depending on the function's goals. When you get to Hour 13's lesson, "Understanding How Procedures Work" (p.301), you'll learn more about the single return value that all functions return.

Next Step

Don't confuse the return value with the button you select. For example, the return value might be 3, meaning that users clicked the Abort button and you may have used 3 (better indicated by the `vbYesNoCancel` named constant) to describe the buttons that you want displayed. Therefore, when the message box appears with the buttons you've selected, the return value might overlap one of your message box values but the number's meaning is now totally different. After the program gains control from the message box function, you test against Table 9.4's values to determine what users did.

If users press Esc at any dialog box that contains a Cancel button, Visual Basic acts as though they chose the Cancel button and returns the value 2 from the `MsgBox()` function. In Hour 10, you learn how to test the return value of `MsgBox()` and execute code depending on which button the users choose.

Topic 3: The *InputBox()* Function

The `InputBox()` function gets data from users by displaying an input box. Of course, the `MsgBox()` function also gets data from users, but the data is only the button number that the users clicked. The `InputBox()` function is the opposite of the `MsgBox()` function; whereas `MsgBox()`'s primary purpose is to display data for users, the `InputBox()` function's purpose is to receive user input.

Overview

You're well aware of the ease with which forms allow users to enter data. When you begin to create powerful Visual Basic applications, however, you must have a way to ask users questions interactively so that your programs can act on their responses. Input boxes do just that.

Figure 9.4 shows an example input box. As you can see, an input box contains a title bar, a prompt, command buttons, and a text box area to receive user input.

FIG. 9.4
The input box asks users for information.

The *InputBox()* Syntax

Here is the syntax of the input box function:

```
strAnswer = InputBox(strPrompt,[ strTitle],[ strDefault][,
➥intXpos][, intYpos])
```

When users answer the input box and close it, the variable indicated at *strAnswer*, a string variable, will hold the users' answer.

strPrompt is a string that you want displayed so that users know what you're asking for. Always ask users a question or describe the input you want; otherwise, users will have no way of knowing what to enter in response to the input box. The *strPrompt* value can be as long as 1,024 characters.

The optional *strTitle* string value becomes the input box's title. Visual Basic displays the application's name for the title if you don't specify one yourself.

The optional *strDefault* value is a default string that appears inside the typing area. Figure 9.4 showed no default string, but if the input box asks for a predictable response, you can speed the users' operation by displaying a default response that users can accept or change. Users accept the default string by pressing Enter if they don't want to enter a new value.

▼ **NOTE**
If you leave out *strTitle* or *strDefault* (or both), their commas are still required in the code as placeholders. ▲

The optional *intXpos* and *intYpos* variables indicate the numeric value of the twips where you want the input box to appear on-screen. If you've displayed a message, table, or form somewhere on-screen, you can position the input box wherever you want it to appear (as opposed to the middle of the screen, if you specified no position). *intXpos* is the x coordinate (the horizontal position), and *intYpos* is the y coordinate (the vertical position).

▼ **NOTE**
A twip is 1/1440 of an inch and 1/567 of a centimeter—very small indeed. ▲

Example Figure 9.5 shows an input box generated from the following `InputBox()` function (assume that `strUserName` is declared to be a `String` variable):

```
strUserName = InputBox("What is your name?", "Ask a name",
"John Doe")
```

FIG. 9.5
Input boxes wait for the user's response.

The `InputBox()` function always offers a typing area for users to enter a value and an OK button so that they can indicate when the input is completed. After users enter a name (or press Enter to choose OK and use the default `John Doe`), the variable `strUserName` holds the users' answer.

Next Step Unlike message boxes, you can't control which command buttons appear inside input boxes. Remember that the goal for input boxes is to get an answer of some kind. If you just need to know the answer to a yes or no question, use a message box and get users to click the Yes or No command button. If you need more of a response, however, use the `InputBox()` function so that users can enter a response into a string variable or control.

If you want Visual Basic to display the input box in the center of the screen, omit the *intXpos* and *intYpos* values. If you want the input box to appear at a particular location on-screen, you can specify the exact placement by specifying the x- and y-coordinates like this:

```
strUserName = InputBox("What is your name?", "Ask a name",
➥"John Doe", 100, 50)
```

Pt **II**

Hr **9**

If you want to use the screen's physical coordinates based on the `Screen` object's `Left` and `Top` properties, you can embed expressions for the two placement values.

▼ **NOTE**
You learned about the `Screen` object in Hour 4's lesson, "Activating Controls." ▲

Summary

You can now display professional-looking dialog boxes from within Visual Basic. If you ever want to give users a little extra message or get their attention in a way that a regular form control can't do, display a dialog box with `MsgBox()`, a built-in function. If you need to test to see which buttons the users choose, you can call the `MsgBox()` function and test the return value.

You also learned how to write programs that accept input from the keyboard. Before this hour's lesson, you had to assign variables values at the time you wrote the code. You can now write programs that prompt for variable data, and users then enter data when the procedure runs.

Often you see `MsgBox()` and `InputBox()` functions next to each other in code. The `MsgBox()` function displays information, and the `InputBox()` might ask the users questions about that information.

Now that you can get user responses to your questions, Hour 10's lesson explains how to act on that response. Being able to control a program's execution based on data is vital for true data processing. Your program must be able to respond and make decisions based on values in tables and variables. Hour 10's lesson introduces you to *conditional programming,* a fancy term for writing programming statements that use the conditional operators to test data values and act according to the results of the test.

Hour 9 Quiz

You can find the answers for the following questions on the accompanying CD-ROM and on the Virtual Classroom Web site.

On the CD

1. What's the difference between a message box and an input box?

2. Which of the following can you not do with a message box?

   A. Display output for users

   B. Test to see which message box button the users clicked

   C. Receive an answer string

   D. Display warnings to users

3. **True or false:** A sound can accompany a message box.

4. Which function do you use to get an answer from the user—
   `MsgBox()` or `InputBox()`?

5. **True or false:** Tables 9.1, 9.2, and 9.3 provide the values for three
   different `MsgBox()` values.

6. What is a twip?

7. Why does the `InputBox()` function let you display output
   (*strPrompt*) when the function is an input-only function?

8. If you don't specify your own title string, what happens when Visual
   Basic executes a `MsgBox()` function?

9. If you don't specify your own title, what happens when Visual Basic
   executes an `InputBox()` function?

10. Where does the `InputBox()` window appear on-screen if you don't
    specify placement coordinate values?

Homework 9 Exercises

1. Write a `MsgBox` statement that displays your name and an OK button.

2. Write a procedure that asks users for their first names, and then asks
   for their last names. After users enter the two names, concatenate
   the names, store them in a string variable, and display the full name
   (with an appropriate separator space) in a message box.

3. Write the `MsgBox()` needed to generate the message box shown in
   Figure 9.6.

FIG. 9.6
*How was this
dialog box
generated?*

Pt **II**

Hr **9**

Creating Logical Programs

THIS HOUR YOU'LL SEE how to use the conditional and logical operators that you mastered in Hour 8's lesson. When you finish this lesson, you'll understand how a Visual Basic program can make a decision and execute certain program instructions based on that decision's result.

This hour's lesson teaches not only new decision-making statements, but also decision-making functions that come with Visual Basic. Although you won't fully master Visual Basic's built-in functions until Hour 14's lesson, you can put these data-testing functions to use right now, just as you did last hour with the message and input box functions.

Topic 1: Comparing Data with *If*

The If statement appears in every programming language. Computers must be able to make decisions based on the data the program receives. The decision is based on a logical comparison of the data to supplied values. The If statement works to make your programs more powerful and self-reliant.

▶▶ **FAST TRACK**

Have you programmed If logic before? Almost every language supports the If statement. Visual Basic's If is fairly straightforward, so you might want to read through the If statement's format and then skip to the second topic section, "Data Type Inspection, *IIf()*, and *Choose()*" (p. 226), to learn about some of Visual Basic's comparison functions.

Overview Because the If statement takes full advantage of the conditional operators, you can begin to write programs that make decisions based on data.

Most of the time, a Visual Basic procedure executes sequentially, with one line following the next, unless you add control statements that change the order of the instructions being executed. (A VB procedure doesn't execute sequentially when an If statement causes some statements to be skipped.) The If statement is one such control statement that determines the order of statement execution at runtime, depending on the data being worked with.

When you master the If statement and its derivatives, the remaining control statements, such as loops and Select Case, aren't difficult.

If's Format

If has several formats. Here is the syntax of the most fundamental If statement:

```
IF conditional Then
    Block of one or more Visual Basic statements
End If
```

▼ **NOTE**

The Block of one or more Visual Basic statements can contain one or more lines with any valid Visual Basic statements, including additional (*nested*) If statements. ▲

Before you get to the programming side of `If`, think for a moment how you use the word *if* in real life. When you begin a sentence with *if*, you're setting up a *conditional statement* (a statement that may or may not be true). For example, consider the following statements:

If the day is warm, then I will go swimming.

If the light is green, then go.

If the light is red, then stop.

If I make enough money, then we'll buy a new house.

If and only if these statements are true do you complete the statements. To clarify, you could break down the last statement further to get the following:

If I make enough money, then we'll buy a new house, but if I don't make enough money, we won't buy a new house.

Making enough money, therefore, is this statement's condition, determining whether the last part of the statement takes place.

▼ **NOTE**

Notice from its format that `If` takes more than a single line. You're now into the heart of Visual Basic, where you see several statements that take more than one line of a program. One shortcut `If` statement takes only a single line of code (as you'll see in the third topic section), but the `If` syntax shown earlier requires a matching `End If` somewhere later in the program.

You might see a one-line `If` statement. If the *Block of one or more Visual Basic statements* takes only a single statement, you can put the entire `If` on a single line without `End If` at the end. Nevertheless, using the complete three-line `If` statement format makes it easier to add statements later, even if only a single statement is needed for the `If` now. ▲

Working with Conditionals

Before you put `If` statements together in complete examples, you would be wise to explore exactly how Visual Basic compares different types of values. With Visual Basic, you can compare numbers to numbers, numbers to strings, strings to strings, and variants to either numbers or strings.

Visual Basic compares differently, depending on what you're comparing. For example, if a conditional operator compares two numbers of any data

Pt **II**

Hr **10**

type—such as an integer to a floating-point—a true numeric conditional results. All the following conditionals are true:

```
If (4 < 5) Then...

If (4 < 5.0) Then...

If (4 < 5.4322344433223) Then...

If (67.2322 > 67.2321) Then...
```

▼ NOTE

The `If` statements shown in this example and the next few examples aren't complete `If` statements. Understanding the conditional first makes the rest of the statement easier to understand.

Also, the values being compared (the expression after the `If`) would normally be variables or fields. But because you're learning about the different types of comparisons, this section uses literal conditional values to make these examples clearer.

Finally, the parentheses around the conditional after the `If`s aren't required, but they help pinpoint the conditional and make `If` statements easier to understand. ▲

As you learned in Hour 8's lesson, Visual Basic compares strings according to the presence of the `Option Compare` statement. Generally, Visual Basic performs a *binary compare*, meaning that uppercase letters compare before lowercase, as the following true `If` results show:

```
If ("St. Francis Hospital" > "Saint Francis Hospital") Then...

If ("abc" > "ABC") Then...

If ("tWELVE" < "Twelve") Then...
```

If the `Option Compare` option now is set in the `Declarations` section, string conditionals aren't case-sensitive. The following string conditionals, therefore, result in true:

```
If ("St. Francis Hospital" = "ST. Francis Hospital") Then...

If ("abc" = "ABC") Then...

If ("1a2" = "1A2") Then...
```

If you compare a numeric value (field, constant, or variable) to a variable defined with the `Variant` data type, a numeric conditional is made if the `Variant` data contains a number or a string that "looks" like a valid number.

If a variable named `v` is defined as follows,

```
Dim varV As Variant
```

and you store a number in the variable like so,

```
varV = 45.6
```

then the following conditionals hold true:

```
If (varV = 45.6) Then...

If (varV < 100) Then...

If (-121 < varV) Then...
```

> **CAUTION** Be careful when comparing single- or double-precision numbers with the equality conditional operator (=). Representing exact fractional quantities inside the computer is difficult, and rounding can occur in the extreme decimal places that you don't always see on-screen. Therefore, `45.6 = 45.6` usually compares as true, but `45.6543234 = 45.6543234` doesn't always compare as true even though the numbers appear to be equal.

If you store a string in the variable as follows,

```
varV = "-343.56"
```

Visual Basic compares the following as true because the string stored in `varV` looks like a valid number:

```
If (varV > 0) Then...

If (varV < -500) Then...
```

> **CAUTION** If the `Variant` doesn't contain a valid number and you attempt to compare that `Variant` variable to a number, a `Type Mismatch` error appears.

As you're beginning to see, the `Variant` data type lets you perform some mixed data type comparisons that you sometimes require when comparing controls to each other or to other variables and literals.

Finishing the *If*

The `If` statement's body is the code between the `If` and the `End If` lines. The following rules hold:

- If the conditional test is true, the block of statements following `If` is performed.

- If the conditional test is false, the body of the `If` is ignored.

- Either way, the statement following `End If` takes over when the `If` statement finishes its job.

Suppose that you want your Visual Basic procedure to display a secret message to users if they know a password. The password is read from a file and stored in the string variable named `strSystemPass`. After asking the users' password, the following `If` statement determines whether the users see the message:

```
If (strUserPass = strSystemPass) Then
    Beep          ' Rings the bell
    MsgBox("The key is in the file cabinet.")
End If
```

TIP The `Beep` statement causes the computer to beep.

If users enter the correct password, the computer beeps, and the message box with the secret message appears. If users don't enter the correct password, however, the body of the `If` doesn't execute, and the program continues after the `End If` statement.

Visual Basic contains an `Exit` statement that unconditionally exits the current subroutine or function procedure. Here are two forms of `Exit`:

```
Exit Function
```

```
Exit Sub
```

If, depending on a data's value, you need to exit a procedure before its normal termination, use one of these statements. The following procedure assigns a bonus value to a label if a user's sales have reached $5,000 or more:

```
Private Sub CalcBonus ()
  If (txtSales.Text < 5000) Then
    Exit Sub      ' Terminate the procedure now
  End If
```

```
        lblBonus.Caption = txtSales.Text * .05  ' Display bonus
    End Sub
```

If the `If` test is true, the `Exit Sub` executes. When Visual Basic runs an `Exit Sub` statement, the entire function immediately terminates. (Without such an `Exit` statement, the procedure continues executing at the statements following the `End If`.) Therefore, Visual Basic calculates and displays the bonus only if the sales warrant the bonus.

▼ **NOTE**

Visual Basic contains additional forms of `Exit` that work with other statements, such as `Exit Do` and `Exit For`. You'll learn more about these `Exit` forms when you learn about the `Do` and `For` statements in the next hour's lesson. ▲

TIP This and the next few hours' lessons show parts of the Visual Basic language. Only after learning the language specifics can you return to full form-based examples throughout the text. Also, you've learned all the controls that you can master without additional statements such as the array data type that you'll learn in Hour 12's lesson. If you want to try some of the sample procedures that you see this hour and the next few hours, you can create a new project and store each procedure that you want to try in a menu item's `Click` event. Or you can add a standard module to the project (by choosing Add <u>M</u>odule from the <u>P</u>roject menu), enter the new procedure, and then type the name of that procedure in a control's event procedure to execute the procedure when the event occurs.

Else Specifies Otherwise

A complete `If` statement contains an `Else` portion that handles conditionals that the `If` without an `Else` can't take care of. By itself, the `If` describes what happens if a conditional is true. The `Else` part of an `If`—if you include an `Else`—specifies what happens if the conditional is false. Here is the format of the `If` with `Else`:

```
IF conditional Then
    Block of one or more Visual Basic statements
[Else
    Block of one or more Visual Basic statements]
End If
```

Pt **II**

Hr **10**

The `Else` portion is enclosed in square brackets to indicate that it's an optional part of `If` (don't include the brackets as part of your actual code). Think of `Else` as meaning *otherwise*. Here is how you might use an *else* as you might use *otherwise* in everyday conversation:

> If I set the VCR correctly, we'll watch our movie; otherwise, we'll read books.

The *otherwise* specifies what happens if the condition following `If` is false.

▼ **NOTE**

It might help to remember that only one of the two blocks of code following `If` executes: the block following `If` or the block following `Else`. Both blocks never execute because the `If...Else` statement is mutually exclusive and ensures that only one of the two blocks of code executes. ▲

▼ **NOTE**

Throughout this hour's lesson, the placement of the ellipsis (...) in the `If` indicates where the body of each `If` statement goes. For example, `If...ElseIf` describes the block of statements defined with this syntax:

```
If
   Block of one or more Visual Basic statements
ElseIf
   Block of one or more Visual Basic statements
End If ▲
```

Last hour's lesson taught you how to use the message functions, but you couldn't determine how users responded to the boxes until you learned `If`. Use `If` to determine exactly which button users clicked. The following simple `If` statement displays a dialog box and tests user response to the dialog box buttons:

```
If (MsgBox("Are you ready?", vbYesNo) = vbYes) Then
   MsgBox("You clicked Yes")
Else     ' You can assume the user clicked No
   MsgBox("You clicked No")
EndIf
```

Checking for *TypeOf*

If you follow an `If` with the `TypeOf` keyword, you can find out exactly what kind of object your code is working with. `TypeOf` is useful if a function is passed a control variable that represents a control on a form or report, and you want to know what kind of control was passed. You also learn ways to save all the controls on a form and then step through each control, one at a time, inspecting each one and making decisions based on what you find.

Here's the syntax of the If TypeOf statement:

```
IF TypeOf object Is objectType Then
    Block of one or more Visual Basic statements
[Else
    Block of one or more Visual Basic statements]
End If
```

The *object* is any control variable name, and the *objectType* can be any one of the following control types (other control types are available as well):

```
CheckBox         Image     OpenButton    Rectangle
ComboBox         Label     OptionGroup   Shape
CommandButton    Line      PageBreak     TextBox
Graph                      ListBox   PictureBox    ToggleButton
```

Example Any statement can reside in the blocks of the If, even additional If statements. Consider the If statement in Listing 10.1.

Listing 10.1 A Sample *If* Statement

```
If Not IsNull(dteAnyDate) Then
  dteResult = DateSerial(Year(dteAnyDate), Month(dteAnyDate) + 1, 1)
  If Weekday(dteResult) = 1 Then          ' Sunday, so add one day.
      dteDueDate = dteResult + 1
  ElseIf Weekday(dteResult) = 7 Then      ' Saturday, so add two days.
      dteDueDate = dteResult + 2
  Else
      dteDueDate = dteResult
  End If
Else
  dteResult = Null
End If
```

You don't have to understand everything in this code at this point. Basically, if the dteAnyDate data being tested isn't a Null value, dteAnyDate contains valid data. A set of nested If statements then tests that data and assigns dteDueDate (which could be the surrounding function's return value) one of two values depending on what dteAnyDate contains.

Concentrate on the nested If statements. (When an If appears inside another If, the internal If statement is a *nested* If statement.) A nested If statement can be confusing to debug, especially if it needs an Else specified and that Else contains another If statement. As this example code shows, Else and If can never go together. You must use the special ElseIf keyword (shown in Listing 10.1) if your Else block of code contains its own If. Be sure that you type the ElseIf keyword as one word and not two.

In this hour's final topic section, you learn about the Select Case statement, which shortens nested If statements and makes them easier to write and test.

Next Step   The following code demonstrates how you might combine If and TypeOf to determine which control you're working with:

```
If TypeOf aControl Is CommandButton Then
    MsgBox("You sent a Command Button")
ElseIf TypeOf aControl Is CheckBox Then
    MsgBox("You sent a Check Box")
ElseIf TypeOf aControl Is TextBox Then
    MsgBox("You sent a Text Box")
End If
```

Although it might seem obvious at this point that you'll always know a control's data type because you created the control and wrote the program, Hour 13's lesson, "Understanding How Procedures Work," shows you how to pass information from one procedure to another. You can use code similar to this If statement to determine the kind of control sent to the current procedure from another.

Topic 2: Data Type Inspection, *IIf()*, and *Choose()*

In the first topic section, you learned about conditional code—that is, code that performs comparison tests and executes one set of statements or another depending on the result of the tests. Your programs can now set up logic that ensures that users have entered correct data, that a table contains enough information, or that the printer is turned on before you print a report.

This topic section extends your knowledge of conditional logic by describing the `Is...()` data-inspection functions and giving you some shortcuts for the `If` statement. So much of programming in Visual Basic or any other language is devoted to looking at data and making decisions about what to do next based on that data.

Overview This topic section introduces these Visual Basic data-testing components:

- The built-in `IsDate()`, `IsEmpty()`, `IsNull()`, and `IsNumeric()` functions
- The `VarType()` function
- The `IIf()` function
- The `Choose()` function

Data plays such an important part of database programming that you should master this topic's content, and you'll be well-rewarded when you begin writing Visual Basic-based applications.

Inspecting Data

The `Is...()` and `VarType()` functions are called *data-inspection functions*. These functions inspect the data *types*, not the contents, of variables. In the first topic section, you learned about the `TypeOf` keyword that inspects data to determine the kind of object you have. You'll typically use `TypeOf` to test for control types.

Your VB programs work with many different kinds of data, and you sometimes don't know in advance what kind of data you have to work with. Before you make a calculation, for example, you want to make sure that the data is numeric.

Table 10.1 lists the data-inspection functions and offers a description of what they do. Each function receives one argument of the `Variant` data type. (An *argument* is a value that you place inside a function's parentheses. Some functions accept multiple arguments separated by commas.)

Table 10.1 The *Is...( )* Data-Inspection Functions

Function Name	Description
IsDate( )	Determines whether its argument is a date data type (or whether the data can be converted to a valid date)
IsEmpty( )	Determines whether its argument has been initialized
IsNull( )	Determines whether its argument holds a `Null` value
IsNumeric( )	Determines whether its argument holds a number (or whether the data can be converted to a valid number)

▼ **NOTE**

Each `Is...()` function accepts the `Variant` data type because they must be able to inspect any data and determine what type it is. ▲

An *empty variable* is one that hasn't been initialized. Perhaps a procedure has declared the variable but has yet to store data in the variable. Newcomers to Visual Basic often wonder why an empty variable is different from a `Null` value and a zero value. At times, you must have some way to tell whether users have entered something into fields; an empty variable signals that nothing has been entered.

On the CD

The code snipped in Listing 10.2 is rather simple and demonstrates what happens when you apply the `IsEmpty()` function to variables that have and haven't been initialized.

Listing 10.2 Ifmsges.bas: Testing for Empty Variables

```
Dim var1, var2, var3, var4 As Variant
Dim msg As Integer   ' MsgBox return
var1 = 0        ' Zero value
var2 = Null     ' Null value
var3 = ""       ' Null string
If IsEmpty(var1) Then
   msg = MsgBox("var1 is empty", vbOKOnly)
End If
If IsEmpty(var2) Then
   msg = MsgBox("var2 is empty", vbOKOnly)
End If
If IsEmpty(var3) Then
   msg = MsgBox("var3 is empty", vbOKOnly)
End If
```

```
If IsEmpty(var4) Then
    msg = MsgBox("var4 is empty", vbOKOnly)
End If
```

The only output from this code is a message box that displays the following:

```
var4 is empty
```

You receive this response because all the other variables have some kind of data (they've been initialized).

> **TIP**   Use `IsNull()` to see whether a control or field on a report or form contains data. Use `IsEmpty()` just for variables.

This `IsNull()` function checks its argument and returns true if the argument contains a `Null` value. The value `Null` is a special value that you can assign to variables to indicate either that no data exists or that there's an error (the way your program interprets a `Null` value depends on how you code the program). On form and report controls, a field is considered `Null` if users enter no data in the field.

> **CAUTION**   Given that you can assign a `Null` value to a variable (as in `varA = Null`), you might be tempted to test for a `Null` value like this:
>
> ```
> If (varA = Null) Then ....
> ```
>
> Be warned that such an `If` always fails. Using `IsNull()` is the only way to check for a `Null` value in a variable.

If your Visual Basic procedure needs to know whether a form's field named Hours Worked has data, the procedure can check it with an `If` statement, as follows:

```
If IsNull(txtHoursWorked) Then
    msg = MsgBox("You didn't enter hours worked!", vbOKOnly)
Else                        ' Thank them for the good hours
    msg = MsgBox("Thanks for entering hours worked!", vbOKOnly)
End If
```

This `If` statement checks to ensure that users typed something in the field before the program continues.

The `IsNumeric()` function checks its argument for a number. Any `Variant` value that can be converted to a number returns a true result in the `IsNumeric()` function and a false result otherwise. The following data types can be converted to numbers:

- Empty (converts to zero)
- Integer
- Long integer
- Single-precision
- Double-precision
- Currency
- Date (returns `False` always)
- String, if the string "looks" like a valid number

Suppose that you place a text box on the form for users to enter a loan amount. The program will use the loan amount to compute past due charges as they accrue. Before you use the amount to compute charges, you should verify that users entered a valid currency value. The text box holds a `Variant` data type when users enter the loan amount, so you can use the `IsNumeric()` to test for the valid number before computing with the number.

The Multitalented *VarType()* Function

If you need to know what data type a variable is, use the `VarType()` function. Table 10.2 lists the return values from the `VarType()` function, and `VarType()` returns no other values than the 16 listed in the table.

Table 10.2 *VarType( )* Return Values

This Value Returned...	Named Literal	If the Variant Contains This Data Type...
0	vbEmpty	Empty
1	vbNull	Null
2	vbInteger	Integer
3	vbLong	Long
4	vbSingle	Single
5	vbDouble	Double
6	vbCurrency	Currency

This Value Returned...	Named Literal	If the Variant Contains This Data Type...
7	vbDate	Date
8	vbString	String
9	vbObject	Object
10	vbError	An error value
11	vbBoolean	Boolean
12	vbVariant	Variant (for Variant arrays, see Hour 12's lesson)
13	vbDataObject	A data-access object
14	vbDecimal	Decimal
17	vbByte	Byte
8192	vbArray	An array (VB adds 8192 to the data type to indicate an array, so 8194 indicates an integer array)

On the CD

The code snippet in Listing 10.3 contains a nested `If` statement, which prints the data type of whatever data is passed to it.

Listing 10.3 Dattype1.bas: Determining the Data Type Passed

```
' varA comes from another routine
If VarType(varA) = vbEmpty Then
  msg = MsgBox("The argument is Empty")
ElseIf VarType(varA) = vbNull then
  msg = MsgBox("The argument is Null")
ElseIf VarType(varA) = vbInteger then
  msg = MsgBox("The argument is Integer")
ElseIf VarType(varA) = vbLong then
  msg = MsgBox("The argument is Long")
ElseIf VarType(varA) = vbSingle then
  msg = MsgBox("The argument is Single")
ElseIf VarType(varA) = vbDouble then
  msg = MsgBox("The argument is Double")
ElseIf VarType(varA) = vbCurrency then
  msg = MsgBox("The argument is Currency")
ElseIf VarType(varA) = vbDate then
  msg = MsgBox("The argument is Date")
ElseIf VarType(varA) = vbString then
  msg = MsgBox("The argument is String")
```

Pt **II**

Hr **10**

continues

Listing 10.3 Continued

```
ElseIf VarType(varA) = vbObject then
  msg = MsgBox("The argument is an Object")
ElseIf VarType(varA) = vbError then
  msg = MsgBox("The argument is an Error")
ElseIf VarType(varA) = vbBoolean then
  msg = MsgBox("The argument is Boolean")
ElseIf VarType(varA) = vbVariant then
  msg = MsgBox("The argument is a Variant array")
ElseIf VarType(varA) = vbDataObject then
  msg = MsgBox("The argument is a Data Object")
ElseIf VarType(varA) = vbDecimal then
  msg = MsgBox("The argument is Decimal")
ElseIf VarType(varA) = vbByte then
  msg = MsgBox("The argument is Byte")
Else
  msg = MsgBox("The argument is an array")
EndIf
```

> **TIP** The `Select Case` statement, which you learn in this hour's final topic, offers a better method of nesting `If` statements like the ones shown here.

An *If* Shortcut: *IIf()*

The `IIf()` function performs a succinct version of a simple `If...Else` statement. Because `IIf()` is a function, it returns a value, and the value returned depends on a true or false test that you put at the beginning of `IIf()`. The syntax of `IIf()` is as follows:

> `IIf(expression, trueResult, falseResult)`

If the expression is true, *trueResult* is returned; if the expression is false, *falseResult* is returned.

Here's a sample code fragment that uses `IIf()`:

```
Dim atrAns As String
strAns = IIf(intN < 0, "Cannot be negative", "Good data")
```

This statement does the following: If whatever is stored in `intN` is less than 0, the string variable `strAns` is assigned the string `"Cannot be negative"`, but if `intN` contains any number equal to or greater than 0, the string "Good data" is stored in `strAns`. Figure 10.1 illustrates the nature of this `IIf()`.

FIG. 10.1
The `IIf()` *function works like the* `If` *statement.*

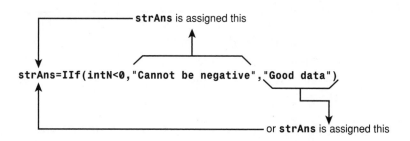

If you rewrite the previous `IIf()` function as an `If` statement, here is what you do:

```
If (n < 0) Then
    strAns = "Cannot be negative"
Else
    strAns = "Good data"
End If
```

`IIf()` is more efficient and easier to write than a multiline `If` statement. However, `IIf()` replaces only simple `If` statements that assign data, and `If` statements with several lines of code in their bodies must remain regular `If` statements.

▶▶ **FAST TRACK**

The `IIf()` function is similar to Lotus 1-2-3's `@IF` function. If you've ever programmed in C, the `IIf()` function works a lot like the conditional operator `?:`.

Choosing with *Choose()*

The `Choose()` function can have many arguments, more arguments than any other built-in function. Depending on the value of the first argument, `Choose()` returns only one of the remaining arguments. Here's the syntax of `Choose()`:

```
Choose(intIndexNum, expression[, expression] ...)
```

Pt **II**

Hr **10**

After the second argument (*expression*), you can have as many expression arguments as needed. The *intIndexNum* must be a variable or field that equates to a number from 1 to the number of expressions in the function.

If, for example, you need to generate a small table of price codes, abbreviations, or product codes, using `Choose()` is more succinct than using an `If` statement. `Choose()`, however, is more limited in scope than `If` because `Choose()` selects on an integer value only, not on a more complete comparison.

> **CAUTION**   `Choose()` returns `Null` if *intIndexNum* isn't between 1 and the number of expressions inclusive.

The first argument of `Choose()` can be an expression. Therefore, you have to adjust the first argument so that it falls within the range of the number of arguments that follow. If the values possible for the index go from 0 to 4, for example, add 1 to the index so that the range goes from 1 to 5 and selects from the `Choose()` list properly.

Suppose that a form contains a Price Code label. When users enter a new product, they should also enter a price code from 1 to 5, which corresponds to the following codes:

1	Full markup
2	5% discount
3	10% discount
4	Special order
5	Mail order

The following `Choose()` function assigns to a description field the correct description based on the price code (type this code all on one line):

```
Descript = Choose(lblProdCode, "Full markup", "5% discount",
➡"10% discount", "Special order", "Mail order")
```

Example   The following code asks users for their age by using a `Variant` variable. The program displays an error message if a user enters a non-numeric number:

```
Dim varAge As Variant
Dim msg As Integer    ' MsgBox() return
varAge = InputBox("How old are you?", "Get Your Age")
If IsNumeric(varAge) Then
    msg = MsgBox("Thanks!", vbOKOnly)
Else
    msg = MsgBox("What are you trying to hide?",
    ➥vbOKOnly+vbQuestion)
End If
```

Next Step You can't divide by zero (division by zero is undefined in mathematics). Therefore, the following `IIf()` function returns an average sale price or a `Null` value if division by zero results:

```
curAveSales = IIf(intQty > 0, curTotalSales / intQty, Null)
```

Remembering that a zero value produces a false result, you can rewrite the preceding statement as follows:

```
curAveSales = IIf(intQty, curTotalSales / intQty, Null)
```

If you rewrite this statement by using an `If`, here is how you do it:

```
If (intQty) Then
    curAveSales = curTotalSales / Qtr
Else
    curAveSales = Null
End If
```

Topic 3: The *Select Case* Statement

You probably shouldn't rely on the `If...ElseIf` block to take care of too many conditions. More than three or four nested `If` statements tend to add confusion (you get into messy logic, such as "If this is true, then if this is true, then do something, else if this is true do something, else if this is true do something," and so on). This topic's `Select Case` statement handles multiple `If` selections better than a long set of `If...ElseIf` statements. The `Select Case` statement is the final logic-control statement left for you to learn in the Visual Basic language.

Overview There are three syntaxes of the `Select Case` statement. `Select Case` is one of the longest statements in Visual Basic. Despite that foreboding

Pt II

Hr 10

length, `Select Case` is one of the easiest statements to master. It exists to make your programming decisions easier, not harder.

This topic section introduces the following subjects:

- Using the `Select Case` statement syntax
- Replacing nested `If` statements with `Select Case`
- Making conditional `Select Case` choices
- Setting ranges of `Select Case` choices

The *Select Case* Format

`Select Case` improves on the `If...Else` block by streamlining the nested "If within an `If`" construction. The format of the primary `Select Case` is as follows:

```
Select Case Expression
Case expressionMatch
    Block of one or more Visual Basic statements
[Case expressionMatch
    Block of one or more Visual Basic statements]
[Case Else
    Block of one or more Visual Basic statements]
End Select
```

As you can see, `Select Case` chooses from among several conditions. As the brackets indicate, you can optionally have two or more sets of `Case` expressions and code following a `Select Case` statement. Your application determines the number of `Case` expressions that follow the `Select Case` line. The expressions can be string or numeric expressions (with constants or variables). The expressions aren't conditional `True` or `False` expressions, but expressions that equate to integer or character values.

The *Block of one or more Visual Basic statements* is similar to the block of statements you saw for the block `If`; you can type one or more statements following each other to make up that block. The `Case Else` line is optional; not all `Select Case` statements require it. You must put the `End Select` line at the end of every `Case Select` statement, however. Otherwise, Visual Basic doesn't know where the last block of `Case` statements ends.

Using `Select Case` is easier than its syntax might lead you to believe. If the `Select Case` expression is the same as any of the `Case` expressions, that matching `Case` code executes. If none of the `Case` expressions match the `Select Case` expression, the `Case Else` code executes. If you don't supply a `Case Else`, the next statement in the program executes.

You can use a `Select Case` anywhere that you can use a block `If...Else`; in fact, `Select Case` is the easier of the two to read.

In the preceding topic section, you learned about the `VarType()` function, which determines the data type of its argument by returning a numeric value. Although nothing is wrong with the procedure as coded in Listing 10.3, nested `If...ElseIf` statements can be confusing. `Select Case` statements do the same thing but are easier to follow. Listing 10.4 shows an equivalent function that uses `Select Case`.

On the CD

Listing 10.4 Seldata.bas: Determining Data Types with *Select Case*

```
Private Sub PrntType(varA)   ' Variant if you don't specify otherwise
  Dim msg As Integer    ' MsgBox() return
  Select Case VarType(varA)   ' VarType() returns an integer
    Case 0
      msg = MsgBox("The argument is Empty")
    Case 1
      msg = MsgBox("The argument is Null")
    Case 2
      msg = MsgBox("The argument is Integer")
    Case 3
      msg = MsgBox("The argument is Long")
    Case 4
      msg = MsgBox("The argument is Single")
    Case 5
      msg = MsgBox("The argument is Double")
    Case 6
      msg = MsgBox("The argument is Currency")
    Case 7
      msg = MsgBox("The argument is Date")
    Case 8
      msg = MsgBox("The argument is String")
    Case 9
      msg = MsgBox("The argument is an Object")
    Case 10
      msg = MsgBox("The argument is an Error")
    Case 11
      msg = MsgBox("The argument is Boolean")
```

continues

Listing 10.4 Continued

```
    Case 12
      msg = MsgBox("The argument is a Variant array")
    Case 13
      msg = MsgBox("The argument is a Data Access Object")
    Case 14
      msg = MsgBox("The argument is Decimal")
    Case 17
      msg = MsgBox("The argument is Byte")
    Case Else
      msg = MsgBox("The argument is an Array")
  End Select
End Sub
```

The long `Select Case` statement, with indented `Case` statements, cleans up the code when your program must select from among many choices. The expression at the end of the `Select Case` line—in this case, `VarType(varA)`—determines which of the subsequent `Case` statements execute. Although only one statement follows each `Case` statement in this example, several statements can execute for a `Case`, and you can trigger the execution of other procedures as well. Instead of numeric literals, you could have used Visual Basic's named literals, such as `vbBoolean`; this example used numbers to help ensure that you master `Select Case`.

▼ **NOTE**

The `VarType()` function always returns a value from 0 to 14, 17, and greater than or equal to 8192. If none of the `Case` values match the expression, use a `Case Else` statement. A `Case Else` executes if none of the other `Case` values match the `Select Case` expression. ▲

Conditional *Select Case* Choices

As with the `If` statement, the expression that `Select Case` tests for can be conditional. You must use the extra `Is` keyword in the conditional `Case`. Because you can put a conditional test after one or more of the `Case`s, you can test for a broader range of values with the conditional `Select Case`. The keyword `Is` is required if you use a conditional test in a `Case`.

▼ **NOTE**

You can't combine And, Or, or Not in a conditional Select Case statement. If you need to make a compound conditional test, you must use a block If...ElseIf. ▲

The procedure in Listing 10.5 asks users for an age and prints an appropriate message. Without the conditional Case testing, it would take too many individual Cases testing for each possible age to make the Select Case usable here.

On the CD

Listing 10.5   Agetest.bas: Testing an Age Value with *Select Case*

```
Private Sub ageTest ()
' Procedure to describe legal vehicles based on age
  Dim intAge As Integer
  Dim msg As Integer  ' MsgBox() return
  intAge = InputBox("How old are you?")
  Select Case intAge
    Case Is < 14
      msg = MsgBox("You can only ride a bike.")
    Case Is < 16
      msg = MsgBox("You can ride a motorcycle.")
    Case Else
      msg = MsgBox("You can drive a car")
  End Select
End Sub
```

The Range of *Select Case* Choices

Another option of Select Case shows that you can test for a range of values on each line of Case. You can use the To keyword in a Case statement to specify a range of values that Visual Basic checks to determine which Case executes. This capability is useful when possibilities are ordered sequentially, and you want to perform certain actions if one of the sets of values is chosen. The first expression (the one to the right of To) must be lower numerically—or as determined by the sort order of its string data—than the second expression.

Pt **II**

Hr **10**

> **TIP** Put the most likely `Case` selection at the top of the `Case` for efficiency. Visual Basic then doesn't have to search down the list as much.

On the CD

Listing 10.6 shows the same age-testing procedure as Listing 10.5, except that a range of ages is tested with the `To` keyword instead of a conditional test.

Listing 10.6 AgeTest2.bas: Testing for an Age with a *Select Case* Range Test

```
Private Sub ageTest ()
' Procedure to describe legal vehicles based on age
  Dim intAge As Integer
  Dim msg As Integer
  intAge = InputBox("How old are you?")
  Select Case intAge
    Case 1 To 13
      msg = MsgBox("You can only ride a bike.")
    Case 14 To 15
      msg = MsgBox("You can ride a motorcycle.")
    Case 16 To 99
      msg = MsgBox("You can drive a car")
    Case Else
      msg = MsgBox("You typed a bad age.")
  End Select
End Sub
```

This procedure ensures that anyone aged 16 or older is told that he or she can drive a car. Any ages that don't match a `Case`, such as 0 and negative ages, trigger an error message.

Example `Select Case` is great for handling user selections. The procedure in Listing 10.7 is a math tutorial, which asks for two numbers and then asks users which type of math to perform with the numbers.

Listing 10.7 Mathtry.bas: Use *Select Case* to Handle Decisions

```
Private Sub mathPractice ()
' Procedure to practice math accuracy
  Dim intNum1, intNum2 As Integer
  Dim strOp, strAns As String
```

```
    Dim msg As Integer    ' MsgBox() return
    intNum1 = InputBox("Please type a number")
    intNum2 = InputBox("Please type a second number")
    ' Find out what the user wants to do with the numbers
    strOp = InputBox("Do you want +, -, *, or / ?")
    ' Perform the math
    Select Case (strOp)
      Case "+"
        strAns = Str(intNum1 + intNum2)   ' Make answer a string
        msg = MsgBox(Str(intNum1) & " plus" & Str(intNum2) & " is" & strAns)
      Case "-"
        strAns = Str(intNum1 - intNum2)   ' Make answer a string
        msg = MsgBox(Str(intNum1) & " minus" & Str(intNum2) & " is" & strAns)
      Case "*"
        strAns = Str(intNum1 * intNum2)   ' Make answer a string
        msg = MsgBox(Str(intNum1) & " times" & Str(intNum2) & " is" & strAns)
      Case "/"
        strAns = Str(intNum1 / intNum2)   ' Make answer a string
        msg = MsgBox(Str(intNum1) & " into" & Str(intNum2) & " is" & strAns)
      Case Else
        Beep
        MsgBox("You didn't enter a correct operator.", vbExclamation)
      End Select
    End Sub
```

This **Select Case** statement demonstrates that string expressions work as well in **Select Case** statements as integer expressions.

Never use a floating-point expression for a **Select Case** match, because it's extremely difficult to store and match exact floating-point quantities. Stick to integer and string expressions for **Select Case**.

The **Str()** expression used in Listing 10.7 is probably new to you here. The **MsgBox()** function requires a string expression, but **MsgBox()** is used in Listing 10.7 to display the result of a mathematical expression. Therefore, the answer to the expression, stored in **strAns**, is converted to a string with **Str()** before being concatenated to other strings in the **MsgBox()** message.

▼ **NOTE**

If users enter an operator other than +, -, *, or /, Case Else takes over and displays an error box. ▲

Pt **II**

Hr **10**

Next Step Visual Basic provides a great deal of customization for `Select Case` statements. You can combine any and all of the previous `Select Case` formats into a single `Select Case` statement.

The following sample `Case` statements show you how you can combine different formats:

```
Case 5, 6, 7, 10

Case 5 To 7, 10

Case "A", "a", "K" To "P", "k" To "p"

Case 1, 5, 10, Is > 100, amount To quantity
```

The `Select Case` statement in Listing 10.8 calculates overtime payroll figures based on the hours worked. Such decision-based calculations are difficult to provide in Visual Basic without your using Visual Basic's control statements such as `Select Case`.

On the CD

Listing 10.8 OTselect.bas: Computing Overtime with *Select Case*

```
Select Case (intHours)
   Case 1 To 40
      sngOverTime = 0.0
   Case 41 To 49
     ' Time and a half
     sngOverHrs = (hours - 40) * 1.5
     sngOverTime = sngOverHrs * sngRate
   Case Is >= 50
     ' Double time for hrs over 50 and
     ' 1.5 for 10 hours
     sngOverHrs = ((intHours - 50) * 2) + (10 * 1.5)
     sngOverTime = sngOverHrs * sngRate
End Select
```

▼ **NOTE**

The `Select Case` variable `intHours` was put in parentheses to make it stand out better. ▲

Summary

You now have tools that you can use to write powerful programming statements. With the `If` statement, you can perform a block of statements only if a certain conditional is true. By adding the `Else` option, you can specify the block of code to execute if the conditional is false.

This lesson described more ways you can test for data values and data types. By using the `Is...()` inspection functions, you can determine whether a data value is a date, empty, `Null`, or a number so that your code can operate accordingly. The `IIf()` is a shortcut form of `If`. Although `IIf()` will never replace the more readable `If` statement, `IIf()` is useful (and efficient) for coding simple decision statements that have a true part and a false part.

The `VarType()` function is extremely useful for functions that can work with more than one data type. By first determining the data type, a subsequent `If` can then select the appropriate code to execute. The `Choose()` function returns a value based on an index, simulating the effect of a lookup table.

`Select Case` has several syntaxes. You can write the statement so that a `Case` match is made based on a single integer or string value. You also can use the `Is` keyword to select from a case based on a conditional expression. With the `To` keyword, you can select from a range of values. Also, you can combine all the formats of `Case` into a multiple-part `Select Case` statement.

Now that you can test data and execute code based on the results of the test, you're ready to learn how to make the computer really work! Next hour's lesson explains how to instruct Visual Basic to repeat lines of code several times when you want to process several occurrences of data.

Hour 10 Quiz

You can find the answers for the following questions on the accompanying CD-ROM and on the Virtual Classroom Web site.

On the CD

1. **True or false:** `Visual Basic is fun!` prints on-screen when the following statement is executed:

```
If (54 <= 50) Then
  msg = MsgBox("Visual Basic is fun!", vbOKOnly)
End If
```

Pt **II**

Hr **10**

2. **True or false:** If a decision (made by a conditional test) has more than one possible result, you can use an `If...ElseIf`.

3. Find the error in the following code:

```
intA = 6    ' a is an integer variable
If (intA > 6) Then
    msg = MsgBox("George", vbOKOnly)
Else If (intA = 6) Then
    msg = MsgBox("Henry", vbOKOnly)
Else If (intA < 6) Then
    msg = MsgBox("James", vbOKOnly)
End If
```

4. What's the shortcut for the `If` statement?

5. **True or false:** You can use a data-inspection function to see whether a variable holds a string value.

6. What happens if the first argument of `Choose()` is less than 1?

7. What's an advantage of `Select Case` over `If...ElseIf` statements?

8. **True or false:** The `Case Else` statement is optional.

9. Which keyword of `Select Case`—`Is` or `To`—lets `Select Case` select from a range of values?

10. **True or false:** The following `Case` statement contains an error:

```
Case Is 34 To 48
```

Hour 10 Homework Exercises

1. Write a simple procedure (using `InputBox()`) that asks users for the previous five days' temperatures (stored in the `Single` variables `sngT1`, `sngT2`, `sngT3`, `sngT4`, and `sngT5`). Compute the average temperature and print (by using `MsgBox()`) "It's cold!" if the average is less than freezing.

2. Rewrite the following `If` statement as an `IIf()` function call:

```
If (total > 10000) Then
    Bonus = 50
Else
    Bonus = 5
End If
```

3. Rewrite the following `If` statement by using a `Choose()` function:

```
If (ID = 1) Then
    bonus = 50
ElseIf (ID = 2) Then
    bonus = 75
ElseIf (ID = 3) Then
    bonus = 100
End If
```

4. Write a `Choose()` function that returns the `VarType()` descriptions based on a data-type number used as the first argument. That is, if the first argument of `Choose()` is 0, add 1 to it to get 1, and return the first expression, `Empty`.

5. Rewrite the following nested `If...ElseIf` by using `Select Case`:

```
If (intA = 1) Then
    MsgBox("Ok")
ElseIf (intA = 2) Then
    MsgBox("No way")
ElseIf (intA = 3) Then
    MsgBox("There's a problem.")
End If
```

6. Write a `Select Case` statement that asks users for the name of the month and prints `Happy Hot Summer!` if the month is a summer month, `Stay Warm!` if the month is in winter, and `Enjoy the Weather!` if the month is a month other than a summer or winter month. (If the users live in Hawaii, they have to suffer through 12 months of bliss, so this application doesn't apply there.)

Adding Loops to Your Programs

THIS HOUR DESCRIBES how your Visual Basic programs can continually execute the same set of instructions. When Visual Basic executes the same instructions over and over, Visual Basic is looping. A *loop* is a series of statements that execute repeatedly. Many times you have to repeat a calculation or print the same message several times.

Visual Basic supports several kinds of loop statements. The looping statements all repeat a section of Visual Basic code until a certain condition is met.

Topic 1: The *Do...Loop* Loop

This topic section introduces the Visual Basic loop statements called the `Do...Loop` loops. There are four different kinds of `Do...Loop`s. In most cases, the `Do...Loop` you select depends more on your preference and not on coding requirements, because you can write almost any loop by using any of the looping statements.

▶▶ **FAST TRACK**

Have you programmed in QBasic or Access Basic? If so, you've already mastered Visual Basic's looping statements. Skip to Hour 12's lesson (p. 273) to learn how Visual Basic supports array handling.

Overview   This topic section introduces the following kinds of loop statements:

- `Do While...Loop`
- `Do...Loop While`
- `Do Until...Loop`
- `Do...Loop Until`
- `Exit Do`

Actually, the first four statements in this list are just specific versions of the more generalized `Do...Loop` statement. The placement of `While` and `Until` determines how the loop behaves.

Introducing Loops

Some desired program repetition just isn't possible without loops. Suppose that you ask users whether they want a report sent to the screen or to the printer by displaying Figure 11.1's dialog box. If users don't press an S or a P, you probably want to tell them that you don't recognize the answer and then repeat the question. In fact, you have to keep asking the same question over and over until the users answer with something that you're expecting. The loop of statements, therefore, contains the `InputBox()` to ask the question, an `If` statement to check the answer, and a `MsgBox()` to issue an error message so that users know what's going on.

FIG. 11.1
Users should answer by pressing either S or P.

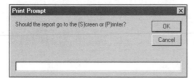

Guard Against Endless Loops

You often write procedures that loop because your procedures are processing sets of data values many times. As you add loops to your programs, you need to guard against writing *endless loops*. A never-ending procedure is no more useful to you than one that doesn't work correctly in the first place. With an endless loop, your users can never regain control of the machine.

> **TIP** Before you go farther, you should learn what to do if you happen to write a procedure with an endless loop. In Visual Basic (as with most dialects of BASIC), you can stop a procedure in mid-execution by pressing Ctrl+Break. The procedure then stops, and you return to the Code window so that you can edit the program.

The General *Do...Loop* Statement

One of the most common ways to perform a loop in Visual Basic is to use the `Do...Loop` statement. `Do...Loop` has several syntaxes. Your choice of syntax has more to do with your own preference and style than with programming requirements. Because the many syntaxes can get confusing, this section presents all the `Do...Loop` syntaxes for your perusal; the following sections explain each one. The syntaxes of the `Do...Loop` statement are as follows:

```
Do While condition
   Block of one or more Visual Basic statements
Loop

Do
   Block of one or more Visual Basic statements
Loop While condition

Do Until condition
   Block of one or more Visual Basic statements
Loop
```

```
Do
    Block of one or more Visual Basic statements
Loop Until condition
```

> **TIP** Indent the inner statements of loops so that you can spot the statements easily inside the loop.

The *condition* is a comparison, `Is...()` function, or any other VB language element that returns a `True` or `False` data type result. As with the `If` statement's comparison, any non-zero value is true, and a zero value is always false. Therefore, the *condition* might be nothing more than a numeric variable or control.

Figure 11.2 gives you an overview of `Do...Loop`'s action within a procedure. The arrow shows you how the `Do...Loop` repeats a section of the procedure. Until this hour's lesson, all procedures that you've seen have flowed sequentially from top to bottom without any repetition.

FIG. 11.2
The `Do...Loop`
*repeats a section
of code.*

```
Private Sub Birthday ()
  Dim strAge As String
  Dim msg As Integer
  'Visual Basic statements can go here

  'The loop is next
Do
   'Possible other statements here
   msg = MsgBox("It's your birthday!")
   strAge = InputBox("How old are you?")
Loop Until IsNumeric(strAge) 'Loop until user enters numeric age
  'Rest of procedure goes here
End Sub
```

These statements repeat until the condition being tested becomes equal to True

▼ **NOTE**

The `While` keyword causes Visual Basic to repeat the loop as long as (while) the condition is true. The `Until` keyword causes Visual Basic to repeat the loop as long as the condition is false (until the condition becomes true). ▲

The *Do While...Loop*

All loops supply ways to control the statements executing through conditional tests. The loops' conditional tests use the same comparison operators you saw in Hour 10 with the `If` statement (refer to Hour 8's lesson for a review of the comparison operators).

If you look at the formats for the Do loops, you see that the condition resides at either the top of the loop or at the bottom. The placement of the
conditional test determines how the Do loop terminates its repetition. Remember to guard against endless loops. You must have some way of quit-
ting every loop you put in your programs; the condition is the way to end
the loop. Basically, the While condition keeps the loop repeating as long as
the relation is true, but as soon as the relation becomes false, Visual Basic
quits repeating the loop and finishes the procedure following the Loop
statement.

On the CD

Listing 11.1 shows a Do While...Loop sample code fragment that tests its
relation at the top of the loop.

Listing 11.1 Docount1.bas: Counting with a *Do While...Loop*

```
Dim intCount As Integer
Dim msg As Integer   ' MsgBox() return
intCount = 1
Do While (intCount <= 10)            ' Count up from 1
   msg = MsgBox("Counting at " & intCount)
   intCount = intCount + 1
Loop
mag = MsgBox("All done now.")
```

If you run a procedure with this code, you'll see message boxes that display
the following output:

```
Counting at 1
Counting at 2
Counting at 3
Counting at 4
Counting at 5
Counting at 6
Counting at 7
Counting at 8
Counting at 9
Counting at 10
All done now.
```

intCount is the variable being tested. As long as the value of intCount
is less than or equal to 10, the body of the loop executes. The body of the
loop executes over and over until the value of intCount is greater than 10.
The only way the loop stops executing (and thereby not becoming an endless loop) is that the body of the loop must change intCount.

The statement `intCount = intCount + 1` is called a *counter statement*—not because the variable is named `intCount`, but because the same variable appears on both sides of the equal sign. When you see the same variable name on both sides of an equal sign, the variable is being changed. One is being added to `intCount` every time your computer executes the statement `intCount = intCount + 1`. (Remember that the assignment statement evaluates whatever is to the right of the equal sign first and then stores that value in the variable on the left.) Every time the body of the loop executes, `intCount` is changed. Eventually, `intCount` will be more than 10, and the loop will stop looping.

> **TIP** A counter statement can also count down by subtracting 1 from a counter variable each time through a loop—for example, `intCount = intCount - 1`.

`intCount` begins at 1. The `Do While...Loop` continues until `intCount` is more than 10. Because the loop tests the condition at the top of the loop, as soon as `intCount` becomes 11, the loop stops and any code that follows the `Loop` statement continues. The loop you saw earlier prints the message 10 times. On the 11th *iteration* (another name for *loop*), the condition becomes false and the loop then ends.

The *Do...Loop While*

The primary difference between the `Do While...Loop` and the `Do...Loop While` is the placement of the conditional test.

On the CD

Listing 11.2 shows the same code as shown in Listing 11.1, with its conditional `While` test at the bottom of the loop.

Listing 11.2   Docount2.bas: Counting with *Do...Loop While*

```
Dim intCount As Integer
Dim msg As Integer   ' MsgBox() return
intCount = 1
Do
   msg = MsgBox("Counting at " & intCount)   ' Print in the message box
   intCount = intCount + 1
Loop While (intCount <= 10)
msg = MsgBox("All done now.")
```

The body of this loop continues as long as `intCount` is less than or equal to 10. The conditional test is located at the bottom of the loop. Therefore, when `intCount` is more than 10, the body of the loop stops looping. In other words, Listing 11.2 produces the same output as Listing 11.1 except that the last message box that displays `Counting at 10` no longer appears.

> **TIP** The difference between the conditional test at the top or bottom boils down to only one real difference: The body of the first loop, `Do While...Loop` (with the test at the top), may never execute because the test might be false before the loop ever executes. The body of the second loop, `Do...Loop While` (with the test at the bottom), always executes at least once. Visual Basic has no idea that the conditional test is false until it performs at least one iteration of the loop.

The *Do Until...Loop*

In each of the two preceding `Do` loops, you learned that the condition being tested is preceded by a `While`. As you can see, the loop continues executing while the condition is true. If you replace `While` with `Until`, the loop continues *until* the condition becomes true.

The choice of loop that you use depends on the type of statements that you feel most comfortable with. You can write any loop with any of the `Do` loops that you've seen.

Here's a `Do...Loop While` that does the same work as the previous ones:

```
Do
   strAns = InputBox("Again?")
Loop While (strAns = "Y")
```

Here is the same code using a `Do...Loop Until`:

```
Do
   strAns = InputBox("Again?"))
Loop Until (strAns = "N")
```

The test being compared in each set of loops is the opposite, even though the output is identical. The first loop prints `Again?` while a certain condition is true, and the second prints `Again?` until a certain condition is true.

You also can write `Do Until...Loop`s that test at the top, such as this one:

```
Do Until (strAns = "N")
   strAns = InputBox("Again?")
Loop
```

If You Need to Exit Early...

The `Exit Do` statement provides a way for you to quit any of the `Do...Loop`s earlier than their normal conclusion. Generally, you use an `Exit Do` in the body of an `If` statement. Therefore, you can write a loop that's controlled by the `Do` condition, but if an extraordinary circumstance arises (such as users entering an unexpected value inside the loop), the `Exit Do` statement forces Visual Basic to terminate the loop immediately and continue with the rest of the procedure, no matter how the `Do` condition tests.

Example

On the CD

One simple but common application of the `Do While...Loop` is ensuring that users enter a proper answer to what your program asks. The section of a program in Listing 11.3 is such a loop. Until users enter a yes or no answer, the program keeps prompting for a correct answer. The `UCase()` function converts the users' answer to uppercase to help the relational test.

Listing 11.3   Yesno.bas: Using a Loop to Get a Yes or No Answer

```
Dim strAns As String
Dim msg As Integer   ' MsgBox() return
' Section of a procedure that asks a yes or no question
strAns = InputBox("Do you want to continue (yes or no)")
Do While (UCase(strAns) <> "YES" And UCase(strAns) <> "NO")

msg = MsgBox("You didn't answer yes or no", vbExclamation)
   Beep   ' Ring the bell
   strAns = InputBox("Do you want to continue (yes or no)")
Loop
```

▼ NOTE

In Listing 11.3, the program requires two `InputBox()` functions to ask for user input so that it can print the error message inside the loop. ▲

Next Step

On the CD

The procedure in Listing 11.4 asks users for a number. A `Do...Loop Until` (which tests the relation at the bottom of the loop) beeps that number of times. Remember that Visual Basic performs an automatic numeric comparison when testing a number against a string that holds a number.

Listing 11.4 Beeploop.bas: The *Do...Loop Until* Controls the Beeping

```
' Beep at the user however many times the user wants
Dim strTimes As String
Dim intCount As Integer
Dim msg As Integer   ' MsgBox() return
strTimes = InputBox("How many times do you want to hear a beep")
intCount = 0   ' Initialize a count variable
Do
   Beep
   intCount = intCount + 1
Loop Until (intCount = strTimes)  ' VB performs numeric compare
msg = MsgBox("That's all the beeps for now!")
```

Topic 2: *For...Next* Loops

In addition to the `Do...Loop` statements you learned in the preceding topic, Visual Basic also offers `For...Next` loops, which are perfect for repeating sections of your programs a fixed number of times. Whereas `Do...Loop`s provide loops that iterate while or until a certain condition is true, `For...Next` loops iterate for a fixed number of times.

Overview This topic section introduces the following:

- Using the `For...Next` statement
- Changing the loop's control values
- Counting up and down with `For...Next` loops
- Nesting `For...Next` loops
- Using the `Exit For` statement

> **TIP** In reality, you can write virtually any loop by using any of the four `Do...Loop`s or the `For...Next` loop. The kind of loop you choose depends as much on style and personal preference as anything. Nevertheless, you may find that the `For...Next` loops generally are easier to code when you need a loop that loops a certain number of times, rather than one that loops based on a condition.

Introducing *For* and *Next*

The `For` and `Next` statements always appear in pairs. If your program has one or more `For` statements, it also should have a `Next` statement following it somewhere. The `For` and `Next` statements enclose one or more Visual Basic statements that form the loop; the statements between `For` and `Next` repeat continuously a certain number of times. You, as the programmer, control the number of times the loop repeats.

The syntax of the `For...Next` loop is as follows:

```
For intCounter = intStart To intEnd [Step intIncrement]
  One or more Visual Basic statements go here
Next [intCounter][, intCounter...]
```

> **TIP** Indent the body of a `For...Next` loop so that you can spot the contents of the loop easily.

intCounter is a numeric variable that you supply to help control the body of the loop (the statements between `For` and `Next`). The *intCounter* variable is initialized to the value of *intStart* before the first iteration of the loop. The *intStart* value is typically 1 but can be any numeric value (or variable) you specify. Every time the body of the loop repeats, the *intCounter* variable changes (increments or decrements) by the value of *intIncrement*. If you don't specify a `Step` value, the `For` statement assumes an *intIncrement* of 1.

The value of *intEnd* is a number (or variable) that controls the end of the looping process. When *intCounter* is greater than *intEnd*, Visual Basic doesn't repeat the loop but continues at the statement following `Next`.

The `Next` statement is Visual Basic's way of ending the loop—the signal to Visual Basic that the body of the `For...Next` loop is finished. If the *intCounter* variable is less than the `intEnd` variable, Visual Basic increments *intCounter* by the value of *intIncrement*, and the body of the loop repeats again.

▼ NOTE

Although the *intCounter* variable after `Next` is optional, most programmers specify one. The *intCounter* variable after `Next` is the same one used at the top of the loop in the `For` statement. ▲

On the CD

The procedure in Listing 11.5 uses a message box to show you how the For...Next loop really works. This procedure uses the intCtr variable to control the loop.

Listing 11.5   Fornext1.bas: Counting Up with *For...Next*

```
Private Sub forNext ()
   Dim intCtr As Integer      ' A local variable
   Dim msg As Integer         ' MsgBox() return
   For intCtr = 1 To 10       ' intCtr starts off with 1 and ends with 10
      msg = MsgBox(intCtr)
   Next intCtr                ' End of the loop
End Sub
```

The loop counts from 1 to 10, printing the numbers each time the count increments once more.

When the loop first begins, the intCtr variable is assigned a 1, the *intStart* value of the loop. Each time through the loop, intCtr is one more than the previous loop.

On the CD

The procedure in Listing 11.6 contains a Do...Loop that works just like the For...Next loop in Listing 11.5. Although the loops in both listings do the same thing, the For...Next loop in Listing 11.5 provides easier syntax and requires less work on your part when a counter variable is involved.

Listing 11.6   Whilefor.bas.ext: Counting Up with *Do...Loop Until*

```
Private Sub whileFor ()
' This procedure simulates the previous one
   Dim intCtr As Integer      ' A local variable
   Dim msg As Integer
   intCtr = 1     ' You must initialize the variable
   Do
      msg = MsgBox(intCtr)
      intCtr = intCtr + 1     ' You must add 1 to Ctr
   Loop Until intCtr > 10 ' You must provide for the loop's exit
End Sub
```

> **CAUTION** Don't confuse the loops with the `If` statement. The `Do...Loop` and `For...Next` statements are loops, and the `If` statement isn't a loop. The body of an `If` statement executes at most one time, whereas the body of a loop can execute many times.

▼ NOTE

A `For...Next` loop will never execute, even once, if the loop's ending value is less than the start value. ▲

Visual Basic assumes an *intStep* of 1 if you don't specify an *intStep* value. You can make the `For` loop increment the counter variable by any value. The procedure in Listing 11.7 displays the even numbers below 10, and then displays the odd numbers below 10. To display, specify a *Step* value of 2, to ensure that 2 is added to the counter variable each time the loop executes, instead of the default of 1 as in the previous example. (Also, the first section's start value is 2, not 1. If it were 1, the number 1 would print first, as it does in the odd-number section.)

On the CD

Listing 11.7 Oddeven.bas: Using *For...Next* to Display Even and Odd Numbers

```
Private Sub oddEven ()
' Prints the first few odd and even numbers
  Dim intNum As Integer
  Dim msg As Integer   ' MsgBox() return
  MsgBox("Even numbers below 10 are about to appear")
  For intNum = 2 To 9 Step 2   ' Start at 2, the first even number
    msg = MsgBox(intNum)
  Next intNum         ' End of first loop

  MsgBox("Odd numbers below 10 are about to appear")
  For intNum = 1 To 10 Step 2
    msg = MsgBox(intNum)
  Next intNum
End Sub
```

This program has two loops. The body of each one consists of the single `MsgBox()`. The first `MsgBox()` isn't part of either loop. If it were, the loop's title would print before each number printed.

The loop's *intStep* value determines just how much `intNum` increments each time through the loops. The first `For` statement is saying, "For each iteration through the loop, with `intNum` starting at 2, step through the loop by adding 2 to `intNum` each time." The second `For` statement is saying, "For each iteration through the loop, with `intNum` starting at 1, step through the loop by adding 2 to `intNum` each time."

> **TIP** So much of this night-school part uses message boxes and input boxes for I/O because the message and input boxes make great vehicles for getting and displaying data. Nevertheless, message and input boxes weren't really designed for output, but for interaction with users. You'll begin to see that such I/O gets tedious, especially when dealing with simple, repetitive loop output, as you've been doing last hour and this hour. Within a few more hours after you master a little more of the Visual Basic language, you'll learn how to generate and display scrolling lists of data on a Visual Basic form and how to print information directly on a form without using controls from the Toolbox.

The Optional *NextVariable*

The variable name after the `Next` keyword is optional; you don't have to specify it. Visual Basic realizes that every single `For` statement in your program requires a `Next` statement. Therefore, whenever Visual Basic encounters a `Next` without a variable, it already knows that `Next` is the conclusion to the loop started with the last `For` statement.

> **TIP** Although the `Next` variable is optional, good programmers recommend that you always specify one. Visual Basic doesn't require the variable name, but it makes your program clearer to those (or yourself) who have to make changes to it later.

To show that Visual Basic doesn't require a variable after `Next`, look at the following counting loop, which counts down from 10 to 1 and then prints a message. Visual Basic knows to match each `Next` with its preceding `For` counter variable, even though the variable name doesn't appear after `Next`.

```
For intCtr = 10 To 1 Step -1
 MsgBox(intCtr)
Next            ' No variable name specified
```

If the last line of this code read

```
Next intCtr
```

the result would have been equivalent.

The preceding example helps show you the programming time and effort the `For...Next` loop saves. Here's a simple loop that shows the time savings as well:

```
For i = 1 To 10
 MsgBox(i*2)
Next
```

This `For...Next` loop serves to shortcut the following 10 statements:

```
MsgBox(1*2)
MsgBox(2*2)
MsgBox(3*2)
MsgBox(4*2)
MsgBox(5*2)
MsgBox(6*2)
MsgBox(7*2)
MsgBox(8*2)
MsgBox(9*2)
MsgBox(10*2)
```

As you can see, you can use the loop's control variables inside expressions.

Nesting Loops

Any Visual Basic statement can go inside the body of a `For...Next` loop—even another `For...Next` loop. When you put a loop within a loop, you're creating *nested loops*. The clock in a sporting event works like a nested loop. You might think this example is stretching an analogy a little far, but it truly works. A clock in a football game counts down from 15 minutes to 0. It counts down four times. The first countdown is a loop going from 15 to 0 (for each minute), and that loop is nested within another loop counting from 1 to 4 (for each of the four quarters).

Anytime your program needs to repeat a loop more than once, use a nested loop. Figure 11.3 shows an outline of nested loops. You can think of the inside loop as looping "faster" than the outside loop. The `For` loop counting from 1 to 10 is the inside loop. It loops fastest because the variable `In` goes from 1 to 10 before the outside loop, the variable `Out`, finishes its first iteration. Because the outside loop doesn't repeat until the `Next Out` statement, the inside `For` loop has a chance to finish in its entirety. When the outside loop finally does iterate a second time, the inside loop starts all over again.

FIG. 11.3

An outside loop controls the inner loop.

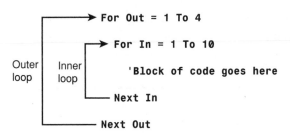

The block of code inside the innermost loop of Figure 11.3 executes a total of 40 times. The outside loop iterates four times, and the inner loop executes 10 times for each of the outer loop's counts.

Figure 11.4 shows two loops within an outside loop. Both loops execute in their entirety before the outside loop finishes its first iteration. When the outside loop starts its second iteration, the two inside loops repeat all over again.

FIG. 11.4

You can nest two loops inside each other.

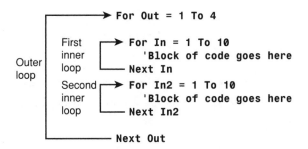

The blocks of code inside the innermost loops of Figure 11.4 execute a total of 40 times each. The outside loop iterates four times, and the inner loop executes 10 times for each of the outer loop's counts.

Notice the order of the Next variables in Figures 11.3 and 11.4. The inside loop always finishes, and therefore its Next must come before the outside loop's Next variable. If no variables are listed after each Next, the loops still are correct and work properly.

Figure 11.5 shows an incorrect order of **Next** statements. The "outside" loop finishes before the "inside" loop. This example doesn't fit the description of nested loops, and you get an error if you try to finish an outside loop before the inside loop finishes.

FIG. 11.5

Be careful how you nest loops.

```
For Out = 1 To 4
  For In = 1 To 10

    'Block of code goes here

  Next Out ◄————————— Too early
Next In ◄
                ————————— Too Late
```

To sum up nested loops, follow this rule of thumb: In nested loops, the order of the **Next** variables should be the opposite of the **For** variables. This arrangement gives the inside loop (or loops) a chance to complete before the outside loop's next iteration.

▼ NOTE

The indentation of **Next** statements has no effect on the order they execute. Indentation serves only to make programs more readable to you and other programmers. ▲

Nested loops become especially important later when you use them for array and matrix processing, as you'll learn in Hour 12, "Handling Large Amounts of Information with Arrays."

On the CD

The procedure in Listing 11.8 contains a nested loop. The inside loop counts and prints from 1 to 4; the outside loop counts from 1 to 3. Therefore, the inside loop repeats, in its entirety, four times; the procedure prints the values 1 to 4 and does so three times.

Listing 11.8 Nested1.bas: Nesting Loops to Control Multiple Counters

```
Private Sub nested1 ()
' Print the numbers from 1 to 4 three times using a nested loop
  Dim intTimes As Integer, intNum As Integer
  Dim msg As Integer  ' MsgBox() return
  For intTimes = 1 To 3        ' Outside loop
    For intNum = 1 To 4        ' Inside loop
      msg = MsgBox(intNum)
```

```
      Next intNum
   Next intTimes
End Sub
```

If you follow the procedure's output, you'll see 12 message boxes that display the following values:

```
1
2
3
4
1
2
3
4
1
2
3
4
```

The *Exit For* Statement

The `For...Next` loop was designed to execute a loop a specified number of times. In rare instances, however, the `For...Next` loop should quit before the `For`'s counter variable has reached its end value. You can use the `Exit For` statement to quit a `For` loop early.

The syntax of `Exit For` is simple:

```
Exit For
```

Although `Exit For` can appear by itself, it generally doesn't. `Exit For` almost always follows the true condition inside the body of an `If` test. If the `Exit For` appears outside an `If` statement, the loop always quits early, defeating the purpose of the `For...Next` statements.

▼ **NOTE**

If you nest one loop inside another, the `Exit For` terminates the "most active" loop—that is, the innermost loop that the `Exit For` resides in. ▲

TIP The conditional `Exit For` (an `If` followed by an `Exit For`) is good for missing data. When you start processing data files or large amounts of user data entry, you may expect 100 input numbers but get only 95; you can use `Exit For` to terminate the `For...Next` loop before it cycles through its 96th iteration.

Example The count variable can count down instead of up if you specify an *intStep* value with a negative amount. With a negative *intStep* value, the initial value assigned in the For statement must be greater than the ending value so that the loop can count down.

On the CD

The procedure in Listing 11.9 counts down from 10 to 1 and then prints Blast Off! at the end of the loop. To accomplish the countdown, you must use a large beginning value (10) and a negative *intStep* value (–1). The For statement requests that intCnt loop from 10 to 1. Each time through the loop a –1 is added to intCnt, causing the backward counting.

Listing 11.9   Countdn.bas: Producing a Countdown to Blast Off with a Negative *Step* Value

```
Private Sub countDown ()
' A procedure that counts down
  Dim msg As Integer   ' MsgBox() return
  For intCnt = 10 To 1 Step -1
    msg = MsgBox(intCnt)
  Next intCnt
  msg = MsgBox("Blast Off!")  ' The loop is done
End Sub
```

If you run this program, you'll see the numbers 10, 9, 8, and so on appear in the message boxes, one at a time. The final message box will display the words Blast Off!

Next Step Nested loops are so important to computing that you need to practice a bit before continuing. If the inside loop's control variable is based on the outside loop's variable, you see an effect such as that shown in Listing 11.10.

On the CD

Listing 11.10   Nest2.bas: Nested Loops Can Help You Analyze Variables

```
Private Sub nested2 ()
' An inside loop controlled by the outer loop's variable
' just a practice drill to follow the variables' values
  Dim intOuter As Integer, intIn As Integer
  For intOuter = 5 To 1 Step -1
    For intIn = 1 To Outer
```

```
    Next intIn
  Next intOuter
End Sub
```

No output appears in this procedure because no code in the procedure fills up a control or uses a message or input box. Instead, the code gives you some practice "playing the computer." Table 11.1 traces the two variables `intOuter` and `intIn` through this program's execution. Sometimes you have to play computer when you're learning a new concept such as nested loops. By stepping through the program a line at a time, as though you were the computer writing down each variable's contents, you produce this table.

Table 11.1 Tracing the Program's Output

intOuter	*intIn*
5	1
5	2
5	3
5	4
5	5
4	1
4	2
4	3
4	4
3	1
3	2
3	3
2	1
2	2
1	1

Topic 3: Using Loops with Forms

The looping statements you've seen last hour and this have been simple statements to teach the mechanics of the Visual Basic language. Now is a good time to begin merging your knowledge: forms and loops. Although this topic section only skims the surface of using loops with forms, it teaches some form fundamentals that you build on throughout the rest of this course.

Overview A form is often known as an object. Visual Basic supports several kinds of objects, such as controls, forms, and objects that reside outside your application, such as an OLE object. (OLE stands for *Object Linking and Embedding*; you learn more about OLE in Hour 22's lesson.)

All your form objects comprise the `Forms` collection, which changes as you create and remove forms within your project. The `Forms` collection contains the name of every form. Therefore, `frmAboutBox` might be the name of one of your forms within the `Forms` collection. (A predefined object named Form—without the s—defines the currently open form.)

Accessing the *Forms* Collection

Before accessing the `Forms` collection, you should realize that Visual Basic lets you refer to all the forms within the `Forms` collection without specifying the names of the individual open forms. If you have open three forms named `frmAcPay`, `frmAcRec`, and `frmAcReview`, for example, the predefined object `Forms` contains these three forms. Each form is numbered, starting at zero, and you can refer to the forms by number instead of by name. This number, called a *subscript*, follows after the `Forms` predefined object enclosed by parentheses. Table 11.2 shows you how you can refer to the three forms by using the subscript.

Table 11.2 Referring to Three Forms by Their Subscripts

Form Name	*Forms* Subscript Notation
`frmAcPay`	`Forms(0)`
`frmAcRec`	`Forms(1)`
`frmAcReview`	`Forms(2)`

▶▶ **FAST TRACK**

Visual Basic lets you specify a specific form within a collection by using yet another notation if you know the form name. `Forms![frmAcPay]` refers to the form named `frmAcPay` inside the current collection. (Unlike statement syntaxes, these brackets are required.) You can also use parentheses to refer to a collection's form by name as follows: `Forms!("frmAcPay")`.

Subscripts for Controls

You may also refer to individual controls, such as fields, inside your forms by a subscript number instead of by name. Therefore, your programs can step through all the fields in a form without having to access the fields' individual names. As you learn more about data collections (especially after next hour's lesson, which covers arrays), you'll see additional ways to refer to groups of objects.

Suppose that a form named `frmStore` contains five controls: three label fields named `lblStoreNum`, `lblStoreName`, and `lblStoreLoc`, and two list box controls named `lstStoreEmps` and `lstStoreMgrs`. Your Visual Basic procedures can refer to each control by a subscript number, starting at 0, as shown in Table 11.3. Notice that you separate the control name from the `Forms` collection with an exclamation point to get an individual control within that collection.

Table 11.3   Referring to Five Form Controls by Their Subscripts

Control Name	*Forms* Subscript Notation
`lblStoreNum`	`Forms!frmStore(0)`
`lblStoreName`	`Forms!frmStore(1)`
`lstStoreLoc`	`Forms!frmStore(2)`
`lstStoreEmps`	`Forms!frmStore(3)`
`lstStoreMgrs`	`Forms!frmStore(4)`

▼ **NOTE**

Don't confuse the subscripts used with specific form names with those in a `Forms` collection. If `Forms` precedes the subscript, the subscript refers to a particular form or subform. If the form name appears before the subscript, as seen in Table 11.3, the subscript refers to a control on that form. ▲

The *Count* Property

Controls have properties, as you know, and so do collections. The `Count` property is available to you when you need to work with the `Forms` collection. `Count` simplifies your programming so that you don't have to know how many individual forms reside in the collection. By using `Count`, you can write generalized procedures that work on all the forms now open.

The `Count` property always contains an integer.

▼ **NOTE**

`Count` also contains the number of controls on a form if you apply the property to a specific form name, such as `frmAcPay.Count`, which contains the number of controls on the form named `frmAcPay`. `Count` includes hidden and visible controls. ▲

Example

The following code declares an integer variable, `intC`, and then stores the number of open forms in `intC`:

```
Dim intC As Integer
intC = Forms.Count      ' Save the number of open forms
```

If you want to know the number of controls on a specific form, you can use the `Count` property as well. The following code declares an integer variable, `intCC`, and stores the number of controls on the form named `MyForm` in `intCC`:

```
Dim intCC As Integer
intCC = MyForm.Count    ' Save the number of controls on the form
```

Next Step

A `For...Next` loop is the perfect tool for stepping through all the open forms in the current project. Always remember to start the controlling loop with a beginning value of 0, as done here, because 0 is the subscript of the first form.

The following code steps through all the open forms and hides the forms:

```
For intI = 0 To Forms.Count - 1
  Forms(intI).Visible = False    ' Hide each form
Next intI
```

You may want to hide all forms when performing a system task that requires no user I/O. After your work is done, you can then repeat the loop and set each form's `Visible` property to `True`.

Visual Basic supports a special `For...Next` loop called `For Each...Next`, which steps through a collection without requiring that you control a loop variable. Here is identical code that hides all the open forms:

```
Dim varFrmObj As Variant
For Each varFrmObj In Forms
   varFrmObj.Visible = False    ' Hide each form
Next
```

The only loop variable you need to declare for the `For Each...Next` loop is a `Variant` variable that holds each form name as the loop iterates through the forms in the collection. In the same manner, the following `For Each` loop's first statement sets up a loop that steps through every control on the form named `frmMyForm`:

```
For Each varControl In frmMyForm
```

Summary

After you learn to write looping control statements, you can repeat sections of code over and over. Without loops, you have to write the same code back to back; even if you do that, some loops *iterate* (a fancy term for repeat) several thousand times, depending on the amount of data being manipulated.

Throughout this section of the book, you learn about several loop constructions. The first presented in this hour's first topic is `Do...Loop`s, of which there are four kinds. They center around the `While` and the `Until` keywords. The location of the conditional test determines how the loops behave; if the test is at the top of the loop, the loop may never execute because the condition might be false to begin with. If the test is at the bottom of the loop, the loop always executes at least one time.

The `For...Next` loop allow you to control a loop when you know how many iterations are supposed to be performed. Although you can write `Do...Loop`s to behave exactly like `For...Next` loops (and the reverse is true as well), `For...Next` loops reduce the amount of coding you have to do when you iterate through loops by using control variables that count up or down. By changing the value of the `Step` option, you can force the `For...Next` loop to count up or down by any increment or decrement you want. If you don't specify a `Step` value, the `For...Next` loop assumes a `Step` value of 1.

You can nest `For...Next` loops so that an outer loop can control one or more inner loops. Any statement can appear in the body of a `For...Next` loop, including `Do...Loops`. Toward the end of this lesson, you learned about combining `For...Next` loops with subscripted form names and controls. By using the `For...Next`, you can work with forms and controls without having to refer to each of them by name.

In Hour 12 you learn how to declare a large amount of variable storage that you'll often use in programs that process numerous data values.

Hour 11 Quiz

You can find the answers for the following questions on the accompanying CD-ROM and on the Virtual Classroom Web site.

On the CD

1. What is a loop?

2. Describe the following statement's action:

   ```
   intCounter = intCounter + 1
   ```

3. What's the keystroke to terminate an endless loop if you accidentally execute one?

4. How many times does the following `MsgBox()` execute?

   ```
   intN = 0
   Do While (intN > 0)
      intN = intN + 3
      msg = MsgBox("**")
   Loop
   ```

5. What, if anything, is wrong with the following loop?

   ```
   intN = 10
   Do
      msg = MsgBox("**")
   Loop Until (intN > 100)
   ```

6. How many times does the following code beep?

```
For intC = 1 To 5
   Beep
Next intC
```

7. What's the value of the first subscript when working with predefined object collections?

8. Why should the Exit For statement follow an If rather than appear by itself?

9. **True or false:** A For...Next loop may never execute, depending on the start and ending values.

10. What, if anything, is wrong with the following nested loop?

```
For intOut = 1 To 3
  For intIn = 1 To 10
    MsgBox(intIn)
  Next intOut
Next intIn
```

Hour 11 Homework Exercises

1. Write a **Do** loop that beeps and displays a message box with "Happy Birthday" 10 times.

2. Write a procedure that prints your name three times, beeps four times, and then prints That's all folks! five times. Use three For...Next loops.

3. Write a procedure that computes and prints the total number of controls and all open forms within the current application.

Handling Large Amounts of Information with Arrays

HOUR *12*

During this hour you will learn

▶ *How arrays and non-array data values vary*

▶ *How to declare arrays*

▶ *What array subscripts do*

▶ *When array notation works with collections*

▶ *Which data makes a good matrix candidate*

THIS HOUR, YOU'LL LEARN how to store many occurrences of data in your Visual Basic programs. Most of the code you've seen so far has worked with very little data. Up to this point, you were learning about variables and controlling statements; lots of data would have hindered your learning how to program, especially if you were unfamiliar with programming languages before learning Visual Basic.

This hour's topics teach about arrays. An array isn't much more than a list of variables. You see in this topic how the naming conventions for array variables vary a little (but not much) from the naming conventions for regular non-array variables. With arrays, you can store many occurrences of data. With non-array variables, each piece of data has a different name, and it's difficult to track many occurrences of data.

Before you learn how to read and process table data with Visual Basic, you must have a way to store the many data items that you read from a table into your programs. Arrays provide the containers for several data values, such as those you get when reading from a table into your program.

▼ **NOTE**

Conquering arrays is your next step toward understanding advanced uses of Visual Basic. This hour's examples are some of the longest programs you've seen in the book. Arrays aren't difficult, but their power lends them to advanced programming. ▲

Topic 1: Arrays and Non-Array Variables

Although arrays vary from variables, they vary only in the way you declare and access them. Arrays contain multiple occurrences of variable data, and your program can treat an array's variable contents as though those array variables were regular non-array variables. The only requirement is that you properly declare and reference the array variables.

▶▶ **FAST TRACK**

Have you programmed with arrays in other programming languages? If you've worked with COBOL tables or BASIC matrixes, you've worked with arrays. You now only need to know how to declare and access arrays. After you read this topic section, skim the remaining topics for follow-up and then move onto Hour 13's lesson, "Understanding How Procedures Work" (p. 301), where you'll learn how Visual Basic subroutines and functions really work.

Overview An *array* is a list of more than one variable with the same name. Not every list of variables is an array. The following list of four variables doesn't count as an array:

```
curSales      sngbonus98      strFirstName      intCtr
```

This list doesn't define an array because each variable has a different name. You may wonder how more than one variable can have the same name; this convention seems to violate the rules of variables. If two variables have the same name, how does Visual Basic know which one you want when you use its name?

In this topic section, you'll learn that you distinguish array variables from each other by a subscript. A *subscript* is a number, inside parentheses, that differentiates one element of an array from another. (You first saw the concept of subscripts in Hour 11's final topic.) Elements are the individual variables in an array.

Good Array Candidates

Suppose that you want to process 35 people's names and monthly dues from your local neighborhood association. The dues are different for each person. All this data fits nicely in a table of data, but suppose that you also want to hold, at one time, all the data in variables so that you can perform calculations and print various statistics about the members by using Visual Basic.

Without arrays, you find yourself having to store each of the 35 names in 35 different variables, and each of their dues in 35 different variables. But doing so makes for a complex and lengthy program. To enter the data, you have to store the data in variables with names such as the following:

```
strFamilyName1  curFamilyDues1  strFamilyName2  curFamilyDues2
strFamilyName3  curFamilyDues3  strFamilyName4  curFamilyDues4
```

The list continues until you use different variable names for all the 35 names and dues.

Every time you use Visual Basic to display a list of members, calculate average dues, or use this data in any other way, you have to scan sets of 35 different variable names. The steps required in this procedure are why arrays were developed; it's too cumbersome for similar data to have different variable names. The time and typing required to process more than a handful of variables with different names is too much. Not only that, imagine if the neighborhood grew to 500 households!

With arrays, you can store similar data, such as the neighborhood data, in a single variable. In effect, each data value has the same name. You distinguish the values (elements in the array) from each other by a numeric subscript. For instance, instead of a different variable name (`strFamilyName1`, `curFamilyDues1`, `strFamilyName2`, `curFamilyDues2`, and so on), give the similar data the same variable name (`strFamilyName` and `curFamilyDues`) and differentiate them with subscripts as shown in Table 12.1.

Table 12.1   Using Arrays to Store Similar Data

Old Names	Array Names
strFamilyName1, curFamilyDues1	strFamilyName(1), curFamilyDues(1)
strFamilyName2, curFamilyDues2	strFamilyName(2), curFamilyDues(2)
strFamilyName3, curFamilyDues3	strFamilyName(3), curFamilyDues(3)
: :	:
: :	:
strFamilyName35, curFamilyDues35	strFamilyName(35), curFamilyDues(35)

> **TIP**   Many Visual Basic programmers like to use an additional variable name prefix for array names, such as strar for a string array or curar for a currency array.

"Where's the improvement?" you might ask. The column of array names has a major advantage over the old variable names. The number inside the parentheses is the subscript number of the array. Subscript numbers are never part of an array name; they're always enclosed in parentheses and serve to distinguish one array element from another.

How many arrays are listed in Table 12.1? If you said two, you're correct. There are 35 elements in each of the two arrays. How many non-array variables are in Table 12.1? Seventy—35 family name variables and 35 dues variables. The difference is very important when you consider how you process them.

Because the subscript number (the only thing that differentiates one array element from another) isn't part of the array name, you can use a `For...Next` loop or any other counter variable to input, process, and output any and all elements of arrays. To input every single family name and their dues into the two arrays by using a loop, for instance, you don't need 70 statements as you do when each variable has a different name. You need only four statements, as shown here:

```
For intSub = 1 To 35
  strFamilyName(intSub) =
  ➡InputBox("What is the family member's name?")
```

```
      curFamilyDues(intSub) = InputBox("What are their dues?")
   Next intSub
```

This code offers a major advantage over using non-array variables. Notice that the `For...Next` loop keeps incrementing `intSub` throughout the data input of all 70 values. The first time through the loop, users enter a value into `strFamilyName(1)` and in `curFamilyDues(1)` with the `InputBox()` function (`intSub` is then equal to 1). The loop then increments `intSub` to 2, and the input process starts again for the next two variables.

These four lines of code are much easier to write and maintain than a set of 70 individual `InputBox()` function calls, and the `For...Next` loop does exactly the same thing. You can't use the `For...Next` loop to process a bunch of differently named variables, even if they have numbers in their names, as they do with `strFamilyName1`, `curFamilyDues1`, and so on.

Any time you're working with a list of data with similar meanings, an array works best. Arrays make your input, process, and output routines much easier to write. Most importantly to Visual Basic, you can read table data into large arrays if needed and work with the data in memory.

▼ NOTE

On the CD

Visual Basic supports two kinds of arrays: static and dynamic. This book discusses static arrays, which are fixed in size and can't be changed at runtime. (You can change dynamic array sizes during the program's execution.) If you want to learn more about dynamic arrays, check out Que's advanced Visual Basic book, *Special Edition Using Visual Basic 5*. **▲**

Not all of your Visual Basic data is stored in arrays. You still use variables (like those you've seen throughout this course) for loop control and user input. When you have multiple occurrences of data that you must track within Visual Basic—such as fields from a table that you read into memory—an array is the perfect holder for that data.

Using *Public* and *Dim* to Set Up Arrays

As you do with non-array variables, you tell Visual Basic that you're going to use an array; you have to declare the array, just as you have to declare other variables. You use the `Public` or `Dim` statements to declare arrays; your choice of statements depends on the kind of array you need and where you want to declare the array.

Declare with a `Public` statement to create a public array that can be used throughout the entire application (across all modules). The `Public` statement must appear in the standard module's `Declarations` section.

If you use a `Dim` statement in a module's `Declarations` section, you create a module-level array that can be used throughout the module.

▼ **NOTE**

You can declare local static variables and arrays with the `Static` keyword. A static array retains its values and when execution returns to the procedure, Visual Basic remembers and uses their values. ▲

For declaring arrays, the format of the `Public` and `Dim` statements varies only in the keyword of the command and its placement in the module. Here are the syntaxes of the two statements:

```
Public arName(intSub) [As dataType][, arName(intSub)
➥[As dataType]]...
```

```
Dim arName(intSub) [As dataType][, arName(intSub)
➥[As dataType]]...
```

You name arrays (*arName*) just as you do regular variables. You can create an array of any data type, so *dataType* can be `Integer`, `Single`, or any of the data types with which you're familiar. The *intSub* portion of the commands describes the number of elements and how you refer to those array elements. In the preceding statement formats, `intSub` can take on the following format:

```
[intLow To] intHigh
```

▼ **NOTE**

You can have more than one set of subscripts, as you learn in this lesson's final topic section. ▲

Unlike other programming languages, Visual Basic's `Variant` data type lets you specify arrays that hold several different kinds of data. All elements of non-`Variant` arrays must have the same data type.

Using *Option Base*

Declaring an array is easiest when you specify only the upper subscript bound. All array subscripts begin at 0 unless the following statement appears in the module's `Declarations` section:

```
Option Base 1
```

The `Option Base` command is rather outdated. If you want to change the lower bounds of an array, you should consider using the more advanced *intLow* To option.

The following `Dim` statement declares seven elements of an `Integer` array named `intAges`:

```
Dim intAges(6)      ' Reserves 7 elements
```

The subscript, 6, is the upper subscript, and the lower subscript is 0 (without an `Option Base 1` appearing elsewhere, which would force the beginning subscript to 1). Figure 12.1 illustrates just what's declared with this statement. An array of seven `Integer` values, all with the same name (`intAges`), is reserved for use. Each variable is distinguished by its subscript number; `intAges(2)` is a completely different variable from `intAges(6)`.

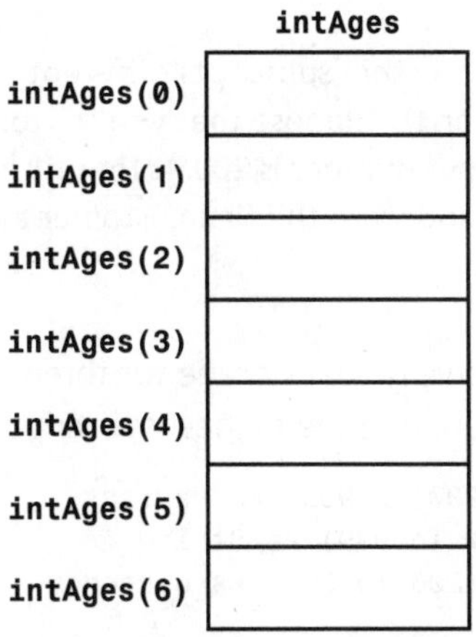

FIG. 12.1
The intAges *array contains seven elements.*

▼ NOTE

Often, programmers ignore the zero subscript. Unless you use `Option Base` 1 or a *intLow* To *intHigh* subscript, Visual Basic reserves an element for the zero subscript, but you don't have to use that zero subscript. ▲

Example Based on the previous discussion, you can declare the `strFamilyName` and `curFamilyDues` arrays as follows:

```
Dim strFamilyName(35) As String  ' Reserves 36 names
Dim curFamilyDues(35) As Currency  ' Reserves 36 dues
```

Actually, the subscript 35 is the upper bound, and the subscript 0 is automatically the lower bound. Therefore, these statements each dimension 36 elements in each array. The previous discussion mentioned 35 members in the neighborhood association, so the 0 subscript isn't used.

Because `Dim` was used here, the arrays have procedure-level scope. Only the code within the procedure that contains these two statements can use the two arrays unless the procedure passes the arrays to other procedures, as explained in Hour 13's lesson.

Sometimes, specifying the lower and upper bounds of the array subscripts makes sense. As you've seen, if you specify `Option Base 1`, the lower array subscript is 1. If you specify `Option Base 0` or nothing at all, the lower array subscript bounds are zero. By using the expanded array declaration statements with the `To` keyword, however, you can specify the upper and lower bounds of your array subscripts.

TIP You may find that your data fits within subscripts different from the defaults (such as those starting at 0 or 1). Suppose that you're storing customer information, and your lowest customer number is 200. It therefore makes sense to begin the array subscripts at 200 and store the first customer at his or her array subscript number 200.

The following statements reserve global storage for three customer-related arrays. The first subscript is 200, and the highest subscript is 999.

```
Public varCustNumber(200 To 999) As Variant
Public strCustName(200 To 999) As String
Public curCustBalance(200 To 999) As Currency
```

CAUTION The high subscript no longer specifies the number of array elements. These three arrays have a total of 800 elements each (subscripted from 200 to 999).

Next Step These `Dim` statements each do the same thing:

```
Dim Amounts(0 To 50)   ' Subscripts 0 to 50

Dim Amounts(50)        ' Subscripts 0 to 50
```

And so do these pairs:

```
Option Base 1
Dim Balances(75)       ' Subscripts 1 to 75

Option Base 0
Dim Balances(1 To 75)  ' Subscripts 1 to 75
```

You can see how the `Option Base` statement affects the arrays you declare. Now that you can declare arrays, you'll now learn how to use them.

Topic 2: Using Arrays

You may see arrays used in calculations, just as non-array variables are, like
the following:

```
curFamilyDues(5) = curFamilyDues(4) * 1.5
```

To use data in an array, you have to use only the subscript of the array element you want to work with.

> **TIP** In one respect, accessing an array value works like a set of boxes in a post
> office. The address of all the boxes is the same (they're all located in the same
> building), but mail is inserted into the appropriate box number.

Overview The rest of this topic uses some code examples to clarify how arrays work.
The earlier examples use arrays to gather and work with user data. After
you understand better how to work with arrays, the later examples in this
topic use arrays with forms.

The Subscript in Use

The best way to learn how to use subscripts is to see examples. Although
the following example shows array elements being filled up by an
`InputBox()` function, most programs get most of their input data from

files and forms. Because arrays can store very large amounts of data, you don't want to have to type that data into the variables every time you run a program. Assignment statements don't suffice either, because they aren't good statements to use for extremely large amounts of data and interactive programs.

In Listing 12.1 is the full program that declares two arrays for the neighborhood association's 35 family names and their dues. The program prompts for the input and then prints the data.

On the CD

▼ **NOTE**

If you run this program, you may want to change the number from 35 down to 5 or so to keep from having to type so much input. ▲

Listing 12.1 Assoc.bas: Arrays Simplify Data Storage

```
Private Sub association ()
' Procedure to gather and print 35 names and dues
  Dim strFamilyName(35) As String ' Reserve the array elements
  Dim curFamilyDues(35) As Currency
  Dim intSub As Integer
  Dim msg As Integer  ' MsgBox() return

  ' Loop getting all of the data
  For intSub = 1 To 35
    strFamilyName(intSub) = InputBox("What is the next family's name")
    curFamilyDues(intSub) = InputBox("What are their dues?")
  Next intSub

  ' You now can display all the data
  ' This example uses a series of message boxes simply
  ' because that's what you know at this point
  intSub = 1 ' Initialize the first subscript
  Do
    msg = MsgBox("Family" & intSub & "is " & strFamilyName(intSub))
    msg = MsgBox("Their dues are " & curFamilyDues(intSub))
    intSub = intSub + 1
  Loop Until (intSub > 35)
End Sub
```

Notice that the program can input and print all the names and dues with simple routines. The input routine uses a `For...Next` loop, and the printing routine uses a `Do...Loop`. The method you use to control the loop isn't critical. The important thing to see at this point is that you can input and print a great deal of data without having to write lots of code. The array subscripts and loop controlling statements make the printing possible.

This example illustrates parallel arrays—two arrays working side by side. Each element in each array corresponds to one in the other array. Parallel arrays work in memory like joined fields work together in tables.

The neighborhood association program is fine for an illustration, but it works only if there are exactly 35 families. What if the association grows? If it were to grow, you would have to change the program. Therefore, most programs don't have a set limit size for data, as the preceding program did. Most programmers declare more than enough array elements to handle the largest array ever needed. The program then allows users to control how many of those elements are really used.

▼ **NOTE**
After you master the fixed-length static arrays discussed here, you may want to learn about dynamic arrays, whose size can change at runtime. If you find that you need more array elements when the program runs, you can get more when using dynamic arrays. ▲

On the CD

The program in Listing 12.2 is similar to the one in Listing 12.1, except that it declares 500 elements for each array. This number reserves more than enough array elements for the association. Users then input only the actual number (from 1 to 500 maximum). The program is very flexible, allowing a variable number of members input and printed each time it's run. It does need an eventual limit, however, but that limit is reached only when there are 500 members.

Listing 12.2 Varynumb.bas: Reserving More Elements Than You Currently Need

```
Private Sub varyNumb ()
' Procedure to gather and print names and dues
  Dim strFamilyName(500) As String    ' Reserve enough array elements
  Dim curFamilyDues(500) As Currency
  Dim intSub As Integer, intNumFam As Integer
  Dim msg As Integer  ' MsgBox() return
  intNumFam = 1

  ' The following loop asks for family names and dues until the
```

continues

Listing 12.2 Continued

```
' user presses Enter without typing a name. Whenever a zero-length
' string is entered (just an Enter keypress), the Do-Loop exits
' early with sub holding the number input to that point.
Do
   strFamilyName(intNumFam) = InputBox("What is next family's name?")
   If (strFamilyName(intNumFam) = "") Then Exit Do      ' Exits early
   curFamilyDues(intNumFam) = InputBox("What are their dues?")
   intNumFam = intNumFam + 1 ' Add one to the subscript variable
Loop Until (intNumFam > 500)

' When the last loop finishes, intSub holds one
' more than the actual number input

' Displays all the input data
For intSub = 1 To intNumFam - 1
   msg = MsgBox("Family" & intSub & "is " & strFamilyName(intSub))
   msg = MsgBox("Their dues are " & curFamilyDues(intSub))
Next intSub
End Sub
```

> **CAUTION** Declare enough array space for your estimated needs, but don't declare more array space than you can possibly use. For every extra array element that you reserve but don't use, memory is wasted.

The empty Enter keypress is a good way to trigger the early exit of the loop. Just because 500 elements are reserved for each array doesn't mean that you have to use all 500 of them.

> **TIP** Alternatively, if users are familiar with the data, you can ask them how many values they want to enter. You then loop until that value is reached. Because users are rarely familiar enough with their data to know how many values they will input, asking for the number of values to enter isn't as common as this example, which allows users to trigger the end of input when finished.

Randomly Accessing Elements

You don't have to access an array in the same order as it was entered. An array works like a table because you can access any element in any order, just like reading a record from file by knowing a record number. You use the subscript to "pick out" items from an array of values.

The program in Listing 12.3 requests salary data for the last 12 months. It then waits until another user types the month he or she wants to see. That month's sales are then printed, without the surrounding months getting in the way. This is how you begin to build a search program to find requested data that's stored in arrays; store the data in an array, and then wait for a request from the users to see only specific pieces of that data.

On the CD

Listing 12.3 Salary.bas: Using Arrays for Data-Searching Code

```
Private Sub salary ()
' Store 12 months of salaries, and print selected ones
   Dim curSal(1 To 12) As Currency    ' Reserve elements for 12 salaries
   Dim intSub As Integer      ' Loop subscript
   Dim intNum As Integer      ' User's month number
   Dim msg As Integer         ' MsgBox() return
   Dim strAns As String

   For intSub = 1 To 12
      curSal(intSub) = InputBox("What is salary for month" & Str(intSub) & "?")
   Next intSub

   ' Request the month number
   Do
      intNum = InputBox("For what month (1-12) do you want a salary?")
      msg = MsgBox("The salary for month" & Str(intNum) & " is " & curSal(intNum))
      strAns = InputBox("Do you want to see another (Y/N)?")
   Loop While (strAns = "Y")
End Sub
```

After users enter the 12 salaries into the array, they can request any or all of them one at a time simply by supplying the month number (the number of the subscript).

The program in Listing 12.4 shows some of the math operations you can perform on arrays. The program asks for a list of temperatures and keeps asking for them until users enter –99 to signal that there are no more temperatures. The program then computes the average temperature by adding them and dividing by the total number.

Listing 12.4 Tempavg.bas: Letting Users Tell Your Program When No More Data Remains

```
Private Sub tempAvg ()
' Prompt the user for a list of temperatures and average them
  Dim sngTemp(1 To 100) As Single ' Up to 100 temps
  Dim sngTotalTemp As Single     ' Holds totals as user enters temps
  Dim sngAvgTemp As Single
  Dim intSub As Integer          ' Subscript
  Dim msg As Integer             ' MsgBox() return

  ' Prompt user for each temperature
  For intSub = 1 To 100    ' Maximum limit
    sngTemp(intSub) = InputBox("What is next temperature (-99 ends)?")
    ' If user wants to stop, decrease count by 1 and exit loop
    If (sngTemp(intSub) = -99) Then
      intSub = intSub - 1   ' Adjust for early exit
      Exit For
    End If
    sngTotalTemp = sngTotalTemp + sngTemp(intSub)    ' Add to total
  Next intSub
  ' Compute average
  sngAvgTemp = sngTotalTemp / intSub
  msg = MsgBox("The average temperature was " & sngAvgTemp)
End Sub
```

▼ **NOTE**

Visual Basic's `MsgBox()` function can convert numeric values to strings when you concatenate numeric values to a string message. ▲

Example In Hour 10's lesson, you learned how to use the **Select Case** statement with the **VarType()** function. **VarType()** returns a number that represents the data type of its argument. Anytime your programs use lists of data, you can almost always use arrays to improve on the code.

On the CD

Listing 12.5 shows the routine as you saw it in Hour 10's lesson. Listing 12.6 shows the same routine, using arrays.

Listing 12.5 Seldata2.bas: Determining Data Types with *Select Case*

```
Private Sub PrntType(varA)  ' Variant if you don't specify otherwise
Dim msg As Integer    ' MsgBox() return
```

```
    Select Case VarType(varA)   ' VarType() returns an integer
      Case 0
        msg = MsgBox("The argument is Empty")
      Case 1
        msg = MsgBox("The argument is Null")
      Case 2
        msg = MsgBox("The argument is Integer")
      Case 3
        msg = MsgBox("The argument is Long")
      Case 4
        msg = MsgBox("The argument is Single")
      Case 5
        msg = MsgBox("The argument is Double")
      Case 6
        msg = MsgBox("The argument is Currency")
      Case 7
        msg = MsgBox("The argument is Date")
      Case 8
        msg = MsgBox("The argument is String")
      Case 9
        msg = MsgBox("The argument is an Object")
      Case 10
        msg = MsgBox("The argument is an Error")
      Case 11
        msg = MsgBox("The argument is Boolean")
      Case 12
        msg = MsgBox("The argument is a Variant array")
      Case 13
        msg = MsgBox("The argument is a Data Access Object")
      Case 14
        msg = MsgBox("The argument is Decimal")
      Case 17
        msg = MsgBox("The argument is Byte")
      Case Else
        msg = MsgBox("The argument is an Array")
    End Select
End Sub
```

Listing 12.6 Arraytst.bas: Using *VarType( )* to Test an Array's Data Type

```
Private Sub PrntType(varA)   ' Variant if you don't specify otherwise
' varA comes from another routine
' Prints data type names using an array
```

continues

Listing 12.6 Continued

```
Dim strTypeNames(17) As String   ' Will use 18 subscripts, 0 to 17
Dim msg As Integer
' Fill the array with data type names
strTypeNames(0) = "Empty"
strTypeNames(1) = "Null"
strTypeNames(2) = "Integer"
strTypeNames(3) = "Long"
strTypeNames(4) = "Single"
strTypeNames(5) = "Double"
strTypeNames(6) = "Currency"
strTypeNames(7) = "Date"
strTypeNames(8) = "String"
strTypeNames(9) = "Object"
strTypeNames(10) = "Error"
strTypeNames(11) = "Boolean"
strTypeNames(12) = "Variant Array"
strTypeNames(13) = "Data Access Object"
strTypeNames(14) = "Decimal"
strTypeNames(15) = "N/A"   ' No VarType value matches
strTypeNames(16) = "N/A"   ' these
strTypeNames(17) = "Byte"
If (VarType(varA) <= 17) Then  ' An array
  msg = MsgBox("The argument is " & strTypeNames(VarType(varA)))
Else
  msg = MsgBox("The argument is an array of type " &
  ➥strTypeNames(VarType(varA-8192)))
  End If
End Sub
```

Shorter code doesn't always mean better code. Your goal should always be writing easy-to-read code, not short, tricky code that works but is hard to maintain later. Nevertheless, many times shorter code does produce easier maintenance because you have fewer lines to understand when you have to make changes later.

The code in Listing 12.6 first stores all the data type names in a string array. The array's subscripts match those of the data types. Therefore, the **VarType()** function's return value can be used as the subscript to print the appropriate data type title. Although Listing 12.6 doesn't seem to be a big improvement over Listing 12.5, Listing 12.6 doesn't contain all the **Case** statements that Listing 12.5 contains. Although the code in Listing 12.6 is, therefore, more efficient, the goal of this code wasn't efficiency but just to show you the capability of an array subscript to select data from an array.

If `VarType()` returns a value that's greater than or equal to 8,192, it is testing an array. To determine the array's data type, subtract 8,192 from `VarType()`'s return value to find the data type.

Next Step In Hour 11's lesson, you learned how forms and controls can be referenced by subscripts. Hour 11 introduced the concept of arrays to you without your knowing about arrays. By using the `Forms` collection, you can refer to all the forms inside an application by its subscript number. Within an individual form, you can refer to controls on that form with a subscript as well, just as you do with array variables.

On the CD

The procedure in Listing 12.7 stores all open form names in an array called `strOpenForms` and then prints the contents of that array in the immediate window.

Listing 12.7 Storefrm.bas: Using an Array to Store Form Names

```
Private Sub storeForms ()
' Function that stores all form names in an array
  Dim intSub As Integer
  Dim strOpenForms(10) As String
  Dim msg As Integer   ' MsgBox()'s return
  ' Save all open forms in the array
  For intSub = 0 To Forms.Count - 1
    strOpenForms(intSub) = Forms(intSub).Name
  Next intSub

  ' Display the names of the open forms
  For intSub = 0 To Forms.Count - 1
    msg = MsgBox(strOpenForms(intSub))
  Next intSub
End SubScx
```

If you have four forms open when this procedure executes, the code displays four message boxes that display those form names. The most important things to study about Listing 12.7 are that the open form names are stored in an array and the array's contents are displayed, one at a time, in message boxes.

After you master arrays, the next topic section is easy. It shows how you can keep track of arrays in a format different from the format you saw here. Not all lists of data lend themselves to multidimensional arrays, but you should be prepared for them when you do need them.

Topic 3: Multidimensional Arrays

Some data fits in array lists like those you saw in the first two topic sections; other data is better suited to a table of data. The second topic section introduced *single-dimensioned arrays*, which are arrays that have only one subscript. Single-dimensioned arrays represent a list of values. This topic section explains how to use arrays of more than one dimension, called *multidimensional arrays*. Multidimensional arrays, sometimes called *tables* or *matrices*, have rows and columns.

Overview   This topic section introduces the following:

- What multidimensional arrays are
- Putting data into multidimensional arrays
- Using nested `For...Next` loops to process multidimensional arrays

If you understand single-dimensional arrays, you should have no trouble understanding arrays with more than one dimension.

What Multidimensional Arrays Are

A multidimensional array is an array with more than one subscript. A single-dimensional array is a list of values, whereas a multidimensional array simulates a table of values or even multiple tables of values. The most commonly used table is a two-dimensional table (an array with two subscripts).

Suppose that a softball team wants to keep track of its players' hits. The team played 8 games, and 10 players are on the team. Table 12.2 shows the team's hit record.

Table 12.2 A Softball Team's Hit Record

Player	Game1	Game2	Game3	Game4	Game5	Game6	Game7	Game8
Adams	2	1	0	0	2	3	3	1
Berryhill	1	0	3	2	5	1	2	2
Edwards	0	3	6	4	6	4	5	3
Grady	1	3	2	0	1	5	2	1
Howard	3	1	1	1	2	0	1	0
Powers	2	2	3	1	0	2	1	3
Smith	1	1	2	1	3	4	1	0
Townsend	0	0	0	0	0	0	1	0
Ulmer	2	2	1	1	2	1	1	2
Williams	2	3	1	0	1	2	1	1

Do you see that the softball table is a two-dimensional table? It has rows (the first dimension) and columns (the second dimension). Therefore, you call it a two-dimensional table with 10 rows and 8 columns. (Generally, the number of rows is specified first.)

Each row has a player's name, and each column has a game number associated with it, but these headings aren't part of the data. The data consists of only 80 values (10 rows times eight columns). The data in a table, like the data in an array, always is the same type of data (in this case, every value is an integer). If the table contains names, it's a string table, and so on.

The number of dimensions—in this case, two—corresponds to the dimensions in the physical world. The first dimension represents a line. The single-dimensional array is a line, or list, of values. Two dimensions represent both length and width. You write on a piece of paper in two dimensions; two dimensions represent a flat surface. Three dimensions represent width, length, and depth. You may have seen three-dimensional movies; not only do the images have width and height, but they also (appear to) have depth.

It's difficult to visualize more than three dimensions. You can, however, think of each dimension after three as another occurrence. In other words, you can store a list of one player's season hit record in an array. The team's hit record (as shown in Table 12.2) is two-dimensional. Its league, made up of several teams' hit records, represents a three-dimensional table. Each team (the depth of the table) has rows and columns of hit data. If there's more than one league, you can consider leagues another dimension.

Visual Basic lets you work with up to 60 dimensions, although real-world data rarely requires more than two or three dimensions.

Dimensioning Multidimensional Arrays

As you do with single-dimension arrays, use the `Dim` or `Public` statement to reserve storage for multidimensional arrays. Rather than put one value in the parentheses, you put a value for each dimension in the table. The basic syntaxes for reserving multidimensional arrays are as follows:

```
Public taName(intSub) [As dataTtype][, taName(intSub)
➥[As dataType]]...
Dim taName (intSub) [As dataType][, taName (intSub)
➥[As dataType]]...
```

The table's *intSub* values can take on this general syntax:

```
[intLow To] intHighRow[, [intLow To] intHighColumn][,
➥[intLow To] intHighDepth][,...]
```

As with single-dimensions, actually reserving storage for tables is easier than the formats lead you to believe. To declare the team data from Table 12.2, for example, you can use the following `Dim` statement:

```
Dim intTeams(1 To 10, 1 To 8) As Integer
```

This statement reserves a two-dimensional table in memory with 80 elements. Each element's subscript looks like the ones shown in Figure 12.2.

FIG. 12.2
The softball team table requires two sets of subscripts.

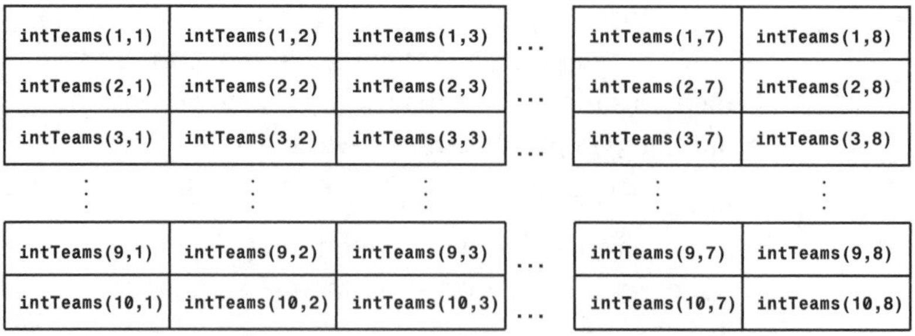

intTeams(1,1)	intTeams(1,2)	intTeams(1,3)	...	intTeams(1,7)	intTeams(1,8)
intTeams(2,1)	intTeams(2,2)	intTeams(2,3)	...	intTeams(2,7)	intTeams(2,8)
intTeams(3,1)	intTeams(3,2)	intTeams(3,3)	...	intTeams(3,7)	intTeams(3,8)
⋮	⋮	⋮		⋮	⋮
intTeams(9,1)	intTeams(9,2)	intTeams(9,3)	...	intTeams(9,7)	intTeams(9,8)
intTeams(10,1)	intTeams(10,2)	intTeams(10,3)	...	intTeams(10,7)	intTeams(10,8)

If you have an entire league of 15 teams to track, you add yet another subscript,

```
Dim intTeams(1 To 15, 1 To 10, 1 To 8) As Integer
```

where the first subscript indicates the team, the second subscript indicates the number of players in each team, and the third subscript indicates the number of games each player plays.

The following statement reserves enough memory elements for a television station's shows for one week:

```
Dim strShows(1 To 7, 1 To 48) As String
```

This statement reserves 7 days (the rows) of 30-minute shows (because there are 24 hours in a day, this table holds up to forty-eight 30-minute shows).

Every element in a table is always the same type. In this case, each element is a string variable. You can initialize some of the elements with the following assignment statements, for example:

```
strShows(3, 12) = "As the Hospital Turns"
strShows(1, 5) = "Guessing Game Show"
strShows(7, 20) = "Raspberry Iced Tea Infomercial"
```

Reserving space for several multidimensional arrays quickly consumes memory space. The following statements reserve a lot of space:

```
Public ara1(10, 20) As Single
Dim ara2(4, 5, 5) As Double
Public ara3(6, 10, 20, 30) As Integer
```

ara1 consumes 200 single-precision memory locations, ara2 consumes 100 double-precision memory locations, and ara3 consumes 36,000 memory locations. As you can see, the number of elements adds up quickly. Be careful that you don't reserve so many array elements that you run out of memory in which to store them.

By reading table data into multidimensional arrays and working with the data in the arrays instead of in database tables, you can speed your program's running times. Anything you can do in memory is faster than doing the same thing reading and writing to disk every time you access values. However, you have much more disk space than memory space. When you're working with large files, you have to forsake the efficiency of memory for the disk capacity.

Tables and *For...Next* Loops

As you see in some of the next few program samples, nested `For...Next` loops are good candidates for looping through every element of a multidimensional table. For instance, the section of code

```
For intRow = 1 To 2
  For intCol = 1 To 3
    MsgBox("Row: " & intRow & ", Col: " & intCol)
  Next intCol
Next intRow
```

produces the following output in the message boxes (you'll learn better ways to display lists of data shortly):

```
Row: 1, Col: 1
Row: 1, Col: 2
Row: 1, Col: 3
Row: 2, Col: 1
Row: 2, Col: 2
Row: 2, Col: 3
```

If you were to print the subscripts, in row order, for a two-row by three-column table dimensioned with the following `Dim` statement, you'd see the subscript numbers shown by this program's nested loops.

```
Dim intTable(1 To 2, 1 To 3)
```

Notice that there are as many `For...Next` statements as there are subscripts in the `Dim` statement (two). The outside loop represents the first subscript (the rows), and the inside loop represents the second subscript (the columns).

For now, you can use `InputBox()` statements to fill tables, although you rarely fill tables this way. Most multidimensional array data comes from forms or—more often—from disk file data. Regardless of what method actually stores values in multidimensional arrays, nested `For...Next` loops are excellent control statements to step through the subscripts. The following examples further illustrate tables and also show how nested `For...Next` loops work with multidimensional arrays.

Example   So many of these past few topic sections have needed to display lists of data, but message boxes simply aren't enough to do the job. I've used message boxes simply as vehicles to teach a concept.

Hour 16's lesson teaches you about a special Visual Basic command called `Print`, which sends output to an object that you associate `Print` with. For example, `frmMyForm.Print` sends output to a form (form output is taught fully in Hour 16's lesson). Visual Basic also contains a special window named the Immediate window to which you can send variables and strings by using `Print`. The syntax is

```
Debug.Print dataToPrint
```

Therefore, if a procedure contained the statement

```
Debug.Print "Hello"
```

Visual Basic prints `Hello` in the special Immediate window that appears when the code executes. The following example will use `Debug.Print` to display a small table of information.

▼ **NOTE**

Don't worry too much about the `Debug.Print` statement. I'm using it just to get past the tedious message boxes that just don't work well to show tables of data. You'll see the Immediate window's figure following the code to describe exactly what the debug window will look like when the procedure terminates. To see the Immediate window, you may have to close some of your development environment's windows or possibly choose Immediate Window from the View menu to show the window if it's hidden. ▲

Suppose that a computer company sells two diskette sizes: 3 1/2 inch and 5 1/4 inch. Each diskette comes in one of four capacities: single-sided low-density, double-sided low-density, single-sided high-density, and double-sided high-density. The diskette inventory is well suited for a two-dimensional table. The company determined that the diskettes have the following retail prices:

	Single-Sided Low-Density	Double-Sided Low-Density	Single-Sided High-Density	Double-Sided High-Density
3 1/2"	$2.30	2.75	3.20	3.50
5 1/4"	$1.75	2.10	2.60	2.95

The procedure in Listing 12.8 stores the price of each diskette in a table and prints the values to the debug window by using a nested `For...Next` loop. You can put this procedure in a standard module or event procedure to trigger its execution.

Listing 12.8 Disks.bas: Inventory Items Often Appear in a Table

```
Private Sub disks ()
' Assigns and prints diskette prices
  Dim curDisks(1 To 2, 1 To 4) As Currency
  Dim intRow As Integer, intCol As Integer
  ' Assign each element the price
  curDisks(1, 1) = 2.3      ' Row 1, Column 1
  curDisks(1, 2) = 2.75     ' Row 1, Column 2
  curDisks(1, 3) = 3.2      ' Row 1, Column 3
  curDisks(1, 4) = 3.5      ' Row 1, Column 4
  curDisks(2, 1) = 1.75     ' Row 2, Column 1
  curDisks(2, 2) = 2.1      ' Row 2, Column 2
  curDisks(2, 3) = 2.6      ' Row 2, Column 3
  curDisks(2, 4) = 2.95     ' Row 2, Column 4
  ' Print the prices in table format
  Debug.Print "          Single-sided, Double-sided, ";
  Debug.Print "Single-sided, Double-sided"
  Debug.Print "          Low-density   Low-density   ";
  Debug.Print "High-density  High-density"
  For intRow = 1 To 2
    If (intRow = 1) Then
      Debug.Print "3-1/2 inch  ";
    Else
      Debug.Print "5-1/4 inch  ";
    End If
    For intCol = 1 To 4
      Debug.Print curDisks(intRow, intCol) & "            ";

    Next intCol
    Debug.Print    ' Moves the cursor to the next line
  Next intRow
End Sub
```

This procedure produces the output shown in Figure 12.3's Immediate window after you resize the window to show the entire table.

FIG. 12.3
The table of diskette prices appears in a table form.

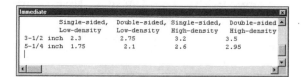

Next Step   Visual Basic includes a special built-in function called `Array()`, which lets you declare and initialize an array quickly.

> **TIP**   The `Array()` function works somewhat like the old BASIC READ and DATA statements. You can quickly initialize small arrays if you know the array data values at programming time.

A `Variant` can contain any other data type, including arrays. Suppose that you want to store the number of days in each month (ignoring leap year) in an array named `Days`. You can declare a `Variant` variable like this:

```
Dim Days As Variant
```

> **TIP**   Remember that if you omit `As Variant`, Visual Basic assumes `Variant`. Typing the data type makes your code as clear as possible, however.

You can then initialize the array in one step (rather than use a `For...Next` loop) like this:

```
Days = Array(31, 28, 31, 30, 31, 30, 31, 31, 30, 31, 30, 31)
```

If the `Option Base 1` statement appears in the module's `Declarations` section, the first subscript of `Array()` is 1 and 0 otherwise. You can declare and initialize strings and dates as well by using the simple `Array()` function assignment to a `Variant` value.

Summary

This lesson covered a lot of ground. You learned about arrays, which are a more powerful way to store lists of data than using individual variable names. By stepping through arrays with subscripts, your procedures can quickly scan, print, and calculate with a list of values.

You also know how to create, initialize, and process multidimensional arrays. Although not all data fits in the compact format of tables, much does. Using nested `For...Next` loops makes stepping through a multidimensional array straightforward.

In Hour 13 you learn how to call procedures from other procedures. You also learn the detailed differences between function procedures and subroutine procedures.

Hour 12 Quiz

You can find the answers for the following questions on the accompanying CD-ROM and on the Virtual Classroom Web site.

On the CD

1. **True or false:** Arrays hold more than one variable with the same name.

2. How do Visual Basic programs tell one array element (value) from another if the elements have identical names?

3. Can array elements within the same array be different types?

4. How many array elements are reserved in the following dimension statement? (Assume an `Option Base` of 0.)

   ```
   Dim varAra(78) As Variant
   ```

5. What's the preferred way to specify the beginning subscript in an array—using `Option Base` or using the `To` keyword?

6. How many elements are reserved by the following `Dim` statement?

   ```
   Dim varStaff(-18 To 4) As Variant
   ```

7. Given the statement

   ```
   Dim strNames(5, 10) As String
   ```

   which subscript (first or second) represents rows and which represents columns?

8. How many elements are reserved with the following statements?

   ```
   Option Base 1
   Dim ara(4, 7)
   ```

9. Given the table of integers called `ara`

4	1	3	5	9
10	2	12	1	6
25	43	2	91	8

   what values do the following elements contain? (Assume that no `Option Base` statement appears in the program.)

   A. `ara(1, 1)`

   B. `ara(1, 2)`

   C. `ara(2, 3)`

10. Given the code

```
Dim intGrades(1 To 3, 1 To 5) As Integer
For intRow = 1 To 3
  For intCol = 1 To 5
    intGrades(intRow, intCol) = intRow + intCol
  Next intCol
Next intRow
```

what values do the following elements contain?

A. `intGrades(1, 2)`

B. `intGrades(2, 2)`

C. `intGrades(2, 3)`

Hour 12 Homework Exercises

1. Write a procedure to store six of your friends' names in a single string array. Use **InputBox()** to initialize the arrays with the names. Print the names on-screen inside message boxes.

2. Write a simple program to track the names of a radio station's top 10 hits. After you store the array, print the songs in reverse order (to get the top 10 countdown) in message boxes.

3. Write a **Dim** statement that dimensions enough string space for the names in a women's basketball league of 5 teams, 25 players, and 6 games per player.

4. Write a procedure that reserves storage for three years of sales data for five salespeople. Use assignment statements to fill the matrix with data and display the table one value per message box.

Understanding How Procedures Work

During this hour you will learn

▶ *Why variable scope is critical*

▶ *What two ways Visual Basic passes data*

▶ *How* Sub *procedures and* Function *procedures vary*

▶ *Why functions return single values*

THIS LESSON FINALLY GIVES the details of Sub and Function procedures. Until now, you've worked with procedures and have had little trouble with them, but you've never had the full reason for the parentheses or the implications of subroutine and function differences explained to you. When you learn to write your own subroutine and function procedures, you'll better understand the built-in functions that Visual Basic supplies, such as InputBox().

This lesson reviews data storage and explains more about local and public variables. You don't see the need for separate subroutine and function procedures until you see that local variables require extra work when you need to use the same local variable in two different procedures.

Topic 1: Variable Scope Revisited

As you've seen, modules often contain multiple procedures. A form module might hold several event procedures—one or more event procedures for each control on the form. Also, the form module might contain general procedures. The standard modules that also appear in applications usually contain multiple procedures. These procedures might be functions or subroutines.

When a module contains multiple procedures, those procedures often have to share data among each other. Creating a variable in one procedure with `Dim` doesn't automatically make that variable available in other procedures. You must understand how procedures share data when needed.

▶▶ FAST TRACK

Do you understand local and global variable scope? If so, jump to the second topic section, "Passing Data Between Procedures" (p. 309), to learn how Visual Basic programs transfer data from one procedure to another. If you've already mastered the local, module-level, and public variable details, as well as written Visual Basic function procedures, you may as well go right on to next hour's lesson, "Using the Supplied Functions" (p. 323).

Overview   As a Visual Basic programmer, you have to know how your module and procedure variables interrelate. This lesson explains how multiple procedures locate variables that are available to them. Although you already know to use the Project menu's Add Module option to add new standard modules to a project, this topic section explains more about why you'd need additional modules within an application's project. When you more fully understand the need for multiple modules and procedures here, the next topic section will show you how to communicate between procedures through shared variables.

A Code Review

A simple application contains a single form with event procedures. Those event procedures appear when you choose Code from the View menu (or when you click the Project window's View Code toolbar button). The code you see might appear all together, separated by dividing lines, as Figure 13.1 shows. The code's procedures might also appear one at a time in the

Code window as you press Page Up and Page Down or select the procedure you want to display from the drop-down list boxes at the top of the
window.

FIG. 13.1
*A Code window
displays the form
module's
procedures.*

Procedure drop-
down list box

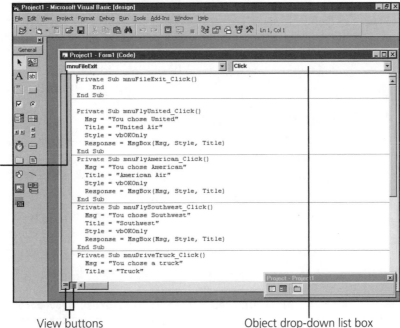

View buttons   Object drop-down list box

Pt **II**

Hr **13**

▼ **NOTE**
Remember that you can switch between the Full Module View and the
single Procedure View by clicking the appropriate button at the bottom
of the Code window. ▲

If a form module contains only event procedures, you don't have to worry
about sharing data between the procedures. All modules, including form
modules, contain a `Declarations` section that you can view by selecting
General from the Object drop-down list box and Declarations from the Procedure drop-down list box. You often have no need to declare data in the
`Declarations` section if your application includes only one form with procedures that are only event procedures.

As you've seen throughout the earlier lessons, a `Declarations` section
might contain special code other than variable declarations, such as the
`Option Explicit` statement. A `Declarations` section, however, can't

contain anything other than variable declarations and these special `Option` statements. All your executable code that contains loops and `If` statements must appear in procedures within the modules and outside the `Declarations` section.

▼ **NOTE**

All modules contain a `Declarations` section even before you add procedures to the modules. You never have to add a `Declarations` section yourself because one will always be available to you. ▲

Adding More to Procedures

If you begin to expand the code inside the event procedures—by declaring variables and adding looping instructions—you may find that you want two or more procedures to work with the same variable. For example, one command button's `Click` event procedure might store a **True** value in a Boolean `blnWasClicked` variable so that another event procedure will know if the command button was ever clicked. Suppose that you declare the variable inside the procedure like this:

```
Private Sub cmdSalesOver ()
  Boolean blnWasClicked
  blnWasClicked = True    ' Let other procedures
                          ' know about the click
  ' Rest of event procedure goes here
End Sub
```

No other procedure can know about the variable! `blnWasClicked` is local just to that procedure because you declared it inside the procedure. If you want certain other procedures to know about `blnWasClicked`, you must move its declaration out of the procedure and into the module's `Declarations` section.

When you declare variables inside a procedure's `Declarations` section, that variable is available to all the procedures in the module. Therefore, with only one form module, if you declared `blnWasClicked` in the form module's `Declarations` section, every event procedure can use `blnWasClicked` and they will all know what value `blnWasClicked` holds at any time.

Adding Complexity

You now can declare two kinds of variables:

- Local variables that are available only with a procedure
- Global variables that are available to any procedure within the module

It's actually more accurate to call these global variables *module-level variables* because the variables you declare with `Dim` in the `Declarations` section is available to all procedures within that module.

If you begin to add additional modules to your project, such as additional forms that contain their own form modules and additional standard modules that hold general-purpose routines that you might use in several applications, you may find that the module-level sharing of variables isn't wide enough in scope for your needs. You may want to access one module's variable from another module. If so, you need to declare truly global variables, called *public variables* in Visual Basic, with the `Public` keyword.

Although Hour 8 explained the format of `Public` (the format is identical to `Dim`), you didn't understand the true purpose for `Public` until now. `Public` declares application-wide global variables. Therefore, if you declare the Boolean variable inside one of your module's `Declarations` section like this:

```
Public blnWasClicked As Boolean
```

the `blnWasClicked` variable is available for use within any procedure and from any module in the entire application.

▼ **NOTE**
You can declare public variables only inside a module's Declarations section. ▲

Applications with Multiple Projects

Visual Basic supports the `Declarations` section statement `Option Private Module`. Not only can any procedure from within any module access public variables normally, but any other project can as well. Visual Basic supports the creation of host applications that can work with multiple projects at one time. If `Option Private Module` is present, however, the public variable you declare is available only to its specific project and not to any outside projects. Generally, even the most advanced and powerful applications don't use multiple projects so you'll rarely, if ever, need to bother with the `Option Private Module` statement.

Problems Now Arise

It's been said that with power comes responsibility. The more public a variable becomes—from local to module-level to public—the more easily your programs get cluttered and bugs enter the picture. Although public variables sound useful, rarely does an application need to use public or even module-level variables. More typically, only two or a few procedures need to share the same data values, and the other procedures don't need access to those variables. If, for example, a report procedure prints values read from the disk in another procedure, only those two procedures need to know the values.

Too often, reusing the same variable name for two different purposes (such as a `For...Next` loop's counting variable) is too easy. If that variable is declared with `Public` or even as a module-level variable, you can replace a value that was assigned and is still in use in another location in the application.

Local variables are *visible* (usable) only from within the procedures in which you declare them. If you use the same local variable name in one procedure as a variable local to another procedure, you don't damage the other's copy of the variable. Keep in mind that without `Option Explicit` in a module's `Declarations` section, you don't even have to declare a variable but you can just begin using one. Visual Basic will assume that the variable is of the `Variant` data type. Therefore, you may be lulled into thinking that you're using a variant variable but in reality you had already declared that same public variable name elsewhere and you're changing the variable's contents instead of using a newly formed variant variable.

▼ **NOTE**

Even procedures have scope. Generally, procedures have private scope (indicated by the `Private` keyword that precedes function and procedure declarations), meaning that only procedures within that same module can use the procedure. If you declare a procedure by using `Public` instead of `Private`, all variables in all modules can use that procedure. Generally, procedures within a standard module (as opposed to a form module) are public so that any application you add the module to can use the routines inside that module. ▲

Declaring local variables and private procedures becomes especially critical when you work on a Visual Basic program with other developers. If you and another programmer are writing modules that operate on the same data in the same application, you could write a procedure or create a variable that has the same name as the other programmer's code. If, however, all your data is local and your procedures are private, name clashes never occur because your module's variables and procedures are accessible only within the module that you write. Despite the name-clash advantage, however, some of your standard module's procedures can't be private because such procedures can't be triggered from a form's event procedures; instead, they can be triggered only from other procedures in the standard module.

The Local versus Public Implications

Here's where you now are: You've seen that variables can be very local or very public. You've seen that routines often need to share data. You've also seen, however, that sharing data publicly or even on a module level is dangerous and that you should avoid declaring anything other than local variables.

The dilemma is this: You need to share data between those procedures that need to share data, but you're not supposed to include module-level and public variables in your applications! How can you share data and still keep your data local? The next topic section explains how to give variable-sharing access only to those procedures in the application that need access. Your variables will then receive shared data values only on a need-to-know basis.

Example Suppose that you run across an application with the following `Declarations` section:

```
Dim a As Integer
Public b As Single
```

You know that **a** is a module-level variable and that only that module can use **a**. All procedures within the module have access to **a** and can change or display the value in **a**.

You also know that **b** is a public variable whose scope is broader than that of **a**'s. Any procedure within the module can access **b** as well as any other module's procedure! In fact, without the `Option Private Module` statement before the variables, any project in a multiple-project application (as mentioned earlier, these are rare) has access to **b**. Therefore, **b** is in potential trouble due to its widespread exposure. Sure, all procedures can share **b**, but that also makes **b** susceptible to inadvertent damage.

Next Step Figure 13.2 illustrates all the scoping possibilities that variables and procedures can posses. Notice that both modules' public variables are accessible from within both modules.

FIG. 13.2
Different variables can have different scope.

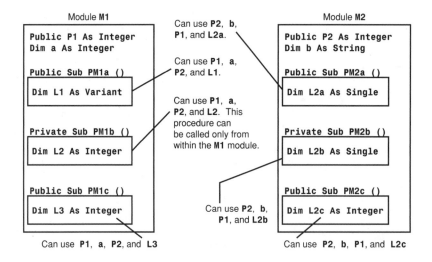

TIP Keep all your public variable declarations together (if you use any at all) within one module—unlike the illustrative example in Figure 13.2—so that you can keep track of them more easily. Remember, however, to limit your use of public variables. Local variables don't get in each other's way as easily as public variables, and public variables consume memory for the entire module's life rather than during a single procedure's execution; that's why you can declare public variables only in the standard module.

In Figure 13.2, the variables **a** and **b** have module-level scope and are visible and usable only from within their module's procedures. Each procedure contains its own local variable (such as `L1` and `L2a`) and, because they're local, only those procedures can access those local variables.

The `PM1b` procedure is a `Private` procedure, as is `PM2b`, so they can be called only from another procedure within their own modules.

Topic 2: Passing Data Between Procedures

Local data is much safer than global data. In the first topic section, you learned that the location of the variable's declaration is the primary determinant of a variable's scope. When you're writing a system with other programmers, using local variable data becomes even more critical. If two of you use many global (public) variables, and you both happen to use the same names, a name clash occurs.

Overview   Given the premise that local variables are good, and given that local variables can be used only in the procedure in which you define them, a problem arises when you need to write modules that contain multiple procedures. Just because procedures are separate doesn't always mean they have to work with separate data.

Suppose that one procedure calculates an array of data that another procedure is to print. Yet, if the array is local to the first procedure, the second procedure can't use the variable. Neither subroutine nor function procedures can use each other's local data—at least, not until you set up a sharing mechanism between them. This topic explains how you can share only certain variables while maintaining the safety of locality.

Name Clashes

If two public variables named `pi` are declared—one for your procedure and one for someone else's procedure who is working on your same application—Visual Basic can't know which `pi` you're initializing when you type the following:

```
pi = 20
```

If you use a public variable and another programmer on the same application uses a local variable with the same name, the local variable always hides the scope of the public variable. When the local variable goes *out of scope* (which means the variable is no longer available for use when the procedure ends), the public variable is then used whenever the name is referred.

Figure 13.3 helps illustrate what happens when a local and a public variable have the same name.

FIG. 13.3
Local variables overshadow public variables with the same name.

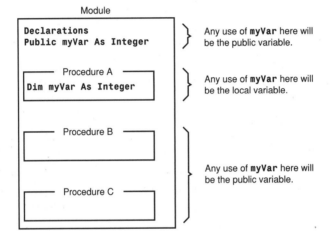

TIP   Use only local variables to solve the problems of name clashes and local variables hiding the scope of public ones.

Two or more local variables residing in two separate procedures can have the same name. You never have a problem with name clashes if you stick to local variables. The variables are known only in the procedures in which they should be known, and one procedure doesn't have improper access to other procedure's variables.

▼ **NOTE**
These local versus global issues apply to you even if you don't work in a team environment and write full applications yourself with Visual Basic. Too often programmers reuse a variable name that they've already declared. If the variable is local, using that same name for local variables in other procedures hurts nothing. If the variable is public, however, using the name will almost surely damage another procedure's value. ▲

Sharing Data

When two procedures share local data, one procedure (called the *calling procedure*) passes data to the second procedure (called the *receiving procedure*). Figure 13.4 shows what you do when you need a local variable to appear in two or more procedures. If the receiving procedure computes or modifies a value that the calling procedure needs, the receiving procedure can return that value back to the calling procedure.

FIG. 13.4
Calling procedures pass local data, and receiving procedures work with that data.

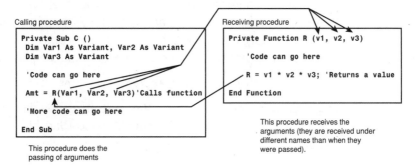

Calling procedure

```
Private Sub C ()
  Dim Var1 As Variant, Var2 As Variant
  Dim Var3 As Variant

  'Code can go here

  Amt = R(Var1, Var2, Var3)'Calls function

  'More code can go here

End Sub
```

This procedure does the passing of arguments

Receiving procedure

```
Private Function R (v1, v2, v3)

  'Code can go here

  R = v1 * v2 * v3;  'Returns a value

End Function
```

This procedure receives the arguments (they are received under different names than when they were passed).

The receiving function named **R( )** returns a computed value back to **C( )**.

CAUTION Never pass a public variable, because Visual Basic will get confused. There's no reason to pass public variables anyway because they're already visible to all functions.

When you pass a local variable from one procedure to another, you pass an argument from the calling procedure to the receiving procedure. You can pass more than one *argument* (variable) at a time if you want several local variables sent from the procedure that sends them. The receiving function is said to receive a *parameter* (variable) from the sending procedure.

▼ **NOTE**
You shouldn't worry too much about whether you call these passed variables arguments or parameters. The important thing to remember is that you're sending local variables from one procedure to another. ▲

▼ **NOTE**
You've already passed arguments to procedures—you did so when you passed data to the MsgBox() and InputBox() functions. The constants,

continues

continued

variables, expressions, and controls that you passed inside the parentheses are arguments. The built-in `MsgBox()` and `InputBox()` functions receives these values (called *parameters* on the receiving end) and displays them. ▲

The parentheses work to hold either the sent data for sending procedures or the received data values for receiving procedures. To pass a local variable from one procedure to another, you must place the local variable in parentheses in the calling procedure and in the receiving procedure. If the parentheses are empty, nothing is being passed to the procedure. The receiving procedure might declare the incoming data inside the parentheses as so,

```
Private Function  R(v1 As Variant, v2 As Variant, v3 As Variant)
```

or the receiving code will assume **Variant** unless the data types you specify vary. All received data is treated like local variables in the receiving procedure.

Sub Procedures versus *Function* Procedures

`Sub` procedures work just like `Function` procedures, with the following exception: A `Sub` procedure never returns a value and a `Function` procedure always returns a value. Therefore, subroutine procedures receive data in one direction only, whereas function procedures receive as well as return data.

The built-in function's arguments work exactly like procedure arguments but because the code for the built-in functions isn't part of your module, you must pass all data to built-in functions. The built-in functions even require that you pass public data. For example, you must pass whatever data you want `MsgBox()` to display, even if that data appears in a public string inside your procedure. `MsgBox()` can't read your mind and needs to know what kind of data to display.

> **TIP** If you need to exit a procedure earlier than its normal `End Function` or `End Sub` would exit, use the `Exit Sub` and `Exit Function` statements. Generally, you'll use `Exit Sub` and `Exit Function` inside the body of an `If` statement that exits only if certain conditions (such as missing data) occur.

By Reference, By Value

If Figure 13.4's `R ()` procedure changes any of its arguments (`v1`, `v2`, or `v3`), the corresponding variables in `C ()` are also changed by their receiving procedure. By default, all Visual Basic procedures pass data *by reference*, meaning that the passed arguments can be changed by their receiving procedure. If you want to keep the receiving procedure from being able to change the called procedure's arguments, you must pass the arguments *by value*. To pass by value, precede the receiving variable arguments with the `ByVal` keyword or by enclosing the passed arguments in parentheses.

Example   The following short examples test your knowledge at recognizing calling and receiving procedures. Being able to recognize the differences is half the battle of understanding them.

`Private Sub doIt()` is the first line, called the *procedure declaration line*. The keywords `Private` and `Sub` let you know that. No arguments are ever to be passed to `doIt()`. If you omit the `Private` keyword, Visual Basic assumes private as in

```
Sub doIt()
```

The statement

```
Call doIt2(curSales)
```

calls a procedure named `doIt2()` and passes that procedure the value of `curSales`. Visual Basic supports an optional `Call` keyword alternative; if you omit `Call`, you must also omit the parentheses, as in

```
doIt curSales
```

> **TIP**   Always use `Call` for procedures to clarify the argument list. You don't use `Call` for built-in functions, such as `InputBox()`. Always use parentheses around the arguments when calling built-in functions unless the functions require no arguments.

The following statement is a receiving procedure named `doIt3()`:

```
Private Sub doIt3(ByVal curSales As Currency)
```

The procedure receives one argument—a `Currency` data type. If `doIt3()` changes `curSales` from the passed value, the calling procedure's value doesn't change due to the `ByVal` keyword (only the value of `curSales` is passed, not the variable itself).

The following statement works just like `doIt3()`, except its argument is received by reference:

```
Private Sub doIt4(ByRef curSales As Currency)
```

Because `ByRef` is the default, the following statement is identical to the previous one:

```
Private Sub doIt4(curSales As Currency)
```

If you omit the `As Currency` option, `doIt4()` will assume that it's receiving a `Variant` data type, which, in many instances, works just fine.

Next Step Suppose that you're writing a procedure that needs to call the following subroutine procedure:

```
Public Sub Area (Radius)
  Dim sngCirArea As Single
  sngCirArea = 3.14159 * Radius * 2  ' Compute area of a circle
  MsgBox ("The area is " & sngCirArea)
End Sub
```

To call this subroutine, you can do the following from another procedure:

```
Call Area (3.4)     ' Call the sub procedure
```

Visual Basic supports a shortcut for calling subroutine procedures. You can omit both `Call` and parentheses like this:

```
Area 3.4     ' Call the sub procedure
```

Such calling statements can be confusing, however, so stick with `Call` when you can.

Topic 3: Returning Values from Functions

You know how to pass data but don't yet know how to return data back from function procedures. Until now, most procedures in this book have been **Sub** procedures, which are called from another procedure but don't return any values. A function procedure returns only one value back to the calling procedure.

Overview   Functions that return values offer you a new approach to programming. In addition to passing data one way—from calling to receiving procedure—you can pass data back from a receiving function procedure to its calling procedure. In Visual Basic, the way you return a value is to assign that value to a variable named the same as the procedure.

Why Only One Return Value?

A function can, as can a subroutine, receive zero, one, or multiple arguments. That is, you can write a function that accepts no arguments by typing empty parentheses after the function name. You can write a function that accepts one or more arguments by specifying those arguments in the parentheses as indicated in the preceding topic sections. The same can be said of subroutine procedures as well.

The distinction between functions and subroutines, as you now know, is that a subroutine never returns a value but a function does. Other than the return value, functions and subroutines are procedures, both can contain any Visual Basic statement, both can call other procedures, and both can be called.

A Sub procedure is useful for routines that perform common work. Suppose that you display a special series of input boxes that set up users' data-entry sessions for a bookstore. The input boxes might ask users for an employee ID, a password, and a shift code; then the application might display an empty form that accepts the first book's data. Although your application could have asked users for the three initial values with a second form that contains text boxes, the extra form would be overkill; the input boxes seem to make the most sense for those three values.

Suppose that you want to use this same series of input boxes in several of your bookstore's applications. If you write the code that manages the input boxes and store the code as a Sub procedure inside a standard module, you then can add that module to whatever application needs the three input boxes. That application could then, from different places in the application, call the subroutine. Four places in the code might call the subroutine to trigger its execution, but the subroutine's code appears only once.

A function is useful when a calculation or data manipulation must occur. Suppose that your bookstore's accounting records require a long series of calculations to be performed to come up with a day's total net adjusted sales. Perhaps the calculations required four values: gross sales, tax rate, gross returns, and the average daily store expense. Although you could pass these four values to a subroutine procedure, how would the calling procedure know the result of the calculated answer? If you use a Sub procedure, you have only two inelegant ways to get the answer back from the procedure:

- Pass a fifth variable by reference (the default). When the Sub procedure finishes, that fifth variable will contain the calculation's answer. Before you call the Sub procedure, the calling procedure's fifth variable would be declared but not used. On return from the Sub, that fifth argument would then have the answer. (As stated, this is inelegant at best and makes for awkward coding and maintenance, because the variable has no use in its declared procedure until the subroutine's return.)

- Make the calculation's answer public and declare that public variable in the **Declarations** section of the calling code. You already know that public variables are frowned on, so by their very nature you should avoid them when you can. Also, the Sub procedure can't be as general-purpose as you might like because it must use the same variable name as the calling procedure's public variable.

A function procedure takes care of the problems nicely. You can pass the four argument values to the function as you would with a subroutine. The function, however, would specifically return the calculated value back to the calling code. No name matches would need to take place; your calling code can grab the return variable and store the value in any variable needed.

Functions always return only single values. As you'll see in the next topic section, you can't really set them up to return more than one value because there would be no way to capture multiple return values from a function.

▼ **NOTE**

If you've studied mathematics, you've no doubt studied functions that take on the notation f(x). Mathematical functions return only one value no matter how many arguments (the x and additional parameters that might be needed) you pass to them. ▲

Setting Up Function Procedures

A `Function` procedure declaration requires only a slight difference from a `Sub` procedure. You must tell Visual Basic the data type of the function's return value. Here is the general syntax:

```
Public Function FunName([Arg As DataType][, ...]) As FunDataType
```

Many functions are public, especially the ones in standard modules, so you can call them from elsewhere in the module. Notice the final two components, `As FunDataType`. When writing function declarations, you must indicate the function's return data type. The function will then return a value based on that data type.

Therefore, the preceding section's net adjusted sales calculation function's declaration line might look something like this (the line is long to hold all the arguments):

```
Public Function CalcNetAdj(curGrSls As Currency,
➥sngTaxRt As Single, curGrRet As Currency,
➥curStrExp As Currency) As Currency
```

The final `As Currency` tells Visual Basic that the function's purpose is to return a single currency value.

Making the Return

Visual Basic uses a simple method to set up the return value. Somewhere in the function, you'll assign the return value to a variable that has the same name as the function name. You won't declare this variable, but you can use it. Therefore, if the final calculation inside the `CalcNetAdj()` function subtracts the average daily store expenses from a local variable named `curTempHold`, you can assign that expression directly to the function name like this:

```
CalcNetAdj = curTempHold - curStrExp
```

This line tells Visual Basic to send back the value, stored in `CalcNetAdj`, to the calling procedure. Although one or more statements might follow this assignment in the function, the assignment to the function name is usually the final line in a function. When the function ends at the `End Function` statement, the value is sent back to the calling procedure.

The calling procedure, therefore, must supply a place for the return value. Generally, you'll assign the returned value to a variable. In the calling procedure, it's not unusual to see a statement such as this:

```
curDailyNet = CalcNetAdj(curGrSls, sngTaxRt, curGrRate, curStrExp)
```

The calling procedure runs along until it gets to this assignment statement. Visual Basic then puts the calling procedure on hold and executes the function named `CalcNetAdj()`, passing the values to the function. When the function returns the calculated value, the calling procedure then gets the function's return value and stores that value in `curDailyNet`. The calling procedure can then keep executing. In other words, to complete this assignment, the function must execute and get a return value.

▼ NOTE

The calling procedure doesn't have to use the same variable names in the argument list as listed in the function argument list. A calling procedure might pass variables, literals, named constants, control values, and expressions in the argument list. The names often match in the calling and receiving argument lists, but not always. ▲

Example The module in Listing 13.1 doesn't contain all of its needed code, but only enough so that you can focus on the function's construction and operation. The variable r is received by reference, whereas v is received by value in the second procedure, RF (). If the RF () receiving function changes r, the CF () calling function's r is changed as well. If the RF () receiving function changes v, however, the CF () calling function's argument retains its original value.

Listing 13.1 Practice Passing and Receiving Values

```
Option Explicit

' Calling function is next
Private Function CF ()
  Dim r As Variant v As Variant   ' Declare local variables named r and v
  Dim i As Integer                ' to hold the return value of the function

  i = RF(r, v)          ' Call the function and pass r and v
                        ' i gets RF ()'s return value
End Function
```

```
' Receiving function is next
Private Function RF(r As Variant, ByVal v As Variant)
  ' Received r by reference and v by value
  r = 50       ' Changes r in both procedures
  v = 20       ' Changes v just here
  RF = r * i   ' Returns a value
End Function
```

Next Step Think of how the `InputBox()` function works. To produce an input box, you issue a statement that looks something like this:

```
strUserName = InputBox("What is your name?", "Ask a name",
➥"John Doe", 100, 50)
```

As you can now understand, the built-in functions work just like the functions you write. This statement calls the `InputBox()` function and passes five arguments to the function: three string literals and two numeric literals. The assignment can't take place until the `InputBox()` function completes, so the calling procedure is put on hold until users supply the input. After the `InputBox()` function completes, the user response—the string returned from `InputBox()`—must go somewhere. That somewhere is the variable named `strUserName`. You couldn't call `InputBox()` without supplying the capturing variable because Visual Basic would have no place to put the returned value.

`InputBox()` is just one of numerous Visual Basic built-in functions. Visual Basic supplies these built-in functions that not only work with I/O but also perform mathematical and string operations.

Summary

This lesson explained the significance of variable scope. You now understand the differences between local, module-level, and public variables. Keeping variables local—or perhaps at times on a module level—helps maintain their integrity. Understanding when a variable is visible is the prelude to writing programs with many procedures. Although keeping variables local is suggested, local variables present a problem that you haven't, until now, had to address: They are visible only within the procedure in which you declare them. Therefore, you should keep all variables local for safety, but you need to transfer data between procedures only when needed and not all the time publicly.

When you pass and return variables between procedures, you ensure that only those procedures that need access to those variables have access. Also, you protect the variables from inadvertent change that can take place with too many public variables floating around the application.

Visual Basic lets you use the same public and local variable names in different procedures. Although you don't want to overdo this practice, using the same variable name for simple processing—such as in counters and for loop control—helps document your code and simplifies the number of variables you have to keep track of. If, however, you have a public variable and a local variable with the same name, the local variable always hides the public's value. Think of Visual Basic as always using the "most local" variable if two variables in the same module have the same name.

When you use local variables, your procedures must be able to communicate with each other. When one procedure contains data that another needs, pass the data argument from the calling procedure to the receiving procedure. The receiving procedure (if it's a function procedure) can return a single value back to the calling procedure. Normally, you pass arguments by reference, meaning that if the receiving procedure changes the arguments, the arguments are changed in the calling procedure also. If you pass arguments by value (by using `ByVal`), the receiving procedure can't change the calling procedure's arguments. Any changes made to the by-reference arguments inside the receiving procedure don't appear when the calling procedure regains control.

Hour 14, "Using the Supplied Functions," explores many of Visual Basic's built-in functions that will greatly simplify your work. Rather than write a common calculation or string-manipulation procedure, you can call one of the built-in functions that Visual Basic supplies. After the lesson, you'll be able to write your own functions and use Visual Basic's supplied functions to add power to your programs.

Hour 13 Quiz

You can find the answers for the following questions on the accompanying CD-ROM and on the Virtual Classroom Web site.

On the CD

1. **True or false:** Every module contains a `Declarations` section.

2. What kind of variable—local, module-level, or public—has the broadest scope?

3. What kind of variable—local, module-level, or public—poses the most probable danger?

4. How do name clashes occur?

5. How many values can a `Function` procedure return?

6. How many values can a `Sub` procedure return?

7. If your program uses only local variables, name clashes don't occur. Why then must you be able to pass data between procedures?

8. What are the two ways to pass values?

9. **True or false:** The keyword `ByRef` is optional.

10. Suppose that a module contains a public variable named `sngSales` and a procedure within the same module creates a local variable named `sngSales`. Which variable—local or public—is changed by the following statement inside the procedure?

    ```
    sngSales = curPrice * intQuantity
    ```

Hour 13 Homework Exercises

1. By using Figure 13.2's outline box-notation, draw the following scenario: You're writing three modules. The first module, `Mod1`, contains a public `Proc1` procedure with two local variables. The second of `Mod1`'s procedures, `pProc2`, is private. The second module, `Mod2`, contains a module-level variable named `m1` and a single procedure named `Proc2a` that contains a local variable named `i`. The third procedure declares a variable named `s` that's public to all the other modules and also contains one procedure named `Proc3` that declares no variables.

2. How can you change the code in Listing 13.2 so that `v` is passed by reference and `r` is passed by value?

Listing 13.2   Change the Passing Methods

```
Option Explicit

' Calling function is next
Private Function CF ()
  Dim r As Variant v As Variant    ' Declare local variables named r and v
  Dim i As Integer                 ' to hold the return value of the function

  i = RF(r, v)           ' Call the function and pass r and v
                         ' i gets RF ()'s return value
End Function

' Receiving function is next
Private Function RF(r As Variant, ByVal v As Variant)
  ' Received r by reference and v by value
  r = 50        ' Changes r in both procedures
  v = 20        ' Changes v just here
  RF = r * i    ' Returns a value
End Function
```

3. Write a module that contains two subroutine procedures. The first procedure asks for a name and the second prints the name. Don't use any module-level or public variables in the module.

Using the Supplied Functions

During this hour you will learn

▶ The numeric functions Visual Basic provides

▶ Which string functions come in handy

▶ When to use the time and date functions

▶ How to make data look good

THIS LESSON EXPLORES the many built-in functions that Visual Basic provides so that you have less to code. You'll learn all about the numeric, string, date, time, and formatting functions that make up Visual Basic's library.

Topic 1: Numeric Functions

Visual Basic includes many built-in numeric functions that convert and calculate with your data. Although some of the built-in functions are highly technical, many of them are used daily. Most of the built-in functions reduce your programming time. Rather than have to "reinvent the wheel" every time you need Visual Basic to perform a numeric or string operation, you can use one of the many built-in functions to do the job for you.

Overview As with built-in functions and functions that you write, all the functions in this topic return a value of some kind, and most of them require arguments. Not all functions require arguments, such as the **Now** function, and those that don't shouldn't have the parentheses after their name when you call them.

The Integer Conversion Functions

The `Int()` and `Fix()` functions return whole numbers. Here are their syntaxes:

```
Int(numericValue)
Fix(numericValue)
```

`Int()` returns the integer value of the number you pass in the parentheses; `Fix()` returns the truncated whole number value of the argument. *Truncation* means that the fractional part of the argument is taken off the number.

`Int()` and `Fix()` return the numeric data type as their argument or `Null` if you pass them a `Null` argument.

CAUTION If you pass to `Int()` or `Fix()` a non-numeric argument (such as strings that can't be converted to numbers by the functions), you get a `Type mismatch` error.

The primary difference between `Int()` and `Fix()` appears when you pass them negative arguments.

Both of the following statements store 8 (the function's return value) in `intAns`:

```
intAns = Fix(8.93)
intAns = Int(8.93)
```

The following line of code stores –8 in `intAns`:

```
intAns = Int(-7.6)
```

`Int()` returns the highest integer that's less than or equal to the argument in parentheses.

For negative numbers, `Fix()` and `Int()` return very different return values. `Fix()` simply drops the fractional part of the number—whether it's positive or negative—from the argument.

```
intAns1 = Fix(-8.93)
intAns2 = Fix(-8.02)
```

`Int()` doesn't truncate but returns the closest integer less than or equal to the argument.

The Data Type Conversion Functions

Table 14.1 describes the data type conversion functions, denoted by their initial letter C (for *convert*). Each function converts its argument from one data type to another.

Table 14.1   The Data Type Conversion Functions

Function Name	Description
`CBool()`	Converts its argument to the `Boolean` data type
`CByte()`	Converts its argument to the `Byte` data type
`CCur()`	Converts its argument to the `Currency` data type
`CDate()`	Converts its argument to the `Date` data type
`CDbl()`	Converts its argument to the `Double` data type
`CDec()`	Converts its argument to the `Decimal` data type
`CInt()`	Converts its argument to the `Integer` data type
`CLng()`	Converts its argument to the `Long` data type
`CSng()`	Converts its argument to the `Single` data type
`CStr()`	Converts its argument to the `String` data type
`CVar()`	Converts its argument to the `Variant` data type

> **CAUTION** You must be able to convert the argument to the target data type. You can't convert the number 123456789 to `Integer` with `CInt()`, for example, because an `Integer` data type can't hold an integer that large.

Unlike `Int()` and `Fix()`, `CInt()` returns the closest rounded integer to the argument. Look at the remarks to the right of each of the following statements to see what's stored in each variable:

```
cA1 = CInt(8.5)       ' Stores an 8 in cA1
cA2 = CInt(8.5001)    ' Stores a 9 in cA2
```

For negative numbers, `CInt()` also rounds to the closest whole integer.

The following code declares a variable of four different data types and then converts each argument to those data types. Remember that you also can pass to these functions expressions that produce numeric results so that you can control the data types of your calculated results before storing them in a field or variable.

```
vVar1 = CCur(123)     ' Converts 123 to currency data type
vVar2 = CDbl(123)     ' Converts 123 to double-precision data
                        ➥type
vVar3 = CSng(123)     ' Converts 123 to single-precision data
                        ➥type
vVar4 = CVar(123)     ' Converts 123 to the variant data type
```

The Absolute Value Function

`Abs()` often works with the sign of a number instead of the value itself. `Abs()` returns the absolute value of its argument.

Absolute value is the positive value of the argument. The absolute value of 10 is 10, and the absolute value of −10 is also 10. You may find some good uses for absolute value, such as distance and age/weight differences (the distance between two cities is always positive).

Suppose that you want to know how many years' difference in two employees' ages. The following statement stores the difference in ages between `intEmp1Age` and `intEmp2Age`:

```
intAgeDiff = Abs(intEmp1Age - intEmp2Age)
```

The Math Functions

You don't have to be an expert in math to use many of the mathematical functions that come with Visual Basic. Often, even in business applications, the following functions come in handy:

- `Exp()`, which returns the natural logarithm (*e*, approximately 2.718282) base
- `Log()`, which returns the natural logarithm of a number
- `Sqr()`, which computes the square root of its argument.

`Sqr()`'s argument can be any positive numeric data type. (Square root isn't defined for negative numbers.) The code

```
intVar1 = Sqr(4)
intVar2 = Sqr(64)
intVar3 = Sqr(4096)
```

stores 2, 8, and 64 in the three respective variables.

Pt **II**

Hr **14**

The Randomizing Tools

Two randomizing tools are available in Visual Basic. You never use the `Randomize` statement by itself. If a module includes `Randomize`, you find the `Rnd()` function later in the procedure. Here is the format of the `Randomize` statement:

```
Randomize [number]
```

The format of the `Rnd()` function is as follows:

```
Rnd[(number)]
```

Notice that neither the `Randomize` statement nor the `Rnd()` function requires values after them (as the square brackets indicate). The purpose of `Rnd()` is to generate a random number between 0 (inclusive) and 1 (1 is never generated by `Rnd()`). You can use the random number function for games, such as simulating dice rolls or card draws.

If you run a procedure with four `Rnd()` numbers printed, each number is different (random) if you include no number argument. If, however, you specify 0 as the argument to `Rnd()`, such as x = `Rnd(0)`, the four numbers are the same number. If you specify a number greater than 0 as the argument to `Rnd()`, a different random number is produced (the same as leaving off the argument altogether). An argument less than zero, such as `x = Rnd(-3)`, always produces the same random number if you specify the same negative argument, and a different random number if the negative argument is always different.

If you want a different random number generated with `Rnd()` every time it executes, don't specify an argument. If you want the same set of random numbers produced from a series of `Rnd()` function calls (such as a scientific simulation that you want to repeat several times), specify the same negative argument.

`Rnd()` always produces the same set of values between procedure runs unless you provide a `Randomize` statement before the first `Rnd()`. In other words, if you run a procedure 20 times, the same set of random numbers results no matter what argument (or lack of argument) you use with the `Rnd()` function calls. The `Randomize` statement reseeds the *random-number generator*, a fancy term meaning that `Randomize` ensures that `Rnd()` produces a new set of random values each time you run a program.

If you don't specify a number after `Randomize`, the value of `Timer` is used. (`Timer` returns the number of seconds since midnight.) Because the value of `Timer` changes every second, the `Randomize` statement ensures that a new seed value is used for the next occurrence of `Rnd()`.

> **TIP** If you want truly random values every time `Rnd()` appears—even between program runs—put the `Randomize` statement (with no arguments) at the top of the first procedure in the module and leave off all arguments to `Rnd()` in subsequent `Rnd()` calls.

The following procedure always produces the same three random numbers every time you run it (assuming that no `Randomize` statement has executed yet within the module):

```
Private Sub randIt()
    Dim b As Integer      ' For button clicked
    b = MsgBox(Rnd)       ' A random number
    b = MsgBox(Rnd(0))    ' The same random number
    b = MsgBox(Rnd(0))    ' The same random number
End Sub
```

If you put a `Randomize` statement anywhere in the module so that it executes before the three `Rnd()` statements shown in the preceding example, you still get the same three random numbers due to `Rnd()`'s zero argument.

If you want three different random numbers always generated (as you usually do), don't specify an argument after `Rnd()`.

You rarely want a random number from 0 to 1, as produced by `Rnd()`. By using the following simple formula, however, you can generate a random number from low to high (assuming those two variables have been initialized):

```
Int((high - low + 1) * Rnd + low)
```

Suppose that you want to offer a special discount to a different customer each month. If your customer numbers fall between 1000 and 6456 (meaning that you have a total of 5,457 customers), you can do something like the following:

```
intLow = 1000      ' Lowest customer number
intHigh = 6456     ' Highest customer number
intSpecialCustNum = Int((intHigh - intLow + 1) * Rnd + intLow)
```

Example The following procedure uses the `Abs()` function to compute and display the difference between two ages. The ages come from a calling procedure.

```
Private Sub (intAge1 As Integer, intAge2 As Integer)
  ' Computes and displays the age difference
  lblAdeDiff = Abs(intAge1 - intAge2)
End Sub
```

Without `Abs()`, the procedure would print a negative age difference if the first age passed happened to be smaller than the second.

Next Step You can even write games with Visual Basic! With the procedure in Listing 14.1, you actually can use Visual Basic to write a number-guessing game. The computer generates a random number from 1 to 100, and then uses control statements to offer users hints until they correctly guess the number.

On the CD

Listing 14.1   Guess1.bas: Guessing Game

```
Private Sub Guessing ()
' Number-guessing game
  Dim intRNum As Integer
  Dim intUserNum As Integer
  Dim strTitle As String
  Randomize     ' Ensure that the number is always different
  intRNum = Int(100 * Rnd + 1)   ' Generates a number from 1 to 100
  intUserNum = InputBox("Welcome to a game! Guess a number...", strTitle)
  ' Keep looping until the user guesses correctly
  Do While (intUserNum <> intRNum)
    If (intUserNum < intRNum) Then
      intUserNum = InputBox("Too low, try again...", strTitle)
    Else
      intUserNum = InputBox("Too high, try again...", strTitle)
    End If
  Loop
  Beep
  intRNum = MsgBox("Congratulations! You guessed my number!", vbInformation)
End Sub
```

Topic 2: String Functions

In the preceding topic section, you learned about the numeric functions. In this topic section, you learn about the built-in functions that work with strings. Some functions described in the following sections convert between strings and numbers.

Overview   Visual Basic provides better string-handling capabilities than most programming languages. Your data is often composed of string data. You may need to test various string values and change string values, and you'll find those tasks easy after you learn the string functions.

▼ **NOTE**

Some of the items taught in this topic section are statements, not functions. However, these statements work hand in hand with string functions, and this topic section is the most logical place to group this material together. ▲

The *Len( )* Length Function

Len( ) is one of the few functions that can take either a numeric variable or a string for its argument. Len( ) returns the number of memory bytes needed to hold its argument. Here's the syntax of Len( ):

Len(*Expression*)

▼ NOTE

Len( ) accepts any string value (variable, literal, or expression). However, only numeric variables, not numeric literals or expressions, work as Len( ) arguments. ▲

If you're getting ready to store 200 single-precision variables and want to see how much memory the data takes, you can code the following:

```
Dim sngTestIt As Single
sngTestIt = 0      ' A sample single-precision variable
intStorage = (Len(sngTestIt) * 200.0)
```

This code stores the amount of memory needed to hold 200 single-precision values.

Len( ) also returns the length (number of characters) of the string variable, string constant, or string expression inside its parentheses. The following MsgBox( ) function displays a 6 as its output:

```
b = MsgBox(Len("abcdef"))
```

> **TIP** If the string contains Null, Len( ) returns a value of 0. Testing for a null string lets you test to see whether a user entered data in response to an InputBox( ) function or a control value.

The String Conversion Functions

Several conversion functions work with string data. Table 14.2 describes each string-conversion function used in the following examples.

Table 14.2 The String-Conversion Functions

Function Name	Description
CStr( )	Changes its argument to a string
Str( )	Converts its numeric argument to a string (actually, to a Variant data type that you can use as a string)

continues

Table 14.2 Continued

Function Name	Description
Val()	Converts its string argument to a number, assuming that you pass Val() a string-like number

▼ **NOTE**

Although they're easier to use, neither CStr() nor Str() are as powerful as Format(), which you learn about in the next topic section. ▲

CStr() and Str() convert their arguments to string values. The only difference is that CStr() doesn't add a leading blank before positive numbers converted to strings; Str() does. The following code displays the difference between CStr() and Str():

```
Private Sub convStr ()
   Dim s1 As String, s2 As String
   Dim b As Integer    ' For button clicked
   s1 = CStr(12345)
   s2 = Str(12345)
   b = MsgBox("***" & s1 & "***")
   b = MsgBox("***" & s2 & "***")
End Sub
```

Figure 14.1 shows the first message box displayed; Figure 14.2 shows the second. Notice that no blank appears before the first string because the CStr() function was used, not Str().

FIG. 14.1
This string was created with CStr().

FIG. 14.2
A blank appears before the number.

The ASCII Functions

Appendix B, "The ASCII Table," lists the ASCII characters used with the ASCII functions. You use the `Chr()` and `Asc()` functions to convert strings to and from their numeric ASCII values. The ASCII table lists every possible character available on the PC and assigns a sequential number (an *ASCII code*) to each character.

By putting a number inside the `Chr()` parentheses, you can produce the character that corresponds to that number in the ASCII table. By using `Chr()`, you can generate characters for variables and controls that don't appear on your computer's keyboard but that do appear in the ASCII table.

The `Asc()` function is a mirror image of `Chr()`. Whereas `Chr()` takes a numeric argument and returns a string character, `Asc()` requires a string argument and converts that argument to its corresponding ASCII table number.

Therefore, an A is stored in `aVar` in the following assignment statement because the ASCII value of A is 65:

```
aVar = Chr(65)     ' Stores an A in aVar
```

Of course, it makes more sense to store an A directly in the `aVar` variable in the preceding example's statement. What, however, if you want to ask a Spanish question inside a message box? Spanish questions always begin with an upside-down question mark, and no upside-down question mark appears on your keyboard. Therefore, you can resort to using `Chr()` as follows:

```
' Chr(241) produces an n with a tilde over it
strMyQuest = Chr(191) & "Se" & Chr(241) & "or, como esta?"
b = MsgBox(strMyQuest)
```

Figure 14.3 shows the message box displayed from this code.

FIG. 14.3
Use ASCII characters to display characters not on the keyboard.

`Asc()` returns the ASCII number of the character argument you give it. The argument must be a string of one or more characters. If you pass `Asc()` a string of more than one character, it returns the ASCII number of the first character in the string. For example, the statement

```
b = MsgBox(Asc("A") & " " & Asc("B") & " " & Asc("C"))
```

produces the following output in a message box:

```
65 66 67
```

Look at the ASCII table in Appendix B to see that these three numbers are the ASCII values for A, B, and C.

Now look at the following example:

```
strAns = InputBox("Do you want to see the name")
If ((Asc(strAns) = 89) Or (Asc(strAns) = 121)) Then
   b = MsgBox("The name is " + aName)
End If
```

The user can answer the prompt with y, Y, Yes, or YES. The `If...Then` test works for any of those input values because 89 is the ASCII value for Y, and 121 is the ASCII value of y. `Asc()` returns the ASCII value of its string argument's first letter.

The Substring Functions

The substring functions return parts of strings. `Right()` returns characters from the right side of a string. `Right()`'s cousin, `Left()`, returns characters from the left side of a string. `Mid()` takes up where `Right()` and `Left()` fail—`Mid()` lets you pick characters from the middle of a string.

Here are the syntaxes of the substring functions:

```
Left(stringValue, numericValue)
Right(stringValue, numericValue)
Mid(stringValue, startPosition[, length])
```

The following section of code demonstrates `Left()`:

```
strA = "abcdefg"
partSt1 = Left(strA, 1)     ' Stores a
partSt2 = Left(strA, 3)     ' Stores abc
partSt3 = Left(strA, 20)    ' Stores abcdefg
```

▼ **NOTE**

If you try to return more characters from the left of the string than exist, `Left()` returns the entire string. ▲

Pt II

Hr 14

`Right()` works in the same manner as `Left()`, except that it returns the rightmost characters from a string:

```
strA = "abcdefg"
partSt1 = Right(strA, 1)    ' Stores g
partSt2 = Right(strA, 3)    ' Stores efg
partSt3 = Right(strA, 20)   ' Stores abcdefg
```

`Mid()` accomplishes what `Left()` and `Right()` can't—it returns characters from the middle of a string. `Mid()` uses three arguments: a string followed by two integers. The first integer determines where `Mid()` begins stripping characters from the string (the position, starting at 1), and the second integer determines how many characters from that position to return. If you don't specify two integers, `Mid()` uses 1 as the starting position.

`Mid()` can pull any number of characters from anywhere in the string. The following example shows how the `Mid()` function works:

```
strA = "Visual Basic FORTRAN COBOL C Pascal"
lang1 = Mid(strA, 1, 12)   ' Stores Visual Basic
lang2 = Mid(strA, 14, 7)   ' Stores FORTRAN
lang3 = Mid(strA, 22, 5)   ' Stores COBOL
lang4 = Mid(strA, 28, 1)   ' Stores C
lang5 = Mid(strA, 30, 6)   ' Stores Pascal
```

If you don't specify the *length* argument, VB returns all the characters to the right of the starting position. If the length is longer than the rest of the string, VB ignores the *length* argument.

▼ **THE *Mid()* STATEMENT**

`Mid()` is a command and a function. It works as a command when it appears on the left side of an assignment statement's equal sign; it's a function when it appears anywhere else.

When you use the `Mid()` statement, it changes the contents of the string used inside the statement's parentheses. The following code initializes a string with three words and then changes the middle word with `Mid()`:

```
strSentence = "Rain in Spain"
' Change the middle word
Mid(strSentence, 6, 2) = "on"
' After the change
b = MsgBox("After change: " & sentence)
' Prints Rain on Spain ▲
```

Converting to Uppercase and Lowercase

The UCase() function returns its string argument in all uppercase letters. LCase() returns its string argument in all lowercase letters. The following MsgBox() function displays VISUAL BASIC:

```
b = MsgBox(UCase("Visual Basic"))
```

Justifying and Trimming Strings

LTrim() and RTrim() trim spaces from the beginning or end of a string. LTrim() returns the argument's string without any leading spaces, whereas RTrim() returns the argument's string without any trailing spaces. The Trim() function trims leading and trailing spaces.

Here are the syntaxes of the string-trimming functions:

```
LTrim(stringExpression)
RTrim(stringExpression)
Trim(stringExpression)
```

Example

On the CD

The following ReverseIt() function procedure in Listing 14.2 includes several of the string functions described in this topic section. This function reverses a certain number of characters within a string.

Listing 14.2   Reverse.bas: A Function That Reverses a String

```
Public Function ReverseIt (s As String, ByVal n As Integer) As String
' Accepts: a string and an integer indicating the number of
'          characters to reverse
' Purpose: reverses the specified number of characters in the
'          specified string
' Returns: the modified string

' Reverses the first n characters in s.

    Dim strTemp As String, intI As Integer

    If n > Len(s) Then n = Len(s)
    For intI = n To 1 Step -1
        strTemp = strTemp + Mid(s, intI, 1)
    Next intI
    ReverseIt = strTemp + Right(s, Len(s) - n)
End Function
```

Suppose that the **ReverseIt()** function were called with the following statement:

```
newStr = ReverseIt ("Visual Basic", 6)
```

If all goes well, the string named **newStr** will hold the characters **lausiV Basic** (the first 6 characters are reversed).

Here is how the function works. The first statement, **Dim**, declares two local variables, the first of which, a string variable named **strTemp**, holds the reversed string as it's being built. The second variable, **intI**, is used in the **For** loop.

The **If** statement ensures that the integer passed to **ReverseIt()** isn't larger than the length of the string passed. It's impossible to reverse more characters than exist in the string. If more characters are passed, the **If** statement ensures that the entire string is reversed by changing the length to reverse to the exact length of the string via the **Len()** function.

Pt II

Hr **14**

The **For** loop then counts down, from the position to reverse (stored in n) to 1. By using the **Mid()** function, Visual Basic concatenates one character from the string, at position n, to the new string being built. As n reaches 1, the reversed characters are sent to the new string. After all the characters that need to be reversed are reversed, the rightmost portion of the passed string is concatenated as is to the reversed characters.

Next Step The following statements trim spaces from the beginning, end, or both sides of strings:

```
st1 = LTrim("     Hello")   ' Stores Hello
st2 = RTrim("Hello     ")   ' Stores Hello
st3 = Trim("   Hello   ")   ' Stores Hello
```

Without the trimming functions, the spaces are copied into the target variables as well as the word *Hello*.

Earlier, you learned how to use **Str()** to convert a number to a string. Because **Str()** always converts positive numbers to strings with a leading blank (where the imaginary plus sign appears), you can combine **LTrim()** with **Str()** to eliminate the leading blank. The first of the following two statements stores the leading blank in **st1**. The second uses **LTrim()** to get rid of the blank before storing the string into **st2**.

```
st1 = Str(234)          ' Stores " 234"
st2 = LTrim(Str (234))  ' Stores "234"
```

Topic 3: Special Functions

The time and date functions are critical when processing data, especially in a database environment. It might be important to record exactly when a field was edited for security or verification purposes. Also, all printed reports should have the date and time (often called *date-* and *time-stamping*) printed on the report, showing exactly when the report was produced. In a stack of like reports, the date and time stamps show when the latest report was printed.

In addition to the time and date functions, Visual Basic supports a special data-formatting function that you can use to display formatted strings.

Overview The date and time functions help you add such values to your code. The `Format()` function isn't just for dates or times, but after you learn the date and time functions, you'll know about all the data types available with `Format()`.

Retrieving the Date and Time

Inside most computers are a clock and calendar that Visual Basic programs can read. You may have used the `Date` and `Time` functions in your forms. These functions don't require arguments and don't use parentheses, so they don't always look like functions.

Your Windows settings determine the format of the `Date` and `Time` return values. For example, on many systems `Date` will return the system date in the `Variant` data type in the following format:

   mm-dd-yyyy

where *mm* is a month number (from 01 to 12), *dd* is a day number (from 01 to 31), and *yyyy* is a year number (from 1980 to 2099).

`Time` returns the system time in the `Variant` data type in the following format:

   hh:mm:ss

where *hh* is the hour (from 00 to 23), *mm* is the minute (from 00 to 59), and *ss* is the second (from 00 to 59).

`Date` uses a 24-hour clock. Therefore, all hours before 1:00:00 in the afternoon equate to a.m. time values, and all times from 1:00:00 until midnight have 12 added to them (so 14:30 is 2:30 in the afternoon).

`Now` combines the `Date` and `Time` functions. `Now` returns a `Variant` data type in the following syntax (if you were to print the `Variant` return value of `Now` in a message box, you'd see this syntax):

> *mm/dd/yy hh:mm:ss* AM¦PM

where the placeholder letters correspond to those of the `Date` and `Time` functions, with the exception that a 12-hour clock is used and either AM or PM appears next to the time. The vertical line in the syntax indicates that AM *or* PM appears—not both.

The most important thing to remember about all three date and time retrieval functions is that they return date and time values that are stored internally as double-precision values (with enough precision to ensure that the date and time values are stored accurately). The best way to format date and time values is to use `Format()`, which you learn about later in this topic discussion.

Assuming that it's exactly 9:45 in the morning, the statement

> `currentTime = Time`

stores 9:45:00 in the variable `currentTime`. If the date is 2/23/99, the statement

> `currentDate = Date`

stores 2/23/99 in the variable `currentDate`. The statement

> `currentDateTime = Now`

stores 2/23/99 9:45:00 AM in the variable `currentDateTime`.

Setting the Date and Time

By using the `Date` and `Time` *statements*, you can set the current date and time from within Visual Basic. After you set your computer's date and time, they remain in effect until you change them again. The placement of `Date` and `Time` in an expression indicates whether you want to use the functions or statements.

Here are the formats of the `Date` and `Time` statements:

```
Date = dateExpression
Time = timeExpression
```

The Date Expression Format

You must enter the *dateExpression* with pound signs enclosing the date, as follows:

```
Date = #11/21/1993#
```

Because there are several date formats, just about any way you're used to specifying the date is recognized by Visual Basic.

`Date` can recognize the following formats:

mm–dd–yy
mm–dd–yyyy
mm/dd/yy
mm/dd/yyyy
monthName dd, yyyy
mmm dd, yyyy (where *mmm* is an abbreviated month name, as in *Dec*)
dd monthName yy
dd–mmm–yy (where *mmm* is an abbreviated month name, as in *Dec*)

The following code tells users the currently set date and lets them enter a new date. If users press Enter without entering a date, the previous date is kept.

```
Dim newDate As Variant
b = MsgBox("The current date is " & Date)     ' Calls function
newDate = InputBox("What do you want to set the date to?")
If IsDate(newDate) Then
   Date = newDate
End If    ' Don't do anything if a good date isn't entered
b = MsgBox("The date is now " & Date)
```

The Time Expression Format

Here are some of the ways you can express the time:

hh
hh:mm
hh:mm:ss

You must use a 24-hour clock with `Time`.

Computing the Time Between Events

The `Timer` function returns the number of seconds since your computer's internal clock struck midnight. The syntax of `Timer` is simple:

```
Timer
```

As you can see, `Timer` is another function that uses no parentheses.

On the CD

`Timer` is perfect for timing an event. For example, you can ask users a question and determine how long it took them to answer. First, save the value of `Timer` before you ask users; then subtract that value from the value of `Timer` after they answer. The difference of the two `Timer` values is the number of seconds users took to answer. Listing 14.3 shows a procedure that does just that.

Listing 14.3   Comptime.bas: Time the Users' Response

```
Public Sub CompTime ()
' Procedure that times the user's response
  Dim b As Integer    ' MsgBox() return
  Dim Before, After, timeDiff As Variant
  Dim mathAns As Integer
  Before = Timer     ' Save the time before asking
  mathAns = Inputbox("What is 150 + 235?")
  After = Timer      ' Save the time after answering
  ' The difference between the time values
  ' is how many seconds the user took to answer
  timeDiff = After - Before
  b = MsgBox("That took you only" + Str(timeDiff) & " seconds!")
End Sub
```

More Date Arithmetic

`Timer` finds the number of seconds between time values, but only for those time values that fall on the same day. `DateAdd()`, `DateDiff()`, and `DatePart()` take up where `Timer` leaves off. Table 14.3 lists these three date arithmetic functions and their descriptions.

Table 14.3 The Date Arithmetic Functions

Function Name	Description
DateAdd()	Returns a new date after you add a value to a date
DateDiff()	Returns the difference between two dates
DatePart()	Returns part (an element) from a given date

All three date arithmetic functions can work with the parts of dates listed in Table 14.4. Table 14.4 contains the parts of dates these functions work with, as well as their interval values that label each part. You use the interval values inside the date arithmetic functions to get to a piece of a date or time.

Table 14.4 The Time Period Interval Values

Interval Value	Time Period
yyyy	Year
q	Quarter
m	Month
y	Day of year
d	Day
w	Weekday (Sunday is 1, Monday is 2, and so on, for Day(), Month(), Year(), and DateDiff())
ww	Week
h	Hour
n	Minute (*careful*—not m)
s	Second

The *DateAdd()* Function

Despite its name, DateAdd() works with both dates and times (as do all the date functions) because the date passed to DateAdd() must appear in a Date data type format. Here's the syntax of DateAdd():

```
DateAdd(interval, number, oldDate)
```

The *interval* must be a value (in string form) from Table 14.4. The interval you specify determines what time period is added or subtracted (a second value, minute value, or whatever). The *number* value specifies how many of the interval values you want to add. Make *interval* positive if you want to add to a date; make *interval* negative if you want to subtract from a date. The *oldDate* is the date or time from which you want to work (the date or time you're adding to or subtracting from). The *oldDate* doesn't change. The `DateAdd()` function then returns the new date.

Suppose that you buy something today with a credit card that has a 25-day grace period. The following statement adds 25 days to today's date and stores the result in `intStarts`:

```
intStarts = DateAdd("y", 25, Now)
```

The date stored in `intStarts` is the date 25 days from today.

▼ **NOTE**
You can use either `"y"`, `"d"`, or `"w"` for the interval if you're adding days to a date. ▲

Suppose that you work for a company that requires 10 years before you're vested in the retirement program. The following statement adds 10 years to your start date and stores the vested date in `vested`:

```
vested = DateAdd("yyyy", 10, hired)
```

Notice that the interval string value determines what's added to the date.

TIP For any of the date arithmetic functions, if you don't specify a year, the current year (the year set on the system's clock) is returned.

The *DateDiff()* Function

The `DateDiff()` function returns the difference between two dates. Embed `DateDiff()` inside `Abs()` if you want to ensure a positive value. The difference is expressed in the interval that you specify. Here's the syntax of `DateDiff()`:

```
DateDiff(interval, date1, date2)
```

The following statement determines how many years an employee has worked for a company:

```
beenWith = Abs(DateDiff("yyyy", hireDate, Now))
```

The *DatePart()* Function

`DatePart()` returns a part of a date (the part specified by the interval). With `DatePart()`, you can find on what day, month, week, or hour (or whatever other interval you specify) a date falls. Here's the syntax of `DatePart()`:

```
DatePart(interval, date)
```

The following statement stores the day number that an employee started working:

```
DatePart("w", hireDate)
```

Working with Serial Date and Time Values

Although you may not know about serial values, the date and time functions you've been reading about work with serial values. A *serial value* is the internal representation of a date or time, stored in a `VarType 7` (the `Date` data type) or a `Variant` data type. These values actually are stored as double-precision values to ensure the full storage of date and time and that accurate date arithmetic can be performed.

Here's the syntax of the `DateSerial()` function:

```
DateSerial(year, month, day)
```

year is an integer year number (either 00 to 99 for 1900 to 1999, or a four-digit year number) or expression; *month* is an integer month number (1 to 12) or expression; and *day* is an integer day number (1 to 31) or expression. If you include an expression for any of the integer arguments, you specify the number of years, months, or days from or since a value. To clarify the serial argument expressions, you use the following two `DateSerial()` function calls, which return the same value:

```
d = DateSerial(1998, 10, 6)
```

```
d = DateSerial(1988+10, 12-2, 1+5)
```

The `DateSerial()` functions ensure that your date arguments don't go out of bounds. For example, 1996 was a leap year, so February 1996 had 29 days. However, the following `DateSerial()` function call appears to produce an invalid date because February, even in leap years, can't have 30 days:

```
d = DateSerial(1996, 2, 29+1)
```

Nothing is wrong with this function call because `DateSerial()` adjusts the date evaluated so that **d** holds March 1, 1996, one day following the last day of February.

The `DateValue()` function is similar to `DateSerial()`, except that `DateValue()` accepts a string argument, as the following syntax shows:

```
DateValue(stringDateExpression)
```

stringDateExpression must be a string that VB recognizes as a date (such as those for the **Date** statement described earlier in this topic section). If you ask the user to enter a date a value at a time (asking for the year, then the month, and then the day), you can use `DateValue()` to convert those values to an internal serial date. If you ask the user to enter a full date (that you capture into a string variable) such as October 19, 1999, `DateValue()` converts that string to the serial format needed for dates.

The `TimeSerial()` and `TimeValue()` functions work the same as their date counterparts. If you have three individual values for a time of day, `TimeSerial()` converts those values to an internal time format (the **Variant** or **VarType 7**). Here's the syntax of `TimeSerial()`:

```
TimeSerial(hour, minute, second)
```

`TimeSerial()` accepts expressions for any of its arguments and adjusts those expressions as needed, just as `DateSerial()` does.

If you have a string with a time value (maybe the user entered the time), `TimeValue()` converts that string to a time value with this syntax:

```
TimeValue(stringTimeExpression)
```

`Day()`, `Month()`, and `Year()` each convert their date arguments (of **Variant** or **VarType 7** data type) to a day number, month number, or year number. These three functions are simple:

```
Day(dateArgument)
Month(dateArgument)
Year(dateArgument)
```

Also, `Weekday()` returns the number of the day of the week (refer to Table 14.4) for the date argument passed to it.

Pass today's date (found with **Now**) to `Day()`, `Month()`, and `Year()` as shown here:

```
d = Day(Now)
m = Month(Now)
y = Year(Now)
```

The current date's day of week number (refer to Table 14.4), month number, and year are stored in the three variables.

The *Format()* Function

One of the most powerful and complex functions, `Format()`, returns its argument in a different format from how the argument was passed. Here's the syntax of `Format()`:

```
Format(expression, format)
```

`Format()` returns a `Variant` data type that you'll almost always use as a string. The expression can be any numeric or string expression. You can format all kinds of data—numbers, strings, dates, and times—to look different. For example, you might want to print check amounts with commas and a dollar sign.

The format is a string variable or expression that contains one or more of the display-format characters shown in Tables 14.5 through 14.7. The table that you use depends on the kind of data (string, numeric, or date) that you want to format. The tables are long, but after looking at a few examples, you'll learn how to use the display-format characters.

Table 14.5   The String Display-Format Characters

Symbol	Description
@	A character appears in the output at the @ position. If there's no character at the @'s position in the string, a blank appears. The @ fills (if there are more than one) from right to left.
&	This character is just like @, except that nothing appears if no character at the &'s position appears in the string being printed.
!	The exclamation point forces all placeholder characters (the @ and &) to fill from left to right.
<	Less-than forces all characters to lowercase.
>	Greater-than forces all characters to uppercase.

Table 14.6 The Numeric Display-Format Characters

Symbol	Description
Null string, " "	This string displays the number without formatting.
0	A digit appears in the output at the 0 position if a digit appears in the number being formatted. If no digit is at the 0's position, a 0 appears. If not as many zeros in the number are being formatted as there are zeros in the format field, leading or trailing zeros print. If the number contains more numeric positions, the 0 forces all digits to the right of the decimal point to round to the display-format's pattern and all digits to the left print as is. You mostly use this display-format character to print leading or trailing zeros when you want them.
#	The pound-sign character works like 0, except that nothing appears if the number being formatted doesn't have as many digits as the display format has #'s.
.	The period specifies how many digits (by its placement within 0 or #'s) are to appear to the left and right of a decimal point.
%	The number being formatted is multiplied by 100, and the percent sign (%) is printed at its position inside the display-format string.
,	If a comma appears among 0's or #'s, the thousands are easier to read because the comma groups every three places in the number (unless the number is below 1,000). If you put two commas together, you request that the number be divided by 1,000 (to scale down the number).
E-, E+, e-, e+	The number is formatted into scientific notation if the format also contains at least one 0 or #.
:	The colon causes colons to appear between a time's hour, minute, and second values.
/	The slash ensures that slashes are printed between a date's day, month, and year values.
-, +, $, space	All these characters appear as is in their position within the formatted string.
\	Whatever character follows the backslash appears at its position in the formatted string.

Table 14.7 The Date Display-Format Characters

Symbol	Description
c	Displays either the date (just like the **ddddd** symbol if only a date appears), the time (just like **ttttt** if only a time appears), or both if both values are present.
d	Displays the day number from 1 to 31.
dd	Displays the day number with a leading zero from 01 to 31.
ddd	Displays an abbreviated three-character day from **Sun** to **Sat**.
dddd	Displays the full day name from **Sunday** to **Saturday**.
ddddd	Displays the date (month, day, year) according to your settings in the International section of your Control Panel's Short Date format (usually *m/d/yy*).
dddddd	Displays the date (month, day, year) according to your settings in the International section of your Control Panel's Long Date format (usually *mmmm dd, yyyy*).
w, ww	See Table 14.4.
m	Displays the month number from **1** to **12**. The **m** also means minute if it follows an **h** or **hh**.
mm	Displays the month number with a leading zero from **01** to **12**. The **mm** also means minute if it follows an **h** or **hh**.
mmm	Displays the abbreviated month name from **Jan** to **Dec**.
mmmm	Displays the full month name from **January** to **December**.
q	Displays the quarter of the year.
y	Displays the year's day number from 1 to **366**.
yy	Displays the two-digit year from **00** to **99** (when the year 2000 hits, **yy** *still* returns only the 2-digit year).
yyyy	Displays the full year number from **1000** to **9999**.
h, n, s	See Table 14.4.
ttttt	Displays the time according to your settings in the International section of your Control Panel's Time format (usually *h:nn:ss*).
AMPM	Uses the 12-hour clock time and displays **AM** or **PM**.
ampm	Uses the 12-hour clock time and displays **am** or **pm**.
AP	Uses the 12-hour clock time and displays **A** or **P**.
ap	Uses the 12-hour clock time and displays **a** or **p**.

The following statements demonstrate the string display-format characters. The remarks to the right of each statement explain that the target variable (the variable on the left of the equal sign) is receiving formatted data.

```
strS = Format("AbcDef", ">")   ' ABCDEF is assigned
strS = Format("AbcDef", "<")   ' abcdef is assigned
strS = Format("2325551212", "(@@@) @@@-@@@@") ' (232) 555-1212
```

As the last statement shows, you can put string data into the format you prefer. If the data to be formatted, such as the phone number in the last line, is a string variable from a table's text field, the `Format()` statement works just the same.

Suppose that it's possible to leave out the area code of the phone number that you want to print. `Format()` fills from right to left, so the statement

```
strS = Format("5551212", "(@@@) @@@-@@@@")
```

stores the following in `strS`:

```
(   ) 555-1212
```

If you had included the area code, it would have printed inside the parentheses.

Only use the `!` when you want the fill to take place from the other direction (when data at the end of the string being formatted might be missing). The statement

```
strS = Format("5551212", "!(@@@) @@@-@@@@")
```

incorrectly stores the following in `strS`:

```
(555) 121-2
```

Example   The function in Listing 14.4 contains an interesting use of the `DateSerial()` function:

Listing 14.4   Duedate.bas: Calculate the Next Weekday Value After a Specified Date

```
Function DueDate (anyDate)
' Accepts: a Date value
' Purpose: Calculates the first non-weekend day of the month
```

continues

Listing 14.4 Continued

```
'            following the specified date
' Returns: the calculated date

    Dim Result

    If Not IsNull(anyDate) Then
        Result = DateSerial(Year(anyDate), Month(anyDate) + 1, 1)
        If Weekday(Result) = 1 Then      ' Sunday, so add one day.
            DueDate = Result + 1
        ElseIf Weekday(Result) = 7 Then  ' Saturday, so add two days.
            DueDate = Result + 2
        Else
            DueDate = Result
        End If
    Else
        Result = Null
    End If
End Function
```

When this function is called, it's passed a date value stored in the `Variant` or `VarType 7 Date` data type. As the remarks tell, the function computes the number of the first weekday (2 for Monday through 6 for Friday) of the next month (the first business day of the month following the argument).

Next Step The following statements demonstrate how numeric formatting works. The remark to the right of each statement describes how the data is formatted.

```
strS = Format(9146, "¦######¦")   ' ¦9146¦ is stored
strS = Format(2652.2, "00000.00") ' 02652.20 is stored
strS = Format(2652.2, "#####.##") ' 2652.2 is stored
strS = Format(2652.216, "#####.##") ' 2652.22 is stored
strS = Format(45, "+###")  ' Stores a +45
strS = Format(45, "-###")  ' Stores a -45
strS = Format(45, "###-")  ' Stores a 45-
strS = Format(2445, "$####.##")   ' Stores a $2445.
strS = Format(2445, "$####.00")   ' Stores a $2445.00
strS = Format(2445, "00Hi00")  ' Stores 24Hi45
```

The following statements demonstrate how date and time formatting works. The remark to the right of each statement describes how the data is formatted.

```
Dim d As Variant
d = Now       ' Assume the date and time is
              ' May 21, 1999 2:30 PM
strND = Format(d, "c") ' Stores 5/21/99 2:30:02 PM
strND = Format(d, "w") ' Stores 6 (for Friday)
strND = Format(d, "ww")' Stores 22
strND = Format(d, "dddd") ' Stores Friday
strND = Format(d, "q") ' Stores 2
strND = Format(d, "hh") ' Stores 14
strND = Format(d, "h AM/PM") ' Stores 2 PM
strND = Format(d, "hh AM/PM") ' Stores 02 PM
strND = Format(d, "d-mmmm h:nn:ss")  'Stores  21-May 14:30:02
```

Summary

Pt **II**

Hr **14**

As you've seen this hour, Visual Basic supplies many built-in functions. These functions save you work; you don't have to take the time to write the code yourself, but instead can call on these functions to do the work for you. You may not use all these functions, but some prove useful as you program in Visual Basic.

Most of the built-in functions require parentheses after their names. The parentheses are where you pass to the function the data (the arguments) to work on.

Several numeric functions work with integers. These functions primarily round non-integer data to integer results. Other numeric functions exist to convert data to different data types for you. The random statement and function generate random numbers for you.

The Len() function serves as a bridge between the numeric and string functions. It's the only function that works with string and numeric arguments by returning the length (the number of characters of storage) of the argument. Many string functions return portions (such as the leftmost or rightmost characters) of strings. These functions are sometimes called *substring functions*.

The functions and statements described this hour almost all work with an internal Date data type. Visual Basic recognizes most date formats, and whether you spell out a month name when entering a date is up to you because Visual Basic can interpret the date. The last part of this lesson explained how to format your data so that it appears on-screen the way you want. Formatting doesn't change the data itself, but the `Format()` function changes the way your data looks to the user.

Hour 15 begins a new part of the book, "Intermediate VB Programming." Now that you have the language details out of the way, it's time to have fun working with advanced controls on forms.

Hour 14 Quiz

You can find the answers for the following questions on the accompanying CD-ROM and on the Virtual Classroom Web site.

On the CD

1. What happens if an argument is too big to be converted with a data type conversion function?

2. What value does the following function call return?

   ```
   CVar(Null)
   ```

3. Why do you usually need the `Randomize` statement when you use `Rnd()`?

4. **True or false:** If the following statement appeared in the first procedure executed within a module, the next `Rnd()` function call would produce a different result virtually every time the module is run.

   ```
   Randomize Timer
   ```

5. **True or false:** Both `UCase()` and `LCase()` change their arguments.

6. How can you tell whether the use of `Mid()` is a function or a statement?

7. Without looking at the ASCII table in Appendix B, what's stored in n after the following statement finishes?

   ```
   n = Asc(Chr(192))
   ```

8. What's the difference between the `Now` function and the `Time` function?

9. What's stored in the variable named `strS` in each of the following statements?

   ```
   A. strS = Format("74135", "&&&&&-&&&&")  ' Too short
                                            ' ZIPcode?

   B. strS = Format(d, "h am/pm")

   C. strS = Format(12345.67, "######.###")
   ```

Hour 14 Homework Exercises

1. Create a new project with a blank form named `frmNums`. Write a `For...Next` loop that passes the following series of numbers to `Int()`, `Fix()`, and `CInt()`:

   -2.0   -1.5   -1.0   -0.5   0   0.5   1.0   1.5   2.0

   Use a `Step` value of 0.5 and print each result directly on the form in the immediate execution window with a `Print` statement like this:

   ```
   frmNums.Print Int(val), Fix(val), CInt(val)
   ```

   Study the results to learn how each function varies from each other.

   This is the first time you've sent output directly to a form. The `Print` command is called a *method*; by applying the `Print` method to a form, separating the components with a period, you can write directly to a form. Such output is usually too messy for an application, but this exercise is only printing a list of values, so printing to the form was much easier than trying to display the results in a list of labels. Hour 16, "Using Form Types," explains more about printing data directly onto forms.

2. Change the number-guessing procedure to add a counter that begins at 1 and increments every time the user guesses incorrectly. In the ending message box, print the number of times the user guessed. Concatenate the number of guesses to the message.

3. Write a function that encrypts whatever string is passed to it and returns the encrypted string. Use `Asc()` and `Chr()` to add 1 to the ASCII value of each character before concatenating the encrypted character to the return string.

► **PART**

Intermediate VB Programming

Interacting with Users

THIS LESSON BRINGS YOU back to the really fun stuff! You deserve congratulations because you got through the hard-core language section of this night-school course. Your only requirement now is to master as many controls as you can so that you can combine the new controls with the programming language tools to build extensive applications.

This hour's lesson takes you on a tour of several new controls. Many of the controls that you have yet to master require some programming. For example, you can't fill a drop-down list box with items until runtime. You can initialize some controls, such as labels, but you can't initialize many of the multivalued controls. The multivalued controls (such as list boxes) require some programming.

Even some of the single-valued controls require some background work on your part if you place them on your form's applications. The Check Box and Option Button controls require that your program check their status and maintain order as needed.

Topic 1: Option Buttons and Check Boxes

Although somewhat similar to the command button, option buttons and check boxes require some additional programming to make them functional in working applications. The nature of a Check Box control is that it's on or off like a light switch. When a Check Box control is selected, it contains a check mark; when not selected, a check box is empty. Option buttons work the same way because they show either an on or off state. Unlike check boxes, however, two or more option buttons in a set can never be on at the same time. Whereas users can click as many check boxes as needed, they can't click multiple option buttons that appear together in the same set on the same form.

▶▶ FAST TRACK

Have you programmed check boxes and option boxes in earlier versions of Visual Basic? If so, jump to the next topic section, "List Box Controls" (p. 371). Have you worked with all of Visual Basic's list controls in the past? If so, Visual Basic 5 doesn't add much functionality to these controls (except for the DownPicture property, which you should check out on the online help), so you can move onto the next hour's lesson, "Creating VB Forms" (p. 387).

Overview   Check boxes and option buttons naturally go well together in the same topic section when you learn Visual Basic. Their similarities are more common than other controls. Nevertheless, their slightly different nature requires that you, in the background with program code, make sure that users have checked the appropriate button or box when needed. You'll learn how to place and manage check boxes and option buttons in this topic section. You'll also learn how to use code to test and modify their behavior.

Working with Check Boxes

Remember that a check box is either on or off. The check mark that appears inside the check box indicates its status. Actually, you use check boxes to indicate one of two states that may be on or off but might also represent other kinds of binary possibilities. Check boxes indicate the following kinds of conditions:

- On or Off
- Yes or No
- True or False

A check box's `Value` property is set to 1 or 0 depending on whether the check box is checked. The descriptive label you use next to the check box lets users know why and when to check the box.

▼ NOTE

Remember that your application can contain multiple check boxes on the same form. Users can check as many or as few as needed. **▲**

Pt **III**

Hr **15**

Figure 15.1 shows a sample form from the Controls sample application that comes with Visual Basic. In Figure 15.1, both check boxes are clicked, indicating in this case that users want to see the text boldfaced and italicized. If you run this application yourself (look in the \VB\Samples\PGuide folder for the Controls application), you'll see that as you click the check boxes on and off, the text format changes to reflect the check boxes you've set. When you click a check box, the check mark appears or disappears, depending on the check box's state at the time you click the control.

FIG. 15.1

Two check boxes are checked.

TIP You don't have to click over the actual check box; you can click the check box's caption to mark or unmark the check box.

You don't have to supply a label for the check boxes. The check box Properties window contains a `Caption` property that you can initialize at design time. Also, Visual Basic takes care of displaying the check mark or removing the check mark as users click the check box. Your only programming requirement is to respond to the check box's `Click` event (in the `Click` event procedure) and make the adjustment necessary when the check box changes.

Here's the complete event procedure from Figure 15.1's sample code that executes every time users click the check box labeled <u>B</u>old:

```
Private Sub chkBold_Click()
' The Click event occurs when the check box changes state.
' Value property indicates the new state of the check box.
    If chkBold.Value = 1 Then      ' If checked.
        txtDisplay.FontBold = True
    Else                           ' If not checked.
        txtDisplay.FontBold = False
    End If
End Sub
```

The check box's `Name` property contains `chkBold`, so the event procedure that executes when users click the check box is named `chkBold_Click()`. All check boxes have a `Value` property that contains 1 if the check box is now checked, 0 if the check box isn't checked due to the event's click. This code simply changes the text box's `FontBold` property to `True` or `False` depending on whether users marked the check box.

Table 15.1 lists a few of the Check Box control's most important properties that you'll work with.

Table 15.1   Important Check Box Properties

Property	Description
Alignment	Determines whether the caption appears to the left or right of the check box
Caption	Holds the caption displayed next to the check box (you can insert an ampersand, &, before the hotkey letter)
DownPicture	Contains a path name of a graphic image to display when users click the check box
Value	Holds 0 for unchecked or 1 for checked; you can change this at runtime by assigning a different value to the Check Box control

The example at the end of this topic section walks you through the creation of an application that uses several check boxes.

Working with Option Buttons

Option buttons work much like Check Box controls. Each button is a two-state button indicating whether an option is selected or not. Figure 15.2 shows the sample Controls application with two option buttons selected.

Pt **III**
Hr **15**

FIG. 15.2
Two option buttons are selected.

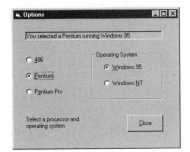

The primary difference between option buttons and check boxes is that only one option button can be selected at any one time. (The option buttons are said to be *mutually exclusive*.) Visual Basic takes care of the selection—that is, when your application's users click an option button and then click another option button, Visual Basic deselects the first one and allows only one single button to be selected at one time.

▼ NOTE

Rarely, if ever, would you need to place only a single option button on a form. When a single option button is selected, users have no way to deselect it. One option button is always selected on a form. If you need a single yes-or-no decision to be added to a form, use a Check Box control. ▲

TIP Some people call option buttons *radio buttons* because of their similarity to some car radios, whose pushbutton channel selector allows for only one station at a time to play.

But wait, doesn't Figure 15.2 show two option buttons selected? The figure shows two sets of option buttons! More accurately, the figure contains a *frame* that holds option buttons. Only one option button can be selected within a single frame at any one time. Therefore, you can put multiple sets, or frames, of option buttons on a form, and Visual Basic makes sure that users can select only one option button from a frame at a time.

In Figure 15.2, the frame is the boxed area labeled Operating System that holds option buttons. Therefore, Visual Basic allows only one of these two option buttons to be selected at one time. The three option buttons labeled 486, Pentium, and Pentium Pro appear outside the frame on the form. When option buttons don't reside in a frame but just on the form, every one of those option buttons is considered one set. Therefore, only one of those option buttons can be selected (set to `True`) at once.

▼ **NOTE**

Through the option button's `Value` property, to which you can assign `True` or `False` at runtime or design time, you can set up option buttons so that none are selected. After users select the first one, however, Visual Basic won't let them deselect all of them again. ▲

Before you add an option button, add a Frame control to your form everywhere you want a set of option buttons. The frame forms the background for the option buttons. In Visual Basic, a frame is known as a container. After you add a Frame control that will contain option buttons, you can then add the option buttons. As the example at the end of this topic section will show, you can't add an option button control directly to a frame. After you add an option button to the form, you must cut it from the form and then paste it onto the frame. You'll add additional option buttons to the frame in this manner until you've completed the form.

Because the Option Button control supports the same properties as the Check Box control, you can refer to Table 15.1 for properties to use with the Option Button control.

Example This example creates a series of check boxes that display various icons of countries. From the File menu choose New Project to create a new project. Increase the size of the Form window and the form so that the form consumes most of the screen space, fitting comfortably within the Form window while still giving room to the Toolbox.

Follow these steps to create the application:

1. Double-click the Check Box control to add a check box to the center of the form (see Figure 15.3). (You'll have to move the check box to another location.) Check boxes first appear with the name `Check1`.

FIG. 15.3
The check box appears in the center of the form.

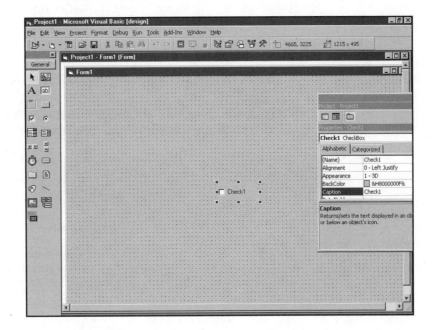

2. Change the control's name to `chkEngland` by entering the new name in the Properties window's `Name` property. If you don't see the Project window, press Ctrl+R (to choose Project Explorer from the View menu) and adjust the window so that you can see enough properties to work in the window.

3. Type **&England** for the check box's `Caption` property.

4. Click the Image control.

5. Click and drag the new Image control to the left of the `chkEngland` check box. Make the image's outline approximately the same height as the check box and draw a square image.

6. Name the Image control `imgEngland`.

7. Set `imgEngland`'s `Visible` property to `False` to hide the image when the program begins.

Pt **III**

Hr **15**

8. Click the Image control's `Picture` property's ellipsis to display the Load Picture dialog box. Select the Visual Basic folder (if it isn't already open), the Graphics folder, the Icons folder, and then the Flags folder. Double-click the CTRUK.ICO icon file. (You, in effect, entered \DevStudio\VB\Graphics\Icons\Flags\CTRUK.ICO in the Image control's `Picture` property to point the property to the icon.) Your Form window should look something like the one in Figure 15.4.

FIG. 15.4

England's picture appears in the Image control.

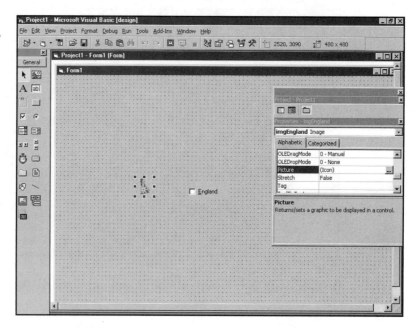

9. Double-click the check box to open its `Click` event procedure. Enter the following code (Visual Basic writes the first and last line for you):

```
Private Sub chkEngland_Click ()
   ' Displays the flag if checked
   If chkEngland.Value = 1 Then
     imgEngland.Visible = True
   Else
     imgEngland.Visible = False
   End If
End Sub
```

10. Run the application and click the England check box. The picture of England alternatively appears and disappears due to the `If` statement in the body of the event procedure.

One simple check box doesn't demonstrate check boxes as well as a series of check boxes would. If you want to add to this lesson's project, you can add additional check boxes and images to the form to display additional foreign country flags.

To add additional check boxes, create five more check boxes and five more image boxes according to the information in Tables 15.2 and 15.3 (the tables include England's check box and image that you've already added). Make certain that you set the **Value** property of all the check boxes to 0 so that the application begins with no checked boxes.

Table 15.2 Check Box Properties for More Countries

Control Type	Control Name	Value	Caption
Check Box	chkEngland	0	&England
Check Box	chkItaly	0	&Italy
Check Box	chkSpain	0	&Spain
Check Box	chkMexico	0	&Mexico
Check Box	chkFrance	0	&France
Check Box	chkUSA	0	&USA

Table 15.3 Image Properties for More Countries

Control Type	Control Name	Visible	Image*
Image	imgEngland	False	CTRUK.ICO
Image	imgItaly	False	CTRITALY.ICO
Image	imgSpain	False	CTRSPAIN.ICO
Image	imgMexico	False	CTRMEX.ICO
Image	imgFrance	False	CTRFRAN.ICO
Image	imgUSA	False	CTRUSA.ICO

*All pictures come from the directory \DevStudio\VB\Grahics\Icons\Flags.

After you assemble these controls into the order and placement shown in Figure 15.5, you're ready to add the event procedures for the controls. Notice that Figure 15.5 shows the check boxes to the left of the images.

FIG. 15.5
The completed form appears with six sets of controls.

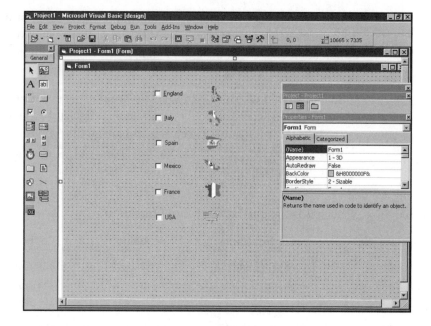

 On the CD Listing 15.1 contains the complete event procedure listing for each control (including England's control set, which you've already added).

Listing 15.1 Checked.bas: Code for the Check Box Control Application

```
Private Sub chkEngland_Click()
  ' Displays the flag if checked
  If chkEngland.Value = 1 Then
    imgEngland.Visible = True
  Else
    imgEngland.Visible = False
  End If
End Sub

Private Sub chkItaly_Click()
  ' Displays the flag if checked
  If chkItaly.Value = 1 Then
    imgItaly.Visible = True
  Else
    imgItaly.Visible = False
  End If
End Sub
```

```
Private Sub chkSpain_Click()
  ' Displays the flag if checked
  If chkSpain.Value = 1 Then
    imgSpain.Visible = True
  Else
    imgSpain.Visible = False
  End If
End Sub

Private Sub chkMexico_Click()
  ' Displays the flag if checked
  If chkMexico.Value = 1 Then
    imgMexico.Visible = True
  Else
    imgMexico.Visible = False
  End If
End Sub

Private Sub chkFrance_Click()
  ' Displays the flag if checked
  If chkFrance.Value = 1 Then
    imgFrance.Visible = True
  Else
    imgFrance.Visible = False
  End If
End Sub

Private Sub chkUSA_Click()
  ' Displays the flag if checked
  If chkUSA.Value = 1 Then
    imgUSA.Visible = True
  Else
    imgUSA.Visible = False
  End If
End Sub
```

TIP   One of the easiest ways to add the code is to copy England's code to the Clipboard, paste the Clipboard below the last event procedure, and then modify the code to fit the next country.

Figure 15.6 shows the running application. You can check more than one check box, as shown in the figure.

FIG. 15.6
*Running the
program shows
multiple check
boxes selected
at once.*

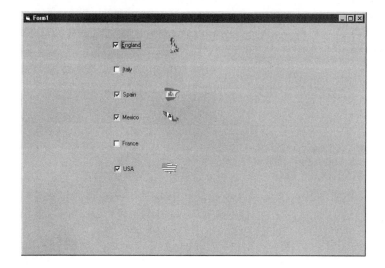

Next Step Suppose that you showed the preceding example's application to a friend
who wanted to see only one flag at a time. Although you can add substantial logic to check for multiple selected check boxes and allow only the
most recent check box to remain selected, you can more easily change the
check boxes to option buttons (on a frame). Although the application contains only a single set of option buttons, the frame will give you practice in
placing controls on a frame.

Follow these steps to convert the application to an option button-based
application:

1. From the Form window, delete all the check boxes. You can click each
   one and press Delete, or select all of them by "lassoing" them with
   the mouse (to select all of them) and then press Delete once.

2. From the <u>V</u>iew menu choose <u>C</u>ode to display the form module code.
   When you delete controls, Visual Basic doesn't delete the event procedure code associated with those controls but moves such code into
   the General section of the form module. Highlight all the code (by
   pressing Ctrl+A, the shortcut key) and press Delete.

3. Add a Frame control to the form. Size the frame to the approximate
   area and location of the check boxes that you deleted. You'll place
   option buttons on the frame now.

4. Add the six option buttons. For each button, click the Option Button tool and then drag a small rectangle onto the frame at the location of the control. (If you double-click the control to place the control in the center of the form, you'll have to cut and paste the control onto the frame, as mentioned at the end of this topic section.)

5. Change the frame's name to `fraCountries` and the frame's `Caption` to Countries.

6. Change the option buttons' properties to those in Table 15.4.

Table 15.4 Option Button Properties for the Countries

Control Name	Caption	Value
optEngland	England	False
optItaly	Italy	False
optSpain	Spain	False
optMexico	Mexico	False
optFrance	France	False
optUSA	USA	False

Pt **III**

Hr **15**

7. Add a new event procedure for each control. Inside England's event procedure, the code will look like this:

```
Private Sub optEngland_Click()
  ' Displays appropriate flag
  Clear_Flags    ' Calls the Clear_Flags proc
  If optEngland.Value = True Then
    imgEngland.Visible = True
  End If
End Sub
```

`Clear_Flags` is a subroutine procedure call. (The `Call` keyword is optional if you're passing no parameters. Also, you don't use parentheses when you omit `Call`.) You'll write the `Clear_Flags` general procedure in step 9.

8. By using the Clipboard, make five more copies of the code and change the country name in each to finish the option button control code.

9. Although Visual Basic takes care of setting and resetting option button values when users click the buttons, VB hasn't connected the option buttons in any way to the images. Therefore, each event procedure first clears all images from the form by calling the `Clear_Flags()` procedure. Type the following code at the top of the module before the first event procedure:

```
Private Sub Clear_Flags()
   imgUSA.Visible = False
   imgSpain.Visible = False
   imgMexico.Visible = False
   imgFrance.Visible = False
   imgEngland.Visible = False
   imgItaly.Visible = False
End Sub
```

Visual Basic automatically puts `Clear_Flags()` in the form module's General section.

10. Run the application and click different option buttons. As you click one, Visual Basic deselects any other that might already be clicked, and you'll see the appropriate icon thanks to this application's code. Figure 15.7 shows the result of clicking one of the option buttons.

FIG. 15.7
You can select only one option button at a time.

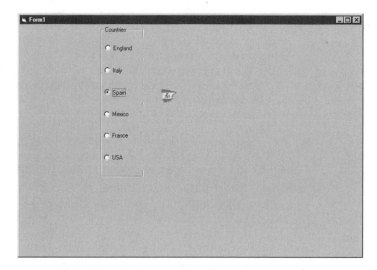

Topic 2: List Box Controls

The List Box and Combo Box controls both work to relieve users from typing. These controls vary from the other controls you've seen because they display multiple values in a list. The controls let you exercise a greater degree of power over the data that users input. Certain kinds of list boxes let users not only select items from a list, but also add items to the list.

Overview   The List Box and Combo Box controls both operate on a principle that mirrors that of arrays. Therefore, you can use the knowledge you now possess with arrays to understand lists more quickly. Here's an overview of these two important controls:

- *List boxes* provide a simple list of choices. The programmer initializes the list, and users aren't allowed to enter data into the list.

- *Combo boxes* offer a cross between text boxes and list boxes. Users can select from the list and, optionally, add items to the list. Visual Basic supports three kinds of combo boxes: drop-down combo boxes act like text boxes that open by dropping down their list when selected; simple combo boxes act like text boxes that remain open just as list boxes do; and drop-down list boxes let users select from a list but not edit any items in the list.

Pt **III**

Hr **15**

List Box Controls

The simplest list control is the regular list box. To add a List Box control to your form, click the List Box tool on the Toolbox. The list box gives your users a way to select one or more items from a list of choices. The only requirement is that you initialize the list box's choices with Visual Basic code.

Consider the following code:

```
Private Sub Form_Load()
  ' Executes when the form loads
  lstFirstList.AddItem "Chicago"
  lstFirstList.AddItem "Dallas"
  lstFirstList.AddItem "Seattle"
  lstFirstList.AddItem "Washington"
  lstFirstList.AddItem "Houston"
  lstFirstList.AddItem "Dayton"
End Sub
```

When you run your application, the runtime module initially loads the form (or forms, if you have multiple forms). Forms support a `Load` event that occurs when the form loads. Through the `Load` and `Unload` Visual Basic form commands, you can specify exactly when in an application a form is to load or to go away from the application to free up resources. (Hour 16 explains the form `Load` and `Unload` events in more detail.)

The form's `Load` event procedure is a nice place to initialize your form's list box items. If you wait much longer, the list box appears on the form empty. You use the `AddItem` method to add items to the list box.

A *method* is kind of like a built-in function. Visual Basic supplies all the methods you'll use. All methods, unlike functions, appear with certain objects. The list box object supports several methods, as do the other controls. You'll always trigger an object's method with this format in your Visual Basic code:

```
ObjectName.MethodName
```

The `AddItem` method is one of the most important list box methods because it adds items to the list. Therefore, if your list box is named `lstFirstList`, you specify that list box's `AddItem` method, as shown in the preceding `Form_Load()` subroutine; add the item you want to put in the list with the `AddItem` method followed by the item to add. Visual Basic adds the items to the list in the order your code adds the items, unless you change the list box's `Sorted` property to `True`, in which case Visual Basic sorts the items in the list alphabetically or numerically as you add items.

The dot (.) notation is common for methods in other languages such as C++. The dot tells the method to operate on the object to the left of the dot. In other words, this line

```
lstFirstList.AddItem "Seattle"
```

makes Visual Basic add Seattle to the next item in the list box named `lstFirstList`.

▼ **NOTE**
Sometimes, one of Visual Basic's most difficult aspects is distinguishing between commands, declarations, methods, properties, and controls. Things heat up even more when you learn about classes in Hour 20, "Understanding Objects and Using the Object Browser" (p. 469). Think of methods as requests that an item makes to itself. `lstFirstList.AddItem` `"Seattle"` is saying, "Add an item named Seattle to me." As a list box,

`lstFirstList` knows how to fulfill this request because Visual Basic's designers added this method to the list box's repertoire of methods. (Most controls have their own set of methods available.) ▲

Assuming that a List Box control named `lstFirstList` appears in the center of the form that contains the previous `Form_Load()` form procedure, the list box will appear, with its city names, like the one shown in Figure 15.8.

FIG. 15.8
The list box holds the added items.

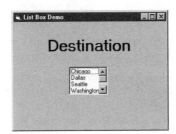

Figure 15.8 shows a label with the caption Destination. Because list boxes don't include such a caption, you must add one when you want to label the list box's contents.

Vertical and possibly horizontal scroll bars appear in the list box if you place the list box control on the form and the height (or width) of the list box isn't sufficient to display all the list items that you add. Also, if the list box can display all the items but the application later adds more items, Visual Basic adds the scroll bars when they become needed.

So far, you've learned only how to display the list box with items inside the list. Although adding items to the list and displaying them is important, your program needs to know which item, if any, users select. The whole purpose of a list box is to let users select an item from a list of choices rather than have to type a value.

When users select an item in the list, the following things happen:

- The item changes color to highlight the selection.
- Visual Basic copies the selection into the list box's `Text` property. Therefore, `lstFirstList.Text` changes during the application's execution, depending on which item users click.

To demonstrate the list box's **Text** property, consider what would happen if you added a text box to the application shown previously in Figure 15.8. If the text box were named **txtCity**, the following procedure sends the selected list box item to the text box as soon as users click (to select) an item in the list box named **lstFirstList**:

```
Private Sub lstFirstList_Click()
  ' Copy the selected item to the text box
  txtCity.Text = lstFirstList.Text
End Sub
```

If you were writing such an application, you would want to erase the text box's **Text** property in the Properties window at design time so that nothing appears in the text box until users select an item. Also, the text box's default **Font** property almost always needs to be changed because the default **Font** property setting is too small.

Figure 15.9 shows the result of selecting one of the list box items and sending that selected item to the text box.

FIG. 15.9

The selected item appears in the text box.

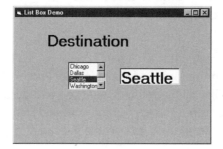

List box items have index values that work like array subscripts. The index starts at 0 for the first item and increases. The list box's **ListIndex** property holds the value of the currently selected list box item. You can, therefore, determine which value is selected. Often, you may fill a list box with values from an array and the one-to-one correspondence to arrays make the selected index item useful for analysis. Other list box methods, such as the **RemoveItem** method, use the **ListIndex** property to remove items you want removed from the list. For example, to remove the third list box item, your program would do this:

```
lstFirstList.RemoveItem 2
```

To demonstrate the `ListIndex` property, Figure 15.10 shows the same application as before with one additional text box that holds the index of the selected item.

FIG. 15.10
*The selected
item's*
`ListIndex`
now appears.

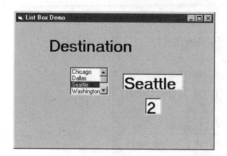

The modified `lstFirstList_Click()`'s code that will send the index to the new text box appears here:

```
Private Sub lstFirstList_Click()
  ' Copy the selected item to the first text box
  ' Copy the selected index to the second text box
  txtCity.Text = lstFirstList.Text
  txtIndex.Text = lstFirstList.ListIndex
End Sub
```

Pt **III**

Hr **15**

Example Some list boxes provide lists from which users may need to select multiple items. For example, you might display a list box with a list of schools in your area, and users are to select one or more of the schools attended.

The List Box control contains the `MultiSelect` property. When you set this property to `1 - Simple` (as opposed to the default value, `0 - None`), users can select multiple values. If you set the `MultiSelect` property to `2 - Extended`, users can Shift+click to select a range of items and Ctrl+click to select disjointed items (just as you can do inside Windows Open dialog boxes).

Figure 15.11 shows an enhanced application from the one the preceding section showed. The enhanced application contains several new text boxes that display `Selected` when the corresponding list box item is selected, and `Not Selected` when the list box item isn't selected. The original list box now has its `MultiSelect` property set to `2 - Extended`.

FIG. 15.11
*Multiple selec-
tions in the list
box are now
possible.*

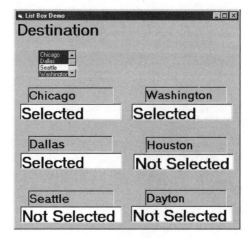

 On the CD The list box's `click()` procedure must be changed to reflect the changed text box format, as shown in Listing 15.2.

Listing 15.2   Clicktb.bas: Extending the Selection in a List Box

```
Private Sub lstFirstList_Click()
  ' Copy the selected item to the first text box
  ' Copy the selected index to the second text box
  If lstFirstList.Selected(0) Then
    txtChicago.Text = "Selected"
  Else
    txtChicago.Text = "Not Selected"
  End If

  If lstFirstList.Selected(1) Then
    txtDallas.Text = "Selected"
  Else
    txtDallas.Text = "Not Selected"
  End If

  If lstFirstList.Selected(2) Then
    txtSeattle.Text = "Selected"
  Else
    txtSeattle.Text = "Not Selected"
  End If

  If lstFirstList.Selected(3) Then
    txtWashington.Text = "Selected"
  Else
```

```
      txtWashington.Text = "Not Selected"
   End If

   If lstFirstList.Selected(4) Then
      txtHouston.Text = "Selected"
   Else
      txtHouston.Text = "Not Selected"
   End If

   If lstFirstList.Selected(5) Then
      txtDayton.Text = "Selected"
   Else
      txtDayton.Text = "Not Selected"
   End If

End Sub
```

When multiple selections are possible, Visual Basic must create a property array called `Selected`. In this case, the array ranges from `Selected(0)` to `Selected(5)` because six selections appear in the list box. The array values are `True` or `False`, depending on the selection. When the program first executes, all the `Selected` values are `False` because users haven't had a chance to select an item from the list box. As users select items, more values in the `Selected` array become `True`. The list box's `Click()` procedure updates all six text boxes every time users select another item.

▼ **NOTE**

If users deselect an item by clicking a selected item, that item's `Selected` value goes back to `False`. ▲

TIP Notice how the labels show a 3-D indented appearance. You can get this same label look by adding a fixed border around the label (change the `BorderStyle` property to `1 - Fixed Single`) and by changing `BackStyle` from `1 - Opaque` to `0 - Transparent` so that the form color shows through.

Next Step Users can't add values to a list box. A list box gains items only when the code inside the application uses the `AddItem` method to add additional items. Users also can't delete items. The code's `RemoveItem` method has to do the removal.

Suppose that you needed the application to remove all the items added so far to a list box. Although you could apply the `RemoveItem` method to each list box item, a `For...Next` loop makes more sense because you can code the loop as follows (given the previous example's list box):

```
' Removes the first 5 items from the list
For intI = 0 To 5
  lstFirstList.RemoveItem 0
Next intI
```

When using a `For...Next` loop, you must keep track of how many items are in the list. Because your code is what adds those items to the list, you should have no trouble keeping track of the count.

If, through programming, you give users a chance to add items to the list (by giving a data-entry text box and a command button that, when clicked, triggers the `AddItem` method), the list could grow but you can still keep track of the count through a variable that you add to or decrease every time an item goes to or comes off the list.

Fortunately, Microsoft thought of virtually everything. You really don't have to keep track of your list's items because Visual Basic internally keeps a count of the number of items in every list box within the application. The `ListCount` property keeps a running total of the number of items in the list. `ListCount` is always one greater than the highest `ListIndex` because `ListIndex` starts at 0. Therefore, any time you want to reference the entire list box with a `For...Next` loop, or any time you need to know the current total of list box items, you can use the `ListCount` property, as done in this loop:

```
' Removes all the items from the list
intTotal = lstFirstList.ListCount   ' Save number
For intI = 0 To intTotal
  lstFirstList.RemoveItem 0
Next intI
```

TIP The List Box control's `Clear` method clears all items immediately without requiring a loop. Therefore, if you want to clear all the contents at once, instead of a range that you'd use a `For...Next` loop for normally, you can erase the entire list box by doing this: `lstFirstList.Clear`.

Topic 3: Combo Box Controls

As stated in this lesson's introduction, Visual Basic supports several kinds of list controls. This lesson explores the combo box that comes in three varieties: the drop-down list combo box, the simple combo box, and the drop-down combo box. The best part of these controls is that they're all similar to the list box in the way you initialize and access them from your code. Their primary differences lie in the fact that your users can select and enter data in two of the three combo boxes.

Overview All three types of combo boxes comes from a single source: the Toolbox's Combo Box control. When you place a Combo Box control on a form, you must then tell Visual Basic, through the combo box's `Style` property, which combo box you want to use. The default `Style` when you first place a combo box on a form is `0 – Dropdown Combo`. The simplest combo box to begin with is the drop-down list combo box, which is the first of the three that this topic section explains.

Pt **III**

Hr **15**

> **TIP** Throughout this topic section, remember that the `Sorted` property automatically keeps lists sorted for you, alphabetically or numerically, even when users add new values to the list. If you don't specify `True` for the `Sorted` property, the list remains unsorted in the order that you put items into it.

The Drop-Down List Combo Box

The drop-down list combo box acts and works just like list boxes, except that list boxes commonly take up more room on a form than a drop-down list combo box. Whereas a list box appears on the form in the size you designate for the list box, the drop-down list combo box always takes a single line on the form. When users click the drop-down list combo box's arrow, however, the drop-down list combo box opens up to display a list of values.

Figure 15.12 shows a form with two drop-down list combo boxes. Before the right combo box was pulled down, both boxes took the same amount of space on the form. Users, by clicking the right drop-down list combo box's arrow, opened the combo box to see the entries and to select one or more values from the combo box.

FIG. 15.12
Drop-down list combo boxes take only a small part of the form until users drop down a box.

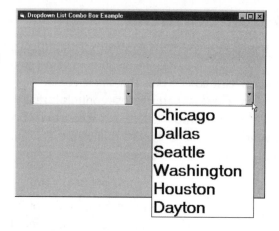

> **TIP** Use drop-down list combo boxes when you need to offer a list of choices but need to save room on the form.

As you can see, a drop-down list combo box displays no text until users select the control. Therefore, you need to make sure that you explain to users, with a label or a message box, exactly what the drop-down list combo box contains.

Use the `AddItem` method to add entries to the drop-down list combo box just as you did with the list box. The following code adds the six city names to the left control on Figure 15.12:

```
Private Sub Form_Load()
    ' Add the left-hand combo items
    cboClosed.AddItem "Chicago"
    cboClosed.AddItem "Dallas"
    cboClosed.AddItem "Seattle"
    cboClosed.AddItem "Washington"
    cboClosed.AddItem "Houston"
    cboClosed.AddItem "Dayton"
End Sub
```

The drop-down list combo box uses the same methods and properties as the list box.

The Simple Combo Box

The simple combo box works like a list box with a text box at the top of the list. In other words, users can select from a list or enter new values in the list. When you add a Combo Box control to a form and set its `Style` property to `1 – Simple Combo`, Visual Basic changes the control so that you can size it the same way you'd size a list box. If you don't give the simple combo box more width and height than is needed to display its values at any time during the application's execution, the simple combo box displays scroll bars to let users scroll through the items.

Figure 15.13 shows the city names listed in a simple combo box control. Your code can load the box with names by using the `AddItem` method, and users can enter additional items. Be sure to blank out the simple combo box's `Text` property when you place the control on the form; otherwise, the control's name will appear in place of the users' data-entry space. If you specify a `Text` property at design time, the simple combo box control uses that value for the default, which users can accept or change.

FIG. 15.13

Users can select a value or enter a new value.

▼ **NOTE**

A simple combo box doesn't add users' entries automatically. You must supply code that adds the entries to the combo box. ▲

Although most programmers place simple combo boxes on forms to let users select or enter a new value, if you want to add the users' values to the simple combo box list, you must provide the following code inside the simple combo box's `LostFocus ()` event procedure:

```
Private Sub cboSCB.LostFocus ()
   cboSCB.AddItem cboSCB.Text
End Sub
```

The LostFocus () event procedure executes when the control loses the focus, which happens when users click another control or move the focus from the simple combo box with the Tab key. Right as the focus moves to another control, the LostFocus () event procedure executes and the code saves the simple combo box's value entered by users (stored in the Text property) into the simple combo box's list with the AddItem method.

Figure 15.13's application shows a command button because after users enter a new city name, they must shift the focus to another control. Otherwise, the simple combo box won't be able to add the new entry.

The Drop-Down Combo Box

The best of all worlds seems to be the drop-down combo box. The drop-down combo box saves screen space by remaining closed until users select the control. Then, it opens to display a list of items. Users can select from the list or enter a new value. The Selected, ListCount, and all the usual list box properties work for drop-down combo boxes, so your code can always determine whether users entered a new value or selected an existing one. Unlike the drop-down list combo box, users can add to a drop-down combo box.

Make sure that the combo box's Style property is 0 – Dropdown Combo (the default) when you want to work with a drop-down combo box. To continue using this lesson's familiar city list example, Figure 15.14 again shows the city list—except that the list appears as a drop-down combo box.

FIG. 15.14
Users can select a value or enter a new value.

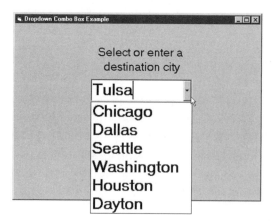

As with the simple combo box, be sure to clear the drop-down combo box's `Text` property when you place the control on the form so that nothing appears in the text box at the top of the drop-down combo box. Users can enter new values (adding those values when the focus leaves the control, as done in the previous section), or open the drop-down combo box to display and select from the list.

Example The `ListCmbo` sample application project that comes with Visual Basic (in the \VB\Samples\PGuide\ListCmbo folder) well demonstrates the distinction between a list box and a combo box. The application displays a list of publishers (you can scroll through the list by clicking the horizontal scroll bar at the bottom of the window).

The nice part of the application is that it switches between a list box and a combo box during the program's execution so that you can see the distinction. Figure 15.15 shows the running application with a list box used for the state abbreviation.

Pt **III**

Hr **15**

FIG. 15.15
*Users select a
state from the
ordinary list box.*

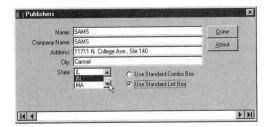

Figure 15.16 shows the same application after users click the option labeled Use Standard Combo Box. Notice that the list remains closed and will remain closed, taking up less room on the form than the list box, until users select the combo box.

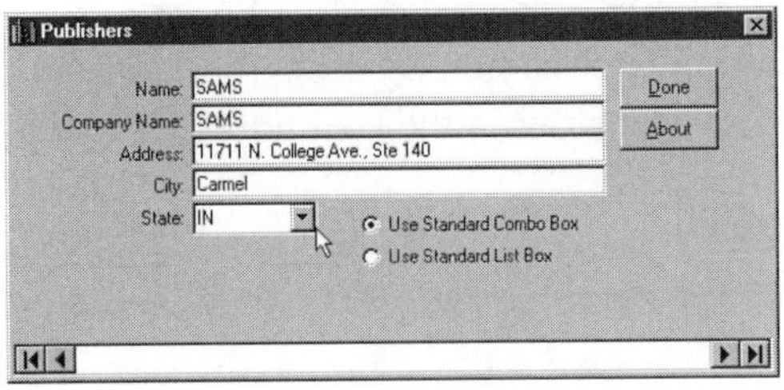

FIG. 15.16
*Users must open
the combo box
before seeing
additional states.*

In neither case can users enter additional states, because all 50 states reside in the list already.

Next Step   Which kind of list do you need? The wide range of choices Visual Basic gives can confuse as much as help. Table 15.5 will help you determine which choice is best for you.

Table 15.5   Determining the Right List Control

Use This Control	If You Want This on the Form
List box	A list from which users can select but not enter values.
Drop-down list combo box	A list that remains closed until users are ready to select values from the list.
Simple combo box	A list that appears on the form and remains open at the size you place the list on the form at design time. Users can select a value or enter a new list value.
Drop-down combo box	A list that remains closed until users are ready to select or enter new list values.

Summary

This lesson showed you how to work with special selection controls. You've learned about the two-choice option buttons and check boxes. Option buttons let users select one value, whereas check boxes let users select zero, one, or more controls.

The list box controls offer several ways to work with data lists. You can add a drop-down list box to display a list of values. The combo boxes let users gain the additional advantage of entering new values into the control.

In Hour 16 you learn how to work with different kinds of application forms. As you already know, forms support properties, and you'll learn the reason for many of those properties in the next hour's lesson.

Hour 15 Quiz

You can find the answers for the following questions on the accompanying CD-ROM and on the Virtual Classroom Web site.

On the CD

1. What's the primary difference between an option button and a check box?

2. What property makes a control, such as the Image control, disappear during program execution?

3. Why do you have to include a frame on which to put some option buttons?

4. How do you initialize a list control?

5. How does a method vary from a function?

6. What are the differences between the three types of combo boxes?

7. How do you enable multiple selection of items in a list box?

8. How does a program determine which item or items users have selected?

9. Describe the purpose of the `Selected` list array.

10. When using a Combo Box control that lets users enter new values, why must you offer at least one additional focus control on the form?

Pt III

Hr 15

Hour 15 Homework Exercises

1. Remove the subroutine named `Clear_Flags()` from the first topic section's "Next Step" example. Run the application and notice what's now different. You'll have to remove not only the procedure named `Clear_Flags()`, but also the calls to `Clear_Flags()` in each of the application's event procedures.

2. Create a radio front containing option buttons for each radio station you listen to. Create an event procedure for each button that displays the call letters of that station in a text box when you click one of the option buttons.

3. Write a program that lists your family members in a list box. Include enough members to require scroll bars. Allow for multiple selections and keep the list sorted at all times.

4. Modify the application you wrote in exercise 3 so that all three kinds of combo boxes appear on the form and display the same data. When one combo box changes—when users enter a new value in the list— reflect that change in the other combo boxes.

Creating VB Forms

THIS LESSON ANALYZES FORMS more thoroughly than has been done to this point. Forms support several methods and events that help you produce better programs that respond to users the way you intend.

Besides study form specifics, you'll learn more about the effects of adding multiple forms to your applications. As your application needs grow, you'll need additional forms to hold secondary data and controls. When you create the MDI forms described here, your applications will be able to support several sets of data, and your users can work with all the sets at once.

Topic 1: Working with Forms

You learned early in Part I of this course that forms have properties just as other controls have properties. Now that you've mastered a number of Visual Basic's language features, this topic section will explore more of the form properties. Also, form methods, such as the `Form.Load` method you saw in Hour 15, provide advanced application control that you may need.

Overview Some programmers rarely change their application's form properties, other than the `Caption` property that appears at the top of the application screen. Nevertheless, you should know which properties come in handy in certain situations, because forms provide the application's backdrop, and the forms' appearance and responses can be a meaningful part of the application.

Form Properties Revisited

In earlier lessons, you learned about some form properties. For example, you learned about `Caption`, which determines the title in the form's title bar, and `MaxButton` and `MinButton`, which specify whether users can maximize and minimize the form during the application's execution.

You might want to display a form that users can resize at runtime. If so, you have to adjust the form's `BorderStyle` property. Table 16.1 describes each `BorderStyle` property value that you can select at design time by using code assignments. (You can't change the `BorderStyle` property at runtime, but you can read and use the numeric value stored in this property.)

▼ **NOTE**
When users resize your application's Form window during program execution, Visual Basic doesn't provide any automatic shrinkage of your form's contents. Therefore, your form's controls, if centered before users resize the form, won't remain centered because they don't automatically move when the window shrinks.

If you want full functionality and uniform appearance when users resize your form, you need to program that uniform appearance into the application. You have to work with the form's `Resize` event procedure to adjust all the controls and their font sizes if the `Resize` event takes place. Such an event procedure is a great deal of work! Most programmers either disallow resizing or let users see only part of the form's controls if they reduce the form size. ▲

Table 16.1 *BorderStyle* Property Values for a Form

Value	Description
0 - None	No border appears—therefore, no control menu, title bar, or resizing window buttons appear.
1 - Fixed Single	A single line appears around the form, with the title bar and locations for resizing window buttons.
2 - Sizable	Users can resize the form window with menu commands, by dragging the form's edge, or by clicking the resizing window buttons. This is the default BorderStyle property value for forms.
3 - Fixed Dialog	The form includes a control menu and title bar but no resizing window buttons. This setting is great for dialog box forms.
4 - FixedToolWindow	This is a miniaturized form with a title bar and a Close button, sometimes used for Windows program launchers. No Windows 95 taskbar button appears for this kind of form window, making it a great style to use for toolbox windows.
5 - SizableToolWindow	This form is identical to the one FixedToolWindow creates, except that users can resize the window. It's also great for toolbox windows.

▼ NOTE

When you change a form's BorderStyle value, other property values may change automatically. For example, the ShowInTaskbar property automatically changes to False for a BorderStyle value of 4 or 5. ▲

The WindowState property determines how the form now appears. If you select 0 - Normal, the form appears at the design-time Height, Left, Top, and Width settings that you set when you created the application. During the program, your code can check the WindowState property to see whether users now have the form minimized or maximized. If WindowState contains 1 - Minimized, users have the form minimized. If WindowState contains 2 - Maximized, users have the form maximized.

You can use `WindowState` to change the startup state of the form. If you set `WindowState` to `1 - Minimized` at design time, the form will appear minimized when users first start the application. An icon will represent the minimized form if you've specified an icon file in the form's `Icon` property. If you set `WindowState` to `2 - Maximized`, the form will appear maximized when users first start the application.

If you want the form to maintain a certain size at all times, just set the appropriate properties as described here. You should, however, make sure that the `Movable` property is set to `True`. (If users can't resize the form, they should be allowed to move it, because they may be running your application while working with several other windows on-screen.)

The `StartupPosition` property proves handy when the placement of your form is critical. Table 16.2 lists the values possible for `StartupPosition`. This property lets you specify a startup screen position without having to calculate screen coordinates to center the form.

Table 16.2 *StartupPosition* Property Values for a Form

Value	Description
`0 - Manual`	No specific placement
`1 - CenterOwner`	Center the form on its parent form
`2 - CenterScreen`	Center the form on-screen
`3 - Windows Default`	Position the form in the screen's upper-left corner

The final appearance property, `Visible`, is set to `True` or `False`. The default value, `True`, specifies that the form will appear on-screen at runtime (and all the controls residing on the form will also appear). At design time or runtime, you can change the `Visible` property setting to hide or display the form at appropriate times.

▼ **NOTE**

Don't confuse the `Visible` property with the `Load` and `Unload` events. A hidden form is loaded into memory but is temporarily hidden from view, so it's not visible even though it's loaded. The `Visible` property, however, mimics the form's `Show` and `Hide` methods. Setting a form's `Visible` property to `True` performs the same operation as executing the form's

Show method, and setting a form's Visible property to False performs the same operation as executing the Hide method. ▲

Many form properties become even more important when you create applications that contain multiple forms, as explained in the next topic section.

Important Form Events and Methods

The first event that occurs for all forms that appear in an application is the Load event. This event occurs when the runtime module loads the form into memory for display. You should place all of a form's control initialization inside the Load event.

Figure 16.1 shows the Project Properties dialog box that appears when you choose Properties from the Project menu. In most cases, you leave the form name in the Startup Object combo box. If you want the runtime module to execute a procedure before loading the initial form, however, you must add a procedure named Main to the module and select Sub Main from the Startup Object list. You can load the form from that procedure when the application is ready.

FIG. 16.1
Specify the startup form or startup procedure.

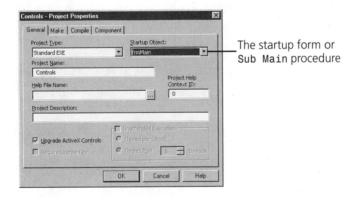

The startup form or
Sub Main procedure

▼ NOTE
The Startup Object combo box becomes especially critical when you add multiple forms to the project. Visual Basic must know which form you want to appear first when users execute the application. ▲

As mentioned earlier, the Resize event occurs whenever users resize the form to be smaller or larger. You must decide whether you want to move or resize the controls located on the form when users trigger the `Resize` event. Although such programming isn't a trivial task, you can create a `Form_Resize ()` event procedure if you want to rearrange or resize some (or all) of a form's controls whenever users resize the form.

> **TIP** If your form's contents can't be resized due to the complexity or nature of the form, you can display a message box whenever users resize the form. This box can warn users that certain controls may be hidden after the resizing, and can mention that users need to resize the form to its original size to access those controls.

The opposite of the `Load` event, `Unload` occurs when your code contains a statement that unloads the form, such as the following:

```
Unload frmMyForm
```

More often, however, `Unload` takes place when users click the form window's Close button (or close the form from the window's control menu or double-clicks the form's title bar). Unlike the form's `Hide` method or a `Visible` property value of `False`, the `Unload` event completely removes the form from memory and reinitializes all controls on the form. Therefore, if your application later reloads the form with the `Reload` statement, all the controls are in their original state and don't remember any settings from the application's earlier load.

Lastly, the `Activate` and `Deactivate` events occur when users change which form is the active window. If your application contains only one form, the form is always active and the `Activate` event occurs only once—when the form first loads. If the application contains multiple forms, however, the `Deactivate` event for a given form occurs whenever users leave that form window to make another form window active.

▼ **NOTE**
Other applications don't affect a form's `Activate` or `Deactivate` events while your Visual Basic application is running. If users switch to another program window and then return to your VB application, neither `Activate` nor `Deactivate` occurs. ▲

If you apply the `Show` or `SetFocus` method to one of an application's forms, the previous form's `Deactivate` event occurs, and the new form window's `Activate` event occurs. Therefore, both statements trigger the `Activate` event procedure for the `frmAccForm` form:

```
frmAccForm.Show
frmAccForm.SetFocus    ' Sets the focus to this form
```

Example One of the places where form-related bugs appear in an application is at program termination. An application's execution is finished when both of the following actions occur:

- The application's forms are all unloaded
- Code no longer executes

A problem can occur if users (or your code) have hidden any forms during the application's execution. Users might think that the application has finished executing, although the application is still running with hidden forms.

To eliminate this problem, add an Exit command to the File menu of the application's primary form. (In every application, one form is the primary form—you'll learn more about this in the next topic section.) If your code or users trigger events that hide other forms before users exit the program from the primary form, the Exit menu command (or an exit command button added to the last form users will use) can contain code similar to the following:

```
Private Sub Form_Unload
  Dim intI As Integer
  Dim intCt As Integer
  intCt = Forms.Count  ' Save the count
  ' Loop through the forms collection and unload
  ' each form.
  For intI = 0 To intCt - 1
   Unload Forms(intI)
  Next intI
End Sub
```

This code unloads all forms, including any that are still hidden.

When your application contains multiple forms, the application keeps track of a `Forms` collection that acts like the control collections you saw in previous lessons. The total number of forms in the application is returned by the `Forms.Count` method, and then you can loop through the forms by subscripting the `Forms` collection as you unload each form. When the procedure ends, you can make sure that the application has completely finished executing and that no hidden forms are left behind to trouble users later.

Next Step Remember that you can assign form and other control property values in code at runtime. If the possible property values appear in a drop-down list in the Properties window at design time—as they do, for example, for the MousePointer property—you can assign the property either a numeric literal or its Visual Basic named literal. The following assignments for the MousePointer property are both valid:

```
frmMyForm.MousePointer = 1

frmMyForm.MousePointer = vbArrow
```

The named literal is easier to maintain later because you can tell what value you're assigning. Nevertheless, the numeric literal is easier to type when you write the program. Visual Basic's online help provides the named literals you can use. To read the online help to learn the named literals, highlight the property within the Properties window and then press F1. Figure 16.2 shows the named literals that appear on the MousePointer help page.

FIG. 16.2
The named literals are listed on the online help screens.

Named literals ⎯

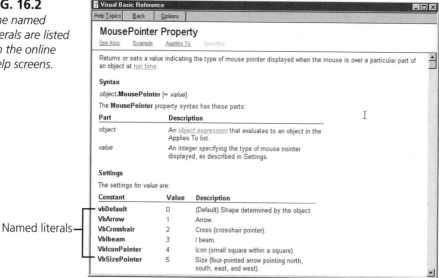

Topic 2: Multiple Forms and SDI/MDI

The preceding topic section discussed applications with multiple forms. Until now, all your applications had a single form. Not much mention was made of multiform applications because, for simple applications, multiple forms are unnecessary. You now are ready to add additional forms to your applications, so you need to know how to distinguish and program SDI (Single-Document Interface) and MDI (Multiple-Document Interface) applications.

▶▶ FAST TRACK

Do you already understand SDI and MDI applications? If so, skip to the next topic section, "Printing Directly to Forms" (p. 402).

Overview Multiple forms generally require that you keep track of two or more sets of forms. Because you assign each form a meaningful name, your programming burden shouldn't increase too much. The form name determines which set of controls you're working with at any given time, and you can hide and show forms as needed while the application runs (or users can switch between the forms).

▼ NOTE

Even when two or more forms appear on a user's screen, only one can be active. Users can activate an inactive form by clicking any part of the form that shows from beneath the currently active form. Also, your application code can activate a form when the time is right. The `frmForm.Show` method activates the form window referenced by the name `frmForm` and hides other windows if the newly active form happens to consume more screen space than the other forms. ▲

Pt **III**
Hr **16**

MDI development allows you to create very complex-looking applications. Almost all major software applications contain multiple document interfaces. As this course begins to describe more powerful programs that use files and additional controls, you'll see more need for an MDI application.

Adding Forms

When you want to add another form to your application, choose Add Form from the Project menu. Visual Basic displays the Add Form dialog box shown in Figure 16.3. You can select from several kinds of new forms to display, or you can select an existing form by clicking the Existing tab and then selecting from the list of forms.

FIG. 16.3

This is where you select the type of form to add.

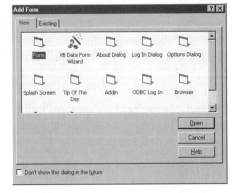

If you want to add another standard form, double-click Form to have Visual Basic open the new form. Visual Basic names your subsequent forms `Form2`, `Form3`, and so on—you should assign better names as soon as you add new forms.

▼ **NOTE**

Hour 26, "Using Form Templates," explains how to incorporate the other kinds of forms offered in the Add Form dialog box. ▲

VB Interface Styles

Visual Basic supports the following interface styles:

- **Single-document interface.** An SDI application contains a single data window. In Windows Notepad, for instance, you can open only one document at a time. An SDI application usually doesn't contain a Window menu on its menu bar because you can't move between data windows. Figure 16.4 shows Notepad's SDI interface.

- **Multiple-document interface.** An MDI application contains multiple data windows (often called *document windows*). Microsoft Word, for example, lets you open as many documents as you want; Word's MDI ensures that each document resides in its own window (see Figure 16.5). You can switch between windows by clicking the desired window with the mouse or by selecting choices from the Window menu. When users switch between document windows (which are forms, from the developer's point of view), the selected window becomes the active form and has the *focus*.

FIG. 16.4

Notepad is an SDI application because you can open only one document window at a time.

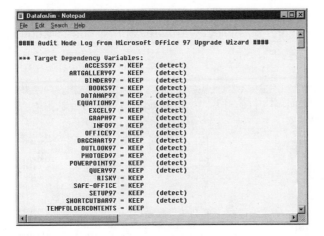

FIG. 16.5

Word is an MDI application because you can open several document windows at once.

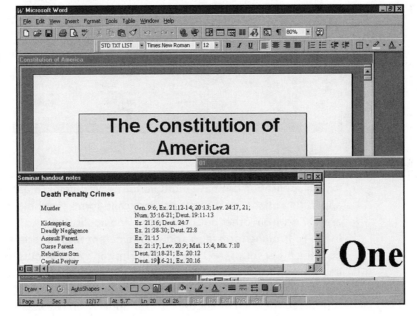

- **Explorer-style interface.** If you've used Windows Explorer (see Figure 16.6), you've seen Visual Basic's third interface. An application that supports the Explorer-style interface has two windows: the left window displays a hierarchical view of the data detailed in the right window. Select an Explorer-style interface when you're working with an application that manages data files and graphics. Such applications include `TreeView` and `ListView` controls that help you traverse the Explorer-style windows (these controls normally don't appear in the Toolbox).

FIG. 16.6

The Explorer-style interface always contains two window panes: a hierarchical view and a detail view.

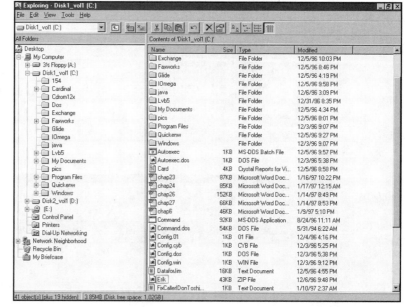

▼ **NOTE**

An SDI application can have multiple forms. MDI simply means that your application might contain one or more child forms that hold data sets that are distinct from other data sets within the application. An MDI application uses a *controlling form* (also known as a *parent form* or *primary form*) to hold the other forms, and the other forms can't appear outside the controlling form's boundaries. If you create an SDI application—which most applications are—your application can have multiple forms, yet no form is considered the child of another. If your application works with only one set of data at a time (such as one customer file or one employee payroll file), or if your application doesn't work with any data except for program control information, the application should be an SDI application. ▲

Example   If you want to create an application that works with multiple data files, you must know the MDI terminology. The primary form used as the backdrop holding the other forms is often called the *parent form* or *parent window*.

The parent form acts like a form container that contains one or more child windows (also forms). In Microsoft Word, for example, the Word background with the menu bar, status bar, and toolbar is the parent window. As you open Word documents, these documents appear in child windows within the parent window, and the child windows never go outside the parent window's boundaries.

The parent window that provides boundaries for the child windows supports only these types of controls:

- Controls that support the `Align` property
- Controls without a visible interface (you learn more about such interfaces in Hour 26, "Using Form Templates")

▼ **NOTE**

If users minimize any of the child windows, these windows appear minimized at the bottom of the parent window but not on the taskbar. Child windows are bound to their parent window and can't appear outside the parent window at all; the parent window defines the application's absolute boundaries. ▲

The primary distinction of a child window form is that its `MDIChild` property is set to `True`. Also, an MDI application might contain non-child forms. For example, the application might contain an About dialog box (which users would reach by choosing About from the Help menu); this dialog box isn't an MDI child because the dialog box window doesn't hold program data.

When you want to create an MDI application, choose Add MDI Form from the Project menu and then add child window forms with an `MDIChild` property of `True`.

Next Step Rather than build an MDI application from scratch, you can start with the Application Wizard. This wizard makes MDI applications much easier to produce than creating the forms and setting the `MDIChild` properties by hand.

When you create a new project and select the VB Application Wizard option, the second dialog box that appears (see Figure 16.7) lets you select the kind of interface style you prefer.

FIG. 16.7
*Select the
appropriate
interface style
from the
Application
Wizard.*

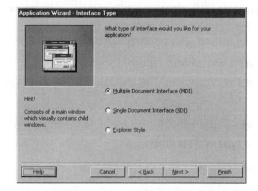

The Application Wizard creates a project that supports the creation of multiple child windows through the File menu's New command. The following code is executed when you choose New from the File menu in the generated MDI application (the `mnuFileNew.Click ()` event procedure executes this):

```
Private Sub LoadNewDoc()
    Static lDocumentCount As Long
    Dim frmD As frmDocument

    lDocumentCount = lDocumentCount + 1
    Set frmD = New frmDocument
    frmD.Caption = "Document " & lDocumentCount
    frmD.Show
End Sub
```

The code is tricky but contains nothing you can't figure out with the background you already have. The *static variable* named `lDocumentCount` is local to the procedure, yet never goes out of scope. The first time this procedure executes, `lDocumentCount` is 0. If the procedure changes the value of `lDocumentCount` (which it does by adding 1 every time the procedure executes), Visual Basic remembers the new value. Although no other procedure can access `lDocumentCount`, its value remains intact inside this procedure. The value doesn't go away as it would if the variable were local and *automatic* (the opposite of static; all variables you've declared locally so far have been automatic).

The line after that adds an interesting twist to the declaration statements you've seen before. Rather than declare a variable, this statement declares a form!

The application contains, at startup, a child form named `frmDocument` created at design time. This `Dim` statement declares a new variable named `frmD` to be a variable that contains the same object as `frmDocument`; in other words, rather than refer to an `Integer` or `String` data type, `frmD` refers to a document that contains the same properties as `frmDocument`.

After updating the static variable that keeps track of all the newly created documents, the `Set` statement creates a new document and sets `frmD` as a reference to the document. For all intents, `frmD` is the new document. The next statement sets the new document's caption to `Document` followed by the document number, and the last statement uses the `Show` method to display the new document on the parent window.

No matter how many times users choose New from the File menu, the `LoadNewDoc()` procedure is executed and creates another child window. The code for the File menu's Close command, if you run the Application Wizard and then execute the resulting MDI application, does nothing—the Application Wizard places no code there. You have to add code that will unload the active child window when users choose Close from the File menu. As you can see, programming MDI applications can be a bit confusing.

Pt **III**

Hr **16**

> **TIP** Child forms are useful for the dialog boxes you might want to add to your applications. Although the next lesson explains how to display common dialog boxes, such as the File Print dialog box, you also can create your own dialog boxes by displaying a child form with controls that make up a dialog box. You can set the default command button with the command button's `Default` property and initialize text box controls with default text if you want to help users with common entries. If you set the command button's `Enabled` property to `False`, the command button can be grayed out and unavailable, depending on user action leading up to the dialog box's display.
>
> When users need to see the dialog box, show the dialog box with the `Show` method this way: `frmDialog.Show vbModal, Me`. `vbModal` produces a modal dialog box that users must respond to with OK or Cancel before they can do anything else in the application. `Show`'s second option is the name of the parent form, but you can use `Me` if the parent form is the standard application form.

Topic 3: Printing Directly to Forms

Until now, all your form I/O has taken place inside controls. Visual Basic offers the `Print` method, which you can apply to forms to print directly to them without using controls. Using `Print` to write text to forms often isn't as clean as using controls, and the form can get cluttered fast. Nevertheless, the `Print` method is good for titles and for testing programs as you learn Visual Basic programming.

Overview This short topic section explains how to use the `Print` method so that you can write data to forms without worrying first about placing a label or text box control on the form and writing to one of those controls. Although you *should* use controls for most I/O, you'll be able to debug your programs more easily if you print directly to the form with `Print`.

▼ **NOTE**
The more powerful Microsoft makes the Visual Basic debugger, the less often you'll need `Print`. `Print` is handy, however, for printing lists of variables that you want to analyze. ▲

Using the *Print* Method

If you want to print a line of text, Visual Basic provides the `Print` method for all objects that can support text. The `Print` method applies to forms, picture boxes, the Printer object, and the Debug object (which is a special *Immediate window* to which you can send test results as a program runs). The easiest of all objects to write to with the `Print` method is the form.

If you open a new project and double-click the `Form1` window, you see the Code window. Because you've just opened the project, no objects are available to use other than `Form1` and the General procedure where the `Declarations` section resides. All predefined procedures that the form can recognize are shown in a drop-down list box. Choose `Click` from the list and then type the following code between the `Form_Click ()` procedure's opening and closing lines:

```
Dim strString As String
strString = "Visual Basic"
Form1.Print strString      ' Print value of the string
```

You now can run the sample program. The form will appear and nothing will happen. Remember that you entered code into the `Form_Click ()` subroutine—until you click the form, nothing should happen. Click the form several times. You should see results similar to those shown in Figure 16.8.

FIG. 16.8
This is simple output from the form's Print *method.*

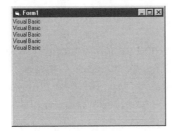

`Print` is the one of simplest methods you can use to output information from your program to the form. To print on any form in your program, you just need to reference the form name and the `Print` method, separated by a period. The syntax is

```
frmFormName.Print DataToPrint
```

`frmFormName` is the form on which you want to print, and `DataToPrint` is the data you want to print. You can print literals (numeric, string, or date), variable values, or controls.

Pt **III**
Hr **16**

Adding Formatting to *Print*

You can format the `Print` method's output by including either the `Spc()` function or the `Tab()` function. Each works inside the `Print` method to add spacing to the data you're printing.

Consider the following code, which uses `Spc()` and the semicolon (`;`) to print two strings on the same line. `Spc(5)` tells the `Print` method to skip five blanks before the text string begins printing in the sixth column. If you end a `Print` statement with a semicolon, the next `Print` prints where the current one left off rather than print on the next line, as would happen without the semicolon.

```
Private Sub Form_Click ()
  Dim strString As String
  strString = "Visual Basic"
```

```
      Form1.Print "*"; Spc(5); strString;    ' Notice semicolon.
      Form1.Print Spc(2); strString
   End Sub
```

The output will appear on the form like this as you click the form several times to trigger the code:

```
   *      Visual Basic   Visual Basic
   *      Visual Basic   Visual Basic
   *      Visual Basic   Visual Basic
```

The code forces the `Print` method to print an asterisk and then skip 5 spaces before the first `Visual Basic` appears. After two more spaces, the second `Print` also prints `Visual Basic`. The next time you click, you force the event procedure to execute again, repeating the process.

If you use `Tab()` instead of `Spc()`, Visual Basic moves to the column argument located inside the parentheses and prints the next data item there. `Spc()` forces the next print to begin a certain number of spaces over, whereas `Tab()` forces the next print to begin in a specific column. Consider the following code:

```
   Private Sub Form_Click()
      Dim strString As String
      strString = "Visual Basic"

      Form1.Print "*"; Tab(5); strString; Tab(20); strString
      Form1.Print "*"; Spc(5); strString; Spc(20); strString
   End Sub
```

`Tab()` keeps the printing in specific columns, but `Spc()` moves the printing over by a certain number of spaces.

Here is the output from this procedure:

```
   *      Visual Basic   Visual Basic
   *       Visual Basic                      Visual Basic
```

Example You can use the `Print` method to print blank lines on a form by not specifying any data. Consider this code:

```
   Private Sub Form_Click()
      Dim strString As String
      Dim CurLine As Integer

      CurLine = 1
```

```
    strString = "Visual Basic"

    Form1.Print strString & " is on Line #" & CurLine

    For CurLine = 2 To 6
      Form1.Print      ' Print blank lines!
    Next CurLine

    Form1.Print strString & " is on Line #" & CurLine
  End Sub
```

The output contains five blank lines between the lines printed:

```
Visual Basic is on Line 1




Visual Basic is on Line 7
```

Next Step By experimenting with the different keywords available to the `Print` method, you can place information on a form to inform your users or alert them when something significant happens.

Visual Basic supports several other properties that can be used to place text onto a form. These properties use the current position of the text cursor, which Visual Basic moves as the `Print` method executes. Information containing the location of the cursor is stored in the `CurrentX` and `CurrentY` properties. These properties let you determine exactly where you want your output to appear.

Another property, `ScaleMode`, affects how `CurrentX` and `CurrentY` behave. A form can recognize several different modes depending on the `ScaleMode` property you set. This mode refers to the scale used for drawing graphics and text on the form.

The most common `ScaleMode` property for text is *character mode*. This means that when `CurrentX` and `CurrentY` are both set to **5**, the next `Print` method will begin at column 5, row 5. The starting position of the `ScaleMode` property is the upper-left corner of the form (with the coordinates 0,0). The following example `Click` event procedure uses the `ScaleMode`, `CurrentX`, and `CurrentY` properties:

```
Private Sub Form_Click()
  ' Set up for characters
  Form1.ScaleMode = vbCharacters   ' Character (4)

  Form1.CurrentX = 20    ' Move across 20 chars
  Form1.CurrentY = 6     ' Move down 6 lines
  Form1.Print "Down and across"

  Form1.CurrentX = 0     ' Move back to the left
  Form1.CurrentY = 0     ' Move back up
  Form1.Print "Upper left"
End Sub
```

Study the output in Figure 16.9. Notice that the output of the second **Print** method appears higher on the form than the first **Print** method's output due to the coordinate placement.

FIG. 16.9
Use CurrentX *and* CurrentY *to position the* Print *method's text cursor.*

Summary

Form properties, methods, and events all work together to serve as the foundation for your application. The form is the backdrop for the entire application, and Visual Basic supports several properties and methods that display the form in the manner you want. You can control exactly how much ability users have to change and resize the form.

Visual Basic supports three interface styles: SDI, MDI, and Explorer-style. Most of your programs will use SDI style unless you want users to be able to work with multiple sets of data within the same application. (Such an application lets users cut and paste between data files easily.)

The final topic section taught you how to use the **Print** method to send output directly to the form. **Print** is one of the oldest elements of the Visual Basic language, because it has been around since the original BASIC from decades ago. Unlike the original PRINT command, however, Visual Basic's Print is a method that applies to objects such as forms.

In Hour 17 you'll learn how to add dialog boxes to your application so that users can specify options and values required by the application to complete its tasks.

Hour 16 Quiz

You can find the answers for the following questions on the accompanying CD-ROM and on the Virtual Classroom Web site.

On the CD

1. How can you keep users from resizing a form?
2. How can you keep users from moving a form?
3. What's the easiest way to place a form in the center of the screen when your application first starts?
4. What's the difference between the Activate and Load form events?
5. What's the difference between SDI and MDI applications?
6. **True or false:** An SDI application can contain, at most, one form.
7. Name the three interface styles that the Application Wizard can create.
8. What method sends output directly to a form?
9. What's the difference between Spc() and Tab()?
10. What is the output from the following Print methods?

```
Form1.Print "Line 1";
Form1.Print "Line 2"
```

Pt **III**

Hr **16**

Hour 16 Homework Exercises

1. Run the Application Wizard to generate an MDI application.
2. Run the Application Wizard to generate an Explorer-style application.
3. Create code to write the numbers from 1 to 100 on a form. Separate the numbers with one space. Don't use any controls for the output. Trigger the output in the form's Click event procedure.

Adding Control Containers: Dialog Boxes

During this hour you will learn

▶ *Why the Common Dialog Box control adds consistency to applications*

▶ *How to add a tool to your Toolbox that creates the Common Dialog Box control*

▶ *Why Common Dialog Box controls don't appear in the Form window*

▶ *How to turn a Common Dialog Box control into a specific dialog box*

THIS LESSON EXPLAINS how to add dialog boxes to your programs. A *dialog box* is a container that holds a set of controls. Common dialog boxes are the type you see when you open files, save files, and print documents. To streamline your programming efforts and to ensure application consistency, Visual Basic includes the *Common Dialog Box control*, which produces a standard dialog box that performs these and other common dialog box operations.

Before the Common Dialog Box control, you had to tediously design dialog boxes by placing controls on each dialog box that you wanted to create. Virtually every programmer created a slightly different dialog box, so applications lost the consistency so important in the Windows environment. The Common Dialog Box control not only maintains this consistency but is easy to use.

Topic 1: Introducing Common Dialog Boxes

Although Visual Basic includes file-related controls such as the Directory List Box and File List Box controls, you don't have to deal with these controls if you want to provide a file-related dialog box for your users. All you need to do is place the Common Dialog Box control on your form and set the properties that specify the dialog box's purpose. The same is true for many other dialog boxes you've seen used in various applications.

▶▶ **FAST TRACK**

Even if you've already used the Common Dialog Box control in other Visual Basic versions, you need to read the section "Getting Ready" (p. 411) to learn how to add the Common Dialog Box tool to your Toolbox. After you add this tool, you can jump to Hour 18, "Using Additional Controls" (p. 431x).

Overview   The Common Dialog Box control is a multi-talented control. It lets you place several types of dialog boxes on your form:

- **Color selection**, which lets users select from a palette of colors without having to enter numeric codes to indicate a color
- **Open**, which lets users select from a common dialog box that traverses disks, directories, and files
- **Save**, which lets users specify file names for data while saving your application's data
- **Font selection**, which lets users select from the fonts available on their computers
- **Print selection**, which lets users select a printer and printer options from the standard Print dialog box
- **WinHelp**, which starts the Windows help engine

▼ **NOTE**

Hour 29, "Building a Help Subsystem," explains more about the WinHelp common dialog box feature. ▲

The topic sections in this lesson explain how to produce common dialog boxes in the applications you distribute so that your users can more quickly adapt to your programs and conveniently provide input responses when needed.

Getting Ready

Tools for all controls that you place on a form reside in the Toolbox. Therefore, you can't add the Common Dialog Box control to any forms until the Common Dialog Box tool appears in the Toolbox. This tool normally isn't in the Toolbox, so you have to add it by following these steps:

1. Choose Components from the Project menu to display the Components dialog box shown in Figure 17.1.

FIG. 17.1
You can add tools to the Toolbox by using the Components dialog box.

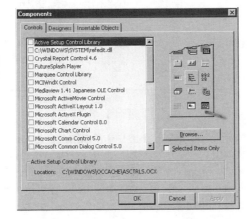

2. Scroll down to the control named Microsoft Common Dialog Control 5.0 if you don't already see this control in the dialog box, and then click it.

3. Click OK. The tool now appears in your Toolbox (see Figure 17.2).

▼ **NOTE**

You might wonder why you have to add certain tools to the Toolbox. As you can see from the Components dialog box, Visual Basic comes with many controls. If the Toolbox held a tool representing every available control, the Toolbox would be flooded with tools and would consume far too much of your development environment's screen. Therefore, Microsoft puts the most common controls in the default Toolbox and allows you to add other controls when and if you need them. ▲

Pt **III**

Hr **17**

FIG. 17.2

The Common Dialog Box tool now appears in the Toolbox.

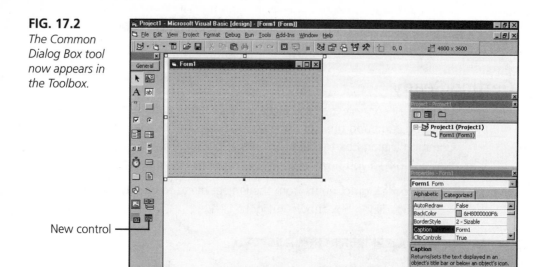

New control —

TIP   Many software vendors offer additional Visual Basic controls. Be on the lookout for useful controls that perform tasks you may need, such as reporting, communicating, or displaying graphics. Although Visual Basic's tool set is powerful and fairly complete, other tools sometimes offer flexibility and usefulness that can come in handy in certain situations. Check your online service or the Internet for additional tools that you can purchase (or sometimes even download for free).

Dialog Box Response

Your running application will display the dialog boxes that the Common Dialog Box control provides, and Visual Basic will receive information based on user input or selected values within the dialog box. Your application then acts on the dialog box information. Your application, in other words, won't open a file just because you've displayed an Open dialog box and users have selected a file. The Common Dialog Box controls simply provide a standard mechanism that your program can use to find out what users really want.

When your application is ready to open a data file, for example, you display the Open dialog box (assume that users have triggered the file opening, perhaps by choosing the File menu's Open command). Users then select the file to open or cancel the operation. Your program then determines what to do based on what happened in the dialog box. You can tell whether users have canceled the operation (by clicking the dialog box's Cancel button) or selected a file (by using the dialog box's file-selection features). If users have selected a file, your application knows the exact file location and name, but your code must then open the file and read the data by using standard file-access procedures. Without follow-up code, an Open dialog box would just go away when users selected a file, and no file activity would take place.

Dialog Box Placement

When you first place a dialog box on your form, you don't see anything that looks like a dialog box. For example, you never see the Open dialog box in the Form window. The Common Dialog Box control appears only as a small icon in the Form window. You can move the Common Dialog Box control icon out of the way to see other, more important controls.

As long as you've placed a Common Dialog Box control somewhere on the form, your application can display the appropriate dialog box when needed. The Common Dialog Box control acts like a general-purpose control that can turn into a specific dialog box as often as needed.

▼ **NOTE**
You can place as many Common Dialog Box controls on your form as you want. If you plan to display an Open dialog box, a Save dialog box, and a Print dialog box at various times, you can place three Common Dialog Box controls on your form and set up each one in the Properties window to do a specific job. Alternatively, you can place just one Common Dialog Box control on the form, and then set the appropriate options at runtime each time you're ready to produce one of the specific dialog boxes. ▲

Example Figure 17.3 shows a new form window that contains a single Common Dialog Box control. As you can see, the control doesn't look at all like an actual dialog box.

FIG. 17.3
The Common Dialog Box control takes up very little room.

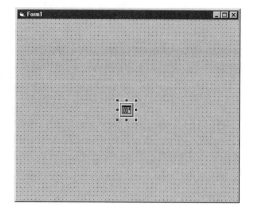

When you place a Common Dialog Box control on a form, Visual Basic won't let you resize the control. The control's size depends on what you turn the control into with properties. All you can—and should—do is move the control out of the way of your other controls. The Common Dialog Box control just sits there and waits for your running program to trigger its execution.

▼ **NOTE**
The Common Dialog Box control is invisible at runtime, so the control's location on the form doesn't matter. ▲

Next Step Your code will use one of these methods to trigger the display of one of the common dialog boxes:

- `ShowColor` displays the Color selection dialog box.
- `ShowFont` displays the Font selection dialog box.
- `ShowHelp` displays the Help engine's dialog box.
- `ShowOpen` displays the Open dialog box.
- `ShowPrinter` displays the Print dialog box.
- `ShowSave` displays the Save dialog box.

For example, if you name a Common Dialog Box control **dbPrint**, your code to display the Print dialog box (which might be found in the `mnuFilePrint_Click ()` event procedure for the File menu's Print command) would be the following:

```
dbPrint.ShowPrinter        ' Activate the Print dialog box
```

Now that you understand how to place and activate the Common Dialog Box control, you need to understand that you must set up dialog boxes before you activate them. Therefore, the remaining two topic sections describe the normal process you go through to set up specific Common Dialog Box controls. After you set up a control, you'll learn how to access user responses for the dialog box.

▼ **NOTE**

All the common dialog boxes are *modal*. Users must close the dialog box by clicking OK or Cancel before they can continue with any other part of the application. ▲

Topic 2: Working with Color and Fonts

The Color and Font dialog boxes are fairly easy to generate and respond to. Your users will appreciate that you've used standard dialog boxes in your application. Also, the standard dialog boxes make it easier to write your application because you don't have a different set of rules for several different-but-similar dialog boxes that you might have created without the standard.

Overview Using Color and Font dialog boxes in your applications requires these fundamental steps that subsequent sections explain in more detail:

1. Place the Common Dialog Box control on your form.
2. Before any code displays the dialog box, set up the dialog box's default values.
3. Include code that shows the dialog box.
4. When control returns to your application, inspect the user's values and respond accordingly.

The Color Dialog Box

Figure 17.4 shows the Color dialog box that the Common Dialog Box control produces.

FIG. 17.4

The Color dialog box provides a color selection palette.

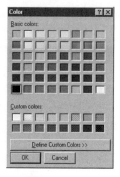

Colors provide an interesting challenge to many Windows programmers. Windows supports thousands of color shades, and a different number represents each possible color. Inside Windows programs, the number often appears as a hexadecimal (base 16) number called the *RGB number* (it's RGB because a particular Red/Green/Blue combination produces the specific shade). Fortunately, the Color dialog box means that you don't have to worry too much about RGB numbers. When users close the Color dialog box, the chosen number appears in the Common Dialog Box control's `Color` property.

▼ NOTE

Users have the option of clicking the Color dialog box's Define Custom Colors button to display the color spectrum tool (see Figure 17.5). The color spectrum tool lets users select an exact color from a prism of colors, and then adds that color to the basic colors in the Color dialog box for subsequent selection. ▲

FIG. 17.5

Users can select from a color spectrum.

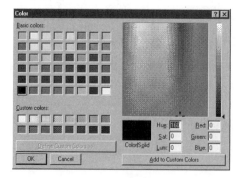

Two properties that you should set before displaying the Color dialog box are `DialogTitle` and `Flags`. `DialogTitle` displays a title in the Color dialog box's title bar. `Flags` determines how the dialog box appears. Table 17.1 lists the flag values you can use for the Color dialog box. You can combine these values by adding them together if you want to specify several values in the same dialog box.

Table 17.1 Color Dialog Box *Flags* Values

Named Literal	*Flags* Value	Description
cdlCCRGBInit	1	Sets the initial color value
cdlCCFullOpen	2	Displays the entire dialog box, including the Define Custom Colors section
cdlCCPreventFullOpen	4	Prevents users from defining custom colors
cdlCCHelpButton	8	Displays a Help button in the dialog box

The Font Dialog Box

Figure 17.6 shows the Font dialog box that the Common Dialog Box control produces.

FIG. 17.6

The Font dialog box provides a font selection.

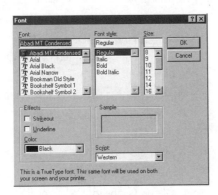

The fonts vary depending on the computer on which your application is running. The Font dialog box ensures that the font is available to your application, because the fonts come from the current machine and not from the computer that produced the program. Before you print or display certain text, you may want to give each user a chance to format the text (perhaps with the Format menu's standard Font command), so display the Font dialog box and then assign the selected values to the user's text.

You must set the proper Font dialog box **Flags** value from Table 17.2. Otherwise, the Font dialog box won't appear.

Table 17.2   Font Dialog Box *Flags* Values

Named Literal	*Flags* Value	Description
cdlCFANSIOnly	&H400	Ensures that the dialog box allows only fonts from the Windows character set and not a symbol-based font
cdlCFApply	&H200	Enables the dialog box's Apply button
cdlCFBoth	&H3	Lists the available printer and screen fonts in the dialog box; the **hDC** property identifies the device context associated with the printer
cdlCFEffects	&H100	Lets the dialog box enable strikethrough, underline, and color effects
cdlCFFixedPitchOnly	&H4000	Ensures that the dialog box selects only fixed-pitch fonts
cdlCFForceFontExist	&H10000	Displays an error message box if users try to select a font or style that doesn't exist
cdlCFHelpButton	&H4	Displays the dialog box's Help button
cdlCFLimitSize	&H2000	Ensures that the dialog box selects only font sizes within the range specified by the **Min** and **Max** properties
cdlCFNoFaceSel	&H80000	No font name is selected as the default
cdlCFNoSimulations	&H1000	Disallows graphic device interface (GDI) font simulations
cdlCFNoSizeSel	&H200000	No font size is selected as the default
cdlCFNoStyleSel	&H100000	No font style is selected as the default
cdlCFNoVectorFonts	&H800	Disallows vector-font selections
cdlCFPrinterFonts	&H2	Lists only the fonts supported by the printer, specified by the **hDC** property
cdlCFScalableOnly	&H20000	Allows only the selection of scalable fonts
cdlCFScreenFonts	&H1	Lists only the screen fonts supported by the system

Named Literal	*Flags* Value	Description
cdlCFTTOnly	&H40000	Allows only the selection of TrueType fonts
cdlCFWYSIWYG	&H8000	Specifies that the dialog box allows only the selection of fonts available on the printer and on-screen (if you set this flag, you should also set cdlCFBoth and cdlCFScalableOnly)

> **CAUTION** You must set at least one of the following values before the Font dialog box appears correctly: cdlCFScreenFonts, cdlCFPrinterFonts, or cdlCFBoth. Otherwise, Visual Basic issues an error message.

You may need to set more than one **Flags** value, such as **cdlCFNoStyleSel** and **cdlCFScreenFonts**. Use the logical **And** or **Or** operator to combine these **Flags** values, as in the following assignment:

```
cdbFontDB.Flags = cdlCFNoStyleSel And cdlCFScreenFonts
```

After you set the **Flags** property, apply the **ShowFont** method to the dialog box to display the Fonts dialog box. You can't set multiple **Flags** at design time, only at runtime.

Example Suppose that you've added two Common Dialog Box controls, **cdbColor** and **cdbFont**, to a form. To activate and respond to the Color dialog box, you might code a procedure section that looks something like this:

```
' Set the Color Flags property.
cdbColor.Flags = cdlCCFullOpen  ' Display complete Color DB
' Display the Color dialog box.
cdbColor.ShowColor
' Set a label's foreground color
' to the dialog box's selected color.
lblMessage.ForeColor = cdbColor.Color
```

You might set up and respond to the Font dialog box like this:

```
' Set the Font Flags property.
CdbFont.Flags = cdlCFBoth Or cdlCFEffects
CdbFont.ShowFont  ' Display the Font DB
' Set a label's properties to the
' user's selected font information
LblMessage.Font.Name = CdbFont.FontName
LblMessage.Font.Size = CdbFont.FontSize
```

Pt **III**

Hr **17**

```
LblMessage.Font.Bold = CdbFont.FontBold
LblMessage.Font.Italic = CdbFont.FontItalic
LblMessage.Font.Underline = CdbFont.FontUnderline
LblMessage.FontStrikethru = CdbFont.FontStrikethru
LblMessage.ForeColor = CdbFont.Color
```

Pay attention to the multipart assignments of the first five properties when this code returns from the dialog box display. There are several values, each of which indicates a different kind of font. Read such multipart names from right to left. Consider the following statement:

```
LblMessage.Font.Bold = CdbFont.FontBold
```

This tells Visual Basic to assign the dialog box's `FontBold` property (which is either `True` or `False`) to the `Bold` attribute of the `Font` property of the label named `lblMessage`.

One problem with the code presented here is that no provision is made for a Cancel click in the dialog box. To test to see whether users have clicked Cancel, you need to learn a new Visual Basic command—the `On Error Goto` statement. This statement jumps the program execution down to a code label if an error occurs during subsequent statements. Therefore, the statement

```
On Error Goto dbErrHandler
```

tells Visual Basic to jump to the code labeled `dbErrHandler` if an error occurs during any line that follows the `On Error Goto` statement (until the end of the procedure).

A *code label* is a label inside your Code window's code that you name using the same naming rules used for variables. A label, however, must end in a colon to distinguish it from a variable name. With the example just given, the procedure must have the following code label somewhere after the `On Error Goto` statement (generally, programmers put the error code label toward the bottom of the procedure):

```
dbErrHandler:
```

The statements after the error-handling code label are executed if an error occurs in the procedure and an `Exit` statement terminates the procedure early. Visual Basic triggers an error condition if users click the Cancel button and you've set the `CancelError` property to `True`. Although clicking Cancel isn't a real error, treating it like an error condition lets you write code like that in Listing 17.1 to handle it.

On the CD

Listing 17.1 Cancel.bas: Controlling the User's Cancel Selection

```
Private Sub cmdMessage_Click()
   cdbFont.CancelError = True   ' Causes an error if
                                ' user clicks Cancel
   On Error Goto dbErrHandler   ' Jump if an error occurs

' Set the Font Flags property.
   CdbFont.Flags = cdlCFBoth Or cdlCFEffects
   CdbFont.ShowFont   ' Display the Font DB
   ' Set a label's properties to the
   ' user's selected font information
   LblMessage.Font.Name = CdbFont.FontName
   LblMessage.Font.Size = CdbFont.FontSize
   LblMessage.Font.Bold = CdbFont.FontBold
   LblMessage.Font.Italic = CdbFont.FontItalic
   LblMessage.Font.Underline = CdbFont.FontUnderline
   LblMessage.FontStrikethru = CdbFont.FontStrikethru
   LblMessage.ForeColor = CdbFont.Color
   Exit Sub
dbErrHandler:
   ' The user clicked cancel so ignore the proc
   Exit Sub
End Sub
```

Rather than end the procedure if users click Cancel, you might choose to set default values for the label rather than retain the current values and exit the procedure.

Next Step Although you can set all the Common Dialog Box control properties at runtime, Visual Basic provides an ingenious way to set some properties at design time.

The Common Dialog Box control contains a property named Custom. When you click the ellipsis for this property setting in the Properties window, Visual Basic displays the Property Pages dialog box (Figure 17.7 shows the dialog box's Font page).

The Property Pages dialog box makes it easy for you to set some initial dialog box properties. Here you can review the most important properties for each style of common dialog box. For example, if you want the Font dialog box's default font to be 12-point Bold, type **12** in the FontSize text box and click to select the Bold check box.

FIG. 17.7

You can set properties at design time from the Property Pages dialog box.

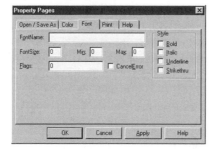

Topic 3: The Remaining Dialog Boxes

Now that you've mastered the Color and Font dialog boxes—including the necessary handling if Cancel is clicked—the remaining dialog boxes are simple.

Overview   The Open and Save common dialog boxes are virtually identical, and you set them up in almost the same manner. The key difference is that the Open dialog box displays a list of files from which users select one (or more) to open, whereas the Save dialog box lets your users select a single file name (and location) to use for saving data. You need to worry only about setting certain default values.

The Print dialog box prepares users for printing to whatever printer (or fax) they select. Your program can read the Print dialog box responses to know how many copies users want and where they want the printed output sent.

The Open Dialog Box

Figure 17.8 shows the Open dialog box that the Common Dialog Box control produces. The Open dialog box ensures that users select a valid computer (in a networked environment), drive, path name, and file name.

Although you don't have to set any `Flags` values before displaying the Open dialog box, Table 17.3 lists the optional `Flags` values that you might want to set before triggering the dialog box's `ShowOpen` method.

FIG. 17.8

The Open dialog box lets users select a file to open.

Table 17.3 The Open and Save Dialog Boxes' *Flags* Values

Named Literal	*Flags* Value	Description
cdlOFNAllowMultiselect	&H200	Lets the File Name list box accept multiple file selections. The FileName property then returns a string that contains all the selected file names (names in the string are delimited by spaces).
cdlOFNCreatePrompt	&H2000	Prompts users to create a file that doesn't currently exist. This flag automatically sets the cdlOFNPathMustExist and cdlOFNFileMustExist flags.
cdlOFNExplorer	&H80000	Uses the Explorer-like Open a File dialog box template.
cdlOFNExtensionDifferent	&H400	Indicates that the extension of the returned file name is different from the extension specified by the DefaultExt property. This flag isn't set if the DefaultExt property contains Null, if the extensions match, or if the file has no extension. You can inspect this flag's value after the dialog box is closed.
cdlOFNFileMustExist	&H1000	Lets users enter only names of existing files. If this flag is set and users enter an invalid file name, a warning is displayed. This flag automatically sets the cdlOFNPathMustExist flag.
cdlOFNHelpButton	&H10	Displays the dialog box's Help button.
cdlOFNHideReadOnly	&H4	Hides the read-only check box.

Pt **III**

Hr **17**

continues

Table 17.3 Continued

Named Literal	*Flags* Value	Description
cdlOFNLongNames	&H200000	Allows long file names.
cdlOFNNoChangeDir	&H8	Forces the dialog box to set the current directory to what it was when the dialog box was opened.
cdlOFNNoDereferenceLinks	&H100000	Disallows dereferencing of *shell links* (also known as *shortcuts*). By default, choosing a shell link causes it to be dereferenced by the shell.
cdlOFNNoLongNames	&H40000	Disallows long file names.
cdlOFNNoReadOnlyReturn	&H8000	Specifies that the returned file won't have the read-only attribute set and won't be in a write-protected directory.
cdlOFNNoValidate	&H100	Allows invalid characters in the returned file name.
cdlOFNOverwritePrompt	&H2	Causes the Save As dialog box to generate a warning message box if the selected file already exists (users then choose whether to overwrite the existing file).
cdlOFNPathMustExist	&H800	Lets users enter only valid paths. If this flag is set and the users enter an invalid path, a warning message is displayed.
cdlOFNReadOnly	&H1	Selects the read-only check box when the dialog box is created. This flag also indicates the state of the read-only check box after the dialog box is closed.
cdlOFNShareAware	&H4000	Indicates that possible sharing violation errors will be ignored.

When you display an Open dialog box, you may want to specify a filter for the file-name extensions that the box shows. This determines the file types that the users see in the Files of Type text box, but they can override these extensions. To specify the filter, type the desired extensions in the `Filter` property. The file types appear in the Files of Type text box, separated by semicolons. The filter, if you specify one, is a string and must conform to this format:

```
"FilterDescrip1 ¦ extension1 ¦ FilterDescrip2 ¦ extension2 ¦
➥FilterDescrip3 ¦ extension3"
```

For example, the following statement assigns a filter that shows only Word and Excel documents when the Open dialog box appears:

```
cmdFiles.Filter = "Word Docs (*.doc)¦*.doc¦
➥Excel Docs (*.xls)¦*.xls"
```

▼ NOTE

Don't confuse the file extensions in the description with the actual extensions in the filter. In the example, Word Docs (*.doc) is text to be displayed to users, and the *.doc following the first pipe symbol is the dialog box's first actual filtering instruction. ▲

You can supply multiple filters by including multiple strings for the `Filter` property. If you specify more than one filter, you must set the `FilterIndex` property to the filter you want to use for the current Open dialog box. The first filter has a `FilterIndex` of 1; this number is incremented if you supply additional filters.

The Common Dialog Box control's `FileName` property holds the selected file name after users close the dialog box.

The Save Dialog Box

Figure 17.9 shows the Save dialog box that the Common Dialog Box control produces when you apply the `ShowSave` method to the control's name.

Pt **III**

Hr **17**

FIG. 17.9
The Save dialog box lets users select a file name to use for saving data. (It becomes the Save As dialog box if you've yet to name the file you are saving.)

▼ **NOTE**
Review the differences between the Save and Open dialog boxes. They're both used to help users select a file name, but although users can save data to only one file name, they can—if your application and the `Flags` property allow—select multiple files to open from the Open dialog box. Also, the Save dialog box grays out all existing file names and displays only the directory paths to files. ▲

The Save dialog box uses the same `Flags` values as the Open `Flags` values you saw in Table 17.4.

The Print Dialog Box

Figure 17.10 shows the Print dialog box that the Common Dialog Box control produces when you apply the `ShowPrinter` method to the control name. Users can select the printer type, number of copies, range of pages, and several other printing options. Each printer setup for the users' system displays a different set of Print dialog box options. When users enter the desired values, your application can use that information (taken from the Common Dialog Box control's properties) to direct the print output properly.

FIG. 17.10
The Print dialog box lets users select printer options.

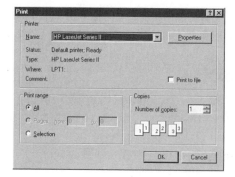

▼ **NOTE**
Your Print dialog box will vary from Figure 17.10, depending on your printer type. ▲

  Figure 17.11 shows the Open dialog box that results from the procedure in Listing 17.2.

Listing 17.2 Filter.bas: Creating Advanced Open Dialog Boxes

```
Private Sub mnuFileOpen_Click ()
' Assumes CancelError is True
  On Error Goto dbErrHandler
  ' Determine what appears in
  ' the Files of type text box
  cdbFile.Filter = "Text Files (*.txt) ¦ *.txt"
  ' Specify default filter
  cdbFile.FilterIndex = 1

  ' Display the Open dialog box.
  cdbFile.ShowOpen

  ' *****
  ' You must place code here or call
  ' a procedure to open the file
  ' selected by the user
  ' *****
  Exit Sub   ' Don't fall through

dbErrHandler:
  ' User clicked the Cancel button
  Exit Sub   ' Don't open a file
End Sub
```

FIG. 17.11

*You can limit an
Open dialog box
to show only
text files.*

Next Step The code in Listing 17.3 displays a Print dialog box and checks to see
whether Cancel is clicked.

Listing 17.3   Printdb.bas: Using the Common Dialog Box to Direct Printed Output

```
Private cmdPrintIt_Click()
  Dim intBegin As Integer, intEnd As Integer
  Dim intNumCopies As Integer, intI As Integer
  ' Assumes Cancel is set to True

  On Error Goto dbErrHandler
  ' Display the Print dialog box
  cbdPrint.ShowPrinter
  ' Get user-selected values from the dialog box
  intBegin = cbdPrint.FromPage
  intEnd = cbdPrint.ToPage
  intNumCopies = cbdPrint.Copies
  For intI = 1 To intNumCopies
    ' Put code here to send data to your printer
  Next intI
  Exit Sub

dbErrHandler:
  ' User pressed Cancel button
  Exit Sub
```

Summary

In this lesson, you mastered the Common Dialog Box control. This control becomes any of the following specific dialog boxes: Color, Font, Open, Save, Print, and Help.

The Common Dialog Box control is invisible on your form when the application runs. At design time, you can place the control anywhere that's out of the way of other controls you want to work with in the Form window.

When users trigger a situation that requires a dialog box, you use code to set appropriate dialog box properties and display the dialog box (you have no control over where the dialog box appears). The resulting dialog box is a standard Windows dialog box that will be familiar to your users. When users make selections in the dialog box and close it, your code uses the information by accessing the Common Dialog Box control properties.

In Hour 18, you'll add a few more controls to your repertoire so that you can customize your applications to their fullest.

Hour 17 Quiz

You can find the answers for the following questions on the accompanying CD-ROM and on the Virtual Classroom Web site.

On the CD

1. What must you do to your Toolbox before you can work with the Common Dialog Box control?

2. Name the specific dialog boxes that the Common Dialog Box control displays.

3. What purpose does the Common Dialog Box control serve?

4. Why can't you adjust the size of the Common Dialog Box control on your form?

5. **True or false:** The Open dialog box doesn't really open anything.

6. What role does the `Filter` property play in the file-related dialog boxes?

7. What does the `Flags` property do?

8. **True or false:** You must set a `Flags` value, or Visual Basic won't display the Fonts dialog box.

9. **True or false:** You must set a `Flags` value, or Visual Basic won't display the Print dialog box.

10. **True or false:** The `Show` method displays a Common Dialog Box control.

Pt **III**

Hr **17**

Hour 17 Homework Exercises

1. Write a filter that displays an Open dialog box showing files with these extensions and descriptions:

Description	Extension
Microsoft PowerPoint	*.ppt
ASCII Text Files	*.asc
Visual Basic Project Files	*.vbp

2. Create a text box that displays the words *Your Text*. Before displaying the text box, ask users for font information that will determine the way the text box displays its contents.

3. Write a small application that contains one command button and one Common Dialog Box control. When users click the command button, ask them for a color and then change the form background to that color.

Using Additional Controls

THIS HOUR'S LESSON explores more controls in the Toolbox, so you can expand your Visual Basic knowledge and begin to add these new controls to your applications. You'll see that manipulating new controls doesn't require many additional programming skills, because all VB controls support a set of properties that you can set at design time with the Properties window or at runtime with code. Some controls do require extra coding, but that coding generally only initializes and manages the control.

During this hour you will learn

▶ *What scroll bar controls Visual Basic supports*

▶ *How the Slider control improves user input*

▶ *When the Picture Box control adds power over the Image control*

▶ *Which file list controls Visual Basic supports*

Topic 1: Scrolling Along

Many times, Visual Basic adds scroll bars to your applications for you. For example, when you programmed multiline text boxes in Hour 4, "Activating Controls," Visual Basic displayed a horizontal or vertical scroll bar (or both) if the multiline text box wasn't large enough to display all the text. In addition to the automatic scroll bars that appear when necessary, you can place vertical and horizontal scroll bars anywhere on your forms when you want to give users more control over a list, volume, or position within a document.

▶▶ FAST TRACK

Do you want to scroll past scroll bars? If you already know how to program them or want to return to them later, you can jump to the next topic section, "The Picture Box Control" (p. 439), to learn the advantages and disadvantages of using a Picture Box control instead of an Image control. (On your way to the next topic section, check out this topic's "Next Step" section on p. 437 if you want to learn about the Slider control.)

Overview Scroll bars allow users to shift their position within a text area, a graphic, or any of a number of other form objects. Unlike the built-in scroll bars that automatically appear—such as those on the multiline text box shown in Figure 18.1—you must carefully control the scroll bars that you choose to place on the form.

FIG. 18.1
Visual Basic controls automatic scroll bars such as these.

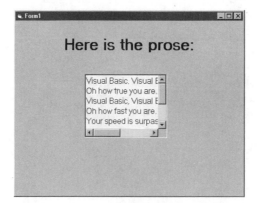

▼ **NOTE**
Visual Basic offers the vertical scroll bar and horizontal scroll bar individually because you won't always want to place both of them on the form at the same time. ▲

The scroll bars that you place on your forms conform to the Windows 95 standard that automatically adjusts the size of the scroll bar's *thumb* (the moving bar inside the scroll bar shaft) to display the relative size of the scrolling area. The thumb is small when the scroll range is large to show your users that the scroll bar controls many values; the thumb is large when the scroll range is small to show your users that the scroll bar controls only a few values.

Scroll Bar Setup

When you place scroll bars on your form, you'll be most concerned with setting the scroll bar properties described in Table 18.1.

Table 18.1 Important Scroll Bar Properties

Property	Description
LargeChange	The amount the scroll bar changes when users click it on either side of the thumb (if you were scrolling text, for example, LargeChange might scroll a full screen)
Max	The maximum value returned from the scroll bar when users scroll the scroll bar to its most extreme position (the far right for horizontal scroll bars and the bottom for vertical scroll bars)
Min	Specifies the minimum value returned from the scroll bar when users scroll the scroll bar to its least extreme position (the far left for horizontal scroll bars and the top for vertical scroll bars)
SmallChange	The amount the scroll bar changes when users click a scroll bar arrow to move the thumb either direction (if you were scrolling text, for example, SmallChange might scroll a single line)
Value	The scroll bar's current value, bounded by the Min and Max properties as well as the increment

As you can see from Table 18.1, a scroll bar is a general-purpose control that returns values based on minimum and maximum values. For example, you can set up a scroll bar that steps through (as users scroll) the returned values 1 through 1,000 with a `LargeChange` increment of 25, steps through the returned values 100 through 200 with a `LargeChange` increment of 1, or steps through the returned values 1,000 through 32,000 with a `LargeChange` increment of 5,000. In other words, you can control all aspects of the scroll bar's returned value range and increment by setting the appropriate properties at design time or runtime.

CAUTION The scroll bar can return only positive integer values (from 1 to 32,767), so you can't increment or set maximum and minimum fractional values. If the scroll bar is to select fractional values, you have to apply an appropriate calculation to the scroll bar's `Value` property to convert the integer value to a fractional value.

You can set the height and width of a scroll bar at design time or runtime. The scroll bar's default thickness is a standard Windows size, and you'll generally want only to adjust the length.

Example Scroll bars allow you to pan across graphic images. When you pan across a large picture, only a portion of the picture appears at any one time. Although scroll bars themselves don't do anything to the graphic display, you can use the scroll bar values to adjust images.

To experience one panning method, create a new project and adjust the form's `Width` and `Height` measurements to 7,155 and 5,535 respectively. Add a Frame control that takes the entire form, but leave enough room at the right and below the frame for vertical and horizontal scroll bars (make the frame's `Caption` property blank).

Add the vertical and horizontal scroll bars (named `vsbMoney` and `hsbMoney`). Set the `vsbMoney.Min` property to 850 and the `hsbMoney.Max` property to 1200. Set each scroll bar's `LargeChange` property to 50. Your form window should look something like the one shown in Figure 18.2.

FIG. 18.2

You can create a control that pans the window.

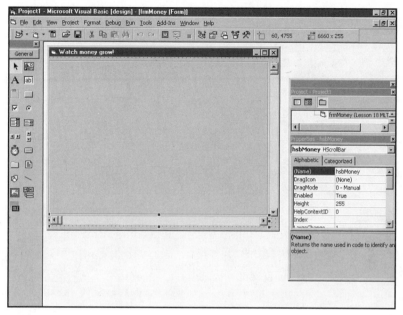

Now add an Image control named `imgMoney` to the frame. To place the image on the frame, double-click the Image control to place an image on the form, cut the image, and then paste the image back onto the frame area. This seems redundant, but you want to ensure that Visual Basic considers the image part of the frame. Expand the image to the size of the frame.

Set the image's `Picture` property to this file in your VB directory: \Graphics\ Metafile\Business\Dollar.WMF. The .WMF extension indicates that the file is a Windows *metafile*, meaning that you can enlarge the image to a width of 12,000 twips and a height of 8,500 twips. (A *twip* is a Windows pixel measurement that is a twentieth of a pixel.) The dollar bill won't completely fit within the frame's width (this is good). Move the image so that you see only the right edge of the bill. Users will pan the bill into view at runtime.

Name the Image control `imgMoney`. Figure 18.3 shows how your screen should look.

Pt **III**

Hr **18**

Add the following two event procedures that adjust the image's area when users change a scroll bar:

```
Private Sub vsbMoney_change()
   imgMoney.Top = vsbMoney.Value * 10
End Sub
Private Sub hsbMoney_Change()
   imgMoney.Left = hsbMoney.Value * 10
End Sub
```

When you run the application, the first time you scroll the image to the right with the horizontal scroll bar, the bill comes into view. The bill moves up and out of the way when you click the vertical scroll bar. Due to the image's original negative Left property value (because you moved the image so that only the right edge showed), the horizontal scroll bar doesn't put the image back where it first appeared but instead places the bill so that its edge touches the left window edge. Through code, you could adjust the scroll bar's Value property to position the bill back at a negative location if you wanted users to be able to scroll the bill off the window as it first appeared.

▼ **NOTE**
Several panning methods exist. You can control whether you want to move the application window over an image, or pan an image over an application's window (as is done here). The calculations inside the code handle the panning movement you want. ▲

Next Step If you use Visual Basic Professional Edition, you can add a tool representing the Slider control to your Toolbox. Choose Components from the Project menu and then click the control set named Microsoft Windows Common Controls 5.0. When you close the dialog box, your Toolbox will contain new controls (as shown in Figure 18.4), including the Slider control.

FIG. 18.4
The Slider Control now appears in your Toolbox.

The Slider tool

▼ NOTE

You must use the Professional or Enterprise Edition of Visual Basic to create this example. ▲

The Slider control works like the Horizontal Scroll Bar control, except that Microsoft recommends using the Slider control for user input when the input can span a range of values. For example, if users are to enter a number from 1 to 1,000, you could ask them to enter the number from within an input box, a text box, or with a scroll bar that moves through that range. Microsoft recommends that if you have access to a Slider control, you use it for such user input. The Slider control displays optional tick marks (through the TickStyle property) that you can control.

Pt **III**

Hr **18**

To consider the differences between a slider and a scroll bar, start a new project and place a horizontal scroll bar, a slider, a command button (with the `Caption` property set to `E&xit`), and two labels on the form, as shown in Figure 18.5.

FIG. 18.5
This form contains a scroll bar, a slider, a command button, and two Label controls.

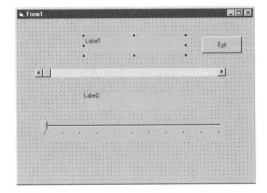

Name the first label `lblScroll` and set its `Font` size to 18. Name the second label `lblSlide` and set its `Font` size also to 18.

Name the command button `cmdExit` and complete this `Click` event procedure in the Code window:

```
Private Sub cmdExit_Click()
    Unload Me    ' Unloads the current form and ends program
End Sub
```

Name the scroll bar `hsbScroll` and name the Slider control `sldSlide`. Type the following event procedures:

```
Private Sub Form_Load()
    hsbScroll.Max = 150
    hsbScroll.Min = 0
    hsbScroll.LargeChange = 15
    hsbScroll.Value = 50
    lblScroll.Caption = hsbScroll.Value
    ' Now do same for slider
    sldSlide.Max = 150
    sldSlide.Min = 0
    sldSlide.LargeChange = 15
    sldSlide.Value = 50
    lblSlide.Caption = sldSlide.Value
End Sub
```

```
Private Sub hsbScroll_Change()
  lblScroll.Caption = hsbScroll.Value
End Sub

Private Sub sldSlide_Change()
  lblSlide.Caption = sldSlide.Value
End Sub
```

Run the application and click the shaft of the scroll bar to see what happens to its position. Then click the scroll bar arrows to study the difference in movement between the large change and small change values. Now, click the slider's line or drag the slider pointer to see how it works. Figure 18.6 shows the running application. You should note that `SmallChange` has no effect on the slider when used with the mouse, because the slider never has end buttons. The arrow keys, however, will work to move the slider incrementally in small steps when the slider has the focus.

FIG. 18.6
This simple application introduces you to the Slider control.

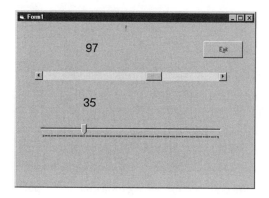

Topic 2: The Picture Box Control

You've already used the Image control to place images on the form. The Picture Box control works almost the same as the Image control does, except that the Image control isn't as flexible as the Picture Box control. Also, the Picture Box control is less efficient than the Image control, but today's fast computers should offer no speed problems. The Picture Box control supports more properties and methods than the Image control does.

Pt **III**

Hr **18**

▶▶ **FAST TRACK**

Are you far beyond displaying simple graphic images on your forms? Do you want more jazz in your applications? Check out the lessons in Part IV, "Adding Power to VB Programs" (beginning on p. 533), to read about multimedia and advanced graphics tools.

Overview This topic section reviews the Picture Box control and its properties. You'll have no trouble understanding the Picture Box control now that you've used the Image control. The key task you need to master is the `LoadPicture()` function, which lets you set Picture Box control images at runtime.

The Picture Box Control Setup

When you need to display a graphic image, you'll select the Picture Box control or the Image control. Both support the same fundamental set of properties, methods, and events, but you'll find that the Picture Box control offers a better choice of property options. Table 18.2 lists the most important Picture Box control properties.

Table 18.2 Important Picture Box Properties

Property	Description
Align	Determines the relative location where the picture appears on the form
AutoSize	Specifies whether the control is to expand or contract in size to display the entire picture, or whether the control is to display only a portion of the image
BorderStyle	Draws an optional border around the picture
FontTransparent	Determines whether background text will show through the image
Picture	Contains the path and file name of the graphic image

▼ **NOTE**

The Picture Box control doesn't support the Image control's `Stretch` property that you used in earlier lessons. The Picture Box control uses the `AutoSize` property to stretch the underlying control's size to the image being loaded. `AutoSize` allows this automatic resizing during runtime as you load different pictures into the image. ▲

You can specify at design time the initial image to be displayed in the Picture Box control by entering the path and file name in the control's

Picture property. Use the built-in `LoadPicture()` function when you want to display or change an image during runtime. Here is the syntax for using `LoadPicture()`:

```
picPictureCtl.Picture = LoadPicture(strExpression)
```

You can't directly assign the path and file name of the picture to the `Picture` property at runtime. You must enclose the path and file name inside the `LoadPicture()` function's argument. The following assignment statement replaces the Picture Box control's picture with a new image loaded from the root directory:

```
Picture1.Picture = LoadPicture("c:\planes.bmp")
```

Picture Box File Types

Table 18.3 lists the graphic file types you can load with the Picture Box control.

Table 18.3   File Types Supported by the Picture Box Control

Type	Extension
Bitmap	.BMP
Graphic Image File	.GIF
Icon	.ICO
JPEG	.JPG
Metafile	.WMF, .EMF

Example   Create a new project and place a Picture Box control in the center of the form window. Expand the form to a height of 6,825 and a width of 7,650. Expand the Picture Box control to a height of 3,540 and a width of 4,020.

Click the ellipsis (…) for the Picture Box control's `Picture` property, and then select the \Graphics\Metafile\Business\Dollar.WMF file used in the last topic section's example. The bill will appear shrunken (see Figure 18.7) because the Picture Box control's `AutoSize` property is set to `False`.

FIG. 18.7
`AutoSize` *is set to* `False`, *so the image appears shrunken.*

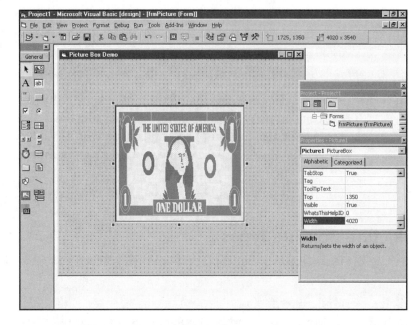

Change `AutoSize` to `True`, and the control immediately expands to the size of the file's image (see Figure 18.8).

FIG. 18.8
When `AutoSize` *is set to* `True`, *the image expands.*

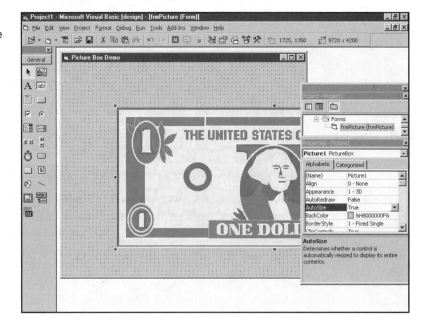

Change the `AutoSize` property back to `False` to see that the image doesn't shrink to its original size. When you set `AutoSize` to `True` at design time or runtime, the control's size increases or decreases to hold the entire image. Therefore, you now have to manually change the `Height` and `Width` properties back to 3,540 and 4,020. Name the Picture Box control `picPicture`.

Next Step   Add a command button named `cmdChangePic` to the previous example's form. Type `&Change Picture` for the `Caption` property of the command button. Add the following event procedure for the command button:

```
Private Sub cmdChangePic_Click()
    picPicture.Picture = LoadPicture("VB\Graphics\MetaFile\
                         ⇒Business\Computer.WMF")
End Sub
```

▼ NOTE

You have to insert the exact path of your computer's Computer.WMF file in the `LoadPicture()` function. If the line becomes too long to fit easily in the Code window, you can end the line early with Visual Basic's code-continuation character, an underscore (_) that follows a single space, and then continue it on the next line. ▲

When you run the program, you see the original dollar image. Click the command button to see the image shown in Figure 18.9.

FIG. 18.9
The picture has changed!

Topic 3: File-Related List Boxes

This topic section introduces some new kinds of list boxes. You already know how to work with simple list and combo boxes. You also know how to use the Open and Save dialog boxes. The Toolbox also contains three special list boxes that work with file data.

Overview

Visual Basic's three special list boxes help you manage directories, drives, and files. Here are descriptions of these special list boxes:

- **Directory.** Lets users select a directory.
- **Drive.** Lets users select a disk drive.
- **File.** Lets users select a file name.

Figure 18.10 shows a form window that contains all three kinds of special list boxes.

FIG. 18.10

You can work with these three special list boxes.

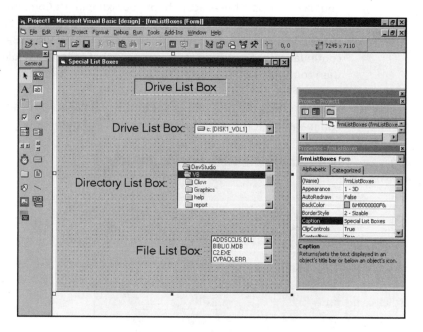

▼ **NOTE**
You might wonder why Visual Basic supplies these file-related controls, because you've already seen the Common Dialog Box control that supports the full use of these controls as a set without requiring you to place the controls individually on a form. Well, these special list controls let you place specific kinds of lists on a form whenever you need just one or two aspects of a file. For example, you might need to write data to users' disks. Although your application will handle the file name and directory, you need to ask the users which disk drive should receive the application's data. ▲

CAUTION These lists don't work in tandem with each other unless you program them to do so. For example, if you place the three controls on one form and run the application, changing the disk drive doesn't change the directory or file name shown in the other two controls.

The Drive List Box

Use the Drive List Box control to let users select a disk drive. This control is smart enough to search the host computer and determine which drives—local and remote, floppy, hard, and CD-ROM—exist on each user's system. The control then displays these choices graphically when users open the drive list box (see Figure 18.11).

FIG. 18.11
Users can select from the drive list box.

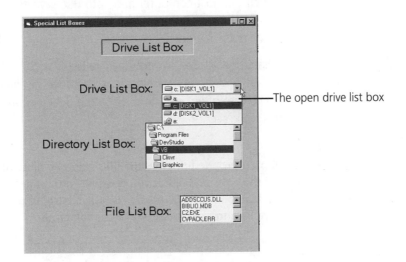

The open drive list box

▼ **NOTE**

The Drive List Box control first displays the drive from which users launched the application, but you can override this default drive by using Visual Basic code to point the control to another drive. ▲

The Directory List Box

Use the Directory List Box control to let users select a directory folder. This control is smart enough to search the host computer and determine which directories exist in the system. The directory list box displays these choices graphically by using the standard Windows format.

Remember that the Directory List Box control can't determine which drive is selected in the drive list box. You have to take care of linking the drive to the directory, as explained at the end of this topic section.

▼ **NOTE**

The Directory List Box control first displays the directory from which users launched the application, but you can override this default directory by using Visual Basic code to point the control to another directory. ▲

The File List Box

Use the File List Box control to let users select a file. This control is smart enough to search the host computer and determine which files exist in the file system. The file list box then displays these choices graphically by using the standard Windows format.

As with the Directory List Box control, the File List Box control can't determine which drive (or directory) is selected in the drive (or directory) list box. You have to take care of linking the drive to the directory, as explained at the end of this topic section.

▼ **NOTE**

The File List Box control first displays the files from the directory in which users launched the application, but you can override this default directory by using VB code to point the Directory List Box control to another directory before linking the file list box to the folder. ▲

Example Visual Basic supports several drive and directory commands that prepare the file list controls, as described in Table 18.4.

Table 18.4 Drive and Directory Commands

Command	Description
ChDrive *strDrive*	Changes the default drive to the drive in the string expression
ChDir *strDirectory*	Changes the default directory to the directory in the string expression (if you specify no drive inside the string, Visual Basic selects the directory on the current drive)
Kill *strFileSpec*	Erases the file or files specified with wild cards by the string expression
MkDir *strDirectory*	Creates the directory specified by the string expression
RmDir *strDirectory*	Erases the directory specified by the string expression

▼ **NOTE**
RmDir produces an error if you try to remove a directory that still contains files. ▲

In addition to the statements shown in Table 18.4, Visual Basic supports the Dir() function, which checks whether files exist, and the CurDir() function, which returns the name of the current directory.

Suppose that you want to point the Drive List Box and Directory List Box controls to the directory C:\MyFiles. You can insert the following code in the Form_Load() procedure:

```
ChDrive "C:"
ChDir "\MyFiles"
```

The Drive List Box, Directory List Box, and File List Box controls now point to the C:\MyFiles directory when they appear on the form, rather than to the application's current directory.

The Dir() function requires a little more explanation. Suppose that you want to know if a file named SALES98.DAT exists in the root directory on drive D. You can check for such a file this way:

```
If (Dir("c:\SALES98.DAT")) = "SALES98.DAT" Then
  msg = MsgBox ("The file exists")
Else
  msg = MsgBox ("The file does not exist")
End If
```

The `Dir()` function returns the file name you pass as an argument. The file name is returned only if that file resides inside the directory argument you provide. If `Dir()` doesn't return the file name, the file doesn't exist on the drive.

You can pass `Dir()` a wild-card file specification like this:

```
Dir("c:\Sales*.DAT")
```

`Dir()` will return the first file found that meets the wild-card specification—if any files meet the specification. After you pass the first file specification, you can make subsequent calls to `Dir()` by specifying `Dir` without parentheses or any argument. Visual Basic keeps returning files that match your wild-card file specification until the last file is found. When `Dir` returns a null string (`""`), you must include a file specification in the next call to `Dir()`; otherwise, `Dir` will return an error.

Next Step If you want to set the Drive List Box control's drive to a specific disk drive, set the control's `Drive` property this way:

```
drvDisk.Drive = "d:\"
```

The Drive List Box control then will display with D: at the top of the list. If users change the drive list box to a different drive, the drive list box's `Change()` event occurs. You can set the users' selected drive to the default drive with the following statement inside `drvDisk_Change()`:

```
ChDrive drvDisk.Drive
```

Use the following code to set the `Drive` property of the Directory List Box control to the drive the control is to display:

```
dirDirect.Drive = drvDisk.Drive
```

This assignment statement sets the directory's drive to the directory selected by the users. You can add the Directory List Box control's disk assignment to the `drvDisk_Change()` event procedure.

After users change the Directory List Box control to a different directory, the control's `Change` event occurs. In the `Change` event procedure, you can set the current directory to the users' directory this way:

```
ChDir dirDirect.Path
```

The Directory List Box control supports a rather unusual access scheme—it supports a property named `ListIndex`. The value of `ListIndex` is –1 for the selected directory, –2 for the directory immediately above the selected one, –3 for the directory immediately above that, and so on. The `ListIndex` property is 0 for the first subdirectory of the selected directory, 1 for the next subdirectory, and so on.

If you want to display only certain files in the file list box, assign a string file specification, as follows, to the File List Box control's `Pattern` property:

```
filFiles.Pattern = "*.vbp; *.frm"
```

You can include as many file specifications as you like, indicated with wild cards within the string's quotation marks. The File List Box control immediately changes to reflect the new pattern by showing only those files. When users select a file, the File List Box control's `Change` event occurs and the selected file appears in the `FileName` property. As with the Drive List Box control, the selected file also appears as the `ListIndex` value of –1.

After users select a path, you can change the File List Box control to reflect files in that path, as follows:

```
filFiles.Path = dirDirect.Path
```

Summary

This lesson explained how to use the scroll bar controls as well as the Slider, Picture Box, and file list controls to add more processing capability to your forms. As you learn more controls, you increase your Visual Basic programming bag of tricks and can add extra I/O capability for your users.

The scroll bar controls give users a way to pan, select, and enter values with the mouse or keyboard. Visual Basic supports horizontal and vertical scroll bars. You can adjust all the scroll bar attributes so that the scroll bars return the values you need when users change the scroll bar. If you use the Professional or Enterprise Edition of Visual Basic, you can offer Slider controls so that your users can more easily enter values without the keyboard.

Pt **III**

Hr **18**

The Picture Box control displays images just like the Image control does. Unlike the Image control, however, the Picture Box control adds flexibility so that you can automatically adjust the size of the picture box based on the size of the image you want to display.

The last topic section taught you the individual file list controls available from the standard Toolbox. Although you almost always will use the Open and Save dialog boxes for user control of file selections (the dialog boxes require less programming work), the individual file list controls provide a way for you to let users select individual files, directories, or drives when needed.

In Hour 19, you'll learn how to integrate the users' printers into your Visual Basic applications.

Hour 18 Quiz

You can find the answers for the following questions on the accompanying CD-ROM and on the Virtual Classroom Web site.

On the CD

1. What's the difference between a scroll bar's `LargeChange` and `SmallChange` properties?

2. What must you do before using the Slider control?

3. Which control is better for user input: the scroll bar or slider?

4. Which is more efficient: the Image control or the Picture Box control?

5. What's wrong with the following assignment?

   ```
   Picture1.Picture = "c:\planes.bmp"
   ```

6. What property does the Picture Box control use in place of the Image control's `Stretch` property?

7. What does the Picture Box control's `AutoSize` property do to the control's size measurements?

8. Look at the following code and determine what the contents of the text box's `Text` property will be after users change the drive:

   ```
   Private Sub drvDrive_Change ()
     txtAns.Text = drvDrive.Drive
   End Sub
   ```

9. Explain the difference between the `Dir()` function with an argument and the `Dir` function without an argument.

10. What's the likely cause of an error that arises from the following statement? (Assume that the directory named Bills exists and resides in the root directory of C.)

```
RmDir "C:\Bills"
```

Hour 18 Homework Exercises

1. Change the Picture Box control application you created in the second topic's "Next Step" section (p. 443) to display the Open dialog box when users want to change the image in the Picture Box control. When users select a graphic file, display the selected file in the image. Be sure to write the supporting code that sets the default file type to .wmf metafile graphic images and that handles the users' click of the Cancel button by keeping the original image in the Picture Box control.

2. Create a dialog box that mimics the Open dialog box. Use only drive, directory, and file-selection lists as well as OK and Cancel command buttons. Write code so that an application that uses this dialog box will change the directory or file lists whenever users select a different drive or directory.

Printing with VB

NOW THAT YOU'VE mastered Visual Basic's development environment, learned a lot of the language, and can develop working applications, you should know how Visual Basic deals with printed output. Obviously, you'll want your applications to print things sometimes. Until now, you've had no way to send information to the printer.

Be forewarned—Visual Basic's printer interface isn't as simple as most of the other VB components you've mastered. Printing data from a VB program usually isn't a trivial task. This lesson explains how to work with the several printer interfaces available to VB programmers.

Topic 1: Printing Forms

One of the easiest ways to send output to your printer is to print a form. VB includes the `PrintForm` method that applies to any form in your project. To get output to the printer, simply write to the form by using the standard controls that you've already mastered with the `Print` method, and then print the form.

Overview This topic section explains the `PrintForm` method. Like the `Print` method, you apply `PrintForm` to your project's forms. When you issue a `PrintForm` method, Visual Basic begins printing the form immediately. Therefore, you must have the form ready for output before issuing `PrintForm`. This topic section explains how to use `PrintForm` to achieve the best results. You'll see that `PrintForm` won't suffice for much of your Visual Basic printing, but that the method works well for outputting forms to the printer.

TIP Perhaps the biggest benefit of `PrintForm`, as well as VB's other printer-output capabilities, is that VB uses Windows printer objects. Thus, you never need to worry about specific printing instructions that are unique to a certain printer brand and model.

The *PrintForm* Method

Here is the syntax for the `PrintForm` method:

```
[frmFormName.]PrintForm
```

Notice that *frmFormName* is optional; if you don't specify a form name, Visual Basic applies the `PrintForm` method to the current form.

To print a form named `frmAccPayable`, you would issue the following command at the event procedure or module procedure that requires the printing:

```
frmAccPayable.PrintForm     ' Print the Accounts Payable form
```

If `frmAccPayable` is the current form (the form with the focus whose title bar is highlighted), you can omit the form name as follows:

```
PrintForm     ' Print the Accounts Payable form
```

Me refers to the current form, so you can also issue the following statement to print the current form:

```
Me.PrintForm    ' Print the Accounts Payable form
```

> **TIP** You can return to Hour 16, "Creating VB Forms," to review the Print method. Print sends text output directly to the form. You can send output to a form with Print and then print the form with PrintForm. Remember, though, that all controls that appear on the form will also appear on the printed output.

PrintForm Warnings

PrintForm's strength lies in its simplicity. PrintForm definitely provides the most useful and simplest printer output within Visual Basic. Unfortunately, along with PrintForm's simplicity come a few problems that you should know about.

No matter how high a resolution a user's printer can print, PrintForm prints the form at the screen's current resolution. This resolution generally goes no higher than 96 DPI (*dots per inch*). Printer resolutions often range as high as 600 DPI, so the form won't look as good on paper as the form looks on-screen. (96 DPI is plenty adequate for screen resolution but isn't high enough for quality printout resolution.)

You must always make sure that the form's AutoRedraw property is set to True before you print any form that contains controls and other non-text graphic elements. By default, a form's AutoRedraw property is False, meaning that the Print method prints directly atop graphical controls. If you set AutoRedraw to True, the graphic image stays in the foreground while Print does its thing behind the image and doesn't overwrite part or all of the graphic. You might use AutoRedraw's False property to create background graphics first. You can later write text on top of it, but then set the AutoRedraw property to True immediately before printing the form, so the output appears correctly on the printer.

Be careful, because PrintForm prints those objects placed on the form at design time (and their runtime control values for controls such as labels and text boxes) only if AutoRedraw is False. Therefore, if you add graphics and pictures to a form at runtime and then want to print the form with

`PrintForm`, be sure to set the form's `AutoRedraw` property to `True` before adding the additional items. Otherwise, the runtime additions won't appear on the printed form.

> **CAUTION** Printing is sometimes the bane of the Windows programmer. Test your application on as many different printers as possible to make sure that you're getting adequate results. You can't ensure that your printed output will look great on every printer, but you should have an idea of the results on a few common printer types if you distribute your applications to a wide range of users. Your application is dependent, of course, on users' printer drivers being properly installed and set up. Your application also depends on users selecting an appropriate printer.
>
> Your application can do only a certain amount of work toward good printing results, because the Windows printer interface takes over much of your printer interface job. Windows is only trying to help by putting this interface buffer between your application and the printer—and you certainly have to code much less than the MS-DOS programmers of old, who had to take into consideration every possible printer in existence (an impossible task because printers often came out after the code was written but before the application was distributed).

Example You could print a text message to a blank form and then send that message to the printer like this:

```
Dim blnAutoRedraw As Boolean    ' Holds value of AutoRedraw
'
frmBlank.Print "This is a Division Listing"
frmBlank.Print     ' Blank line
frmBlank.Print "Division"; Tab(20); "Location"
frmBlank.Print "--------"; Tab(20); "--------"
frmBlank.Print "North"; Tab(20); "Widgets"
frmBlank.Print "South"; Tab(20); "Presses"
frmBlank.Print "East"; Tab(20); "Dye Tools"
frmBlank.Print "West"; Tab(20); "Grinders"
'
' Save the form's AutoRedraw Property
'
blnAutoRedraw = frmBlank.AutoRedraw
'
' Now print the form
'
frmBlank.AutoRedraw
frmBlank.PrintForm
```

```
'
' Restore the AutoRedraw Property
'
frmBlank.AutoRedraw = blnAutoRedraw
```

This code demonstrates saving the form's `AutoRedraw` property before triggering the `PrintForm` method. Although in this case you're probably safe
setting the `AutoRedraw` property to `True` at design time (assuming that
you'll never send graphics to the form elsewhere in the application), you
can use this property-saving feature before you print any form.

TIP   Create a standard module property that receives a form as its argument
(you can send and receive forms just as you do variable data types), saves the
`AutoRedraw` property, and prints the form with `PrintForm`. This general-purpose
procedure will save you from having to code the `AutoRedraw`-saving property
each time you print with `PrintForm`.

Next Step   Any time you print, check for error conditions. The user's printer might not
be turned on, might not be connected to the computer, or might not have
paper. Use the **On Error Goto** command, as follows:

```
Private Sub cmdPrintForm_Click ()
   Dim intBtnClicked As Integer
   On Error Goto ErrHandler      ' Set up error handler.
   frmAccPayable.PrintForm       ' Print form.
   Exit Sub
ErrHandler:
   intBtnClicked = MsgBox("A printer problem exists",
                  ➥vbExcalamtion, "Print Error")
End Sub
```

TIP   When you need to print a fill-in-the-blank form from a VB application,
there's no better way to do so than to create the form and then issue the
`PrintForm` method.

▼ NOTE
You'll probably want to remove the form's title bar, control menu icon,
and window buttons before printing most forms. You can temporarily hide
a form and display another while your code removes these extras by
setting the appropriate display property values to `False`. **▲**

Pt **III**

Hr **19**

Topic 2: The *Printers* Collection

The printer that Visual Basic selects for `PrintForm`'s output is your user's Windows default printer. What if you don't want to print to the default printer? You have access to all printers on the system. Some Windows users connect multiple printers to their systems via multiple printer ports. Also, internal faxes often act as just another printer. You can print to any printer or fax from your application by selecting the appropriate printer as Visual Basic's default printer. After you set Visual Basic's default printer, Visual Basic will route all output to that printer and ignore the system's default printer until the application ends or you designate yet another default printer.

> **TIP** To set a different Windows default printer from the system's Printers window, click the Windows Start button and choose Settings and then Printers.

Overview The `Printers` collection is the list of all printers on the system running your application. This collection obviously changes from system to system. A user might run your application one minute, add or remove a system printer, and then run your application again, causing the application's `Printers` collection to vary between the two runs. This topic section explains how to access the printers in the current collection.

▼ **NOTE**
The `Printers` collection is the same list of printers that appears in the system's Print dialog box when you open the <u>N</u>ame drop-down list box. ▲

Accessing the *Printers* Collection

As with most lists within Visual Basic, you can reference the `Printers` collection from your application by using an index value. The first printer (the system default printer) has an index value of 0, the second printer has an index value of 1, and so on. If you want to use a `For...Next` loop to step through the printers, you can determine the number of properties now on the system by referencing `Printers.Count-1`. Alternatively, you can use the `For Each` statement to step through the printers without having to determine the number (as seen in this topic's example section).

Use the Set Printer statement to set Visual Basic's default printer to one of the printers on the system. The following statement sets Visual Basic's default printer to the second printer on the system:

```
Set Printer = Printers(1)  ' Change the default printer
```

Of course, determining the printer you want to print to at runtime isn't always easy. How can you even know what kind of printer you're testing for? You can test only for specific properties. For example, if you need to print to a printer that has a certain page size, you can loop through every printer on the system, looking for one that has that page size.

Printer Properties

Table 19.1 lists many important printer properties that you'll commonly use in determining which printer your application now needs. Most of these properties have named literal values associated with them. Therefore, rather than test for property values of 1 and 2 for a page size, you can test by using named literals such as vbPRPSLetter and vbPRPSLetterSmall. These are easier to understand later when you maintain the program (but they take longer to type).

> **TIP** If you look up a property in the online help reference, you'll find a list of the named literals that Visual Basic supports for that property.

Table 19.1 Common Printer Object Properties

Property	Description
ColorMode	Determines whether the printer can print in color or black and white
Copies	Specifies the number of copies users want (set at runtime by users from the Print dialog box that your application displays, or by your code setting this property)
CurrentX, CurrentY	Returns or sets the X and Y coordinates where the next character (or drawing) will appear
DeviceName	Holds the name of the printer, such as Canon BubbleJet IIC
DriverName	Holds the name of the printer (multiple printers from the same company may use the same printer driver)

Pt **III**

Hr **19**

continues

Table 19.1 Continued

Property	Description
Duplex	Determines whether the printer can print to both sides of the paper or to only a single side
Font	Returns certain font subproperty values that are set, such as `Printer.Font.Bold` and `Printer.Font.Underline`
FontCount	Returns the number of fonts supported by the printer
Height	Returns the height of the printed page for the selected printer (in `ScaleMode` measurements)
Orientation	Determines or sets the printer's portrait or landscape orientation
Page	Returns the current page number
PaperBin	Returns or sets the paper bin used for printing (keep in mind, though, that not all printers support multiple bins)
PaperSize	Returns or sets the paper size now being used
Port	Returns the name of the printer's port
PrintQuality	Returns or sets the printer's resolution value
TrackDefault	If `False`, keeps the current printer property settings when you change default printers; if `True`, changes the printer property settings at runtime when you select a different default printer
Width	Returns the width of the printed page for the selected printer (in `ScaleMode` measurements)
Zoom	Returns or sets the percentage of scaling used for the printed output; for example, if you set `Zoom` to 75, subsequent output appears on the page at 75 percent of its regular size (not all printers support the `Zoom` property)

When your application runs, the printer properties for the `Printer` object match those of the Windows system default printer. If you select a new default printer for VB, the properties change accordingly. At runtime, you can change many of these properties as described in Table 19.1.

▼ **NOTE**
You'll use many of the properties from Table 19.1 to access the specific printer-output methods introduced in the next topic section. Also, you'll learn about the `Printer` object's graphics-related properties in the next part of this tutorial. ▲

The next topic section explains how to use the methods related to the `Printer` object.

Example The following code demonstrates how you might step through the system's current printers:

```
Dim prnPrntr As Printer
For Each prnPrntr In Printers  ' Steps through each
  frmMyForm.Print prnPrntr.DeviceName
Next
```

The code simply prints each printer's name on the current form.

Notice the first line that declares a variable with the data type `Printer`. As you learn more about Visual Basic, you'll notice that you can declare variables of virtually any data type, including `Printer` and `Form`. The `prnPrntr` variable lets you walk through each printer on the system. An equivalent `For` statement would be

```
For prnPrntr = 1 to (Printers.Count - 1)
```

▼ **NOTE**
Remember that `Printer` and `Form` are Visual Basic *objects*. You learn more about VB objects in Hour 20, "Understanding Objects and Using the Object Browser." ▲

Rarely, if ever, would you want to print every printer's name on a form. Nevertheless, the loop shown in this example will form the basis for much of your printer processing.

Next Step The following code searches through all printers on the system, looking for a color printer to output a colorful chart:

```
Dim prnPrntr As Printer
For Each prnPrntr In Printers
  If prnPrntr.ColorMode = vbPRCMColor Then
    ' Set color printer as system default.
    Set Printer = prnPrntr
    Exit For  ' Don't look further
  End If
Next    ' Step through all of them if needed
```

Pt **III**

Hr **19**

Topic 3: Printing with the *Printer* Object

The `Printer` object exists so that you can send data to the default printer without worrying about specific printer types and ports. You apply methods to the `Printer` object to route output—such as reports and graphics—to the printer. Although programming with the `Printer` object can be tedious, you'll develop general-purpose output procedures that can help you print more easily in subsequent programs.

> **TIP** Before sending output to the `Printer` object, set the default printer by using the previous topic section's `Set Printer` statement if you want the `Printer` object to point to a printer other than the system default printer.

Overview After you select a default printer, use the `Printer` object to route text and graphics to the user's printer. This topic section explains how to control the `Printer` object and route text to the printer. In the next part of the book, you'll learn graphics commands and methods that you can also apply to the `Printer` object.

In this topic section, you'll see how to *build* your output. This means that you send output to the `Printer` object, but nothing actually prints. When you've completed the output and are ready to send the completed output to the printer, you issue the `NewPage` or `EndDoc` method to start the actual printing. (Printing also begins when your application ends if you don't first issue the `EndDoc` method.)

Printing to the *Printer* Object

One of the easiest ways to route output to the `Printer` object is to use the `Print` method. The following lines send a message to the printer:

```
Printer.Print "This report shows sales figures for"
Printer.Print dteStart; " through "; dteFinish; "."
Printer.Print "If you need more information, call ext. 319."
```

You used the `Print` method to send output to a form in Hour 16, but as you can see here, `Print` is a general-purpose method that sends output to any valid object that can accept text.

You can move the print output to the top of the next page at any point by using the `NewPage` method:

```
Printer.NewPage  ' Go to top of next page
```

Scaling Output

When printing, you may want to scale the output to create margins on the page that subsequent printing-related methods will respect. Table 19.2 lists the properties you can set to produce a scaling effect.

Table 19.2 Scaling Properties

Property	Description
ScaleLeft	Defines the printable area's extreme left X coordinate. For example, a `ScaleLeft` value of 10 moves the subsequent left margin to 10 `ScaleMode` measurements.
ScaleMode	Determines the measurement value used for scaling. Generally, a `ScaleMode` of `VbPoints` (the value 2), `vbCharacters` (the printer's default character width), `VbInches`, or `VbCentimeters` is used for text printing.
ScaleHeight	Changes the `Printer` object's vertical coordinate system.
ScaleTop	Defines the printable area's extreme top Y coordinate. For example, a `ScaleTop` value of 5 moves the subsequent top margin to five `ScaleMode` measurements.
ScaleWidth	Changes the `Printer` object's horizontal coordinate system.

To set a top margin of five characters and a left margin of eight characters, you would issue the following methods:

```
Printer.ScaleMode = VbCharacters   ' Set scale to chars
Printer.ScaleTop = 5
Printer.ScaleLeft = 8
```

Subsequent `Print` methods would respect these boundaries.

CurrentX and *CurrentY* Positions

Unless you change the coordinate system from an upper-left page coordinate of 0,0 to another X,Y system with the `ScaleHeight` and `ScaleWidth` properties, the `Printer` object's `CurrentX` and `CurrentY` values begin at

0,0. (The coordinates always use the measurement set by `ScaleMode`.) You can change these values to different X and Y coordinate values if you want to print the next item at a specific location on the page.

▼ NOTE

The `CurrentX` and `CurrentY` properties always respect the margins you have set with `ScaleLeft` and `ScaleTop`. Therefore, the coordinate pair `CurrentX`,`CurrentY` refers to the first character at the upper-left corner of the current page within any margins that you've defined. ▲

To print a message 15 lines down the page and 25 characters to the right, you would use code like this:

```
Printer.ScaleMode = VbCharacters
Printer.CurrentY = 14    ' Remember the starting value = 0
Printer.CurrentX = 24
Printer.Print "Warning, warning, there's danger ahead."
```

Example Visual Basic's `Printer` object supports several methods that let you control the printing process. You can move the printing to the top of the next page at any time by using the `NewPage` method:

```
Printer.NewPage  ' Go to top of next page
```

At any point during the preparation for printing, issue the `KillDoc` method if users want to cancel the print job:

```
Printer.KillDoc  ' Don't send the output to the printer
```

`KillDoc` completely removes your output from the `Printer` object. If you need to reissue the printed document later, you have to re-create the output.

▼ NOTE

`KillDoc` can't cancel anything that has already started printing, nor can it kill `PrintForm` jobs. ▲

Next Step Microsoft recommends creating a general-purpose printing subroutine inside a standard module that you can call from subsequent applications—as long as you include the standard module in those applications. You can use this routine to print form graphics. The following subroutine accepts two arguments of the `Object` data type. Because it receives the `Object` data type, you can pass the subroutine either a `Form` or `Printer` object.

```
Sub PrintAnywhere (Src As Object, Dest As Object)
  Dest.PaintPicture Src.Picture, Dest.Width / 2, Dest.Height / 2
  If TypeOf Dest Is Printer Then
    Printer.EndDoc
  End If
End Sub
```

Suppose that your application contains a form with a picture box or image that you want to display and also send to the printer. Perhaps you display a blank form for users to enter data, and then send the completed form to the printer.

This subroutine requires source and destination arguments. The source will always be the form you want to print. The destination can be `Printer`. You can call the procedure like this whenever you're ready to print the form:

```
Call PrintAnywhere (frmUserForm, Printer)   ' Print form
```

This subroutine uses the `PaintPicture` method to output the form. `PaintPicture` draws a form on the object to which you've applied the method. The `PaintPicture` method requires three values: the form to draw, the destination width, and the destination height. This code simply paints a form that's one-half the size of the destination area. To ensure that the form prints at the end of this method, the `If` statement immediately outputs the form with the `EndDoc` method if the destination is the `Printer` object and not another form. (You could pass a second form for the destination.)

The `If TypeOf` statement demonstrates a kind of `If` you haven't seen before. The `If TypeOf...Is` command lets you test objects for certain data types.

▼ **NOTE**
The `If...Is` statement does more than just test for specific objects, as you'll find out in Hour 20, "Understanding Objects and Using the Object Browser." ▲

Summary

You now can route output to your printer. The easiest way to get printer output is to use `PrintForm` to direct an entire form to the printer; all the form's controls, text, and graphics go to the printer. Be sure to adjust the `AutoRedraw` property if you want the printed output to include all the form's graphics.

Before printing non-form output, you'll want to access the `Printers` collection, which includes an indexed list of the printers on the system. Your program can analyze the printer properties to determine which printer best meets the needs of the application. After you find an appropriate printer, you can set the default printer that the remainder of the application uses.

The `Printer` object accepts all output for the default printer. You can apply methods to the `Printer` object to scale and position printed output. The output you route to the `Printer` object goes into a waiting area and then goes to the printer when the application ends or when you issue the `EndDoc` method.

You'll learn more about objects in Hour 20. You'll learn how to build object classes to increase your programming power and decrease your effort.

Hour 19 Quiz

You can find the answers for the following questions on the accompanying CD-ROM and on the Virtual Classroom Web site.

On the CD

1. What determines whether a form is the current form?

2. At what resolution does a `PrintForm` method usually print?

3. What value should you assign to the `AutoRedraw` property before you print forms?

4. How can your application determine the number of printers installed on the system?

5. **True or false:** The following declaration declares two variables:

   ```
   Dim intI As Integer, prnP As Printer
   ```

6. Which property determines the measurement of the `Printer` object's properties?

7. How can you force printing to begin on a new page?

8. Which form of `If` tests objects for specific data types?

9. **True or false:** You can pass objects—not just variables—to procedures.

10. **True or false:** `KillDoc` cancels all printed output, including `Printer.Print` commands and form `PrintForm` methods.

Hour 19 Homework Exercises

1. Write a procedure that prints the numbers 1 through 150 to the printer, one number per line, down the left side of each page. Print exactly 50 numbers per page and place a page number formatted as *Page* # in the upper-right corner.

2. Change the code at the end of the second topic section that searches for a color printer. Add a Boolean variable that you'll set to `True` only if a color printer is found. As the code now operates, the default printer remains the same if no color printer is found. The new Boolean variable will inform subsequent code whether the loop has properly found a color printer.

Understanding Objects and Using the Object Browser

THIS LESSON RETURNS to some theory and hones your knowledge of Visual Basic objects. After this hour, you'll have a better understanding of objects and will better understand how they relate to arrays and collections.

The *control array* is nice to use when you need to place several similar controls on a form. You need to create only one control, adjust its property values, and then create additional controls from that one (at runtime or design time). The subsequent controls contain the same property values—until you change one or more of the values. You reference the individual controls in the control array the same way you reference elements in arrays.

In this hour you also will master the *Object Browser*, which is a repository of object data. The Object Browser gives you an organized view of your project as well as Visual Basic's language.

Topic 1: Objects

In Hour 19, you learned how to use the `If...Is` statement to test for an object's form. This lesson further explains what `If...Is` does—it actually determines an object's *class*. If you're new to objects and classes (these terms are used in other programming languages, especially object-oriented languages), you'll learn all you need to learn in this lesson.

Overview An *object* can be just about anything in Visual Basic. You've already worked with objects such as controls, forms, and the `Printer` object. Also, you passed the `Object` data type to a procedure in Hour 19.

This topic section explains some object-related terminology and helps you view Visual Basic objects from a new perspective.

Object Terms

You've already seen that *control objects* contain properties, methods, and events. The controls contain code and data items. In a way, an object—such as the Command Button control—is like a package handed to you by the Visual Basic programmers. You don't have to write code to trigger a command button, declare variables that describe how a command button looks or what caption it has, and write code to perform work with a command button. The command button methods do all the work for you.

> **TIP** Objects are *encapsulated*. Like a capsule that contains medicine or lunar astronauts, an object encapsulates methods, events, and properties. This encapsulation lets you work with objects from a higher perspective than if you had to write all the code needed to support the objects.

The Object Class

Objects not only bring encapsulation to your programming fingertips, but they're also part of an object hierarchy called an object *class*. The benefit of a class is that all objects in the class share the same features. (A single object is said to be an *instance* of the class.)

▼ **NOTE**

You can create your own objects. By making them part of an existing class, your objects automatically gain, or *inherit*, many properties, methods, and events from that class. ▲

When you test an object with `If...Is`, Visual Basic returns the object's class. Therefore, the following returns `True` or `False`, depending on whether the object named `myObj` is a part of the `CommandButton` class:

```
If TypeOf myObj Is CommandButton   ' Check the class
```

TIP VB also supports the `TypeOf()` function that returns the class name. For example, `TypeOf(myObj)` might return `CommandButton` or `Form`.

Classes make programming with objects more flexible than it would be without the class structure. For example, the `With...End With` statement lets you easily assign multiple properties for a single object. Notice the following code's redundancy:

```
chkMaster.Caption = "Primary Source"
chkMaster.Alignment = vbLeftJustify
chkMaster.Enabled = True
chkMaster.Font.Bold = False
chkMaster.Left = 1000
chkMaster.RightToLeft = False
chkMaster.Top = 400
```

When you enclose an object inside a `With...End With` block, you can eliminate the repetition of the object name. The following code is identical to the previous code:

```
With chkMaster
  .Caption = "Primary Source"
  .Alignment = vbLeftJustify
  .Enabled = True
  .Font.Bold = False
  .Left = 1000
  .RightToLeft = False
  .Top = 400
End With
```

Pt **III**

Hr **20**

▼ NOTE

Using `With...End With` for two or three property settings requires more typing than using straight assignments. When you need to assign more than three properties, however, the `With...End With` block is an appealing coding statement, because it requires less typing and is easier to maintain if you add properties and require more assignments later. ▲

The System Objects

Unlike the objects you declare, *system objects* are the `Printer` and `Debug` objects you've already used in this book. Although you can't pass system objects (they're already global in nature), you can treat them much like the objects you create. System objects represent specific elements of your application.

Table 20.1 describes the system objects and lists some important methods that you can apply to them.

Table 20.1   System Objects and Their Key Methods

Object	Description	
App	The current application. Key methods:	
	EXEName	Returns the application's file name
	Path	Returns the application's path
	Title	Returns the primary startup form's title bar text
	Previnstance	Returns `True` or `False` indicating whether another copy of the application is now running
Clipboard	The Windows Clipboard region. Key methods:	
	Clear	Erases the Clipboard
	GetData	Returns the graphic image stored on the Clipboard
	GetFormat	Returns the format of the Clipboard object
	GetText	Returns the text from the Clipboard
	SetData	Copies a graphic image to the Clipboard
	SetText	Copies text to the Clipboard
	SelStart	Used for Clipboard selection operations
	SelLength	Used for Clipboard selection operations
	SelText	Used for Clipboard selection operations

Object	Description
Debug	The Immediate window. Key method:
	Print Copies information at runtime to the Immediate window (only possible in non-EXE VB programs that are run from VB's development environment)
Printer	The system printer. Hour 19, "Printing with VB," introduces the methods of the **Printer** object and demonstrates how they provide printer support.
Screen	The user's screen. Key methods:
	FontCount Returns the number of fonts the current screen supports
	Fonts Contains a list of all the screen's possible font names
	Height Returns the height of the screen area in twips
	MousePointer Holds (or determines if you specify a new one) the shape of the mouse cursor
	TwipsPerPixelX Returns the number of possible horizontal twips
	TwipsPerPixelY Returns the number of possible vertical twips
	Width Returns the width of the screen in twips

You've worked with most of the system objects, especially the **Printer** and **Screen** objects, before this lesson. The **App** object is useful for determining runtime information about the program path and file name. The **Clipboard** object provides some interesting functionality you may want to use.

Depending on your application's needs, the **Clipboard** object is relatively simple to program. The **Clipboard** object is the same Clipboard that Windows uses; therefore, your application can copy or cut information to the **Clipboard** object and users can paste it in another Windows application. Also, your application can paste information that's contained in the Windows Clipboard into the **Clipboard** object.

You can use the **Clipboard** object and its properties to select text from within your program and to determine the text selected by users. For example, the **SelStart** property marks the starting position of the selection cursor in the text box (or whatever control receives the selection). A value

Pt **III**

Hr **20**

of 0 for `SelStart` places the cursor before the first character. `SelLength` determines how many characters are selected for Clipboard work. If you select text by setting `SelStart` and `SelLength` values, that text goes to the `Clipboard` object when users press Ctrl+C or Ctrl+X for copy or cut. `SelText` is a string that contains the selected text you've bounded with `SelStart` and `SelLength`.

If you've selected text in a Text Box control (or you've asked users to select text), that text appears in the `SelText` string value. You can clear the Clipboard of its current value (the Clipboard can hold only one value at a time) and send the selected text to the Clipboard with this code:

```
Clipboard.Clear    ' Erase current Clipboard
Clipboard.SetText txtName.SelText  ' Copy text
```

If you want to copy the Clipboard text into a variable, you can use `GetText()` this way:

```
strInfo = Clipboard.GetText()
```

If you want to replace selected text in a control with the text on the Clipboard, you can do so this way:

```
txtName.SelText = Clipboard.GetText()
```

The `GetText()` method sometimes uses arguments, and requires parentheses even if you specify no arguments. For text-based Clipboard work, you don't need to supply any arguments.

▼ **NOTE**
If you use Microsoft Word, notice that the last statement mimics Word's Replaces Selection feature. ▲

Object and Control Arrays

One of the most interesting things you can do with objects is declare an array of objects. For example, you can declare an array of command buttons or forms. Moreover, these objects don't even have to exist. For example, you *don't* have to declare all forms at design time, but at runtime you can still create an array of forms.

You already know about the `Forms` and `Printers` collections. Visual Basic also supports the `Controls` collection that lets you step through all your `Controls` as though they were array variables. For example, the following code hides all controls:

```
For intCtr = 0 to Controls.Count - 1
   Controls(intCtr).Visible = False
Next intCtr
```

If your application contains multiple forms, you can hide all controls on all forms by nesting the loop like this (notice that the **For Each** eliminates the **Count - 1** requirement):

```
Dim frmAForm As Form
Dim ctlAControl As Control
For Each frmAForm In Forms     ' Step through all forms
   For Each ctlAControl In frmAForm.Controls
      ctlAControl.Visible = False
   Next ctlAControl
Next frmAForm
```

CAUTION A menu is considered a control in the `Controls` collection. In many situations, you'll want to omit the menu controls in such a loop by testing with the `TypeOf()` function to determine whether the control is a `Menu` object before setting its visibility to `False`.

Whereas the **Controls** collection holds *all* controls on your current form, you can declare a control array to hold one specific type of control. Declare an array of controls as follows:

```
Dim ctlManyLabels(1 To 4) As Label
```

The next topic section discusses collections further. Collections work a lot like arrays in that you can access individual elements in the collections just as you can with arrays. You might want to create an array of objects such as forms and controls. Rather than create the objects at design time, you can create the objects in an array as follows (notice the **New** keyword):

```
Dim frmArray(1 To 10) As New frmFirstForm
```

This **Dim** statement assumes that one form, **frmFirstForm**, exists. After the declaration, 10 new forms exist, subscripted from **frmArray(1)** to **frmArray(10)**. Subsequent code can then change the form properties of the forms in the array to make each form different from the base form named **frmFirstForm**.

▼ NOTE
None of these forms will appear until you invoke their Show methods. **▲**

Example Suppose that you want to decrease the font size of a form's controls if users resize a maximized form. You can use the `Controls` collection to decrease the font size of all controls:

```
Private Sub Form_Resize ()
  ' Decrease all the controls' font size
  Dim intCtr As Integer
  For intCtr = 0 to Controls.Count - 1
    Controls(intCtr).FontSize = Controls(intCtr).FontSize * .75
  Next intCtr
End Sub
```

Each control's font size will now be 25 percent smaller than it was before users resized the form.

Next Step You won't see many VB programmers using control arrays when a collection exists for the same object. VB supplies predefined collections such as `Forms`; if you want to use control arrays, however, you have to declare array memory to hold the array contents and initialize the arrays.

VB supports one technique for control arrays that you'll find yourself using a lot, even though collections are always available to you. When you copy a control and paste that control back onto the form, VB displays the message box shown in Figure 20.1.

FIG. 20.1
VB can automatically create a control array at your request.

You might wonder why you'd ever copy and paste a control, but if you need to place several command buttons or labels that all have the same format—perhaps the same font size and caption alignment—it's a helpful technique. You just create one control, set all its properties, copy that control to the Clipboard, and then paste the Clipboard contents onto the form to add as many controls as you need.

As soon as you paste the copied control, VB displays the message box asking if you want to create a control array. If you answer Yes, VB automatically creates a control array with a name that matches the first control.

For example, if the first control is a check box named `Check1`, the array is named `Check1`, and the elements begin at `Check1(0)` and increment as long as you keep pasting the control. Your code then can step through all the control array elements from `Check1(0)` through `Check1(n)` where *n* is the total number of `Check1` controls on the form, and set properties for them.

Topic 2: Collections

Collections play a vital role in VB programming, as you've seen in earlier lessons and in the preceding topic section. Collections are always present. VB updates collections automatically; for example, if you add a form at runtime with the `New Form` declaration, VB updates the `Forms` collection's `Count` property accordingly.

The predefined collections are helpful, so why not create your own? This brief topic section introduces some factors involved in declaring your own collections.

Overview If you create a collection, you'll need to manage the collection yourself—this takes more effort than managing the predefined collections. This topic section explains what you need to know to declare your own collections and manage them properly.

As you learned in the previous topic section, all objects belong to a class. If you know something about a class, you know something about all objects within that class. For example, if a control is a member of the `CommandButton` class, you know that the control supports the `Click` event because all `CommandButton` class members support the `Click` event.

Your own collections must be objects of the `Collection` class. You define collections at the module level by using the `Private` or `Public` keyword, depending on the range of procedures that need access to your collection. The following statement declares a collection named `colMyCol`:

```
Private colMyCol As New Collection
```

A collection works like an empty bookcase. You can add objects (such as books), remove objects, count objects, and so on. Of course, a bookcase can hold more than just books. A collection can hold only one kind of item, but you can declare multiple collections that each hold different kinds of items. Here are the methods your collections can access:

- Add   Adds an item to your collection
- Count   Returns the number of items in your collection
- Item   Serves as an index number for the items in the collection
- Remove   Removes an item from the collection

As the following example shows, Visual Basic takes care of updating Count and adding items to your collections.

Example   The code in Listing 20.1 creates a collection named Cities and adds four items (city names) to the collection.

Listing 20.1   Using *Add* to Add Items

```
Dim Cities As New Collection
Dim intCtr As Integer

' Add items
Cities.Add "Tulsa"
Cities.Add "Miami"
Cities.Add "New York"
Cities.Add "Seattle"

' Show that there are four cities
frmMyForm.Print "There are"; Cities.Count; " cities:"

' Print each city name
For intCtr = 1 To Cities.Count
  frmMyForm.Print "  "; Cities(intCtr)
Next
```

If you run this code, the following output appears on the form:

```
There are 4 cities:
  Tulsa
  Miami
  New York
  Seattle
```

Next Step This lesson only scratches the surface of collection power. Nevertheless, you should know that you can insert items into and remove items from your collections easily and in whatever order you prefer. Remember that each item in the collection contains a subscript, starting at 1, that you use to reference a particular item. In the preceding example, `Cities(1)` is the first city listed in the collection named `Cities`. Remember that your collection index value begins at 1, not **0** as the control arrays require.

You can use a *named argument* (an argument in which you include the argument name followed by `:=`, a special named argument assignment operator) named **Before** to add items to a collection at the exact location you want. The following line adds a city to the beginning of the `Cities` collection, no matter how many cities reside in the collection to begin with:

```
Cities.Add "St. Louis", Before:=1
```

A **Before** position of 1 adds the items to the front of the collection. In other words, VB inserts the new item *before* the specified indexed item in the collection. If you included this **Add** method statement at the end of the code shown earlier, the output would change to this:

```
There are 5 cities:
   St. Louis
   Tulsa
   Miami
   New York
   Seattle
```

If you added the code line without the `Before:=1` named argument, St. Louis would appear at the end of the collection.

You can remove specific items by using the **Remove** method. As you remove items, the remaining subscripts adjust so that they always begin at 1. The following statement removes the second item (Tulsa) from the collection:

```
Cities.Remove 2
```

Topic 3: The Object Browser

As your VB knowledge improves, your need for better tools grows. VB includes the *Object Browser*, a tool that lets you inspect variables, controls, and other objects throughout your application. VB programmers new to the Object Browser often use it much more than they initially realize they will, because its features make programming with VB much simpler.

Overview The Object Browser is a comprehensive online reference, but it's not online in the same sense as the online help reference. The Object Browser gives you a one-stop location to hunt for objects and object information, and to jump directly to the code you need to work with next.

> ▼ **NOTE**
> The Object Browser describes your application's *type libraries*, which are the repositories of your class information. You can use the Object Browser to access all object properties, events, and methods for your application—including objects you've created. ▲

The Object Browser Window

When you first choose O<u>b</u>ject Browser from the <u>V</u>iew menu or click the toolbar's Object Browser button, you see the Object Browser window (see Figure 20.2). You may have to expand your window and close the Properties window and Toolbox to see the full Object Browser.

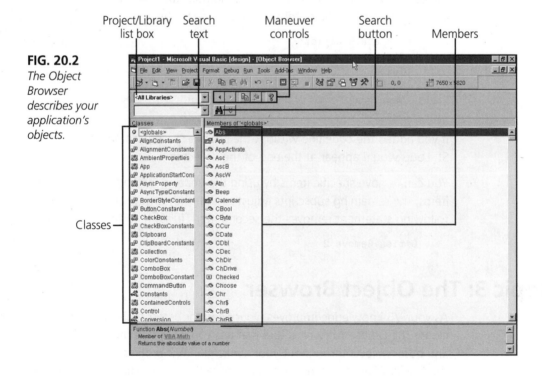

FIG. 20.2
The Object Browser describes your application's objects.

Table 20.2 describes the parts of the Object Browser window.

Table 20.2 Parts of the Object Browser Window

Component	Description
Project/Library list box	Describes the source of the objects you want to browse (you'll generally browse the <All Libraries> option, but you can browse, for example, the objects in a particular project by selecting your project's name)
Search text	Lets you enter an object, event method, or property to search for
Maneuver controls	Used to jump back and forth along a browsing path that you've previously traveled
Classes	Holds the class names from the project or library you've selected
Members	Contains the members for the class you've selected

Traversing the Object Browser

The Object Browser contains much of the same information as the online help system. The Object Browser, however, specifically targets the VB programmer and offers succinct information that's needed often. For example, the <globals> entry in the Classes list describes all of VB's built-in functions. Scroll down to the Left entry to learn about the Left() function.

▼ **NOTE**
As you learned in Hour 14, "Using the Supplied Functions," the Left() function returns the left part of a string. ▲

When you highlight the Left entry, VB describes the function at the bottom of the Object Browser window. The text not only describes the function's purpose but also shows the function's syntax. You can tell the nature of each object listed in the Members drop-down list by its icon. The small green icon indicates that the member is a function. You can spot collections (look at the Forms entry) and named literals by their respective icons. Scroll down to see the entire list of named literals that appears below the functions and collections in the Members scrolling list.

If you right-click either list and select Group <u>M</u>embers from the pop-up menu, Visual Basic groups all members and classes by their purpose. Therefore, rather than have the literals appear in alphabetical order, the Object

Browser displays all the named literals together, all the events together, and so on.

> **TIP** After you highlight any entry in an Object Browser window, click the toolbar's Help button (the icon is a question mark) to get online help on that object.

You can get even more specific with the Object Browser. For example, the Classes list contains several entries that reference *constants* (another term for literals). When you click the ColorConstants entry, for example, only VB's color constants appear in the Members list (see Figure 20.3).

FIG. 20.3
The object search has been narrowed to particular constants.

Color named constants

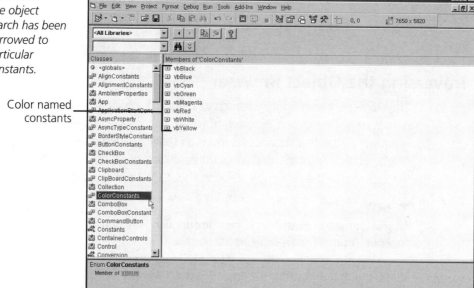

> **TIP** You may use these named literals anywhere in code that you need a color. For example, you can set a form's background color this way:
>
> ```
> frmMyForm.BackColor = vbRed    ' Set form to red
> ```

Notice that all the controls available in the Toolbox also appear in the Classes list. If you click on ComboBox, for example, the Object Browser displays all pertinent information for combo boxes, including properties, events, and methods. If you click one of the combo box entries in the Members list, you get a description of that method, event, or property.

Example People use the Object Browser for many different purposes. Keep in mind that the Object Browser displays object information in an organized manner. In addition to objects, it coordinates all your programming specifics. For example, if you're writing code that takes advantage of the built-in date and time functions, click the Object Browser's Classes entry labeled DateTime. As Figure 20.4 shows, the Members list is updated to show you only those built-in functions related to dates and times.

FIG. 20.4
It's easy to find the built-in functions for a certain topic.

The date and time functions

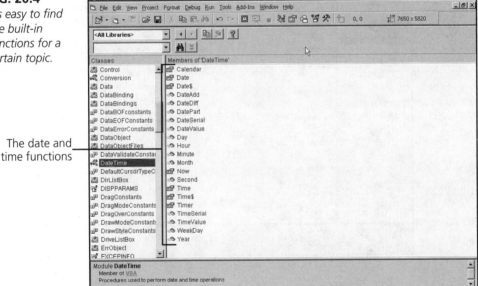

Although these functions are listed in the online help guide and are also available from other locations in the Object Browser (such as in the Classes entry named <globals>), reviewing the group of date and time functions makes programming with those functions simple because all the functions are referenced here in one location.

TIP Remember that the Go Back maneuver button retraces your steps through the Object Browser, so it's easy to move back and forth with the mouse.

Pt **III**

Hr **20**

Next Step   The Object Browser is very useful for describing your own project. As you add objects, variables, and event procedures to your application, the Object Browser sits in the background filing everything. Figure 20.5 shows the Object Browser with `Project1` selected for the Project/Library. When `Form1` (the only user-placed object in this project so far) is clicked, the Object Browser displays a list of all the event procedures, methods, and properties for that form. Only one entry, `Command1_Click`, is boldfaced, meaning that code has been added only to that event procedure so far.

FIG. 20.5

The Object Browser shows only active features of the application.

The only event
procedure
with code

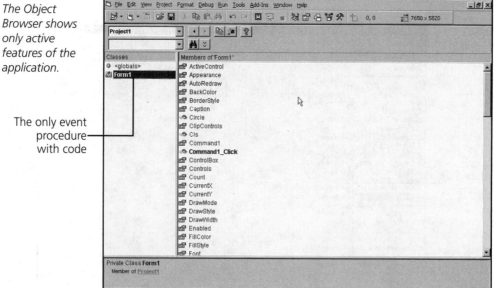

One of the most powerful aspects of the Object Browser is the View <u>D</u>efinition option. If you highlight a member that's one of your own objects, such as an event procedure you've written or an object you've declared, right-click the object and choose View <u>D</u>efinition. VB jumps directly to the code where you've defined that object! Therefore, you can use the Object Browser to locate specific code within a large application. You don't have to know which project an object was defined in, as long as you can locate the object in the Object Browser.

When you search for an item with the Object Browser, you get a list of every reference to that item within your entire application. For example, if you search for Click, VB displays an extra window (see Figure 20.6) that contains every relevant reference in the entire project (and in the entire VB repertoire, because the <All Libraries> option is selected in the Library/ Project drop-down list).

FIG. 20.6
The search feature has found all occurrences of Click.

Search topic

Found window

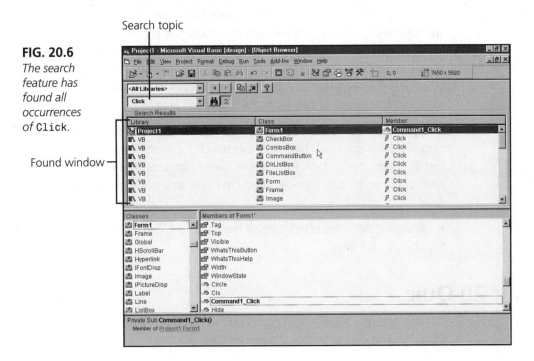

The Click event occurs for several objects, so the Object Browser displays a window that contains every referenced object that supports Click. You then narrow the search by clicking the object or project that contains the Click you wanted.

Summary

This lesson described some theory behind VB objects and collections. Objects are more than variables in VB. Although this hour's lesson didn't go into a lot of depth about objects, you're now better prepared to program with objects and to learn more about them when you're ready.

In addition to collections, Visual Basic allows you to declare control arrays, which often act like object arrays. You can replicate controls on a form so that all the controls share common features, leaving you the task of changing only the distinguishing features such as captions or colors.

The system objects provide common predefined objects through which your application can interact with resources outside the typical program environment. By accessing the **App** object, your application at runtime can determine the path from which users started the application. The `Clipboard` object lets your application interact with the Windows Clipboard by copying and pasting text to and from the Clipboard area.

To organize things, VB supplies a tool called the Object Browser, which is basically a repository of data. You can search for specific events, properties, and methods, or can look for a whole class of objects. The Object Browser even tracks your code for objects you initialize and event procedures you write.

In Hour 21, "Accessing Files," you'll learn about file I/O and see how VB interacts with file data.

Hour 20 Quiz

You can find the answers for the following questions on the accompanying CD-ROM and on the Virtual Classroom Web site.

On the CD

1. Why is `With...End With` probably a bad idea here?

```
With chkMaster
   .Caption = "Primary Source"
   .Alignment = vbLeftJustify
End With
```

2. Name two ways to test for an object's class.

3. What do objects of the same class share?

4. What's the difference between a control array and the `Controls` collection?

5. Which usually takes less memory: an object array or that object's collection?

6. Name the four methods that all collections share.

7. **True or false:** You must pass system objects if you need to access them in multiple procedures.

8. Name three kinds of items that often appear in the Members list in the Object Browser.

9. What happens if you group the Members list in the Object Browser?

10. **True or false:** The Object Browser won't search for objects you've created.

Hour 20 Homework Exercises

1. Write an application with six labels. Place the first label on the form. Use `January` for its `Caption` property. Change its `Font.Size` property to 18. Change its `Font.Bold` property to `True`. Make its background color blue. Place this label in the upper-left corner of the form.

   Now, create a control array that contains five more labels identical to the first one. (Use the Clipboard to hold the first label and paste the five new ones.) Write code in the project's `Form_Load()` event procedure to make two changes for each subsequent label: make the color a different named literal color and make the caption a new month. (Look in the Object Browser for a list of named literal colors.)

2. Write an application that copies the text contents of the Windows Clipboard into a text box control when users click a command button.

3. By using the Object Browser, find out the use of the form's `Picture` property.

4. Locate the properties and methods associated with the `Printer` object by searching the online help file.

Accessing Files

THIS LESSON EXPLAINS the fundamentals of file I/O. Although professional VB programmers don't use the file I/O commands you'll learn in this lesson (because they generally work with the more flexible data and database controls that you'll master later), all programmers should understand file fundamentals and should understand every concept in this lesson before using those other database tools.

You'll learn all about the kinds of file processing possible and the commands that VB supports to work with such processing. At the core of every advanced file I/O routine and database control lie the fundamental concepts you'll learn this hour.

Three file types exist: *sequential*, *random*, and *binary*. Sequential access is the simplest file access, but prone to some drawbacks; although sequential

files are simple to create and read, they can be slow and cumbersome. Random access is a much faster and more useful method of access, but programs that use random-access files are often more complex than sequential-access programs. Binary files are special, compacted forms of random-access files. (Binary files are difficult to work with but are discussed briefly in Hour 22, "Adding OLE to a Program.")

Like random-access memory, you can access random-access files in any order. Random-access files work with any kind of data you can declare. When you learn how to declare user-defined data types at the end of this hour, you'll be able to use the `Put #` command to write (or read) an entire set of information to (or from) a data file in one statement.

Topic 1: Basic File-Handling Concepts

Virtually every program in existence today uses files. At the very least, even if a program doesn't use files, the program itself is a file that executes when users run the program. Whether a program saves data into a database or just keeps information for its own use (such as a user's preferred color scheme or window position), most programs do rely on files.

▶▶ **FAST TRACK**

If you understand flat-file processing concepts, you can skip to Hour 22, "Adding OLE to a Program" (p. 513).

Overview Several Visual Basic commands are common to all forms of file input and output. These commands open the files, specify the file modes, close the files, and check for free file numbers to be used as file associations. This topic section explains how fundamental file processing operates. One way you can better understand file concepts is to begin with the first statement of any file-based project: the `Open` statement.

The *Open* Statement

Sequential files and random-access files share common features. You use `Open` for both file types. The kind of file access you achieve with `Open` depends on the arguments you use in the `Open` statement.

Open initiates a channel for reading from and writing to a file. When this channel is open, the data stream can flow. The mode for which you open the channel—read, write, or both—dictates how the data stream can flow between the file and the computer.

Here is the **Open** statement's syntax:

```
Open strFileName [For Mode] [AccessRestriction] [LockType] As
➥[#]Channel% [Len = intRecordLength]
```

▼ **NOTE**

The *Channel* value is commonly called the *file number* or *file handle*. When you open a program and assign a data file to a number, the program will use that file number to access that file. Your program never again has to use the file name to get to the file. This chapter refers to the *channel value* and *file number* interchangeably because of their common uses in the data-processing industry. ▲

All **Open** statements must include the file-name and file-number arguments, but the other arguments are optional. A simple call to **Open** with only the required parameters might look like this:

```
Open "aFile.Txt" As #1
```

This statement opens a file named aFile.Txt as file number 1. To reference this file for input or output, you reference the file number. This file has been opened in random-access mode, because the default when you omit the **For** *Mode* portion is **Random**. All of this lesson's commands work with text files. This lesson uses the file-name extension .txt or .dat, two commonly used extensions for text files.

The Modes

Table 21.1 explains the optional settings for *Mode* values.

Table 21.1 *Open* Statement Modes

Mode	Description
Append	Opens a file number to a file for sequential output, beginning at the end of the file if the file exists. If the file doesn't exist, VB creates the file. **Append** never overwrites existing files.

continues

Table 21.1 Continued

Mode	Description
Binary	Opens a file number to a file for binary data access. In `Binary` mode, you can access a file at the byte level, meaning that you can write and read individual bytes to and from the file.
Input	Opens a file number to a file for sequential input, starting at the beginning of the file. Data is read in the same order that it was sent to the file.
Output	Opens a file number to a file for sequential output, starting at the beginning of the file. If the file doesn't exist when you issue the `Open` statement, VB creates the file; otherwise, VB overwrites the file.
Random	Opens a file number to a file for random read and write access. This mode allows data to be read from and written to a file at any specific record boundary.

For *Mode* isn't required when using the `Open` statement. If you don't include the mode, Visual Basic assumes `Random` and inserts the `For Random` mode for you. The following examples show how to use various modes for opening a file:

```
Open "filInpdt.txt" For Input As #1

Open "Append.txt" For Append As #1

Open "Output.txt" For Output As #1

Open "Random.txt" For Random As #1
```

The last statement is equivalent to the following:

```
Open "Random.txt" As #1
```

> **TIP** Be sure to set up error-handling logic using the `On Error Goto` statement that you learned about in Hour 17. Anytime you open or access a file, an error might result. Good error-handling logic will help your application exit gracefully from the problem rather than burden users with nasty runtime error messages.

AccessRestriction

The optional *AccessRestriction* in an `Open` statement lets you restrict the access to `Read`, `Write`, or `Read Write`. This access restriction is often used when writing programs that will run across a network.

Specifying read-only access with Read lets users see the contents of the file, but leaves them unable to modify the file. Specifying Write access lets users modify the file, and specifying Read Write lets users do both (read and modify).

LockType

Use a *LockType* to specify the operations permitted on the open file by other processes. This parameter is useful when writing network applications. You can restrict access to a file so that only one user at a time has access to the file or can write to the file. This helps prevent two users from trying to make changes at the same time (which would inevitably lose the changes that one of the users made).

The valid options for *LockType* are Shared, Lock Read, Lock Write, and Lock Read Write. Shared lets all users access the file simultaneously. Lock Read locks the file so that only the person with the file open for reading can access the file. Lock Write locks the file so that only the person who has the file open for write access can write to the file. Lock Read Write locks the file from all users except the one who has the file now open for read and write access.

Len = intRecordLength

The length specified by the Len = *intRecordLength* option is used by random-access files as the size of data records that will be passed from VB to the file. This size is necessary when accessing records from a file. The first record in a file begins at location 1, and all subsequent records are written at locations in increments of 1. The actual location in the file of any given record is $N \times intRecordLength$, where N is the record number.

This record access might seem similar to the way you access arrays. Although the first element in an array is stored in Array(0), the first element in a file is stored at record number 1. To make index coordination between arrays and files easy, use Option Base 1 in your Declarations section, or define your arrays to begin with element 1 and ignore the 0 subscript.

The *FreeFile* Function

Visual Basic lets you open multiple files at once, as long as you assign each file a different file number. You need to keep track of the next available number, especially if you open files in a function that has no way of knowing whether other functions have opened files. VB provides the `FreeFile` function, which can be used to determine the next available file number. By using this function, you're guaranteed that the file number you use hasn't already been used by an open file. Here is the syntax of `FreeFile`:

```
FreeFile[(RangeNumber)]
```

The optional *RangeNumber* parameter lets you specify that you want the returned file number to be in a specific range: 1–255 or 256–511. The default range, if you specify no *RangeNumber* parameter, is 1–255. Almost all Visual Basic programmers keep the default because rarely, if ever, do programs need to open more than 256 files. The following lines use `FreeFile` to obtain a file number and then open a file with that number:

```
intFileNumber = FreeFile
Open "AccPay.Dat" For Output As intFileNumber
```

Use `FreeFile` whenever you want to ensure that a file number isn't already in use. This may not be necessary for small applications that use only several files. Even in small applications, however, it helps to use `FreeFile` to ensure that you don't accidentally use the same file number for more than one file at a time.

> **CAUTION**   Avoid the shortcut of using `FreeFile` within the `Open` statement, as shown here:
>
> ```
> Open strFileName For Output As FreeFile
> ```
>
> Although this works, you have no way to know the file number for later operations on the file.

The *Close* Statement

You need to close all files that you open with `Open`. The statement for closing a file is—not surprisingly—`Close`. This statement takes the open file number as its only parameter. The complete syntax is as follows:

```
Close # intChannelNumber[, intChannelNumber2][,
➥...intChannelNumberX]
```

You can specify any number of channels (file numbers) to close in a single `Close` statement. If you don't specify a file number, all open channels are closed. This can be useful for terminating your applications.

Example The code in Listing 21.1 opens two sequential files—one for reading and one for writing—on the next available channels, and closes both files when done.

Listing 21.1 Using *FreeFile* to Request a File Number from Visual Basic

```
Dim intReadChan As Integer, intWriteChan As Integer
' Handle input file
intReadChan = FreeFile    ' Get first channel #
Open "AccPay.Dat" For Input As intReadChan
' Handle output file
intWriteChan = FreeFile    ' Get next channel #
Open "AccPayOut.Dat" For Output As intWriteChan
'
' Code goes here to send the contents
' of the input file to the output file
' (You'll learn how to do this later in the lesson)
Close intReadChan
Close intWriteChan
```

You never have to use an actual file number in this example, because `FreeFile` returns available channels and the code stores those values as named integers.

▼ **NOTE**
If you don't close all open files, you run a risk—albeit a small one today due to improved hardware—that damage will occur to the file. Generally, if power goes out when a file is open, the file's contents might be in jeopardy. Therefore, don't keep a file open longer than you need it to be open. If you don't close a file, the system closes the file when your application terminates. ▲

Next Step You can close as many files as you want with a single `Close` statement. The following simple line closes all open files:

```
Close
```

The following lines would, instead, close only two files that might be open:

```
Close 3
Close 6
```

You may want to close certain files in the middle of a program when you're finished with those files but still need access to other open files.

Topic 2: Sequential-Access Files

Now that you've seen the basic statements required for opening files, closing files, and setting file-access modes, this topic section looks at several examples that output to and input from sequential-access files. You'll see that a form of `Print`, which you used earlier for form and printer output, can output text to a file.

Overview *Sequential file access* means just that—you access the file sequentially. When you create a sequential-access file, you're creating a file that your application must read from and write to sequentially (that is, in order from the file's beginning to end). This sequential read and write limitation is the biggest weakness of a sequential file.

To use the file, you must process the entire file from beginning to end. If you need to update only 1 byte of information in a 1,000-byte file, you must process 999 extra bytes every time you want to perform the update.

Sequential file access can be very useful if you need to process a text file, such as a settings file, or if you're storing small amounts of data where access speed isn't an issue. This topic section looks at the VB functions that handle sequential files.

The *Print* # Statement

You must open files to use them in your program. After you open the files, you must put information into them. One common approach is the `Print #` statement. `Print #` writes only to a sequential-access file. Here is the syntax of `Print #`:

```
Print #intChannelNumber, [OutputList]
```

intChannelNumber is the open file number to which you want to write. *OutputList* can consist of the following:

[Spc(*intN1*) ¦ Tab[(*intN2*)]] [*Expression*] [*charPos*]

The vertical bar (¦) indicates that you can use either Spc() or Tab(), but not both together. Table 21.2 explains the components of *OutputList*.

Table 21.2 The *Print* # Statement Contents

Component	Description
Spc(*intN1*)	Used to insert spaces in the output, where *intN1* is the number of spaces to insert.
Tab(*intN2*)	Used to position the insertion point to an absolute column number, where *intN2* is the column number. Use Tab with no argument to position the insertion point at the beginning of the next print zone (a *print zone* occurs every 14 spaces).
Expression	A numeric or string expression that contains the data you want to send to the file.
charPos	Specifies the insertion point for the next character to print. Use a semicolon to specify that the next character should appear immediately following the last printed character.

▼ NOTE

You can use Tab() in *charPos*; the functions that Tab() performs at the beginning of a Print # statement also apply here. If you omit *charPos*, the next character appears on the next line in the file. **▲**

On the CD

The procedure in Listing 21.2 opens a file named Print.txt, writes the numbers 1 through 5 to the file, and then properly closes the file.

Listing 21.2 Writeseq.bas: Using *Print* # to Write to a Sequential File

```
Private Sub cmdFile_Click()
  Dim intCtr As Integer     ' Loop counter
  Dim intFNum As Integer    ' File number
  intFNum = FreeFile

  ' Change the path if you want
  Open "C:\Print.txt" For Output As #intFNum

  ' Describe this proc
  Debug.Print "File Print.txt opened"
```

continues

Listing 21.2 Continued

```
For intCtr = 1 To 6
  Print # intFNum, intCtr      ' Write the loop counter
  Debug.Print "Writing a " & intCtr & " to Print.txt"
Next intCtr

Close # intFNum

Debug.Print "File Print.txt closed"
End Sub
```

If you run this procedure, you see the Immediate window output shown in Figure 21.1. The procedure tells you that it has opened the file, and then proceeds to write to the file and show you what has been written. Finally, the procedure closes the file and tells you that the file has been closed.

FIG. 21.1

It's easy to monitor the progress of the Print # *statement.*

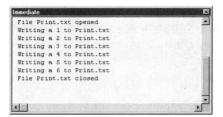

To verify that the procedure worked, open Notepad and look at the Print.txt file. You should see the numbers 1 through 5 printed inside the file, as shown here:

```
1
2
3
4
5
```

Listing 21.2 demonstrates a simple Print # statement. No statements existed to position the output, so the procedure defaulted to printing each number on a new line. An example at the end of this topic section explains how you can embed formatting codes in the Print # command.

Creating and writing to a file won't do you much good if you can't retrieve the information when you want to. The following section covers retrieving information from a file.

The *Input* # Statement

After you write data to a file, you eventually will need to retrieve that data. For sequential files, use the `Input #` statement to read sequential data. You must read the data in exactly the same order and format as you wrote it, due to the nature of sequential file processing. Here is the syntax of `Input #`:

```
Input # intChannel, Variable1[, Variable2][, ...VariableN]
```

`Input #` requires an open file number and variables to hold the data you are reading. The `Input #` statement and the `Print #` statement that originally wrote the data to the file should use the same format. If you used comma delimiters to write the data, you should use the same delimiters for `Input #`.

▼ NOTE

If you write a series of variables on one line and want to be able to read them reliably with `Input #`, you must either use `Write` instead of `Print #`, or manually include comma delimiters. `Input #` reads up to the first space, comma, or end of line if it reads into a numeric variable. It reads up to the first comma or end of line when reading a string, unless the string contains quotation marks. ▲

The following statement reads five variables from an open sequential file. The variables all reside on the same file line:

```
Input # intChannel V1, V2, V3, V4, V5
```

The `Print #` statement that created the file has to match the `Input #` statement's format and use the same variable data types; otherwise, `Input #` can't read the data.

`Input #` is fairly simple because it performs the mirror-image task of `Print #`. As the next section explains, `Write #` often outputs file data in a more general format than `Print #`, reducing your worry about matching the `Input #` statement to its original output code.

The *Write* # Statement

`Write #` is another command that writes information to a sequential file. `Write #` and `Print #` vary only slightly. All data that `Write #` writes to a file is comma-delimited, not space-delimited. Also, `Write #` automatically encloses all string data inside quotation marks (the quotation marks appear in the file), encloses all date data within pound signs, writes Boolean data as #TRUE# or #FALSE#, and sends null data and error codes to the file as #NULL# and #Error *errorcode*#, respectively. (*errorcode* represents an error number that explains the output error that has occurred, such as a disk not found.)

Comma delimitation is required for files that certain mail-merge or spreadsheet programs read. The commas also make reading the data less error-prone because subsequent `Input #` statements don't have to match the `Write #` exactly.

▼ **NOTE**

To read data correctly from a file into variables, always use `Write #` instead of `Print #`. ▲

Here is the syntax for `Write #`:

```
Write # intChannel, [OutputList]
```

OutputList is the list of one or more variables you want to read from the file opened on the file number.

The upcoming "Next Step" section demonstrates the use of `Write #`.

Example   The earlier section "The *Print #* Statement" showed how to output one value per line with the `Print #` statement. You can include the same formatting options in `Print #` that you can include in the regular `Print` method.

On the CD

For example, if you want to print the values one after another on the same line, you include a semicolon after the `intCtr` variable, as is done in Listing 21.3.

Listing 21.3   Oneline.bas: Using the Semicolon to Write Multiple Values on a Single Line

```
Private Sub cmdFile_Click()
  Dim intCtr As Integer      ' Loop counter
  Dim intFNum As Integer     ' File number
  intFNum = FreeFile
```

```
' Change the path if you want
Open "C:\Print.txt" For Output As #intFNum

' Describe this proc
Debug.Print "File Print.txt opened"

For intCtr = 1 To 6
  Print # intFNum, intCtr;      ' Notice semicolon!!
  Debug.Print "Writing a "; intCtr; " to Print.txt"
Next intCtr

Close # intFNum

Debug.Print "File Print.txt closed"
End Sub
```

When you run this procedure, the created file contains the following:

    1 2 3 4 5

Notice the spaces between the numbers when they're printed to the same line. Print # inserts these spaces so that the different data elements you write to the file can be distinguished from each other. This space is referred to as a *delimiter*. When you attempted to read the data later, it would be difficult to know how many elements were written if the file contained 12345... instead of 1 2 3 4 5 . . . .

You should experiment with the different Print # parameters to see what results you get when creating a file.

Next Step

On the CD

After you write data to a file, reading back the data often takes place in another procedure—or even another application—that needs the data. The procedures in Listing 21.4 provide examples of how you can write to a file and then read the information back into variables.

Listing 21.4 Readwrit.bas: Reading and Writing to a File in the Same Procedure

```
Private cmdFileOut_Click ()
  ' Create the sequential file
  Dim intCtr As Integer   ' Loop counter
  Dim intFNum As Integer  ' File number
  intFNum = FreeFile

  Open "Print.txt" For Output As #intFNum
```

continues

Listing 21.4 Continued

```
   For intCtr = 1 To 5
     Print # intFNum, intCtr;     ' Write the loop counter
   Next intCtr

   Close # intFNum
End Sub

Private cmdFileIn_Click ()
   ' Read the sequential file
   Dim intCtr As Integer    ' Loop counter
   Dim intVal As Integer    ' Read value
   Dim intFNum As Integer   ' File number
   intFNum = FreeFile

   Open "Print.txt" For Input As #intFNum

   For intCtr = 1 To 5
     Input # intFNum, intVal
     ' Display the results in the Immediate window
     Debug.Print "Retrieved a " & intVal & " from Print.txt"
   Next intCtr

   Close # intFNum
   Debug.Print "The Print.txt file is now closed."
End Sub
```

Figure 21.2 shows the Immediate window that appears when you run this code and click the buttons assigned to the file output and file input tasks.

FIG. 21.2

The Immediate window here monitors writing and then reading the same file.

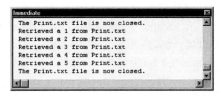

Now look at the procedure in Listing 21.5, which creates a file named Write.txt.

Listing 21.5 Writeout.bas: Writing Output to Sequential Files

```
Private cmdFile_Click ()
  Dim intCtr As Integer    ' Loop counter
  Dim intFNum As Integer   ' File number
  intFNum = FreeFile

  Open "Write.txt" For Output As #intFNum

  For intCtr = 1 To 5
    Write # intFNum, intCtr;     ' Write the loop counter
  Next intCtr

  Close # intFNum
End Sub
```

After this procedure creates the Write.txt file, use Notepad to look at its contents. You'll immediately notice the difference between the `Print #` and `Write #` statements. Here are the contents of Write.txt:

```
1,2,3,4,5,
```

If you didn't use the semicolon after the data you wrote, each piece of data would be on its own line and no commas would separate the data, because the single value per line would make the commas unnecessary. (In that case, `Write #` and `Print #` would behave identically.)

> **TIP** If you use sequential files often, you'll soon gain insight into ways you can improve your code. For example, you might want to write (as the first piece of data in the file) the number of values that appear in the file, so subsequent programs that read the data will know how many values exist and can loop accordingly.

▼ **NOTE**
Keep in mind that VB programmers rarely use sequential file processing! You're not wasting your night-school lesson this hour, however, because all the more common file-access methods and controls use the fundamentals that sequential file processing teaches you. ▲

Topic 3: Random-Access Files

Whereas you must read and write sequential files in order, you can read and write random-access files (often just called *random files*) in any order. For example, you can write customer records to a random-access file and then read one or more customer records later in any order you want. If the customer file were sequential, you would have to read every record in the file that preceded the records you wanted.

Overview   This topic section explains how to perform I/O with random-access files. As with sequential access, programmers don't use random access in its strictest form today as much as in the past because of the increased availability of data-access controls and advanced file-processing procedures. Nevertheless, most file access is based on the concepts you'll learn here.

Random-access files offer a good opportunity to learn about *user-defined data types*. A user-defined data type is one that you define and use instead of one of the built-in data types (such as `Integer` and `String`). Random-access files often read and write data records, and VB's user-defined data types let you define data items that look exactly like the records you need to write to (and read from) the random file.

Working with Random Access

In the second topic section, you learned about statements that you can use with sequential files. The `Open` and `Close` statements work the same for sequential- and random-access files. The only difference between the two is in the access mode.

▼ NOTE

If you don't tell Visual Basic what mode to use to open a file, VB assumes `For Random` and fills in the mode for you. Suppose that you type the following:

```
Open "Random.Txt" As #1
```

Visual Basic changes the line to the following:

```
Open "Random.Txt" For Random As #1 ▲
```

The following statement opens a file for random access:

```
Open "Random.Txt" For Random As #1
```

You can open a file as a random-access file and then use it for sequential access. You sacrifice the benefits of a random-access file during the processing, but you may want to do this sometimes—especially if you've entered the records in a predefined order and you now want to print a report or display the file data in that exact order.

Consider an example of the difference between sequential and random access. Suppose that you create a file that contains 10 lines of inventory totals. To read the sixth line (*record*) of the file in sequential mode, you have to read the first five items to get to the sixth, and then have to read the last four items. If you access the file in random mode, you can go straight to record six, read the data, and close the file.

The same holds true for writing to a file. If you have the same 10-line file and you want to change the eighth record with sequential access, you have to read all 10 records in the file, change the eighth record, and write all 10 records back to the file. In random mode, you can just write the changes to the eighth record.

When a file contains only 10 records, you don't benefit much from a random file, but when the file contains 10,000 records, you save a lot of time and decrease system overhead when you use random access.

Using *Get* and *Put*

Two statements are used for random access files: `Put #` and `Get #`. These statements are similar to the `Print #` and `Input #` statements you used for sequential file access. The major difference between these two sets of statements is that `Print #` and `Input #` handle one piece of data at a time and work all the way through the file. There's no way for these statements to position to a specific record and update only that record.

The syntax for `Put #` and `Get #` is a little different from those of `Print #` and `Input #`:

```
Put [#]intChannel, [intRecNum,] Variable

Get [#]intChannel, [intRecNum,] Variable
```

As you can see, these statements use a record number. By specifying the record number you want to work with, you can update or read only certain data. Record numbers begin with 1. The variable you read or write can be of any data type—even an array or a user-defined variable (see the next section). The freedom to handle any type of variable as a single unit is one of the most powerful features of random-access files.

The examples at the end of this topic section include procedures that read and write particular records in a random-access file.

User-Defined Data Types

You already have learned about variables and arrays in this book. You'll now learn how to create your own data types consisting of other data types grouped together. These user-defined data types are sometimes called *structures* or *records*.

If you wanted to create a program that would allow you to maintain an address book for all your contacts, you could use individual variables for each field you needed. For example, you could use a string named `strFName` for the first name, a string named `strLName` for the last name, and so on. These separate variables would work; however, such programming would become cumbersome when you had a large number of contacts to manage. It would be much easier to have one user-defined data type that contained all the same information and that you could handle as one entity just as you handle individual variables.

A user-defined data type is one that contains other existing data types grouped together to form a new data type. This grouping is referred to as a *composite declaration*.

▼ **NOTE**
A user-defined data type is composed of pre-existing data types (VB's built-in data types, other user-defined types, or both). ▲

You use the `Type` statement to create your own data types. The format is as follows:

```
[Private ¦ Public] Type TypeName
  VarName1[(ArraySize)) As ExistingType [* StringLength]
  VarName2[(ArraySize)] As ExistingType [* StringLength]
     ⋮
     ⋮
End Type
```

Notice that the name of the user-defined data type you want to create follows the `Type` keyword. This name can be any word that isn't a reserved word, keyword, or declared variable name. If you've already declared a variable named `Client`, for instance, you can't create a user-defined data type named `Client`.

You must declare all user-defined types at the module level; it's invalid to declare them inside procedures. You can declare a type in a form module, but this declaration must be `Private`, and the data type will be private to the form's module code only.

Examine the following code:

```
' Module Page of the Project
Type UserType
   strFName As String
   strLName As String
End Type
Public Names As UserType
```

This code creates a user-defined data type named `UserType`. It contains two strings, `strFName` and `strLName`. It also creates a variable named `Names` of type `UserType`.

▼ NOTE

`UserType` isn't a variable, but a type you've defined. `Names` is the variable name and `strFName` and `strLName` are called *members* or *fields* within the variable. You've added a new data type to the Visual Basic language for the duration of the program's execution. In addition to `Integer` and `Boolean`, you now can declare variables of the data type `UserType`. **▲**

TIP To access the individual fields that make up the data type, use the variable name, a period, and then the field name.

The following statements initialize and work with the variable just declared:

```
Names.strFName = "John"
Names.strLName = "Doe"
lblFName.Caption = "First Name: " & Names.strFName
lblLName.Caption = "Last Name: " & Names.strLName
```

You can limit the size of string variables used in a structure by adding the *StringLength* option to the declaration after an `As String` field type. The fixed-length string sets the absolute length of the string to *StringLength*. This usually is required when you're going to be randomly reading and writing your structures to a file. A fixed string length is needed to ensure that each record written to the file is the same size so that you can safely access records randomly.

To change the previous example to make the string sizes constant, consider the following code:

```
' Module Page of the Project
Type UserType2
  strFName As String * 8
  strLName As String * 20
End Type
Public Names As UserType2
```

The fixed-length strings limit the string length to an inflexible maximum. Although the string data may not consume the entire string space you've reserved, Visual Basic pads the remaining length with spaces to ensure that any variables declared with UserType2 and written to a random-access file will consume the same record length—no matter what data the variable holds.

Example   The procedure in Listing 21.6 demonstrates the basics of working with random files.

Listing 21.6   Random.bas: Writing to Any Record Number You Want

```
Private Sub cmdCreate_Click()
  ' This procedure creates the file
  Dim intChan As Integer    ' Free channel
  Dim intCtr As Integer     ' Loop counter

  intChan = FreeFile
  Open "c:\Random.Txt" For Random As #intChan Len = 5

  ' Loop through numbers and write file
  For intCtr = 1 To 5
    Put # intChan, intCtr, intCtr  ' Record # same as data
  Next intCtr

  Close intChan
End Sub

Private Sub cmdChange_Click()
  ' This procedure changes 3rd record
  Dim intChan As Integer    ' Free channel
```

```
   intChan = FreeFile
   Open "c:\Random.Txt" For Random As #intChan Len = 5

   ' Write a new 3rd record
   Put # intChan, 3, 9    ' Record 3, value: 9
   Close # intChan
End Sub

Private Sub cmdDisplay_Click()
   ' This procedure displays the file
   Dim intChan As Integer    ' Free channel
   Dim intVal As Integer     ' Read value
   Dim intCtr As Integer     ' Loop counter

   intChan = FreeFile
   Open "c:\Random.Txt" For Random As #intChan Len = 5

   Debug.Print "File Random.Txt opened..."

   ' Loop through records and write file
   For intCtr = 1 To 5
     Get # intChan, intCtr, intVal
     Debug.Print " Retrieved a " & intVal & " from Random.Txt"
   Next intCtr
   Close # intChan

   Debug.Print "File Random.Txt is now closed"
End Sub
```

Notice that the random-access Open statement uses the Len = option. The procedure uses Put # to create a random-access file with a record length of 5; the Len = option specifies the record length. The record length is very important; if you didn't know the record length, Put # and Get # wouldn't know how far into the file to search for a particular record. (The formula for finding a record is *RecordNumber * RecordLength*.)

This example assumes that the form has three buttons. One creates the file, another displays the file, and a third changes the file. You can easily create such an application and run it. Click the Create button, and then click the Display button. Your Immediate window should look like Figure 21.3.

Click the Change button and then click the Display button again. Your results now should look like those shown in Figure 21.4.

FIG. 21.3
Here are the results after writing the values to Random.txt.

FIG. 21.4
The third record is different now.

This record used to show a 3

The third record in the file now holds 9 instead of 3. The subroutine that made this change simply wrote the 9 to record number 3, using Put # to access the correct record.

Next Step

You've seen how to create your first user-defined data type, but what if you want to include a user-defined data type inside another user-defined data type? One of the fields needs to be a user-defined data type rather than one of the built-in VB data types. Just be sure to declare the user-defined data type you want included *before* you declare the user-defined data type you want to include it in.

Here's an example of one user-defined data type used as a field inside another:

```
'  Entered into the Code module
Type Address
  strStreet As String
  strCity As String
  strZip As String
End Type

Type UserType3
  strFName As String * 10
  strLName As String * 25
  typAddr As Address   ' Another data type
End Type

Public Names As UserType3  ' Declare a variable
```

The following code initializes these fields and shows you how to get to the fields within fields:

```
Names.strFName = "Jonathan"
Names.strLName = "Doe"

Names.typAddr.strStreet = "AnyStreet"
Names.typAddr.strCity = "AnyTown"
Names.typAddr.strZip "12345-9876"

' Work with the data
lblFName.Caption = "First Name: " & Names.strFName
lblLName.Caption = "Last Name: " & Names.strLName
lblAddr.Caption = "Street: " & Names.strAddr.strStreet
lblCty.Caption = "City: " & Names.strAddr.strCity
lblZip.Caption = "Zip: " & Names.strAddr.strZip
```

Summary

In this lesson, you learned how to create and access files. Visual Basic supports three file modes, and you practiced working with the two most common—sequential and random. Sequential file processing is easier to code, but random file processing lets you access data that you need when and where you need it, without tediously reading and writing all other records in the file.

In Hour 22, you'll learn about OLE and see how to embed objects from other sources in your applications.

Hour 21 Quiz

You can find the answers for the following questions on the accompanying CD-ROM and on the Virtual Classroom Web site.

On the CD

1. How many open files can you close with a single **Close** statement?
2. What function returns the next unused file number?
3. What happens if you open a file for sequential output access and the file already exists?
4. What happens if you open a file for sequential append access and the file already exists?
5. What type of file does the following statement open?

```
Open "TestFile.Dat" For Append As #1
```

6. Why do random-access files need to know the record length of their data?

7. Why should you specify the absolute length of strings within a user-defined data type if you're going to read and write those strings to a random-access file?

8. What statement do you use to define your own data types?

9. **True or false:** The following code declares a new user-defined variable named `CustRec`:

```
Type CustRec
    strFName As String * 10
    strLName As String * 15
    curBalance As Currency
    blnDiscount As Boolean
End Type
```

10. **True or false:** You can't embed one user-defined data type within another user-defined data type.

Hour 21 Homework Exercises

1. Write a program that creates a sequential file that holds the following information: name, age, and favorite color. Fill this file with five units of information (each unit should contain one name, one age, and one color). Use three `For...Next` loops to write this information to the file. *Hint:* You need to initialize three arrays, one for each kind of value you're writing.

2. Write a program that creates a random-access file to store 20 numbers. Use an input box to query users for two things: the number of the record that should be updated next and the new value for that record. Then modify the record.

3. Write a program that creates a random-access file that stores 100 names and addresses stored as the user-defined data type `UserType3` presented at the end of this lesson's final topic section. Display a form for users with Save and Done command buttons. Put text boxes on the form to represent each piece of the record data. When users click Save, check the text boxes to see whether they contain data; if so, write the record to the random-access file. When users click Done, print the records *backward* (use `Get #`) in the Immediate window.

Adding OLE to a Program

HOUR 22

During this hour you will learn

▶ *What OLE is*

▶ *How to use the OLE Container control*

▶ *What in-place activation is*

▶ *How to add insertable OLE Toolbox tools*

THIS LESSON EXPLORES Visual Basic's OLE capabilities. If you've read much about the latest version of Visual Basic, you may wonder why a discussion of OLE appears in this tutorial before ActiveX. (Hour 30, "Enhancing Programs with ActiveX," begins ActiveX coverage.) The new ActiveX technology is supposed to replace OLE in Visual Basic 5. OLE is still vitally important, however, because only some Visual Basic programmers will have access to ActiveX. If you use the Standard Edition, you won't have access to primary ActiveX control creation and usage (except for a subset of ActiveX tools) and will have to rely on the OLE control if you want to embed outside objects in your applications. Also, although OLE is less powerful than ActiveX, OLE provides some groundwork learning before you master ActiveX.

If all these OLE and ActiveX terms confuse you, read on. You'll soon see that these controls add capabilities that help eliminate coding, not increase your workload. OLE (which stands for Object Linking and Embedding) lets you reuse objects from other software applications. Therefore, you don't have to reinvent the wheel every time you need, for example, to add a painting program's features to your application. You'll be able to borrow from an existing program such as Microsoft Paint.

▶▶ FAST TRACK

If you've used OLE in other applications, you'll appreciate the added power ActiveX gives your applications. See Hour 30, "Enhancing Programs with ActiveX" (p. 681), for more information.

Topic 1: Introducing OLE

Microsoft introduced Object Linking and Embedding a few years ago to take advantage of software reuse. By designing their applications according to the OLE standard, independent software vendors can create programs that fit seamlessly into Visual Basic and other Microsoft products. This strategy greatly increases programmer productivity by allowing the integration of these components into Visual Basic applications. OLE lets your applications connect to outside applications by using either *linking* or *embedding* technologies.

▼ NOTE

If you have Visual Basic's Standard Edition, you can still use ActiveX controls. When working with OLE controls, such as a Microsoft Excel worksheet, you actually are working with an ActiveX control if you're using Microsoft's latest version of Excel, from Office 97. The ActiveX technology works and acts like OLE technology, but ActiveX *extends* that technology, as you'll see in Hour 30.

The rest of this lesson sticks with the term *OLE* to teach the OLE control, but you'll know that some of the "OLE controls" you embed in your Standard Edition applications are really ActiveX controls. If you use the Professional or Enterprise Edition, you'll be able to take ActiveX technology further than you can with OLE. ▲

Linking to an application means that your OLE control contains a link to another application's document (a data file). In fact, an OLE control is often called a *container control* because it holds an outside application's functionality. If the other application changes that document, your application will reflect the changes. The object is known as a *persistent object* because you can keep the object's contents up-to-date via the link.

Embedding a document means that your container control contains a document that was created by using an OLE-compliant application. It does not, however, maintain any links back to the external document. Therefore, if the outside application changes the external document, your application won't reflect that change.

Overview When you place an OLE object on a form, you must make the linking or embedding decision. The primary difference between the two kinds of objects is that an embedded object appears to be part of the application (almost as though it were a custom control placed on the form); on the other hand, a linked object, when activated, calls up another program (the source program it's linked to). By using the source program, users can then work with the document's data. When finished, users close the source application and return to the VB application.

This topic section explains more about what you can expect from an OLE object, and subsequent topic sections demonstrate OLE objects within applications.

An OLE Tutorial

The only way to change a document contained in your OLE control is to open your application and activate the control. Normally, users do this by double-clicking the control itself. When the OLE application appears, you can alter the contents of the document, and then choose Close and Return to <VB Application> from the File menu. Users then see the changed document in the changed window. You'll see how this works throughout the rest of this lesson.

Any object that supports *Automation* (or *OLE Automation*) is available as an OLE object. Many of today's Windows applications support Automation, so you'll often be able to use the OLE control to integrate your applications with other applications.

The OLE Container Control

The OLE Container control that you can double-click to add to the form (see Figure 22.1) holds your application's OLE object. You can link or embed as many OLE objects as your application requires by placing multiple OLE Container controls on your form. (Generally, simple applications contain only a single OLE Container control.)

FIG. 22.1

The OLE Container control appears in the standard Toolbox.

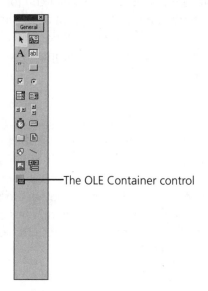

The OLE Container control

The OLE Container control displays a rectangle on the form when you place it. The control can display data from another application. You can resize the OLE Container control to adjust the size of the embedded or linked object.

Example   When you place an OLE Container control on the form by double-clicking the Toolbox control, you don't see the OLE Container control rectangle immediately. Instead, VB displays the Insert Object dialog box (see Figure 22.2).

FIG. 22.2

The Insert Object dialog box lets you describe the OLE object.

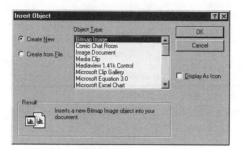

The initial Insert Object dialog box has the Create <u>N</u>ew option button selected. This option lets you create a brand new OLE object to place on the form.

> **TIP** If you inadvertently close the Insert Object dialog box, you can reopen it by right-clicking the OLE Container control and selecting Insert Object from the pop-up menu.

The Object <u>T</u>ype list box contains the OLE-compliant application controls you have to select from. The list varies according to the software installed on your system. An application updates your Windows Registry database with the application's OLE objects when you install the application. Normally, one shrink-wrapped Windows application can yield two, three, or more custom controls. For example, if you have PowerPoint 97 installed, you'll find two PowerPoint controls in the list.

▼ NOTE

The list box displays true controls. Your application can borrow these controls from the listed applications. ▲

When you select the Create <u>N</u>ew option, VB embeds a generic object into your OLE Container control. You then specify the kind of object you want to embed.

If the OLE object already exists, you can click the Create from <u>F</u>ile option button, which results in the Insert Object dialog box in Figure 22.3.

FIG. 22.3
You can select a current object to link or embed.

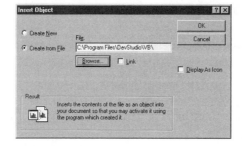

▼ **NOTE**

Notice the Link check box below the File text box. If you mark this check box, Visual Basic links rather than embeds the object. However, when you create an object from scratch by using the Create New option, the object is embedded in your application because you're creating the object just for your application. ▲

If you want to follow along throughout this lesson and add an OLE object to an application, open a new project and double-click the OLE Container control. Keep the Create New option selected.

Next Step   Although you'll have a different set of applications installed on your system, this section will select the Windows Paint program's tools, which should always appear in the Insert Object dialog box. If you select Paintbrush Picture (*Paintbrush* is a synonym for Windows Paint) and click OK, Visual Basic closes the Insert Object dialog box and displays the object's rectangle in the center of your form, as Figure 22.4 shows.

FIG. 22.4
Your application now displays a container for a Paint picture.

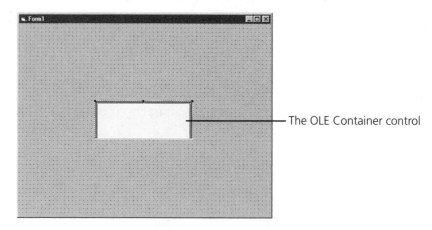

———— The OLE Container control

▼ **NOTE**

You have *not* imported an actual Paint picture—instead, you've inserted a mini-application version of Windows Paint directly inside your own application. Your own application will be able to communicate with the Paint object, but your users will be able to access Paint's capabilities when they run your application. ▲

Topic 2: The OLE Control

Look back at your screen if you followed the first topic's example. Where are your Visual Basic menu commands and toolbar buttons? Where did the form location and size coordinate section go? Where is Visual Basic's status bar? This topic section begins by explaining more about OLE objects and their properties. You'll then complete the simple OLE project that you began in the preceding topic section and see why the OLE Container control caused some of VB's screen, menu, and toolbars to go away.

Overview The OLE Container control lets you create something called a *document-centered application*. The document, as alluded to in the first topic section, is actually data from one or more other applications. The OLE Container control holds the document you want to bring in from the outside application. This topic explains the OLE objects you link or embed in depth.

Linking and Embedding Revisited

One of the nice advantages of linking is that the data resides in only one location on your computer. No matter how many applications link to the object, such as a Microsoft Excel worksheet, the object takes up only a single location and consumes less disk space than if you embedded the object in the various applications.

Linking does pose its share of problems, however, especially in networked environments and in distributed applications. Users must have the source application that created the linked object, or they won't be able to modify the object. Also, if you want your application to reflect the linked object's current state (in case someone used the source application to modify the object after you link to the object), you must use the `Update` method to update the object, like this:

```
oleWorkSheetSales.Update
```

Without the `Update` method, the object retains the form and data contents that it contained when you first linked the object to your application. The updating might slow your application somewhat, because the update has to occur, but the object container will always be linked to the most recent version.

When you embed an object, the object appears frozen in time. Subsequent changes users make to the object from another application won't affect your Visual Basic application's copy of the embedded object.

▼ NOTE

Be aware of the increased file size that comes with embedded objects. Not only must Visual Basic store the embedded object with your application, but VB must also keep track of the source application that controls the object. (For example, Visual Basic can't manipulate an Excel worksheet, but Excel can, so Visual Basic has to remember the Excel connection to the object.) ▲

One of the greatest benefits of OLE objects is that your application's users can double-click the object, and the running VB application starts the source application and lets users manipulate the control. Actually, the double-click is the default mechanism that starts the source application. You can change the OLE Container control's `AutoActivate` property to start the source application when the OLE Container control gets the focus. When your code triggers the object with the special VB `DoVerb` OLE Container control method, or when the object receives its normal activation event, the control gets the focus.

The Paste Special Object

If you want to use only part of an object, such as a selected range of cells from a worksheet, you can't use the Insert Object dialog box. Instead, you must use VB's Paste Special command available from the right-click menu. Paste Special uses the Windows Clipboard to make the transition from the original application's object to the OLE Container control.

This topic section's "Next Step" section explains how to use Paste Special instead of the Insert Object dialog box to insert part of existing objects into your application.

Runtime OLE

You can place an OLE Container control on your form without using the Insert Object dialog box or Paste Special to place the object in the container. The OLE Container control supports several methods, such as `CreateLink` and `CreateEmbed`, that let your VB code create a link at runtime. If your VB application is part of an overall system that uses worksheets, documents, and databases from other applications, it may have to create a link to an OLE-compliant application at runtime after certain conditions are met.

Through coding, you can create linked and embedded objects at runtime. VB even includes methods that display the Insert Object or Paste Special dialog box at runtime so that your application's users can control the object coming into the application. Generally, you won't be writing such applications, and some VB programmers never have the need to let their users interactively select objects—but VB makes this option possible. This tutorial doesn't go into such programming logic because of how rarely most programmers need to display the Insert Object dialog box at runtime.

Example   In the previous topic section, you included an OLE Container control in a project and created a new Paint picture object in the OLE Container control. The OLE Container control still looks like an empty rectangle, however. You'll add more to the OLE Container control in this example.

When you placed the OLE Container control and set up the container to embed a Paint picture, the Visual Basic menus and toolbars went away. You were left with a smaller set of menu items above the Form window. If you were to click one of the menu bar options, such as View, you may be surprised at what you see. Figure 22.5 shows that the View menu doesn't contain any familiar Visual Basic options.

You aren't viewing the Visual Basic View menu; you're viewing the Windows Paint View menu! (Sometimes, minor menu differences between Visual Basic's object menus and the true source application's menus appear.) If you move your mouse pointer to the OLE Container control, the pointer changes to a drawing pencil. If you click and drag the pencil inside the OLE Container control, you can draw on the control just as you would draw on the Paint window. Figure 22.6 shows a simple line drawing inside the OLE Container control.

FIG. 22.5
The <u>V</u>iew menu doesn't look like a VB <u>V</u>iew menu!

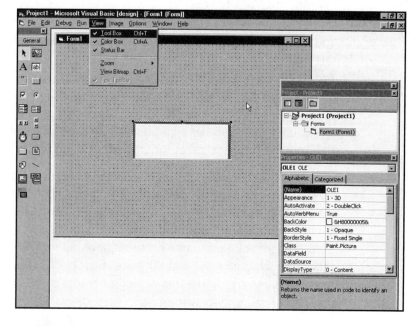

FIG. 22.6
You can draw something with Paint inside the Visual Basic Form window.

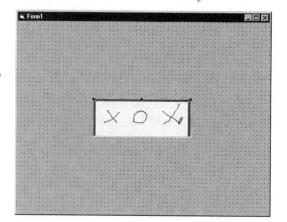

> **TIP** The OLE Container control won't expand to display the object you want to display. Change the control's `SizeMode` property to `2 – AutoSize`. `SizeMode` expands the control to show the normal OLE document size. The drawing area won't be limited to the size of the OLE container control that you used to place the control on the form.

Run your application to see what users see. Figure 22.7 shows the running application. Not much is really happening here, is it? A user (you in this case) sees the simple drawing that you made at design time. If you hadn't drawn the lines, users wouldn't know that the center of the application window even includes a Paint object except that they would see the blank rectangle. (You could have left the OLE Container's Paintbrush picture blank so that users start with a clean slate.)

FIG. 22.7
Add labels to describe objects; otherwise, users might not know what the object is for.

Obviously, you'll have to include labels and form text to let your users know what the objects you embed or link contain. Perhaps this application's form might be part of an engineer's application that tracks jobs, and the embedded Paint object lets the engineer make simple drawings that go with current building plans. You'll need to label the application and perhaps even write a user manual to let users know that they can activate the object.

When users activate the embedded object, the object's original purpose becomes obvious because the original application's menu and tools become available within your own application. Remember that you can change the object's `AutoActivate` property to change the activation requirement. In other words, you can change the object so that the object immediately activates (its application's menus and toolbars automatically appear) as soon as users bring the object into focus or at runtime.

▼ **NOTE**
Two forms of activation take place. In this case, you're seeing a separate window with the Paint application embedded within your OLE document.

continues

continued

With a compound document (described in this hour's final topic section), the application's toolbars and menus actually change to Paint's, Excel's, or those of whatever kind of source application created the object. ▲

You'll need to change one of the property values to activate the entire Paint program's tools and menu options. Close the application and click the OLE object to display its Properties window. Set the `MiscFlags` property to 2. The flags determine how the OLE object responds. When you set `MiscFlags` to 2 for the Paint object, Visual Basic starts Paint and places the embedded picture in the Paint window when the OLE object is activated.

Run the program, and you'll see nothing has changed since you ran the program previously. When you double-click the object, however, the application starts Windows Paint and places the object in the Paint window (see Figure 22.8).

FIG. 22.8
Paint opens so you can edit the object.

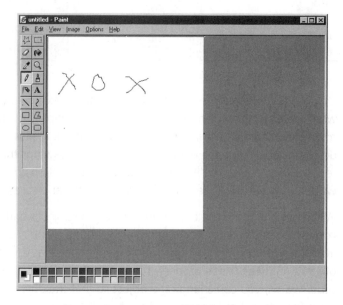

Before you changed `MiscFlags` to 2, you could use Paint somewhat and edit the drawing in place, but you had no access to Paint's Toolbox and Color box. When the full Paint application begins, your users have complete access to these tools.

If you edit the object and close Paint's window by choosing E̲xit and Return to <VB Application> from the F̲ile menu, the changes you made will then be in place inside your application's form. When you close the application, your changes aren't saved with the application, however. You'll learn how to save changes in the next topic section.

Next Step When you want to link or embed part of an object, such as part of an Excel worksheet, you must use the Paste Special OLE option. With Paste Special, you can create embedded and linked objects in your Visual Basic application.

If you have Excel, you can follow these steps to create an OLE object out of a partial Excel worksheet:

1. Open a new project in Visual Basic and create a standard .EXE application.

2. Start Microsoft Excel. Enter three columns of random numbers six rows deep.

3. Highlight the first five rows in the first two columns (the worksheet range goes from cell A1 to B5).

4. From the E̲dit menu, choose C̲opy to copy the selected range to your Windows Clipboard.

5. Double-click Visual Basic's OLE Container control tool to place a control in the center of the form. Click Cancel to get rid of the Insert Object dialog box.

6. Change the OLE Container control's `SizeMode` property value to `2 - AutoSize`.

7. Right-click over the OLE Container control and choose Paste Special. Visual Basic instantly recognizes the kind of object you've copied to the Clipboard and displays the dialog box shown in Figure 22.9.

FIG. 22.9
Get ready to paste the special Clipboard contents as an Excel object.

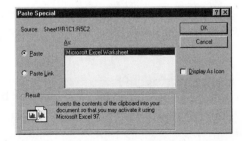

8. Click Paste Link to insert the OLE link (if you left the Paste option selected, Visual Basic would embed the object).

9. Switch back to the Excel worksheet and save the worksheet.

10. Exit Excel.

11. Run your application and double-click the object. Visual Basic instantly starts Excel and displays the full worksheet with the partial data that you pasted still highlighted. The object looks like a pasted section from the worksheet.

12. If you make changes to the worksheet and save it, those changes will be reflected in your project. Because you embedded objects, however, the changes won't remain in the worksheet object the next time you start the application.

Topic 3: Working with OLE

This topic section discusses some OLE extras that you'll need when working with OLE objects. For example, you may not want the embedded application's object to appear as a worksheet or as a picture but to appear as an icon. Users can double-click the icon and then start the source application. Also, you need to learn how to save changes so that the next time users run your application, the changes will reside with the application.

Overview This topic wraps up this quick OLE discussion by describing some important properties and methods that may come in handy as you learn more about OLE's ActiveX replacement. Due to OLE's decrease in popularity now that the more powerful and extendible ActiveX controls have come out, you'll learn more powerful ways to accomplish OLE-like feats beginning in Hour 30 if you use the Professional or Enterprise edition of Visual Basic. If you use the Standard edition, you will, at the end of this topic section, understand OLE fundamentals that you'll be able to build on later after you master ActiveX. This topic provides the groundwork for ActiveX controls that you'll master in the future.

OLE as an Icon

Figure 22.3 shows the Insert Object dialog box. If you look back at the figure now, you'll see the check box labeled Display As Icon. If you click this option when you embed, link, or paste special into an OLE Container control, Visual Basic doesn't display the object's contents but instead displays an icon that represents the object. Figure 22.10 shows the running Excel-based object displayed as an icon (with a `SizeMode` property set to `AutoSize`).

FIG. 22.10
An icon repre-sents the Excel data.

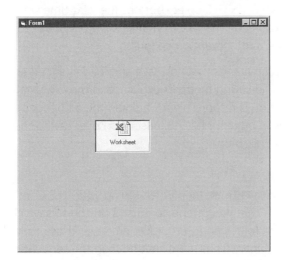

The icon represents the application for the embedded object. When users double-click the icon, the application opens Excel and loads the original worksheet for editing.

TIP You can change the OLE Container control's `DisplayType` property from `0 - Content` to `1 - Icon` at design time as long as you haven't embedded, linked, or pasted special an object into the control. After you change `DisplayType` to represent an icon when the application runs, you can embed or link an object to the control and its startup state will reflect the `DisplayType` entry.

In-Place Activation

One nice feature of some OLE objects is *in-place activation*. The running application's menus and toolbars change to the OLE object's source application's menus and support tools. Users don't feel as though they have left your application but that only the application's menus and tools changed. You'll learn about in-place activation in Hour 30 when you learn about ActiveX. Although OLE often supports in-place automation, the ActiveX controls provide better in-place activation support.

Saving Object Contents

When you make a change to a linked data item, the source application makes the actual change because the object doesn't exist inside your application. Therefore, you use Excel's or Paint's (or whatever application's) <u>S</u>ave command on the <u>F</u>ile menu to save your changes. The changes will reflect in your application's OLE object but not the next time you start the application unless you issue the OLE Container control's `Update` method (such as in the `Form_Load()` event procedure).

Microsoft recommends that you save and load changed embedded objects with several file-saving methods explained in the next example section. Your application is responsible for holding the embedded object, so the source application really has no jurisdiction over saving the object's content inside your application.

Example Use the `SaveToFile` method when saving your OLE Container control data. Suppose that you offer a command button to save changes made to an object. The following event procedure saves those changes in a special binary file. A binary file is more limiting than the sequential or random-access files that you learned about in Hour 21. Nevertheless, binary files provide a fast and efficient method for storing objects, as long as you later read objects in the same order you save them.

The following code saves your OLE Container control object:

```
Dim intFileNum as Integer

' Get next free file number
intFileNum = FreeFile

' Open output file
Open "TEST.OLE" For Binary As #intFileNum

' Save file
oleObj1.SaveToFile intFileNum

' Close the file
Close
```

The next time your application starts, the application should read the object's latest values (from the previous run) into the OLE Container control by using the `ReadFromFile` method as follows:

```
Dim intFileNum as Integer

' Get next free file number
intFileNum = FreeFile

' Open input file
Open "TEST.OLE" For Binary As #intFileNum

' Read file into object
oleObj1.ReadFromFile intFileNum

' Close the file
Close
```

Next Step   As you learn more about OLE and eventually ActiveX, you'll need to master the following terms:

- **Compound Documents.** Documents that contain embedded or linked objects and that overlay the running application's menu and tools with the embedded or linked application's menu and tools when in-place activation begins.
- **OLE Automation.** Controlling one application from another.
- **OLE Container.** A holder of objects, such as an application that holds a Paint object and an Excel object.
- **OLE Server.** An OLE-compliant application that you can use in a Visual Basic compound document (with overlaid menus and tools).

If you press Ctrl+T and click the Insertable Objects tab, Visual Basic displays a list of objects that you can insert into your applications. The object list comes from the Windows Registry that your applications update when you install them.

If you select one of the listed objects (such as the one labeled Microsoft Excel Worksheet) and click OK, Visual Basic updates your Toolbox as shown in Figure 22.11. Visual Basic actually inserted a new tool in your Toolbox that lets you insert Excel objects without going through the usual OLE Container control selection process from the Insert Object dialog box.

FIG. 22.11

The in-place activation Excel OLE tool appears.

The MS Excel tool

These tools provide for in-place activation, not just simple activation. When you embed, for example, an Excel object by clicking the Excel tool, you've inserted a special OLE object that supports in-place editing. If you were to add the Excel object tool to the center of a new project's Form window (assuming that you have Excel on your system) and then run the application, you would see the form in Figure 22.12 with a complete Excel worksheet in the middle of the Form window. All of Excel's functionality is now available, including Excel's primary menu options, even if the Form window didn't originally contain a menu.

Generally, you'll want to offer in-place editing when it's available so that your users don't have to go outside the application to access the OLE data. You may not have the right in-place editing tool available (you'll find far more OLE objects in the Insert Object dialog box list than in the Insertable Objects dialog box), so you'll have to offer the next-best thing as described throughout the earlier sections of this lesson: the OLE Container control that supports activation of the source application and, possibly, also supports in-place editing if the OLE object's source application supports in-place activation.

FIG. 22.12
Users can now use Excel from within your applications.

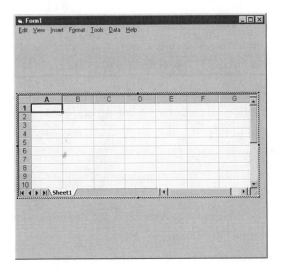

Summary

You've only scratched the OLE surface. OLE offers a wide assortment of features that go beyond linked and embedded applications. Nevertheless, OLE is dying out and ActiveX is taking its place. ActiveX isn't fully dominant in the software development industry, so you may not have to make the switch to ActiveX soon, but someday you'll have to make that switch.

In the meantime, the OLE objects provide a starting location that lets you practice the same fundamental operations that you'll use with ActiveX. You can link, embed, and paste special objects, as well as create compound documents in which your users can access the object's tools and menus as though they were running the actual external application instead of one you wrote.

Next hour's lesson, "Enhancing Your Program," starts a new part of the book, "Adding Power to VB Programs." You'll learn more Toolbox tools, as well as master the installation of new tools in your Toolbox.

Hour 22 Quiz

You can find the answers for the following questions on the accompanying CD-ROM and on the Virtual Classroom Web site.

On the CD

1. What does *OLE* stand for?

2. What's the difference between linking and embedding?

3. Which kind of OLE insertion lets you insert only a portion of an outside application's object?

4. Which kind of OLE usually takes the most disk space: embedding or linking?

5. What's the difference between in-place OLE activation and the simple OLE activation?

6. **True or false:** Visual Basic automatically saves your users' changes to the OLE embedded object.

7. What is a compound document?

8. Which property lets the OLE object appear when users change the focus to the OLE object?

9. Which method saves an OLE object to a disk file?

10. Which method reads an OLE object to a disk file?

Hour 22 Homework Exercises

1. Write a program that contains one OLE Container control for each type of program on your computer.

2. Embed an in-place Word control on a form and run the application to work with Word within Visual Basic. Obviously, you must have Microsoft Word installed on your system, or you'll have to use a different word processor. If you use a Windows word processor, such as WordPerfect, you should see its object control that you can add to your Toolbox.

During this hour you will learn:

▶ *What the Timer control does*

▶ *How to add toolbars*

▶ *Why to use image lists*

▶ *When pop-up menus help*

Enhancing Your Program

THIS LESSON IMPROVES on your programming skills by teaching you ways to improve the usability of your applications. The Timer control lets you generate responses to the internal computer clock. You'll be able to write code that executes after a certain amount of time passes and use the Timer control to perform background processing.

To brighten up your applications, you can add toolbars. Toolbars not only make your applications look more professional, but also give your users additional ways to execute commands. You can paint your toolbar buttons with graphic icons.

Finally, this lesson finishes by explaining how to incorporate pop-up menus into your application. If you embed one or more pop-up menus, your users can perform context-sensitive operations depending on the object they right-click.

▶▶ **FAST TRACK**

Toolbars have been around for a long time. If you've already mastered toolbars and want to learn a topic that is new to Visual Basic 5, jump to Hour 26, "Using Form Templates" (p. 595), to learn about the form template wizard access that comes with Visual Basic 5.

Topic 1: The Timer Control

One event that users don't trigger is a timer event. Your computer's internal clock ticks off 18 beats a second. The clock is vital to the workings of your CPU and memory, and the clock helps synchronize all the hardware and software interaction that must take place.

Fortunately, you can take advantage of these clock ticks. Your Visual Basic application can respond to the clock. You can set up a preset interval of time, after which Windows sends an event message to your application. As with all events, you can write event procedures that execute each time the timer event takes place. The bottom line is that you can write code that executes whenever a fixed amount of time passes.

Overview When you place Visual Basic's Timer control on a form, you set up the time interval that determines the frequency of timer events. That time interval is one of the Timer control's properties. When the interval of time passes, the Timer control triggers the event procedure that you've set up to handle the timer events.

▼ **NOTE**

You can add multiple Timer controls to your application just as you can add several instances of the other controls. Therefore, your application can perform an event procedure every minute, every half hour, and every hour (as might be required of a time and billing application) if you send three Timer controls to the application's form and set up the three intervals. ▲

This topic section explains how to use the Timer control to write code that responds to time passing. After you learn the Timer control, you'll have learned all of Visual Basic's standard tools (called the *intrinsic controls*) that appear in the Toolbox. Although you can add more tools to the Toolbox, the intrinsic tools are the ones you'll use most frequently. Therefore, you will have mastered the basics of Visual Basic after you master the Timer control.

▼ MULTIPLE TOOLBOX CONTROLS

You've now seen three kinds of controls: the intrinsic controls that appear in the Toolbox, the *insertable object controls* such as the Excel control you added to the Toolbox in Hour 20, and ActiveX controls, such as the Common Dialog Box control you added in Hour 17. (All three Visual Basic editions contain extra ActiveX controls, but you can't work with ActiveX inside your code—except for the ActiveX controls in the Toolbox—unless you use the Professional or Enterprise Edition.)

When you need to add controls to the Toolbox, use the Project menu's Components command as you did in Hour 17 when you added the Slider control. If you add third-party controls to VB, you'll add those extra controls to the Toolbox by using the Project menu's Components command as well. Don't add more controls than you need for the current project, however, to keep your application file sizes small. ▲

TIP You'll think of many uses for the Timer control as you become more familiar with it. For example, you can use timer event procedures to perform background processing. Also, you can animate graphics by redrawing the graphic image every time your preset timer event occurs, such as every half second.

Placing the Timer Control

The best way to place a Timer control on your form is to double-click it in the Toolbox and move the control that appears on the form out of the way of the other objects. You can't resize a Timer control, and it doesn't appear on your form at runtime.

▼ NOTE

You've already seen another control that you could neither resize nor see at runtime: the Common Dialog Box control (Hour 17, "Adding Control Containers: Dialog Boxes"). ▲

Figure 23.1 shows a Timer control placed in the center of a new form.

FIG. 23.1

You can move a Timer control around on the form, but you can't resize it.

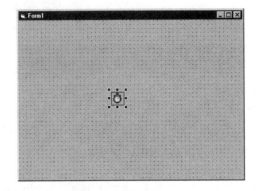

The Timer Control Properties

The Timer control supports very few properties. Of the six design-time properties you can set, five aren't particularly unique:

- `Left` and `Top` determine the Timer control's location.
- `Enabled` determines the timer's activated state.

> **TIP** If you set the Timer control's `Enabled` property to `False` at design time, the Timer control won't begin responding to events until your code later sets `Enabled` to `True`.

- `Tag` holds remark information that you may want to include with the control.
- `Index` determines the control's subscript in a control array.

The only property critical and truly unique to the Timer control is the `Interval` property, which determines the frequency with which you want the Timer control to generate events. You'll enter (at design time or runtime) the number of milliseconds that have to pass before the Timer control responds to an event. For example, if you set the `Interval` property to a value of 1000, the timer events will occur every 1,000 milliseconds, or roughly once per second.

The Timer's Accuracy

The Timer control seems to have some drawbacks at first. The `Interval` property can hold values only from 0 to 64,767. Therefore, you can set a time interval that spans only about 65 seconds and no more. If you need to set an event interval greater than 65 seconds, you simply can't do so. However, in the Timer control's event procedure (described in the next section), you can ignore events and return to the application without responding to the event until a certain amount of time passes. In other words, although the event procedure you've set up for the Timer control might trigger every 60 seconds, you can place code at the top of the event procedure to return to the application and not respond to the event unless a fixed amount of time has passed (such as an hour or whatever) since the previous execution of the event procedure.

CAUTION The Timer control isn't actually extremely accurate. Although the crystal inside your computer's clock is highly accurate, by the time Windows sends a timer event to your application, some accuracy is lost. Also, other events that occur can slow down the timer, such as a network access or modem update. Your computer can't do two things at once, and a Timer control inside a running VB application doesn't always get high priority. Therefore, the Timer control works well when time sensitivity is important to the nearest second, but no control exists in Visual Basic that provides higher precision.

The Timer's Single Event

The Timer control supports only a single event: the `Timer` event. Therefore, if you name a Timer control `tmrClock`, you'll write only a single event procedure for the Timer control, named `tmrClock_Timer()`. Therefore, you'll put the code inside `tmrClock_Timer()` that you want Visual Basic to execute once every time interval that passes.

Example Follow these steps to create a simple application that demonstrates the Timer control:

1. Create a new project and place a Timer control on the form.

2. Set the Timer control's `Interval` property to 1000 so that the control responds to the timer event procedure every second.

3. Name the timer `tmrTime1` and move it to the lower-left portion of the screen.

4. Place another Timer control named `tmrTime2` on the form next to the first one. Set its `Interval` property value to 500 so that it responds to its timer event procedures every half second.

5. Add two text boxes to the form named `txtTime1` and `txtTime2`. Position the text boxes close to the positions in Figure 23.2.

FIG. 23.2
The application is almost finished.

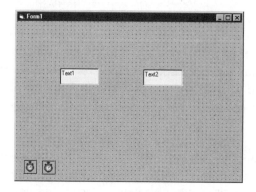

6. Enter **1** for both text box controls' `Text` properties and set the text box font size to 18. Set both text-box `Alignment` properties to 2 – `Center` so that their text appears centered inside the boxes at runtime. Set both text box `Width` properties to 1000.

7. Double-click the first timer to switch to the Code window and enter the following code for the `tmrTime1_Timer()` procedure:

```
Private Sub tmrTime1_Timer()
  ' Add one to the display
  txtTime1.Text = txtTime1.Text + 1
End Sub
```

8. Add the following code for the second timer's event procedure:

```
Private Sub tmrTime2_Timer()
  ' Add one to the display
  txtTime2.Text = txtTime2.Text + 1
End Sub
```

This code adds a numeric 1 to the text box values because Visual Basic stores the values with the `Variant` data type.

9. Run the application. Your form should look something like Figure 23.3. Two things are happening: The first text box updates every second, but the second updates every half a second. Depending on the accuracy of the timer events, the second text box, therefore, should update twice as fast as the first text box.

FIG. 23.3

The two timers update at different times.

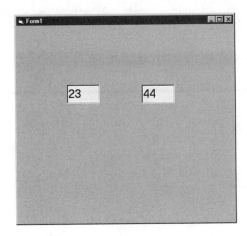

Next Step   In the next lesson, you'll learn how to create and display simple line graphics. You can use the Timer control to animate graphics. Although you have yet to master Visual Basic's graphics components, you can try your hand at animating Picture Box controls with the timer. Animated pictures are more fun to watch than two numbers updating every half second and every second.

This example incorporates a Picture Box control in a form. In this example, the Timer control manipulates the picture to make it appear and disappear, and then animates the picture. Follow these steps:

1. Create a new project and place a Picture Box control named `picAni` on the form. Set the `BorderStyle` property to `0 - None`.

2. Set the `Picture` property to the icon file named Mail01a.ico (in the \Graphics\Icons\Mail subdirectory within your Visual Basic directory).

3. Add a Timer control to the form by double-clicking the Toolbox's Timer control. Name the Timer control `tmrAni` and set its `Interval` property to 1000. Move the timer out of the way.

4. Add the following code to the `tmrAni_Timer()` event procedure:

```
Private Sub tmrAni_Timer()
  ' Turn the picture either on or off
  If picAni.Visible = True Then
    picAni.Visible = False
  Else
    picAni.Visible = True
  End If
End Sub
```

5. Adjust your form size to look something like the one in Figure 23.4.

FIG. 23.4

The timer and envelope icon are placed on the form.

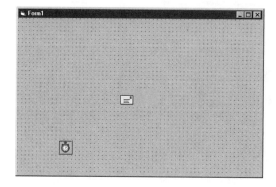

If you run the application, you'll find that the envelope disappears for one second and then appears the next second. This process continues until you stop the program.

Now that you have the basics down, complicate the project somewhat by animating the opening and closing of the envelope in alternating seconds. To do this, you need to create a Picture Box control array and name the two new pictures `picAni2(0)` and `picAni2(1)`.

▼ **NOTE**

Hour 20, "Understanding Objects and Using the Object Browser," explained what control arrays are. As a review, to create the control array, create the two controls for the array and name them the same, `picAni2`. (You can also place one Picture Box control and then copy and paste the control to a second occurrence on the form.) VB asks whether you intend to make the controls a control array. If you answer Yes, the new control is assigned an `Index` property value that's different from the other members of that array. The control is then referenced by the name and the `Index` property combined, and the `Index` property acts like a subscript. ▲

The Picture Box controls will contain the individual cells of the animation. Set the `Picture` property of `picAni2(0)` to the same picture as the first icon, Mail01a.ico. Set the `Picture` property of `picAni2(1)` to the icon named Mail01b.ico located in the same directory. Now, set both picture boxes' `Visible` property to `False`. Set both picture boxes' `BorderStyle` property to `0 – None`. Move the controls to the positions shown in Figure 23.5.

FIG. 23.5
All the animation icons now reside on the form.

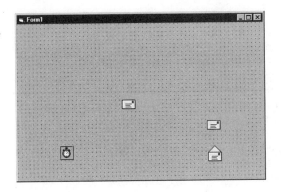

Switch the code in the `tmrAni_Timer()` event procedure with this code:

```
Private Sub tmrAni_Timer()
  ' Determine the correct picture to display
  If intCounter = 1 Then
    picAni.Picture = picAni2(1).Picture
    intCounter = 0
  Else
    picAni.Picture = picAni2(0).Picture
    intCounter = 1
  End If
End Sub
```

Declare the integer variable named `intCounter` in the form module's `Declaration` section. The counter variable is to "remember" which icon was last displayed so that the other icon can display on the next iteration. The program now causes the timer and the two `picAni` controls to disappear and the envelope icon to open and close in a very simple animation.

Although it's great to have a timer that runs continuously, it would be better for some applications to start and stop the timer according to user input. Visual Basic has provided a way to do exactly that with the `Enabled` property. When the `Enabled` property is set to `True`, the timer's event procedure executes just as you've seen. When `Enabled` is set to `False`, no timer event procedure can execute for that timer.

Add a command button to the application and call it `cmdAni`. Set its caption to `Animate`, and then add the following code to the `Click` event procedure for this button:

```
Private Sub cmdAni_Click()
  ' Use the command button to control the animation
  If intCounter2 = 0 Then
    cmdAni.Caption = "Stop"
    tmrAni.Enabled = True
    intCounter2 = 1
  Else
    cmdAni.Caption = "Animate"
    tmrAni.Enabled = False
    intCounter2 = 0
  End If
End Sub
```

From the Properties window, set the `Enabled` property on `tmrAni` to `False`. Also, add the variable named `intCounter2` to the form's `Declarations` section. After you move the command button, your form should look something like Figure 23.6.

FIG. 23.6

The form now contains the starting command button.

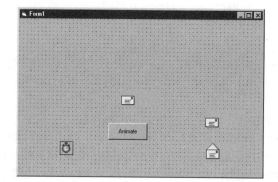

Run the program to see what happens. The envelope sits still until you click the Animate command button. When you click the button, the animation starts and the caption on the command button changes to Stop. When you then click the Stop command button, the animation stops. If you click the button again (when the command button reads Animate), the motion begins again.

You're probably already thinking of a new video game that uses these techniques. You can build on this application's fundamental animation principles to create moving objects by changing their form locations each timer event.

Topic 2: Toolbars

Toolbars give users one-button access to several common application features. Most often, the toolbar buttons provide the same functionality as menu commands. You can use several different methods to add toolbars to your application. Add toolbars so that your users can quickly access the most important and common menu commands without opening a menu. Toolbars require that you first set up a list of the toolbar button icons by using the Image List control. This topic section explains one of the most common methods.

▼ LOCATING THE TOOLBAR-RELATED CONTROLS

Several vendors provide Visual Basic custom controls (get the ActiveX-compatible ones) that supply toolbars. VB's Professional and Enterprise editions supply the Toolbar control inside the ActiveX custom control named Microsoft Windows Common Controls 5.0. Press Ctrl+T and select this control to add the control to your Toolbox. Figure 23.7 shows the Toolbar control that appears (other new tools appear, as well).

If you use VB's Standard edition, you don't have this control. Check out online services for custom toolbar controls (make sure that they don't end in the older .VBX file extension) that you may be able to download for free or for a small charge. Although you can manually create toolbars with the Standard Edition, doing so is painstaking and you'll be glad you found a control to do the dirty work.

Creating a toolbar manually without a Toolbar control requires that you place a wide Picture Box control on the form the size of the toolbar (the toolbar area generally spans an entire ribbon across the form) and then add command buttons that do the job you want done. The command buttons should use the Picture property to hold the toolbar button's icon. Each command button will then have its own Click() event procedure that performs the work. ▲

FIG. 23.7
*The Toolbox now
contains the
Toolbar control.*

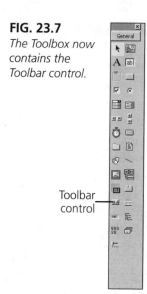

Toolbar
control

Overview After you add the Toolbar control to your Toolbox, adding a toolbar to your application is simple. You'll add the toolbar to the top of your primary Form window. If you write MDI applications, you can add toolbars to one or more forms within the project. This topic explains how to add a toolbar to your Form window and connect the toolbar buttons to their event procedure code.

Creating the Toolbar

You can easily add a toolbar to the top of the animated envelope application you created at the end of the last topic section. Open the application, display the Form window, and double-click the Toolbar control to add the toolbar to the top of the form. The toolbar doesn't show up well yet because you haven't added buttons to the toolbar. If you have the grid turned on, you'll see the toolbar at the top of the form because the toolbar covers up the grid dots.

▼ NOTE
You can't adjust the toolbar's size with the mouse or by changing the `Left`, `Top`, or `Width` property settings. The toolbar will consume the entire area across the top of the form. If you adjust the form, the toolbar automatically adjusts with the form. (The toolbar's `Width` property always matches the form's `Width` property.) ▲

You can change the toolbar's `Align` property value to `vbAlignBottom` so that the toolbar rests on the bottom of the Form window. The standard location for toolbars, however, is at the top of the form or directly beneath a menu bar if the form uses a menu. In most cases, you should stay with the standard so that your users have no trouble adapting to your application's features.

Adjusting the Toolbar Settings

The Toolbar control provides some unusual property values that you haven't seen with the standard intrinsic controls. For example, the Toolbar control supports the `About` property. When you click the `About` ellipsis, a small dialog box opens that describes the control's copyright information. When you insert a control, the control's vendor (in this case, Microsoft) often includes copyright information about the control, so you'll always be able to determine the source.

When you click the `Custom` property's ellipsis, the dialog box in Figure 23.8 appears and makes it easier to set the remaining property settings. Rather than use the Properties window to set up toolbars, most programmers prefer the `Custom` property's dialog box. Therefore, you'll also probably want to use this dialog box to set up the toolbar.

FIG. 23.8

*Toolbar proper-
ties are easier
to set in the
Property Pages
dialog box.*

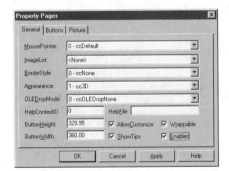

Most toolbar buttons display graphic icon images. Although you can set up toolbar buttons to display captions, a picture is worth a thousand words, especially because virtually every toolbar in every Windows program displays buttons without captions. The buttons that use picture icons require that you add another new control to your Form window. That control, found on the same insertable set of controls that contains the Toolbar control, is called the *Image List control*, which holds a series of one or more images. The Image List control does *not* display these images, but merely holds the image list for other controls that need such a list as your toolbar will need for its buttons.

The Image List control acts somewhat like the Timer control in that the Image List control never shows up on the form when you run the application. The Image List control is a container for the toolbar icons. Therefore, when you place the Image List control on your form, move it away from the other controls. After you load the Image List control with icons (as explained in the example at the end of this topic section), you then can link each toolbar button to each icon in the Image List control.

Here are the general guidelines to follow when creating the toolbar:

1. Load the Microsoft Windows Common Controls 5.0.

2. Add an Image List control to your form. Move the Image List control away from the other form controls.

3. Set up the Image List control to hold the toolbar button icons.

4. Click the Toolbar control to add the toolbar to the top of your Form window.

5. Add buttons to the Toolbar control. Place an icon on the buttons and adjust the other property values to make the toolbar look and act the way you want.

6. Program the toolbar's event procedure so that the toolbar responds to users.

The example at the end of this topic section demonstrates toolbar creation.

The Toolbar Button's Job

If your toolbar button mimics one of the menu commands, the rest of your programming job is simple. An event procedure can trigger another event procedure simply by calling that event procedure just as it would any other procedure. For example, if an Open toolbar button is to mimic the <u>O</u>pen command on your application's <u>F</u>ile menu, the following statement is the only one needed inside that toolbar button's event procedure (assuming that you named the <u>O</u>pen command `mnuFileOpen`):

```
Call mnuFileOpen.Click    ' Trigger the menu command
```

▼ NOTE

Remember that you don't include the parentheses when using `Call` if the called procedure requires no arguments. **▲**

The toolbar's most important event procedure is `ButtonClick()`. Unlike command buttons that support the `Click()` event procedure, toolbars support their own unique event procedure, `ButtonClick()`. You'll have to code `ButtonClick()` to respond to a user's toolbar click. The `ButtonClick()` procedure is one of the few event procedures that requires arguments. Your event procedure will have to check `ButtonClick()`'s argument to determine which toolbar button the user clicked.

Example With the first topic section's animation application still open, follow these steps to add a toolbar to the form:

1. Add an Image List control to the Form window. Move the control to the edge of the form.

2. Name the Image List control `imlIcons`.

3. Click the Image List control's `Custom` ellipsis to display the control's Property Pages dialog box.

4. Click the Images tab. This page is where you'll specify the images the toolbar buttons are to hold.

5. Click the Insert <u>P</u>icture button and browse to the \Graphics\Icons\ Traffic subdirectory in your Visual Basic directory.

6. Select the icon named trffc10a. VB displays the image in the Image List control's <u>I</u>mages area. Continue clicking Insert <u>P</u>icture to add two more images, named trffc10c and trffc14. Figure 23.9 shows the resulting dialog box. As you add each image, VB assigns it an index value, beginning with 1 and ending with 3. The Toolbar control uses these index values to place the appropriate images on the toolbar buttons.

FIG. 23.9

The images are ready for the three toolbar buttons you'll add.

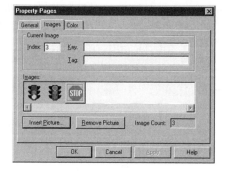

7. Close the Image List control's Property Pages dialog box and add a Toolbar control to the form. The Toolbar control appears at the top of the Form window. (You may have already added the Toolbar control earlier in this topic section.)

8. Change the toolbar's Name property to `tlbAni`.

9. Click the `Custom` property's ellipsis to display the toolbar's Property Pages dialog box.

10. Change the `BorderStyle` property to 1 – `ccFixedSingle` to add the line border around the toolbar. You can see the result immediately by clicking the Apply button.

11. Open the ImageList drop-down list and select `imlIcons`. You've just connected the image list that holds the icons to this toolbar.

TIP You can add multiple toolbars to your application and adjust their visibility by setting each one's `Visible` property to `True` or `False` to show or hide them as needed. Multiple toolbars that appear at the same time appear beneath one another.

12. Click the Buttons tab to add the toolbar buttons. When you click the Insert Button command button, you'll see the first button appear on the toolbar.

13. Type **1** in the Image text box to link the first image to the first button. Click Apply to see the results.

14. Click the Insert Button twice more to add two more buttons. Set the new buttons' `Image` property to 2 and 3, respectively. Close the dialog box.

You've now added three toolbar buttons and placed images on them. Your final job is to connect proper event-procedure code to the buttons so that they respond properly.

Double-click the toolbar to open the `tlbAni_ButtonClick()` event procedure. Notice that the parentheses include an argument. This argument, `Button`, passes as the toolbar button users click to generate this event. You can use the button's `Index` property to respond to the correct button. Listing 23.1 shows the event procedure that turns on the animation if users click the first button, turns off the animation if users click the second, and stops the running program if users click the third.

On the CD

Listing 23.1 Tlbutton.bas: Connecting Actions to Toolbar Buttons with the *Index* Property

```
Private Sub tlbAni_ButtonClick(ByVal Button As ComctlLib.Button)
  ' Respond to the correct toolbar button
  Select Case Button.Index
    Case 1: tmrAni.Enabled = True      ' Turn on animation
            cmdAni.Caption = "Stop"
    Case 2: tmrAni.Enabled = False     ' Turn off animation
            cmdAni.Caption = "Animate"
    Case 3: End
  End Select
End Sub
```

Run the application to see the toolbar in Figure 23.10. You now can click the red light and green light toolbar buttons or the Animate command button to start and stop the animation. You also can terminate the program by clicking the Stop toolbar button.

FIG. 23.10
The toolbar gives users extra control.

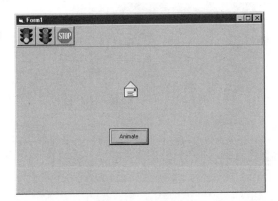

Next Step When placing toolbars, you may want to take advantage of some of the extra features available with the control. Two of the features are incredibly easy to implement and add professionalism to your application.

A *ToolTip* is a pop-up description that appears when you let your mouse pointer hover over a button or other object. If you move your mouse pointer to VB's toolbar icon that resembles a diskette, the ToolTip that appears (after a brief pause) will read `Save Project`. To add ToolTips to your toolbar buttons, open the Toolbar control's Property Pages dialog box and click the Buttons tab; then, in the ToolTipTe<u>x</u>t text box, enter the pop-up description that you want your users to see as a ToolTip. For example, you could add the description `Start Animation` to the first toolbar button's ToolTip. Click the <u>I</u>ndex button to switch to the next toolbar button and add ToolTips text for it, and then do the same for the third button. When you subsequently run the application, your ToolTip automatically appears when you place your mouse pointer over a button.

▼ NOTE
You'll learn more about applying ToolTips to other controls in Hour 29, "Building a Help Subsystem." ▲

Topic 3: Pop-Up Menus

Figure 23.11 shows a pop-up menu (sometimes called a *context menu*). When users right-click the form, the pop-up menu can appear. Your applications can contain several pop-up menus that appear depending on where users right-click.

FIG. 23.11
A pop-up menu is there when your users need it.

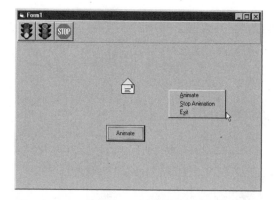

Overview You'll create the menu that appears in a pop-up menu just as you create regular menus that appear at the top of some applications' menu bars. The PopupMenu method provides the control that initiates the pop-up menu. Therefore, you use the Menu Editor to create the menu that appears at the user's right-click.

When creating pop-up menus, you must make sure that you create a regular menu item that contains at least one submenu. The submenu is the menu that appears when users right-click. Figure 23.12 shows the Menu Editor with the pop-up menu from Figure 23.11 defined.

FIG. 23.12
The Menu Editor creates the pop-up menus.

While looking at Figure 23.12, consider the following points:

- The caption for the top menu item is meaningless and happens to be the same name as the menu name. The top-level caption doesn't appear on the pop-up menus because only the submenu appears. Therefore, the first item's Caption value is unimportant.

- The menu has a submenu with three items, which appear when users request the pop-up menu.

- The menu items have shortcut keystroke underlines (from the ampersands that you typed before the appropriate hotkey) so that users can, after they display the pop-up menu, press a key to activate that command.

- The Visible check box isn't selected. If you left Visible selected, the menu would appear in its normal position atop the Form window. When users activate the pop-up menu, the PopupMenu method displays the menu at the mouse pointer.

You must decide where you want the pop-up menu to appear. For example, you can create multiple pop-up menus (as long as the top menu level has a different name) and pop one up if users right-click a command button, pop another up if users right-click a form, and pop another up if users right-click over a label.

Example

Load the toolbar example you created at the end of the previous topic section, and then press Ctrl+E to display the Menu Editor. Enter the values shown earlier in Figure 23.12. Name the three submenu options `mnuAni`, `mnuStop`, and `mnuExit`. The menu name is `mnu` because the top level's name is `mnu`. It's vital that you deselect the Visible check box so that the menu doesn't appear at the top of the form.

Open the Code window (choose Code from the View menu). Enter a new event procedure that contains the following code (if you select `Form` and `MouseUp` from the Code window's two drop-down lists, VB writes the first and last lines for you):

```
Private Sub Form_MouseUp(Button As Integer, Shift As Integer,
➥X As Single, Y As Single)
  If Button = 2 Then
    Form1.PopupMenu mnu
  End If
End Sub
```

Generally, you'll insert the pop-up menu code inside the `MouseUp` event for whatever object you want to use for the pop-up trigger. This example assumes that the pop-up menu will appear when users right-click the form. (No example in this lesson renamed the form from `Form1`.) The `Button` argument contains 2 if the right mouse button caused this event (you can ignore the remaining arguments for this example). If the `Button` argument is a 2, apply the `PopupMenu` method to the form and designate the top-level name of the menu you want to display at the pointer. In this example, you've defined only one menu, `mnu`.

▼ **NOTE**
If code follows the `PopupMenu` method, the code doesn't execute until users finish with the menu. ▲

You'll have to write the event procedures for the menu options as you need to do with a regular menu. Therefore, the event procedures in Listing 23.2 take care of the menu selections.

Listing 23.2 Menuopts.bas: Adding Code for Pop-Up Menu Options

```
Private Sub mnuAni_Click()
  ' The user clicked the Animate menu item
  tmrAni.Enabled = True
  cmdAni.Caption = "Stop"
End Sub

Private Sub mnuExit_Click()
  ' The user clicked the Exit menu item
  End
End Sub

Private Sub mnuStop_Click()
  ' The user clicked the Stop Animation menu item
  tmrAni.Enabled = False
  cmdAni.Caption = "Animate"
End Sub
```

Next Step Adding a pop-up menu to another object is just as easy. In the Menu Editor, create another menu option. To do so, open the Menu Editor and click the last item in the menu (in this case, the **E&xit** item). Click the Next button to add another menu. Click the left arrow to make the new menu item another high-level item and enter **mnu2** in the Caption and Name text boxes. Be sure to deselect the Visible check box.

Enter two more items subordinate to mnu2. Enter **&Hide Toolbar** for the first Caption and **mnu2Hide** for the Name. Enter **&Display Toolbar** and **mnu2Display** to the second item's Caption and Name text boxes. Click OK to close the Menu Editor.

Enter the following MouseUp event procedure for the toolbar:

```
Private Sub tlbAni_MouseUp(Button As Integer, Shift As Integer,
➥x As Single, y As Single)
  If Button = 2 Then
    Form1.PopupMenu mnu2
  End If
End Sub
```

Your only job now is to add the menu option code. Type the following event procedures to display and hide the toolbar in response to the pop-up menu:

```
Private Sub mnu2Display_Click()
  ' Display the toolbar
  tlbAni.Visible = True
End Sub

Private Sub mnu2Hide_Click()
  ' Hide the Toolbar
  tlbAni.Visible = False
End Sub
```

CAUTION Hiding a toolbar makes the toolbar unable to generate a response to a mouse click.

If you run the program, you now can display two pop-up menus. If you right-click the form, you get the menu that turns the animation on and off. If you right-click the toolbar, you get the menu that hides and displays the toolbar.

The application has a problem, however; if you turn off the toolbar, you can never turn it back on again! This demonstrates that a toolbar and pop-up menus should never take the place of a regular menu bar. The regular menu bar can contain options that hide and display the toolbar (perhaps with a check mark if the toolbar shows), as well as options that turn the animation on and off.

Summary

This lesson explained how to use the Timer control to add time-sensitive processing to your applications. The Timer control keeps track of the milliseconds that pass and triggers an event when a preset amount of time goes by. The Timer control supports only one event, so your programming is relatively light when using the control.

The Toolbar control adds another dimension for your users. Toolbars give your application one-button access to the most common controls. Before you can place icons on toolbar buttons, however, you must insert those icons inside the Image List control.

You now can give your users another way to issue commands besides the menu bar and toolbar. Your users can right-click certain objects to display a pop-up menu. You'll want to create pop-up menus that help users do what's most common on the object they right-click.

In the next hour, "Shaping Up Your Applications with Graphics," you'll learn how to place graphics on the Form window.

Hour 23 Quiz

You can find the answers for the following questions on the accompanying CD-ROM and on the Virtual Classroom Web site.

On the CD

1. **True or false:** There's only one computer internal clock, so you can place at most one Timer control on the Form window.

2. **True or false:** The Timer control is an intrinsic control.

3. What's the only event produced by the Timer control?

4. How can you set up an event procedure to respond to a time interval greater than 65 seconds (the approximate limit for the Timer control)?

5. Where do most toolbars appear on a form?

6. Which control stores the toolbar's button icons?

7. How do you add ToolTips to toolbar buttons?

8. What's the difference between a pop-up menu and a menu bar?

9. **True or false:** An event procedure can call another event procedure with the `Call` statement.

10. Which event procedure do VB programmers generally use for pop-up menu display?

Hour 23 Homework Exercises

1. Change the first topic section's animation example so that the envelope not only opens every second, but a piece of paper flies out. (*Hint:* Use `Left` and `Top` properties and another Picture Box control.)

2. Correct the example at the end of this lesson's third topic section by adding a menu bar with the following menus and commands: File, Exit; Animate, On and Off; and Toolbar, On and Off. Change the toolbar's pop-up menu so that it contains only one option: Hide Toolbar. Users can now use the menu bar to display the hidden toolbar.

During this hour you will learn

▶ How to place lines

▶ How to place shapes

▶ How to draw with methods

Shaping Up Your Applications with Graphics

THIS LESSON INTRODUCES YOU to Visual Basic's fundamental graphic controls and routines. You have already seen how to embed pictures onto your forms with the Image and Picture Box controls. This lesson explains how to draw your own graphic lines, circles, and drawings.

VB programmers use this lesson's line-drawing controls a lot, but generally they don't use the controls to draw final, complex graphic images. Instead, they often use lines and circles to accent form elements, draw dividing lines, and add shapes to highlight areas of the form. These line-drawing controls are fairly primitive for creating complex graphic images.

▶▶ **FAST TRACK**
Do you want more action than simple graphics give? Check out the
multimedia topics in Hour 25, "Adding Multimedia to Your Programs"
(p. 577).

Topic 1: The Line Control

The Line control supports no events, so its usefulness is limited. Nevertheless, the Line control makes underlining and separating form items easy because it's so simple. Placing lines on a form requires only the placement of
the Line control and adjusting its length and thickness.

Overview The Line control draws lines of any length in any direction on the form.
Your VB code can change the Line control's properties, but you'll generally
place lines when you design your form and not adjust the lines later at
runtime. The control doesn't support a large number of properties, but
you'll learn all there is to know about the Line control in this topic. Also,
you can't connect two lines together to form a single line-drawn image
object. Nevertheless, for underlining and dividing forms, the Line control
works well.

Placing Lines on Forms

When you double-click the Line control, Visual Basic places the control in
the center of your form (see Figure 24.1). The line has two sizing handles,
so you can lengthen or shorten it. Also, you can drag a handle to change
the line's orientation so that the line points in a different direction. If you
click and hold your mouse button over the line, you can drag the line to a
different location.

Four property values define the line's size and placement: X1, Y1, X2, and
Y2. X1 and Y1 specify the line's starting coordinates; X2 and Y2 specify the
line's ending coordinates. The coordinates measure in twips. Remember
that the 0, 0 coordinate X1, Y1 is the upper-left hand twip position in the
Form window.

FIG. 24.1
The line appears at an angle.

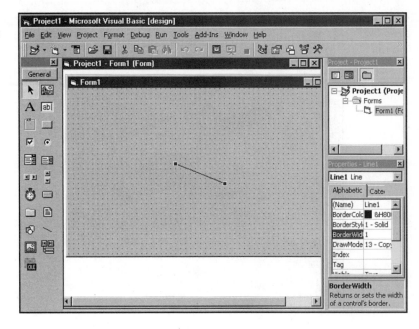

The Line Control Properties

Table 24.1 describes the most important Line control properties.

Table 24.1 The Line Control Properties

Property	Description
BorderColor	Determines the line's color
BorderStyle	Determines the line's format (see Table 24.2)
BorderWidth	Specifies the line's width; if 1, you can set a BorderStyle value from 1 to 6
X1, Y1, X2, Y2	Determines the line's starting and ending coordinates

As Figure 24.2 shows, the BorderWidth property determines the width of the line, but the width can alter the line's appearance dramatically.

The BorderStyle property value can range from 0 to 6, as described in Table 24.2. Figure 24.3 shows the various line BorderStyle values.

Pt **IV**

Hr **24**

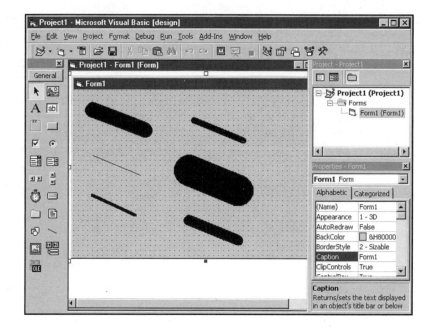

FIG. 24.2
The line widths affect the lines' look.

Table 24.2 The Line Control's *BorderStyle* Values

Value	Description
0 - Transparent	Background color will show through the line
1 - Solid	Line is solid
2 - Dash	Line is made up of dashes
3 - Dot	Line is made up of dots
4 - Dash-Dot	Line is made up of dashes and dots
5 - Dash-Dot-Dot	Line is made up of dashes and double dots
6 - Inside Solid	Same as 1 - Solid

▼ NOTE
BorderStyle property values greater than 1 work only if the line's BorderWidth is greater than 1. ▲

FIG. 24.3
`BorderStyle` *determines the line's style.*

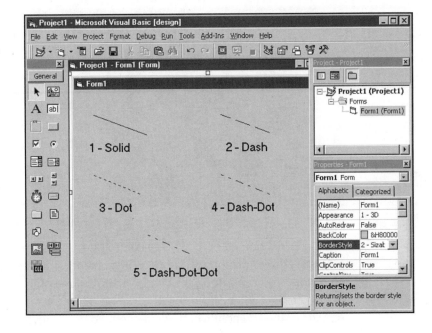

Example Figure 24.4 shows a caption underlined with the Line control and with separating lines on the form. You can see how the Line control accents form components.

FIG. 24.4
You can use lines and underlining for titles and separation.

Next Step Figure 24.5 shows that you can use the Line control to draw primitive pictures. You can learn two things from the figure: the Line control isn't flexible for high-resolution graphics, and the author can't draw.

FIG. 24.5
The Line control doesn't produce advanced pictures.

To draw a line, double-click the Line control. Visual Basic places a line in the middle of the Form window. Notice that each end of the line contains a sizing handle. You can extend the line by dragging one of its handles farther away from the center of the line. If you drag a sizing handle up or down the screen, the line points in that direction. You can move the line by dragging the center of the line to any location on the Form window.

Topic 2: The Shape Control

Unlike the Line control, the Shape control draws several shapes, including boxes and circles. The Shape control's properties determine the shape that the Shape control produces. Like the Line control, however, the Shape control doesn't lend itself to a lot of advanced graphic programming. Nevertheless, it can be nice for highlighting certain form components.

Overview The Shape control's properties determine its many forms. The Shape control is one of the most interesting controls in that its look changes considerably when you modify a single property—**Shape**.

The Shape's Shapes

Figure 24.6 shows the six shapes you can draw with the Shape control. You can enter the following six values in the Shape control's **Shape** property to display the shapes:

```
0 - Rectangle
1 - Square
```

```
2 - Oval
3 - Circle
4 - Rounded Rectangle
5 - Rounded Square
```

FIG. 24.6
The Shape control can display one of six shapes.

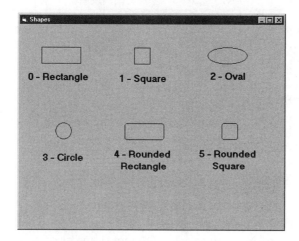

The Shape's Properties

The Shape control has other properties in addition to the **Shape** property. Table 24.3 lists the more important properties.

Table 24.3   The Shape Control's Properties

Property	Description
BackStyle	Determines whether the form background shows through the shape
BorderColor	Specifies the color of the shape's border
BorderStyle	Specifies the form of the line that outlines the shape (see Table 24.2)
BorderWidth	Specifies the shape's border width in twips
FillColor	Specifies the color of the **FillStyle** pattern
FillStyle	Determines the pattern that fills the shape
Height	The height, in twips, of the highest point in the shape
Width	The width, in twips, of the widest point in the shape

Example   Figure 24.7 shows the fill patterns you can use for your application's shapes. The patterns can greatly affect the way your shapes look.

FIG. 24.7
Set the `FillStyle` *pattern to the interior you need to see.*

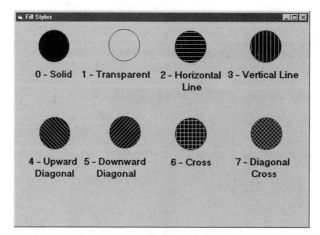

Next Step The application described here demonstrates the Shape control and its fill patterns. The application displays a shape on the form and fills the shape with a pattern. You can select a different shape or pattern from the two drop-down lists to change the shape and learn the available patterns better.

Follow these steps to create the application:

1. Create a new application.

2. Place a Shape control on the form. Name the shape `shpSample`. Keep the shape a rectangle.

3. Adjust the shape's size and location properties to these values: `Height`: 4,560, `Left`: 1,710, `Top`: 720, and `Width`: 4,560. (You may need to expand the Form window's width to see the whole shape.)

4. Add a list box named `lstShape` and assign these properties: `Left`: 690, `Top`: 3,840, and `Width`: 2,130.

5. Add a label above the list box named `lblShape` with a `Caption` property of `Shape` and assign these properties: `FontSize`: 18, `Left`: 1170, `Top`: 3270, and `Width`: 1215. Your screen should look something like Figure 24.8.

6. Add a list box named `lstPattern` and assign these properties: `Left`: 5070, `Top`: 3840, and `Width`: 2130.

7. Add a label above the drop-down list box named `lblPattern` with a `Caption` property of `Pattern` and assign these properties: `FontSize`: 18, `Left`: 5505, `Top`: 3285, and `Width`: 1215.

FIG. 24.8
Your application is shaping up!

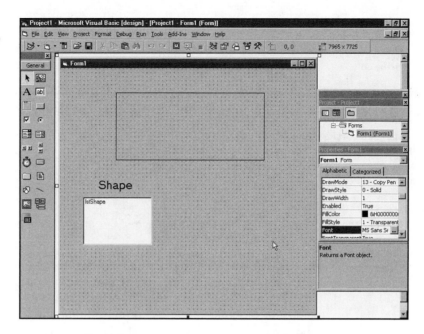

On the CD

8. You must initialize the two list boxes at runtime. Add the `Form_Load()` event procedure shown in Listing 24.1.

Listing 24.1 Listshp.bas: Giving Users Entries for the List Boxes

```
Private Sub Form_Load()
  ' Initialize the shape drop-down list box
  lstShape.AddItem "0 - Rectangle"
  lstShape.AddItem "1 - Square"
  lstShape.AddItem "2 - Oval"
  lstShape.AddItem "3 - Circle"
  lstShape.AddItem "4 - Rounded Rectangle"
  lstShape.AddItem "5 - Rounded Square"

  ' Initialize the FillStyle pattern drop-down list box
  lstPattern.AddItem "0 - Solid"
  lstPattern.AddItem "1 - Transparent"
  lstPattern.AddItem "2 - Horizontal Line"
  lstPattern.AddItem "3 - Vertical Line"
  lstPattern.AddItem "4 - Upward Diagonal"
  lstPattern.AddItem "5 - Downward Diagonal"
  lstPattern.AddItem "6 - Cross"
  lstPattern.AddItem "7 - Diagonal Cross"
End Sub
```

Pt IV

Hr 24

9. When users select a value in either drop-down list, you want to update the shape. Therefore, add the two list-box event procedures shown in Listing 24.2.

On the CD

Listing 24.2   Pattshap.bas: Specifying the Control's Pattern and Shape

```
Private Sub lstPattern_Click()
  ' Change the pattern according to the selection
  shpSample.FillStyle = lstPattern.ListIndex
End Sub

Private Sub lstShape_Click()
  ' Change the shape according to the selection
  shpSample.Shape = lstShape.ListIndex
End Sub
```

---

10. Add a graceful exit routine by including a File menu Exit option that stops the program's execution. When you run the program, you can see the results of changing the shape's Shape and Pattern properties (see Figure 24.9).

FIG. 24.9

Users can select from shapes and patterns.

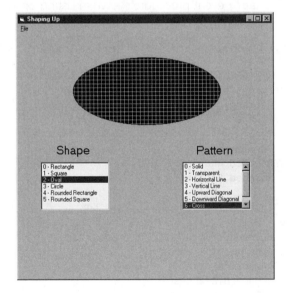

Topic 3: A Few Graphic Methods

Visual Basic supports a few graphic methods that are fairly primitive, but they do provide some graphics capabilities that you can display at runtime. Although you could animate the Line and Shape controls that you place on a form by setting and resetting their properties, you may be able to use this topic's graphic methods as better animation tools, especially when you need to set individual screen pixels. (A *pixel* is another name for *picture element* and represents a dot on your screen.)

▼ NOTE

This topic section assumes that the form's ScaleMode measurement is set to pixels and not the default twips. If you want to work with pixels (which many graphics programmers prefer to do), set the form's ScaleMode property to 3 - Pixel. ▲

Pt **IV**

Hr **24**

Overview This topic explains the graphic methods that you can apply to forms. You'll learn how to turn individual pixels on and off, draw lines, and produce other shapes. Remember that in today's world of graphical environments, you may want to incorporate graphic images and animation files inside your applications rather than work with these more primitive methods, but these methods often suffice well for simple line- and dot-oriented graphics.

Drawing with Pixels

The most fundamental graphics method, **PSet**, turns screen pixels on and off. Here is the syntax of **PSet**:

```
frmFormName.PSet [Step] (intX, intY) [color]
```

intX and *intY* represent the pixel column-and-row intersections that you want to turn off. (The **ScaleX** and **ScaleY** properties determine how the coordinates operate, but coordinate 0, 0 generally represents the upper-left hand pixel on the form.) The *intX* and *intY* coordinates are absolute and reference the exact form pixel coordinates unless you specify the optional **Step** keyword. In other words, the statement

```
frmForm.PSet (30, 67)
```

turns on the pixel at graphics x-coordinate (column) 30 and y-coordinate (row) 67. If you include the optional `Step` keyword, as in

```
frmForm.PSet Step (30, 67)
```

Visual Basic turns on the form's pixel located 30 and 67 pixel positions away from the last `PSet` method. If you performed no other `PSet` before this `PSet Step` method, VB turns on the pixel that's 30 and 67 pixels away from the upper-left hand corner of the form.

If you don't specify a color value, Visual Basic uses the form's `ForeColor` color-property value. You can turn a pixel off by specifying the form's `BackColor` property in the `PSet` method like this:

```
frmForm.PSet (300, 200) frmForm.BackColor
```

▼ **NOTE**
Although you can use `PSet` to draw lines and circles, the following sections describe additional methods that draw these shapes. ▲

Drawing Lines and Boxes

Although `PSet` is good for individual pixels, it's slow at drawing lines and boxes because it requires that your program first calculate each pixel in the line or box. Visual Basic provides a `Line` method that makes drawing lines easier and faster. Rather than collect a group of `PSet` methods to draw a line or box, the `Line` method does all the work at once.

The `Line` method draws lines and boxes, depending on the syntax you use. The simplest syntax draws a line from one coordinate to another:

```
frmFormName.Line [Step] (intX1, intY1) - [Step] (intX2,
  ➡intY2), [Color] [B][F]
```

The *intX1* and *intY1* values define the beginning point (coordinates) of the line; the *intX2* and *intY2* coordinates define where the line ends. Remember that the coordinates can't exceed the resolution of the form. The following method draws a line from pixel 100, 100 to pixel 150, 150:

```
frmForm.Line (100, 100) - (150, 150)
```

In a manner similar to `PSet`, the `Line` method's `Step` option draws the line relative to the starting location (the last pixel drawn or turned off). You don't have to include the starting coordinate pair because the new option knows where to begin. When you use `Step`, therefore, some of the coordinates may be negative, as in the following example:

```
frmForm.Line -Step (-15, 0)
```

This option tells Visual Basic to draw a line from the last pixel drawn to a point 15 pixels to the left.

▼ NOTE

`Line`'s arguments have no mandatory order. You can draw up, down, to the left, or to the right. ▲

If you omit the *Color* value, Visual Basic uses the form's `ForeColor` property value.

When you want to draw a box, you don't have to issue four `Line` methods. You can use the `B` option at the end of the `Line` method to draw a box. The two coordinate pairs, when you specify the `B` box option, specify the upper-left corner of the box and the lower-right corner of the box. For example, the following `Line` method draws a box on the form:

```
frmForm.Line (20, 20) - (300, 300) , , B
```

CAUTION Be sure to type the extra comma if you don't include a *Color* value. Without the comma, Visual Basic issues a syntax error.

If you add the `F` option to the end of the `Line` method (`F` can appear only after `B`), Visual Basic fills in the box with the same color as the box's outline. The following, therefore, draws a solid box on your form:

```
frmForm.Line (20, 20) - (300, 300) , , BF
```

Drawing Circles

You can use the `Circle` method to draw circles and *ellipses* (elongated circles). If you want to draw circles on your form, use this syntax:

```
frmForm1.Circle [Step] (intX, intY) sngRadius, [Color], , , ,
➥sngAspect
```

▼ NOTE

The commas are required for rare placeholder values that this lesson doesn't need to discuss. ▲

The *intX* and *intY* coordinates determine the center point of the circle. *sngRadius* is the distance, in pixels (or whatever the form's `ScaleMode` dictates), between the circle's center and its outer edge. If you include the `Step` keyword, the *intX* and *intY* coordinates are relative (and can be negative) from the current (last-drawn) pixel. If you don't specify a *Color* value, Visual Basic uses the form's `ForeColor` value.

The following `Circle` method draws a circle on the form with a center point at 320, 100 and a radius of 100 pixels:

```
frmForm.Circle (320, 100), 100
```

To draw an ellipse, you must add the *sngAspect* value to `Circle`. The aspect value has either of two effects, depending on its value. If the aspect is less than 1, the aspect stretches the circle on the vertical x-coordinate axis; and if the aspect is greater than 1, the aspect stretches the circle vertically on the y-coordinate axis.

> **TIP** The aspect ratio acts like a height and width measurement through the center of the ellipse. The ratio also acts as a multiplier of the radius in each direction. An aspect of 4, for example, means that the ellipse is vertically stretched four times the regular circle's height. An aspect ratio of 4/10/2 (or .2) means the circle is horizontally stretched five times its regular radius (one-half of 40 percent).

The following methods draw two ellipses (the first with a stretched x-radius, and the second with a stretched y-radius):

```
frmForm.Circle (300, 100), 50, , , , (4 / 10 / 2)
frmForm.Circle (150, 100), 50, , , , 4
```

Example The procedure in Listing 24.3 randomly draws dots on the form. The form's width and height twip values are used to keep the dots within the boundaries of the form.

Listing 24.3   Randmdot.bas: Using *PSet* to Draw Dots On-Screen

```
' Randomly draw pixels
Dim intCtr As Integer
Dim intX As Integer
Dim intY As Integer
```

```
' First, set the internal randomness
Randomize Timer

' Loop to write random dots
For intCtr = 1 To 500
  intX = Int(Rnd * Form1.Height) + 1
  intY = Int(Rnd * Form1.Width) + 1
  Form1.PSet (intX, intY)  ' Turn on dot
Next intCtr
```

Next Step The procedure in Listing 24.4 draws multiple boxes on the form so you can see how to draw more than just pixels.

Listing 24.4 Boxdraw.bas: Drawing Boxes On-Screen with *Line*

```
Private Sub cmdBoxes_Click()
  Dim intStartX As Integer
  Dim intStartY As Integer
  Dim intLastX As Integer
  Dim intLastY As Integer
  Dim intCtr As Integer

  intStartX = 0
  intStartY = 0
  intLastX = 1000
  intLastY = 800

  For intCtr = 1 To 20
    frmBoxes.Line (intStartX, intStartY)-(intLastX, intLastY), , B

    ' Prepare for next set of boxes
    intStartX = intStartX + 400
    intStartY = intStartY + 400
    intLastX = intLastX + 400
    intLastY = intLastY + 400
  Next intCtr
End Sub
```

Figure 24.10 shows the boxes running diagonally down the form.

FIG. 24.10
Line *draws boxes more easily than setting individual pixels for boxes.*

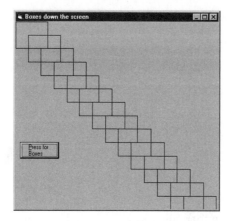

Summary

You now have a basic understanding of Visual Basic's graphic tools and methods. Although you'll not use this lesson's information to draw extremely detailed graphics, you can draw stick figures, underline titles, and enclose other controls inside customized boxes and ovals.

The Line control draws lines on your form. The Shape control draws one of several shapes, such as boxes and circles, on your form. Neither the lines nor shapes you place on the form can accept event processing, but you can place such graphics on a form to highlight special controls.

The graphic methods turn on and off screen pixels, squares, and circles on the form. As with the Line control and the Shape control, the graphic methods don't draw form elements that can accept events, but the simple graphics do accent forms.

In the next hour, "Adding Multimedia to Your Programs," you'll learn about adding multimedia capabilities to your applications. Whereas this lesson explained simple graphics, you'll be able to improve on those graphics and other multimedia components that reside in your code.

Hour 24 Quiz

You can find the answers for the following questions on the accompanying CD-ROM and on the Virtual Classroom Web site.

On the CD

1. What does *pixel* stand for?
2. What control draws circles on forms?
3. What control draws squares on forms?
4. What method draws lines on forms?
5. What method draws boxes on forms?
6. Which of the following methods is used for drawing boxes?
    A. `PSet`
    B. `Line`
    C. `Box`
    D. `Draw`
7. **True or false:** The Line and Shape controls produce graphics that support properties but not events.
8. How does the form's `ScaleMode` property affect the graphic coordinates that you draw?
9. What `Line` method option adds a solid interior to boxes?
10. How does the aspect ratio affect circles?

Hour 24 Homework Exercises

1. Add a fill-color drop-down list box and a border color drop-down list box to the application at the end of Topic 2's "Next Step" section and see how the colors affect the look of your shapes.
2. Write a simple application that asks users what they want to see from a menu. Give them a choice of a box, a rectangle, a circle, or an ellipse.
3. Write a program that draws a picture of books on a shelf.

Adding Multimedia to Your Programs

During this hour you will learn

▸ *What the Multimedia control is*

▸ *What Multimedia control properties are required*

▸ *How audio programming varies from video programming*

THIS LESSON WILL BE a lot of fun! You'll learn how to use the Multimedia control to place multimedia capabilities into your applications. Your users will be able to hear sound clips and watch videos if you want to add those features to your applications.

The Multimedia control is extremely simple to use. You'll need to write only a small amount of code to use multimedia in your applications. The differences between a compact disc player and a video clip player are almost nothing to a programmer, as you'll learn in this lesson. The Multimedia control takes care of the tedium and lets you worry about the other aspects of your application.

▶▶ **FAST TRACK**
If you want to concentrate more on getting advanced user input at this time rather than learn how to output multimedia files, you may want to skip to Hour 28, "Using Keyboard and Mouse I/O" (p. 643).

Topic 1: The Multimedia Control

Microsoft's Multimedia control provides simple and advanced multimedia capabilities for your applications. The Multimedia control supports the following kinds of multimedia objects:

- Animation files
- CD audio player
- Digital audio tape player
- Videotape player and recorder
- Videodisk player
- MIDI sequencer (.MID)
- Video file player and recorder (.AVI)
- Audio file player and recorder (.WAV)

The last three categories list file-name extensions associated with those kinds of multimedia capabilities. The first five kinds of multimedia capabilities are called *simple multimedia devices* because no data file is necessarily associated with those items. For example, if you use a VB application to control a CD playing in your CD-ROM drive, the data comes from the CD, not from a file.

The last three kinds of multimedia capabilities are called *compound multimedia devices* because of the extra file needed for data, as well as the play or record capabilities. If you want to play a wave audio file, for example, you must have access to the .WAV file, and your VB application gets its data from the .WAV disk file.

▼ **NOTE**
Most computers sold today are multimedia ready and conform to the industry standard called *MPC* (Multimedia Personal Computer). Nevertheless, the computer that runs your multimedia application must have the

appropriate hardware before the multimedia software inside your application works. Obviously, if the computer doesn't have the .WAV file your application needs to play or if the computer has no CD-ROM, your application won't be able to perform audio file or compact disc playing. ▲

Overview Visual Basic uses the Multimedia control to perform multimedia operations. This section explains some of the Multimedia control's capabilities and prepares your system for the control.

Loading the Multimedia Control

The Multimedia control doesn't exist in your Toolbox's intrinsic tools, so you must add it. You must have VB's Professional or Enterprise Edition to have access to the Multimedia control.

Add the Multimedia control to your Toolbox as you do other new tools. From the Project menu choose Components to display the Components dialog box. Select the control named Microsoft Multimedia Control 5.0 and click OK. The Multimedia control is loaded when you see it appear in your Toolbox, as shown in Figure 25.1.

Pt **IV**

Hr **25**

FIG. 25.1
The Multimedia control must reside in your Toolbox before you can use it.

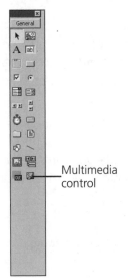

Multimedia
control

Preparing for the Multimedia Control

The Multimedia control is formally called the Multimedia Control Interface (MCI). If you have the correct hardware, the MCI connects your software to that hardware to control multimedia devices. The Multimedia control looks a lot like the panel of buttons on the front of a tape recorder (see Figure 25.2).

FIG. 25.2

The placed Multimedia control looks like a tape recorder's control buttons.

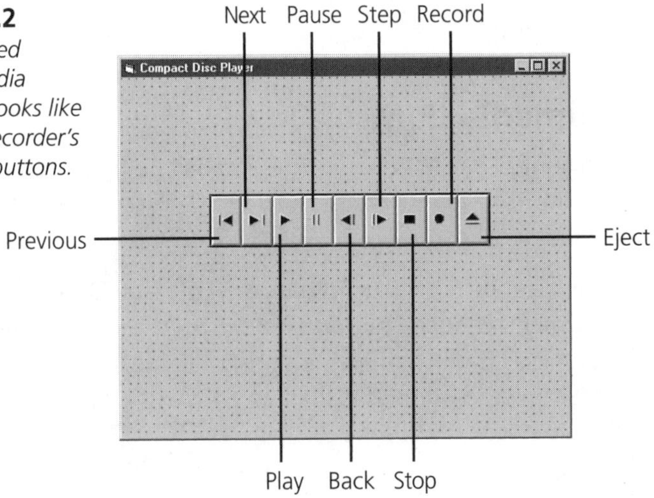

As your application uses the Multimedia control to play a device, such as a compact disc, VB updates the buttons according to the available functions. For example, if you click the Eject button, VB disables the other buttons, such as Play, until you close the CD door again.

You can control the number of buttons that appear on the Multimedia control and which ones are enabled at any one time. Some multimedia devices don't require all the buttons. For example, you can't record onto a compact disc, so you would hide the Record button if you were writing a CD interface to play an audio CD.

▼ **NOTE**
When you first place the Multimedia control on a form, none of the buttons are enabled. ▲

Example Prepare to use the Multimedia control by creating a new project. Add the Multimedia control to your Toolbox by pressing Ctrl+T to open the Components dialog box. Click the control named Microsoft Multimedia Control 5.0, and then click OK to add the control to your Toolbox. Double-click the control to place a control in the center of your form. Name this Multimedia control `mciCD`.

Now make a few modifications: Change the form's caption to `Compact Disc Player` and the form's name to `frmCD`. Add a label named `lblCD` with a `Caption` property that reads `My CD`. Center the text and change the point size to 24.

▼ **NOTE**
You can resize the Multimedia control to increase or decrease the button width, although you should leave the control at its default size for this application. You can expand the form, however, to make more room for the control and its title. ▲

Your Form window should look something like the one in Figure 25.3.

FIG. 25.3
You've now placed the Multimedia control and a title.

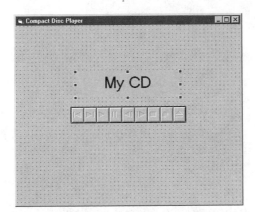

Place a right-justified label named `lblTrack` on the form beneath the buttons with an 18-point `Caption` that reads `Track:`. Add another label named `lblTrackValue` to the right of the previous label, left-justify its `Caption`, adjust the width to 810, and change the point size to 18 also.

Place a fixed-single border around the last label. Your CD player not only will be able to play compact discs, but also will tell users which track is now playing.

Although you can enable the individual Multimedia control buttons, the Multimedia control supports a property called `DeviceType` that, when initialized with the device you want to use (such as `CDAudio`), automatically enables the correct buttons. Therefore, your job is to tell the application that the Multimedia control is to be a CD Audio player.

Click the `Custom` property to display the Property Pages dialog box. The value property you need to enter now is `DeviceType`, so that the control will know which buttons to enable. Enter the Multimedia-control named literal **CDAudio**. Although `DeviceType` is the only value you need to adjust, click the Controls tab to see the button controls you can set from this dialog box (see Figure 25.4). Setting individual buttons (for example, if you ever want to hide or enable specific buttons) is much easier to do here than from the regular Properties window.

FIG. 25.4

The Property Pages dialog box makes enabling buttons simple.

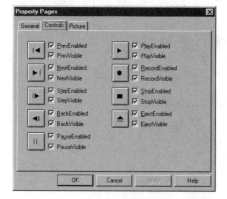

Click OK to close the dialog box. Now that you've set up your CD player, you have to add a little bit of code in the next section.

Next Step The Multimedia control contains its own little programming language and can accept commands in a special property named `Command`. While you're learning more of the Multimedia control language, this lesson will teach you the commands you need. The only two commands you need to implement a compact disc player are Open and Close.

When your application begins, you need to tell the Multimedia control to open whatever device you specified in the DeviceType property. Perhaps the best place to open the Multimedia control device is in the Form_Load() event procedure. Double-click the form and enter the following:

```
Private Sub Form_Load()
   ' Tell the Multimedia control to open the CD
   mciCD.Command = "Open"
End Sub
```

The most important Multimedia control event is StatusUpdate. Every time the status changes on your CD, such as a track change, the StatusUpdate event takes off. To update the track numbers, place the following code in the StatusUpdate event procedure:

```
Private Sub mciCD_StatusUpdate()
   ' Update the tracks
   lblTrackValue.Caption = mciCD.Track
End Sub
```

The Multimedia control supports several commands your applications can use to inform users of the Multimedia control's status. The Track property monitors the current track number. If users click the Next button while a compact disc is playing, the StatusUpdate event occurs and updates the label for the track number.

Finally, when the application ends, the Multimedia control will close. Nevertheless, you should begin to get in the habit of unloading all your forms and performing any final cleanup of your application before the application abruptly ends. In some rare MDI cases, a form may not unload properly if you don't specifically unload it in the Form_Unload() event procedure (the final procedure that executes when an application ends). Code the following property:

```
Private Sub Form_Unload(Cancel As Integer)
   ' Clean up the CD and form
   mciCD.Command = "Close"
   Unload Me
End Sub
```

The `Close` command tells the Multimedia control to stop playing the CD. If your application contains only a single form, `Unload Me` unloads the form from memory so that the application can gracefully exit and release all of its resources properly. If your application contained several forms, you would unload each form by name (or step through the `Forms` collection).

You can now play an audio CD. Insert a compact disc in your CD-ROM caddy. Close the Windows CD Player accessory program if it begins. When you run your application, the appropriate buttons will appear, along with the first track number. Figure 25.5 shows the CD player you just embedded within your application. As you click on the Next and Previous buttons, notice that the track value changes to reflect the current track (due to the Multimedia control's `StatusUpdate` event). Stop and pause the music to see how the Multimedia control adjusts itself. Eject the CD when you're done and close the application.

FIG. 25.5
You are playing beautiful music!

Topic 2: Making Waves

You'll learn more about the Multimedia control by creating a wave music player. A *wave file* (with the file name extension .WAV) contains audio music that someone digitally recorded for play by a device such as your sound card powered by the Multimedia control software. You'll set up the wave music player in roughly the same way as you set up the CD player.

Overview In this topic section, you'll not only learn how to manage a compound multimedia device (the wave player), but you'll also learn about the Multimedia control's `Mode` property. `Mode` contains lots of helpful information about the status of the control, and your program can access the `Mode` property to learn that information. Fortunately, Microsoft defined named literals to represent the various `Mode` values.

The *Mode* Values

Table 25.1 lists the `Mode` values that you'll need for the Multimedia control. These `Mode` values don't just work for the wave music audio player but for all the Multimedia control functions. For example, you could have tested `MCI_MODE_PLAY` in the preceding topic section's application and displayed a message on the form when the CD was playing. (`MCI_MODE_PLAY` is a system variable that the Multimedia control updates as it plays a multimedia clip.)

Table 25.1 The Multimedia Control *Mode* Values

Value	Description
mciModeNotOpen	Multimedia device isn't open
mciModeStop	Multimedia device is stopped
mciModePlay	Multimedia device is playing
mciModeRecord	Multimedia device is recording
mciModeSeek	Multimedia device is seeking past information
mciModePause	Multimedia device is paused
mciModeReady	Multimedia device is ready

The Wave Player

When creating an application that demonstrates playing a .WAV audio file, you must tell the Multimedia control that you want the wave audio play function and tell it which .WAV file to play. Unless your application plays background music or an opening music sequence during startup, you'll probably want to add an Open dialog box to let users select a .WAV file to play.

The following example creates a wave audio file multimedia player. You'll be able to use the `Mode` values in Table 25.1 to display status information about the file being played. The Visual Basic system comes with a .WAV file named Mcitest.wav in VB's \Samples\CompTools\mci directory, and that's the file the next example plays.

Example Save your previous project if you still have it open, and then use that project as the basis for this one. To keep both projects separate, save the project again under a new name (perhaps *Lesson 25 MCI Proj*) and modify the project according to these steps:

1. Change the top label's name to `lblWav` and change the `Caption` property to `Wave Player`.

2. Change the form's name to `frmWav` and the form `Caption` to `Wave Music Player`.

3. Change the Multimedia control's name to `mciWAV` and change its `DeviceType` property to `WaveAudio`. (You can change the property in the Properties window or from the Property Pages dialog box that appears when you click the `Custom` property's ellipses.) Change `Filename` to the Mcitest.wav file located in your \VB\Samples\CompTools\mci directory.

4. Wave files don't have tracks like CDs do, but you can still use the labels beneath the multimedia control buttons. Change the left label's name from `lblTrack` to `lblStatus` and change its `Caption` to read `Status`.

5. Change the right label's name from `lblTrackValue` to `lblStatusValue` and blank out the `Caption`. Change the `Width` property to 2565.

6. Add another pair of labels beneath the two you just modified with the same width and font properties. (You could copy them to create a set of label arrays.) Name the first label `lblFile` (unless you created a control array) and change the `Caption` to `Filename:`. You'll have to extend the left edge to make room for the caption.

7. Change the left label's `Name` property to `lblFileValue` (unless you created a control array). Leave the label blank. After you center the

labels beneath the buttons, your application should look like Figure 25.6.

FIG. 25.6
The wave music player is almost complete.

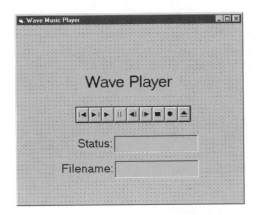

Change the `Form_Load ()` event procedure to the following:

```
Private Sub Form_Load ()
    ' Tell the Multimedia control to open the WAVE player
    mciWAV.Command = "Open"
End Sub
```

You must also change the `Form_Unload()` event procedure as follows:

```
Private Sub Form_Unload(Cancel As Integer)
    ' Clean up the WAVE and form
    mciWAV.Command = "Close"
    Unload Me
End Sub
```

Run the application. When you click the Play button, you'll hear a cuckoo sound.

Next Step

On the CD

The wave player isn't quite complete. The labels beneath the buttons don't display the status or file-name information. You can supply these labels with their values in the `StatusUpdate()` event procedure (see Listing 25.1). You'll need to use the `Mode` values to determine the proper play mode.

Pt **IV**

Hr **25**

Listing 25.1 Status.bas: Adding Status Information to the Labels

```
Private Sub mciWAV_StatusUpdate()
  ' Display the status
  If mciWAV.Mode = mciModeNotOpen Then
    lblStatusValue(0).Caption = "Not Ready"
  ElseIf mciWAV.Mode = mciModeStop Then
    lblStatusValue(0).Caption = "Stopped"
  ElseIf mciWAV.Mode = mciModePlay Then
      lblStatusValue(0).Caption = "Play"
  ElseIf mciWAV.Mode = mciModeRecord Then
    lblStatusValue(0).Caption = "Record"
  ElseIf mciWAV.Mode = mciModePause Then
    lblStatusValue(0).Caption = "Paused"
  ElseIf mciWAV.Mode = mciModeReady Then
    lblStatusValue(0).Caption = "Ready"
  End If
  ' Display the filename being played
  lblStatusValue(1).Caption = "Mcitest.Wav"
End Sub
```

> **CAUTION**   Change the label names to the actual names that you used in steps 6 and 7 of the previous topic section's example if you didn't create control arrays to hold the labels. Otherwise, your application won't run correctly because the code uses a control array for the labels, not individual label names.

When you run the player, your Form window should look like the one in Figure 25.7.

FIG. 25.7
The cuckoo is working.

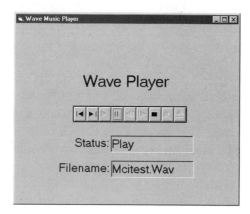

As you play the wave file, consider the following:

- The wave player doesn't display a Stop button except during the quick play of the audio file. The file stops playing when it comes to its end. If the wave file were longer, you would have more of a chance to stop the play.
- The file plays only once, and then the player's position points to the end of the file. Click the Rewind button to return to the beginning of the audio file to replay the sound.
- The Record button is active. You can record at the beginning or end of the file and then rewind the file to play back the original sound plus your recording.
- Don't save your recorded audio in the file. You'll instead want to pre- serve the sample .WAV file that comes with Visual Basic. Also, before saving the file, you would need to give users a way to enter a new file name with the Save dialog box.

Topic 3: Playing Video Clips

You've already mastered the Multimedia control! Believe it or not, playing a video clip isn't much different from playing a wave audio file, as you'll see in this topic section. You must supply the video file name to play (the Multi- media control as a video player is a compound device, so the file name is critical). Then set up the Multimedia control to handle video playing, and your application will be showing the latest in multimedia entertainment.

Overview Your Multimedia control requires a bit of help when playing video clips. Rather than keep only a simple panel of buttons, you need a projection screen from which to show the video. The most common control to display videos with is the Picture Box control. Therefore, you'll add a Picture Box control to every application that needs to display a video file.

Device Type Values

So far, you used a Multimedia control `DeviceType` property value of `CDAudio` to play compact discs and of `WaveAudio` to play .WAV audio files. Table 25.2 lists all the `DeviceType` properties that the Multimedia control supports. Although you can enter these in the `Custom` property's Property Page dialog box, you may need to set these values at runtime with assignment statements if you need your Multimedia control to perform double duty and play different kinds of media files.

Table 25.2   The Multimedia Control *DeviceType* Values

Value	Description
AVIVideo	.AVI video file
CDAudio	CD audio
DAT	Digital tape
DigitalVideo	Digital video
MMMovie	Multimedia movie clip (.MM extension)
Other	Newly supported multimedia device files
Overlay	An audio clip that overlaps another
Scanner	Scanned image import and management
Sequencer	MIDI sequencer file (.MID extension)
VCR	Video tape recorder
Videodisc	Videodisc player
WaveAudio	Wave audio file (.WAV extension)

Connecting the Picture Box Control

Your application might contain several Picture Box controls, so the Multimedia control must know to which Picture Box control to send the video output. You must tell the Multimedia control the name of the Picture Box control in which to show the video in the Multimedia control's hWndDisplay property.

hWnd is a common Windows programming prefix that represents a *handle* or, more accurately, a *device context*. Output from Visual Basic doesn't represent true screen output but windowed output. (Actually, you can send output to any Windows device with the same basic set of commands, so Windows devices are more virtual than real to your program. Windows performs all the complicated conversions to get output printed on a printer or color screen.) The bottom line is that your program doesn't send video clip output to your screen, but to a device context. That device context is almost always your screen, but the Multimedia control needs to know the proper device context so that it knows which window to play the file inside and can manipulate borders appropriately so that the video stays within the window.

Example   Create a new application. Name the form `frmVideo` and specify `Video Player` for the form's `Caption`. Add a Multimedia control to the top center of the form. (You'll have to add the Microsoft Multimedia Control 5.0 to your Toolbox window first, if you haven't already.) Name the Multimedia control `mciVideo`.

Add a Picture Box control to fall below the Multimedia control buttons and size the Picture Box control to the size you see in Figure 25.8. Name the Picture Box control `picVideo`.

FIG. 25.8
The Picture Box control will display the video.

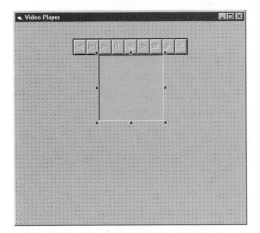

Change the Multimedia control's `DeviceType` to `AVIVideo`. Select the .AVI file named Blur24.AVI that you'll find in the \VB\Graphics\AVIs directory.

You're almost finished! As you can see, setting up video isn't any different from setting up a normal audio player. Add the following `Form_Load()` event procedure:

```
Private Sub Form_Load()
    ' Open the video player
    mciVideo.Command = "Open"
    ' Connect the video player to the Picture Box
    mciVideo.hWndDisplay = picVideo.hWnd
End Sub
```

Run your program to see the numbers, one of which is shown in Figure 25.9, flash by in the video.

FIG. 25.9
The video plays flawlessly!

Next Step As you work with the Multimedia control, you'll learn more shortcuts. For example, you don't have to specify the device type, such as `AVIVideo`, when programming compound devices because Visual Basic will look at the compound device's file extension to determine the device type needed.

Also, you probably noticed that the status labels don't always update right on time. In other words, when running Topic 2's wave file player, the status label didn't always display `Play` until the clip was almost finished. The `StatusUpdate` event occurs every few milliseconds. If you want to update such labels more frequently to gain more accuracy, change the `UpdateInterval` to a smaller value (1,000 is the default, so the status updates once each second).

CAUTION Don't make the `UpdateInterval` value too small, or your Multimedia control application will consume too much time and slow down your system. Often, this slowdown results in shaky playback of Multimedia control files.

Summary

If you're like me, you're surprised at how simple the Multimedia control makes adding multimedia to applications. The Multimedia control, available in VB's Professional and Enterprise editions, makes quick work of multimedia and takes care of such tedious details as the buttons that should be enabled, and such device mechanics as ejecting the CD caddy properly.

Your biggest job is to open the Multimedia control, select the device type, and specify a file name for compound devices that need files. The control does the rest of the work. After you set up the control, users will then determine what happens next by clicking the Multimedia control buttons.

Although you learned the fundamentals of the Multimedia control, you might want to browse the online help for additional Multimedia control properties and methods. You can keep track of and display the time and tracks as the clip plays, as well as the position within the file that's now playing. Also, you can adjust the playback so that only part of the file plays from the start and stop positions you specify.

In the next hour, "Using Form Templates," you'll learn how to use the templates that provide common functionality between applications.

Pt **IV**

Hr **25**

Hour 25 Quiz

You can find the answers for the following questions on the accompanying CD-ROM and on the Virtual Classroom Web site.

On the CD

1. What's the difference between a simple multimedia device and a compound multimedia device?

2. Why doesn't Visual Basic enable every button when you first place the Multimedia control on a form?

3. What does the `Mode` property do?

4. Why does a wave player need to supply a Rewind button?

5. What extra programming effort is required to record audio?

6. What does the Picture Box control do for video clips?

7. What's another name for a *handle*?

8. How does the Multimedia control know which Picture Box control to send the video to?

9. **True or false:** You must set the `DeviceType` property when programming the Multimedia control for compound devices.

10. How can you update the status of a Multimedia control device more frequently?

Hour 25 Homework Exercises

1. Although the Multimedia control takes care of enabling the buttons that need to appear (depending on the events taking place), you may want to hide unneeded buttons. For example, you need no Record button when playing compact discs. Change the first topic section's project so that the project displays only the buttons needed to play and manage compact discs.

2. Modify the first topic section's CD player application to show the total number of tracks on the CD (stored in the `Tracks` property), as well as the track length (stored in the `TrackLength` property).

3. Change Topic 2's wave player to ask users for a file to play and play that file. Use the File Open button. You can add a menu option or command button to trigger users' file-name entries.

Using Form Templates

AS YOU BUILD MORE advanced applications, you'll begin to add standard forms to your applications that perform routine tasks. For example, if you choose <u>A</u>bout from virtually any Windows application's <u>H</u>elp menu, a dialog box appears that describes information about the application, such as contact information, and some system statistics that users may find useful.

This hour's lesson describes some of the predefined forms that come with Visual Basic that you can use and customize so that your applications share these common dialog boxes with other applications. Often called *form templates* (a template is a pattern for something), these sample forms take the tedium out of manually adding such forms to your applications.

▶▶ **FAST TRACK**

Do you already work with multiple forms? If so, you may want to skip to Hour 33, "Developing and Designing Forms" (p. 735), to learn more about form design and usage.

Topic 1: Start Easy with Help About

One of the most common dialog boxes that appears in almost all Windows applications is the About dialog box, which pops up when users choose About from the Help menu. Figure 26.1 shows the About dialog box that appears in VB.

FIG. 26.1

VB's About dialog box describes the system.

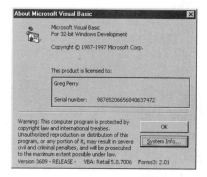

Overview This topic section examines the process needed to add one of the form templates to your project. These are the general steps you follow:

1. Add the form.

2. Modify the form's content to match your application.

3. Hook the form to your project with code.

Adding Form Templates

When you use the VB Application Wizard to create a new project's shell, you see the dialog box shown in Figure 26.2. This dialog box lets you select up to four *standard forms* (also called form templates) in the project. As you'll see in this lesson, you don't need to run the VB Application Wizard to include these forms in your project because you can add them at any time.

FIG. 26.2
You can add forms from VB's Application Wizard.

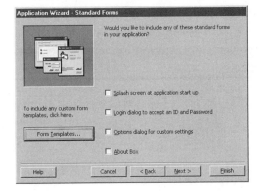

▼ **NOTE**
This lesson's final topic section discusses the form templates that appear when you click the wizard's Form Templates command button. ▲

If you want to add one or more of these forms outside the wizard, choose Add Form from the Project menu to display the Add Form dialog box (see Figure 26.3). Then select one of the form templates listed there.

FIG. 26.3
You can insert a form template in your project at any time.

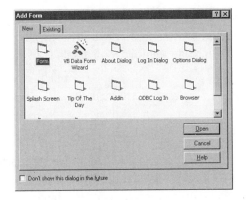

Changing the Form Templates

The form templates contain suggested controls that you can use. For example, the About dialog box template holds labels where you can place the application's title, version number, a description, and any warning text (such as copyright violation warnings) that you want your users to read. Also, the form template's About dialog box contains two command buttons and an icon.

In most cases, you should follow the suggested control layout. In other words, don't rearrange the labels so that the title appears beneath the description. The form templates are common dialog boxes that your users are used to seeing. Users will accept your application more quickly if you provide them with a standard set of auxiliary dialog boxes. If a particular form template control doesn't apply, you can delete that control. For example, you may not have any warnings to display, so don't include the warning Label control in your application's About dialog box.

Activating the Form Templates

Your application must be able to activate the form template when needed. For example, if you add an About dialog box, you'll certainly want an About option on the Help menu. Even if your application doesn't support online help, add the one Help menu option so that users can display the About dialog box by using the standard approach.

> **TIP** When working with a project that contains more than one form, use the Window menu to switch between form windows that you want to edit.

Use the `Show` method to display a form template. For example, the form template's About dialog box is named `frmAbout`. The About option's click event procedure might include the following single statement to display the dialog box:

```
frmAbout.Show       ' Display the About dialog box
```

Form Template Code

The form templates don't just provide guidelines for standard forms. They also provide you with a lot of code that goes with the form. For example, the About dialog box comes into your application bringing with it *five* event procedures, plus a `Declarations` section in its form module.

The About dialog box contains a command button labeled System Info. Clicking the button requests information on the current hardware, such as memory and the processor type. You don't have to write code to detect the hardware; the form template contains all the necessary code to display users' computer hardware information by using a standard hardware description window. Figure 26.4 shows the System Information window that the form module's code produces when you add the About dialog box to your application.

FIG. 26.4
The About dialog box produces detailed system information.

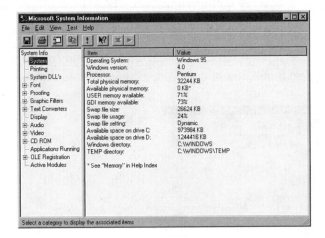

Example This example gives you practice in adding the About dialog box form template. Create a new project and follow these steps to hook up an About dialog box:

1. Open the Menu Editor, add <u>H</u>elp to the menu bar, and list <u>A</u>bout as the only option on the <u>H</u>elp menu. Name the <u>A</u>bout option `mnuHelpAbout`.

2. Name the project's form `frmTestAbout` and supply the following form `Caption`: `Demonstrate the About Dialog Box`.

3. From the <u>F</u>ile menu choose Save Form <u>A</u>s, and then type **Lesson 26 About Form** for the form's file name.

4. Choose Sav<u>e</u> Project As from the <u>F</u>ile menu, and then type **Lesson 26 About Proj** for the project's file name. (The About dialog box that you add will use the project name.)

5. From the <u>P</u>roject menu choose Add <u>F</u>orm to display the Add Form dialog box. Double-click About Dialog to add the About dialog box to your form. A dialog box is nothing more than a form with controls, and the About dialog box comes to your application as a new form named `frmAbout`.

6. Use the <u>W</u>indow menu option to switch back to your original form named `frmTestAbout`. Add the following event procedure to the `mnuHelpAbout_Click()` procedure:

```
Private Sub mnuHelpAbout_Click()
    frmAbout.Show
End Sub
```

7. You can now run the application. When you choose <u>A</u>bout from the <u>H</u>elp menu, the About dialog box appears as shown in Figure 26.5.

FIG. 26.5

The About dialog box responds to the menu selection.

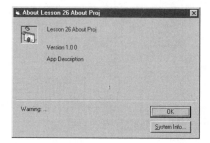

8. Click OK to close the About dialog box, and close the primary form's window to shut down the application.

As you can see in Figure 26.5, the About dialog box knows the name of the project and displays the name in its title area. The About dialog box gets the name from the **App** object (see Hour 20, "Understanding Objects and Using the Object Browser," for an explanation of **App**'s properties). The dialog box's **Form_Load ()** event procedure contains the following code that initializes the title from the **App** object:

```
Private Sub Form_Load ()
    Me.Caption = "About " & App.Title
    lblVersion.Caption = "Version " & App.Major & "." &
    ➥App.Minor & "." & App.Revision
    lblTitle.Caption = App.Title
End Sub
```

You can set the application's major, minor, and revision numbers at runtime in the primary form's **Form_Load ()** event procedure if you choose to use these values. You can also delete the About form module's reference to these values (and the labels that display the values) if you don't need version numbering.

The About dialog box's form module contains code that initializes these values (the title and version number) for you. The About dialog box, however, can't initialize such labels as the application's description or warning area. You have to initialize the description yourself in the description label's (named `lblDescription`) `Caption` property. If you don't need a warning or copyright area, delete the About dialog box's Warning label (named `lblDisclaimer`). You could, in its place, insert an icon or Picture Box control that grabs users' attention.

Next Step The About dialog box involves more code than just the application's name and version numbers. Obviously, the dialog box's form module contains the code to look for the application's name and version numbers. Also, the dialog box's form module contains code that unloads the dialog box if users click OK. The real power of the About dialog box, however, lies in the System Info command button's event procedure:

```
Private Sub cmdSysInfo_Click()
  Call StartSysInfo
End Sub
```

`StartSysInfo` is a general procedure listed below the event procedures in the About dialog box's form module. `StartSysInfo`'s code runs a system program named MSINFO32.EXE located in your Windows directory. Although you could override this program with your own, why not stick with a standard system information program that users will see in other Windows programs?

Pt **IV**

Hr **26**

If you were to rerun the program, display the About dialog box, and click the System Info button, the System Information application would start. (The application is known to be a *child process* of your application. Your application will continue when users close the System Information window.)

Topic 2: Other Standard Form Templates

Now that you've built a project that uses the About dialog box, you'll have no trouble placing the other three primary form templates. When you choose Add Form from the Project menu, you have the chance to add several form templates to your current project. This topic section looks at these three form templates:

- Splash screen
- Login dialog box
- Custom Options dialog box

Overview   Not all applications should include all the form templates. Most Windows applications do include the About dialog box, so you should make it a habit to include About in your applications. The remaining form templates may or may not fit into your application, depending on your application's goals and requirements. This topic section looks at these three standard form templates in detail, so you can determine whether you need to add one or all of them to your own projects.

> **TIP**   Throughout this section, you'll learn how to connect the various form templates to your application. If you add one or more of these templates while using the VB Application Wizard, the wizard will take some of the work off your shoulders so that you won't have to do as much to integrate the templates into your project.

The Splash Screen

A *splash screen* is an introductory screen that displays an opening message and perhaps copyright and contact information about a project. (Although it's called a screen, the splash screen is actually another form window in your project's Forms collection.) The splash screen's primary purpose is to greet your users. Unlike the About dialog box, users won't see the application's splash screen again unless they run your application again.

The splash screen often displays a graphic image with introductory text. Figure 26.6 shows one splash screen that appears when you start the Enterprise Edition of Visual Basic. The splash screen contains an attention-getting graphic image and information about the product for the user.

A splash screen often goes away after a brief period. Generally, you can add a command button or check for a keypress so that users can get rid of the splash screen at their leisure. You also could use a Timer control (see Hour 23, "Enhancing Your Program") to display the splash screen for a fixed amount of time. A splash screen can mask a startup delay that might occur if the application initializes files and data by displaying a splash screen for a few moments while the initialization takes place.

FIG. 26.6
Some VB users see this splash screen on VB startup.

The splash screen does pose one requirement that the About dialog box didn't. You must tell your application to display the splash screen *before* the normal form appears. Set the splash screen as the startup form in the Properties dialog box (which you access by choosing Properties from the Project menu). You also must add a command button or a Timer control event to the splash screen to display the next window when it's time to do so.

The Login Dialog Box

As online computer use grows, the need for security grows with it. The Login dialog box is an interesting form template that you can add to your project that asks for the user name and password and returns the values to your application for processing. Figure 26.7 shows the Login dialog box.

FIG. 26.7
Use the Login dialog box to request a user's name and password.

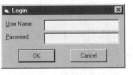

On the CD

When users enter their name and password, the actual user name appears but the password displays as asterisks thanks to the dialog box's `PasswordChar` property. Although the asterisks display as users enter the password (to protect the password from snooping eyes), your program will have access to the real password that's being typed. The initial password is `password`, and you can use it to test your program's Login dialog box. Listing 26.1 shows the form module's code behind the Login dialog box.

Listing 26.1 Login.bas: Letting Users Log In

```
Option Explicit
Public LoginSucceeded As Boolean

Private Sub cmdCancel_Click()
    'set the global var to false
    'to denote a failed login
    LoginSucceeded = False
    Me.Hide
End Sub

Private Sub cmdOK_Click()
    'check for correct password
    If txtPassword = "password" Then
        'place code to here to pass the
        'success to the calling sub
        'setting a global var is the easiest
        LoginSucceeded = True
        Me.Hide
    Else
        MsgBox "Invalid Password, try again!", , "Login"
        txtPassword.SetFocus
        SendKeys "{Home}+{End}"
    End If
End Sub
```

The form module uses a global variable named LoginSucceeded, which your code can test for True or False on return from the dialog box. If users click the Cancel command button, the cmdCancel_Click() event procedure sets LoginSucceeded to False.

To adapt the code for your own users, follow these steps:

1. Change the password string literal in the cmdOK_Click() event procedure to the password your application requires. Often the password will be stored in a file and encrypted. If you store the password in a random, binary, or database file, nobody will be able to detect the password by studying the password file with a text editor.

2. Change the message box text to the message that you want to show if users enter the wrong password.

3. For security reasons, consider putting the password-check routine in a `For...Next` loop to give users a fixed number of tries before the application refuses to display the Login dialog box again. This will make it more difficult to break the password.

> **CAUTION** Just because Microsoft supplied the Login dialog box code with a global variable doesn't make the global good to use. As the `cmdOK_Click()` event procedure's remark explains, the global variable is the *easiest* way to inform the surrounding application of the success of the login, but good programming practice recommends that you replace the global with local variables. Perhaps the best way to modify this code to improve its maintainability is to turn the subroutine procedure into a function procedure and set the function's return data type to `Boolean`. The surrounding application can then test the function's return value for `True` or `False`.

The code at the end of the `cmdOK_Click()` routine might look confusing because it varies in style from what you're used to—plus you'll find a few new statements. Until now, `MsgBox()` has been a function, but the code contains this `MsgBox` *statement*:

```
MsgBox "Invalid Password, try again!", , "Login"
```

Although VB5 still supports this `MsgBox` statement format, Microsoft is trying to get programmers to use the `MsgBox()` function. To turn this statement into a function, you need to assign the function to a variable (a `Variant` will do) and add parentheses like this:

```
varKeys = MsgBox("Invalid Password, try again!", , "Login")
```

Pt **IV**
Hr **26**

▼ **NOTE**

The `MsgBox` statement can't determine which command button users clicked to close the message box. On the other hand, the `MsgBox()` function returns the button clicked. If OK is the only `MsgBox()` button you choose to display, you don't need to test for a button click because users must click OK to close the message box. ▲

The next statement returns the focus to the <u>P</u>assword text box (this occurs only if users enter an invalid password) with the `SetFocus` method. When you apply `SetFocus` to a control that can receive the focus, the application sets the focus to that control. Although the focus might ordinarily move to another control, such as the OK command button, the `SetFocus` method moves the focus back to the <u>P</u>assword text box because users have to re-enter the password.

The final statement uses the `SendKeys` statement to highlight the text that appears in the <u>P</u>assword text box. No matter what users type as the incorrect password, the `SendKeys` statement moves the text cursor to the beginning of the text box and then to the end of the text box—in effect, highlighting the entire text box contents so that the user's next keypress replaces the selected text.

▼ **NOTE**
Hour 28, "Using Keyboard and Mouse I/O," explains the `SendKeys` statement in more detail. ▲

The Options Dialog Box

The form template called the Options dialog box is perhaps the template that does the least work but has the most potential uses. When you add an Options dialog box, you'll see the dialog box template shown in Figure 26.8. The dialog box contains four pages, with tabs at the top of each page and a frame on the body of each page. You can add pages and controls to the inside of the page frames for the options you require.

FIG. 26.8
The Options dialog box displays pages for various options.

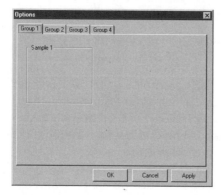

Many Windows programs contain an Options dialog box accessed from the <u>T</u>ools menu that looks a lot like the Options dialog box this form template produces. The Options dialog box is a starting point, albeit just a dialog box shell, from which you can build a more complete dialog box.

The Options dialog box uses a special ActiveX control called TabStrip, which produces this multiple-page tabbed dialog box. If you want to add a TabStrip control to one of your applications—that is, if you don't want to use this form template—you'll have to add the control from the Project Properties dialog box's Microsoft Custom Controls 5.0 option (choose Properties from the Project menu).

When you want to use the Options dialog box, follow these general guidelines:

1. Add as many pages to the Options dialog box as you need. The easiest way to modify the tabs and pages is to click one of the tabs and then click the ellipsis for the `Custom` property. The Property Pages dialog box that appears (see Figure 26.9) helps you set up the pages, tabs, and ToolTips that you want to use in the Options dialog box.

FIG. 26.9

Use the Property Pages dialog box to set up the dialog box pages.

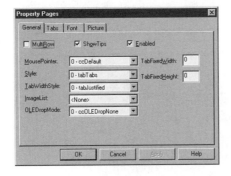

2. Add a general procedure that reads all the controls in the Options dialog box and sets whatever options the dialog box contains.

3. Call the options-setting procedure from the `cmdApply_Click()` procedure so that the options go into effect when users click the Options dialog box's Apply button. (You can also remove the Apply button and its associated event procedure if you don't want users to have the Apply feature.)

4. Replace the following statement that appears in the `cmdOK_Click()` with a procedure call to your own options-setting procedure:

    `MsgBox "Place code here to set options and close dialog!"`

5. Modify the `Form_KeyDown()` event procedure to handle the focus order that the dialog box supports as users press Ctrl+Tab. This code isn't trivial, and you'll probably need to master Hour 28's subject matter before you fully understand the `KeyDown()` event procedure.

▼ **NOTE**
The `tbsOptions_Click()` event procedure shows the appropriate page (and hides the other pages) in the TabStrip control as the program runs. ▲

Example Follow these steps to create a project that contains a splash screen:

1. Create a new project. You won't do anything with the form named `Form1`.

2. From the Project menu choose Add Form, and then select the splash screen. VB displays the sample splash screen.

3. Change the labels to match those of Figure 26.10.

FIG. 26.10
The splash screen is now modified.

4. Choose Properties from the Project menu. Change the Startup Object to `frmSplash` (the name of the splash screen) and click OK.

5. Add the following line to both the `Form_Keypress()` event and `Frame1_Click()` (place the line after the `Unload Me` statement in both procedures):

```
Form1.Show    ' Display the regular form
```

6. Run the application. The first form that appears is your splash screen. When you press a key or click the mouse button, the splash screen will disappear and the normal form named `Form1` will appear. Close the form window to return to VB's development environment.

Next Step   Create a new project and run the VB Application Wizard. Accept the application's default values until you get to the Standard Forms dialog box. Click all four standard forms, click <u>N</u>ext twice, name the application `Project26`, and click <u>F</u>inish. Visual Basic builds the application shell while you wait. After the Application Wizard finishes, click OK and read the setup instructions before closing the instructions' dialog box.

As you might recall from Hour 2, "Creating Your First Application," the VB Application Wizard creates only a shell of an application. You must fill in the details. Nevertheless, the shell you now can study includes every one of the four standard form templates described in this lesson's first two topic sections.

To begin with, run the application to see how the application has already created quite a bit for you. Don't enter a password (the default password is blank until you add one to the code module), but you can see that the splash screen grabbed the user's name (*your name* in this case!) from the **App** object and displayed the name automatically in the <u>U</u>ser Name text box.

The splash screen appears but goes away quickly before the regular form appears. The About dialog box appears when you choose <u>A</u>bout from the <u>H</u>elp menu, and the Options dialog box appears when you choose <u>O</u>ptions from the <u>V</u>iew menu. This project, although only a shell, gives you a lot of good code to study when implementing your own application that requires one or more standard form templates.

Pt **IV**

Hr **26**

▼ **NOTE**
The form templates all reside in the \VB\Forms directory. This lesson describes the most common form templates, but you can create your own and add those forms to the \VB\Forms directory if you want more forms to be used as templates. ▲

Topic 3: Additional Form Templates

All the form templates described in the first two topic sections appear as options in the VB Application Wizard. If you click the Form <u>T</u>emplates button on the wizard's Form Template dialog box, the wizard lets you add these three additional forms (others may appear if your \VB\Forms directory contains additional forms):

- Tip of the Day dialog box
- Add In dialog box
- ODBC Log In dialog box

Overview This topic section explains how to access these three additional form templates. Unlike the first two topic sections' forms, these three don't routinely appear in every application. You'll want to use these form templates only on special occasions and only if your application requires the features.

> **TIP** These extra forms don't appear just at the Application Wizard's prompting. Whenever you add a form file, Visual Basic gives you a list of form choices, and these three form templates will be among the choices Visual Basic gives you in the Add Forms dialog box. Depending on the forms listed in your \VB\Forms directory, you may have more form templates than those described in this lesson.

Tip of the Day

Do you sometimes start software and get greeted with a tip of the day? Windows 95 offers such a tip (see the Welcome Screen in Figure 26.11) until you turn off the option. Every time you start Windows 95, you'll see the tip until you deselect the check box and turn off the tip of the day.

FIG. 26.11
The Windows 95 Tip of the Day dialog box offers help for newcomers.

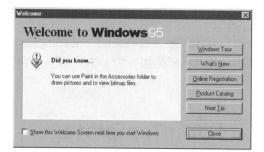

When you add the Tip of the Day dialog box to a form window, Visual Basic adds the Tip of the Day form to your Forms collection. Depending on your screen size and default font settings, you may have to extend the text box that holds the text labeled Show Tips at Startup. Click under the Did you know... label to display the label named `lblTipText`. This label holds the tips that you display.

The code inside the form module sets up the form to display a daily tip each time users start the application. The following guidelines help you understand and modify the code to fit your application:

1. The code creates a new collection called `Tips`. The procedure grabs the startup tips from this collection.

2. Obviously, the `Tips` collection needs to read the tips into the collection from a file that you create and supply with the project. The file should hold one tip per line.

3. The code loads the file name in the named literal `TIP_FILE` in the `LoadTips()` function. The procedure uses the `Add` method to add each tip to the collection as the file data is read. Your only real job is to create this tip file by using a text editor such as Windows Notepad.

4. The `DoNextTip()` procedure randomly selects a tip from the collection and displays it by using a special method named `DisplayCurrentTip` (which is actually a subroutine procedure located at the bottom of the code).

5. The most technical part of the code is the shortest in the procedure named `chkLoadTipsAtStartup()`. Fortunately, Microsoft supplies this code. The code uses the `SaveSetting` command to change your system Registry. The `SaveSetting` command, in this case, stores the value that determines whether users want to see startup tips. If users deselect the check box labeled Show Tips At Startup, the Registry is updated accordingly and the code won't display tips in subsequent sessions.

Pt **IV**

Hr **26**

The Add-In Dialog Box

An *add-in* is a supplemental program to enhance the current application. Visual Basic supports add-ins that modify the development environment. For example, you may locate a VB add-in that adds a spelling checker to literals within VB code. VB contains a special feature called the Add-In Manager that manages these add-in programs.

If you need to supply an add-in manager to your own application, the Add-In dialog box gives you the place to start. Although this dialog box is fairly simple, its form template gives you a start. When you add the Add-In form template to your Form window, you'll see the My Add In form in Figure 26.12.

FIG. 26.12
The Add-In form template lets you specify new templates.

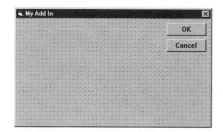

After you change the Add-In form's `Caption` property, you must hook your add-in code to the form module. Writing add-in code isn't a trivial task. You should get to know VB's Add-In Manager (see the A̲dd-Ins menu option) thoroughly and master all of Visual Basic before trying to write your own add-ins.

The ODBC Logon Dialog Box

ODBC stands for a special database access called Open Database Connectivity. ODBC provides a standard command set for accessing different kinds of data stored on different kinds of computers. The ODBC standard lets your program access data that it otherwise wouldn't be able to access. ODBC's goal is to let a number of different systems access data stored elsewhere.

Figure 26.13 shows the form template that appears when you insert the form on your Form window.

FIG. 26.13
The ODBC Logon dialog box form template lets you set up external database access.

The ODBC Logon dialog box is one that you can add to your application so that users can select and access an ODBC database source. The source indicates the location and type of data the application is to access. Table 26.1 describes each ODBC field.

Table 26.1 The ODBC Logon Dialog Box's Text Boxes

Name	Description
DSN	The *Data Source Name* that lists (in a drop-down list box) the currently registered ODBC sources in the user's system Registry
UID	The User ID that supplies the connection with the user's identification so that the ODBC database can validate the user's access
Password	The user's password to access the system
Database	The name of the database to connect to
Driver	A drop-down list box that lists all the drivers on the system and lets users register a new ODBC driver
Server	The name of the server supplying the database if the DSN isn't available

The code necessary to connect the ODBC Logon dialog box's values to the proper ODBC-compatible database is fairly extensive. You must understand the ODBC API (Application Program Interface) commands necessary to connect to the outside database. Such commands are beyond the scope of this book because Visual Basic programmers rarely have to resort to API-based routines, except in system-related applications.

Example   As you've learned from this topic section, the extra form templates don't appear as routinely as the ones described by the first two topic sections. Nevertheless, your applications may require one or more of these form template services.

The Tip of the Day form template is perhaps the most common of the three described in this topic. Follow these steps to set up a Tip of the Day dialog box on your system:

1. Start the Windows Notepad editor. Create a file called Tipofday.TXT (the default file name used by the tip's dialog box) and store the file in your application's directory. After you enter the following contents, save the file and exit Notepad:

```
Brush your teeth daily.
Save money for retirement.
Get plenty of sleep.
Read good books.
Don't speed.
Exercise often.
Remember to floss.
```

2. Create a new application and display the standard Form window. Before doing anything else, save the form and project in the same application directory as you saved the tip file. If these files aren't in the same directory, the code won't be able to locate your tips.

3. From the Project menu choose Add Form, and then select the Tip of the Day form.

4. Change the label with the **Caption** *Did you know...* to *Be sure to....*

5. Run the application to see the results.

Where did the Tip of the Day dialog box go? Although you've set up the tip file and added the Tip of the Day dialog box to your application, you must remember that VB first displays your project's primary form (called **Form1** unless you change it) at startup. The following section explains how to set the Tip of the Day form for the initial form's startup and set up the code to display your regular form when users close the Tip of the Day dialog box.

Next Step From the Project menu choose Properties, and set the Startup Object to **frmTip**. Click OK to close the dialog box. The application is now set to display the Tip of the Day dialog box when users run the application.

You must connect the regular form (named **Form1** still) to the Tip of the Day dialog box form module so that the regular form appears when the Tip of the Day dialog box disappears. Change the **cmdOK_Click()** procedure as follows:

```
Private Sub cmdOK_Click()
    Unload Me      ' Unloads the tip dialog box
    Form1.Show     ' Show the regular form
End Sub
```

You must attend to one more item. If users decide not to see the tips in subsequent startup sessions, there's no way now for the tip's form module to display the regular form. Therefore, add the **Form1.Show** statement to the **Form_Load()** procedure as follows:

```
Private Sub Form_Load()
    Dim ShowAtStartup As Long

    ' See if we should be shown at startup
    ShowAtStartup = GetSetting(App.EXEName, "Options",
    ➥"Show Tips at Startup", 1)
    If ShowAtStartup = 0 Then
        Unload Me
        Form1.Show  ' Show the regular form  ** New statement
        Exit Sub
    End If      ' Rest of code is not shown here
```

You now can run the application and read the tips randomly by clicking the Next Tip command button. When you click OK, the regular form appears, although the form is blank and boring because you've added nothing to it. If users decide not to see the tips in subsequent sessions, the application will show the regular `Form1` form at startup.

▼ NOTE

You can set up the application to display the tip or the regular startup form in other ways, as well. If you add proper `Show` methods to a subroutine procedure named `Main`, you can add this `Main` subroutine to the startup object. ▲

Pt **IV**

Hr **26**

Summary

The form templates exist to save you time. By adding them to your project, you won't have to take the time to create the forms and add the routine code that they need to integrate with your applications. The form templates contain all the code you need to begin connecting them to your applications. You'll have to modify the code slightly and adjust the control properties that appear on the forms, but your job is made much lighter than would otherwise be the case without the form templates.

In Hour 27, "Accessing Databases," you'll learn about VB's extensive set of data controls. The data controls let your applications access data that resides in outside database files.

Hour 26 Quiz

You can find the answers for the following questions on the accompanying CD-ROM and on the Virtual Classroom Web site.

On the CD

1. What's the purpose of the form templates?
2. Describe two ways to add form templates to applications.
3. Describe the code needed to connect the About dialog box to your project.
4. **True or false:** You must write the code to display system information if users click the About dialog box's <u>S</u>ystem Info command button.
5. What's the difference between a splash screen and your regular form?
6. Would you consider the Tip of the Day dialog box to be a splash screen?
7. What does *ODBC* stand for?
8. What's the purpose of the `SaveSetting` command?
9. What must you do in the Properties dialog box before your application can properly display a splash screen or a Tip of the Day dialog box?
10. Describe the format of the tip file required by the Tip of the Day dialog box.

Hour 26 Homework Exercises

1. Follow the recommendation in Topic 2's Login dialog box section that turns the Login dialog box code into a better set of routines. Replace the global variable with local variables.
2. Create an application that displays a different PC tip every time the application starts. (You can modify the tip file at the end of the third topic section and you're there.) Add a menu option to the regular form to make the tips appear again at startup. *Hint:* Check out the `chkLoadTipsAtStartup_Click()` procedure and use the `SaveSetting` command to reset the tips. Although you haven't mastered `SaveSetting`, you have all the tools you need to complete this project quickly.

Accessing Databases

THIS LESSON EXPLAINS how to access databases. A *database* is a collection of files that work together to form a complete data-management system. A database system, such as Microsoft Access, creates the database that your VB applications may need to connect to. By using the Data controls, DAO programming, and the Data Form Wizard, your applications can manage and access a database without disturbing its integrity.

Topic 1: The Data Controls

Visual Basic includes the Data control and some cousin controls that perform application access to data outside the realm of ordinary data files. Although you learned how to read, write, and update files in Hour 21, "Accessing Files," the concepts presented there didn't help you interact with database-created data. A *database system* is a program, such as Microsoft Access or Paradox, that creates and manages data for you in a special format. As you'll learn in this lesson, VB's Data controls interact with databases and lighten the programming required to access such databases.

▼ NOTE

The Data control and its related controls are difficult to cover in a single hour because they're difficult to cover in a single book! This lesson provides you with the guidance you need to get started with the Data control and related controls. All editions of Visual Basic support the Data control and additional controls that you'll find helpful in accessing data from external database files. The Professional and Enterprise editions include an advanced set of database controls called *DAO* (for *Data Access Objects*) that perform faster and more advanced database interaction. ▲

Overview   This topic section examines the Data controls. You'll learn to place the primary control (the Data control) and other forms of the Data control, and also learn how to *bind* (connect) those controls to your form's application. The Data controls take care of most of your database access. You can be concerned with your application's goals and not worry so much about the tedium of file access when you begin using the Data controls.

Database Data

This lesson assumes that you want to connect your applications to a database file. Not every VB programmer has access to a database system, so you may wonder where your application's database data will come from.

Visual Basic includes a sample Microsoft Access database file named Biblio.mdb, and this lesson will use that file. Therefore, you can practice with this lesson's exercises even if you don't have access to an outside database source. Remember, however, that this lesson offers only a small overview of the whole VB-to-database picture, and you must master fairly advanced concepts in database theory to use all of VB's database concepts.

Visual Basic does include an add-in tool called *VisData* that lets you create, edit, and manage database files for the following database programs, even if you don't have those database programs on your computer:

- Microsoft Access
- dBASE
- FoxPro
- Paradox
- ODBC
- Text files (a text file generally isn't considered to be a true database)

From the Add-Ins menu, choose Visual Data Manager to start VisData. You can create your own database files with VisData and, if you ever get one of the listed database applications, you can load your VisData files directly into the database.

TIP VB's Professional and Enterprise editions come with the source code for VisData. The VisData add-in program is a Visual Basic application that you can study to learn more about advanced coding.

Terminology

In database terminology, a *table* is a file, and the *fields* and *records* relate to columns and rows in the file. A database varies greatly from a normal file because a database file generally contains multiple tables, as well as access techniques (called *queries*) that return data in a predetermined format. A database file also can contain predefined report and screen form definitions so that database users can see the data needed.

Pt **IV**

Hr **27**

▼ **NOTE**
Today, most database systems are *relational*, meaning that no two records are exactly alike and file redundancy is eliminated as much as possible. Microsoft Access is such a relational database. For database files that aren't relational, such as pre-dBASE 4.0 files, you have to add fairly complex VB code to change the database to relational access before performing I/O with the database. ▲

Database tables usually have at least one index defined. An *index* is a key field with unique values for every record. The index works just as a book's index works; when you need to access a particular row in the table, you can specify the index value and the database can jump directly to the row without having to search the entire table as you would have to do when writing sequential file-access routines.

When working with selected data, you'll often define or use a *recordset*, which is a subset of the actual table. For example, a customer balance recordset might contain only those customers from the customer file who owe more than $100 to the company. Often, a database query creates this recordset.

Bound Controls

Bound controls are controls bound to your database data in a way that makes traversing the database simple for your program. In a nutshell, you can bind many VB controls, such as a text box, to a database; when users step through the database, the text box displays the field you've set up. When you bind the control to the database, you don't have to worry about displaying the field data because Visual Basic does all the work.

▼ NOTE

If you need to perform a unique operation on the data before displaying the data in a bound control, you'll have to use VB's database commands to process the database. **▲**

In particular, if you want to display one record at a time, use bound controls. Bound controls usually display only the current record, or a field within the current record. (As a user traverses the database, the current record changes to reflect the user's position within the selected table.)

TIP Use the special bound grid control named DBGrid to display multiple records at one time, as well as DBList and DBCombo. The DBGrid control is the only control that lets users update the displayed data, however.

A Data control has five parts:

- The inner arrows let you move forward and backward through the table one record at a time.
- The outer arrows with the vertical lines move you to the first or last record in the table.

- Between these arrows, the `Caption` displays any information you want to display.

You'll see the Data control's parts when you add the control to a form in the next example.

Example This example creates an application that uses it. Create a new project and perform these steps to add the Data control:

1. Double-click the Data control to add it to the form. Change the Data control's `Width` to 4620 to make room for text that will appear on the control. Move the control to the bottom of the Form window. Your Form window should look like the one in Figure 27.1.

FIG. 27.1
The Data control is now on the form.

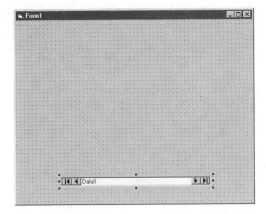

2. Name the Data control **dtaBooks**.

3. Use the **DatabaseName** property to connect the Data control to the database. Click the **DatabaseName** ellipsis and select the file named Biblio.mdb from the VB folder. Biblio.mdb is the Microsoft Access database that comes with Visual Basic.

4. Remember that a database file can hold multiple tables, so you must tell the Data control which table the control should access within the database. Open the **RecordSource** property to display a list of tables (see Figure 27.2) that appear in the selected database. Select Titles.

FIG. 27.2

Tell the Data control which table to access from the database.

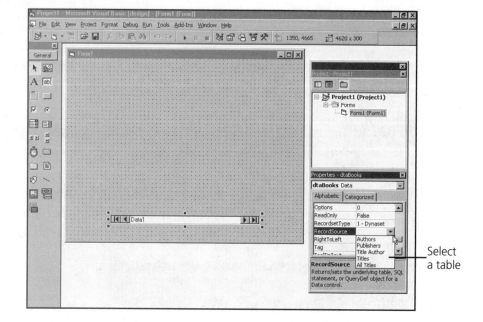

Select a table

5. Change the Data control's `Caption` property to `Click to change titles`.

6. Add a Label control to the form with these properties: `Font.Size`: 18, `Height`: 2115, `Name`: `lblBooks`, `Top`: 1275, and `Width`: 4200.

7. Open the label's `DataSource` property drop-down list and select `dtaBooks`. If the form contained multiple Data controls, you would have to select the one that targets the label.

8. Not only must you tell Visual Basic which data control provides the data, but you also must tell Visual Basic the field to display. Open the label's `DataField` property drop-down list to display a list of all the fields with the Data control's selected table. Select Title.

9. You're ready to run the application. As soon as you execute the application, the first title appears in the label. Click the various Data control buttons to traverse the database table. As you click, the label bound to the Data control updates to show the current row's title (see Figure 27.3).

FIG. 27.3
*The Data control
does all the
work.*

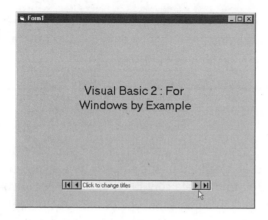

Next Step If you choose Components from the Project menu, you can add additional
Data controls by selecting the options labeled Microsoft Data Bound Grid
Control and Microsoft Data Bound List Controls 5.0. Three new tools—
DBCombo, DBList, and MSFlexGrid—will appear in the Toolbox when you
click OK. Remember these controls if you want to display multiple records
at one time, so users can select from a drop-down list rather than click the
Data control to retrieve the fields you need.

▼ NOTE
Be sure to use a check box to display Yes/No database data. The check box
indicates that the Yes/No value is Yes when selected and No when not
selected. ▲

If you display the field data in a text box, users can modify the data. When
users then click the Data control, the changes stay recorded in the database
file. If you use a Label control, users will only be able to see the data but
not change it.

You should know that you can accomplish a lot more with the Data control
than is taught in this topic section. Nevertheless, the section has introduced
you to the power and ease that the Data control and its related data controls bring to applications that must interact with databases. As your programming skills improve, you'll begin to use some of the Data control
methods to perform the database traversal. For example, the `Move...`
methods move the current record pointer to the same locations as the Data

Pt **IV**

Hr **27**

control's buttons. The following methods would move the record pointer to the first, last, next, and previous records in the database table pointed to by the Data control's `DataSource` property:

```
dtaBooks.Recordset.MoveFirst    ' Move to the 1st record
dtaBooks.Recordset.MoveLast     ' Move to the last record
dtaBooks.Recordset.MoveNext     ' Move to the next record
dtaBooks.Recordset.MovePrevious ' Move to the previous record
```

Remember that a *recordset* is a collection of records from a table. The Data control's recordset is defined by the property values you set. If you added a command button to the Data control example that included a `Click` event procedure which in turn contained one of these methods, the label would display that record selected by the method every time users clicked the control. In addition to the record-movement controls, methods exist that add and delete records.

> **TIP** Use the `BOF` and `EOF` Boolean properties to see whether the record pointer is at the beginning or end of the table. VB programmers often use a `Do...While` loop to step through every table record, and the loop terminates when `dtaBooks.Recordset.EOF` is equal to `True`.

Topic 2: Data Access Objects (DAO)

If you use either the Professional or Enterprise editions, you can learn how to program Visual Basic by using *DAO (Data Access Objects)*. Data Access Objects are database objects that you create and manage with your program code.

The primary reason for mastering DAO is because it offers several advantages over the Data control. DAO gives you more control and speed in accessing databases. Although using DAO takes a little more knowledge than using the Data control and its related controls, DAO is the choice among most VB programmers due to its powerful advantages.

Overview In the first topic section, you learned some recordset methods that apply to the Data control. Data Access Objects also use recordset methods, as you will see in this topic section. This section discusses the advantages and disadvantages of using DAO over the Data controls, so you can more easily determine whether DAO is for you.

DAO Advantages and Disadvantages

The Data control is simple to use but doesn't offer extremely fast database access. Although today's computers run quickly, you'll notice speed degradation when you use the Data control in large database tables, especially ODBC-based databases.

When you use DAO, you must write more program code than you have to write with the Data control. As you saw in the first topic section, you can program the Data control primarily through setting property values. Although you can write code that accesses various Data control methods, straightforward database access is less involved with the Data control.

DAO lets you control data access in a much stricter way than with the Data control. The ease of the Data control reflects its inability to be flexible. Also, the overhead of the Data control doesn't burden DAO-based programs. DAO uses the recordset concept for most of its operations, and you can create a recordset variable just as you can create other kinds of object variables in Visual Basic.

Database Variables

When you need to work with a database, you'll need to declare a variable of the data type named `Database`. The following statement declares such a variable:

```
Dim dbBooks As Database    ' Declare a database variable
```

The database variable will provide the connection to the database throughout your code.

▼ NOTE
You'll also need to create `Dynaset` and `Snapshot` variables from time to time. A *dynaset* is a recordset that remains active; if the recordset data changes, the corresponding dynaset data changes also. Think of a dynaset as being a link to the database table's records. A *snapshot* is a one-time picture of the recordset. The recordset works like a copy of a selected recordset; when the original recordset changes, the copy doesn't change. ▲

The *OpenDatabase()* Function

When you declare a database variable, you must specify the `OpenDatabase()` function to open the selected database. Remember that a database contains many tables. Before you can access one of the tables, you must open the database. The `OpenDatabase()` function informs Visual Basic that you want to access the database.

The following code declares a database variable and opens a database:

```
Dim dbBooks As Database
Set dbBooks = OpenDatabase("Biblio.mdb")
```

After `OpenDatabase()` completes its task, Visual Basic has prepared the database and connected the database file to your **Database** data-typed variable. The **Set** command works *almost* like an assignment statement. **Set** is used to create a reference to an object. The **dbBooks** variable can't really hold the entire database, but **dbBooks** is a reference to the database.

> **CAUTION** The `OpenDatabase()` function generates an error if the database file doesn't exist or if a hardware error occurs when the function executes. Also, you may want to search the online help for the `OpenDatabase()` function options that exist for particular database types. For example, you can include a password if the database is protected, and you can open a database for exclusive access so that others on the network can't access the database until you complete your work.

▼ NOTE

The global `Database` data-typed variables are the few exceptions to the rule of local variable usage. The database resides outside your entire application. In every real respect, the database is global to your application due to its separation from your application. Variables, on the other hand, are internal to your program, so local variables provide safety barriers to keep some parts of the code away from some variables. ▲

The `OpenDatabase()` function opens both ODBC databases and Jet engine databases. A *Jet engine database* is a Microsoft-designed database specification that provides quick access to databases. The database can reside in any folder and on any computer networked to yours.

Working with Dynasets

A dynaset, being a selected subset of a database, lets you work with a smaller set of data than the entire database table. The nice thing about dynasets is that as soon as you make a change to a dynaset, the linked table updates in the database.

▼ NOTE

One problem is that the creation of dynaset variables often requires a full working knowledge of *SQL* (pronounced *sequel*), a database-access language that works among many database products. This and subsequent sections will show you some recordset and dynaset object creation and manipulation by example, but much more can be involved in the coding of DAO. As stated earlier, DAO can be much tougher to code than the Data controls, but DAO provides speed and flexibility that you don't get with the Data controls. ▲

One common dynaset variable you can create references an entire table from the database. The following code defines a database and sets a dynaset variable named `dsTitles` to the Titles table inside the Biblio.mdb database:

```
Dim dbBooks As Database
Dim dsTitles As Recordset    ' A dynaset is a special recordset
' Create reference to database
Set dbBooks = OpenDatabase("Biblio.mdb")
' Create reference to dynaset (the entire table)
Set dsTitles = dbBooks.OpenRecordset("Titles", dbOpenDynaset)
```

When you supply a table name for `OpenRecordset()`'s first argument, as done here, the entire table is referenced from the dynaset variable named `dsTitles`. Therefore, subsequent code can access information from the dynaset that corresponds to the entire table. `vbOpenDynaset` makes the recordset a dynaset, as opposed to a snapshot that would result if you used the `vbOpenSnapshot` option. You can also pass `OpenRecordset()` the name of an existing *query*. Many database systems, such as Microsoft Access, let you specify queries that retrieve records and fields based on a criterion. You can save those queries and reference them in the `OpenRecordset()` function. The existing named query sets the dynaset variable to that subset of data generated by the query.

Pt **IV**

Hr **27**

▼ **NOTE**

A big query advantage is that a query can access data from multiple tables within the database. The recordset acts as though the data all came from a single location. ▲

Also, if you know SQL, you can place SQL language directly in the `OpenRecordset()` function, like this:

```
Set dsTitles = dbBooks.OpenRecordset("Select * FROM " _
    & "Titles WHERE Year Published = '1998'"), dbOpenDynaset)
```

The ampersand (the concatenate operator) lets you break the `OpenRecordset()` more easily into two lines.

After the `OpenRecordset()` finishes its task, the dynaset associates with its variable. To assign the dynaset's current record field value to a control such as a Label control, use this code:

```
If IsNull(dsTitles!Title) Then      ' Don't assign Null
    lblBookTitle.Caption = ""
Else
    lblBookTitle.Caption = dsTitles!Title
End If
```

You can shorten the code by using the `IIf()` function, like this:

```
lblBookTitle.Caption = __
    IIf(IsNull(dsTitles!Title), "", dsTitles!Title)
```

Consider the following when studying these `If` tests:

- You separate the field name from the dynaset with an exclamation mark.

- You must know the table's field names. You won't be able to manipulate the database through DAO if you're unfamiliar with the database table structure.

- A field might hold a `Null` value, but you should assign an empty string instead of the `Null` value. You can't assign `Null` to some controls.

Example This example works with the Biblio.mdb database through DAO object code. Create the form shown in Figure 27.4. All the buttons at the bottom of the form are command buttons that let you manage the database.

You've worked with the Titles table from the Biblio.mdb database throughout this lesson, and this example uses DAO to access that same data. The text boxes on the form correspond to the seven fields from the Titles table. Set the title's Text Box control to a `Multiline` value of `True`, and add vertical scroll bars so that users can see long book titles. Draw the lines that separate some of the controls with the Line control.

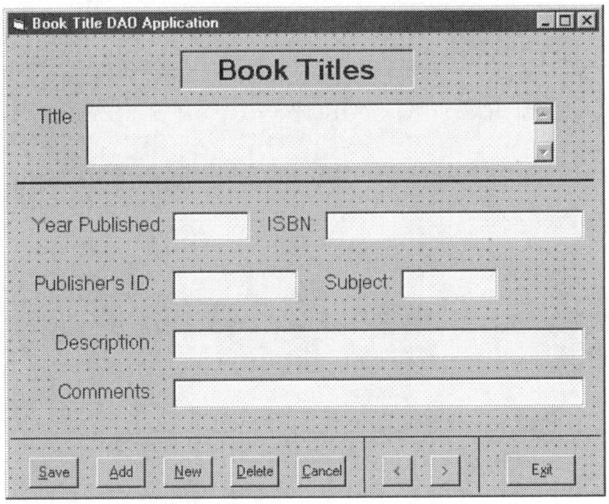

FIG. 27.4

You can create a form that accesses and manages a database.

The first task is to declare your database variables. Enter the following code in the form module's `Declarations` section:

```
Dim dbBooks As Database
Dim dsBooks As Recordset      ' Dynaset
Dim blnNewRec As Boolean      ' Adding a new record?
```

The global variable named `blnNewRec` will come in handy in this project and later if you expand the project. The variable keeps track of the users' add or edit modes so that an appropriate update can be made to the database. Again, the database is global to your program, and such a variable attached so closely to the database is best left global so that all the routines accessing the database will know the database status.

You must open the database and create the dynaset. In the `Form_Load()` procedure, code this:

```
Private Sub Form_Load()
   ' Open the database and initialize the dynaset
   ' Set a path in the following line if needed
   Set dbBooks = OpenDatabase("Biblio.mdb")
   Set dsBooks = dbBooks.OpenRecordset("Titles", dbOpenDynaset)
   Call DispForm   ' Display the form and its data
End Sub
```

Pt **IV**

Hr **27**

Although you must display the first data record on the form when the form first appears, you should code a separate procedure named `DispForm ()` to display the data inside the form's text boxes. Although you could enter the text box initialization inside `Form_Load()`, you need to initialize the text boxes elsewhere when users move to other records in the table. Therefore, good coding principles dictate that you put the code in a separate procedure so that you can call the record-displaying routine from elsewhere. When the application first opens the database and creates the recordset, the record pointer points to the first record in the file, so you can call the record-displaying routine without adjusting the record pointer.

The `DispForm ()` procedure in Listing 27.1 assigns the current record's fields to the text boxes.

Listing 27.1 Tbrecord.bas: Assigning Record Fields to Text Boxes

```
Private Sub DispForm ()
  ' Fill the text boxes with the initial record
  Dim varButton As Variant   ' MsgBox() return
  If Not dsBooks.EOF Then    ' If not at end of file
    ' Use default Text property
    txtTitle = _
      IIf(IsNull(dsBooks!Title), "", dsBooks!Title)
    ' Place multiple word field names inside brackets
    txtYear = _
      IIf(IsNull(dsBooks![Year Published]), "", dsBooks![Year Published])
    txtISBN = _
      IIf(IsNull(dsBooks!ISBN), "", dsBooks!ISBN)
    txtPubID = _
      IIf(IsNull(dsBooks!PubID), "", dsBooks!PubID)
    txtSubject = _
      IIf(IsNull(dsBooks!Subject), "", dsBooks!Subject)
    txtDescription = _
      IIf(IsNull(dsBooks!Description), "", dsBooks!Description)
    txtComments = _
      IIf(IsNull(dsBooks!Comments), "", dsBooks!Comments)
  Else
    varButton = MsgBox("No records exist in the file")
  End If
End Sub
```

The assignments demonstrate several programming aspects. The lines are long, so the underscore (_) works as a line-continuation character in the assignment statements. As stated earlier in this topic section, you shouldn't assign null values to fields, so the `IIf()` function guards against assigning nulls. If the field contains `Null`, an empty string goes into the text box. Notice also that if a field name contains blanks, you must enclose the field name inside brackets.

The code does *not* list the Text Box control's `Text` property in the assignment. In other words, the control named `txtYear` is assigned the table's year, not `txtYear.Text`, which is the Text Box control value that you usually assign. All controls have default property values that are the most common properties usually assigned to the control. Therefore, the following statements are identical, but the first one is simpler to type because the `Text` value is understood:

```
txtFName = "Laura"        ' The Text property is assumed
txtFName.Text = "Laura"
```

Before running the application, you should code the Next (>) and Exit command buttons so that you can step through the table and exit the program. Enter the event procedures in Listing 27.2.

Listing 27.2 Nextend.bas: Coding the Next and Exit Command Buttons

```
Private Sub cmdExit_Click()
  dbBooks.Close     ' Close the database
  ' A great idea in case user hides the form
  End
End Sub

Private Sub cmdNext_Click()
  ' Display the next record
  Dim varButton As Variant   ' MsgBox() return
  If Not dsBooks.EOF Then
    dsBooks.MoveNext    ' Updates the pointer
    ' Check to see if at end of file and a blank rec
    If dsBooks.EOF Then
      dsBooks.MovePrevious  ' Re-adjust pointer
    End If
  End If
  Call DispForm
End Sub
```

The extra `If` inside `cmdNext_Click()` keeps the next record button from displaying `DispForm()`'s message box that indicates no records exist in the file.

Run the application to display the form in Figure 27.5, and look through the titles. You still have some coding left to do, but the fundamentals are already in the application. Some Biblio.mdb fields contain strange values, such as empty braces in the Comments field, but the title and other fields generally contain valid data.

FIG. 27.5

The book titles appear, thanks to DAO.

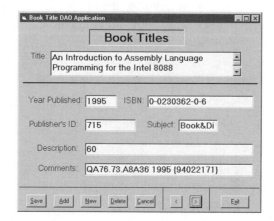

Next Step   The code in Listing 27.3 takes care of the previous record command button (<).

Listing 27.3   Previous.bas: Code for the Previous Record Button

```
Private Sub cmdPrevious_Click()
  ' Display the previous record
  If Not dsBooks.BOF Then     ' Check for file beginning
    dsBooks.MovePrevious
    ' Keep DispForm()'s No Data message box out
    If dsBooks.BOF Then
      dsBooks.MoveNext  ' Back to beginning
    End If
  End If
  Call DispForm
End Sub
```

The Data control automatically updates the underlying database record if users make a change in a bound text box, but you must do the edit processing for DAO data. The event procedure in Listing 27.4 is just a start for updating the record when users make a change to a field and click the Save button to save those record changes.

Listing 27.4   Recsave.bas: Saving the Record's Changes

```
Private Sub cmdSave_Click()
  ' Assign all the text boxes to the fields
  ' First you must prepare the DAO for editing
  If blnNewRec Then
    dsBooks.AddNew  ' Prepare to add a record
  Else
    dsBooks.Edit    ' Prepare for editing
  End If

  ' Assign non-null values to fields
  dsBooks!Title = _
    IIf(txtTitle = "", "N/A", txtTitle)
  ' Don't save
  dsBooks![Year Published] = _
    IIf(txtYrPub, txtYrPub, Empty)
  dsBooks!ISBN = _
    IIf(txtISBN = "", "N/A", txtISBN)
  dsBooks!PubID = _
    IIf(txtPubID = "", "N/A", txtPubID)
  dsBooks!Subject = _
    IIf(txtSubject = "", "N/A", txtSubject)
  dsBooks!Description = _
    IIf(txtDescription = "", "N/A", txtDescription)
  dsBooks!Comments = _
    IIf(txtComments = "", "N/A", txtComments)

  ' Make the actual update to dynaset
  dsBooks.Update

  If blnNewRec Then  ' If adding a record
    dsBooks.MoveLast ' Add to end of dynaset
    blnNewRec = False
  End If
End Sub
```

Pt **IV**

Hr **27**

The dynaset's **Edit** method prepares the database for an edit. If another networked user has the record, you won't be able to edit it, and an error will occur. Although this tutorial omits most error-processing code to focus on the current topic, you should add an **On Error Goto** routine to the code to handle such potential problems. This procedure only begins to handle data errors. You probably don't want to write `Null` values back to the database, so the procedure writes either `N/A` (for *not applicable*) or `Empty`, depending on the data type (string or numeric) of the field being updated.

As you can see, programming with DAO isn't a trivial task. You've been working on this example for a while and the functionality—although getting closer to being final—is incomplete. Consider the following issues required to complete the task:

- When writing the Add command button code, you must blank all fields showing on the form and reset the focus to the first field so that users can enter the record.

- The `AddNew` and `Update` methods update the database table with new record additions.

- Use the `MoveLast` method to move the record pointer to the end of the file before you add the new record.

- Be sure to program the Cancel button so that users can click Cancel and not save edits or new record data if they change their mind before clicking Save. The Cancel event procedure needs to call the `DispForm ()` procedure again to return the record to its prior settings.

> **TIP** To really master DAO, consider getting Que Publishing's *Special Edition Using Visual Basic 5*, which explains DAO in detail and completes your study of the subject.

Topic 3: Visual Basic Wizard

The preceding topic section only scratched the surface of DAO, but you now know the fundamental requirements and issues that surround DAO programming. You deserve a break, so this final topic section demonstrates a way that you can let Visual Basic do all the work—writing a database application by responding to a few dialog boxes from the VB Application Wizard.

Overview   The VB Application Wizard lets you add database capabilities to your project without extensive programming. As you'll see when you follow this topic section's example, the resulting code is fairly complete and forms the basis for a true database application.

The New Project dialog box contains the VB Application Wizard that you've used a few times throughout this book. When you get to the dialog box shown in Figure 27.6, you can click the Yes option to add database support to your application.

FIG. 27.6
The VB Application Wizard creates database-based applications.

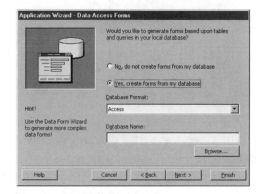

After you select the database option, the rest of the wizard changes dramatically from the dialog boxes that you've seen so far. The next "Example" and "Next Step" sections describe the wizard in more detail.

Pt **IV**

Hr **27**

TIP   Before writing a DAO application, create the initial shell with the VB Application Wizard and modify the application to suit your specific needs. You won't have to write as much code if you start with the wizard's shell.

Example   From the File menu choose New Project, double-click the VB Application Wizard icon, and click Next six times to accept all the VB Application Wizard defaults and to display the dialog box you saw earlier in Figure 27.6. Perform these steps to begin the database-aware application:

1. Click Yes to request that the wizard add a database form to the application. You must now select a database on which the wizard will base the form's fields.

2. Click the Browse button and locate the Biblio.mdb database located in the VB directory. Notice that you can select from a wide variety of database systems by opening the Database Format drop-down list. (For this application, retain the default database, Access.) Click Next to display the Select Tables dialog box (see Figure 27.7).

FIG. 27.7
Visual Basic must know the table you want to access.

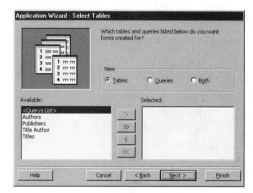

Your application can retrieve data directly from the database tables or from any defined queries. As you might recall from earlier in this lesson, a query is a predefined selection criterion for records and fields. A query is just a named instruction set that produces a subset of the database data. The big advantage of queries over table access is that a query, if predefined by users of the database system that generated the database file, can contain data from multiple database tables. The Biblio.mdb database contains only one query, named All Titles (you can click the Queries option to see the query name).

This dialog box lets you add multiple tables, so you can select data from more than one table even if no query exists, but the query is often more efficient if defined properly. For this application, however, you'll select two tables: Authors and Titles.

3. Click the Authors table and then click the > button to send the table to the Selected list. Now send the Titles table to the Selected list.

4. Click Next and Finish to finish the wizard and create the project.

The wizard generates a substantial amount of database code for you and designs forms that make the two tables available to the application. When you run the application, choose Authors from the View menu to display the Form window shown in Figure 27.8.

FIG. 27.8
The wizard created the form that updates the Authors table.

From the View menu, choose Titles to open the Titles dialog box. Perhaps the most surprising feature of the application appears when you click Grid. Visual Basic formats the table's data into the worksheet-like format shown in Figure 27.9. You can resize columns, sort on columns (by clicking a column title), and scroll through the grid to view multiple records at one time. The grid comes from the DBGrid control that the wizard added to the application's Toolbox window during the project's creation.

FIG. 27.9
The grid shows more information at one time.

Pt **IV**

Hr **27**

Next Step   Visual Basic contains a special Data Form Wizard that lets you design advanced forms that you can insert into your applications. These forms offer unique DAO and *RDO* (*Remote Data Objects* that might appear on a network) capabilities that you can select by answering the wizard's dialog box questions. The Data Form Wizard is an add-in program that you have to set up before you can use it. (You must also have the Professional or Enterprise VB editions before you can add the Data Form Wizard.)

Perform these steps to add the Data Form Wizard to your Add-Ins menu:

1. From the Add-Ins menu, choose Add-In Manager to display the list of add-ins you can add to your Visual Basic development environment.

2. Select the Data Form Wizard and click OK. When you open the Add-Ins menu again, the Data Form Wizard appears on the menu.

3. From the Add-Ins menu choose Data Form Wizard to start the wizard. After reading the opening dialog box, click Next to select a database type. You'll connect the Microsoft Access Biblio.mdb database to the wizard, so keep Access selected and click Next again.

4. Select the Biblio.mdb database and click Next to display the Form dialog box in Figure 27.10. The three options determine the style of the form you want the wizard to generate.

FIG. 27.10
Select the kind of form you want the wizard to create from the data.

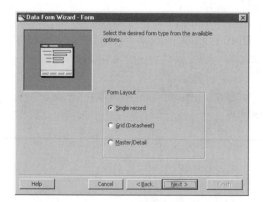

The Single Record style displays records one form at a time and is most useful for adding new records to the database from the application. Grid (Datasheet) presents the grid view (called the *datasheet view*) of the data in a worksheet format like you saw in Figure 27.9. The Master/Detail view provides an interesting combination for the data display. As you click each option, the dialog box updates its icon to show you what the resulting form will look like.

5. Select Master/Detail and click Next. The next dialog box determines which table and fields you want to see in the resulting application's form. Select the Publishers table and then move the following fields to the Selected Fields list: PubID, Company Name, and State.

You've entered the Master section of the form, and you must now click <u>N</u>ext to move to the next dialog box and enter the Detail section of the form. The Master section will show one selected record, and the Detail section will list the multiple records beneath the Master record.

6. Select the Titles table for the Detail section. A title list will appear beneath the publisher shown in the upper half of the form. Send these fields to the <u>S</u>elected Fields list: Title, Year Published, ISBN, and PubID.

7. Select the Titles field in the <u>C</u>olumn to Sort By list box. The form will display the titles in alphabetical order by title and not in the table's actual order, which may be different. Click <u>N</u>ext to move to the next dialog box.

8. The Record Source Relation dialog box lets you connect the Master section to the Details section by selecting a common field. Click the PubID field in each column, and then click <u>F</u>inish to complete the wizard and generate the project.

The Data Form Wizard generates only the form, not a complete project. Therefore, you can add the form to whatever project needs the form. To try the form, choose Prope<u>r</u>ties from the <u>P</u>roject menu and change <u>S</u>tartup Object to `frmTitles`. When you run the application, you'll see the resulting Master/Detail form. As you click through the records, publishers with multiple titles in the database will appear as shown in Figure 27.11. Although you normally wouldn't show the PubID field (because the field will contain the same value for each record), you can see now how the PubID field connects the Master record to the Detail record.

Pt **IV**

Hr **27**

FIG. 27.11
The Master and Detail record are synchronized.

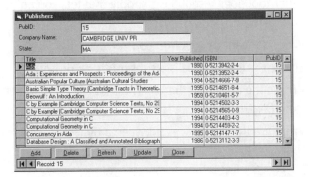

After designing the form, you can save it and add it to future projects that need access to the data.

Summary

This lesson walked you through the ins and outs of database access with Visual Basic. The simplest way to access a database (assuming that you don't use a wizard) is to add the Data control to your form. The Data control takes care of updating the underlying database and changing the bound controls as you move between records.

The DAO VB interface requires extensive programming, but you get much more control and flexibility over your database access. Your application must update controls and move between records as users trigger these events, but you gain much faster database applications.

After you create database forms with the Data Form Wizard, your applications immediately take on a professional form appearance. The forms that the wizard creates will take care of all the tedious updating and maneuvering between records in the underlying tables.

In Hour 28, "Using Keyboard and Mouse I/O," you'll learn how your applications can take control of the keyboard and the mouse.

Hour 27 Quiz

You can find the answers for the following questions on the accompanying CD-ROM and on the Virtual Classroom Web site.

On the CD

1. What tool does Visual Basic supply that lets you edit and look at database files?

2. What is meant by a *bound control*?

3. **True or false:** A table is a subset of a recordset.

4. What's the difference between the `Set` statement and the assignment statement?

5. What are the differences between a dynaset, a recordset, and a snapshot?

6. Name two advantages of DAO over a Data control.

7. Unlike variable names, a database field name can contain spaces. How do you specify field names inside DAO statements that include spaces in their names?

8. What do the EOF and BOF values determine?

9. What must you do to your development environment before using the Data Form Wizard?

10. What's the difference between a Master view and the Detail view in a data form?

Hour 27 Homework Exercises

1. Change the example program from Topic 1 to show three additional fields from the Titles table in the Biblio.mdb database. Make sure that all fields change when users change the position of the Data control. You can load the example from this book's CD-ROM if you didn't enter the code during this lesson.

2. Add error correction to Topic 2's example DAO database access.

3. Create a Master/Detail database form from the Biblio.mdb database that presents author information in the Master view and the author's books in the Detail view.

Pt **IV**

Hr **27**

Using Keyboard and Mouse I/O

THIS LESSON EXPLAINS how to use the keyboard and mouse to exercise more user interface control. Although the controls you've seen provide for excellent I/O, your programs may need to respond to the keyboard differently from the ways you've seen so far. For example, you may want to know whether users have pressed a key, even if no keyboard-based control (such as a text box) now has the focus. You can determine exactly when users press a key and even when users release that key.

After you master the mouse, you'll not only be able to respond to mouse movements and clicks, you'll also be able to support drag-and-drop operations. Surprisingly, no mouse control exists. The mouse (as with the keyboard's keystrokes) generates events that your procedures can test for and respond to.

Topic 1: Programming the Keyboard

Keyboard events let your applications monitor the keyboard's input. After your application receives keyboard input, the application can then modify the input or ignore the pressed key if it isn't an expected keystroke. Keystroke testing is useful for triggering a splash screen's closing, validating input, and even playing some types of games.

Overview Mastering the keyboard requires that you master the following events:

- KeyPress
- KeyDown
- KeyUp

In addition to these events, the Form control's `KeyPreview` property determines the way your application responds to keystrokes. This topic section explains how to use these events and the `KeyPreview` property to manage the user's keyboard.

▼ NOTE
Users can combine certain keys, such as Alt, Shift, and Ctrl, with mouse clicks. This lesson's second topic explains how to check for these keystrokes if they happen at the same time as a mouse event. ▲

The *KeyPress* Event

The `KeyPress` event occurs when users press any key that corresponds with one of these characters:

- Uppercase and lowercase letters
- Numeric digits
- Punctuation
- Enter, Tab, and Backspace

When describing the `KeyPress` event, most programmers say that `KeyPress` tests for ASCII characters (those characters that appear in Appendix B's ASCII table). As you can see, `KeyPress` doesn't test for *all* ASCII characters (such as the horizontal tab or the arrow keys), but it certainly does test for most of them. Use `KeyPress` to determine exactly which key users pressed. For example, `KeyPress` will return a letter A if users press that key.

▼ **NOTE**

The `KeyPress` event occurs on the downstroke and will repeat as the keyboard auto-repeats characters. ▲

An event, as you know, is always associated with an object, such as a command button or the form. The `KeyPress` event always associates with whatever object now has the focus when users press the key. If no object has the focus, the `KeyPress` event associates with the form. (An exception can occur, depending on the `KeyPreview` property explained at the end of this topic section.)

CAUTION Don't use a keystroke event to test for a menu shortcut key. The Menu Editor supports shortcut keys for you and sets up the response automatically by triggering the menu item's `Click()` event procedure. If you test for keystroke events, your program won't be able to respond to menu selections.

The `KeyPress` event procedure always contains an integer argument. Therefore, if you were to write a `KeyPress` event for a Text Box control, the event procedure might begin and end like this:

```
Private Sub Text1_KeyPress (KeyAscii As Integer)
   '
   ' Code goes here to test and respond to keystroke
   '
End Sub
```

The `KeyAscii` argument is an integer that represents the ASCII code of the character the user pressed. You can use `If` or a `Select Case` statement to see whether the character is an expected keystroke.

One of the most important tasks you can perform with `KeyPress` is to *change* users' keystrokes. The `KeyPress` event occurs as soon as users press the key and *before* a control gets the keystroke. Normally, for example, a Text Box control immediately displays whatever key users pressed when the Text Box control has the focus. If, however, you write a `KeyPress` event procedure for a text box control, the `KeyPress` event procedure can change the key, as is done in the following code:

```
Private Sub txtTryIt_KeyPress(KeyAscii As Integer)
  ' Change any uppercase A to an uppercase B
  If KeyAscii = 65 Then   ' 65 is ASCII for A
    KeyAscii = 66         ' 66 is ASCII for B
  End If
End Sub
```

If the text box named `txtTryIt` has the focus, the text box will accept and display any keystroke the user presses *until* the user presses an uppercase A with an ASCII code value of 65. The `If` statement changes the keystroke's `KeyAscii` value to a letter `B` (ASCII 66), and the Text Box control shows the `B` and not the `A` because the `KeyPress` event gets the keystroke before the text box gets the `KeyAscii` value.

TIP   Search VB's online help for *Key Code Constants*. The online help displays named literals that you can use in keyboard testing. For example, you can test for a Backspace press by checking `KeyAscii` for `vbKeyBack`, test for an Enter press by checking for `vbKeyReturn`, and test for Tab press by checking for `vbKeyTab`. (Remember that `KeyPress` tests for only these three controls, in addition to letters, numbers, and punctuation.) Although the text box will respect the other keystroke controls (such as Home and End), `KeyPress` reliably responds only to Enter, Tab, and Backspace.

The *KeyDown* and *KeyUp* Events

Whereas `KeyPress` tests for a wide range of keystrokes, the `KeyDown` event is more specific. `KeyDown` occurs when users press a key down just as `KeyPress` does, but `KeyDown` gives you a more detailed—albeit slightly more complicated—status of your keyboard. For example, `KeyPress` returns a different ASCII value for the uppercase T and the lowercase t keypresses. `KeyDown` returns the *same* value, as well as another value called the *state* argument that describes the state of the Shift key.

▼ NOTE
The `KeyDown` event occurs whenever users press a key. Therefore, both the `KeyDown` and `KeyPress` events can occur at the same time (assuming that users press an ASCII key). ▲

TIP   Use `KeyPress` if you want to test for an ASCII keystroke, because `KeyPress` is simpler to program than `KeyDown`.

Here are the opening and closing statements of a **KeyDown** event procedure:

```
Private Sub txtTryIt_KeyDown(KeyCode As Integer,
➥Shift As Integer)
    '
    '  Keyboard code handler goes here
    '
End Sub
```

KeyCode contains the keystroke, and the **Shift** argument determines the
state of the control keys such as Shift, Ctrl, and Alt. The **KeyCode** matches
the *uppercase* equivalent of the key pressed. Therefore, if users press a lowercase t, the **KeyCode** argument contains 84 (the ASCII value for an uppercase T).

CAUTION KeyDown's ignorance of the lowercase keys can cause confusion if
you're not careful. If you receive a number keypress, you *must* check the **Shift**
argument. If **Shift** indicates that users pressed Shift at the same time as the
number, users actually wanted the corresponding character above the number
(such as the caret, ^, above the 6).

The primary advantage of **KeyDown** over **KeyPress** is that, despite
KeyDown's Shift problems, you can check for virtually *any* keystroke, including the arrow keys, Home, End, and so on. Again, check online help for the
key-code constants that VB uses to test these special keystrokes.

The *shift state* is the key—either Shift, Ctrl, Alt, or none—that users press
with the other key. The internal binary pattern of the shift argument determines the kind of shift state. To check the shift state, you must perform an
And against a number 7. (This special kind of **And** is called a *bitwise And*, as
opposed to the more common logical **And** that works as a compound comparison operator.) The code in Listing 28.1 is the shell that performs the
common shift state test.

Pt **IV**

Hr **28**

Listing 28.1 Code That Tests for the Shift State

```
Private Sub Text1_KeyDown(KeyCode As Integer, Shift As Integer)
  Dim intShiftState As Integer
  intShiftState = Shift And 7  ' Special bitwise And
```

continues

Listing 28.1 Continued

```
Select Case intShiftState
  Case 1
    ' Code for Shift combinations
  Case 2
    ' Code for Ctrl combinations
  Case 3
    ' Code for Alt combinations
  Case 4
    ' Code for Shift+Ctrl combinations
  Case 5
    ' Code for Shift+Alt combinations
  Case 6
    ' Code for Ctrl+Alt combinations
  Case 7
    ' Code for Shift+Ctrl+Alt combinations
  End Select
End Sub
```

The KeyUp event occurs whenever users release a pressed key. You can test for the specific key released (such as the A if users release half of a Shift+A keystroke) by analyzing the argument passed to KeyUp(). Therefore, KeyUp occurs after both KeyDown and KeyPress events.

Using *SendKeys*

The SendKeys statement sends keystrokes to your application as though users were typing those keystrokes. SendKeys is useful for controlling the placement of the text cursor because you can send keystrokes such as the Home and End keys to position the text cursor in a text box or other data-entry control. Here is the syntax of SendKeys:

```
SendKeys strKeystrokes[, blnWait]
```

strKeystrokes is often a string literal, such as "Widgets, Inc.", if you want to type the value for users. The Boolean *blnWait* option is usually omitted and, if False (the default if you omit *blnWait*), control returns to the executing procedure as soon as the keystrokes are sent. If *blnWait* is True, the system processes the keystrokes before the code continues, meaning that the keystroke events are active during the keystroke entry.

You must enclose the following special characters inside braces ({}) if you send them with SendKeys: caret (^), plus sign (+), percent sign (%), tilde

(~), and parentheses. Therefore, to simulate typing **7 + 6**, the `SendKeys` statement must embed the plus sign in braces, like this:

```
SendKeys "7 {+} 6"
```

Several special keystroke characters, such as the Home and function keys, require a `SendKeys` code and the braces. For example, to send the Home keypress to an application, you must use the `{Home}` literal as follows:

```
SendKeys "{Home}"
```

All these special keys have code equivalents you can use. You can look up `SendKeys` in online help to learn which keystroke codes are defined for the special keys.

▼ **NOTE**
You can't send the Print Screen keystroke to an application with SendKeys. ▲

Form or Control Response

When users press a key, either the form or the control with the active focus gets the keystroke. If no control currently has the focus, the form gets the keystroke event. If, however, a control has the focus, either the control or the form gets the focus, depending on the result of the form's `KeyPreview` property.

If the form's `KeyPreview` property is `True`, the form receives the keystroke event. Therefore, if you had coded two event procedures named `frmAcct_KeyDown()` and `txtEntry_KeyDown()`, and if the form's `KeyPreview` property contains `True`, the `frmAcct_KeyDown()` event procedure executes when users press a key. If the form's `KeyPreview` property contains `False`, the `txtEntry_KeyDown()` control executes (assuming that the text box has the current focus).

Pt **IV**

Hr **28**

Example The following code shows an event procedure for a text box. The code converts any lowercase letters the user types into the Text Box control to uppercase:

```
Private Sub txtTry_KeyPress(KeyAscii As Integer)
   ' Convert any lowercase letters to uppercase
   If (KeyAscii >= 97) And (KeyAscii <= 122) Then
```

```
            KeyAscii = KeyAscii - 32    ' Adjust to upper
         End If
      End Sub
```

The ASCII value range for lowercase letters, as you can verify from Appendix B, is 97 (for a) to 122 (for z). The ASCII value difference between the uppercase letters and their lowercase counterparts is 32. Therefore, if the KeyPress event procedure successfully gets a lowercase letter ASCII value, the procedure subtracts 32 from the value to convert the value to its uppercase equivalent.

▼ NOTE

Don't use the keyboard events to write your own masked edit routine if you use the Professional or Enterprise Edition of VB. Both editions let you add the Microsoft Masked Edit Controls 5.0 to the Toolbox, and the Masked Edit control lets you set up input fields, such as phone numbers with area codes and automatic parentheses and hyphens. ▲

Next Step Hour 26, "Using Form Templates," described the Options dialog box form template that contained the code shown here in Listing 28.2.

Listing 28.2 Formtemp.bas: Handling Options Dialog Box Selections

```
Private Sub Form_KeyDown(KeyCode As Integer, Shift As Integer)
  Dim i As Integer
  'handle ctrl+tab to move to the next tab
  If Shift = vbCtrlMask And KeyCode = vbKeyTab Then
      i = tbsOptions.SelectedItem.Index
      If i = tbsOptions.Tabs.Count Then
          'last tab so we need to wrap to tab 1
          Set tbsOptions.SelectedItem = tbsOptions.Tabs(1)
      Else
          'increment the tab
          Set tbsOptions.SelectedItem = tbsOptions.Tabs(i + 1)
      End If
  End If
End Sub
```

You can now understand this complete event procedure, whereas you really didn't possess all the tools before now. The code's purpose is to move the focus between tabbed pages in the Options dialog box. As users press Ctrl+Tab, the next tabbed page is to display and the previously displayed page is to disappear behind the new one. The `If` statement shows an interesting way to check for Ctrl+Tab. If users haven't pressed the Ctrl+Tab combination, nothing executes and the event procedure ends.

Topic 2: Mouse Events

Controlling the mouse is one fundamental task that Windows applications must be able to do. A number of events can result from user interaction with the mouse. By mastering the mouse events, you'll be able to sense the user's mouse movement, clicks, and double-clicks. Also, you'll be ready to master drag and drop.

Overview This topic section teaches you how to monitor the mouse movements and button clicks. Before responding to the mouse, you may want to change the mouse pointer to reflect the current activity. For example, you might change the mouse pointer to an hourglass shape during a long update or disk read. Also, you might want to change the mouse pointer to a different shape (such as the international Not symbol, the circle with a slash) if users move an object over a control that doesn't accept the moved object. After you set the mouse pointer, you can monitor the mouse-generated events so that you can respond to various mouse actions.

The Mouse Cursor

Table 28.1 lists the possible mouse pointers that you can set. Almost every control that you place on the form contains a special property called `MousePointer`. The `MousePointer` property can take on any of Table 28.1's values. If you'd like to display an icon graphic in place of one of the predefined mouse pointers in Table 28.1, set the `MouseIcon` property to an icon file and then set the `MousePointer` property to `99 - Custom`.

Pt **IV**

Hr **28**

Table 28.1 Mouse Pointer Named Literals

Literal	Description
VbArrow	Regular mouse-pointer arrow
VbCrosshair	Crosshair

continues

Table 28.1 Continued

Literal	Description
VbIbeam	I-beam
VbIconPointer	Small square within a square
VbSizePointer	Four-pointed arrow pointing up, down, left, and right
VbSizeNESW	Double-arrow pointing northeast and southwest
VbSizeNS	Double-arrow pointing up and down
VbSizeNWSE	Double-arrow pointing northwest and southeast
VbSizeWE	Double-arrow pointing left and right
VbUpArrow	Up arrow
VbHourglass	Hourglass (indicating wait)
VbNoDrop	No drop (the international Not sign)
VbArrowHourglass	Arrow with an hourglass
vbArrowQuestion	Arrow with a question mark
vbSizeAll	Size all for resizing operations
vbCustom	The shape indicated by the **MouseIcon** property

▼ NOTE

You can set these values at runtime by assigning the named literals or at design time by selecting one of the values in a control's MousePointer property. ▲

Mouse Moves and Clicks

You'll use mouse events to check for a mouse movement or click. Windows generates these events and sends them to your program. Although your program might choose to ignore the events, you can place code in any of the events that you want to respond to. Table 28.2 describes each mouse event.

Table 28.2 Windows Generates These Mouse Events

Event	Description
Click	The user clicked a mouse button.
DblClick	The user double-clicked a mouse button.

Event	Description
MouseDown	The user pressed and held a mouse button.
MouseMove	The user moved the mouse.
MouseUp	The user released the mouse button.

All the mouse events associate with controls. You'll find the mouse events listed for almost every control, as well as for forms. For example, if you wanted to test for a mouse button click event on your form that's named `frmTest`, the event procedure would be named `frmTest_MouseDown()`.

When users double-click a mouse button, the `DblClick` and `MouseUp` events occur. (Windows doesn't trigger a `MouseDown` event if users double-click the mouse.)

The `MouseDown`, `MouseMove`, and `MouseUp` event procedures always require these four arguments:

- `Button`   Describes the button pressed: 1 for the left button, 2 for the right button, or 4 for both buttons (or for a center button if you have a 3-button mouse).
- `Shift`   Describes the shift state and works the same way as the first topic section explained. Use the `Shift` argument to determine which shift key (Alt, Ctrl, or Shift) users pressed while moving or clicking the mouse.
- `x`   The horizontal twip value where users clicked or moved the mouse.
- `y`   The vertical twip value where users clicked or moved the mouse.

Visual Basic generates a movement event after users move the mouse every 10 to 15 twips. Although 15 twips is an extremely small portion of the window, VB doesn't get a mouse movement event for each twip movement.

Pt **IV**

Hr **28**

Example   Suppose that you want the mouse pointer to change to a happy face when users move it over a command button named `cmdHappy`. From the `cmdHappy` Properties window, you would click the ellipsis to select an icon file from the \VB\Graphics\Icons\Misc directory. Select the file named Face03.ico.

Now that you've displayed the mouse icon, change cmdHappy's MousePointer property to 99 – Custom. The customized value tells VB to check the MouseIcon property for the file to display if users move the mouse over the command button. Figure 28.1 shows the resulting happy mouse pointer.

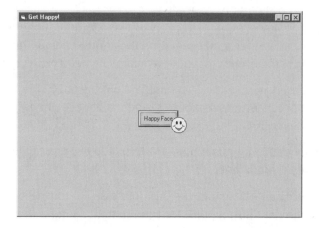

FIG. 28.1
The mouse pointer now looks happy.

Next Step

Create a new project and then place an Image control named imgMouse on the form. Set the value of the image's Picture property to the bull's-eye icon, which can be found in the \VB\Graphics\Icons\Misc directory. Move the image to the upper-center portion of the Form window.

On the CD

Add to the form a text box named txtMouse that lets a message be written on-screen. Adjust the text box to look something like Figure 28.2's Form window. Blank the text box's Caption and add the code shown in Listing 28.3.

Listing 28.3 Caption.bas: Testing for Various Mouse Events

```
Private Sub Form_Click()
  txtMouse.Text = "You clicked the form"
End Sub

Private Sub Form_DblClick()
  txtMouse.Text = "You double-clicked the form"
End Sub
```

```
Private Sub Form_MouseDown(Button As Integer, Shift As Integer,
➥X As Single, Y As Single)
  ' Clicked over the form
  txtMouse.Text = "Clicked over the form at " & X & ", " & Y
End Sub

Private Sub Form_MouseMove(Button As Integer, Shift As Integer,
➥X As Single, Y As Single)
  txtMouse.Text = "Moving the mouse..."
End Sub

Private Sub imgMouse_Click()
  txtMouse.Text = "You clicked the image"
End Sub

Private Sub imgMouse_DblClick()
  txtMouse.Text = "You double-clicked the image"
End Sub

Private Sub imgMouse_MouseDown(Button As Integer,
➥Shift As Integer, X As Single, Y As Single)
  ' Clicked over the image
  txtMouse.Text = "Clicked over the image at " & X & ", " & Y
End Sub

Private Sub imgMouse_MouseMove(Button As Integer,
➥Shift As Integer, X As Single, Y As Single)
  txtMouse.Text = "You moved over the image"
End Sub
```

FIG. 28.2
*Users will click
this image.*

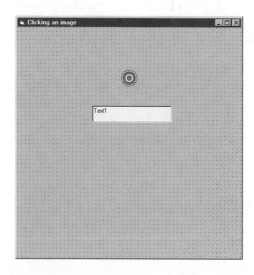

The code tests for the various mouse-based event procedures and changes the text box according to user actions. If the `MouseDown` event doesn't seem to occur, click and hold your mouse button to read the `MouseDown` description. As you click, the x- and y-coordinates describe the mouse's twip location at the time of the click.

Topic 3: Dragging and Dropping

Now that you've mastered the standard mouse events, you're ready to master dragging and dropping. One of the most important features you can add to a visual graphics-based program is drag-and-drop support. Visual Basic makes drag-and-drop support extremely simple to implement.

Overview *Drag-and-drop* is the process of the user clicking an object on-screen, holding down the mouse button, and dragging that object to another location on-screen. Visual Basic gives you the choice of automatic drag-and-drop or manual drag-and-drop; the method you select depends on the needs your application has at the time.

Automatic Drag-and-Drop

Almost every control in the Toolbox contains the property named `DragMode`. This property lets users move the control with the mouse. When users move the control, Visual Basic displays an outline of the control. Your job is to move the control to the place where users release the mouse button. Although the automatic mode shows the moving control's outline, the automatic mode doesn't actually move the object.

The form's `DragDrop` event controls the placement of the drop. To set up the drag, you only need to change the control's `DragMode` property to `1 - Automatic`. The control then can allow the drag and show the moving outline. The `Form_DragDrop()` event procedure takes care of the second half of the drag-and-drop operation by placing the dragged control in its new location.

Completing the Drag

Although the control's dragged outline appears as users move the mouse, you can change the outline to any icon file (such as the icon files in the

\VB\Graphics\Icons directory). When you drag the control, the icon replaces the mouse pointer during the drag.

After users complete the drag, you should code the following `Form_DragDrop()` procedure to take care of moving the object to its final location. The `DragDrop` event takes care of removing the first location and moving to the placed location. Here's the code that performs the placement:

```
Private Sub Form_DragDrop(Source As Control, X As Single,
➡Y As Single)
  Source.Move X, Y
End Sub
```

> **TIP** The `DragOver` event procedure occurs when the user drags one control over another. `DragOver` receives four arguments:
>
> - The control
> - The mouse pointer's x-coordinate
> - The mouse pointer's y-coordinate
> - The state of the drag that takes on one of three possible values: 0 when the drag first covers the object, 1 when the drag leaves the object, and 2 when the control is being dragged through the object

Manual Drag-and-Drop

Manual drag-and-drop works just like automatic, except for these three differences:

- You must set the `DragMode` property to `0 – Manual`.
- Manual drag-and-drop lets the control respond to a `MouseDown` event before beginning the drag, so you can record the control's original location coordinates.
- You must add code to `MouseDown`'s event procedure to invoke the drag.

Pt **IV**

Hr **28**

The `MouseDown` event procedure can perform the special `Drag` method on the object if you want to continue the drag-and-drop process. The following code drags the image if the image control's `DragMode` property is set to `0 – Manual`:

```
Private Sub imgMouse_MouseDown(Button As Integer,
➥Shift As Integer, X As Single, Y As Single)
   ' Clicked over the image
   txtMouse.Text = "Clicked over the image at " & X & ", " & Y
   imgMouse.Drag
End Sub
```

The `Drag` method turns on drag-and-drop. Without the `Drag` method, the `MouseDown()` event procedure couldn't initiate the drag-and-drop operation. Use manual drag-and-drop operations if you want to perform processing and drag-and-drop limitations before and during the drag-and-drop process.

Example   Open the project you created in the second topic section. This example modifies the project somewhat to let you drag the bull's-eye icon around the form and drop the icon somewhere else.

Perform these steps to add drag-and-drop capabilities to the project:

1. Change the image's `DragIcon` property by clicking the ellipsis and selecting the Clock02 icon from \VB\Graphics\Icons\Misc. The bull's-eye image will turn into a clock during subsequent drag-and-drop activities.

2. Change the image's `DragMode` to `1 – Automatic` so that VB takes care of the dragging details for you.

3. Open the Code window and add the following event procedure to the form's event procedures:

```
Private Sub Form_DragDrop(Source As Control, X As Single,
➥Y As Single)
   Source.Move X, Y  ' Drop the image
End Sub
```

The `DragDrop` event's `Source` argument is the control you're dropping onto the form, and the `X` and `Y` coordinate values tell the control where the drop is occurring. The `Move` method actually moves the control (the image in this case) to the location of the drop.

4. Run the application and drag and drop the bull's-eye image around the form. When performing most drag-and-drop operations, you'll want to use automatic drag and drop so that VB handles the details of the drag.

Next Step You can see how easy it is to implement manual drag-and-drop by following these steps to turn the previous example into a manually controlled (via code) drag-and-drop application:

1. Change the image's `DragDrop` property to `0 - Manual`.

2. You must now initiate the dragging when users click over the image. Change the image's `MouseDown` event procedure to the following code:

```
Private Sub imgMouse_MouseDown(Button As Integer,
➥Shift As Integer, X As Single, Y As Single)
  ' Clicked over the image
  txtMouse.Text = "Clicked over the image at " & X & ", " & Y
  imgMouse.Drag      ' Initiate the drag and drop
End Sub
```

The only new statement is the `imgMouse.Drag` statement. Your `MouseDown` event must initiate the drag-and-drop operation. The advantage is that you can now perform other kinds of processing in response to the `MouseDown` click, if needed, before starting the drag-and-drop operation. Without the manual drag mode, the drag would take place outside your control.

3. Run the application. You'll be able to drag-and-drop the image as easily as you did in the previous example.

Summary

Because of this lesson, you can now analyze the keyboard and respond to keyboard events that don't associate with a specific control's events. Therefore, you can decide exactly which keystrokes to allow or ignore when users enter text in a Text Box control. The keyboard events also let you respond to immediate keystrokes.

Pt **IV**

Hr **28**

Controlling a mouse is simple due to the mouse-related events that VB supports. The mouse events are relatively simple because you can perform only four basic tasks with a mouse: click, double-click, multi-button click, and move. The mouse events inform your code, with appropriate arguments, of the mouse pointer's location.

This lesson's final topic section explained how to implement drag-and-drop. VB's automatic drag-and-drop mode is the easiest kind of drag-and-drop to implement, although you can manually control drag-and-drop if you need more control over the operation.

In Hour 29, "Building a Help Subsystem," you'll learn how to add help files to your application so that your users can request assistance when needed.

Hour 28 Quiz

You can find the answers for the following questions on the accompanying CD-ROM and on the Virtual Classroom Web site.

On the CD

1. What's the difference between the `KeyPress` and `KeyDown` events?
2. Describe how the ASCII table is invaluable for keyboard interpretation.
3. **True or false:** The `KeyDown` event occurs before a text box control can display users' text as they type text.
4. What's the difference between `KeyPress` and `KeyPreview`?
5. Which mouse events respond to specific mouse buttons? Which mouse events respond to *either* mouse button?
6. How can you determine the button clicked when a `MouseDown` event occurs?
7. How do you program the outline that appears for some drag-and-drop operations?
8. How can you change the icon that appears during a drag operation?
9. What happens when users drag one control over another?
10. Name two differences between an automatic drag-and-drop operation and a manual drag-and-drop operation.

Hour 28 Homework Exercises

1. Write the code that changes all uppercase letters to lowercase letters as users type text in a Text Box control.
2. Add a splash screen (such as a form with the message *Press any key...*) to the application you wrote in exercise 1. Keep the splash screen on-screen until users press any key on the keyboard.

3. Play musical mouse! Write a simple application that plays a wave file when users click anywhere on the form and stops playing the file as soon as users release the mouse button.

4. Write a drag-and-drop application that drags a letter into an envelope (let the envelope seal on its own). Use the icons in \VB\Graphics\Icons.

Building a Help Subsystem

During this hour you will learn

▶ *Where to create help files*

▶ *How to add hypertext jumps*

▶ *Where to compile help files*

▶ *How to add context-sensitive help*

▶ *When ToolTips and What's This help helps*

THIS LESSON EXPLAINS HOW to help your users. By the time you finish this lesson, you'll know how to add a help system to your applications so that your users can read online documentation to help them better understand your application. The online help system that you can use with Visual Basic is nice because it mimics the online help found in virtually all other Windows programs. Therefore, your users won't have a startup learning curve ahead of them when learning how to use your application's online help system.

In addition to the standard online help, this lesson teaches you how to add help in other ways. You've already seen how to add ToolTips to toolbars (in Hour 23, "Enhancing Your Program"), but this lesson explains how to add ToolTip help to all your applications' controls. You can also add the all-important What's This help to your application forms.

▶▶ **FAST TRACK**

Do you want to forego learning about creating a help system and go straight to an application's design? Check out Hour 33, "Developing and Designing Forms" (p. 735).

Topic 1: Online Help

Although writing an online help system might be a daunting task, you can borrow the Windows help system for your applications. All you really have to do is write the text that becomes the help text and then use the Windows help system to display that help text at the right time and place. Your users won't have a learning curve because they already know how to use the Windows help system.

> **TIP** Don't wait until your application is completely finished before designing the online help system. The best time to write the help text is when you design and create the application. At design time, you have a better working knowledge of the application than at any subsequent time, and you'll be better equipped to write the kind of help your users need.

Overview This topic section explains how to build and link the help topic file to your application. Not only must you write the help topic file, you must also build a help project that you then compile into a help system that links to the application. The text that goes in your help topic file must be in the special RTF (Rich Text Format) format, which the application can use to embed hypertext jumps from topic to topic when appropriate.

▼ **NOTE**

You must have access to a word processor or text editor that creates RTF files. Microsoft Word is perhaps the most popular word processor used for help files. ▲

Preparing for the Topic File

When you use Word to create the help file, you should turn on the hidden formatting codes. Although most people write documents without the codes showing, the hypertext jumps require hidden text, which you need to be able to see even though that text will be hidden from all eyes but yours at the word processor keyboard. Click the Show/Hide button (the paragraph symbol) on Word's toolbar to display hidden codes.

Creating Hypertext Jumps

Most of your help file will consist of regular text that describes the help topics. Regular help text requires no special formatting, but you can vary the font size and style as much as you want to. The hypertext jumps require some special formatting, however, so that the help system can recognize hypertext jump keywords and the help system will know where the linked topics reside.

The more you cross-link your help file topics with hypertext jumps, the more useful your help system will be to your users. When you add hypertext jumps, you keep users from having to use a menu to select every topic that might benefit them; rather than use a menu, they can jump directly to the topic they want to read.

The requirements for creating hypertext jumps are as follows:

- Double-underline all hypertext jump phrases. Hypertext jump phrases appear in green text when users see the jump phrases in the help window. You can double-underline in Word by highlighting the word or phrase, choosing Font from the Format menu, and selecting Double from the Underline drop-down list box. You can also press Ctrl+Shift+D to double-underline selected text, as well as customize Word by putting a double-underline icon on the toolbar.

- Follow the hypertext jump phrase with a unique tag called the *context string*, which holds the jump target topic, formatted as hidden text. Don't add a space between the hypertext jump and the context string. Be sure to format only the context string as hidden text and nothing else (not even punctuation or paragraph marks). You can hide text from the Format menu by choosing Font and clicking the Hidden check box. You can also press Ctrl+Shift+H to hide selected text, as well as customize Word by placing a hidden text icon on the toolbar.

- Separate the topic page that contains the hypertext jump from the target jump page with a page break. You can insert a page break from the Insert menu when you choose Break, Page Break (or press Ctrl+Enter).

Pt **IV**

Hr **29**

- Connect the text for the hypertext jump to the jump page with at least one of three custom footnote symbols:

Symbol	Description
#	To connect to the jump page via the context string
$	To place the jump page title in the help system's Locate text box and to connect the hypertext to the jump page's title
K	To connect to a topic search on one or more particular keywords

Many help topics link to their jump pages with all three footnote symbols, because you want users to be able to jump from topic to topic, the topic titles to appear in the help system's Locate text box, and users to find the topic by searching with multiple keywords.

- Display pop-up help descriptions and definitions by underlining the topic to define with a single underline. You can underline text from the F_ormat menu by choosing F_ont and then choosing Single from the U_nderline drop-down list box. You can also press Ctrl+U or click the toolbar's underline button to underline selected text.

Describing the help file is much more involved than showing you an example. Therefore, the Example section appears next, to illustrate the different ways you can set up the hypertext jump and the jump target.

TIP If you use the K footnote symbol to designate a topic search, add as many search topics as you can. As you'll see in the example, K footnotes often contain multiple entries separated by a semicolon. The following footnote entry tells the help system that the help topic should appear in four entries in the help index:

```
KChange Options;Menu commands;Change;Changing text
```

Example This example begins to build a help system for the sample program that comes with Visual Basic called MDI Notepad. The application uses MDI forms to manage a tiny multi-windowed text editor. Although the text editor is fairly complete and extends past the Windows Notepad editor (because MDI Notepad supports multiple windows), the MDI Notepad application supports no online help.

▼ NOTE

This example uses Microsoft Word to create the help file. You might need to use a different word processor depending on the contents of your system. ▲

Figure 29.1 shows a sample opening help screen in Word for the MDI Notepad application. Remember that the double-underlined phrases are the hypertext jump phrases that will appear in green on the user's help system. All hidden text is turned on, so the dotted underline text represents the hidden text that holds the context strings.

FIG. 29.1

MDI Notepad's opening help text screen contains hypertext jumps.

Underlined text —

Double-underlined text —

Hidden text —

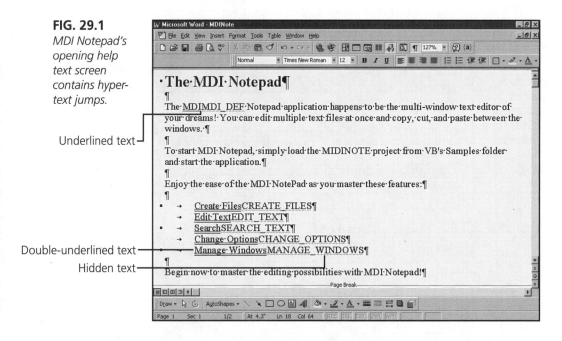

Figure 29.1 shows six jump-phrase context strings: `MDI_DEF`, `CREATE_FILES`, `EDIT_TEXT`, `SEARCH_TEXT`, `CHANGE_OPTIONS`, and `MANAGE_WINDOWS`. Therefore, at least six more Word pages must appear below the opening help screen. You connect these pages to their original hypertext jump links with one or more of the special footnote symbols. The first jump, `MDI_DEF`, will be a pop-up definition box for the term *MDI*.

Pt **IV**

Hr **29**

The entire help file needs a help context ID value so that the underlying application can reference this opening help screen when needed. Figure 29.2 shows two footnotes created for the opening help text. To add a footnote, you would move the text cursor before the first character in the title, choose Footnote from the Insert menu, and type # for the custom symbol that indicates the hypertext jump page location. Repeat these steps to enter the $ footnote for the hypertext jump link's title. The two footnote symbols appear to the left of the opening text as well as next to their respective footnote text in the bottom window. The application can use the help context ID to reference this help screen, and the help engine's search tools can display the title that appears next to the $ footnote symbol.

FIG. 29.2
The entire opening help window now appears when its context ID or title is called for.

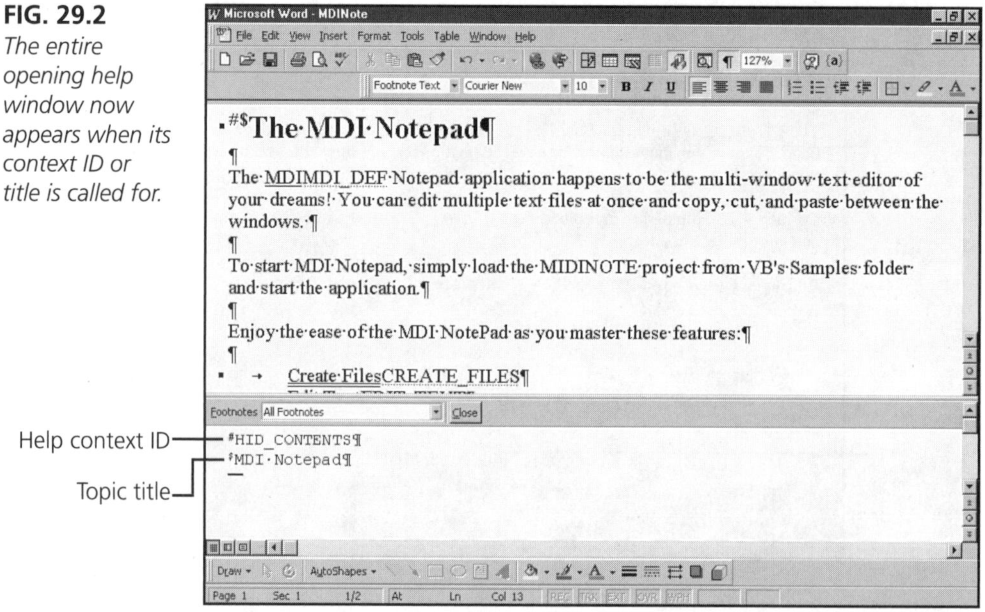

Help context ID ── #HID_CONTENTS¶

Topic title ──┘ $MDI·Notepad¶

CAUTION Don't use the K footnote symbol for the opening help window. Remember that K is reserved for those times when you want a pop-up help box to appear if users click an underlined help topic. Also, you'll use a K footnote with # and $ so that every topic appears on the help dialog box's Index list of topics.

In the next few paragraphs, you'll learn that the RTF document contains a different kind of help context ID than Visual Basic wants to use. As a result, you'll have to map the RTF file's textual context ID values to numeric values before an application can use context-sensitive help.

The remaining help hypertext jumps now need corresponding help pages and footnotes to connect the pages to the opening screen. The first help topic to create is the pop-up definition for MDI. The page below the opening help screen must contain the following information:

- The MDI title on the first line
- A separating blank line
- The definition of MDI

Figure 29.3's footnote completes the connection between this page and the opening page's MDI location by adding a help context ID to the definition. Also, the **K** footnote symbol indicates that the connected page is a pop-up definition and not a hypertext jump.

FIG. 29.3

The definition will now pop up thanks to the **K** *footnote symbol.*

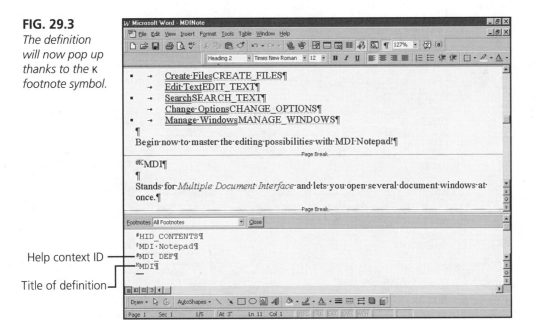

Help context ID

Title of definition

▼ **NOTE**

This lesson's help file typically uses the same help context ID (in uppercase) as the topic title that the context ID links to, but these values don't have to be the same. ▲

Finally, Figure 29.4 shows the first part of the remaining help hypertext jump topics. The # footnote connects the opening page's hyperjump topics to the subsequent jump pages.

FIG. 29.4

Subsequent jump pages are now linked to the opening help page.

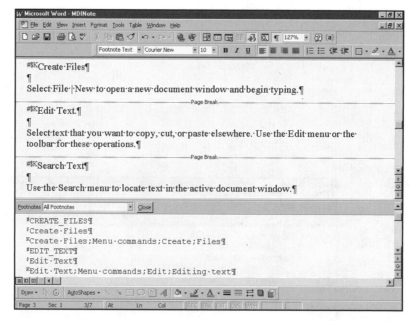

TIP Any of these subtopics can contain additional links to additional pages (and to each other) as well as pop-up help definitions.

As soon as you finish your RTF help file, you must save the document. Be sure to select the Rich Text Format file type when saving the file. Now you must create the help project file by using yet another file type, the ASCII text file type. Word can save ASCII text files, and you can even use the MDI Notepad sample application to create this file. The following project file was used for the help file described here:

```
[OPTIONS]
contents=HID_CONTENTS
title=MDI Notepad Help
```

```
[FILES]
MDINote.rtf
```

The [OPTIONS] section describes the opening help page context ID and the title bar text. The [FILES] section describes the help file being compiled (you might need to specify a path name if the file resides in a special location). Enter the name of the RTF help file you created and saved earlier. You can set other help project file options from within the help compiler.

Save the project file under any file name (the name of the application file is perhaps the best project file name). Use the .HPJ extension, however.

You need to install the help compiler from your Visual Basic installation CD-ROM because the help compiler doesn't install with the normal Visual Basic installation. At this writing, you must install the help system by following these steps:

1. Insert the Visual Basic Installation CD-ROM in your CD-ROM drive.

2. Select the Start menu's Run option.

3. Execute the Setup.exe program, \Tools\HCW, located in VB's CD-ROM folder. Follow the instructions, and the Setup program installs your help compiler on the Start menu's Microsoft Help Workspace option.

Start the Microsoft Help Workshop program and load your help project file when you want to compile the project. After you click the Compile toolbar button and accept all the default values, the compilation will begin. Read the warnings and errors that the compiler might display after the compilation finishes. Often, warnings occur that won't affect your help system, but you should attempt to eliminate all warnings completely to perfect your help file under all conditions. If errors exist, the compiler will be unable to compile the file.

Next Step After you compile the help system, you can run it to test your help entries. You won't learn how to connect the system to the application until the next topic section, but you can follow these steps to test the help file:

1. Start the Windows Explorer.

2. Locate the help file's folder. You'll see the help file in the list of files with a help icon.

3. Right-click the help file and choose Open. The Windows online help system begins, and you can check out your help file.

Figure 29.5 shows the help window that appears with the help system described in this topic section. The first window (which you can return to by clicking the Contents button at any time) displays the opening help page. The Index page, shown in Figure 29.6, shows a complete listing of all κ footnote values that cross-reference help topics.

FIG. 29.5

The opening help window looks good and provides ample help for the program.

Pop-up definition —

Hypertext jump topics —

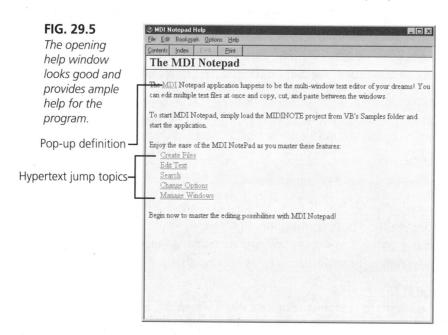

FIG. 29.6

The Index values generated from the κ entries provide an index of topics that users can search.

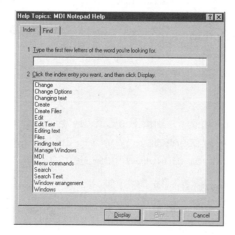

Topic 2: Hooking Up the Help File

After you generate the help file, you need to connect the application to the file. The help context IDs associate the various help topics to controls and parts of the application. Also remember to add a <u>H</u>elp menu option so that users can request help at any time on any subject in the help file.

Overview   The number of help connections varies dramatically from application to application. You can use the depth of the help file as well as the complexity of the application to predict how much help users will need. The rest of this topic section explains some of the ways you can connect the help file to the application. (Visual Basic supports a number of help file connections, but this topic section describes the most common connections.)

The Project Properties Dialog Box

The Project Properties dialog box (see Figure 29.7) is the primary link between your project and the help file. The Project Properties dialog box ensures that the help file connects to the user's F1 keypress.

FIG. 29.7
Connect the help file to your project.

Select a file name ———

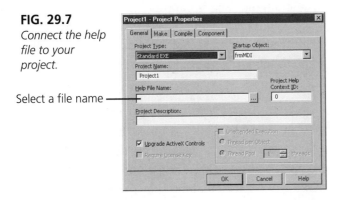

▼ NOTE

You don't need to worry about changing the text box labeled Project Help Context <u>I</u>D. Any help context ID you enter there determines the help that appears when you click this application's Help toolbar button from within the Object Browser. ▲

VB's Help Context ID

Unfortunately, you've taken care of the easiest part of the help system connection: the F1 key that generates the complete help window. If you want to add context-sensitive help to your application so that users can press F1 to see help when a control has the focus or during a menu selection, you must complete a few more steps.

You must trigger the execution of the Windows help engine. You must also tell the help engine exactly which help window page to display when users select context-sensitive help. Starting the help engine requires a special Windows API (for Application Program Interface) function call from a standard module in your project. You then must edit the help file's project file again and map numeric context IDs to your textual context IDs. Here are the basic steps you'll see detailed in the next example:

1. Add a standard code module to the application.

2. Declare the API function. You must declare all API functions inside the application just as you declare variable names. The API function declaration is a long declaration because it must tell your application exactly where the function comes from, how to call it, and what to expect in return. Although the declaration code to start the Windows help engine is messy, you use the identical code in any Visual Basic program that requires context-sensitive help. The declaration will let you use a Help menu to trigger certain help page displays.

3. Edit the help project file and map the textual context IDs to numeric context IDs.

4. Recompile the help file.

5. Select every form and control and menu item in the project to which you want to add context-sensitive help. Change that object's `HelpContextID` to the numeric ID that matches the help page that you want displayed when the user presses F1 and the object has the focus.

6. Add code to the Help menu options to trigger appropriate help pages.

If you fail to add context-sensitive help to all controls, Visual Basic displays the help file's Contents page (the opening help page).

Example   When you want to add context-sensitive help, you must right-click the application's Project window and add a new module file. The file contains only the following API function declaration (you must type it exactly as it appears):

```
Declare Function WinHelp Lib "user32" Alias _
    "WinHelpA" (ByVal hwnd As Long, _
    ByVal lpHelpFile _
    As String, ByVal WCommand As Long,  _
    ByVal dwData As Long) As Long
```

The statement is one continuous statement, and the underscores connect the lines so that Visual Basic views the five lines as a single line of code. The statement allows you to hook up a Help menu system that can display various pages of the help system later.

You now must re-edit the project file and map the textual context IDs to numeric ones. To do so, you'll add a [MAP] section to the project file. Given the MDINote.rtf help file and associated project file described in the last topic section, the following code provides such an edit of the project file.

```
[OPTIONS]
contents=HID_CONTENTS
title=MDI Notepad Help

[FILES]
MDINote.rtf

[MAP]
HID_CONTENTS 1
MDI_DEF 2
CREATE_FILES 3
EDIT_TEXT 4
SEARCH_TEXT 5
CHANGE_OPTIONS 6
MANAGE_WINDOWS 7
```

Make sure that no two context ID numbers are the same. The mapping can begin at 1, but many Visual Basic programmers reserve series of numbers to represent different kinds of help topics. For example, all command button help topics might range from 1000 to 1050. The numbers, therefore, don't have to be sequential. Recompile the project file to embed the new map information in the help file.

Pt **IV**

Hr **29**

Your sleuthing now begins. You must locate every control and form to which you want to add context-sensitive help. For example, in the MDI Notepad application, you could display the `frmFind` form (the form that supports the Find menu option that locates data in the document) and change the <u>F</u>ind command button's `HelpContextID` property to 5. If that were the only change you made, users would always see the standard opening help Contents screen when they run the application and press F1, except when the <u>F</u>ind button has the focus; users would then see the help topic for the Search page. Of course, you would want to add additional context-sensitive help displays to other controls, including some forms, for your user's benefit.

▼ NOTE

As you add the context-sensitive help to controls, you'll likely find other areas of the application that need explanation. Therefore, you might add to your .RTF help file many times before you've provided ample help support to the application. ▲

> **TIP** When you add help pages, try your best to locate every place in the application from which users might need specific help. Every time you add context-sensitive help, your users don't have to search through the help Index or Contents page that otherwise would appear.

Next Step You haven't added a <u>H</u>elp menu to the application yet. You must specifically call the windows help system to add the <u>H</u>elp menu options. If you're following these examples and creating the help file for the sample MDI Notepad application, you can also add a <u>H</u>elp menu item to the primary MDI Notepad form that contains these items: <u>C</u>ontents and <u>I</u>ndex. Assuming that you use the standard menu-naming conventions (described in Hour 5, "Creating Menus for User Ease"), you should add the code in Listing 29.1 to connect those menu items to their appropriate help pages.

On the CD

Listing 29.1 Mnuhelp.bas: Using *WinHelp( )* to Display the Help System

```
Private Sub mnuHelpContents_Click()
  ' You can ignore the return value for now
  Dim varHelpRet As Variant
  varHelpRet = WinHelp(frmNotePad.hwnd, "MDINote.Hlp", cdlHelpContents, CLng(0))
End Sub
```

```
Private Sub mnuHelpIndex_Click ()
  ' You can ignore the return value for now
  Dim varHelpRet As Variant
  varHelpRet = WinHelp(frmNotePad.hwnd, "MDINote.Hlp", 11, CLng(0))
End Sub
```

Although this `WinHelp()` function call code is about as messy as the `WinHelp()` function's declaration code, you can copy and paste this exact code into your menu `Click()` event procedures as long as the second argument is the name of your help file (including a possible path, if needed) and the third argument contains either `cdlHelpContents` or 11 (unfortunately, Visual Basic doesn't provide a named literal for the help index's display), depending on the menu option. (These are named literals that Visual Basic supplies.)

Topic 3: Simple Help: ToolTips and What's This?

As you've seen, the big task of providing online help is creating the help file and project. ToolTips are simple to add to various objects (as you've seen for the toolbar in Hour 23, "Enhancing Your Program"), and the special What's This help relies heavily on your help file. As long as you've created a detailed help file, adding eye-catching What's This help is simple.

Overview You can add ToolTips to a control when you add the control to the form. The Properties window's ToolTips property value holds text that you can enter. When users rest the mouse pointer over any control with the ToolTips property, the ToolTip appears after a brief pause.

In addition to the ToolTips, you can provide What's This help to give users additional information for your applications. What's This lets users see the help text for any object that supports What's This. Figure 29.8 shows one of this lesson's help file pages that appears when users right-click the MDI Notepad's Find button. The What's This help is available whenever a form window contains the What's This question mark button. Users click the What's This button, move the mouse cursor (now a question mark) over any object, and click to see the help that you've set up for that object.

Pt **IV**

Hr **29**

FIG. 29.8

The user can ask, "What's this?"

What's This button

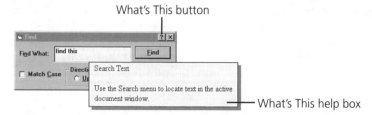

What's This help box

▼ NOTE

Make your What's This help match the objects. Figure 29.8 uses the closest help page available for the <u>F</u>ind button from the pages described in the previous topic sections. This lesson's example doesn't contain enough help pages to describe all the What's This needed for the MDI Notepad, but I wanted to use a page from the examples that you've seen. **▲**

ToolTips

To add ToolTips to any object, you only need to enter the ToolTip text in the object's `ToolTipText` property. Visual Basic does the rest of the work. Look through the MDI Notepad application's controls to see that Microsoft added ToolTips to almost every control on every form. ToolTips are simple to add, and you should get in the habit of adding ToolTip text as you add controls to your applications' Form windows.

What's This Help

You must add a help page for every What's This help feature that you want to support. After you add the pages and connect them to the other help pages in the system through the custom footnotes described earlier in this lesson, you must map the pages to a numeric context ID. The What's This help engine uses those context ID numbers to determine the proper help box to display when users request the What's This help.

The secret to What's This help is twofold:

1. Make sure that the form supports What's This help by setting the form's `WhatsThisButton` property to `True` and by setting the form's `WhatsThisHelp` property to `True`.

2. Enter the help page's context ID in the object's `WhatsThisHelpID` property.

Example The What's This help from the MDI Notepad application (if you've followed the first two topic sections and created a help file with help pages that you can use) requires only that you perform these steps:

1. Open the Project window and double-click the form named `frmFind` to display the Find dialog box's form.

2. Assign `True` to the `WhatsThisButton` and `WhatsThisHelp` properties. When you subsequently display this form when the application executes, you'll see the What's This question mark button on the form.

3. Repeat the assignment for the other two forms in the application.

4. Look through the help project file's `[MAP]` section for context ID numbers and assign these context ID values to various menu options (use the Menu Editor) and form objects that might need the description. Although the help file is far from complete, several of the help pages work well for the objects, especially the menu bar items.

Summary

Several forms of help are available to Visual Basic developers. By using the Windows help engine, you can build a complete hypertext jump system with interconnected help pages and pop-up definitions. Your user can get context-sensitive, access-specific help pages by pressing F1. Although you must include a new module with a special API call to the system help engine, as soon as you include the API call, users receive help at the push of a button.

Adding context-sensitive help allows your users to locate the help they need. You can assign context-sensitive help to various objects so that specific help text appears when users select the object and press F1. The context-sensitive help feature keeps your users from having to search through the index every time they require help.

Two simple help features that you can add quickly are the ToolTips and What's This help elements. ToolTips are extremely simple and require only that you add the ToolTips text in the Properties window. Before you can assign What's This help, you must build a comprehensive help file and assign various numeric context IDs that you can assign to objects.

Pt **IV**

Hr **29**

In the next hour's lesson, you'll learn more about ActiveX controls and how you can implement such controls in your Visual Basic applications.

Hour 29 Quiz

You can find the answers for the following questions on the accompanying CD-ROM and on the Virtual Classroom Web site.

On the CD

1. What file format must you use to create an online help file?
2. How can hypertext jumps improve a help system?
3. Which custom footnote symbol creates pop-up help definitions for underlined help page text?
4. What are some of the features of the help project file?
5. After you compile a help file, how can you attach such a file to an application so that the help file appears when users press F1?
6. How do you connect context-sensitive help to the help file topics?
7. **True or false:** The context-sensitive help uses the textual context IDs in your help file.
8. What's the difference between the What's This help and the ToolTips help?
9. How can you add the What's This button on forms?
10. **True or false:** You can offer What's This help for forms as well as for objects on the form. (*Hint:* Check the form's properties.)

Hour 29 Homework Exercises

1. Create a help file that describes the basic steps for starting an automobile. Connect pages with hypertext jumps and create pop-up definitions for various terms such as *ignition*. Create a help file with at least 10 help pages (including the opening contents page). You can test the help file by right-clicking the compiled file in Windows Explorer and selecting <u>O</u>pen.
2. Add What's This help to every object in MDI Notepad. This task might seen tedious—and it is somewhat—but you'll quickly get the hang of What's This help, context IDs, and help pages.

Enhancing Programs with ActiveX

THIS LESSON EXPLAINS HOW to use ActiveX controls. You may not have realized it, but you've been using ActiveX controls ever since Part I of this tutorial. ActiveX technology is integral to Visual Basic and to almost every other current Microsoft product, especially Microsoft's Internet-related products such as Internet Explorer. An ActiveX control is nothing more than a control like the Common Dialog Box control you used to build dialog boxes in Hour 17.

A general overview of ActiveX is simple because it's a replacement for OLE as well as for the Visual Basic controls you add to your Visual Basic development

environment. If all you did was implement simple OLE as described in Hour 22, "Adding OLE to a Program," and insert new controls you purchase or obtain online with VB's Components dialog box, ActiveX would remain simple. The difficult part of ActiveX appears when you begin tackling the programming behind ActiveX—when you want to create your own controls to add to the development environment, for example.

ActiveX's simple-but-difficult nature prompted two ActiveX lessons in this book. This lesson explains ActiveX in detail and demonstrates uses of ActiveX controls. The next lesson walks you through the somewhat challenging task of creating your own ActiveX control.

▶▶ FAST TRACK

Have you ever tried to create an ActiveX control? Visual Basic 5 makes creating such a control much easier than tools that came before. You learn how to create an ActiveX control in next hour's lesson, "Creating a Simple ActiveX Control" (p. 697).

Topic 1: ActiveX Explained

Before programming ActiveX, you must master ActiveX objects and learn how to use them in programming applications from Visual Basic to end-user applications such as Microsoft Word. ActiveX is today's buzzword in computing, and Microsoft is strongly encouraging the development community to adopt the ActiveX technology.

Overview This topic section explains ActiveX in more detail. This lesson and the next primarily deal with ActiveX from a VB developer's point of view, but this introductory topic section gives you a better ActiveX understanding for users as well as developers.

Benefits

Before getting into the details, here is one of the primary benefits of ActiveX: You can drop (sometimes with drag-and-drop and sometimes by using more procedural methods) ActiveX controls into not only Visual Basic, but also Excel, Access, and many other products. The product doesn't have to be written by Microsoft. ActiveX is an upward-compatible replacement for OLE and OCX controls. Almost every Windows program now supports ActiveX in some way. Although different products support the inclusion of ActiveX differently, the bottom-line reason for using ActiveX is that you can insert ActiveX controls in virtually any program you use.

▼ **NOTE**

A general rule of thumb is that ActiveX controls take the place of Visual Basic controls that used to be known as OCXs (all ActiveX controls retain the OCX file-name extension). The use of ActiveX replaces OLE that used to be the primary source of interobject communication in Windows applications. ▲

CAUTION You can no longer use VBX controls, commonly known as *Visual Basic controls*, inside Visual Basic 5. OCX ActiveX controls completely replace VBX controls because VBXs are 16-bit only, whereas ActiveX controls are exclusively used in 32-bit environments. If you tried to use a VBX, Visual Basic would issue an error message and wouldn't compile your code until you remove the control from the application.

Already, many vendors supply stand-alone ActiveX technology tools. Therefore, as a Visual Basic developer, you can obtain numerous ActiveX controls that you can use immediately in Visual Basic's development environment. After you put the ActiveX control into the Toolbox, the control works just like the intrinsic controls that already appear in the Toolbox. You can set ActiveX properties, respond to ActiveX events, and trigger ActiveX methods.

Today's Internet users benefit dramatically from ActiveX technology if they use an ActiveX-aware Web browser such as Internet Explorer 3 or Netscape Navigator 3 with its ActiveX support plug-in. You can embed ActiveX controls inside Web pages that you create. When other Internet users view your Web page with an ActiveX-aware Web browser, they will see active content instead of a static Web page. Depending on the ActiveX control's capabilities, Web users can interact with the ActiveX control and see results as though the Web page contained a small Visual Basic program in addition to the normal text and graphics.

> **TIP** ActiveX controls are reusable. After you create an ActiveX control in Visual Basic, you can use that control in every other programming platform that also supports ActiveX, such as Visual C++, Visual J++, Borland Delphi, Borland C++, or Java.

The Internet isn't the only reason to use ActiveX, but it's the original reason Microsoft transformed the OLE and OCX technology into ActiveX. OLE controls couldn't function inside a Web page as can ActiveX controls. By tweaking OLE just a bit, ActiveX controls can fully support OLE and OCX technology while extending that technology further.

ActiveX for Java Programmers

If you've never heard of Java (the computer-based Java, not the coffee or the Indonesian island), it's a new technology that activates Web sites. A Java application is an embedded in-place *applet* (a small application) that you insert into a Web page so that users can interact with the Web page and with interactive technology such as multimedia. Of course, that's exactly what the previous section said about ActiveX! ActiveX isn't technically called a replacement for Java applets, but in almost every case, you can replace a Java-based applet with an ActiveX control. What's more, the ActiveX control can be more powerful than the Web-based Java language.

Java programmers can extend their Java Web-based programs with ActiveX controls. In reality, many of today's Java programmers simply write enough Java language to wrap around an ActiveX control. The control remains the focus of the Java applet, even though the ActiveX control may be written in a non-Java language such as Visual Basic or C++.

▼ NOTE
This and next hour's ActiveX lesson won't discuss the Internet much further. Hour 32, "Adding Internet Access to Applications," is devoted entirely to Visual Basic's Internet connection. ▲

Example If you have Internet access, why not browse a few ActiveX-based sites? Point your ActiveX-aware Web browser to Intel's interactive ActiveX site at **http://www.intel.com** (see Figure 30.1). The site contains ActiveX controls that display moving pictures and color-changing icons.

FIG. 30.1
View ActiveX content on Intel's home page.

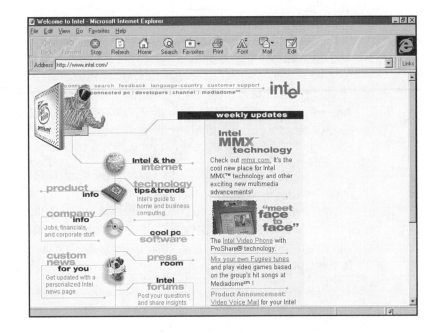

You'll also find some fun ActiveX controls on United Media's Web page at
http://www.unitedmedia.com (see Figure 30.2). The Web site contains
several popular cartoons, and the ActiveX content helps to bring some of
the cartoons to life.

FIG. 30.2
The United Media's site includes several fun ActiveX-based controls.

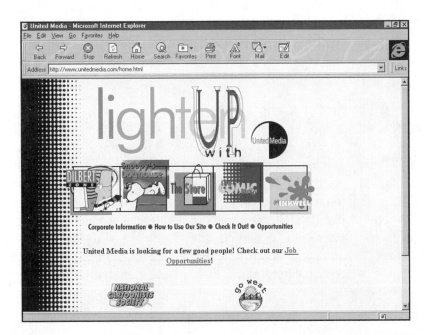

Pt **IV**

Hr **30**

Next Step   Before a Web site can display ActiveX content on your computer, the ActiveX control must download from the site to your Web browser. Therefore, when you connect to a Web page that requires an ActiveX control to view, the Web site checks to see whether your computer has the needed ActiveX control. If your computer doesn't have the control, the Web site sends it to your computer. (Some security measures are in place to ensure that damaging programs don't get on your machine.)

Check out Microsoft's ActiveX site (**http://www.microsoft.com**) for a categorized sample of ActiveX controls that you can download to your computer. When there, the ActiveX control will be in place for subsequent Web sites you visit that require the controls. Microsoft's ActiveX site not only lets you download the controls, but also lets you view the control's features before you download them.

You'll be amazed at some of the things ActiveX controls can do. ActiveX controls act like complete Visual Basic applications in some cases because they can be extremely complex and powerful.

Topic 2: Integrating ActiveX Controls

When you add tools to your Toolbox, those tools are almost always ActiveX controls (for Visual Basic 5). These tools become part of the Toolbox and part of the development environment just like the standard intrinsic controls. After you add the ActiveX control to the Toolbox, you can select and place that control on the Form window just as you place controls such as command buttons.

Overview   ActiveX controls let you extend Visual Basic and even turn VB into a customized programming environment that suits your exact needs. Suppose that you specialize in multimedia programming and use Visual Basic as your development platform to create multimedia applications. Over time, you'll collect multimedia-based ActiveX controls. Although Visual Basic comes with extra multimedia ActiveX controls, other vendors might supply specialized video-coloring controls, video playback tools, and video editing tools. You'll add these tools to your Visual Basic environment, and perhaps eliminate some controls from the Visual Basic directory that you'll rarely, if ever, use.

Be Careful with Older Controls

If you've worked with previous editions of Visual Basic and added several 16-bit VBX controls, the current 32-bit Visual Basic system can't use those controls unless the system comes with 32-bit replacements for those old controls. For example, Visual Basic comes with a 32-bit version of the Gauge control. (16-bit Gauge VBX controls have been around for several versions of Visual Basic.) Therefore, if you load an older VB application that uses the Gauge VBX control, Visual Basic will replace that control with the 32-bit version and things should work fine. If, however, a replacement doesn't exist and the VBX vendor can't supply you with a replacement, you'll have to eliminate that control from the application and substitute a similar one.

Distributing ActiveX Controls

When you distribute your applications to users, you must distribute a runtime copy of the application's ActiveX controls as well. These ActiveX controls go to each user's \Windows\System or \Windows\System32 folders. Therefore, when you create a setup and installation routine for the applications you distribute, you must take into account any external ActiveX controls (those outside the realm of intrinsic controls) your application contains.

▼ **NOTE**
Hour 37, "Packaging Your Application," explains more about setting up an application for distribution and installation. ▲

Example   Although your system may contain several ActiveX controls, Visual Basic doesn't load these controls into its Toolbox window because, by default, only the intrinsic default tools appear there. Also, Visual Basic doesn't automatically locate all ActiveX controls on your system during installation.

Nevertheless, Visual Basic's installation routine does install and locate several ActiveX controls, which you can add to your development environment's Toolbox window. Here's a review of the steps you take when installing ActiveX controls into your Visual Basic's development environment:

1. From the Project menu choose Components to open the Components dialog box (see Figure 30.3).

FIG. 30.3

Add controls to your Toolbox from the Components dialog box.

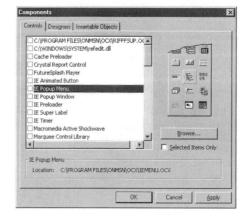

2. Click the check box next to each ActiveX control you want to add to your project.

3. Click OK to close the dialog box. The Toolbox now contains the new controls.

Some ActiveX control groups that you select—such as Microsoft Payment and Address Selector, available with the Professional Edition—contain more than one tool, so multiple tools may appear on the Toolbox after you select just a single ActiveX control title.

TIP The ActiveX control's path name and disk name (with an OCX extension) appear in the Components dialog box when you select a control.

The Components dialog box includes three tabbed pages. You'll use the first page, Controls, most of the time because you'll be adding ActiveX controls to your form. The Components dialog box also supports a Designers page that lets you add *designers*, or class descriptions with which you can build new classes of objects. If you use the Professional or Enterprise editions, the Designers page will show designers for ActiveX controls and documents.

The Insertable Objects page supplies a list of registered insertable objects that you can drop into an application. An insertable object usually comprises more scope than the typical control supports; for example, you can insert an Excel worksheet in the middle of your Form window.

The insertable feature demonstrates ActiveX's upgraded and close relationship to OLE technology. The insertable object's icon appears on your Toolbox window when you click OK in the Component dialog box. However, the insertable object becomes much more active and typically requires that you select a data document, such as a worksheet or graphic image, before the object appears in your Form window. For example, if you insert the insertable object named Microsoft Clip Gallery, the Microsoft Clipart Gallery application executes and lets you select a graphic, sound, or multimedia clip to insert into your application. In other words, the program itself (the Microsoft Clipart Gallery) doesn't go into your application, but the program's compatible data file does. The insertable object, therefore, executes rather than embeds itself into your application.

> **TIP** Don't add too many controls at one time until you're sure that you need all of them. Figure 30.4 shows the result of adding far too many controls—the Toolbox window is too big to be useful. If it turns out that you need so many controls at one time, you'll have to hide and display the Toolbox (use the View menu) so that it stays hidden until you need it.
>
> You also can right-click the Toolbox and choose Add Tab to convert the Toolbox into a more organized set of pages. You can then place similar tools on their own pages to group them together.

FIG. 30.4
Don't add too many ActiveX controls to your Toolbox.

Next Step Suppose that ActiveX controls appear on your system in folders other than Visual Basic's primary search folder. When you choose Components from the Project menu, the Components dialog box can't locate the ActiveX controls without your help. Therefore, if you don't see the ActiveX control you want to add to your project, click the dialog box's Browse button to locate the OCX files you want to load. When you double-click a located file, Visual Basic adds that OCX to the Toolbox.

Topic 3: Working with ActiveX

After you add the controls, you know all about setting properties, responding to events, and triggering methods. Some ActiveX controls let you go a step farther, however. You can actually use an embedded control inside your application and borrow that control's functionality for your own application's use.

Overview

In Hour 22, "Adding OLE to a Program," you learned about OLE but were told that ActiveX replaced OLE. You also learned that OLE, in its truest form, exists only in Visual Basic's Standard Edition because other than a few drop-in controls, ActiveX has little support in Visual Basic 5. Although ActiveX is a replacement for OLE, programmers still use OLE terminology when describing such topics as Automation.

When your application uses Automation, your application processes another application's data and manipulates that data with the help of the other application. Users will have no idea that the other application has started, helped, and then gone away. For example, you can open Excel, load a worksheet, manipulate the worksheet data with Excel-based commands, close Excel, and embed the resulting worksheet in your application's Form window without users ever knowing that you borrowed Excel's capabilities.

This topic section is comprised primarily of a long example because you'll best grasp Automation when you see it in action. You're somewhat limited to using Automation only for ActiveX applications registered in your system Registry. Generally, if you use an application that's ActiveX-aware, that application registered its Automation availability in your system Registry when you installed the application.

▼ **NOTE**

Don't expect to master Automation in a single topic section. Automation requires extensive knowledge of the other application's *object hierarchy*, and such a hierarchy can be complex. The following example demonstrates Automation with an ActiveX document more than it teaches Automation, due to Automation's requirement that you be well versed in the borrowed application's internals. This course can't get into the specifics of other applications. Fortunately, most Automation concepts overlap applications, so the example's concepts you see here carry over to other applications in many ways. ▲

Example   You'll use Visual Basic's `Object` data type to create a variable that references the Automation application. First, you must define an application object like this:

```
Dim obExcelApp As Object
```

You must connect the application object variable to the application. If the application isn't running now, you must start the application in the background with the `CreateObject()` function. `CreateObject()` not only starts the application, but also connects your object variable to the application like this:

```
Set obExcelApp = CreateObject("Excel.Application")
```

You'll substitute the application's name in place of the `CreateObject()` function's argument.

▼ **NOTE**

Be sure to use `Set` and not a simple assignment. A variable can't hold an outside application, so you use `Set` to create a reference variable to the outside object. ▲

A problem can occur if the application is already running. As a multitasking, multiuser operating system, Excel can have more than one copy of itself running at the same time on the same computer. Therefore, you can use the `GetObject()` function in place of `CreateObject()` if the application is running, like this:

```
Set obExcelApp = GetObject(, "Excel.Application")
```

Notice the comma at the beginning of the argument list. You omit the first argument in most cases. You can check for failure with the following `If`:

```
If obExcelApp Is Nothing Then
   ' You must use CreateObject()...
```

> **TIP** Automation application object variables are an exception to the rule of local variables. The application is truly outside your application, so you could safely use a global object variable so that your procedures don't have to pass the application variable around.

When you open another application and use Automation, your application must intimately understand the other application's interface. In a way, your application is the user of the other application. Therefore, when you open the Excel application, you interact with Excel by using the normal row and column notation, except that you have to use some object property notation specific to Excel.

Now you must declare a worksheet object so that the application can generate data:

```
Dim obWorkSheet As Object  ' Worksheet object
```

The following code adds data to some worksheet cells:

```
' Enter values in cells
obWorkSheet.Cells(1, 1).Value = "Sales"
obWorkSheet.Cells(1, 2).Value = "Month"
obWorkSheet.Cells(2, 1).Value = 21913.44
obWorkSheet.Cells(2, 2).Value = "April"
```

Next Step

On the CD

If you put everything together that you saw in the preceding section, as well as add some cleanup code and code that expands the end of the code to save the worksheet and closes the Excel object, you would come up with something like Listing 30.1.

Listing 30.1 Automat.bas: Using Excel to Create a Worksheet

```
Dim obExcelApp As Object    ' Application object
Dim obWorkSheet As Object   ' Worksheet object

' Set the Excel application reference
Set obExcelApp = CreateObject("Excel.Application")
```

```
' Add a new workbook
obExcelApp.Workbooks.Add

' Reference the active sheet
Set obWorkSheet = obExcelApp.ActiveSheet

' Enter values in active sheet's cells
obWorkSheet.Cells(1, 1).Value = "Sales"
obWorkSheet.Cells(1, 2).Value = "Month"
obWorkSheet.Cells(2, 1).Value = 21913.44
obWorkSheet.Cells(2, 2).Value = "April"

' Select the second row only to format
obWorkSheet.Rows("2:2").Select
obExcelApp.Selection.NumberFormat = "$##,###.##"

' Save the worksbook
obExcelApp.Save ("c:\temp")

' Don't quit if Excel was already running!
obExcelApp.ActiveWorkBook.Close False
If blnNotRunning Then
  obexcelApp.Quit    ' Quit Excel
End If
```

If you tested to see that Excel wasn't already executing, you can close Excel as done in this final statement. If, however, Excel was running (meaning that the `GetObject()` function didn't come back as `Nothing`), don't quit the application, because it might be running a background process. The code shown in this quick example creates the simple worksheet shown in Figure 30.5.

FIG. 30.5
Your Visual Basic application can create Excel worksheets!

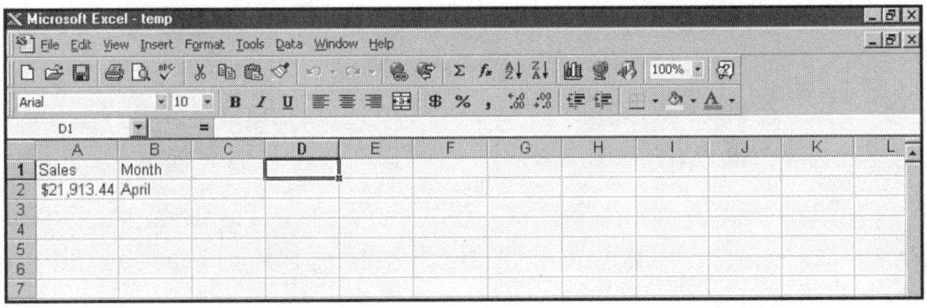

The worksheet is simple just to make the example a reasonable size. Ordinarily, your Visual Basic application would adjust values and perhaps trigger an Excel chart and print a report. The important thing to remember is that Visual Basic used Excel's brains to create a formatted worksheet without users sitting at the keyboard knowing that Excel was involved.

▼ **NOTE**
Excel contains its own Automation language, as does Word and all of the ActiveX-aware, Automation-compatible applications. Nevertheless, most of the applications support the opening and closing features that were used to connect an application and the application's primary data object to Visual Basic object variables in this topic section. Also, the applications support methods and properties such as the ones shown here, so you'll have little problem as long as you understand Visual Basic and have access to the application's internal language used for Automation. Search the application's online help for the application's object hierarchy, which shows the available objects that you can work with. ▲

After you use Excel or Word or some other ActiveX-compatible Automation application, you then have that object in your Visual Basic application.

Summary

You now understand ActiveX more fully, especially how ActiveX relates to VBX, OCX, and the OLE technologies. ActiveX is just an evolved replacement for those older technologies. You can drop ActiveX controls into VB's development environment and control outside applications from a simple Visual Basic program. Application control through Automation lets your Visual Basic application generate data by borrowing the usefulness of an outside application (even if the application is already running in another window) to create the data. Users at the keyboard won't even know that your application uses the other application's functionality. This reuse is one of ActiveX's benefits because after you create a control, you can use that control in many subsequent programs that you write.

In next hour's lesson, you'll see how to create an ActiveX control with Visual Basic. Such a task can be daunting, but you're ready to take on the challenge!

Hour 30 Quiz

You can find the answers for the following questions on the accompanying CD-ROM and on the Virtual Classroom Web site.

On the CD

1. What does ActiveX replace? (*Hint:* At least three answers are possible.)

2. Where can you add new ActiveX controls?

3. What happens if the Components dialog box can't locate the ActiveX control that you want to add to your Toolbox?

4. What can you do if you want to make some old 16-bit VBX controls work in Visual Basic 5?

5. What does *Automation* mean?

6. **True or false:** If you sell your application, you must properly install the application's ActiveX controls on the user's system.

7. Why can't you directly assign applications to object variables?

8. What happens if your application uses `CreateObject()` for a Word document and Word is already running?

9. How can you determine the Automation application's object and property names?

10. What do users see when your application performs Automation?

Hour 30 Homework Exercise

1. Use the Components dialog box to search your disk for ActiveX controls; you'll probably find some that aren't in the Windows folder. For example, if you're a member of Microsoft Network's online service, you'll find several ActiveX controls in the Microsoft Network folder.

2. Write an Excel worksheet-opening routine that checks to see wheth-er Excel is now running. If so, use `GetObject()` to get the Visual Basic worksheet object; if Excel isn't open, open Excel with the `CreateObject()` function. Add message box error messages if needed.

3. What's the difference between an insertable object and an ActiveX control that doesn't appear on the Components dialog box's Insertable Objects page? Insert one and see what happens when you use it.

Creating a Simple ActiveX Control

During this hour you will learn

▶ *What a class is*

▶ *Who needs a Control Creation Edition (CCE)*

▶ *Which ActiveX control types exist*

▶ *When to use the ActiveX Control Interface Wizard*

▶ *How to compile ActiveX controls*

ARE YOU READY FOR a whirlwind tour? This lesson shows how to create ActiveX controls. Just as this tutorial can't teach you Visual Basic in a single lesson, neither can it teach you how to create ActiveX controls in a single lesson. Even a simple ActiveX control is extremely difficult to program, and complicated ActiveX controls add multiple layers of difficulty on top of that. Nevertheless, the more a control does, the less you subsequently have to do in every application in which you use that control.

As you learned from Hour 30, an ActiveX control isn't just for Visual Basic. No matter which programming platform you work with in the future (assuming ActiveX compatibility as most of them possess these days),

you'll be able to use the ActiveX controls that you built with VB without modifying the controls or working the code to insert the control. All you'll need to do is drop in the control by using the platform's normal ActiveX control insertion method (such as VB's Components dialog box).

Topic 1: Control Design Basics

In object-oriented programming languages, such as C++, a *class* is a collection of data properties and procedures that define specific objects. A simple data type, such as `Integer`, isn't a class because the data type has properties (whole-number representations) but not procedures. When you design and create ActiveX controls, you must first design a class that describes the control.

Overview   This topic examines objects in more theoretical detail than Hour 20, "Understanding Objects and Using the Object Browser," because you must work more closely with *classes* (which describe an object's properties, methods, and event procedures) when designing ActiveX controls. You'll now learn how to design classes so that you can create brand-new ActiveX objects—specifically, new controls for the Toolbox window. In most programming languages that support classes, studying class design would comprise half the book. In Visual Basic, studying classes requires a lot less instruction, especially when you have an example to build a simple ActiveX control, as this lesson does.

The Control Creation Tools

Only those of you with VB's Professional or Enterprise editions can create ActiveX controls because the Control Creation Edition (CCE) is included in those editions. If, however, you use the Standard Edition, you're not out in the cold because you can download VB's Control Creation Edition. At the time of this writing, and seemingly for the future, Microsoft is giving away VB's Control Creation Edition that Standard Edition users can add to their system.

To obtain the software, point your Web browser to **http://www. microsoft.com/vbasic/**. The download takes about 30 minutes, so grab a bite to eat while you wait.

Pt IV

Hr 31

▼ NOTE

If you download the Control Creation Edition, you'll have two separate copies of VB on your system: the Standard Edition and the Control Creation Edition. To follow this hour's lesson, you'll work not from VB 5 as you've done throughout this book but from the Control Creation Edition. Fortunately, the two editions' interface and development environments are identical because the Control Creation Edition supports the same toolbars, menu bar, Toolbox, Properties window, Project window, and Form window as the regular VB environment. **▲**

Controls and Classes

A control is nothing more than an example, or *instance*, of a Visual Basic class. Therefore, when you insert a new form in an application, the new form is an instance of the `Form` class. The `Form` class is the definition of a form, and the class distinguishes forms from other objects such as a command button.

The Toolbox holds the class or the definition of controls, and when you place a control onto a form, you *instantiate* the control. You instantiate specific objects. The Toolbox window holds the control's class, and when you double-click a Toolbox tool to add a control to your Form window, the class generates an object on your form. ActiveX controls support the *class* definition because their properties and procedures work together to form controls.

As Figure 31.1 shows, a control has both data (property values) and code (methods and event procedures). Therefore, a control is part of a class that defines those members that are data and code.

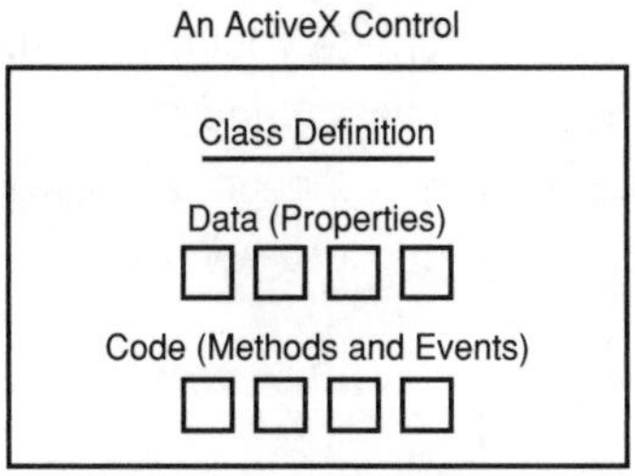

FIG. 31.1
A control is a package of data and procedure members.

There's a great aspect about VB programmers who are new to classes and objects: VB programmers, unlike programmers who work with true object-oriented languages such as C++, have little or no trouble accepting the definition of classes and objects. Using controls has been an integral part of their VB development since they placed their first command button in a Form window. In other words, you already understand that a Text Box control is a package containing data members that are property values that make the control unique. You also know that code members are events and methods that respond to the control or make the control do something.

Subclassing

VB can create ActiveX controls by using three methods:

- **Subclassed simple controls.** An existing ActiveX control forms the basis of your new control. Your new control is said to be *subclassed* from the original (*parent*) control. Your new control can receive all the functionality of the existing parent control and can extend that parent control's features by adding additional features. Subclassing a control is the easiest way to create an ActiveX control, so if you want to create from scratch a new ActiveX control that acts a lot like an existing control, use that existing control to subclass the new one. You'll have to modify the subclassed control's interface to support any new features you want your control to provide.

- **Subclassed aggregate controls.** You subclass your new control from multiple controls that now exist. In other words, if your new control is a dialog box-like control that contains command buttons, text boxes, and labels, use the existing command buttons, text boxes, and labels to reduce the effort you must put into your new control. Then you can concentrate on the added features that your control provides.

- **User-drawn controls.** If your control has nothing in common with existing controls, you'll have to create your control from scratch; define all the control's properties, events, and methods; and draw the control so that it looks exactly as you need. A user-drawn control requires quite an effort to create because you can't borrow functionality from any existing control.

The ActiveX control that you create, with any of the three methods described in the preceding list, will look and act like other controls. You can insert them into the Toolbox window, double-click the control to add the control to the Form window, and select control properties from the Properties window. Also, the control can support special *enumerated properties*, such as the `Alignment` property that drops down a list of choices, and the Property Pages dialog, such as the one that appears when you click the `Font` property's ellipsis. If the control isn't to appear on the running Form window (such as the case with the Timer control), you can set the control's `InvisibleAtRunTime` property to `True`, and the control will work in the background when needed rather than appear on the end user's form.

▼ **NOTE**

Subclassing somewhat *simulates* but doesn't *replace* inheritance in pure OOP languages such as C++ and SmallTalk. VB can't inherit from a parent class, but VB can use the features of a parent class with property-mapping mechanisms. As a result, VB seems to inherit subclassed objects, but the inheritance mechanism is fairly primitive. VB won't be a true object-oriented language, despite the strong OOP ties that VB supports, until Microsoft adds inheritance features to the language. ▲

Example With this example, you begin creating a new control that you'll continue to build throughout the rest of the lesson. As you follow this and subsequent examples, you'll no doubt consider the following:

- The control that this lesson creates is extremely simple.
- The steps required to create this extremely simple control are numerous.

This example is going to subclass the Text Box control to create a new control named the *UL Text Box control*. This control is nothing more than a Text Box control with one addition: The UL Text Box control will contain a property called `ULText` that determines whether the text in the UL Text Box control should appear in all uppercase letters, all lowercase letters, or as the programmer entered the text. The `ULText` will produce a drop-down list box property that includes these three possible values. You'll have to write some code to respond to the property's change—that is, when the programmer changes the `ULText` property, code will have to convert the text to uppercase or lowercase letters.

▼ **NOTE**

After the programmer changes the text to uppercase or lowercase, the original state of the text will be lost. Therefore, any application that uses the UL Text Box control will be able to display the text the way the user or the way the programmer inserted the text in the `Text` property. After the programmer uses the `ULText` property to convert the text to all uppercase or lowercase letters, however, the original state will be lost. From then on, the programmer can only convert the text to uppercase or lowercase letters. ▲

To begin building the new control, open a new project and select ActiveX Control from the New Project dialog box. If you use VB's Control Creation Edition, you also will open a new project and select the ActiveX Control icon. Although Professional and Enterprise Edition programmers can access the Control Creation icon from within Visual Basic, Standard Edition programmers have to start the separate application. All subsequent steps are identical for each edition.

The Visual Basic development environment looks no different from all the other sessions you've seen when creating new projects. Notice the name on VB's title bar: UserControl1. Notice also the type of object described in parentheses on the title bar: (UserControl). You're creating something called a *user control*, and VB assigns the default name of `UserControl1` to the user control. The term *user* is somewhat misleading because programmers rather than end users will use the control in their applications.

Visual Basic generates a default control class called `UserControl` when you begin to create a new control. VB assigns default properties, events, and methods to the control, and the rest of your work session requires modifying these default properties and code-related parts of the instantiated `UserControl1` to make the control behave the way you want it to. All ActiveX controls subclass from this overall class, `UserControl`, hence the name.

▼ **NOTE**

When creating controls, the concept of *runtime* and *design time* can confuse programmers. Whereas a control's design time occurs when you create and edit the control, a control's runtime occurs in two ways. When a programmer inserts the control into an application at the application's design time, the control is a compiled and executing control that responds to the programmer's setup instructions. Also, when the programmer compiles and runs the application, the control is also running, except that the control runs and responds to an end user. Often, programmers distinguish the two kinds of control runtimes by calling them *design time running* and *runtime running*. Generally, the context of the run mode is obvious as you create and work with the control. ▲

Next Step   It's time to customize the control. Therefore, display the Project Properties dialog box and type **ULTextBoxControl** in the Project Name text and **A text box with case-conversion** into the Project Description text box. This description appears in subsequent Project Properties dialog boxes for applications that you insert the control into. Close the dialog box and change the control's Name property to read ULText.

You should now change the default graphic image used for the control. The image will appear on the Toolbox when you insert the tool into subsequent application's Toolbox windows.

To change the image, select the `ToolboxBitmap` property and click the ellipsis that appears. Search VB's \Graphics\Bitmaps\Assorted folder and select the Notebook file. Be warned that a really good graphic doesn't exist that matches this lesson's new control. Instead of a notepad, a modified Text Box control graphic would be more appropriate. You might have to design your own small bitmap images with Windows Paint if you can't find good images for the controls that you create. This lesson uses the Notepad graphic to keep things as simple as possible. The image won't appear in the control's Project Windows but will appear in subsequent applications that use the control.

▼ NOTE
If you create your own bitmap image, size the image down to 15 by 16 screen pixels so that it appears in the same relative size as the other Toolbox control images. ▲

Your Project window changes to reflect the new named status of your project and control (see Figure 31.2).

FIG. 31.2
The Project window now describes your project and control names.

Save your project. Visual Basic asks for the control file name and project name. A control's source application uses the .CTL file name extension, but you'll ultimately compile the control into a usable OCX control before this lesson is over.

Topic 2: Subclassing the Existing Control

Now that you've set the stage for the control's creation by creating a new project and control and naming all the components, you're ready to work with the parent Text Box control so that you can subclass the original Text Box control. Fortunately, Visual Basic supplies an ActiveX Control Interface Wizard that you can run to ease the subclassing requirements.

Overview Most of this topic section consists of the "Example" and "Next Step" sections. Although you could learn all the theory behind the subclassing first, the UL Text Box control lends itself to a fairly streamlined development (compared to more complicated ActiveX controls). This topic section's example will use the wizard to add properties, methods, and events to your new control and to request the properties, methods, and events that you want to keep from the parent Text Box control.

Example Double-click the Text Box control to add the intrinsic Text Box control to your new control's control object window. Name the text box `txtULParent`. You've just embedded the Text Box control into your new UL Text Box control, and the UL Text Box control will use the embedded Text Box control to do its job. The text box will be hidden from view, and the UL Text Box control will use the text box. Programmers who use the UL Text Box control, however, will *not* work with the text box. The embedded text box acts like a local object variable within the UL Text Box control. The text box is hidden from the outside world, but the UL Text Box control has full access to the text box and will borrow abundantly from its properties, events, and methods.

From the Add-Ins menu choose Add-In Manager to include the add-in ActiveX Control Interface Wizard in your development environment. Click OK to close the Add-In Manager dialog box and to add the wizard to the Add-Ins menu. Pull down the Add-Ins menu again and choose ActiveX Control Interface Wizard to start the wizard's Introduction dialog box. When you click Next to move past the Introduction, you'll see Figure 31.3's Select Interface Members dialog box.

FIG. 31.3
The wizard suggests properties, events, and methods that you might want to use.

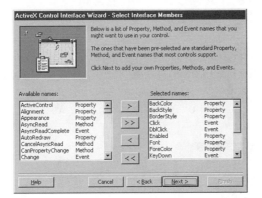

The Available Names list box in Figure 31.3 displays all available properties, events, and methods that you can select for your project. The Selected Names list box lists the new control's selected properties, events, and methods. In other words, the Available Names list box contains those properties, events, and methods that the wizard predicted that you might want to include in your control. The wizard guesses fairly well, but you can change the wizard's guess if needed.

Remove the `MouseMove` property from the Selected Names list by selecting it and clicking the < command button. When building your own controls, you should scan the list and remove whatever properties, events, and methods the wizard selected but that you don't want in the new control. Although you can leave it, the `MouseMove` event isn't an extremely useful event for text box controls, and removing the event gives you some practice with the dialog box. Also, remove the `BackStyle` property that has no bearing on the UL Text Box control.

Often, more difficult than removing items is adding property, event, and method items to the list. You must know which ones your new control needs to support as well as the ones already selected. Select the following items in the Available Names list box and click the > button to move them to the Selected Names list box: `Alignment`, `Change`, `FontBold`, `FontItalic`, `FontName`, `FontSize`, `FontStrikethru`, `FontUnderline`, `MultiLine`, `PasswordChar`, `ScrollBars`, `SelLength`, `SelStart`, `SelText`, `Text`, and `ToolTipText`.

TIP To select multiple items in the Available Names list box, Ctrl+click the items and then click the > button to send all the selected items to the Selected Names list box.

Click the Next button to move to the next dialog box. You must add any new members to the set of events, properties, and methods that the UL Text Box control will support. Click the New button to display the Add Custom Member dialog box (see Figure 31.4).

FIG. 31.4

Add your new properties, events, and methods in the Add Custom Member dialog box.

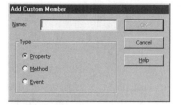

Type **ULText** in the Name text box, leave the Property option button selected, and click OK. `ULText` is the new property you're adding that will distinguish the UL Text Box control from a normal text box, as explained in the previous topic section.

Click Next to move to the next dialog box, where you'll map the properties, events, and methods to the text box equivalents. To map all but the new `ULText` property to the text box named `txtULParent`, select all properties, events, and methods *except* `ULText` in the Public Name list box, and select `txtULParent` from the Control drop-down list box. Your dialog box should look something like the one in Figure 31.5.

FIG. 31.5
All properties, events, and methods except for the new one map to the regular text box.

If you select an individual name in the Public Name list box (except `ULText`), the Control box shows the control that the name maps to. All of these controls map to the text box, of course. The Member box shows the corresponding property, event, or method that the name maps to within the Text Box control. All the names map to corresponding member names. However, you could change the mapping and make a `MouseDown` event in your new control map to a `MouseClick` event if you wanted to change the way that the new control responds from its normal state.

Click Next to show Figure 31.6's Set Attributes dialog box. The dialog box requests information about any unmapped properties, events, and methods that appear in your new control. Obviously, the `ULText` property has no mapping to an existing property, and `ULText` happens to be the only un-mapped property in the control.

FIG. 31.6
Set the mapping for all unmapped properties, events, and methods in the Set Attributes dialog box.

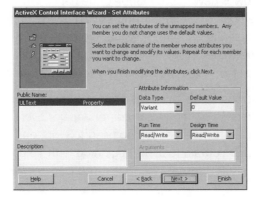

Normally, you might need to change the Data Type, Default Value, Run Time, and Design Time values listed in the Attribute Information section. The default values happen to be correct already, so you need to enter only a description for the new property, which will appear at the bottom of the Properties window when a programmer selects the control. Type the following description in the Description text box:

Sets the text to uppercase, lowercase, or no change

Click Next to display the Finished dialog box, and then click Finish to create the control's shell and display some information about the created control. The information describes the rest of the control's creation process that you must perform. As you'll see in the next section, you must manually work on the rest of the control because the wizard's job is done.

Save the new control's project now so that it's safely tucked away.

Next Step

Notice that the preceding section called the new control a *shell*. Didn't the wizard create the control? The ActiveX Control Interface Wizard is just a guide that helps you map properties, events, and methods to existing properties, events, and methods, and describes any new properties, events, and methods that you might have added to the new control. The wizard did nothing to activate the ULText property because the wizard has no idea what you want to use ULText for. To activate ULText, you must modify the code that the wizard generated for the control.

From the View menu choose Code to look at the Code window. Much of the Code window is devoted to mapping the new control's properties, events, and methods to the underlying txtULParent text box control's properties, events, and methods. In other words, when the programmer who uses this new control sets the BackColor property at design time running, the code actually sets the underlying text box's BackColor property.

Although this lesson keeps things as simple as possible, the wizard's generated code can require either a small edit or a major overhaul. No matter how much overhaul is needed, you do need to work on the parts of the Code window that contain remarks beginning with TO DO because the wizard uses those remarks for placeholders if you later modify the code.

Guard against modifying remarks prefixed with the following so the wizard will be able to modify the code later:

```
'WARNING! DO NOT REMOVE OR MODIFY THE FOLLOWING COMMENTED LINES!
```

▼ **NOTE**

Unless you base your new ActiveX control on a list-based parent control, such as the List Box control, you won't see TO DO remarks. The wizard can't manipulate list-based parent controls, and you'll have to handle the routines that process lists yourself. ▲

You can change the default **ULText** value from 0 to a different value by changing the second line in the Code window. (The first line is a remark.) Also, recall from this lesson's first topic section that a *member* is the property, event, or method that's part of the object. Only one member exists for the UL Text Box control (other than the ones subclassed from the parent), and the fourth line in the Code window names that member. The following provides the opening lines of the Code window that describes the default value and member declaration:

```
'Default Property Values:
Const m_def_ULText = 0
'Property Variables:
Dim m_ULText As Variant
```

▼ **NOTE**

The Const keyword creates named literals. Therefore, m_def_ULText isn't a variable but a constant that, when used in the rest of the program, is the same as 0 (or whatever you change the named literal to). Named literals are sometimes called *named constants*, hence the Const keyword. ▲

The next several lines declare event procedures. The nature of Visual Basic controls requires that all event procedure code within an ActiveX control be declared just as the variables that you declare before you use them. These event procedure declarations are called *prototypes* because they prototype, or model, the procedures that follow. Visual Basic needs to know these prototypes in advance before the event procedure code actually appears inside ActiveX controls.

If the code contains no **TO DO** remarks, as this lesson's code doesn't, your only job is to modify the new control's sizing capabilities and to add the new property's functionality to the control. Before handling the executing code, you need to set up the three drop-down list box values that will appear when the programmer who uses this control clicks the **ULText** property. Set up three values from which the programmer can choose: **AsIs**, **Uppercase**, and **Lowercase**.

To program these values, you need a special declaration block called an *enumeration block*. Before learning the details, enter the following code directly below the declarations in the Code window's **General** section:

```
Public Enum ULTextEnum
  AsIs = 0
  Uppercase = 1
  Lowercase = 2
End Enum
```

The special **Enum** block tells the ActiveX control compiler which items should appear in a property drop-down list box. Code that you add later will use these enumerated values, which will appear as follows when the programmer clicks the **ULText** property in the UL Text Box control's Properties window:

```
0 - AsIs
1 - Uppercase
2 - Lowercase
```

The UL Text Box control's sizing code is extremely simple because the new control should size just as the parent text box would size. Often, a new ActiveX control should size differently from the control or controls that it subclasses from, especially for subclassed aggregate ActiveX controls. If a one-to-one correspondence occurs with the parent's and the new control's size, however, you can add a **UserControl_Resize()** event procedure as follows by selecting the **Resize** procedure from the Code window:

```
Private Sub UserControl_Resize()
  ' Set the height and scaling to the underlying control
  ' Stretch the control to the width and height
  txtULParent.Move 0, 0, ScaleWidth
End Sub
```

Now that the resizing is out of the way, your primary job is to set up the enumerated value display and to convert the UL Text Box control to uppercase or lowercase, depending on the ULText property. The wizard created code for the ULText property, but you must fill in the details. The only two procedures you need to worry about here (because the control's only added functionality is a single property that the programmer can set or use) are the Property Get ULText() and the Property Let ULText() procedures. The Property Get and Property Let keywords define procedures that execute every time the property is set or used. The shell code uses a Variant data type, but you want to work with the enumerated data types. Change the Property Get code to this:

```
Public Property Get ULText() As ULTextEnum
  ULText = m_ULText
End Property
```

This code only assigns the state property the current member's value, and converting the Variant to the enumeration for the property value's return value is the only necessary change. Change the Property Set code as follows:

```
Public Property Let ULText(ByVal New_ULText As ULTextEnum)
    m_ULText = New_ULText
    ' Test the control's state
    ' and change the text box accordingly
    ' (ignore a ULText of 0 which means As Is)
    If New_ULText = 1 Then
      Text = UCase(txtULParent.Text)
    ElseIf New_ULText = 2 Then
      Text = LCase(txtULParent.Text)
    End If
    PropertyChanged "ULText"
End Property
```

The UCase() and LCase() internal functions convert the text value to uppercase or lowercase depending on the value assigned to the property. If the programmer who uses the ActiveX control assigns the ULText property at design time or runtime, this procedure executes. (The next-to-last wizard dialog box gave you a chance to limit the change to design time or runtime, but you kept the default so that programmers will be able to modify the ULText property at runtime or when using the control during an application's design.)

Here's the amazing part: You're through! The next topic section shows you how to compile and test the ActiveX control.

Topic 3: Testing and Running New ActiveX Controls

The fun part begins now. Not only can you insert your new control into another application and place the control on the Form window just as you do other controls, but the new ActiveX control takes on *every single benefit given to intrinsic controls*. Therefore, the control's Properties window will act like other controls. Also, when the programmer who uses the ActiveX control inside a Code window types an assignment to assign a property value, even the Code window's Quick Info pops up to let you select a property. Also, the Toolbox that holds the ActiveX control automatically displays a ToolTip describing the control's name. You'll be proud of your new ActiveX control when you begin using it because the control will act as though it was supplied by Microsoft with Visual Basic!

Overview   When you compile the ActiveX control, Visual Basic compiles the control into an .OCX file that you then can insert into a project just as you can other ActiveX controls. The next "Example" and "Next Step" sections demonstrate the steps you take to compile and use the control.

Example   Save your control before compiling it. Choosing Sa_ve Project from the _File menu saves both the control and the project. You can't run an ActiveX control by using the normal F5 keypress because all ActiveX controls must be compiled before they can execute. If you attempt to run the control, Visual Basic displays Figure 31.7's dialog box.

FIG. 31.7

You must compile an ActiveX control and run it from another environment.

To compile the ActiveX control, choose Ma_ke from the _File menu. Visual Basic displays the Make Project dialog box to request the location of the compiled ActiveX control. You might want to place the control in your

\Windows\ System folder or in a VB work folder that you've created. (This is the folder you search when you want to load the ActiveX control into another Visual Basic application's Toolbox from the Project Properties dialog box.) If the compiler notices errors, Visual Basic won't build the control and will highlight the error lines in the code. As soon as you eliminate the bugs, the compiler returns you to the development environment.

Visual Basic supports two ways to test the control:

- Open a new project and test the control from that project. (You can't open project groups if you use VB's Standard Edition coupled with the Control Creation Edition.) A multiproject development environment is available only for testing ActiveX controls.

- Open a new Standard .EXE project (Standard Edition users will have to start VB's Standard Edition) and drop the control into that new project. The following "Next Step" section does just that.

Next Step   Start Visual Basic if you use the Standard Edition. No matter which edition you use, choose New Project from the File menu and create a new Standard .EXE file. Press Ctrl+T to open the Components dialog box. As Figure 31.8 shows, the UL Text Box control appears at the top of the dialog box.

FIG. 31.8
Your ActiveX control's Project Description text appears in the Components dialog box.

Your new control is here

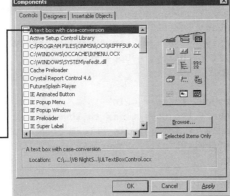

Select the ActiveX control and close the dialog box. The control's bitmap image that you selected when you created the control appears on the Toolbox. To use the control in a simple application, follow these steps:

1. Change the form name to `frmActiveX`, and change the form's Caption to `Test the ActiveX Control`. Expand the form's `Width` and `Height` properties to approximately 7,680 and 6,870.

2. Point to the `ULText` control and read the ToolTip that the ActiveX Control Interface Wizard took care of for you.

3. Double-click the UL Text Box control to add the control to the form. (You could also drag and draw the control onto the Form window.) Size the `ULText` control to approximately 4,815 twips (the `Width` property) by 496 twips (the `Height` property). Change the `FontSize` property to 18 and the `FontBold` property to True.

4. You're changing the properties of the `ULText` control, *not* a normal Text Box control. Click the `ULText` property's arrow to open the drop-down list box. You'll see the three enumerated values—`AsIs`, `Uppercase`, and `Lowercase`—just the way you programmed them. For now, leave the control at its default `AsIs` state. Change the `Name` property to `ULtMyFirst` and blank out the `Text` property.

5. Add two command buttons to the form: `cmdUpper` and `cmdLower`. Place the `cmdUpper` button above the `cmdLower` button so that you can see both fall below the UL Text Box control. Change the first `Caption` to `&Uppercase` and the second `Caption` to `&Lowercase`.

6. Add these two event procedures:

```
Private Sub cmdUpper_Click()
    ' Convert the ULText box to uppercase
    ' simply by setting its ULText property
    ULtMyFirst.ULText = Uppercase
End Sub

Private Sub cmdLower_Click()
    ' Convert the ULText box to lowercase
    ' simply by setting its ULText property
    ULtMyFirst.ULText = Lowercase
End Sub
```

As you type the assignment, notice that Visual Basic helps you locate the UL Text Box control's property when you type the period, as shown in Figure 31.9 with a drop-down list box of choices. The same happens when you assign the `ULText` value the `Uppercase` or `Lowercase` values; `Uppercase` and `Lowercase` (and `AsIs`) are the enumerated values and the only possible values the ActiveX control will let the `ULText` receive. Therefore, the selection list that appears when you type the equal sign is incredible, given that you did absolutely nothing to produce this feature.

FIG. 31.9

Your control supports all the list box Quick Info help that the other controls provide.

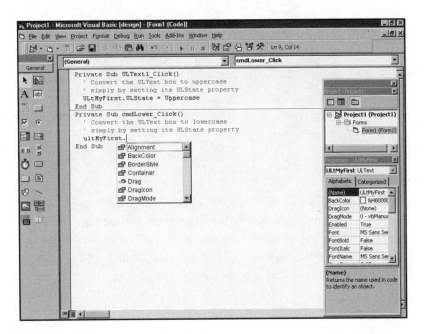

Compile and run the application. Type a value in the UL Text Box control's text box area, using a combination of uppercase and lowercase letters. When you click either command button, the UL Text Box control converts its text to the proper format, as shown in Figure 31.10. Although you didn't need a control to convert the text, the new UL Text Box control supports a built-in conversion property that you can set at any time to convert its contents to uppercase or lowercase letters.

▼ NOTE

Hour 37, "Packaging Your Application," explains how to distribute the ActiveX controls that you create. **▲**

FIG. 31.10
The ActiveX Control's property now performs conversion.

Summary

You've made it through a long ActiveX control example. Although this lesson's ActiveX control was simple and was based heavily on an existing control, the steps required to create the control were numerous. ActiveX control creation is one of the most challenging tasks a Visual Basic programmer can accept. The rewards, however, are an eventual time savings. If you take the time to write an ActiveX control now, you only need to drop that ActiveX control into whatever application uses the control in the future. Also, the market is hot for new ActiveX controls. Just remember: You're not just creating ActiveX controls for Visual Basic programmers, but for all programmers who work on ActiveX control platforms.

In Hour 32, you'll learn the basics of interfacing Visual Basic programs to the Internet.

Hour 31 Quiz

You can find the answers for the following questions on the accompanying CD-ROM and on the Virtual Classroom Web site.

On the CD

1. What is *instantiation* all about?

2. **True or false:** Programmers must have the Professional Edition or Enterprise Edition to create ActiveX controls.

3. What's the name of the class from which all ActiveX controls derive?

4. What are the three types of ActiveX controls?

5. Which type of ActiveX control is the easiest to create?

6. **True or false:** When you subclass a control, the new ActiveX control borrows properties, events, and methods from the parent.

7. What are enumeration blocks used for?

8. How can you control the description text that appears when a programmer displays your ActiveX control in the Components dialog box?

9. What extension does Visual Basic use for compiled ActiveX controls?

10. Which two procedures do ActiveX control properties require?

Hour 31 Homework Exercise

Change the `AsIs` enumerated value to `AsEntered`. Change the UL Text Box control so that, if a program changes the `ULText` from `AsEntered` to either `Uppercase` or `Lowercase`, the control remembers the text as it appeared before the conversion. Write an application that acts like the third topic section's example application, except add a third command button that reads <u>A</u>s Entered. When users click this command button, the text reverts back to its pre-uppercase or pre-lowercase form.

This is the only exercise for this lesson because, as you've seen, even making a minor change to an ActiveX control can be time-consuming.

Adding Internet Access to Applications

During this hour you will learn

▶ *How to add Web browsers to applications*

▶ *Which Internet controls come with VB*

▶ *How encapsulation works*

▶ *What ActiveX documents do*

THINGS CAN BEGIN to slow down after last hour's lesson. You've reached the final hour of the night-school tutorial that follows a three-topic teaching pattern. After you finish this lesson, you can consider yourself graduated from *Visual Basic 5 Night School*'s curriculum of programming arts and, more important, consider yourself primed for the rank of Visual Basic 5 guru. Your next step is to develop as much as you can with Visual Basic to hone the skills you've gained throughout this tutorial. To help get you started, the final part of this book walks you through a complete application's development.

In the meantime, no night-school course about Visual Basic 5 would be complete without some mention of Visual Basic and the Internet. Visual Basic is one of the easiest tools available today to use for Internet access. Bear in

mind, however, that even with Visual Basic, Internet access via programming is challenging. This short hour's lesson only scratches the surface and offers a glimpse of how Visual Basic views and works with the Internet.

Topic 1: The Internet Wizard

The VB Application Wizard does some work for you when you want your application to access the Internet. Simply by your selecting the correct choice within the wizard, Visual Basic automatically adds the access and gives your application worldwide communications capabilities.

▼ **NOTE**

The Internet tools described in this lesson work equally well for Internet and intranet applications. The *Internet* is a worldwide networked system of computers, whereas an *intranet* is a local networked system (perhaps a network inside a single building or even a small area on the same floor) that provides the same features as the Internet. ▲

Overview This topic section explains what the VB Application Wizard does when you use it to add Internet access to your application. Although the wizard describes Internet access, it specifically gives your application the capability to browse World Wide Web pages.

▼ **NOTE**

Your users must already have an Internet service provider (ISP, an account with any organization that connects to the Internet), or they can't access the Web with your application. Also, you must have Internet Explorer 3.0 or later installed on your own development system. Internet Explorer helps the wizard add appropriate code. ▲

Working the Wizard

When you create an application shell with the VB Application Wizard, the fifth dialog box you see (in Figure 32.1) is the Internet Connectivity dialog box, which sets up Internet Web access for the application you're building.

When you select <u>Y</u>es, the wizard actually inserts the engine for a Web browser in the generated application.

FIG. 32.1

You can select Web access from the wizard's Internet Connectivity dialog box.

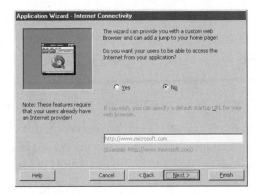

Default URL

An *URL (Uniform Resource Locator)* is a Web site address. Every Web site has a unique URL. If you opt to add the Internet access capability to the wizard's application, you can supply a default URL Web page site for the application's browser. When a user triggers the browser inside the application, the browser logs on (using the user's own Internet provider) and connects to the URL you specify in the wizard.

▼ NOTE

The wizard supplies a default URL—Microsoft's home page—so you need to change this default URL if you want your users to see something else. **▲**

Always begin the URL with **http://**. (The letters *http* stand for *Hypertext Transport Protocol* and designate the standard communications procedure used to access Web pages.)

Example Follow these steps to add an Internet-browsing feature to your wizard's generated application:

1. Create a new project and double-click the icon labeled VB Application Wizard.

2. Click <u>N</u>ext to bypass the opening Introduction dialog box. You can keep the dialog box from appearing in subsequent sessions by clicking the check box labeled <u>S</u>kip This Screen in the Future.

3. Select <u>S</u>ingle Document Interface (SDI) to keep the generated application simple.

4. Click <u>N</u>ext to move through the next three dialog boxes and to accept the default menu options.

5. At the Internet Connectivity dialog box, click <u>Y</u>es. For this example, leave Microsoft's Web site URL in the text box.

6. Click <u>F</u>inish to finalize and generate the application.

When you return to VB's development environment, notice the Toolbox. Figure 32.2 shows the tools that the wizard added to the usual collection of intrinsic controls. You've used these added controls before in this tutorial: Common Dialog Box, Toolbar, Image List, and Slider.

FIG. 32.2
The wizard added a few tools to your Toolbox.

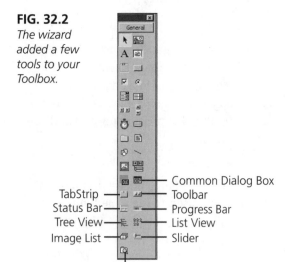

TabStrip
Status Bar
Tree View
Image List

Common Dialog Box
Toolbar
Progress Bar
List View
Slider

WebBrowser

The extra tools give the application's Web-browsing portions the control they need to do their job. Obviously, the WebBrowser control is the primary tool this lesson is concerned with.

▼ **NOTE**
The next topic section, "Internet Controls," explains more about the Internet controls that come with Visual Basic's Professional and Enterprise editions. ▲

Next Step   Get a feel of the application's shell by pressing F5 to run the application. The screen you see looks no different from other wizard-generated applications you've seen. The Internet feature appears, however, when you choose Web Browser from the View menu. In the middle of the application's screen, a Web-browsing dialog box appears and requests that you log on with your typical provider's logon dialog box. After you enter your user name and password, an Internet Explorer-like window appears in the center of your application screen and displays Microsoft's Web site (see Figure 32.3).

FIG. 32.3

Your generated application is hooked into Microsoft's Web site.

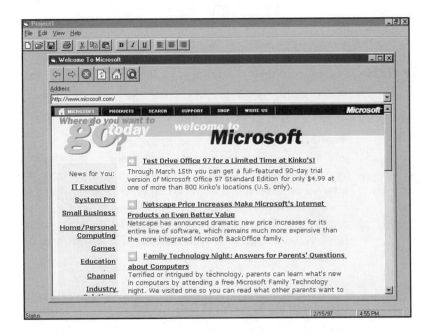

▼ **NOTE**

Internet Explorer is actually a small application wrapped around a huge ActiveX control. The Web browser that Visual Basic's wizard inserted is a sample of such an ActiveX control. Although the application's Web browser is simpler than the full-blown version of Internet Explorer (fewer toolbar buttons appear and no menu bar exists), the embedded browser supplies all the common browser features needed, such as a previous page button, next page button, home page button, and so on. If you click the Search toolbar button, Internet Explorer uses Microsoft's search site to launch the search request. ▲

To log off the Internet, you must close the Web browser, double-click your service provider's taskbar icon, and select the logoff option. Although the Web browser doesn't include a logoff feature, you can add one through programming.

Topic 2: Internet Controls

If you use VB's Professional or Enterprise Edition, you can use several advanced Internet-based ActiveX controls to add and control Internet access from within your applications. The previous topic's example demonstrated the power of one single control, WebBrowser. This topic section explains more about these controls.

Overview Several Internet controls appear when you choose Components from the Project menu. This topic section reviews those controls and explains how and when you can use them in projects that access the Internet.

▼ NOTE
Internet access can mean many different things in today's world, including complete applications that users access and run from the Web. The Internet provides more services than Web page viewing and file downloading these days, especially with the new ActiveX controls that work across the Internet as easily as they work inside single-computer applications. When you activate Web pages with programs, Visual Basic can be the engine that you use. ▲

The Encapsulation Controls

The term *encapsulation* refers to different things, depending on whether you're encapsulating data, code, or both. Nevertheless, in a broad sense, encapsulation always refers to packaging. Visual Basic includes some Internet controls that encapsulate, or package, your existing applications and code into Internet-aware applications. These controls help encapsulate your applications so that they work across Internet technology.

The encapsulation controls are as follows:

- **Internet Transfer control.** Encapsulates the three most popular Internet protocols: HTTP, FTP (File Transfer Protocol), and Gopher (a searching protocol to help you locate information on the Internet). You can download files directly from within your Visual Basic applications by using FTP.

● **WebBrowser control.** Encapsulates a Web browser directly inside your application.

● **WinSock control.** Gives you a Windows common connection and data-exchange control that provides these two protocols: UDP (User Datagram Protocol) and TCP (Transmission Control Protocol).

You saw one of these encapsulation controls—the WebBrowser control—in the previous topic section. The VB Application Wizard uses the WebBrowser control to insert the browser in the generated application. As you saw, the WebBrowser control isn't as full-functioned as Internet Explorer, but it does provide simple and direct access for any user who subscribes to an Internet service.

Internet Explorer Controls

Visual Basic 5 comes with several controls you can add to a project so that the project can interact with the Web. These controls begin with the IE abbreviation in the Components dialog box. The following example describes these controls.

Example Table 32.1 helps you locate the controls described in this topic section. Often, the control names don't describe their capabilities. Table 32.1 describes the control you select from the Components dialog box to get the functionality you need. (To access the Components dialog box, choose Components from the Project menu.)

Table 32.1 The Component Names You Select

Component Name	Description
IE Animated Button	Animated display showing IE's connection
IE Popup Menu	A menu control that appears on the Web page
IE Popup Window	A tabbed window control that opens a new connection window
IE Preloader	Preloads a site before the visible Internet access begins
IE Super Label	A Web page label

continues

Table 32.1 Continued	
Component Name	**Description**
IE Timer	Provides timing operations for Internet services
Microsoft Internet Controls	Web browser control
Microsoft Internet Transfer Control 5.0	The transfer protocol control
Microsoft Winsock Control 5.0	The Windows connection to common Internet protocols

▼ **NOTE**

If you use The Microsoft Network online service, a set of controls comes with Visual Basic 5 that offers Microsoft Network-related services from the applications you write, such as the MSN mail control. These controls begin with the MSN abbreviation in the Components dialog box. ▲

Topic 3: Preview of Advanced Issues

Assuming that you want to interact with the Internet and Visual Basic, you've already seen a start of what's in store. The simplest way to add Internet capabilities is to use the VB Application Wizard to add the wizard as done in this lesson's first topic. If you go further than that, you have a steep learning curve ahead of you.

Overview This short topic discusses some of the terms and concepts you'll first face as you dive into the VB-to-Internet foray. By learning what's in store now, you won't be faced with a completely new environment if and when you learn the details needed to provide comprehensive Internet interaction from your applications.

ActiveX Documents

If you want to develop a pure Internet application, you can use ActiveX documents to get started. An *ActiveX document* acts and looks just like a regular Visual Basic application on a Form window, except that an ActiveX document sends ActiveX controls to the end user's computer if the computer doesn't contain the ActiveX controls used by the document. The document comes to the user looking like a regular HTML page. (*HTML*, or *Hypertext Markup Language*, is the primary language for Web page formatting.) The ActiveX document can contain hypertext links (ActiveX controls that are downloaded or used depending on the end user's machine contents) and an automatic merging of the ActiveX document's menus with its parent application (like OLE servers).

The ActiveX document links to an HTML page that you create or use. When the end user clicks the link to your ActiveX document, your ActiveX document activates, the controls get to the user's computer, and the Web page's ActiveX document code executes as the user views the page.

▼ **NOTE**

The ActiveX document isn't static. The document in *ActiveX document* is, in every respect, a running application. Using a document concept helps programmers see how Web pages use the embedded ActiveX document. ▲

Perhaps the most important reason for creating ActiveX documents is that Internet Explorer can run ActiveX documents as though Internet Explorer were a control program or operating system program launcher. The ActiveX document's menus merge with Internet Explorer's (and override functionality when needed), and you don't have to learn a new language such as Java to activate Web pages.

▼ **NOTE**

The New Project dialog box contains two icons—ActiveX Document EXE and ActiveX Document DLL—which create ActiveX document shells. After you start creating the ActiveX document, you can add whatever features you like to the Form window, just as you do for regular applications. ▲

TIP You can add the ActiveX Document Migration Wizard to the <u>A</u>dd-In Manager menu option. This wizard converts existing applications to ActiveX documents so that you can place whatever applications you've already created onto the Web.

HTML and VBScript

Although you only need to know the Visual Basic programming language to access all the Internet connectivity features found in Visual Basic 5, you need to master two auxiliary languages to tie things together well. HTML is the formatting language behind Web pages. The HTML language is designed to achieve the following goals:

- Format Web pages in columns, with graphics and appropriate titles
- Allow the integration of additional Internet service programs, such as VB ActiveX documents and Java (a small programming language that activates Web pages)

HTML is known as a *scripting* language. The language doesn't compile and become executable as Visual Basic programs do. Instead, HTML formats Web pages, specifies where graphics and dividing frames go, and allows for embedded activated applications such as ActiveX documents and Java programs.

VBScript, as the name implies, is another scripting language, but Microsoft designed VBScript based on the Visual Basic programming language. Therefore, you'll feel right at home with VBScript. It is useful when you want to add key Visual Basic features to a Web page, such as pop-up messages, input boxes, loop-through calculations, and so on. VBScript, despite its foundation in Visual Basic, doesn't replace Visual Basic's ActiveX documents but instead loads the ActiveX documents into an HTML page for execution. Therefore, VBScript is the medium through which HTML documents locate and execute Visual Basic ActiveX document applications.

▼ NOTE

VBScript wasn't originally designed to be used solely as a launcher for ActiveX documents because VBScript was around before ActiveX. The loading of ActiveX documents into HTML pages is one of VBScript's many jobs, but for a VB5 programmer, the ActiveX document is perhaps VBScript's most important job. ▲

VB to Java?

One technology you can look for shortly is VB-to-Java conversion programs. Several vendors have announced their intent to distribute such utilities. The big advantage is that you don't have to worry much with Internet-based controls. If you can write an application that uses any VB controls, the conversion program translates the Visual Basic project into a Java-based project. When in Java, you can embed the application inside your intranet or Internet Web pages, and the application automatically ends up on the end user's screen over the Internet as soon as the end user displays the Web page.

These Java conversion tools don't necessarily replace the ActiveX Document Migration Wizard you read about two sections ago. Some non-Windows systems support Java, but not ActiveX, so active Java applications can be more universally accepted than ActiveX-based applications.

▼ NOTE

If Java is new to you, note that it was designed to provide true active content on Web pages long before ActiveX controls appeared on the scene. Java is a C++-like language that application developers can use to create small applications that travel with Web pages and execute on the end user's machine, even if that user's machine and operating system vary from the developer's. If you want additional information on Java, check out Que Corporation's *Using Visual J++* for one of the best well-rounded introductory texts based on the Java technology. (Visual J++ is Microsoft's Java implementation, and contains an interface that looks and acts a lot like Visual Basic's.) ▲

Example   Listing 32.1 shows an example of the first few lines of HTML code for Microsoft's Web site.

Listing 32.1   A Few Lines of HTML Code

```
<HTML>
<HEAD>
<TITLE>MSN.COM</TITLE>
<meta http-equiv="Content-Type" content="text/html;
  charset=iso-8859-1">
<META http-equiv="PICS-Label" content=
 '(PICS-1.0 "http://www.rsac.org/ratingsv01.html"
 l comment "RSACi North America Server" by
 "Microsoft Network"'>
</HEAD>
<FRAMESET rows="20,*" frameborder="0"
 framespacing="0" border="0">
<FRAME src="/pilot.htm" name="pilot"
 NORESIZE scrolling="no" marginwidth="0"
 marginheight="0" frameborder="0" framespacing="0">
</FRAMESET>
</html>
```

Next Step Log on to the Internet and point your Web browser to Microsoft's home page at **http://www.microsoft.com**. Although the page might vary slightly from the page that Listing 32.1 describes, the page looks *nothing* like Listing 32.1! HTML is a formatting page-description language. Listing 32.1's commands tell your Web browser how to display the informational text and graphics that come to your computer when you point your Web browser to that page.

Summary

This lesson conceptually previewed Visual Basic's role as an Internet player. Obviously, this lesson can't cover even a small fraction of the details needed to truly turn Visual Basic into an Internet programming tool. A huge background is needed just about Internet technology before you tackle Visual Basic's interface. Several good books and online references exist, but your first and best bet is to study the Books Online references that come with Visual Basic 5. There you'll find step-by-step descriptions that detail your role as an Internet programmer.

I don't want to scare you away from learning to write applications that interact with the Internet. Please realize that the promised goal of keeping every lesson in this tutorial under an hour couldn't be met if this lesson were to teach many of the Internet specifics needed to write Internet programs. Nevertheless, Internet programmers are well rewarded for their abilities due to the in-depth study required and the rapid pace they must maintain to keep up with the technology.

You've made it through all the lessons! The next hour begins a tour that walks you through the design and development stages of a full-blown Visual Basic application.

Hour 32 Quiz

You can find the answers for the following questions on the accompanying CD-ROM and on the Virtual Classroom Web site.

On the CD

1. What does the Web-browsing application you generate with the VB Application Wizard do with the URL you supply?

2. **True or false:** Your application's end users must use the Internet Explorer Web browser before your Visual Basic Web browsing control will work.

3. **True or false:** You must use the Internet Explorer Web browser before your Visual Basic Web browsing control will work.

4. What is *encapsulation*?

5. Which online services do some of the Visual Basic controls support?

6. What's the difference between an *intranet* and the *Internet*?

7. What's the difference between an ActiveX document and a regular Visual Basic application?

8. What does Java do?

9. Which scripting language works with HTML to load and execute ActiveX documents?

10. How can you convert existing applications into an ActiveX document?

▼ NOTE

No exercises exist for this lesson due to the general nature of the material. ▲

▶ **PART**

Building a Professional Application

Developing and Designing Forms

THE FINAL PART of this book begins the major Fast Track section that walks you through the building of a complete application from start to finish. Although you've seen applications built throughout this entire course, this part of the tutorial takes things a step further. You'll learn how to design, develop, debug, and package your complete application. This and the next four hourly lessons don't follow the usual three-topic sections that you've become accustomed to. Instead, these lessons raise your application-building skills.

If you've worked with Visual Basic before or are already a strong developer in other languages, you might have jumped directly to this part of the book to see what Visual Basic is all about. You won't be disappointed! If you're brand new to Visual Basic and

jumped to this part of the book, you'll be excited to see the results of what the first 32 lessons will teach you when you go through them sequentially.

If you've followed the book sequentially from the first page to this point, this part of the book doesn't just offer review. Each hour's lesson walks you through an application's development, but also trains you in some advanced development ideas and features that the previous hours couldn't get to. In other words, this part of the book takes you one step beyond your current skill level to initiate you into the ranks of an advanced Visual Basic developer.

The application you learn here is a complete stand-alone application that rivals many applications sold today. The application is fairly simple, but its simplicity is its beauty. The application you develop in this and the next four hours offers an easy-to-use contact management system with an appointment manager. This VBScheduler application will advance your skills.

Looking at the Application

Figure 33.1 shows VBScheduler's form. By the time you complete this and the next four lessons, you'll have completed the VBScheduler application yourself. These lessons, however, don't just walk you through the step-by-step creation—you've had enough of that for now. These lessons teach you about designing, debugging, and distributing your application and use the VBScheduler application for a teaching example.

FIG. 33.1

The VBScheduler application's window forms the appointment scheduler.

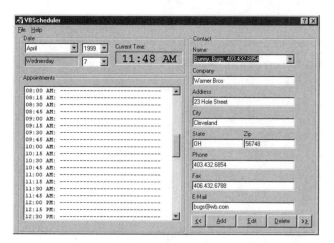

Now that you have a glimpse of the application these lessons describe, you're ready to learn more about application planning and design.

▶▶ **FAST TRACK**

Turn to Hour 2, "Creating Your First Application" (p. 37), to learn how to use Visual Basic's development environment to load and execute programs.

Planning Is Best Done in Advance!

The most difficult part of creating any application is deciding what it will do and how that should be done. The most important part of creating an application is in the design process. If done correctly, the design takes as long or longer to work out than the application itself. Unfortunately, many programmers don't spend as much time designing the application as they should. They would prefer jumping right in and starting to create the application. For every hour that you spend designing your application, however, you can save as much as a day of debugging time. If you start with a good design, you consider more of the situations that might present problems later. You then can head off small problems before they become bigger ones.

▼ **NOTE**

As a general rule, it's always easier to fix a design problem before the program is created. ▲

To arrive at a good design, you need to understand what makes up a good application. Both a house and an application must be built according to a carefully planned set of steps. Following this plan prevents the house's roof from being built before the walls. In a Visual Basic application, you usually shouldn't add any code before you create the forms. Although you might see slight modifications that you want to make to the forms as you add code in a later step, the forms should be fairly solid before you begin to add code. Without the user's interface firmly in mind, your early code is prone to design flaws that consume lots of time to modify.

If you build the application in the wrong order, or leave a part out, it's very hard to code and even harder to test. The application can take longer to complete or might never work at all. To design an application, you must first understand what you want it to do.

Applications comprise the following major components:

- User interface
- Program code
- Database (if required)
- Reports and other printed output (if required)
- Help file

▶▶ FAST TRACK

Turn to Hour 1, "Introducing Visual Basic" (p. 9), to learn more about the program code that comprises many programs.

You should set up your applications in their own Windows folder because applications often require several auxiliary files, such as a Readme.txt file for last-minute documentation fixes and release information. The folder should contain your application with an appropriate matching program icon. (The form's `Icon` property determines the icon displayed on the taskbar when your program runs or is minimized.)

> **TIP** Compile all your applications before distributing them. Keep your applications running interactively inside the development environment only for as long as you create and test the application. Compile the application before distributing the application. Hour 37, "Packaging Your Application," explains application distribution in detail.

Describing the Application

The first step in the application design is to put your application into words. This description phase is usually done by writing a short goal-oriented paragraph that describes exactly what the application is and what it will be able to do. The following is an example of such a description for the VBScheduler:

> *The VBScheduler application keeps track of contact information, such as name, address, and phone numbers. VBScheduler also tracks appointments that you can schedule with the contacts. Users can add and delete contacts as well as obtain online help. Users can view appointments in 15-minute, 30-minute, or one-hour increments. To add*

an appointment with one of the contacts, you only need to open a new appointment and drag a contact's name to the appointment entry.

This description gives you a good idea of what functions the application will do, providing a final goal to aim for as you design the application. The next section discusses application tasks in more detail.

Identifying the Necessary Building Blocks

As you know from earlier lessons, a Visual Basic application's code consists of program building blocks called *procedures*. Although you aren't ready to write procedures when you finish the goal statement, you're ready to begin breaking down your application into smaller tasks that eventually help you determine which procedures are needed.

Pt **V**

Hr **33**

▼ NOTE

Breaking the overall goal into smaller tasks is called *top-down design*. **▲**

One way to determine the tasks the application requires is to ask questions about the application. For example, how complicated will this application be? Will the application print day-planning sheets for the daily appointments? Should users be able to search for an appointment by entering text that might appear in an appointment? Will the application support multiple data files for a project team's usage? Who will the users be—families, small businesses, or both? Also, how many tasks will you include in it, given your time commitments and project costs? The answers to these questions help you build a features list. Some tasks are absolutely required for the application to work, whereas other tasks might be nice to have but aren't required.

Following are some of the more important tasks that must be in a scheduling application:

- Adding, editing, and deleting contacts
- Managing name, address, telephone, fax, and e-mail information
- Offering searching capabilities
- Providing alphabetical, sequential access through the data
- Giving users 15-minute, 30-minute, and one-hour views of the appointments

- Allowing users to select a date and time by clicking
- Letting users drag and drop names from the contact section to an open appointment to ease scheduling with contacts

This is far from a complete list of tasks, but you're headed in the right direction. Already, you're thinking about the form (or forms) required and of coding approaches to such tasks. As the design progresses, you find that you should add more tasks.

When designing in Visual Basic, you should start by designing the forms you might need, and then change them as you go along. This technique, called *prototyping*, lets you create a demo as you design actual programs. Prototyping also lets you decide what should happen when a given button on the form is clicked or when a menu option is selected.

Visual Basic is one of the best programming systems on which to prototype. The Form window makes designing, creating, and testing a user interface simple. After you design your form (or forms), put one of the application's users in front of the running application prototype to make sure that all the controls are placed well and that you've included all the interaction needed for the program to produce its intended result.

You must always realize that the design you come up with isn't set in cement. You should go back over the design several times with several people (preferably end users who will use the eventual application) looking for possible problems in logic *before* you start building the actual application and tying the controls together with code. This critical plan review is an important part of the design process. Also, you learn more about Visual Basic and programming this way as you build the application. Some of these things make the application better, but only if you can go back and rework the application's task list. Allow yourself to go back and change the design, especially this early in the creation, and the application will come out better due to proper prototyping and proper review.

Creating Forms

A Windows application is a collection of related forms that allows users to interact easily with the data. As you might have seen in other Windows applications, some applications can be very useful, but boring to look at or use. Throughout this tutorial, you've brought many Visual Basic objects together to create simple applications that were interesting to look at. By using what you've learned about VB's features, in addition to some design standards that you'll learn here, you can create useful applications that look good and are easy to use. However, no matter how closely standards are followed, an application's forms, to some degree, reflect the personality of the programmer who created them.

For the rest of this hour and the next, I'm going to cover how to design a form, what you should place on the form, and where the objects should be placed. Also, you'll see how the menus are created and how they enhance the application.

▼ **NOTE**
Remember that this part of the book is a Fast Track part. Therefore, some of you are reading this but haven't mastered all the previous hours' topics. Along the way, this and the next four lessons review some of the application-creation process as well as describe application design theory. ▲

Forms: Your User's Interface

The form is the most important part of any application. If the interface isn't easy or just doesn't look good, nobody will want to use it. The GUI (Graphical User Interface) offers a wide variety of ways of making users feel comfortable with the application. The users' experience must be taken into account when considering the layout of the forms.

▶▶ **FAST TRACK**
Turn to Hour 2, "Creating Your First Application" (p. 37), to learn more about forms.

The Principles of Good Form Design

When you design a form, you should maintain as much consistency as possible. Keep the following design concepts and tips in mind:

- **Consistency of forms.** Make all the forms in a multiform application consistent with each other. A good form should display the same information in the same way, all the time. Therefore, don't call a data item Vendor No. on one form or control and then call it Vendor Num elsewhere. This makes the form and application more difficult to understand. If the same information is displayed differently on different forms, it should be for a good reason—not because it looks better. Also, don't change labels on the same command buttons. If one form's command button caption is Cancel, don't change the caption to Quit on another form's command button.

- **Consistency of standards.** Use the same standards throughout the application. Name controls, procedures, variables, and other objects consistently. Prefix variables to help identify their data types, or use data-type suffix characters.

- **Consistency of button location.** When possible, locate similar command buttons in the same positions on all forms. Don't, for example, place an Exit command button in the center of one form and in the lower-right corner of another form.

- **Consistency of color.** Use color to make important information stand out. Set foreground and background colors so that they blend well; don't use clashing colors or try to impress. For the best results, stick to the standard Windows colors used in major applications such as Microsoft Word. (You could add a surprise color for warning purposes, such as a negative balance in a checkbook program.)

- **Consistency of readability.** Make the form easy to read. Don't use all uppercase letters for titles or other labels except in rare cases. Keep lots of *white space* (the blank areas on a form) on the form for clarity. Use a different font for labels and for text boxes that the labels describe, unless the controls' border style and background properties help distinguish them already. Don't mix too many fonts on the same form, however.

- **Consistency of clarity.** Don't clutter the form with too much information. Express but don't try to impress. Although the VBScheduler application form shown earlier in Figure 33.1 is simple, the form is perfect for the application and gives users all available information without too much clutter. VBScheduler requires only a single form, but if the form gets too crowded, using a second form is smarter than squeezing too many more controls on one.

- **Consistency of simplicity.** Make data entry simple. Use a drop-down list box when users need to select from a limited number of choices. Analyze the focus order so that pressing the Tab key sends the focus to the next control in line to receive the focus. Add hotkeys to text-box labels so that users can move directly to the text box. Never let users answer Yes or No questions by typing **Yes** or **No**, but supply check boxes, option buttons, and command buttons for such controls. The simpler you make data entry, the fewer user errors will occur.

What Should Be on Each Form

Look at each form in the application as having a distinct job to do. Most applications have many different types of forms. All applications have a *main form* (also called a *parent form*), which comprises the application's frame. All other objects and forms are selected and displayed from the main form.

Again, VBScheduler is fairly simple, so it has only one form (the main form). If you create a multiform project, however, keep track of the forms you add to the project and document each form's purpose and contents as you go along.

▼ **UPDATING DOCUMENTATION**

As you create your application, update your documentation. Your application might contain different kinds of documentation. You might want to document the application internally with remarks so that you can more easily maintain the project later. Also, you might want to keep a notebook handy with form and control names and their descriptions so that you have a system documentation paper for the project.

End users need documentation as well. You should supply online help and ToolTips where appropriate. Also, write a user manual so that users can learn the program without your help. The best time to write the system and user documentation is during the design and development of the project.

Therefore, documentation is an ongoing task that isn't over until you finish the project. Even then, your users will suggest improvements that you'll want to track so that you can offer updated software and documentation periodically. ▲

Looking at the VBScheduler Form

Whenever you start Visual Basic or open a new project (by choosing New Project from the File menu), Visual Basic displays Figure 33.2's New Project dialog box. You'll almost always double-click the icon labeled Standard EXE because most of the projects you create become a compiled executable program with the .EXE file-name extension.

▶▶ FAST TRACK

Turn to Hour 3, "Adding Controls to a Program" (p. 63), to learn how to create new projects and add controls to forms.

FIG. 33.2
Double-click the Standard EXE icon to build a new project.

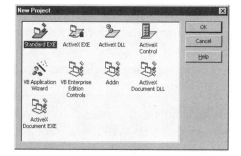

After you select the Standard EXE icon, Visual Basic opens a new project and puts a blank Form window on-screen. This initial form is the main form and provides, for the VBScheduler application, the only form used.

Prepare the form for the VBScheduler application as follows:

1. Change the form's `Name` property to `frmMain`.

2. Set the `BorderStyle` property to `3 – Fixed Dialog` so that users can't resize the form during the application's execution.

3. Change the `Caption` property to `VBScheduler`. As you type the caption, Visual Basic adds it to the top of the form on the title bar.

4. Change the size properties as follows:

Property	Value
Height	6735
Left	885
MaxButton	False

Property	Value
MDIChild	False
MinButton	False
Moveable	True
Top	1095
Visible	False (the application makes the form visible after manipulating some startup objects)
Width	8010

Your Form window should now look like the one in Figure 33.3.

Pt **V**

Hr **33**

FIG. 33.3
Your Form window is now set up properly.

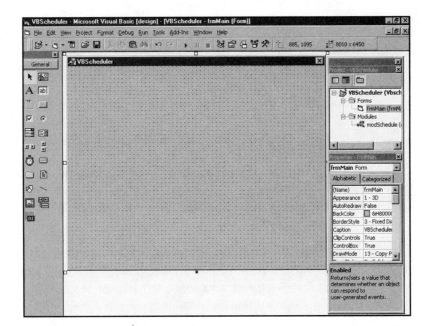

▼ **NOTE**
Users of VB's Standard, Professional, and Enterprise editions can develop the VBScheduler application because it uses no additional controls than what appear by default in the Toolbox. Ordinarily, you choose Components from the Project menu to add new ActiveX controls if you need to work with controls that you don't find on the regular startup Toolbox. ▲

Selecting a Database

Any application must have a way of storing the information that it works with. Selecting the method for storing the data is very important. Some applications use a sequential or random-access file, often called a *flat file*, while other applications use a database created by another application such as Microsoft Access or Borland Paradox. (Visual Basic supports the use of several vendors' databases, including the industry-standard ODBC database format.)

▶▶ **FAST TRACK**

Turn to Hour 21, "Accessing Files" (p. 489), to learn more about data files. Hour 27, "Accessing Databases" (p. 617), discusses how to use Visual Basic's development environment to load and execute programs.

With the inclusion of Visual Basic's Data control that manipulates a data-base—as well as the data-bound controls, such as text boxes, that automatically update the underlying database if users change the data—you will almost certainly want to use a database file for your program's data storage.

Which Database?

Which database should you use? Dozens of commercial databases exist on the market today, such as dBASE, Paradox, and Microsoft Access. Most work with Visual Basic's Data control, as mentioned in the previous section, so compatibility is rarely the determining factor in your database selection.

Although the database selection should primarily rest with the database that best suits your skills (or your company standards), more and more Visual Basic developers are turning to Microsoft Access because of its close relationship to Visual Basic. Using Microsoft Access requires nothing special other than locating the database file that you want to work with.

▼ **NOTE**

Some databases, such as Watcom's, requires special Visual Basic Open Database Connectivity (ODBC) drivers that don't normally install to your PC at VB setup time. Therefore, if you use an ODBC database, you might need to run Visual Basic's Setup program again and add the appropriate drivers. For more information, search the online help for ODBC. ▲

Relational Files

As the amount of stored data increases, the need to have efficient ways of storing and accessing the data becomes a priority. In the sequential-file approach to data, every record needs to have all the data required for the process (for example, name, payee, and so on) included in the record. This duplication of data is a very large waste of disk space and processing time. You need a way to *relate*, or link, several separate files to each other without so much redundancy. This relation ensures that data that needs to appear several times throughout the database can be kept as a single entry in a related table. The *relational database* concept, supported by most of today's database systems such as Microsoft Access, is an organized collection of data tables that your application can access and update in a variety of ways.

Pt **V**

Hr **33**

▼ **NOTE**
Although a sequential file is sometimes still used, most applications today use some form of relational database. ▲

The VBScheduler database is relatively simple. Two related files are needed: one to hold the contacts and one to hold the appointments. Look at the database layout in Figure 33.4 to see how having certain information in separate tables makes it easier to control the data. After the tables are created, the database system links them together to get the data from the separate tables when needed. This linking is called a *table join*. A *table* is one file from a database collection of files. A table is joined by a field or fields in one table matching a field or fields in another table. While the data is processed, an entire record of information can be constructed from the different tables in the database.

FIG. 33.4
Relational tables relate on a common field.

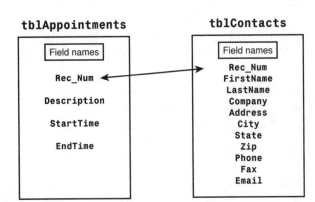

Figure 33.4 describes the database tables needed for VBScheduler. Only two tables are required: the contact table and the appointment table. The appointment table doesn't need to store the contact's name because it can simply hold the contact's record number (in the field named `Rec_Num`). The database format is Microsoft Access.

A big advantage that relational databases offer is the built-in capability to access data by using various queries. A *query* is a way of requesting certain records from database tables. Most relational databases have a standard language used to communicate with the database. This language is called SQL, or Structured Query Language. An example of a SQL request is

```
Select * from tblContacts order by tblContacts.LastName
```

This query retrieves all contact information from the contact table in last-name order. *Indexing* can speed up the retrieval process by putting the records in a particular order before your application searches the table. Your database can take care of the indexing as long as you state the index to use.

Although this lesson doesn't and can't delve into database design, you should understand that you can create just about any database you'll ever need with nothing more than Visual Basic. As Hour 27 explains in greater detail, Visual Basic's add-on tool called VisData (Visual Data Manager) lets you create, analyze, and modify databases in several popular database formats. VBScheduler's database is called VBSched.mdb. You can load and view this database by choosing Visual Data Manager from the Add-Ins menu and opening VBSched.mdb to show the database's format, such as the one in Figure 33.5.

CAUTION The Visual Data Manager doesn't replace a database system, such as Microsoft Access, even though you can work with Access database files from the Visual Data Manager. A full-blown database manager such as Access gives you much better control over your data than the Visual Data Manager can.

On the CD

The VBScheduler application that comes on this book's CD-ROM includes an initial database file with sample data so that you can analyze the database if you'd like from within the Visual Data Manager.

FIG. 33.5
Use the Visual Data Manager to analyze the database file.

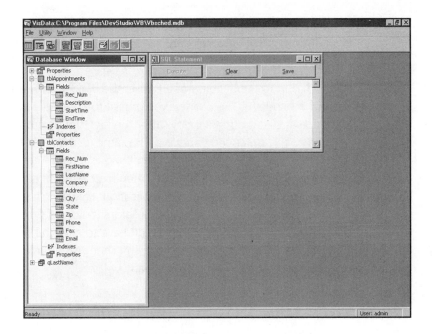

Knowing When to Code

Obviously, much of this book devotes itself to teaching you the Visual Basic programming language—yet the language has not been mentioned to this point in this lesson. The code is the last part of the application that you finalize. If you've followed along through this lesson, you've built an initial form and set some form properties, but you've not added controls yet. You'll add controls in a couple of lessons.

This might seem like a strange topic to include in a chapter on how to create Visual Basic applications; however, knowing what *not* to do when creating an application is just as important as knowing what you *should* do. Why applications begin with design and why standards are important when building the application are discussed in the next two sections.

Don't Write Code Before Designing!

It should be clear by now why it's important to have a good design before starting to create an application. In case it's not, here are the reasons stated another way: Having a good design keeps you from guessing what to do next. Paying attention to the design helps minimize changes to an application after the building of the application begins. Most important, a good design makes the coding process much less tedious.

What if, during the building of a house, the builder forgot to put in the bedroom window? The builder would have to knock the wall down and start again, or cut out a window after the fact, which probably wouldn't look as good as planned windows. The same idea applies to programming. If you find that you've forgotten something in a section of program logic, it can be very difficult to add the forgotten logic without completely rewriting the section of code or the entire application. However, if you find a logic problem early, you can change the program logic and simply move on. Finally, if you find a design problem, you have to alter the design to match the change. To accommodate the design change, you might have to remove some program logic that's already written.

Don't Write Code Before Establishing Standards!

Having programming standards when creating any computer program is very important. The better you name the routines and program variables, the easier it is to understand the code and find errors while you're testing code. You can see, for example, that the routine in Listing 33.1 is harder to follow than the one in Listing 33.2.

Listing 33.1 A Routine That Follows No Conventions

```
Private Function function1 (ByVal var1) As Integer
Dim x as Integer, y As Integer
Dim z As String
If Right$( var1, 1) <> "\" Then
var1 = var1 & "\"
End If
On Error Resume Next
ChDrive var1
If Err <> 0 Then GoTo label1
ChDir "\"var1
x = 3
y = InStr(4, var1, "\")
Do While y <> 0
z = Mid$( var1, x + 1, y - x - 1)
Err = 0
```

```
Mkdir z
If Err <> 0 And Err <> 75 Then GoTo label1
Err = 0
ChDir z
If Err <> 0 Then GoTo label1
X = y
y = InStr(x + 1, var1, "\")
Loop
function1 = True
Exit Function
label1:
If Err = 71 Then
v = MsgBox("Please insert Disk in Drive")
Resume
End If
function1 = False
End Function
```

Listing 33.2 A Routine That Follows Standard Programming Conventions

```
' Create the path contained in DestPath
' First char must be drive letter, followed by
' a ":\" followed by the path, if any.
' -----------------------------------------------------
Private Function CreatePath (ByVal DestPath) As Integer
   Dim intBackpos As Integer, intForepos As Integer
   Dim strTemp As String
   '
   ' Add slash to end Of path if not there already
   ' ---------------------------------------------------
   If Right(DestPath, 1) <> "\" Then
     DestPath = DestPath & "\"
   End If
   '
   ' Change to the drive's root directory
   ' ---------------------------------------------------
   On Error Resume Next
   ChDrive DestPath
   If Err <> 0 Then GoTo errorOut
   ChDir "\"
   '
   ' Attempt to make each directory, then change to it
   ' ---------------------------------------------------
   intBackpos = 3
   intForepos = InStr(4, DestPath, "\")
   Do While intForepos <> 0
```

continues

Listing 33.2 Continued

```
        strTemp = Mid(DestPath, intBackpos + 1, intForpos - intBackpos - 1)
        Err = 0
        MkDir strTemp
        If Err <> 0 And Err <> 75 Then GoTo errorOut
        Err = 0
        ChDir strTemp
        If Err <> 0 Then GoTo errorOut
        intBackpos = intForepos
        intForepos = InStr(intBackpos + 1, DestPath, "\")
    Loop
    CreatePath = True
    Exit Function
    '
errorOut:
    If Err = 71 Then
        varPress = MsgBox("Please insert Disk in Drive")
        Resume
    End If
    CreatePath = False
End Function
```

Although you aren't completely familiar with all aspects of Listing 33.2, the commented and better-structured code should make the routine fairly simple to you.

▶▶ FAST TRACK

Hour 6, "Understanding the VB Program Structure" (p. 133), begins the part of the book that teaches how to understand and write Visual Basic code.

You should be able to tell exactly what a given routine is doing just by its name. Make variable names as long as necessary so that the purpose for each variable is plain. Also, each procedure name should reflect the task that it performs so that each is easy to read and understand.

▼ NOTE

The VBScheduler application follows a standard coding convention that generally matches that described in the rest of this tutorial. Some of the differences are a matter of style preferences. Therefore, you might want to adopt the earlier chapter standards or adopt the VBScheduler standards (many overlap). ▲

Summary

This hour's lesson focused on application and form design. Designing and building an application isn't easy. As you read in this lesson, you need to think about a great many things before you code and watch for many pitfalls as you design. You might have noticed that this lesson avoided the term *coding* as much as possible. Applications are designed, created, and built rather than coded and written. You can never spend too much time up front designing an application. Of course, you must balance design time with the overall schedule and funds to ensure that you finish the project on time, but you'll finish on time more often and more accurately the more up-front time you put into an application.

Hour 34, "Adding the Controls," continues building the VBScheduler application by adding menus and controls to it. You won't add much code, however, until Hour 35, "Integrating Code," because the code is the final step before you test and debug the application.

▼ **NOTE**

No questions or exercises exist for this hour's lesson due to the general nature of the material. ▲

Adding the Controls

THIS LESSON WORKS a lot on the sample application you began building in Hour 33. You'll learn how to create menus and select controls for the application. After you complete the application's design, you must begin creating the user interface as described here. In Visual Basic terms, that means that you must add controls to the form and let users test the running form's prototype to make sure that they're comfortable and that all the input data values are captured when needed.

After you design the user interface with the controls and the menus, you'll be ready to add code in Hour 35. Therefore, this lesson describes the middle cycle of a project's development. If you've followed the tutorial throughout the earlier lessons, this lesson will pose some new concepts related to menu and control placement. If you Fast-Tracked

to this lesson, you'll quickly see how to create menus and place controls so that your application's blank form looks good.

The Scheduler's Menu

Menus provide the mechanism with which your users can select program operations by using the mouse or keyboard. Surprisingly, the tasks of adding menus and hooking the code to menus are fairly simple and don't require in-depth study.

▶▶ FAST TRACK
Turn to Hour 5, "Creating Menus for User Ease" (p. 111), to learn how to create and edit menus.

Many applications supply toolbars as well as a menu so that users can have pushbutton access to many common menu options. The VBScheduler program doesn't provide a toolbar because the program's nature simply doesn't require toolbars. You can learn all about adding toolbars in Hour 23, "Enhancing Your Program" (p. 535), to learn how to use Visual Basic's development environment to load and execute programs.

You use Visual Basic's Menu Editor to add a menu bar and its associated pull-down menu options to your application. The Menu Editor is part of Visual Basic's standard set of features. To add a menu, click the form and then click VB's Menu Editor toolbar button to display Figure 34.1's Menu Editor dialog box.

FIG. 34.1

You build menus with the Menu Editor.

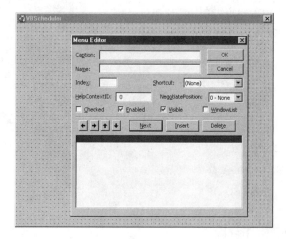

The menu bar across the top of your application is the doorway into the application. To make your application easier to use, you should group the menu selections according to their tasks. More importantly, design your menus to mimic those found in popular Windows applications such as Microsoft Word. Of course, your application will require a different set of menu options than Word's, but your application will need a program-terminating menu option, so use the standard "File menu's Exit option" instead of something less common, such as "Program menu's Quit option."

To add a menu, click the form that will receive the menu and then open the Menu Editor.

▼ **NOTE**
If you create MDI applications, child forms can display menus as well as the main form. Therefore, you must select the form for which you're adding a menu before opening the Menu Editor so that Visual Basic knows to which form you want to add the menu. ▲

Each menu option requires both a Caption and a Name, just as other controls on the form require. The Caption is what users see when the application executes; the Name is how the rest of the application accesses and recognizes the menu options when users select an option.

VBScheduler's menu bar includes the following menus: File and Help. You can add the hotkeys (such as Alt+F to open the File menu) from within the Menu Editor. File and Help menus appear in most other Windows applications. VBScheduler lists these options in the same order as other major Windows applications.

TIP Refer to Figure 33.1 in the preceding hour's lesson to see VBScheduler's menu bar that you design in this lesson.

VBScheduler's File menu contains the Exit option with two other options. Unlike the other options, Exit is a simple option (no submenus open from Exit). Follow these steps to add the File menu and its pull-down Exit option:

1. Type **&File** for the Caption.

   The ampersand (&) before a letter in any Caption indicates the hotkey for that item. Therefore, this menu bar item appears as File on the final menu bar due to the ampersand.

As you enter the Caption property, it appears in the lower half of the Menu Editor, which displays a running list of all the menu options as you add them.

2. Type **mnuFile** for the Name of the first menu bar item.

   Don't worry about the remaining options on the Menu Editor. Most of the default values for the Menu Editor work well, and you won't change them frequently.

3. To add the Exit option on the File menu, click the Next button so that the Menu Editor knows to open a new slot in the lower half of the Menu Editor, beneath File, for a new option.

4. Before entering the Exit option's Caption and Name, click the Menu Editor's right-arrow button. The Menu editor indents the new menu option with an ellipsis. Type **E&xit** for the Caption and **mnuFileExit** for the Name. As Figure 34.2 shows, the Menu Editor indents the new option to show that it's part of the File menu and not the second item on the main menu bar.

FIG. 34.2

The indentation shows one submenu item.

5. The second menu bar item, Help, must appear on the same level of indentation as File so that the Menu Editor knows to place Help on the menu bar. Therefore, click the Next button and then click the left-arrow button to remove the indentation.

6. Type **&Help** for the Caption and **mnuHelp** for the menu's Name.

7. Add the Contents option beneath the Help menu as a submenu item. Name the option mnuHelpContents.

8. A separating bar separates menu items from one another. Separator bars let you group common menu items. To add a separator bar, type **-** (a hyphen) for the item name beneath <u>H</u>elp item and name the separator bar **Sep1**. (You'll never refer to this separator bar from the code; its name simply distinguishes it from other separator bars that can appear.)

9. Add one more option beneath the separator bar with a Caption of **&About...** (notice the ellipsis) and a Na<u>m</u>e of `mnuHelpAbout`. You've now added the full <u>H</u>elp menu shown in Figure 34.3.

FIG. 34.3
The <u>H</u>elp menu is now complete.

▼ **NOTE**

The ellipsis after a menu item name indicates that a dialog box will appear when you select that item. ▲

10. The <u>F</u>ile menu is not yet complete. Add a separator bar above the E<u>x</u>it option and name the separator bar **Sep2**.

The <u>V</u>iew By option will itself be a submenu. Therefore, click the right-arrow button again to add another layer of indentation to the menu options. Add these three options: Quarter Hr, <u>H</u>alf Hr, and H<u>o</u>ur with the names `mnuFileViewQuarter`, `mnuFileViewHalfHr`, and `mnuFileViewHour`. You've just created the cascading menu effect shown in Figure 34.4.

FIG. 34.4
A cascading menu appears.

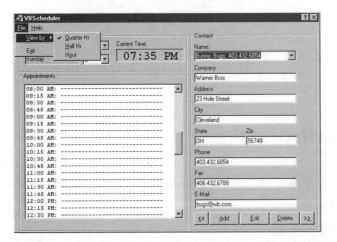

The first cascading menu item, Quarter Hr, has its Checked option set in the Menu Editor. The Checked option puts the check mark you see next to the menu item. The application's code will display the check mark on a different menu item if users want to see half-hour or hourly increments in the appointment pages. The code you add in the next lesson will update the check mark when needed.

11. Add the Contacts menu bar item (with the Name `mnuFileContacts`) to the File menu. Add three items under the Contacts submenu: Add, Edit, and Delete, with the names `mnuFileContactsAdd`, `mnuFileContactsEdit`, and `mnuFileContactsDelete`.

12. Close the Menu Editor and try the form's menu from the development environment. As shown in Figure 34.5, you can view the menu items by clicking the Form window's menu bar.

FIG. 34.5
Try your menu to see how it looks.

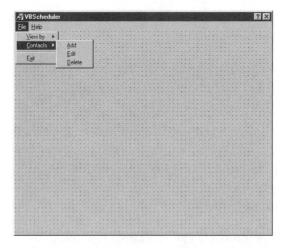

Your application is ready for the controls. The next part of this lesson adds the controls to the form and describes some of the nuances involved with control placement.

Adding Controls

Controls let users interact with the application and are vital to a successful application. As Hour 33 explained, the controls' proper placement and consistency will make your application look professional. You don't want to clutter a form with too many controls, yet you want your form to be functional.

▶▶ **FAST TRACK**

See Hour 3, "Adding Controls to a Program" (p. 63), for information on how to add controls to a form.

VBScheduler's form is about as full as it can be, yet the form doesn't appear to be cluttered. That's because of the nature of this particular application. The appointments list remains clean because only one line shows for each appointment, except when you select or add an appointment to the list.

▼ **CONTROL PLACEMENT: AT DESIGN OR RUNTIME?**

Until now, every lesson in this tutorial has placed the controls at design time where they will eventually appear at runtime. In other words, the design-time look of the form matched the runtime look in most cases. The VBScheduler application shows you a different way to place controls.

VBScheduler doesn't hold all its controls on the form in their proper location at design time. As Figure 34.6 shows, the controls look very cluttered when you look at them in the Form window. (You'll be adding these controls to match this figure shortly.) The controls don't have appropriate Caption and Text properties set and look very little like the runtime application's controls.

The final runtime application, however, doesn't display these controls in such a cluttered fashion. The running application is far more organized, even though a higher number of controls appear on the form at runtime. VBScheduler sets most of its control properties at runtime as well. Therefore, rather than locate the form, select a control, and find the property you want to change, if you need to change a property later, you only need to locate the code location that sets the property.

VBScheduler's designer wanted to show you a different way to place controls. One of the first tasks the code does, when end users run the application, is to move the controls to their proper runtime location. You may wonder why the runtime code performs the same task you could do at design time. By locating the controls at runtime, your application can more easily adapt to form changes. If you add or modify a control later, you only need to change the code that deals with that control's placement. If you can create a good form with proper control placement at design time, by all means do so. VBScheduler is showing you, however, another way to accomplish control placement. ▲

FIG. 34.6
The design time form has controls placed everywhere.

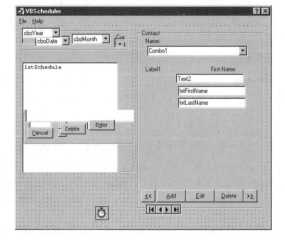

The following sections will review VBScheduler's controls; the final section will describe each control and its properties in a table so that you can add the controls yourself.

The Frames

VBScheduler contains these three frames: a date frame that holds the date and time information; the appointment frame that holds the appointments listed by quarter hour, half hour, or hour (according to the user's menu selection; and the contacts frame that holds the contact information. The frame is a boxed outline around the controls. To place a frame, you double-click the Frame control or click and drag the Frame control onto the form.

The frame lets you move all controls that appear in the frame at one time instead of individually. To add a control to an existing frame, place and size the control onto the frame when you first place the control on the form. If you add a control elsewhere and then drag the control to the form, the control isn't part of the frame and won't move with the frame or be considered part of the framed set of controls.

> **TIP** Only one option button can be True at any one time on a form. However, if you place several groups of option buttons on frames, each frame's group of option buttons can have one True property setting.

The Labels

A label displays text on a form. VBScheduler contains the following labels: the current time label, the date label, a field label control array that holds the captions for the contact information (such as Address and State), and two contact name labels that describe the contact's first and last names.

▶▶ FAST TRACK

A *control array* is a set of multiple controls that are the same type and have the same name. The application distinguishes between the controls in the control array with an index value. See Hour 12, "Handling Large Amounts of Information with Arrays" (p. 273), for information on how to create and use arrays.

Pt **V**

Hr **34**

The Command Buttons

Command buttons let your application's users select options and trigger events by clicking a button. VBScheduler contains these five command buttons that control the display of the contact information: previous contact, add new contact, edit contact information, delete a contact, or next contact.

▼ NOTE

As you work with VBScheduler, the command buttons' Caption properties change to reflect the current state of the application. Therefore, when you click the Edit command button to change a contact's address, the button's Caption changes to Undo Edit so that you can cancel the editing changes if you need to. The code changes the Caption at runtime depending on what users do. ▲

The Data Control

VBScheduler includes one Data control that accesses the contact and appointment database tables. The Data control lets users click the data-bound command buttons to see the database data. If users then edit one of the database records or add a new record, the data control and its corresponding data-bound text boxes change to reflect the update.

VBScheduler uses some SQL commands to select and update the database beneath the application.

The List Box

VBScheduler includes a single drop-down list box that contains a list of all the quarterly, half-hourly, or hourly appointments. The list box doesn't actually look and act like the list boxes you've seen due to the unique way the application initializes the list with the appointment blocks.

One way users will enter an appointment is to click one of the list box's entries. The code displays a text box over the list box with command buttons, as shown in Figure 34.7. When users close the text box, the code updates that item in the list and restores the list box to its usual compact state.

FIG. 34.7

A text box pops up to let users enter a new appointment in the list box.

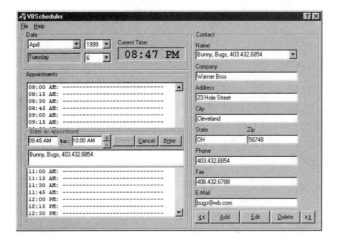

The Combo Boxes

VBScheduler includes four combo box controls. A *combo box* acts like a list box that remains closed until users are ready to select from the combo box's list of items. (Other kinds of combo boxes exist and let users enter new information in the list rather than allow only the selection of list items.) The first three combo boxes let users select the appointment's day, month, and year. The fourth combo box offers a drop-down list of contact names and phone numbers from which users can choose. Therefore, the application lets users search for a contact by choosing Search from the Edit menu or locate the contact by selecting from the drop-down combo box.

The Timer Control

VBScheduler includes one Timer control. The control doesn't appear on the final runtime form, but works in the background to trigger events for a time interval you set. The application uses the Timer control to display the current time of day. The control's `Interval` property is set to 500, so the time is updated every half second.

▶▶ **FAST TRACK**

Turn to Hour 23, "Enhancing Your Program" (p. 535), to learn how to use the Timer control.

▼ **NOTE**

Due to timing problems that can sometimes arise, the half-second interval provides more timing accuracy than a full-second interval could. If you used a full-second interval, the clock could be off as much as a full second. Generally, this lack of precision isn't extremely critical in these kinds of applications. ▲

Pt **V**

Hr **34**

Text Box Controls

VBScheduler contains numerous text boxes that hold specific contact information in a control array, as well as the special pop-up text box that appears when you open a new appointment that the preceding section described. Special first- and last-name text boxes appear when you add a new contact. Notice how Figure 34.8 varies from the regular contacts form when users click the Add command button. Normally, the first and last names appear together when viewing the contacts but, when users add a new contact, the separate first and last name text boxes help them separate the two fields.

TIP One of the neatest features of VBScheduler is that you can drag a contact name to an open appointment text box so that you don't have to type the contact's name and phone number. After you drag the contact name to an open appointment, you can click a plus or minus command button to add to or reduce the ending appointment time.

Last Name
text box

First Name
text box

FIG. 34.8
*First- and last-
name text boxes
appear only
when users enter
a new contact.*

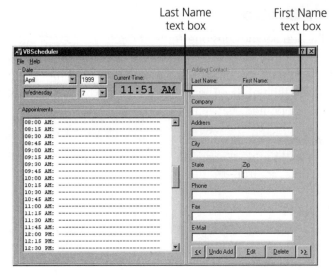

▼ **NOTE**
When you view the Properties window, you'll see all the Menu Editor
items and menu bar options you added at the beginning of this lesson.
Normally, you won't need to access these controls from the Properties
window because the Menu Editor works so well for menu creation. ▲

Placing the Controls

Now that you've seen the control overview, you can place the controls on
the form. As stated earlier this hour, the code will position and size most of
the controls, so you don't have to worry so much about exact placement
when you put the controls on the form. Use Table 34.1 to place the controls on the form and set the properties described in the table. If a property
isn't described in the table, you can be assured that the code will set that
property if the property needs to be changed from its default state.

▼ **NOTE**
The control name's prefix indicates the kind of control. ▲

Table 34.1   Controls Required by the VB Scheduler Application

Control	Properties
Combo Box	Name: cboDate; Height: 315, Left: 420; Style: 2 – Dropdown List; Top: 240; Width: 1095 (on frDate)
Combo Box	Name: cboMonth; Height: 315, Left: 1560; Style: 2 – Dropdown List; Top: 180; Width: 1215 (on frDate)
Combo Box	Name: cboName; Height: 315, Left: 240; Style: 0 – DropdownCombo; Top: 480; Width: 3135 (on frContact)
Combo Box	Name: cboYear; Height: 315, Left: 0; Style: 2 – Dropdown List; Top: 0; Width: 1215 (on frDate)
Command Button	Name: cmdAdd; Caption: &Add; Height: 375; Left: 600; Top: 4800; Width: 900 (on frContact)
Command Button	Name: cmdApptDelete; Caption: De&lete; Height: 315; Left: 1140; Top: 420; Width: 795 (on frEnterAppt)
Command Button	Name: cmdCancel; Caption: &Cancel; Height: 315; Left: 120; Top: 540; Width: 795 (on frEnterAppt)
Command Button	Name: cmdDelete; Caption: &Delete; Height: 375; Left: 2400; Top: 4800; Width: 900 (on frContact)
Command Button	Name: cmdEdit; Caption: &Edit; Height: 375; Left: 1500; Top: 4800; Width: 900 (on frContact)
Command Button	Name: cmdMinus; Caption: –; Height: 210; Left: 1080; Top: 600; Width: 255 (on frEnterAppt)
Command Button	Name: cmdNext; Caption: >&>; Height: 375; Left: 3300; Top: 4800; Width: 435 (on frContact)
Command Button	Name: cmdOK; Caption: E&nter, Height: 315; Left: 2040; Top: 300 Width: 795 (on frEnterAppt)
Command Button	Name: cmdPlus; Caption: +; Height: 210; Left: 1080; Top: 360; Width: 255 (on frEnterAppt)
Command Button	Name: cmdPrevious; Caption: &<<; Height: 375; Left: 120; Top: 4800; Width: 435 (on frContact)
Data	Name: DataMain; RecordSource: tblContacts
Frame	Name: frAppointments; BorderStyle: 1 – Fixed Single; Caption: Appointments; Height: 4095; Left: 180; Top: 300; Width: 3495
Frame	Name: frContact; BorderStyle: 1 – Fixed Single; Caption: Contacts; Height: 5355; Left: 3780; Top: 120; Width: 3915

Pt **V**

Hr **34**

continues

Table 34.1 Continued

Control	Properties
Frame	Name: frDate; BorderStyle: 1 – Fixed Single; Caption: Date; Height: 675; Left: 180; Top: 60; Width: 3315
Label	Name: lblCurrentTime; Caption: Current Time:; Height: 135; Left: 2940; Top: 180; Width: 255
Label	Name: lblDay; Caption: Date; Height: 495; Left: 0; Top: 0; Width: 1215
Label	Name: lblField(0); Height: 255; Index: 0, Left: 240; Top: 1080; Width: 1755 (on frContact)
Label	Name: lblEndTime(0); Height: 315; Index: 0, Left: 1980; Top: 300; Width: 675 (on frEnterAppt)
Label	Name: lblName(0); Caption: Name:; Height: 225; Index: 0, Left: 240; Top: 240; Width: 1215 (on frContact)
Label	Name: lblName(1); Caption: First Name:; Height: 225; Index: 1, Left: 2280; Top: 1080; Width: 1215 (on frContact)
Label	Name: lblStartTime; Height: 315; Left: 180; Top: 240; Width: 675 (on frEnterAppt)
Label	Name: lblTime; Caption: 12:00 AM; Height: 315; Left: 2880; Top: 300; Width: 375 (on frDate)
List Box	Name: lstSchedule; Height: 4710; Left: 1140; Style: 0 – Standard; Top: –540; Width: 3015 (on frAppointments)
Timer	Name: Timer1; Interval: 500; Left: 2460; Top: 5400
Text Box	Name: txtApptEntry; BorderStyle: 1 – Fixed Single; Height: 495; Left: 0; Top: 1440; Width: 3495 (on frAppointments)
Text Box	Name: txtField(0); BorderStyle: 1 – Fixed Single; Height: 285; Left: 240; Top: 1320; Width: 2115 (on frContact)
Text Box	Name: txtFirstName; BorderStyle: 1 – Fixed Single; Height: 315; Index: 0, Left: 300; Top: 1680; Width: 2115 (on frContact)
Text Box	Name: txtLastName; BorderStyle: 1 – Fixed Single; Height: 315; Left: 300; Top: 2040; Width: 2115 (on frContact)

▼ **NOTE**

Be sure to create control arrays for the following controls: lblField and lblName. ▲

After you place all the controls, your screen should look something like Figure 34.9. You've now generated most of the user interface. The code you add to the project in Hour 35 ties everything together and turns this user interface into a working application.

FIG. 34.9
You've now placed the controls and are ready for the coding stage.

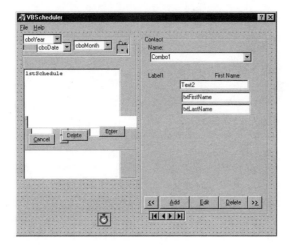

Summary

This hour's lesson added the menu and controls to the VBScheduler application. Although you use the Menu Editor to create and manage the menu items, you'll see the items reside in the Properties window as well because the menu bar and its components are nothing more than controls. Therefore, you can change the menu properties either from the Menu Editor or from within the Properties window.

After you add the controls, you can add the code. This lesson explained that VBScheduler's programmer prefers to adjust final control properties at runtime, even though you can adjust many of the properties at design time. Therefore, your Form window might now look like a busy mess. By studying the sample code that comes with next hour's lesson, you'll see how the code ties in and manages the form properly.

▼ **NOTE**
No questions or exercises exist for this lesson due to the general nature of the material. ▲

Integrating Code

THIS HOUR'S LESSON CONTAINS example code used in the VBScheduler application so that you can get an idea of how code ties things together and finalizes the application. This lesson previews the code that you will ultimately learn to write.

Be warned that the code in the VBScheduler takes the previous 34 lessons one step *beyond* their normal flow. In other words, if you've studied up to this point, you're ready for the more advanced topics that this lesson discusses to code VBScheduler. If you jumped ahead to this fast-track part of the book, you might be surprised at how much you'll learn by going back through the earlier lessons. If the code here seems cryptic, it won't after you finish the earlier lessons in this course book.

Hang on to your thinking caps, because this coding survey of VBScheduler is about to begin!

▶▶ FAST TRACK

To understand code better, refer to the lessons in Part II, "Programs That Do Work," to learn what the code means that you read about here. Part II begins with Hour 6, "Understanding the VB Program Structure" (p. 133).

Startup Code

Before you go further, choose Properties from the Project menu and enter Figure 35.1's Project Properties dialog box values. You enter a value for the Project Name and Project Description.

FIG. 35.1

Prepare the project properties before adding code.

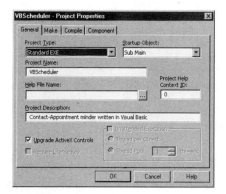

▼ NOTE

The Startup Object is Sub Main, meaning that the primary form's form module (named frmMain) doesn't take over when the application begins. Instead, an external standard module's procedure (named Main) that you add takes over. Sub Main tells Visual Basic to read the external module's code for startup instructions. ▲

Sub Main appears in an external module called the *standard module*. Before you can use the standard module, you must add the module to the project. If you want to follow along, you can add the standard external module by choosing Add Module from the Project menu, double-clicking the Module icon, and then saving the module under the file name modSched.bas.

▼ TO CODE OR TO LOAD?

The complete VBScheduler application is on the accompanying CD-ROM. The code is quite lengthy! This lesson could have listed *all* the code in the project and you could have typed all that code, but you wouldn't have learned a lot from that exercise. Whether you're a programming guru in Visual Basic or any other language or a programming novice, such lengthy code at this point would do little for you.

Therefore, now that you've prepared all of the project except for the code, you can now read the rest of this lesson to get a fast-track approach to understanding the way Visual Basic code interacts and extends the form.

If you want to enter some lines of code, you can do that and become familiar with the editor.

You very easily could find that the fast-track approach this part of the book uses is too advanced at this point because there is no way to explain all the ins and outs of the Visual Basic programming language (that's what the rest of the book does). Study the project from the CD-ROM. Now that you've seen a preview of creating a project and adding controls to the form, load and run the VBScheduler application from this book's CD-ROM. When you go back through the lessons, you'll be better prepared to tackle details such as this project's code. When you load the application from the book's CD-ROM, you can use the Code window's find tools or select from the Object Browser to locate the code being discussed in this lesson. ▲

▼ NOTE

As stated, this part of the book is a fast-track section that shows the process of building a complete application. This part of the book can't begin to explain all the details behind the application's controls or language, or even all the details needed to create the project from scratch. Therefore, this lesson doesn't spend any time describing the fundamentals, such as the need for variables, because you either know those things already or you're here to preview the things you're going to learn when you go study the tutorial's lessons. ▲

As you load this lesson's application into the Code window and follow the short code segments that this lesson duplicates, notice in the Code window that the programmer uses `Option Explicit` at the top of both code modules. The option forces you to declare all variables or otherwise get an error message when you run the program. By requesting that Visual Basic require you to declare all variables, you eliminate misnaming errors that can occur and be difficult to trace without the option set. `Option Explicit` always appears in the General section of a module before any variables (global or local) and before other code begins.

Listing 35.1 shows the code found in the subroutine procedure named Main. Load the VBScheduler application if you haven't done so already. Double-click the Project window's modSchedule object and scroll down a few lines to see Listing 35.1's code. VB code consists of several small routines called *procedures*. Main() is the first procedure executed when you load and run the application (the parentheses after the name indicates that Main() is a procedure and not one of the other kinds of Visual Basic objects).

▶▶ FAST TRACK

To learn more about procedures, turn to Hour 13, "Understanding How Procedures Work" (p. 301).

Listing 35.1 The *Sub Main* Startup Instructions

```
Sub Main()
    'Load the form and let it run the code in the
    ' Form_Load event handler
    Load frmMain
    'Intialize the contact list combo box
    Call InitComboAsDb(frmMain.cboName, frmMain.dataMain)
    'Fill the appointment list with today's appoinments
    Call GetDailyAppointments(CDbl(CDate(frmMain.FormDateString())), _
                             frmMain.lstSchedule, _
                             frmMain.dataMain, _
                             gAppointmentDelta)
    'Show the main form
    frmMain.Show
    'Set the mouse pointer back to an arrow
    frmMain.MousePointer = 0
End Sub
```

Right after the VBScheduler application starts, the frmMain form loads into memory (the form doesn't display just yet, but the code must place and initialize the form's controls), initializes the form's combo box from the database, and finally shows the form on-screen.

This Main subroutine is a little misleading. Although the routine looks short and simple, you must keep in mind that virtually *everything* that happens to objects triggers events. Therefore, the Load statement does load frmMain into memory, but the `Load` statement also triggers the `Form_Load()` event procedure for that form after the form loads. Therefore, you must follow the startup progression even further (throughout the next couple of sections) before you've truly mastered the application's startup process.

> **TIP** Throughout the application's code you'll find *remarks*—messages preceded by an apostrophe that describe the program. The application's author inserted these remarks to help you follow the program and learn from the code. The remarks describe in plain language what the code does.

▶▶ **FAST TRACK**
To learn more about remarks, look at Hour 6, "Understanding the VB Program Structure" (p. 133).

The Initial Literals and Globals

VBScheduler contains several global literals and variables that you need to understand before going much further with the executing code. You've seen examples of Visual Basic's named literals throughout this tutorial, but next you see a list of programmer-defined named literals (remember that *constant* is another name for *literal*). Listing 35.2 contains the `General` section. This code goes above the `Sub Main` procedure in the global section because `Main`, as well as every other procedure in the project, might use these global values and named literals.

▶▶ **FAST TRACK**
To learn more about literals and globals, read Hour 7, "Handling Data" (p. 155).

Listing 35.2 The *Sub Main*'s Global Declarations

```
Option Explicit
'Main Form Width
Public Const FORM_WIDTH = 440

'Control sizing literals
Public Const COLUMN_GUTTER = 1
Public Const COLUMN_MEMO = 48
Public Const FRAME_RATIO = 0.8
Public Const LIST_RATIO_H = 0.95
```

continues

Listing 35.2 Continued

```
Public Const LIST_RATIO_V = 0.9
Public Const GUTTER_HORZ = 6
Public Const GUTTER_VERT = 6

'Move literals for frmMain.PollForDataChanges
Public Const MOVE_NEXT = 1
Public Const MOVE_PREVIOUS = 0

'View increment literals
Public Const QUARTER_HOUR = 15
Public Const HALF_HOUR = 30
Public Const FULL_HOUR = 60

'Database literals
Public Const DATABASE_FILENAME = "vbSched.mdb"
Public Const DQ = """"

'Error literals
Public Const APPOINTMENT_MADE = 0
Public Const ERR_MATCHING_TIME = 1
Public Const ERR_NULL_APPOINTMENT = 2
Public Const ERR_APPOINTMENT_CONFLICT = 3

'Sizing globals
Public gAppointmentDelta As Integer ' Time change granularity
Public gColOneSize As Integer 'Global for size of 1st column
Public gColTwoSize As Integer 'Global for size of 2nd column
Public gColThreeSize As Integer 'Global for size of 3rd column
Public gAppointmentField As Integer 'Global appointment width
Public gComboBox As ComboBox 'The combo box in edit mode
Public gComboText As String 'Global value for gbComboEditOn examination
Public gLeftFramesWidth As Integer 'Global left frame's width
Public gGutterHorz As Integer
Public gGutterVert As Integer

'Appointment String Globals
Public gOpenApptLine As String ' String denoting an open appt
Public gClosedApptLine As String ' String denoting a closed appt

'Semaphores
Public gbAddOn As Boolean 'Indicates a contact ADD in progress
```

```
Public gbEditOn As Boolean 'Indicates an app wide EDIT in progress
Public gbKBEditOn As Boolean 'Indicates that a contact is being edited
Public gbComboEditOn As Boolean 'Indicate a combo dropdown
Public gbInitOver As Boolean 'Indicates that all the controls are loaded
                             'and ready for poplulating

Public gCurrentApptIndex As Integer 'Index of item being edited
Public gcrContactBuffer As ContactRec 'Holds last old record data

Declare Function GetCursorPos Lib "user32" (lpPoint As POINTAPI) As Long

Type POINTAPI
        X As Long
        Y As Long
End Type

Type ContactRec
    fn As String     'First Name
    ln As String     'Last Name
    cmp As String    'Company
    addr As String   'Address
    city As String   'City
    st As String     'State
    zip As String    'Zip
    ph As String     'Phone
    fax As String    'Fax
    em As String     'Email
End Type

Type Appt
    num As Integer
    sTime As Double
    eTime As Double
    Comment As String
End Type
```

Many of the named literals define control and frame placement that other routines will use. Converting numeric literals, such as **15**, for the quarter-hour time intervals helps document the rest of the program that uses the named constant over the literal itself. The uppercase names for the literals help remind you that the value is constant and can't change, unlike variables.

The code does declare a strange-looking function procedure as follows:

```
Declare Function GetCursorPos Lib "user32"
➥(lpPoint As POINTAPI) As Long
```

`GetCursorPos()` is a Windows procedure, not a Visual Basic procedure. Visual Basic can make calls to internal Windows API (Application Programming Interface) routines as long as you know which routines are available. Windows supplies the `GetCursorPos()` function so that applications such as yours can locate the mouse cursor when needed. VBScheduler needs to track when the mouse cursor resides over open appointment. This strange-looking Windows API declaration warns Visual Basic that `GetCursorPos()` is a Windows routine and not one that you forgot to add to your own application's set of procedures.

Do the globals (declared with the `Public` keyword, meaning they're available to the entire project) violate data safety rules that suggest variables should be local? The globals refer to screen-positioning and text-alignment values. Also, the globals define programmer data types so that every routine in the entire project can safely use the defined record data types and declare user-defined variables from those global record types. (For example, the `POINTAPI` user-defined data type holds the x- and y-coordinate values returned from the Windows API `GetCursorPos()` function.) If the record type descriptions weren't global, you could declare such variables only from whatever procedures had access to the descriptions.

> **TIP** Many programmers declare object variables (as done in Listing 35.2 for a combo box variable) globally. Those variables are representing objects on the form, and the global objects make the variables available to the entire project just as the form's controls are available to the entire project.

Looking at *Form_Load()*

Listing 35.3 shows the `frmMain` form's `Form_Load()` event procedure. This code, after the global initialization, does the first real job of the application. Throughout the application, notice that the programmer chose to use data-type suffix characters as well as data-type prefixes. You can compare this variable-naming method to the ones used in earlier lessons and choose

your preference. Many programmers prefer suffixes because they don't
have to type as much as the three-letter abbreviation requires.

Listing 35.3 The *Form_Load()* Event Procedure

```
Private Sub Form_Load()
    Dim FirstLine As Integer ' Location to sync first label to

    MousePointer = 11
    frmMain.Height = FORM_WIDTH * Screen.TwipsPerPixelX

    Call InitGlobalValues
    Call InitHelpIDs
    Call SetDateFrame(frDate, frmMain.ScaleTop, frmMain.ScaleLeft)
    Call InitDateFrame(frDate, cboMonth, cboDate, cboYear, lblDay, _
                       lblCurrentTime, lblTime)
    Call SetAppointmentFrame(frAppointments, lstSchedule, frDate)
    Call SetContactFrame
    Call InitContactFrame(lstSchedule.Top)
    Call PopulateDataCtrls(8)
    Call InitCmdButtons
    gAppointmentDelta = QUARTER_HOUR
    Call SetFrames(frDate, frAppointments, frContact, Me)
    Call InitDataBase
    Call CenterForm(Me)
    gbInitOver = True
End Sub
```

You took the trouble of placing controls on the Form window in Hour 34.
This `Form_Load()` event procedure does the rest of the initial formatting of
the form and its controls. The programmer used good programming techniques. Because the code that executes due to the `Form_Load()` event
procedure is lengthy, the programmer broke the code into many separate
and smaller procedures that the `Form_Load()` simply calls. The smaller procedures help make the application easier to debug because you can narrow
down problems and make bug fixes without adversely affecting surrounding code.

After the `Form_Load()` event procedure initializes the global variables (see
Listing 35.4), the rest of `Form_Load()` concerns itself with initializing the
form's controls.

Listing 35.4 Initializing Global Variables

```
'**************************************************
'Sub/Function Name: InitGlobalValues
'
'Arguments: None
'
'Return: None
'
'Remarks: This Sub is used to initialized the global variables
'          values.
'
'VB concept demonstrated:    Screen.TwipsPerPixelX (Y)
'                            TextWidth()
'                            Variables with global scope.
'
'**************************************************'
Public Sub InitGlobalValues()
    Dim tWidth%

    tWidth% = frmMain.TextWidth("t")
    gGutterHorz = GUTTER_HORZ * Screen.TwipsPerPixelY
    gGutterVert = GUTTER_VERT * Screen.TwipsPerPixelX
    gColOneSize = 9
    gColTwoSize = 34
    gColThreeSize = 4

    gAppointmentField = (gColOneSize + gColTwoSize _
                        + gColThreeSize) * tWidth%
    gLeftFramesWidth = (gAppointmentField * (1 + _
                    (1 - LIST_RATIO_H)))
    ' Used to indicate an open appointment
    gOpenApptLine = String(gColTwoSize - 4, "-")
End Sub
```

▼ **NOTE**
You can't initialize a global variable at the same location (in the
General section) where you declare the global variable. Therefore,
you must initialize the global variables with assignment statements
inside an executable procedure, as done in Listing 35.4. Much of the
InitGlobalValues() procedure initializes the global variables in relation
to the Screen object's properties so that the form centers itself properly
and adjusts its control sizes and labels appropriately depending on the
end user's screen size and resolution parameters. ▲

More important than the code details (at this point), notice how the program's author added helpful remarks at the top of the procedure. The remarks consume almost as much code space as the code itself. The application's author uses these kinds of remarks throughout the entire application for all but the most trivial procedures. The remarks describe these items:

- The arguments received by the procedure, if any

▶▶ **FAST TRACK**

If you want to learn more about how Visual Basic handles arguments, look at Hour 13, "Understanding How Procedures Work" (p. 301). That lesson also describes function return values.

- The value returned by the procedure, if any
- A one- or two-sentence description of the procedure's job
- The concepts demonstrated in the procedure

Throughout the entire project in both code modules, the primary procedures contain this same set of remarks so that you can analyze the procedure's job. The remarks encapsulate an overview of the procedure so that you'll have the tools to then analyze the procedure's details.

▼ **NOTE**

Many of the application's procedures appear in the form module and others appear in the external standard module. You might need to use the Find dialog box (choose Find from the Edit menu) to locate procedures within your application's Code window. Select the Project option before you begin your search so that Visual Basic looks throughout both project code modules when searching for your procedure. ▲

The Event Procedures

The rest of the code handles the runtime execution. Most of the code is taken up by event procedures that respond to users. So now that `Main()` has set the form and controls properly (according to the screen resolution and size), the program just waits and responds to event procedures.

Listing 35.5 contains some event procedure code. An event procedure occurs *only* when users click or otherwise use a control to trigger the procedure's execution. For example, when users click the command

button named `cmdApptDelete`, the event procedure named
`cmdApptDelete_Click()` executes.

▶▶ FAST TRACK

To learn how event procedures work, turn to Hour 6, "Understanding the VB Program Structure" (p. 133).

Listing 35.5   Some Event Procedures

```
Private Sub cboDate_Click()
    If gbInitOver Then
        Call SetDayLabel(lblDay, cboMonth, cboDate, cboYear)
        Call GetDailyAppointments(CDbl(CDate(FormDateString())), _
                 lstSchedule, dataMain, gAppointmentDelta)
    End If
End Sub

Private Sub cmdApptDelete_Click()
    Dim dblStartTime As Double

    dblStartTime = CDbl(CDate(FormDateString) + _
                  CDate(lblStartTime.Caption))

    Call DeleteApptRecord(dblStartTime, dataMain)
    Call GetDailyAppointments(CDbl(CDate(FormDateString())), _
                 lstSchedule, dataMain, gAppointmentDelta)
    frEnterAppt.Visible = False
    cmdApptDelete.Enabled = False
End Sub

Private Sub cmdNext_MouseUp(Button As Integer, _
            Shift As Integer, X As Single, Y As Single)
    If frEnterAppt.Visible = True Then
        cboName.DragMode = 1
    End If
End Sub

Private Sub mnuHelpAbout_Click()
' Menu response for Help, About
    Dim msg As Integer   ' MsgBox() return value
    Dim strMsg As String

    strMsg = strMsg & "VBScheduler" & String(24, " ") & vbCrLf & vbCrLf
    strMsg = strMsg & "Copyright 1997" & vbCrLf
    strMsg = strMsg & "Macmillan Publishing" & vbCrLf
```

```
    strMsg = strMsg & "by Bob Reselman"
    msg = MsgBox(strMsg, , "About")
End Sub
```

To round out this lesson's coding exercise, Listing 35.6 contains two additional procedures. The `InitDataBase()` procedure shows some database programming operations; the `InitHelpIDs()` procedure demonstrates how to add help context ID assignments so that the application can access an external help file.

Listing 35.6 A Few Additional Procedures to Round Out This Lesson

```
'****************************************************
'Sub/Function Name: InitDataBase
'
'Arguments: None
'
'Return: None
'
'Remarks: InitDataBase intializes a Data control to a
'         an Access database file as defined by DATABASE_FILENAME.
'
'VB concept demonstrated: Data control method: Refresh
'                         Data control property: DatabaseName
'                         Data control property: Recordsouce
'                         Assigning an SQL statement as a
'                         recordsource for a data control
'****************************************************
Public Sub InitDataBase()
    Dim db As String       ' Database name variable
    Dim MySQL As String    ' string to hold SQL statement
    Dim msg As String      ' string to hold error message
    ' Define the database name
    db = CurDir & "\" & DATABASE_FILENAME
    ' db = DATABASE_FILENAME
    ' Make sure that it is good
    If IsValidFile(db) Then
        dataMain.DatabaseName = db
        ' Reconnect the new database file
        dataMain.Refresh
    Else
        ' Make and show an error message
        msg = "Cannot find database files. "
        msg = msg & vbCrLf & vbCrLf & "Make sure that the database "
        msg = msg & "file " & DATABASE_FILENAME & " is in the same"
```

continues

Listing 35.6 Continued

```
                msg = msg & " directory as the application file. If you are "
                msg = msg & "running this in app from the VB IDE, make sure that "
                msg = msg & "you copy the MDB file to VB's IDE directory."
                msg = msg & "This also applies to the help file (VBsched.hlp)."
                MsgBox msg, vbCritical, "File Error"
                End
                Exit Sub
        End If
        ' Make an SQL statement that retrieves all the records
        ' from the table, tblContacts and sort them by last name.
        MySQL = "SELECT * FROM tblContacts "
        MySQL = MySQL & "ORDER BY tblContacts.LastName"
        ' Assign the SQL statement to the data control's recordsource
        ' property
        dataMain.RecordSource = MySQL
        ' Reconnect the data control with the new recordsource.
        dataMain.Refresh
End Sub


'**************************************************
'Sub/Function Name: InitHelpIDs
'
'Arguments: None
'
'Return: None
'
'Remarks:    This sub sets the Help Topic IDs as assigned
'            to the constants defined in module, modHelp.bas
'
'VB concept demonstrated: WhatThisHelpID, HelpContextID,
'                         Controls collection, Controls.Count,
'                         TypeOf, Is, And
'**************************************************'
Public Sub InitHelpIDs()
    Dim i%
    Dim MyControl As Control
    ' Assign the WhatsThisHelpID for text fields to
    ' all the text boxes except if it is the appointment
    ' entry text box
    For i% = 0 To frmMain.Controls.Count - 1
        Set MyControl = frmMain.Controls(i%)
        ' If it is a text box. but NOT the text box in from the
        ' appointment entry frame.
```

```
    If TypeOf MyControl Is TextBox And _
            MyControl <> txtApptEntry Then
        ' Then set the Topic ID's
        MyControl.WhatsThisHelpID = IDH_WH_CNTCT_FIELD
        MyControl.HelpContextID = IDH_WH_CNTCT_FIELD
    End If
Next i%

' Name combo box from contract frame
cboName.WhatsThisHelpID = IDH_WH_CNTCT_LIST
cboName.HelpContextID = IDH_CNTCT_NAV
' Appointment List
lstSchedule.WhatsThisHelpID = IDH_WH_APPT_ENTRY
lstSchedule.HelpContextID = IDH_APPT_ADD
' << button
cmdPrevious.WhatsThisHelpID = IDH_WH_CNTCT_PREVIOUS
cmdPrevious.HelpContextID = IDH_CNTCT_NAV
' Add button from contact frame
cmdAdd.WhatsThisHelpID = IDH_WH_CNTCT_ADD
cmdAdd.HelpContextID = IDH_CNTCT_ADD
' Edit button from contact frame
cmdEdit.WhatsThisHelpID = IDH_WH_CNTCT_EDIT
cmdEdit.HelpContextID = IDH_CNTCT_EDIT
' Delete button from contact frame
cmdDelete.WhatsThisHelpID = IDH_WH_CNTCT_DELETE
cmdDelete.HelpContextID = IDH_CNTCT_DELETE
' >> button from contact frame
cmdNext.WhatsThisHelpID = IDH_WH_CNTCT_NEXT
cmdNext.HelpContextID = IDH_CNTCT_NAV
' Enter button from appoinment entry frame
cmdOK.WhatsThisHelpID = IDH_WH_APPT_ENTER
cmdOK.HelpContextID = IDH_APPT_ADD
' Delete button from appointment entry frame
cmdApptDelete.WhatsThisHelpID = IDH_WH_APPT_DELETE
cmdApptDelete.HelpContextID = IDH_APPT_DELETE
' Cancel button from appointment frame
cmdCancel.WhatsThisHelpID = IDH_WH_APPT_CANCEL
' Time increment button from appointment entry frame
cmdPlus.WhatsThisHelpID = IDH_WH_APPT_PLUS
cmdPlus.HelpContextID = IDH_APPT_ADD
' Time decrement button from appointment entry frame
cmdMinus.WhatsThisHelpID = IDH_WH_APPT_MINUS
cmdMinus.HelpContextID = IDH_APPT_ADD
' Start time label from appointment entry frame
' WhatsThisHelp only
lblStartTime.WhatsThisHelpID = IDH_WH_APPT_STARTTIME
' End time label from appointment entry frame
```

Pt **V**

Hr **35**

continues

Listing 35.6 Continued

```
' WhatsThisHelp only
    lblEndTime.WhatsThisHelpID = IDH_WH_APPT_ENDTIME
    ' Current time label from appoinment entry frame
    ' WhatsThisHelp only
    lblCurrentTime.WhatsThisHelpID = IDH_WH_APPT_CURTIME
End Sub
```

▶▶ **FAST TRACK**

To learn more about database programming, turn to Hour 21, "Accessing Files" (p. 489). If you want to know how to add help files to your application, turn to Hour 29, "Building a Help Subsystem" (p. 663).

▼ **NOTE**

Remember that VBScheduler is rather advanced. After you finish this book, you are ready to tackle the entire project. In addition to demonstrating almost every concept taught in this book, the application extends some operations to show you additional ways to use controls. For example, the application applies SQL statements to the Data control to manipulate the appointment database in addition to event procedures that also work to modify the data. ▲

Summary

This lesson reviewed much of VBScheduler's code components that put the brains behind the application. Because the code is lengthy, this lesson didn't even include a fourth of the VBScheduler's application code. As you can see, a major application requires a lot of code despite Visual Basic's visual development tools. You can prototype an application rather quickly by gathering all its I/O controls and placing them on the form. Then you add code to manage the controls and produce the final application's actions.

In next hour's lesson, you learn how to test and debug the application so that you can quickly move from the trial stages to the final stages of your application. After you test and debug the application, the only job left is to compile and distribute it.

▼ **NOTE**

No questions or exercises exist for this lesson due to the general nature of the material. ▲

Debugging and Testing

NO APPLICATION IS EVER complete. You always can add more features, and many times errors appear long after you think you've removed all of them. Therefore, a program's long-term maintenance is part of the programming process. You can take steps to eliminate some of the maintenance headaches, however. Throughout the previous lessons, this tutorial has offered tips to help you better document your code and reduce maintenance problems.

One of the best ways to reduce maintenance problems is to thoroughly debug and test your application before you distribute it to your users. This lesson describes some of the debugging tools that Visual Basic supplies, as well as some testing procedures that you might want to run your application through before you distribute it.

Locating the Bugs

Testing is the process by which you run applications through a series of test-case executions. During the testing, you enter random and extreme values in all the user-entry controls to ensure that the application can handle values outside the typical range. Generally, you find bugs during the testing phase. Debugging is a three-part routine: determine problem bugs and their locations, correct the bugs, and—finally—retest the application to ensure that you eliminated the bugs.

Bugs range from mild errors, such as misspellings or text-alignment mistakes, to serious errors, such as what happens when an application terminates the entire Windows session and results in lost data. To your users, a bug is anything that doesn't match expected program results or prevents the application from running.

Programmers face many debugging problems when looking for bugs. You must decide that you've found as many bugs as you can possibly find, and you must test and retest to ensure that the bugs are gone and don't reappear. Careful planning before, during, and after the coding process helps you reduce the time it takes to debug your application.

TIP Develop and test your application from within the Visual Basic development environment. The development environment contains debugging tools that help you track and locate errors. Only after you're satisfied with your test results should you then compile and distribute your application. (Hour 37, "Packaging Your Application," explains how to compile and distribute your application.)

Windows and the powerful Visual Basic development environment help you locate errors. When you run a Visual Basic application, Visual Basic might find an error during the compilation or preparation for the program's execution, such as a misspelled keyword, and display an error message, such as the one shown in Figure 36.1.

If, when you run an application such as VBScheduler, you see such an error message before you see the first form appear on-screen, you probably embedded a syntax error in your code. A *syntax error* is an error in a programming language's grammar or spelling. Figure 36.1's error is a syntax error.

FIG. 36.1

Visual Basic finds syntax errors for you.

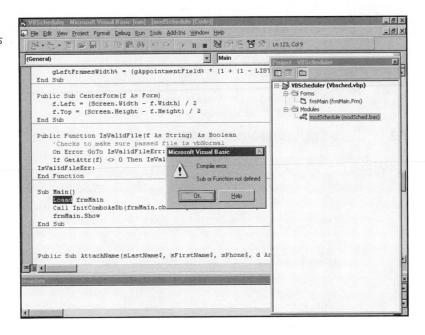

Notice that Visual Basic not only told you about the error in Figure 36.1, but also located the error inside the Code window. Even if the Code window is closed when you try to run the program, Visual Basic highlights the error. The problem is that Load is misspelled as Loaad. After you fix the syntax error, you then can click the Run toolbar button to start the program from the corrected error.

▼ SYNTAX ERRORS AT DESIGN TIME

If you have the Auto Syntax Check check box marked on the Options dialog box's Editor page, Visual Basic checks for syntax errors as you type program code into the Code window. (Choose Options from the Tools menu to access this dialog box.) Some programmers, however, like to have more freedom at design time to sprinkle partial statements here and there that they will repair later in the programming process.

Therefore, you can turn off the automatic syntax check. When the option is off, Visual Basic doesn't check for coding errors, such as a missing parenthesis, until you run or compile the program. Either way, Visual Basic locates these kinds of bugs for you, but the automatic syntax check option gives you the choice of when you want Visual Basic to tell you about the code problem. ▲

More difficult errors appear during the runtime of your application. A syntax error is easy to spot because Visual Basic finds it for you. A runtime error is more difficult to locate and correct. Consider the error shown in Figure 36.2. The error involves program logic. No error message appears, but something is certainly wrong with the application.

FIG. 36.2

Logic errors are more difficult to find.

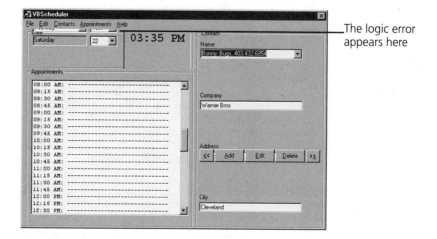

The logic error appears here

The logic error requires that you stop the program. (Visual Basic doesn't recognize the error and stop the program as it does with syntax errors.) You then must track down the problem.

▼ **NOTE**

If you want to duplicate Figure 36.2's error, change the Visual Basic Scheduler's standard module's General section line that correctly reads Public Const GUTTER_HORZ = 6 to Public Const GUTTER_HORZ = 67. Now *that's* a bug that would be hard to trace. See how the extra digit throws off the positioning of the entire frame in Figure 36.2? ▲

You must search through the program code looking for traces where such a runtime logic error might reside and then fix the problem. If the problem involves the form's appearance on-screen, you have to trace all references to that part of the form. Often, but not always, the Object Browser can help you find specific code that goes with an object.

Visual Basic can locate *some* logic errors if the logic error is a request for Visual Basic to do something impossible. For example, Figure 36.3 shows what happens when a program asks Visual Basic to divide a number by zero. Division by zero isn't defined mathematically, so Visual Basic can't accomplish this calculation even if no syntax errors appear in the calculation.

FIG. 36.3
Some logic errors trigger Visual Basic error messages.

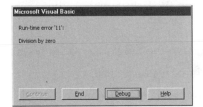

The application runs smoothly without the Code window showing. However, as soon as Visual Basic realizes that the program is requesting an impossible task, Visual Basic displays the Code window and locates the approximate place in the code where the division by zero occurs. You can click the error dialog box's <u>H</u>elp button to get more help on the error message, click <u>E</u>nd to terminate the program's execution, or click <u>D</u>ebug to enter Visual Basic debugging mode.

The Debug Tool

Visual Basic's development environment includes a debugging tool that becomes part of the development environment when you request debugging help. The debug tool lets you do all the following tasks:

- Analyze variable contents at runtime.
- Stop the program at any statement and restart when ready.
- Set *breakpoints* throughout the code that automatically stop the program execution when a breakpoint is reached.
- Change variables during the execution of a program to different values from their current state to test the application.
- Set *watch variables* that halt the program's execution when the watch variables receive a specific value or range of values.

- Skip statements you don't want to execute during a test.
- Use the Debug object's output window to print values during a program's execution. The debug window lets you capture output, such as variable values, without disturbing the normal Form window.

You can enter debugging mode and have access to all the debugger's features (primarily found on the Debug menu) when you do any of the following:

- Press Ctrl+Break to stop the program's execution in midstream.
- Receive a runtime error message dialog box.
- Set a breakpoint, and execution reaches that breakpoint.
- Click a statement in the program and then, from the Debug menu, choose Run To Cursor to execute the program as usual. Visual Basic halts the program and enters debugging mode as soon as execution reaches the cursor.

Breakpoints

One of the easiest breakpoints to set is the *run-to-cursor breakpoint*. Suppose that you suspect that VBScheduler doesn't test for a leap year properly. You can click the first statement in the standard module's `IsLeapYear()` function and select Run To Cursor from the Debug menu. The program starts up as usual, but halts at the breakpoint and highlights the line.

The program isn't halted permanently. Up to this point, all the program variables have been initialized, the code has run, and its effects are available. If output occurred before the cursor's location (none did in this example of VBScheduler), you would have seen the output, such as the Form window, appear on-screen as usual. The program, as indicated by Visual Basic's title bar, is in its *break* state reached due to the breakpoint. The yellow highlight is the line where the cursor rested when you chose Run To Cursor from the Debug menu.

Here is the procedure where this particular example stops:

```
Public Function IsLeapYear(iYear As Integer) As Boolean
    If iYear Mod 4 = 0 Then
        IsLeapYear = True
    Else
```

```
            IsLeapYear = False
        End If
    End Function
```

Perhaps the leap year doesn't work because it receives an incorrect year value from whatever procedure passed `iYear` to the function. Therefore, you can look at the current value of `iYear` to see whether it contains what you expect.

Looking at a variable's contents has never been easier. As Figure 36.4 shows, assuming that the current year is 1997, all you need to do to see the value of `iYear` is rest your mouse pointer over the variable.

FIG. 36.4

Visual Basic pops up the variable's value.

`iYear` contains 1997

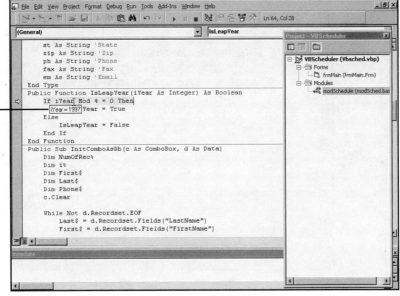

Suppose that the year is *not* 1997. You've just found that the leap year calculation is okay and you have to search back further in the code to see where `iYear` got its value. If the variable has a correct value, however, you might want to run the program a little further.

Retracing Your Steps

Before going further, display the Debug toolbar. From the <u>V</u>iew menu, choose <u>T</u>oolbars and then <u>D</u>ebug to display the Debug toolbar. (As you debug, the toolbar can float, or you can dock the toolbar to the upper toolbar area.) When you need to see where the program's execution has been up to a breakpoint, you can use one of the most useful features—the Call Stack. Click the toolbar's Call Stack button. As Figure 36.5 shows, the Call Stack dialog box appears and shows your program's execution, procedure by procedure, until its current position.

FIG. 36.5

The Call Stack dialog box retraces your program's procedures.

The Debug toolbar

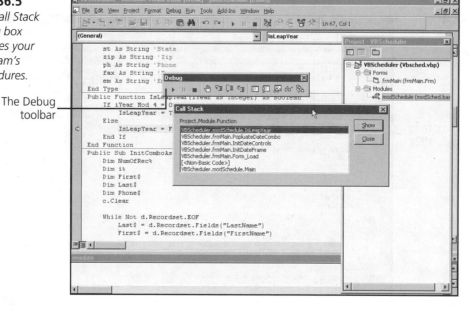

▼ **NOTE**

If you see a Call Stack entry labeled [<Non-Basic Code>], execution occurred from another source, such as the GetCursorPos() Windows API call described in Hour 35, "Integrating Code." ▲

If you want to show one of the Call Stack dialog box's procedures, double-click that entry to move to that procedure. From there, you don't just look at code, but at live values as well. Keep in mind that the application is in a breakpoint stage still, so you can view the values of any variable (or named literal) within that previous procedure.

Single-Stepping Through Code

At any breakpoint, you can click the Debug toolbar's Step Into button to execute the next statement in the program. Whatever statement normally executes next (even if that statement is a call to another procedure) executes when you click Step Into.

The Debug toolbar contains three Step-related buttons; Table 36.1 describes how to use them. You might not want to single-step through *every* statement in an application; the Step buttons give you some options on how you want the program to continue.

Table 36.1   The Possible Step Modes

Step Mode	Description
Step Into	Executes only the next statement. Even if the statement is in another procedure or a return to a previous procedure, the next statement executes and you're placed at that next statement. Therefore, you can single-step through an entire application by pressing F8 continually.
Step Over	Executes the next statement unless the next statement is the call to a different procedure. The new procedure executes in its entirety and execution halts at the statement following the procedure call.
Step Out	Finishes executing the current procedure and then, at the next statement outside the procedure, execution halts again.

▼ **NOTE**
Of course, at any breakpoint, you can click the Start button to continue the execution in its normal manner. If subsequent breakpoints are set, the execution halts at those breakpoints. Otherwise, the program behaves normally as if you'd never stopped it. ▲

TIP   You can terminate debug mode at any time by clicking the Visual Basic Toolbar's End button or by choosing <u>E</u>nd from the <u>R</u>un menu.

Multiple Breakpoints

As your applications execute, you might want to set breakpoints along the way. The breakpoints halt the program's execution so that you can study variables and controls during mid-execution. For example, if you see runtime problems that you want to analyze on the next program run, add a breakpoint by clicking the Debug toolbar's Toggle Breakpoint button at the highlighted statement. You can set multiple breakpoints on additional lines by clicking the Toggle Breakpoint button throughout the code. If you reach a breakpoint (indicated by a red highlight) that you set in a previous session but no longer need, use Toggle Breakpoint again on that line to remove the breakpoint from that location.

> **CAUTION** You can set breakpoints only for lines that execute. You can't set a breakpoint on lines that declare user data types or contain only remarks.

The Debug Window

At any breakpoint, you can display the Debug window to work outside the program's environment. The Debug window is often called the *Immediate window*. When you click the Debug toolbar's Immediate window button, the Immediate window opens at the bottom of your Code window if docked, or in a free-floating location if the immediate window isn't docked to the edge of the screen.

You can type any Visual Basic statement in the Immediate window and see the results of that statement's execution immediately. One of the most common Debug window commands used is `Print`, which prints variable values and control properties. `Print` sends output to different objects (not just to the printer), including the Immediate window. Figure 36.6 shows the form name printed to show that the values you work with in the Immediate window are live values set by the part of the application that's executed to that breakpoint. Also, you can print the results of any expression. If you need to, you can change variable values during execution. After you do that, the rest of the program works with the new value instead of the one assigned originally in the code; that way, you can see the results of the variable's change.

FIG. 36.6
Use the Immediate window to print values and change results.

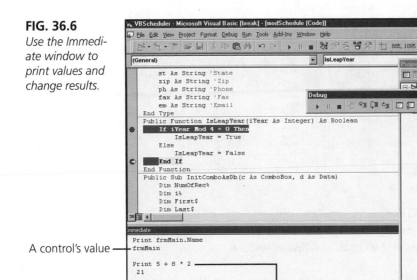

A control's value ———

A variable modification

An expression

The Immediate window

> **TIP** Although the interactive nature of Visual Basic's development environment makes such output less important than it used to be in text environments, your program can write directly to the Immediate window by using the Debug object's Print method. Therefore, if your program includes a statement such as
>
> ```
> Debug.Print frmMain.cmdNext.Caption
> ```
>
> the output goes to the Immediate window, where you can view the output without having to interfere with the normal application's output in the Form window.

The Locals Window

When you click the Locals Window button on the Debug toolbar, Visual Basic displays Figure 36.7's Locals window. The Locals window shows the current value of all variables local to the current procedure (the procedure holding the current breakpoint), as well as global literals and variables.

FIG. 36.7
The Locals window shows all variables local to the current procedure as well as globals.

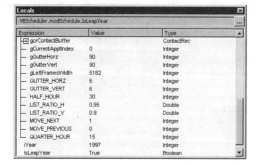

Expression	Value	Type
⊞ gcrContactBuffer		ContactRec
— gCurrentApptIndex	0	Integer
— gGutterHorz	90	Integer
— gGutterVert	90	Integer
— gLeftFramesWidth	5182	Integer
— GUTTER_HORZ	6	Integer
— GUTTER_VERT	6	Integer
— HALF_HOUR	30	Integer
— LIST_RATIO_H	0.95	Double
— LIST_RATIO_V	0.9	Double
— MOVE_NEXT	1	Integer
— MOVE_PREVIOUS	0	Integer
└ QUARTER_HOUR	15	Integer
iYear	1997	Integer
IsLeapYear	True	Boolean

▼ **NOTE**
If you modify a local variable from within the Immediate window, its value changes in the Locals window as well. ▲

In addition to the variable name and value, the Locals window displays the variable's data type. Click the ellipsis button to the right of the Locals window's current procedure name to view a call stack list. When you click one of the call stack procedure names, the Locals window updates to show that procedure's local variables.

The Watch Window

As your debugging process continues, you might find that a bug occurs only when a variable has a certain value. Sometimes problems can't be traced to a single statement, so you have to watch a variable or expression throughout an entire procedure. Visual Basic provides the Watch window in which you can enter values for variables or expressions. You can set up the Watch window with values to watch for at design time or runtime by clicking the Watch window Debug toolbar button. You can use either of the following two methods for adding values to the Watch window:

- From the Debug menu choose Add Watch to display Figure 36.8's Add Watch dialog box.

- Right-click the Watch window (you must first display the Watch window by clicking its Debug toolbar button) and choose Add Watch to display the Add Watch window.

FIG. 36.8
Add values to watch for in the Add Watch window.

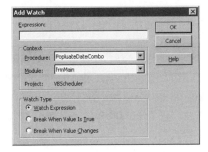

When adding a watch expression, the context of the watch tells Visual Basic the scope of the watch (where it should monitor the expression). Visual Basic can watch a single procedure, a form, a module, or the entire project.

The Watch type lets you specify how you want Visual Basic to respond to the watch value. Visual Basic can display the data in the expression as the value changes at runtime, break the execution when the value is reached, or break *every time* the watched values change. During subsequent execution, Visual Basic updates the Watch window according to your watched values.

TIP Visual Basic includes the Quick Watch window, which lets you add watch values on the fly during any breakpoint. Highlight a variable, expression, or control property, and then click the Quick Watch button on the Debug toolbar. Figure 36.9 shows the Quick Watch window that appears for one of the GetDay() procedure's arguments. You can add this expression to the regular Watch window by clicking Add.

Many programmers find that using Quick Watch during a program's debugging breakpoint is easier to do than trying to collect all the values that you want to watch at design time through the Add Watch dialog box.

FIG. 36.9
At any breakpoint, click Quick Watch to add the highlighted expression to the Watch window.

Summary

This lesson described Visual Basic's powerful debugging tools. Learning how to debug an application such as VBScheduler pays dividends when you need to track bugs. Although Visual Basic's debugging tool can't locate logic errors, the debugger makes it easier for you to locate them. You can trace a program's execution, set breakpoints, and retrace a program's execution from whence it came.

One of the most powerful aspects of the debugger is its interactivity with the program during a breakpoint session. When your program reaches a breakpoint, all the values initialized and computed to that point are still live. Therefore, you can view variables to see whether their intermediate results contain the same values you expect. Also, you can change a variable's or control's value in the middle of the program's execution and watch how the rest of the execution reflects on that change.

Hour 37 completes this part of the book. After you debug your application, you're ready to distribute the application to your users. Application distribution is more involved than simply compiling your application. You must consider the installation routine and ensure that users have all the necessary files related to the application.

▼ NOTE

No questions or exercises exist for this lesson due to the general nature of the material. ▲

Packaging Your Application

YOU'VE CREATED, TESTED, AND debugged your application. The final step is packaging it for distribution to others. If you're creating the application for yourself, you'll probably just compile the application and copy the compiled application and its support files to the folder from where you want to run the program. You can use the Start menu's Settings, Taskbar option to hook the application to your Start menu.

If you want others to use your application, you need to automate the installation so that all the project's files get to their proper location and the Start menu gets the option your program needs. This hour's lesson explains how to distribute the application by using the VBScheduler application as a guide.

Compiling the Application

Visual Basic makes compiling your application simple. The compiled file is a final executable .exe file. All the related modules and forms work together to form the executable file. Although auxiliary files might still be necessary, such as a Microsoft Access database file used for initial data, most of your project's files combine into the executable to make distribution easier.

▼ **NOTE**

The compiled application is more secure than a distributed source project. If you distribute the source code (the project and its related files), anyone with Visual Basic can modify your work. However, most people can't even run your program because they don't have Visual Basic to load and run the program. Therefore, a compiled file is necessary for normal distribution. ▲

Your compiled application runs much faster than the application running within VB's development environment. You want your application to run as quickly and smoothly as possible without your users doing more than necessary. The compiled executable file makes the application's execution simple.

Before you compile your application, make sure that you've debugged the application as much as is feasible and that you've eliminated as many bugs as possible. You can't debug compiled applications with the VB debugger because you run compiled applications from outside the Visual Basic development environment.

When you're satisfied that you have your program running as accurately as possible, choose Make from the File menu. Visual Basic displays Figure 37.1's Make Project dialog box. Select the folder where you want to store the compiled application. (Visual Basic uses the project name as the default executable name.)

Before clicking OK to start the compilation, click the Options button to display Figure 37.2's Project Properties dialog box. (You also can access this dialog box by choosing Properties from the Project menu.) The dialog box lets you specify version information for the compiled application. If you plan to release several versions of the software, the version numbers let you determine the order of versions. You can specify the version information from the development environment's Project Properties dialog box so that you don't have to specify versions just at compile time. The version numbers and description information stay with the project's source code.

FIG. 37.1

You compile the program from the Make Project dialog box.

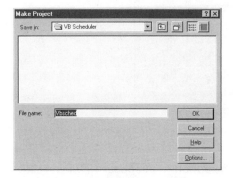

FIG. 37.2

Set the compiled project's options in the Project Properties dialog box.

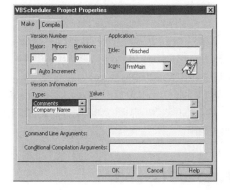

The Icon entry designates the icon that indicates the application on the Windows Start menu and on a taskbar button. Generally, you leave the primary form name in the Icon area. The form's Properties window contains an Icon entry from which you can select an icon for the form and, therefore, for the compiled application.

Click the Compile tab to display the Compile options page (see Figure 37.3). To optimize the compiled project to make it run as quickly as possible, leave the Compile to Native Code option selected. (If you compile to *p-code*, or *pseudocode*, the application requires that your users keep a runtime VB-based .DLL file in their Systems folder. Native code runs faster and requires fewer files.)

FIG. 37.3

Specify the compile options on the Compile page.

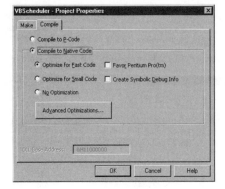

▼ **NOTE**

If you select any of the options that appear when you click the Advanced Optimizations button, you forsake some of the runtime error checking but gain execution speed. ▲

When you close the Project Properties dialog box and click OK, Visual Basic compiles your code. Assuming that no compile errors exist, Visual Basic creates the .exe file (you'll see the compilation status in the upper-right corner). You can exit Visual Basic and run the application by selecting the Start menu's Run option. The form's icon that you selected appears in the taskbar when you run the program.

The Application Setup Wizard

The Application Setup Wizard does a lot of work for you, including the following:

- Compiles the application and compresses the files.

- Creates a setup program that your users can use to install the application.

- Determines the best fit for installation floppy disks, creates the numerous setup disks, and splits files across multiple floppy disks for extra large files. The Application Setup Wizard tells you in advance how many floppy disks the setup requires.

- Copies your compiled application to a hard disk so that you can install the application over a network or onto a CD-ROM creator.

- Sets up your application for distribution across the Internet for Internet Explorer users.

The Application Setup Wizard generates a list of several files needed for the setup. A single Setup.exe doesn't come out of the setup routine. Often, a Visual Basic application requires .dll and .ocx files, and those files reside in the targeted setup area (floppy disks or a hard disk) with the compiled program and the Setup.exe program.

The Application Setup Wizard isn't part of VB's development environment. You need to start the Application Setup Wizard from the Start menu. Use the same Start menu option from where you start Visual Basic and select the Application Setup Wizard to run the program and display its opening dialog box (see Figure 37.4).

FIG. 37.4

Start creating the setup program from the opening Application Setup Wizard dialog box.

The Application Setup Wizard creates a template file that describes the setup routine. In subsequent sessions, you can either modify a setup template that you've already created before, or create the setup from the original project. Therefore, you must select the project or template file from the Application Setup Wizard's second dialog box (see Figure 37.5) so that Visual Basic knows what to set up. Template files end with the .swt file-name extension; previous Visual Basic setup files that used the .vbz extension aren't compatible with version 5 and later. If you want to follow along, select the VBScheduler application (click Browse to locate the file).

TIP If you want to set up an ActiveX control, be sure to mark the Generate Dependency File check box so that the wizard can collect the proper files in the order needed. Also, if your application uses DAO commands, as VBScheduler does, you need to request dependent information.

FIG. 37.5
Select the project and options to set up.

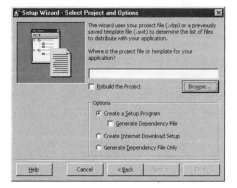

Most of the time, you use the default option, Create a Setup Program, to generate a regular setup program that your users can run to install your application. If your application contains special .ocx ActiveX controls that don't normally appear in the standard Toolbox, you might want to add the dependency information so that the setup routine locates the ActiveX controls properly. Or you can select Create Internet Download Setup to create an Internet-based installation program, or you can create a dependency file only.

Click Next to show Figure 37.6's dialog box, which requests distribution information. The Application Setup Wizard needs to know where your final setup application should go.

FIG. 37.6
Specify the target for the setup files.

TIP If you select the Disk Directories option, the wizard creates multiple disk folders as though they were floppy disks and stores the floppy disk image files in each folder. You can then create floppy disks from the separate folders.

Click Next to specify the location of the setup (such as the directory where you want the setup to go). If you install to a single directory, Visual Basic uses the default name of SWSETUP located beneath your Windows temporary directory, but you can select a different directory.

The directory you select should be empty. Therefore, you'll know when the wizard finishes that all the files in that directory are there as the result of the wizard. When you click Next, the wizard scans your project file to determine which program files your application needs. The wizard can't determine which database drivers are needed if your application contains any data-related controls. You will see Figure 37.7's dialog box if your application requires database access.

FIG. 37.7

You must manually choose the proper data access.

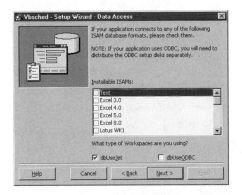

Pt **V**

Hr **37**

> **TIP** If your application uses a Data control that works with a Microsoft Access database, you need to make sure only that the dbUseJet option is set. Microsoft Access requires the Jet database engine, which provides the necessary information for Microsoft Access to work. Click the Jet 2.X option that appears in the list only if you use an older version of the Jet database engine (used in versions 3 and 4 of Visual Basic as well as Microsoft Access 2.0).

Click Next to move to Figure 37.8's ActiveX Server Components dialog box. If your application requires any ActiveX server components, the wizard lists those components. Also, if your application requires any ActiveX controls not found by the wizard and listed in the dialog box, you need to click Add Local (if located on your system) or Add Remote to locate the ActiveX controls and add them to the list. (This list forms part of the dependency list needed by some applications that you set up for installation.)

FIG. 37.8
*Locate ActiveX
controls, if
needed.*

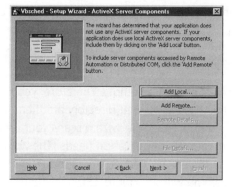

When you click <u>N</u>ext, the wizard displays a list of the dependent files, including your original project and any ActiveX controls it requires. Also, you see data-access files needed for the project if your application uses database commands such as the DAO routines.

> **CAUTION** You might not always have the proper license authority to distribute ActiveX controls unless you created those controls yourself. Therefore, consult your ActiveX control vendor to learn the rules under which you can distribute the controls.

When you click <u>N</u>ext again, the wizard collects all the application's files that you've specified and displays the final dialog box shown in Figure 37.9. Make sure that you look through the files to determine that every file is listed that your application requires. You might need to add (by clicking A<u>d</u>d) more files, such as Readme.txt or a database file. If you are following this lesson by using VBScheduler, add the VBSched.mdb database file to the file list so that the installation routine stores the sample database file along with the installation files.

> **TIP** Click the <u>S</u>ummary Details button to learn how much disk space your final application will consume after users run the setup program you're about to create.

When you click <u>N</u>ext again, the wizard displays its final dialog box, letting you know that the setup information is gathered and that you can click <u>F</u>inish to create the setup program. If you click the <u>S</u>ave Template button, the wizard lets you specify a template file name and saves a template with the setup program. You can, in subsequent Application Setup Wizard sessions, load the template and change the options if you ever need to change the type of setup you want.

FIG. 37.9
The files are prepared for collection into the final setup program.

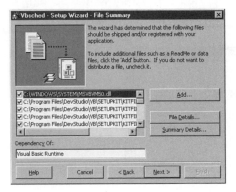

▼ **NOTE**

If you don't save the template file, you can run the wizard in future sessions and create the setup again or with different options, but you have to specify all the setup parameters again. The template keeps you from having to specify every setup option for the same application in subsequent sessions. ▲

After Generating Setup

After the wizard generates the setup routine, test it. To test the routine, run the generated setup program to make sure that no bugs appear and the final application runs smoothly on the computer.

TIP If you really want to test the setup routine, run the setup program on a computer that has never contained your application. Even better, make sure that the computer doesn't even have a copy of Visual Basic installed. By testing your application on such a clean machine, you help ensure that your application installs properly on users' computers.

The Application Setup Wizard creates the setup files in the location you specified during the setup process. If you generated the setup files in a single test directory, you'll find the Setup.exe file among several other files whose file-name extensions end with an underscore (_). The files with the shortened extension are compressed; the Setup.exe routine expands those compressed files onto the target machine or location.

The simplest way to test the generated setup routine is to choose <u>R</u>un from the Start menu and find the Setup.exe file. Click the <u>R</u>un button to start the application's setup. Figure 37.10 shows the opening dialog box that greets you.

FIG. 37.10

Setup warns you to close all running programs before continuing.

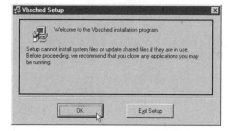

▼ **NOTE**

If you cancel the setup program at any time before it completes, it closes after removing any files copied to that point. Therefore, if you cancel the process at any time, setup removes all traces of the application's setup. ▲

After you click OK, the setup program needs to know where you want the installed software to go. Click the <u>C</u>hange Directory command button if you want to change the path from the default path offered by setup. The default path is a folder with the application's executable name inside the Program Files folder. Any ActiveX controls that the setup installs go to your \Windows\System folder.

▼ **NOTE**

If you specify an installation directory folder that doesn't exist, setup asks whether you want to create that folder or select another one. Most of the time, you create a new one for the installation target folder. ▲

After you change the installation folder or accept the default folder, click the large application installation button to begin setup. Generally, the setup doesn't take a long time if you set up from a hard disk. If the target is floppy disks, however, the setup takes longer and you'll probably have to swap disks.

Assuming that everything worked well, Figure 37.11 appears to let you know that the installation went well. Click OK to return to Windows.

FIG. 37.11
Setup is finished, so now you can test the application.

▼ **NOTE**

Setup uses a smart copy routine to copy files to the installation computer. If setup detects files on the target machine that have the same location and file name as a file about to be installed, and if the target machine's file is newer than setup's, the setup program asks users for permission before overwriting the newer file with the older setup file. Therefore, your users can safeguard against overwriting system ActiveX controls that might be updated and newer versions from your application's. ▲

Changing the Setup Wizard

If you don't like the way the Application Setup Wizard operates, you can change it. The wizard actually runs a Visual Basic project that performs the setup. Microsoft supplies the project's source code, which you can edit. To load the wizard's source code, you must open the project named Setup1.vbp that you can find in your \VB\setupkit\setup1 folder. In the setup project, you can find all of setup's forms, controls, and code modules.

▼ **NOTE**
Consider backing up the setup1 folder before modifying the wizard, in case you inadvertently change something you shouldn't. You can then restore from the backup, if you need to. ▲

Pt **V**

Hr **37**

The setup source code is called the *setup toolkit*. The source code isn't the wizard's source code, but the wizard does use the code and forms in the final generated setup files. For example, if you add your company's logo to the form background of the toolkit's forms, users see your logo on the form during the application's installation because the wizard uses the toolkit's forms in the final setup routine that it creates and compiles.

Uninstalling the Application

The setup wizard not only generates the installable setup routine, but also an application uninstaller that lets users uninstall all the application's files at any time. The Application Setup Wizard hooks to the system Control Panel's

Add/Remove Programs icon. Therefore, if users want to remove the application from the system, they only have to follow these steps:

1. From the Start menu, choose Settings and then Control Panel.

2. Double-click the Add/Remove Programs icon.

3. Select the application from the list of installed applications. After getting verification that the user want to remove the application, the uninstall routine takes over, and removes the program and all its related files from the user's computer.

The Application Setup Wizard stores the uninstall information in the same directory as the application. The file that contains the removal instructions is named ST5UNST.LOG and holds the necessary details for the Add/Remove Programs system utility to do its job. Not all files should be removed, especially system files that might be shared by other programs. Before removing such potentially needed files (such as ActiveX controls), the removal utility displays Figure 37.12's warning dialog box that lets users decide how to remove such files.

FIG. 37.12

Users can decide whether to remove system files.

Summary

This lesson described the considerations necessary to install your application. Visual Basic's Application Setup Wizard does most of the work for you. When you answer a few of the wizard's questions, the wizard builds a complete installation routine that installs your application onto the users' machines.

The Application Setup Wizard is smart and lets you specify dependency information, such as ActiveX controls, that should install with your application's project files. Therefore, after you test, debug, and compile your application, you're ready to generate the installation routine. The Application Setup Wizard generates the installation onto floppy disks or hard disks, and you can install the application onto computers or even onto the Internet from Internet Explorer-based Web pages.

Your application stays on a user's computer until that user wants to remove it. To remove the application, the user only has to select the Add/Remove Programs icon from the Control Panel and then select the application.

▼ NOTE
No questions or exercises exist for this lesson due to the general nature of the material. ▲

Appendixes

The *Visual Basic 5 Night School* Virtual Classroom Web Site

THE MOST UNIQUE feature of *Visual Basic 5 Night School* is its Virtual Classroom Web site, designed to provide you with a comprehensive collection of Visual Basic resource materials. You can visit the site to ask questions, showcase your programs, or complete multiple quizzes to boost your VB5 education. Que has also coordinated IRC's real-time chat capabilities to enhance the Virtual Classroom experience.

Virtual Classroom highlights include

- Real-time discussion with fellow students and VB experts to get immediate response to questions and comments
- Interactive quizzes and exercises
- Visual Basic FAQ (Frequently Asked Questions)
- Book information
- Tips, tricks, and traps
- A showcase area for your programs
- Feedback

Que has made it easy for even novice Web surfers to obtain powerful resource material with a few simple mouse clicks. Just fire up your Web browser, go to **http://www.quenightschool.com**, and you're set! Instructions on how to get the most out of the advanced capabilities of the Web browser, such as real-time discussion groups, are explained on the site. (If you don't have a Web browser, you'll find one provided on the accompanying CD-ROM in the \software\ie directory.)

On the CD
If you aren't connected to the Internet, you still can obtain most of the Web site's capabilities with our offline version included on the CD-ROM!

▼ **NOTE**
Real-time discussion is possible only with an Internet connection. ▲

The ASCII Table

Code	ASCII Character	Code	ASCII Character
000	null	015	☼
001	☺	016	►
002	☻	017	◄
003	♥	018	↕
004	♦	019	‼
005	♣	020	¶
006	♠	021	§
007	•	022	▬
008	◘	023	↨
009	○	024	↑
010	◙	025	↓
011	♂	026	→
012	♀	027	←
013	♪	028	∟
014	♫	029	↔

Code	ASCII Character	Code	ASCII Character
030	▲	056	8
031	▼	057	9
032	space	058	:
033	!	059	;
034	"	060	<
035	#	061	=
036	$	062	>
037	%	063	?
038	&	064	@
039	'	065	A
040	(	066	B
041	)	067	C
042	*	068	D
043	+	069	E
044	'	070	F
045	-	071	G
046	.	072	H
047	/	073	I
048	0	074	J
049	1	075	K
050	2	076	L
051	3	077	M
052	4	078	N
053	5	079	O
054	6	080	P
055	7	081	Q

Code	ASCII Character	Code	ASCII Character
082	R	108	l
083	S	109	m
084	T	110	n
085	U	111	o
086	V	112	p
087	W	113	q
088	X	114	r
089	Y	115	s
090	Z	116	t
091	[	117	u
092	\	118	v
093	]	119	w
094	^	120	x
095	–	121	y
096	`	122	z
097	a	123	{
098	b	124	¦
099	c	125	}
100	d	126	~
101	e	127	Δ
102	f	128	Ç
103	g	129	ü
104	h	130	é
105	i	131	â
106	j	132	ä
107	k	133	à

Code	ASCII Character	Code	ASCII Character
134	å	160	á
135	ç	161	í
136	ê	162	ó
137	ë	163	ú
138	è	164	ñ
139	ï	165	Ñ
140	î	166	ª
141	ì	167	º
142	Ä	168	¿
143	Å	169	⌐
144	É	170	¬
145	æ	171	½
146	Æ	172	¼
147	ô	173	¡
148	ö	174	«
149	ò	175	»
150	û	176	░
151	ù	177	▒
152	ÿ	178	▓
153	Ö	179	│
154	Ü	180	┤
155	¢	181	╡
156	£	182	╢
157	¥	183	╖
158	₧	184	╕
159	ƒ	185	╣

Code	ASCII Character	Code	ASCII Character
186	‖	212	╘
187	╗	213	╒
188	╝	214	╓
189	╜	215	╫
190	╛	216	╪
191	┐	217	┘
192	└	218	┌
193	┴	219	■
194	┬	220	▬
195	├	221	▮
196	─	222	▮
197	+	223	▬
198	╞	224	α
199	╟	225	β
200	╚	226	Γ
201	╔	227	π
202	╩	228	Σ
203	╦	229	σ
204	╠	230	μ
205	=	231	γ
206	╬	232	Φ
207	╧	233	θ
208	╨	234	Ω
209	╤	235	δ
210	╥	236	∞
211	╙	237	ø

Code	ASCII Character	Code	ASCII Character
238	∈	247	≈
239	∩	248	°
240	≡	249	•
241	±	250	·
242	≥	251	√
243	≤	252	^{n}
244	⌠	253	^{2}
245	⌡	254	■
246	÷	255	

Index

Symbols

& (ampersands)
shortcuts, 90
check box caption
hotkeys, 360
suffixes, 165, 169

' (apostrophes), Rem statements, 146

* (asterisks), multiplication operator, 180-182

@ (at signs)
assignment statements, 173
suffix character, 165, 169

/ (backslashes), division operator, 180-182

^ (carets), exponential operator, 180, 182-183

, (commas), numbers, 164

$ (dollar signs), suffix character, 169

. (dots), method notation, 372

... (ellipsis), control properties, 78

= (equal signs), equal to conditional operator, 191

! (exclamation points), suffix character, 165, 169

\ (forward slashes), integer division operator, 180, 182-183

> (greater than) conditional operator, 191

>= (greater than or equal to) conditional operator, 191

- (hyphens), separator lines, 126

< (less than) conditional operator, 191

<= (less than or equal to) conditional operator, 191

- (minus signs), subtraction operator, 180-182

<> (not equal to), conditional operator, 191

( ) (parentheses), event procedures, 93

% (percent signs)
suffix character, 169

+ (plus signs)
addition operator, 180-182
string concatenation, 186

 # (pound signs)
literals, enclosing, 174
date literals, 163
suffix character, 165, 169

"" (quotation marks)
assignment statements, 174
null strings, 172
string literals, enclosing, 162

; (semicolons), Print method code, 403-404

[ ] (square brackets)
assignment statements, 173
command syntax, 4

_ (underscores), 92
code-continuation
characters, 5
variables, naming, 167

0 (zeros)
keywords, converting, 175
numeric variables, 172

3-D labels, list box controls, 377

32-bit VB applications, 40

➥ character, code modules, 4

A

About command (Help menu), 596

About dialog box, 60, 596
adding to projects, 599-601
Form_Load () event, 600
System Info command
button event procedure,
601

R

S

X-Y-Z

Complete and Return this Card
for a *FREE* Computer Book Catalog

Thank you for purchasing this book! You have purchased a superior computer book written expressly for your needs. To continue to provide the kind of up-to-date, pertinent coverage you've come to expect from us, we need to hear from you. Please take a minute to complete and return this self-addressed, postage-paid form. In return, we'll send you a free catalog of all our computer books on topics ranging from word processing to programming and the internet.

☐   Mrs. ☐   Ms. ☐   Dr. ☐

Name (first) ☐☐☐☐☐☐☐☐☐☐☐☐ (M.I.) ☐   (last) ☐☐☐☐☐☐☐☐☐☐☐☐☐☐☐☐

Address ☐☐☐☐☐☐☐☐☐☐☐☐☐☐☐☐☐☐☐☐☐☐☐☐☐☐☐☐☐☐☐☐☐☐☐☐

☐☐☐☐☐☐☐☐☐☐☐☐☐☐☐☐☐☐☐☐☐☐☐☐☐☐☐☐☐☐☐☐☐☐☐☐

City ☐☐☐☐☐☐☐☐☐☐☐☐☐☐☐☐☐☐ State ☐☐ Zip ☐☐☐☐☐ ☐☐☐☐

Phone ☐☐☐ ☐☐☐ ☐☐☐☐ Fax ☐☐☐ ☐☐☐ ☐☐☐☐

Company Name ☐☐☐☐☐☐☐☐☐☐☐☐☐☐☐☐☐☐☐☐☐☐☐☐☐☐☐☐☐☐☐☐☐

E-mail address ☐☐☐☐☐☐☐☐☐☐☐☐☐☐☐☐☐☐☐☐☐☐☐☐☐☐☐☐☐☐☐☐☐

Please check at least (3) influencing factors for purchasing this book.

Front or back cover information on book .... ☐
Special approach to the content .... ☐
Completeness of content .... ☐
Author's reputation .... ☐
Publisher's reputation .... ☐
Book cover design or layout .... ☐
Index or table of contents of book .... ☐
Price of book .... ☐
Special effects, graphics, illustrations .... ☐
Other (Please specify): _____ ☐

How did you first learn about this book?

Saw in Macmillan Computer Publishing catalog .... ☐
Recommended by store personnel .... ☐
Saw the book on bookshelf at store .... ☐
Recommended by a friend .... ☐
Received advertisement in the mail .... ☐
Saw an advertisement in: _____ ☐
Read book review in: _____ ☐
Other (Please specify): _____ ☐

How many computer books have you purchased in the last six months?

This book only .... ☐   3 to 5 books .... ☐
2 books .... ☐   More than 5 .... ☐

4. Where did you purchase this book?

Bookstore .... ☐
Computer Store .... ☐
Consumer Electronics Store .... ☐
Department Store .... ☐
Office Club .... ☐
Warehouse Club .... ☐
Mail Order .... ☐
Direct from Publisher .... ☐
Internet site .... ☐
Other (Please specify): _____ ☐

5. How long have you been using a computer?

☐ Less than 6 months   ☐ 6 months to a year
☐ 1 to 3 years   ☐ More than 3 years

6. What is your level of experience with personal computers and with the subject of this book?

	With PCs	With subject of book
New	☐	☐
Casual	☐	☐
Accomplished	☐	☐
Expert	☐	☐

Source Code ISBN: 0-7897-0921-x

7. Which of the following best describes your job title?

Administrative Assistant .... ☐
Coordinator .... ☐
Manager/Supervisor .... ☐
Director .... ☐
Vice President .... ☐
President/CEO/COO .... ☐
Lawyer/Doctor/Medical Professional .... ☐
Teacher/Educator/Trainer .... ☐
Engineer/Technician .... ☐
Consultant .... ☐
Not employed/Student/Retired .... ☐
Other (Please specify): _____ ☐

8. Which of the following best describes the area of the company your job title falls under?

Accounting .... ☐
Engineering .... ☐
Manufacturing .... ☐
Operations .... ☐
Marketing .... ☐
Sales .... ☐
Other (Please specify): _____ ☐

9. What is your age?

Under 20 ....
21-29 ....
30-39 ....
40-49 ....
50-59 ....
60-over ....

10. Are you:

Male ....
Female ....

11. Which computer publications do you read regularly? (Please list)

_____
_____
_____
_____
_____
_____
_____
_____
_____
_____

Comments: _____
_____
_____

Fold here and scotch-tape to m

What's on the CD-ROM?

On the CD

As one of the exciting features of *Visual Basic 5 Night School*, a CD-ROM is included with this book to serve as a resource for Visual Basic material. The CD-ROM contains all the sample code, and a complete VBScheduler application, an offline version of the Virtual Classroom Web site, and four of Que's top VB-related titles to take you to the next level of the VB programming.

The CD-ROM contains a self-running (for those with Autoplay enabled in Windows 95) index page that explains all the CD's features, and provides links to other valuable VB resources. You can view this index page manually by pointing your browser to the index.html file located in the CD-ROM's root directory.

▼ NOTE

If you don't have a Web browser, the CD-ROM includes Microsoft's Internet Explorer for you (\software\ie302). ▲

Here's an overview of what you can expect:

- All the sample code from the book and the professional-quality VBScheduler application

- A stand-alone CD-ROM version of the Visual Basic 5 Virtual Classroom Web site
- A Visual Basic 5 FAQ (Frequently Asked Questions) document
- Interactive quizzes and exercises
- A glossary of terms in HTML format
- Microsoft's Internet Explorer version 4 (with the enhanced security features)
- Que's *HTML By Example* in HTML format, which provides you with a foundation of HTML knowledge to build on
- Que's *Special Edition Using VBScript* in HTML format, so you can enhance your capabilities with more efficient VBScripts
- Que's *Special Edition Using Visual Basic 5* in HTML format, the logical next step after *Visual Basic 5 Night School* for skilled VB programmers
- Que's *Special Edition Using ActiveX* in HTML format, to enhance your understanding of ActiveX controls

Licensing Agreement

By opening this package, you are agreeing to be bound by the following:

The software contained on this CD is in many cases copyrighted, and all rights are reserved by the individual software developer and/or publisher. You are bound by the individual licensing agreements associated with each piece of software contained on the CD. THIS SOFTWARE IS PROVIDED FREE OF CHARGE, AS IS, AND WITHOUT WARRANTY OF ANY KIND, EITHER EXPRESSED OR IMPLIED, INCLUDING BUT NOT LIMITED TO THE IMPLIED WARRANTIES OF MERCHANTABILITY AND FITNESS FOR A PARTICULAR PURPOSE. Neither the book publisher nor its dealers and distributors assumes any liability for any alleged or actual damages arising from the use of this software. (Some states do not allow exclusion of implied warranties, so the exclusion may not apply to you.)